Emerging Trends in Smart Logistics Technologies

Arbia Hlali
Taibah University, Saudi Arabia

IGI Global
Scientific Publishing
Publishing Tomorrow's Research Today

Vice President of Editorial Melissa Wagner
Director of Acquisitions Mikaela Felty
Director of Book Development Jocelynn Hessler
Production Manager Mike Brehm
Cover Design Jose Rosado

Published in the United States of America by
IGI Global Scientific Publishing
701 East Chocolate Avenue
Hershey, PA, 17033, USA
Tel: 717-533-8845
Fax: 717-533-7115
Website: https://www.igi-global.com E-mail: cust@igi-global.com

Library of Congress Cataloging-in-Publication Data

Names: Hlali, Arbia, 1983- editor
Title: Emerging trends in smart logistics technologies / edited by: Arbia Hlali.
Description: Hershey, PA : IGI Global Scientific Publishing, [2026] | Includes bibliographical references and index. | Summary: "This book aims to enhance logistics and supply chain management by integrating smart technologies, sustainable practices, and digital innovations into a cohesive framework. It addresses critical knowledge gaps by exploring the intersection of smart, green, and digital logistics, fostering interdisciplinary collaboration among researchers in logistics, environmental science, and IT to inspire innovative solutions"-- Provided by publisher.
Identifiers: LCCN 2025007590 (print) | LCCN 2025007591 (ebook) | ISBN 9798337324340 hardcover | ISBN 9798337324357 paperback | ISBN 9798337324364 ebook
Subjects: LCSH: Supply chain management | Business logistics
Classification: LCC HD38.6 .E44 2025 (print) | LCC HD38.6 (ebook) | DDC 658.5002/85--dc23/eng/20250718
LC record available at https://lccn.loc.gov/2025007590
LC ebook record available at https://lccn.loc.gov/2025007591

British Cataloguing in Publication Data
A Cataloguing in Publication record for this book is available from the British Library.

Table of Contents

Detailed Table of Contents

area that has particular logistical problems and a changing technology environment. The study uses a mixed-methods technique to gather qualitative views from industry experts and quantitative data from logistics professionals. The results show that by providing real-time visibility into logistics processes, RTT greatly increases supply chain transparency. Additionally, SLT is recognized as an essential mediator that promotes improved stakeholder communication and data exchange. This study emphasizes how important it is to implement cutting-edge tracking and logistics technology in order to promote openness, establish credibility, and improve overall operational performance.

The fast growth of global supply chains has increased demand for ecologically sustainable, efficient, and intelligent logistics solutions. Because supply chains are constantly changing at a rapid pace, people now require logistics systems that are both sustainable and effective. This chapter examines how green logistics techniques, meant to cut down the environment's impact, can be combined with smart technology. This covers smart logistics, methods for industry sustainability, and how new technology helps achieve both types of goals. Besides, the chapter studies the changes ahead for the logistics industry, how performance is measured, and the difficulties of executing new changes. A growing number of studies give us useful directions on how to create smarter and greener supply chain systems everywhere.

This chapter explores the use of Balanced Scorecards to manage sustainable logistics performance in the retail sector. It aims to integrate the issues of sustainability, digital transformation and crisis management. A literature review identifies four key dimensions (economic, social, environmental, governance) and mechanisms (digital technologies, circular economy, carbon footprint reduction, sustainable governance). The Logistics Balanced Scorecard (LBS) is proposed as a strategic tool for balancing priorities and fostering sustainable value creation. The results of the literature review highlight four main dimensions for steering sustainable logistics performance: economic, social, environmental and governance. Key mechanisms include the integration of digital technologies, the adoption of circular business models, the reduction of the carbon footprint, and the implementation of sustainable governance policies. The corresponding KPIs measure cost efficiency, stakeholder satisfaction, reduction of CO_2 emissions, and transparency in sustainability reporting.

The integration of smart logistics technologies is revolutionizing supply chains by enhancing operational efficiency and promoting sustainability. However, the path to adoption is fraught with technological, financial, organizational, regulatory, and security challenges. This chapter critically examines these hurdles, offering strategic frameworks for overcoming them through targeted training, phased implementation, collaborative partnerships, robust business cases, and stringent cybersecurity measures. Drawing on empirical evidence and real-world case studies, it highlights the importance of leadership, organizational culture, and adaptive strategies. It also outlines future directions shaped by advancements such as autonomous systems and AI-driven logistics, emphasizing the need for interdisciplinary research and ethical governance. By addressing these complexities, the chapter aims to equip practitioners, researchers, and policymakers with actionable insights for fostering resilient and future-ready smart logistics ecosystems.

Logistics acts as a company's bloodstream, organizing supply chains for production and distribution of goods and services to meet customer demands for the right quantity, cost, location, time, and product. Over time, logistics has evolved to encompass economic activities involving the movement of manufactured goods and capital. However, global transformation presents challenges for modern logistics due to growing demand, rapid urbanization, and increased operational costs, particularly under traditional methods. In response, smart logistics technologies like IoT, drones, LiDAR, blockchain, and AI have emerged alongside financial innovations such as cryptocurrencies and agile supply chain finance. This study explores whether key logistics firms should adopt these innovations. Results indicate that diversifying and integrating smart logistics technologies can provide a competitive edge. The findings emphasize the need for logistics management to proactively embrace smart technologies to boost corporate competitiveness.

This chapter examined the transformative role of blockchain technology in enhancing transparency and security within logistics and supply chain management. As global supply chains become increasingly complex and susceptible to issues such as fraud, data silos, and inefficiencies, blockchain offers a decentralized, tamper-proof ledger system that fosters trust, accountability, and real-time visibility across all stakeholders. The chapter explored how blockchain can mitigate long-standing logistical challenges by improving traceability, reducing counterfeiting, and optimizing coordination. Emphasizing both operational and ethical implications, it highlighted how blockchain adoption contributes to regulatory compliance, product authenticity, and sustainability.

The Ports and Maritime industry has long utilized technology interventions. This study examines the relationship between Blockchain technology and shipping operations in Nigerian ports. It evaluates Blockchain's role in the supply chain and its potential to improve information dissemination and efficiency. Two key roles of Blockchain technology are focused: Shipment Tracking and Smart Bills of Lading. The study used the survey method to collect data through questionnaires from a sample size of 120 respondents, including shipping company representatives and port workers in the commercial unit. The study finds a positive correlation between Blockchain technology and shipment tracking and between Blockchain technology and Smart Bills of Lading. It concludes that Blockchain technology is relevant in the Nigerian shipping industry for Shipment Tracking and Smart Bills of Lading. The study integrates various theories to explain adoption trends and supports findings. Government policy support and public-private collaboration can accelerate Blockchain implementation in Nigerian ports.

Ankit Garg, Ajay Kumar Garg Institute of Management, India
Ruchika Nayyar, Amity Business School, Amity University, Noida, India
Surabhi Singh, G.L. Bajaj Institute of Management and Research, India
Himanshu Sharma, Ajay Kumar Garg Institute of Management, India
Rahul Singhal, Ajay Kumar Garg Institute of Management, India

This chapter investigates how foundation models might be incorporated into Logistics 5.0 to support a green strategy that fosters sustainability and long-term financial viability. Through the use of foundation models, the study seeks to improve social responsibility, guarantee sustainable innovation, and organize the environmental framework of the logistics sector. The company ideology, products, processes, and business models are all included in the multi-layered approach, which emphasizes sustainability-oriented innovation (SOI) as a need rather than just a tactic. According to the results, artificial intelligence—in particular, foundation models can achieve social, economic, and governance goals while optimizing a range of logistical processes, such as route planning, packaging reduction, and warehouse management.

Nimit Sharma, REVA University, India
Vijaya Kittu Manda, PBMEIT, India
A. Shivasharana, REVA University, India
Majeed Mohammed, Tamale University, Ghana

Reverse Logistics (RL) has become a critical challenge in supply chain management, especially for retail and e-commerce. With online shopping growth, product returns have increased due to sizing issues, quality concerns, and unmet customer expectations. This study analyzes return causes in online apparel shopping and proposes cost optimization strategies. Our findings show that understanding return drivers—fit issues, quality mismatches, and delivery delays—helps businesses reduce returns and enhance customer satisfaction. The research emphasizes adopting AI, blockchain, and IoT technologies to improve reverse logistics efficiency. Recommendations include implementing centralized return centers, automating supply chains, and educating customers to minimize costs. The study highlights RL's role in sustainability through recycling, refurbishment, and waste reduction practices. This research provides valuable insights for students, academics, and industry professionals seeking to address RL challenges and enhance supply chain sustainability in the apparel industry and beyond.

The chapter will focus on the disruptive aspects of using AI, IoT, Robotics, and Blockchain in transportation today. With the world facing increasing supply chain challenges caused by urbanism, climate change, and technological disruption, smart logistics are providing avenues of increasing efficiency, resilience, and sustainability. It gives a conceptual summary, discusses its applications in road, maritime, and air transport, and is supplemented with case studies. The main themes identified are intermodal integration, digitalization of the supply chain, and significant barriers to implementation, which are cost, cybersecurity, and regulatory problems. Future enablers and emerging technologies such as digital twins, edge AI, and 6G can therefore be identified. The chapter ends with strategic recommendations to policymakers, industry leaders, and researchers by giving a stepwise process by which the digital transformation of logistics in the 21st century can be examined.

Preface

INTRODUCTION

The dawn of the 21st century has witnessed supply chains evolve from linear, transactional pathways into dynamic, intelligent ecosystems, driven by the fusion of artificial intelligence, blockchain, IoT, and fintech, with technologies collectively redefining the global circulation of goods, data, and capital. Emerging at this critical juncture of geopolitical turbulence, climate imperatives, and digital acceleration, this book, ***Emerging Trends in Smart Logistics Technologies***, maps the frontier of this transformation with a dual purpose: to dissect the technological architectures reshaping logistics and to interrogate their profound socioeconomic, ethical, and environmental implications. The urgency of this inquiry is paramount since as supply chains grow increasingly interconnected, their vulnerabilities to cyber threats, regulatory fragmentation, and inequitable access, also intensify their transformation.

As editor my objective is to facilitate a multidisciplinary exploration of smart logistics technologies within synthesizing insights from engineering, economics, data science, and sustainability within a qualified book. In addition, to translate cutting-edge research into actionable strategies that empower policymakers and industry leaders in building supply ecosystems.

This volume is the product of a meticulous editorial journey: 42 chapter proposals were submitted by scholars across several countries (India, Saudi Arabia, Pakistan, China, Ethiopia, Ghana, Morocco, Lebanon, United States of America, Nigeria, Spain, Bangladesh, London, Russia, Oman, Switzerland, etc.), reflecting the global resonance of this field. After initial screening, 38 proposals advanced to full manuscript development. Only 29 full chapters undertook rigorous double-blind peer review by experts. Only 15 chapters were accepted.

The accepted chapters are grouped into three main thematic categories:

1. Smart Logistics Technologies (covering AI, IoT, hyperautomation, and decision systems)
2. Green Logistics and Sustainability
3. Blockchain Applications and Case Studies

Group 1: Smart Logistics Technologies (Chapters 1, 2, 3, 7, 15)

This cluster examines the core technological infrastructure transforming logistics, including hyperautomation stacks integrating AI and robotics (Ch1), AI-IoT convergence for real-time optimization (Ch2), and quadruple-helix frameworks enabling self-regulating networks (Ch3). It further addresses adoption barriers (Ch7) and advances next-gen transportation via digital twins (Ch15), collectively establishing the algorithmic backbone for intelligent, responsive supply chains.

Group 2: Green Logistics and Sustainability (Chapters 5, 6, 12, 13, 14)

Focusing on ecological transformation, this group introduces metrics like the Logistics Balanced Scorecard aligning ESG with operations (Ch6), circular economy models converting waste into value (Ch12), and foundation models for Green Logistics 5.0 (Ch13). It proves sustainability's operational viability through carbon-aware digital twins (Ch5) and AI-optimized reverse logistics hubs (Ch14), demonstrating how environmental stewardship enhances efficiency.

Group 3: Blockchain Applications and Case Studies (Chapters 4, 8, 9, 10, 11)

Centered on blockchain's real-world impact, this segment validates transparency solutions in developing economies (Ch4), fintech integrations synchronizing payments with shipments (Ch8), and anti-fraud protocols for high-risk sectors (Ch9). Emerging market case studies quantify blockchain's efficiency gains in maritime logistics (Ch10) and customs automation (Ch11), offering scalable blueprints for document integrity and trade digitization.

ORGANIZATION

Chapter 1

This first chapter examines the paradigm of hyperautomation as the next evolutionary stage in supply chain management. This comprehensive analysis establishes how the integration of artificial intelligence, robotic process automation, and IoT creates interconnected systems that eliminate operational silos between manufacturing and logistics. The study provides a theoretical framework for implementing cognitive automation stacks that enable predictive self-correction across procurement, production, and distribution workflows.

Chapter 2

This chapter investigates the synergistic potential of artificial intelligence and Internet of Things technologies in revolutionizing logistics operations. Through empirical case studies, the research demonstrates how AI-driven demand forecasting and IoT-enabled real-time monitoring collectively optimize route planning, reduce fuel consumption by up to 30%, and enhance end-to-end supply chain visibility. The analysis further addresses critical implementation barriers including data privacy concerns and legacy system integration challenges.

Chapter 3

Chapter 3 presents a quadruple-helix convergence model where blockchain, IoT, robotics, and artificial intelligence interoperate to create self-regulating logistics networks. The research demonstrates how blockchain provides tamper-proof validation for IoT sensor data, which AI algorithms then process to orchestrate robotic adjustments in warehouse operations. This framework proves particularly transformative for circular economy implementations, where material flows are continuously optimized against sustainability metrics.

Chapter 4

This chapter delivers groundbreaking field research on technology-mediated supply chain transparency in developing economies. Focusing on the Horn of Africa, the study reveals how real-time tracking systems overcome infrastructural limitations through innovative mobile network adaptations. The validated mediation model demonstrates that smart logistics platforms significantly enhance stakeholder trust and operational reliability where traditional systems fail.

Chapter 5

This chapter links ecological sustainability with technological innovation through a comprehensive green logistics framework. The research establishes how digital twins and AI-driven carbon accounting synchronize environmental goals with operational efficiency. By introducing lifecycle assessment methodologies, the chapter debunks the perceived trade-off between emission reduction and cost-effectiveness, also providing actionable models for decarbonizing transport corridors.

Chapter 6

This chapter revolutionizes performance measurement through a Logistics Balanced Scorecard (LBS) designed for large-scale retail operations. This integrated metric system aligns economic objectives with environmental and social governance by tracking carbon intensity, stakeholder equity, and crisis resilience simultaneously. The framework transforms sustainability from compliance obligation into strategic advantage across procurement, warehousing, and distribution functions.

Chapter 7

Chapter 7 conducts a vulnerability mapping of technological adoption barriers across organizational, financial, and regulatory dimensions. The research yields a phased implementation methodology prioritizing cybersecurity infrastructure, workforce reskilling programs, and legacy system migration pathways. Case studies demonstrate how this approach reduces integration risks while accelerating return on investment in smart logistics technologies.

Chapter 8

This chapter decodes the financial innovation-logistics nexus through blockchain-based supply chain finance models. The analysis reveals how smart contracts triggered by IoT-verified shipment events create agile liquidity buffers for SMEs. This synchronization of physical and capital flows significantly reduces payment delays while enhancing transparency between shippers, carriers, and financial institutions.

Chapter 9

This chapter establishes blockchain technology as an anti-fraud mechanism for pharmaceutical and luxury goods logistics. Through tamper-proof digital ledgers, the research demonstrates complete eradication of counterfeit infiltration in validated case studies. The chapter further develops an ethical audit protocol that sets new industry standards for supply chain integrity and regulatory compliance.

Chapter 10

This chapter quantifies blockchain's transformative impact on port operations through rigorous analysis of Nigeria's maritime sector. Results show 40% acceleration in bill-of-lading processing and near-total elimination of documentation fraud. The research provides a replicable digitization blueprint for emerging economies seeking to modernize customs procedures and cargo tracking systems.

Chapter 11

This chapter addresses systemic inefficiencies in maritime logistics through smart contract applications. Research demonstrates how automated customs clearance reduces cargo dwell times by 70% while minimizing human error. The chapter's regulatory sandbox proposal offers a governance framework for accelerating global adoption of blockchain-based trade documentation.

Chapter 12

Chapter 12 studies the positions of IoT and blockchain as catalysts for circular economy transformation in logistics. The “waste-to-value” framework turns return flows into profit centers through AI-powered refurbishment algorithms and material recovery systems. Case studies from electronics and apparel sectors prove how real-time monitoring of reverse logistics can simultaneously boost sustainability and operational margins.

Chapter 13

This chapter introduces a foundation models (large-scale AI) as engines for Green Logistics 5.0. The research demonstrates how generative AI optimizes packaging design, warehouse energy consumption, and circular workflow orchestration. Through the Sustainability-Oriented Innovation (SOI) matrix, the chapter proves that environmental, social, and governance goals can be systematically embedded across logistics operations.

Chapter 14

This chapter describes how to transform reverse logistics from cost center to strategic asset through AI-driven return processing. The study establishes centralized refurbishment hubs that reduce handling expenses by 60% while increasing material recycling rates. By analyzing root causes of apparel returns, the research provides predictive models for minimizing initial product rejection through sizing algorithms and quality verification.

Chapter 15

This chapter simulates next-generation transportation networks through digital twin technology. The research models autonomous intermodal corridors integrating road, rail, and air transport with real-time congestion pricing. Policy simulations demonstrate how edge-AI processors can optimize traffic flow in megacities while reducing emissions through dynamic routing adjustments.

Arbia Hlali
Taibah University, Saudi Arabia

Acknowledgment

As editor of *Emerging Trends in Smart Logistics Technologies*, I extend profound gratitude to all who transformed this project from concept to reality. My deepest appreciation goes to every contributing author whose expertise illuminates these pages. Their pioneering research into smart logistics from AI-driven supply chains to blockchain-enabled traceability represents not just academic excellence but tangible advancement for global logistics ecosystems. Each chapter stands as testament to the author's professional dedication. Special recognition belongs to the peer reviewers who performed extraordinary intellectual service. Their rigorous blind evaluations conducted across time zones with meticulous care ensured scholarly integrity in every published chapter. That many of reviewers simultaneously contributed chapters while reviewing others' work demonstrates exceptional commitment to collective knowledge-building. I extend my sincere appreciation to IGI Global publisher for their expert organization, their e-editorial and e-production teams demonstrated for their exceptional professionalism in guiding books.

Arbia Hlali
Taibah University, Saudi Arabia

Chapter 1
Hyperautomation:
The Next Frontier in Supply Chain (SC) and Manufacturing

Mohammad Kamrul Hasan
https://orcid.org/0000-0003-3866-0090
Tongling University, China

Zahid Latif
https://orcid.org/0009-0007-9096-9489
Allama Iqbal Open University, Pakistan

Arbia Hlali
https://orcid.org/0000-0002-1850-4579
Taibah University, Saudi Arabia

Lei Xunping
https://orcid.org/0009-0000-2899-3428
Tongling University, China

Shah Afrin Billah Aka
https://orcid.org/0009-0005-8750-6411
Beijing Institute of Technology, China

ABSTRACT

The integration of automation within supply chains (SC) and manufacturing has been propelled by technological advancements, with hyperautomation emerging as a transformative paradigm. This paradigm combines artificial intelligence (AI), robotic process automation (RPA), machine learning (ML), and the Internet of Things (IoT) to enhance operational efficiency. Despite its growing relevance, hyperautomation remains unexplored. Thus, this chapter examines hyperautomation

DOI: 10.4018/979-8-3373-2434-0.ch001

through a theoretical framework, analyzing scholarly articles, industry reports, and relevant publications. It presents an understanding of hyperautomation as a pivotal technology for future SC and manufacturing systems. The findings clarify its core principles, operational workflows, and underlying mechanisms, highlighting its capacity to redefine business processes, SCM, production, and logistics. By synthesizing diverse perspectives, this study seeks to address the current knowledge gap, offering theoretical insights that advance scholarly discourse and inform future developments in SC and manufacturing automation.

INTRODUCTION

Technology has changed the pattern of logistics management and manufacturing systems by adding intelligent solutions to operations (Frikha & Hlali, 2023). The essential business functions in today's industrial sector are increasingly automated through the application of machine learning (ML), robotics, and generative AI (GenAI). In addition, the integration of data and ML has driven this development of intelligent solutions (Kusiak, 2024; Surur et al., 2025).

With the advancement of technology and AI, revolutionary approaches are reforming supply chain management (SCM) (Kumar et al., 2022). Organizations are increasingly embracing work environments that prioritize people and leverage intelligent systems (Haleem et al., 2021). This shift marks the beginning of a new phase for organizations that rely on technological innovation and automated solutions to maintain a competitive edge. By integrating automation technologies, organizations can move beyond the isolated benefits of these tools to achieve agility and scalable adaptability (Haleem et al., 2021). This integration of advanced technologies in the field of automation is referred to as "hyperautomation," a term coined by Gartner, a research group. It underpins the autonomy of manufacturing and supply chains' (SC) by focusing on the advancement of digitization and modeling beyond traditional automation frameworks (Haleem et al., 2021; Kusiak, 2024). It enables the integration of AI and ML capabilities into automation processes via pre-built modules (Haleem et al., 2021). With the increasing complexity and globalization in SC (Chen & Hasan, 2023; Hasan et al., 2024), there is a growing demand for improved efficiency, accuracy, and resilience (Kaswan et al., 2025). Hyperautomation can address these needs by facilitating real-time data integration, predictive analytics, and intelligent decision-making.

In today's dynamic business landscape, SC is under increasing pressure to improve adaptability and operational efficiency (Hasan et al., 2025). Industry forecasts indicate that by 2026, approximately 30% of enterprises will automate more than half of their network-related processes, a sharp rise from under 10% recorded in mid-2023. This shift is primarily driven by the adoption of hyperautomation, which is revolutionizing traditional SCM practices (Kusiak, 2024). Over the next ten years, a growing number of firms are anticipated to delegate a significant portion of decision-making responsibilities to advanced technological systems (Gartner, 2021). As a result, SC executives must prepare to leverage these advancements while simultaneously mitigating potential workforce disruptions (Gartner, 2021). Research further indicates that hyperautomation remains a critical strategy for nearly 90% of large corporations, primarily due to its ability to enhance both efficiency and organizational resilience. Additionally, the worldwide market for robotic process automation (RPA) and hyperautomation is projected to expand from $15.0 billion in 2024 to $103.3 billion by 2033, growing at a compound annual growth rate (CAGR) of 23.9%.

The synergistic incorporation of RPA with AI and ML represents a convergence of some of the most transformative technologies in SCM today (Deloitte, 2020). This strategic fusion has led to the emergence of hyperautomation, which enables organizations to undergo digital transformation (Niedzielski et al., 2024) and establish a robust framework for future innovation. Thus, hyperautomation embodies the principle that what is considered disruptive today may become stable tomorrow (George et al., 2023). The notion has evolved into a technological framework that plays a vital role in enhancing digital maturity, which is increasingly recognized as an essential element for the success of organizations undertaking their digital transformation initiatives (Niedzielski et al., 2024).

Although the concept of hyperautomation is gaining prominence within the rapidly evolving business landscape, it is particularly fostering methodical transformations globally while bringing advancements in various industries to improve operational efficiency (Deloitte, 2020). Despite its relative novelty in SCM literature, the concept is still rather new and underutilized (Niedzielski et al., 2024). A plethora of research has explored operationalization and what is contained within the concept of hyperautomation. Table 1 presents a summary of a few related studies. However, scholarly and in-depth investigations to familiarize manufacturers and business leaders with it principles and applications are still limited (Niedzielski et al., 2024), specifically in the context of SCM (Kaswan et al., 2025). Moreover, the expected heavy reliance on hyperautomation initiatives over the next decade and their potential to transform operations demand a more holistic study to explore challenges and future trends to ensure the sustainability of the sector (Srivastava et al., 2025). To address these limitations and research gaps, this chapter seeks to define an approach, particularly on a theoretical basis, as a paradigm for the analysis and enhancement of automation processes. Accordingly, this chapter further aims to provide a comprehensive overview of hyperautomation in the context of SCM, exploring its implications and potential future developments. To explore the dimensions and the influence of hyperautomation on SCM, this chapter aims to underscore the following research questions (RQs):

1. RQ_1 What is hyperautomation?
2. RQ_2 What does it mean to SCM?
3. RQ_3 How does it work for enhancing business processes and transforming SCM?
4. RQ_4 What are the possible influences of hyperautomation for the next frontiers?

Thus, this chapter offers substantial contributions to the evolving domain of SCM. The findings hold considerable relevance for both scholarly discourse and SC operations. To begin with, it enhances the comprehension of the concept of hyperautomation, thus expanding the theoretical landscape for subsequent research endeavors. Furthermore, the insights derived from this study are beneficial for SC professionals and manufacturers, equipping them to design an operational framework to improve process efficiency. Lastly, the creation of conceptual models will be relevant to the hyper-automated ecosystem in manufacturing while facilitating the acceleration of operational strategies.

The rest of the chapter is organized as follows. Section 2 presents a brief concept of hyperautomation and its progress in SCM in the current era. Section 3 describes the approaches of the study. Section 4 details the dynamics of hyperautomation in enhancing SCM, the production process, and manufacturing, and how it transforms the business processes. Section 5 presents the strengths, weaknesses, opportunities, and threats. Finally, Section 6 presents the best practices and the implications. Finally, Section 7 concludes the study with final remarks.

Table 1. Study that utilized the concept hyperautomation

NO.	Author(s)	Research theme	Methods/Research types	Findings/Results/Suggestions
1	Birkbeck & Weston (2024)	Organizational ambidexterity through hyperautomation.	Theoretical approach	AI and RPA to improve efficiency and effectiveness, while also identifying novel ways to adapt to market conditions.
2	Fedosovsky et al. (2022)	Sustainable hyperautomation in high-tech manufacturing industries	Modular design approach	Presents a groundbreaking conceptual business model and technological infrastructure designed to achieve sustainable hyperautomation in the manufacturing industry.
3	Gunisity (2024)	Automation to hyperautomation	Theoretical approach	Delineates the framework of conceptual hyperautomation architecture and guides how organizations can leverage the capabilities of RPA, AI, ML, and NLP to attain maximum operational efficiency.
4	Gartner (2022)	The top 8 supply chain technology trends	Theoretical report	How the most important emerging technologies trends are affecting SC.
5	George et al. (2023)	Hyperautomation in business processes	Theoretical report	Signifies a novel advancement in business process automation, fundamentally transforming the operational, interactive, and decision-making frameworks of organizations
6	Haleem et al. (2021)	Hyperautomation for the enhancement of automation in industries.	Theoretical approach and literature review	Develop theory and conceptualize hyperautomation for industries to increase the efficiency and human enhancement of automated operations.
7	Jiang et al. (2023)	Blockchain-based hyperautomation technology in enhancing corporate performance by the green supply chain.	A qualitative and quantitative approach	Blockchain technology with hyperautomation can impact business performance.
8	Kusiak (2024)	Hyperautomation in manufacturing industry.	Theoretical approach	Conceptualize hyperautomation for the intelligent manufacturing of the future.
9	Lasso-Rodriguez & Winkler (2020)	Hyperautomation in business process management.	Application of Delphi techniques.	It is possible to have an RPA robot fulfill a BPM manager's role.
10	Niedzielski et al. (2024)	Hyperautomation in organizations.	Theoretical study based on a cognitive approach with the use of Euler circles.	To deploy hyperautomation successfully in businesses, industries, and other economic sectors, enterprises must take a distributed and integrated approach.
11	Szelągowski & Berniak-Woźny (2023)	Hyperautomation in business processes.	Theoretical study.	Present a theoretical reflection of hyperautomation how it reduces traditional business process tasks mainly automatically, and enhances the importance of dynamic business processes.

HYPERAUTOMATION AND ITS PROGRESS IN SCM

Hyperautomation: Evolution and Concept

The rise of automation can be traced back to the Industrial Revolution, marked by a complete change in production techniques and technologies intended to reduce human efforts through mechanization. However, the earliest forms of automation focused on simple and repetitive tasks in manufacturing (Mathur et al., 2022). Technological advancement sparked innovative thinking that has led to the current era of intelligent automation that represents a new frontier of process automation, enabling end-to-end digitalization of operations through the integrated suite of emerging cutting-edge technologies like AI, ML, RPA, and IoT (George et al., 2023). This evolution of automation has transformed industry, leading to today's hyperautomation and AI-driven industry. Table 2 represents a timeline highlighting key technologies along with key milestones.

Table 2. Historical timeline of automation: From Industry 3.0 to Industry 4.0 and beyond

Era	Key Technologies	Characteristics	Impact
Industry 3.0 (1970s–2010s) The Digital Revolution	- PLCs - CNC Machines - Early Robotics	Digital control systems, Isolated automation, Rule-based programming	Shift from mechanical to digital automation, improving precision but still requiring human oversight.
Industry 4.0 (2010s–2020) The Smart Factory Era	- IoT - AI/ML - Cloud Computing - Digital Twins	Connected systems, Predictive analytics, Smart factories	Factories become self-optimizing, reducing downtime and improving efficiency.
Industry 5.0 (2021-Present) Human-Centric Automation	- Cobots - Generative AI - Edge Computing	Human-centric design, Sustainable production, AI-augmented creativity	Machines and humans work side-by-side, with AI handling complex decisions.
Beyond Industry 5.0 The Cognitive Automation Era	- Quantum ML - Neuromorphic Computing - Self-reconfiguring Factories	Autonomous decision-making, Real-time global optimization	Near-total automation with self-healing systems and real-time global optimization.

Hyperautomation represents a progressive paradigm in the realm of automation (Kusiak, 2024), which is characterized by the comprehensive automation of organizational functions through the integration of various ML techniques (Gartner, 2022). This is fundamentally business-oriented and emphasizes a human-centric methodology that systematically identifies, evaluates, and automates both business and IT processes. It includes technologies such as AI, RPA, ML, and advanced tools such as the Internet of Things (IoT), chatbots, intelligent document processing (IDP), and blockchain to facilitate the automation of even the most complex business operations (George et al., 2023). The synergistic application of these cutting-edge technologies has led to intelligent process automation that has surpassed traditional automation capabilities, enabling organizations to enhance efficiency, mitigate narrow profit margins, and improve visibility (Gunisity, 2024). Hyperautomation can render customized solutions that can fulfill the needs of any industry or business enterprise, thereby leading to digital transformation. The result is a process of human-machine interaction to achieve autonomy.

However, hyperautomation is distinguished from traditional automation as it seeks to optimize production and business processes through a holistic approach, whereas the latter seeks to improve the execution of individual tasks by implementing robotic collaboration instead of humans (Stankov, 2024). Traditional approaches ordinarily operate in silos and use RPA bots to mechanize tasks, whereas hyperautomation digitally transforms entire operations through AI-driven intelligent solutions and cross-system integration. As per Forrester's study, hyperautomation delivers three times more ROI than traditional RPA, while according to an IDC report, 75% of enterprises integrate AI for automating data analysis and real-time decision-making to achieve enterprise-wide scalability (George et al., 2023). A brief of the core technologies enabling hyperautomation is presented in Table 3.

Table 3. Core technologies enabling hyperautomation

SL.	Core Technologies	In Brief
1	AI & ML	• Backbone of intelligent decision-making, analyzing data, making predictions, accurate demand forecasting, identifying patterns, optimized route planning, and predictive maintenance of equipment.
2	Robotic Process Automation (RPA)	• Automate repetitive and rule-based tasks. It is capable of managing functions like data entry, processing invoices, and responding to customer inquiries.
3	Intelligent Document Processing (IDP)	• Streamline the processing of complex documents particularly for handling invoices, contracts, and shipping manifests, allowing quicker and more precise data extraction and processing.
4	Business Process Management (BPM)	• BPM tools facilitate the design, modeling, execution, and optimization of business processes, ensuring alignment with organizational strategic objectives.
5	Process Mining & Discovery	• These instruments observe process logs to detect trends, inefficiencies, and potential areas for enhancement.

However, this concept in business is not entirely new; numerous organizations like JP Morgan, Pfizer, Uber, and Target have already implemented this strategy to optimize their operations, thereby reducing reliance on human intervention and minimizing the potential for human error (Agbelusi et al., 2024; George et al., 2023). Indeed, many sectors have been actively exploring avenues for process automation using intelligent machines since the onset of the Industrial Revolution. Hyperautomation is revolutionizing the agriculture and farming industry as well by increasing productivity, as the use of smart technologies helps farmers monitor the exact pesticide and fertilizer doses. Agriculture accounts for 70% of worldwide water usage; the implication of these advanced tools helps farmers optimize resource utilization (Ilango, 2025). Moreover, ML techniques have been found effective in monitoring crop health and forecasting yields. The integration of ML with IoT sensors in organizations like John Deere is used to analyze soil conditions and weather patterns, which enables data-driven farming decisions. This transformation has led to improved productivity and reduced resource usage, resulting in sustainable agriculture practices. Similarly, Amazon and Walmart have leveraged automation tools to optimize SC and augment customer experiences. ML algorithms have been used by Amazon to predict demand patterns that ensure efficient warehouse management and timely delivery (Osman et al., 2025).

The Progress of Hyperautomation in SCM

Hyperautomation fueled by technology developments has emerged as a relatively new paradigm that has transformed SC automation. It integrates advanced technologies that have revolutionized the SCM and the movement of goods. It influences all facets of logistics, encompassing warehouse operations and transportation management, with the potential to enhance efficiency and reduce costs to unprecedented levels. As companies endeavor to meet the escalating demands of consumers, it stands out as a pivotal development, capable of fundamentally reshaping the industry. A basic concept of the hyperautomated ecosystem in SCM is shown in Figure 1.

Figure 1. Concept of hyperautomation

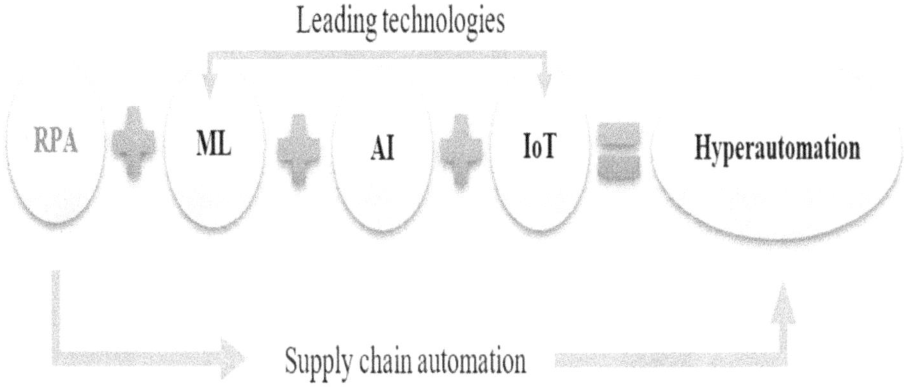

Source: Created by author(s)

The concept of hyperautomation has garnered considerable interest in the field of SCM. The processes associated with SCM and logistics are progressively transitioning toward digitalization, prompting organizations to cultivate capabilities that support a digital ecosystem and agility in their operations (Mubarik & Khan, 2024). A recent projection indicates that in the near future, approximately one-third of organizations will implement a digital ecosystem to improve visibility and collaboration with external partners. A survey conducted by Manufacturing Digital revealed that 42% of enterprises are currently utilizing automation to address risks, a figure expected to double within the next two years. By proactively investing in this technology, organizations can safeguard against future uncertainties, maintain competitiveness, and ensure the continuity of global industry operations, regardless of external challenges.

In addition, Gartner (2019) has recognized hyperautomation as one of the ten most significant strategic technology trends. This trend is poised to enhance process efficiency, improve visibility and transparency, and address challenges related to narrow profit margins in SC. A recent survey by Gartner indicated that 85% of respondents plan to either increase or maintain their investments over the upcoming year, with more than 56% already engaged in four or more simultaneous hyperautomation projects. Another study on SC automation by Deloitte depicts that 78% of 441 interviewed companies have already implemented RPA, which is considered the first step toward hyperautomation, while 16% plan to adopt it in the upcoming three years. A prominent example is Unilever, which has implemented AI-driven automation in the ERP system to improve SC operations and decision-making. This has led to a 15% cost reduction with a 10% increase in on-time deliveries (Agbelusi et al., 2024). According to a McKinsey report in 2024, up to 60% of work activities in the upcoming 20 years are expected to be supercharged by gen AI automation (Atluri et al., 2024). Notably, 23% of SC leaders anticipate the establishment of a digital ecosystem by 2025, a substantial increase from just 1% today, as illustrated in Figure 2.

Figure 2. SC expect to speed up digital maturity by 2025

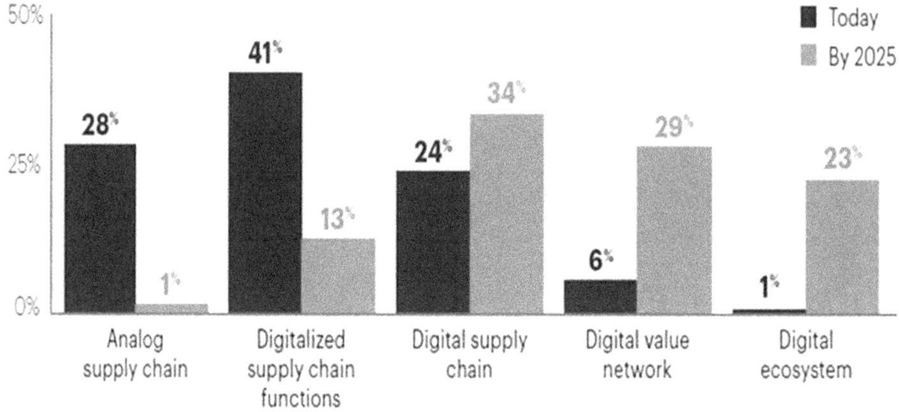

Source: Gartner (2022)

METHODOLOGY

The study employs a qualitative research methodology grounded in theoretical frameworks and informed by an extensive review of various reports, academic literature, online news sources, websites, and working papers. The information gathered from these diverse sources is examined using two primary qualitative research methods: phenomenology, which explores the essential nature and meaning of specific phenomena, and content analysis, which examines specific events or trends to extract insights that help organizations assess the alignment of their current strategies with public or expert perceptions. In addition, a SWOT analysis is used to identify the strengths, weaknesses, opportunities, and threats associated with hyperautomation.

The principal aim of this chapter is to enrich the theoretical understanding of hyperautomation and enhance its representation within the SCM literature. Accordingly, the integration of theoretical frameworks with SWOT analysis serves to illuminate the concept and emphasize its advantages and disadvantages. A summary of the study's outline is presented in Figure 3.

Figure 3. Outline of the study

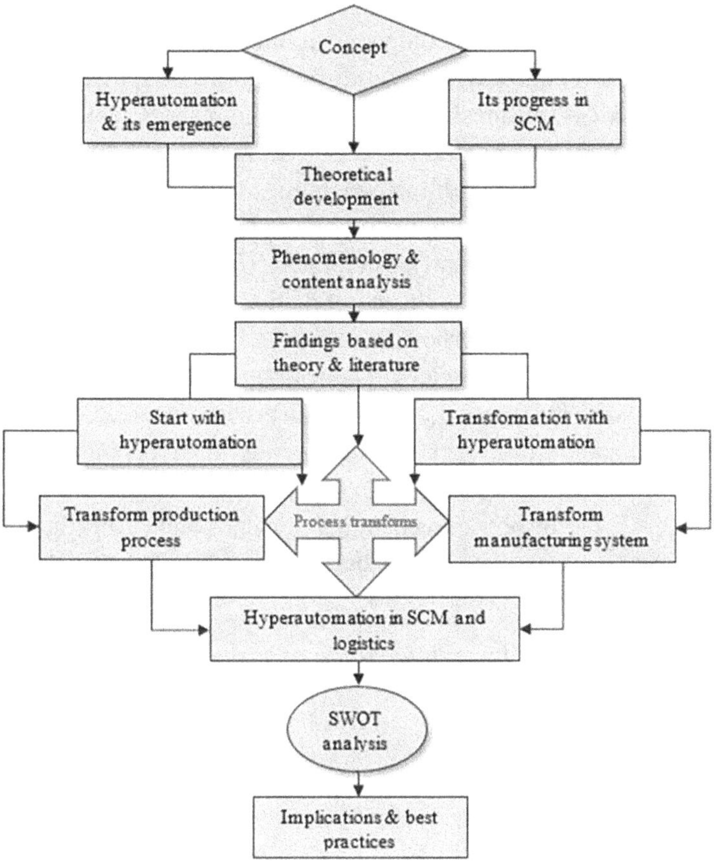

Source: Created by author(s)

DISCUSSION

The theoretical assessment of scholarly articles, editorials, and a range of news reports are presented in this section. The assessment begins with outlining the conceptual steps for starting with hyperautomation along with an explanation of its operational mechanisms. Additionally, our assessment emphasizes the increasing significance of the topic in business process management (BPM), production and manufacturing systems, SC, and logistics processes.

Start With Hyperautomation

Hyperautomation inherently encompasses a combination of various technologies, making it crucial for organizations to carefully choose different appropriate tools. In the selection process, business analysts should emphasize factors such as user-friendliness, scalability, and compatibility across different platforms. It is vital to select a tool that corresponds with the capabilities of the team. Many automation solutions require users to engage with coding, which can pose a considerable obstacle. Organizations require human participation (Haleem et al., 2021) in conjunction with advanced technology, as this combination represents the future strength necessary for hyperautomating processes shown in Figure 4. Opting for a tool that removes this requirement can provide organizations with a competitive edge in the automation landscape. This meticulous selection process is what Gartner, a leading IT research organization, describes as "architecting for hyperautomation." It signifies that organizations must possess the capability to adapt their operations and supporting processes in response to changing demands and competitive pressures. So, future hyperautomation necessitates hyper-agile working practices and tools.

Figure 4. Future strength of hyperautomation in business process

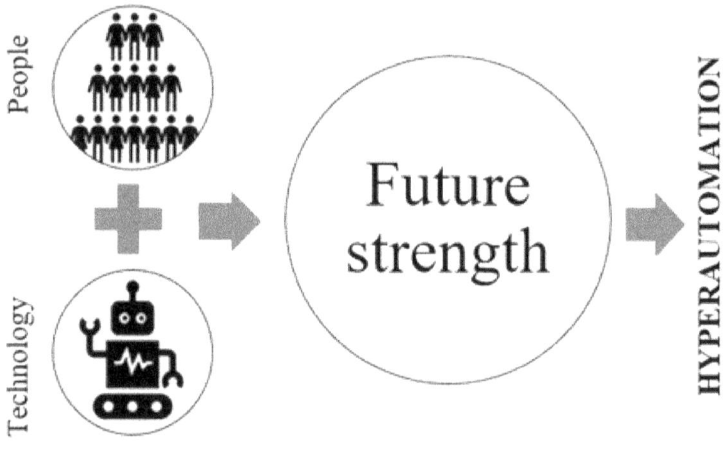

Source: Created by author(s)

By evaluation existing business processes and carefully selecting appropriate tools, organizations can effectively incorporate advanced automation and secure significant benefits. The first steps in embarking on the hyperautomation journey are illustrated in Figure 5. To begin with hyperautomation, companies must conduct an initial assessment and define their core objectives to identify automation opportunities in the existing process (George et al., 2023). It is necessary to identify repetitive and time-consuming tasks that could be improved through automation, and to identify the areas characterized by significant manual effort, frequent errors, or notable delays. Following the objectives, extensive research is required to identify tools and platforms that meet the specific needs of the current business and technology. Organizations can prioritize solutions that are user-friendly, scalable, offer strong interoperability with their current systems, and are easy for the team to use.

Businesses initiate a pilot project to evaluate the selected tools and technologies on a limited scale. This approach enables them to assess their effectiveness and make necessary adjustments prior to wider implementation. The businesses utilize feedback from the pilot project to enhance their strategy and continuously monitor outcomes and adjust to optimize the automation process. In addition, they implement training programs and invest in their development to equip their employees with the knowledge and skills to effectively use new automation tools that will facilitate a smoother transition and maximize the advantages of hyperautomation. Following the success of the pilot project, businesses gradually expanded their automation initiatives to other areas within the organization.

Figure 5. Steps for starting with hyperautomation strategy

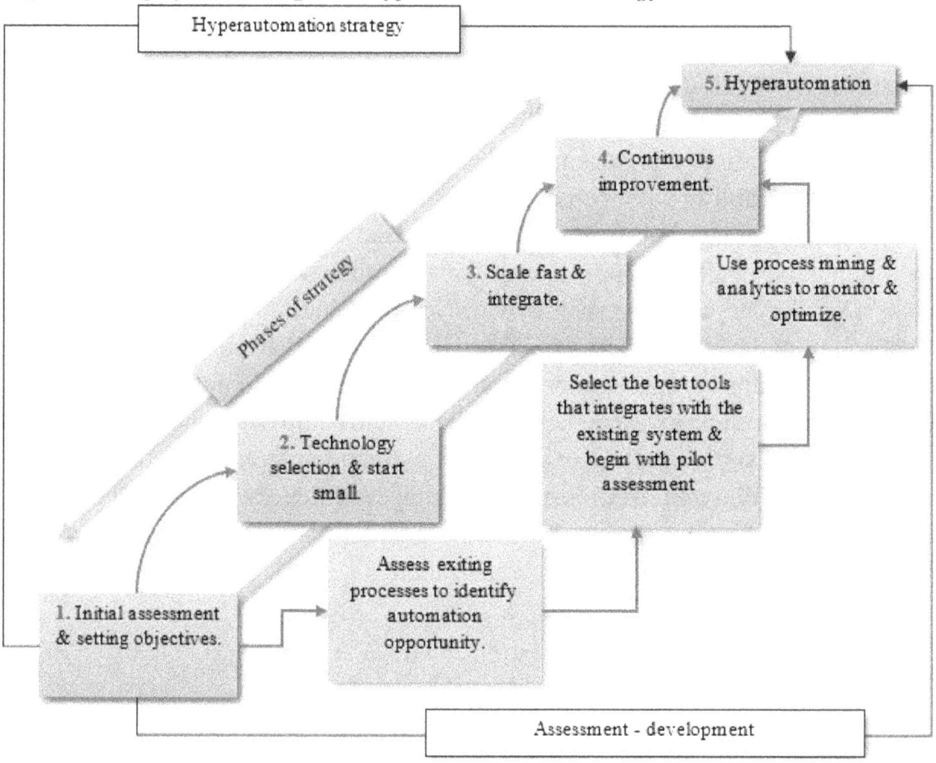

Source: Created by author(s).

Workflow of Hyperautomation and How It Works

Hyperautomation does not focus on a singular, predefined technology or tool; instead, it emphasizes the integration of enhanced intelligence and a comprehensive and systems-oriented strategy. A critical consideration is to determine the individuals or tools accountable for the automation process and the methodologies to be employed. Gartner, an IT research group, added the 'digital twin' idea to this consideration. In generally, the hyperautomation journey within an organization commences with the development of a digital twin, which serves as a virtual model illustrating the operational dynamics of the company's processes. This procedure is generated and refreshed automatically through the integration of process mining and task mining techniques. A brief of how hyperautomation workflow works is presented in Figure 6.

Figure 6. The sequential phases of workflow in hyperautomation.

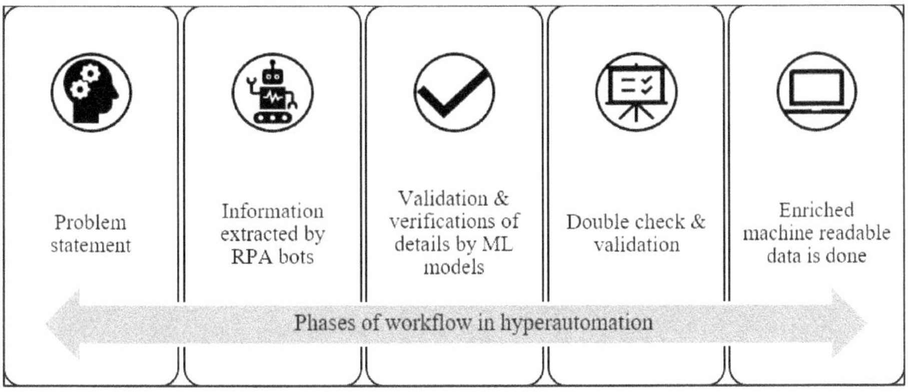

Source: Created by author, concept based on Haleem et al. (2021)

Hyperautomation allows the organization to enhance its understanding of the interrelationships among various problems, processes, and indicators, thereby elucidating how they collectively generate value. Additionally, it provides insights into the problem and how the implementation of hyperautomation may either augment this value or introduce potential challenges. After defining the problem, RPA is implemented to extract information. It enables the programming of virtual bots to handle repetitive tasks, frequently associated with back-office operations. However, the only application of RPA may not inherently support scalability and validation. So, hyperautomation framework requires other tools of no-code or low-code platforms for streamlining development processes. This is addressed by integrating RPA with AI, such as ML, that validates and verifies the automation process (Haleem et al., 2021). Accordingly, this allows enriched data and processes in organizations and enables human employees to allocate more time to engage in creative or complex activities within their organizations. The top ten use cases or examples of the application of hyperautomation and how it works are summarized in Table 4.

Table 4. Top ten hyperautomation examples and use cases in 2024

SL.	Use Cases or Examples	Applications
1	Data entry & processing	• Apply RPA and Optical Character Recognition (OCR) to digitally store, process and use to improve the quality of the service.
2	Supply chain management (SCM)	• Leveraging AI, RPA, ML automate manufacturing, production, and supply management. • Order processing, inventory management, logistics tracking, supplier management, and demand forecasting.
3	Customer service and support	• Automate customer interaction with pre-defined workflow and AI chatbot for instant response. • Enterprises can gain insights from employee communications to understand customer preferences and create personalized customer experiences. • Handling a high volume of inquiries simultaneously.
4	Data analytics and insights	• NLP algorithms can analyze unstructured data sources such as emails, customer feedback, or social media posts to extract relevant information. • Extract data from standardized forms, such as surveys, analyze, and improve the accuracy and speed of processing. • Automate data validation and verification.
5	Financial processes	• Streamline and optimize financial tasks, including invoice processing, expense management, and payment reconciliation, leading to increased efficiency, improved accuracy, and enhanced decision-making.
6	Document management	• Documents digitization. • Information extraction and validation. • Enrichment and routing.
7	Compliance and risk management	• Identify potential risks and use algorithms to detect patterns, and reduce risks. • Improve data security.
8	IT operations and management	• Enhance system performance through automated monitoring. • AI-driven monitoring tools observe system performance, network traffic, and log files in real-time.
9	Sales and marketing automation	• Apply ML and AI to manage customer relationships and track sales opportunities. • Analyzing customer information, tracking interactions, and managing the sales pipeline, thus predicts the market. • CRM platforms such as Salesforce, HubSpot, and Microsoft Dynamics provide a centralized database for managing customer interactions, leads, and opportunities.
10	Claims processing automation	• NLP, OCR, and ML to extract claims data from multiple sources, & formats, and verify them. • Share claim processing assessment with customers using chatbot autonomously. • Clearing execution- valid claims. • Detects fraud in real-time and generates alerts to help in decision-making.

Source: Summarized by author(s)

Transformation With Hyperautomation

- **Transformation of business process management (BPM)**

Hyperautomation possesses the capacity to profoundly alter business operations (George et al., 2023). Technologies such as process mining, task automation, and event processing empower organizations to achieve a holistic view of workflow dynamics across the enterprise (Szelągowski & Berniak-Woźny, 2023). This insight can be utilized to accelerate digital innovation and anticipate potential improvements. To effectively implement automation that boosts performance, it is crucial for organizations to cultivate a comprehensive understanding of the workflows involving personnel, implementation processes, and selection of techniques used in the systems (Szelągowski & Berniak-Woźny, 2023). Currently, traditional automation may not suffice to maintain a competitive edge. As organizations strive to optimize their business processes and enhance speed and agility (Latif, et al., 2023), improved connectivity throughout the enterprise becomes crucial for accelerating advancement, which can be fulfilled by hyperautomation.

Hyperautomation improves operational efficiency and boosts automation in business processes by automating routine and manual activities (e.g., production chains, workflows, marketing processes, etc.). This advancement not only increases productivity but also reduces labor costs and errors. It facilitates collaboration between humans and robots, enabling them to jointly handle tasks ranging from simple operations to intricate business processes.

An automated customer service chatbot can be a remarkable addition to alter business processes. It provides immediate answers to inquiries, which not only increases customer satisfaction but also frees up employees. It enables organizations to scale their operations and respond to changing market dynamics by rapidly changing automated workflows. By eliminating low-value manual tasks and quickly delivering insights and data, hyperautomation enables businesses to make timely, informed decisions and adapt to market fluctuations. This capability enables organizations to adopt data-driven strategies. However, organizations must also work towards the integration of functional and process silos to enhance and automate their business processes. The transformation from a simple business path to hyperautomation is shown in Figure 7.

Figure 7. Business paths to hyperautomation

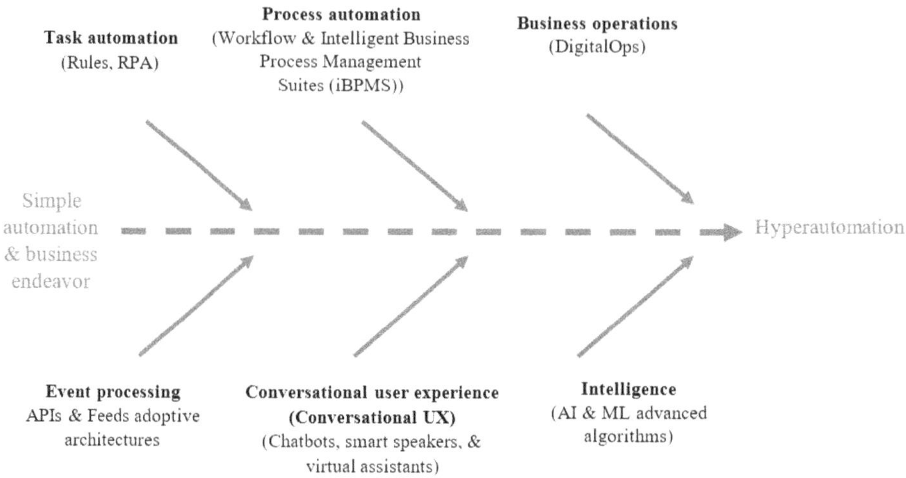

Source: Created by author(s) based on the concept of Gartner

- **Transformation of SCM functions and capabilities**

The implications of hyperautomation within the SC are far-reaching and complex. By leveraging advanced technologies, companies can realize numerous benefits that improve the overall efficiency. According to Gartner (2021), more than 70% of companies are involved in various automation initiatives; however, these initiatives often operate independently and are not aligned with overarching business goals. As a result, achieving a state of SC autonomy requires a cohesive strategy that leverages intelligent technologies to automate as many processes as possible. This approach allows hyperautomation in SCM to benefit from multiple domains. The top SC technology trends that will reshape the industry's operations over the next several years are shown in Figure 8.

The importance of hyperautomation is paramount and impacts many factors of SCM. End-to-end visibility within the SC has become an essential factor in maximizing returns in the SCM. The level of visibility relies on the strategic gathering of data, which acts as a dynamic tool of SC transparency, illuminating present conditions and guiding future actions. This results in a more efficient flow of goods with minimized delays. Hyperautomation is pivotal in facilitating this visibility. By leveraging IoT devices for real-time insights, digital twins for comprehensive monitoring, and integrated systems for seamless collaboration with AI, SC managers can obtain real-time insights into their operations. This capability enables them to pinpoint potential bottlenecks, enhance transportation routes, track assets, assess conditions, predict, and make informed and data-driven decisions.

Figure 8. Top supply chain technology trends over the next several years.

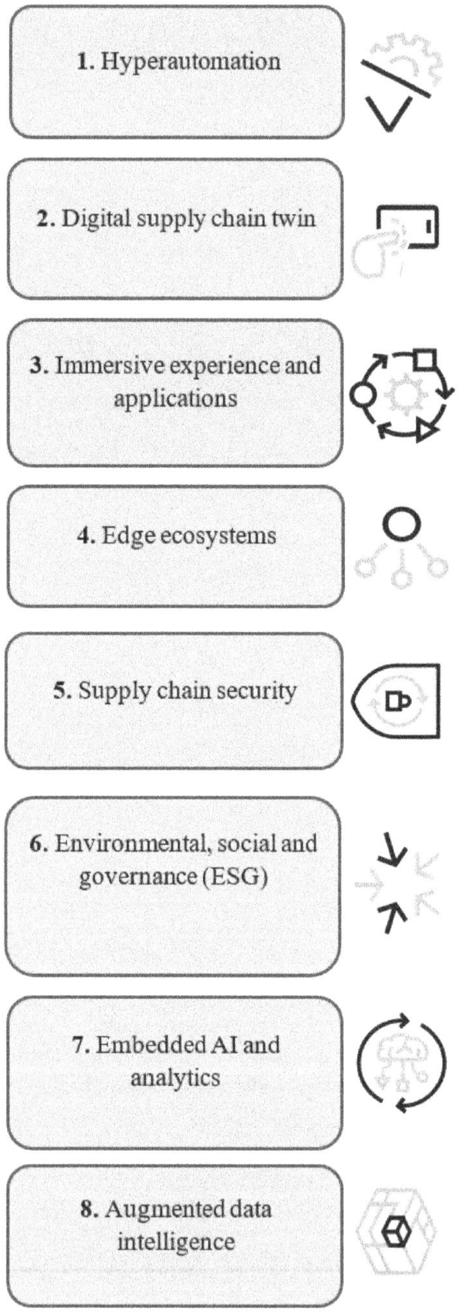

Source: Created by author based on Gartner (2022)

Hyperautomation improves demand forecasting capability in SC using predictive analytics. The ML algorithm is capable of examining historical sales data, market dynamics, and external influences precisely. The accurate anticipation enables organizations to proactively modify their production and inventory levels, thereby minimizing the likelihood of stockouts or mitigating disruptions. This enables these organizations to adopt a more predictive approach, allowing them to proactively identify, assess, analyze, and mitigate risks. So, investment in analytics will effectively tackle the prevalent issue of inaccuracies in demand estimations, which are frequently attributed to insufficient visibility across the SC.

In addition, AI-driven systems will facilitate real-time monitoring of inventory levels, automatically initiating reorders when stock falls below predetermined thresholds. This not only alleviates the manual workload associated with inventory management but also guarantees the availability of the appropriate products at optimal times, thereby reducing lead times and enhancing customer satisfaction. Furthermore, hyperautomation is fundamentally transforming quality control and assurance within manufacturing processes, effectively tackling persistent challenges. By utilizing cutting-edge technologies— AI, ML, and RPA—manufacturers are overhauling their quality management systems, leading to superior product quality, lower costs, and improved customer satisfaction. A summary of the SCM functions through the integration of various integrated tools is illustrated in Table 5.

Table 5. Ways hyperautomation will transformation SCM

NO.	Capabilities/Task	Functions/Ways in Brief
1	Operational function	• Automating repetitive and time-consuming tasks. • Inventory management, route optimization, and shipment tracking.
2	Supply chain visibility and transparency	• End-to-end SC visibility. • Enables organizations to recognize bottlenecks and implement proactive strategies to prevent disruptions. • Data analytics and real-time monitoring facilitate improved insight into SC operations, thereby augmenting transparency.
3	Customer experience	• Real-time visibility of shipment status and delivery. • Anticipating customer needs, and improving support processes.
4	Predictive analytics	• Utilize predictive and prescriptive analytics and AI-driven insights to facilitate real-time decision-making. • Leveraging ML algorithms and real-time data to address potential risks and optimize operations. • Enable organizations to anticipate and mitigate SC disruptions.
5	Operational costs	• Automating routine tasks and optimizing processes, reducing labor costs, energy consumption, and material waste.
6	Agility and responsiveness	• Facilitates greater agility and responsiveness to adapt quickly to changing market dynamics and customer demands.
7	IoT Integration	• Improved asset tracking, condition assessment, and predictive maintenance with IoT technologies.

continued on following page

Table 5. Continued

NO.	Capabilities/Task	Functions/Ways in Brief
8	Autonomous supply chain operations (ASCO)	• Enable organizations to anticipate and mitigate SC disruptions. • ASCO driven by hyperautomation envisions a future to complete tasks such as transportation, warehouse operations, and inventory management with intelligent systems and robotics.
9	Blockchain-enabled transparency	• Leveraging blockchain for secure and immutable record-keeping. • Integration of blockchain technology reduces the risk of fraud and counterfeiting.
10	Human-machine collaboration	• Shift towards enabling seamless collaboration between humans and machines • Leverage the strengths of both human expertise and automated capabilities
11	Enhanced quality control & productivity	• ML algorithms identify defects and deviations from quality standards. • Allows the workforce to focus on higher-value tasks.
12	Flexibility and Scalability	• Hypretautomation is flexible and scalable to make it suitable for both small manufacturers and large enterprises.

Hyperautomation in the Production Process and Manufacturing

Hyperautomation is fundamentally altering the dynamic landscape of manufacturing. This strategy integrates AI, ML, and RPA, thereby transforming production process and enhanes efficiency to unprecedented heights. It elevates the concept of automation by significantly reducing the manual involvement. This advancement enables manufacturers to effortlessly automate complex workflows, creating opportunities to extend automation initiatives across the enterprise and develop intelligent solutions.

- **Transforming production processes**

Hyperautomation transforms production processes in four distinct ways, including ● streamlining workflows, ● leveraging real-time monitoring and control, ● equipping predictive maintenance, and ● employing data-driven quality management. The transformation of production processes is summarized in Figure 9.

Streamlining workflows elevates the concept of automation by significantly reducing the need for manual intervention in repetitive tasks while integrating intelligent capabilities into processes. It allows manufacturers to effectively automate intricate workflows, thereby providing a pathway to expand automation initiatives and develop intelligent solutions. This encompasses the automation of quality control, procurement, inventory management, and quality assurance. Thus, manufacturers are able to execute tasks with greater speed and precision than human operators, leading to marked improvements in reductions of production time and costs.

Figure 9. Transforming production processes

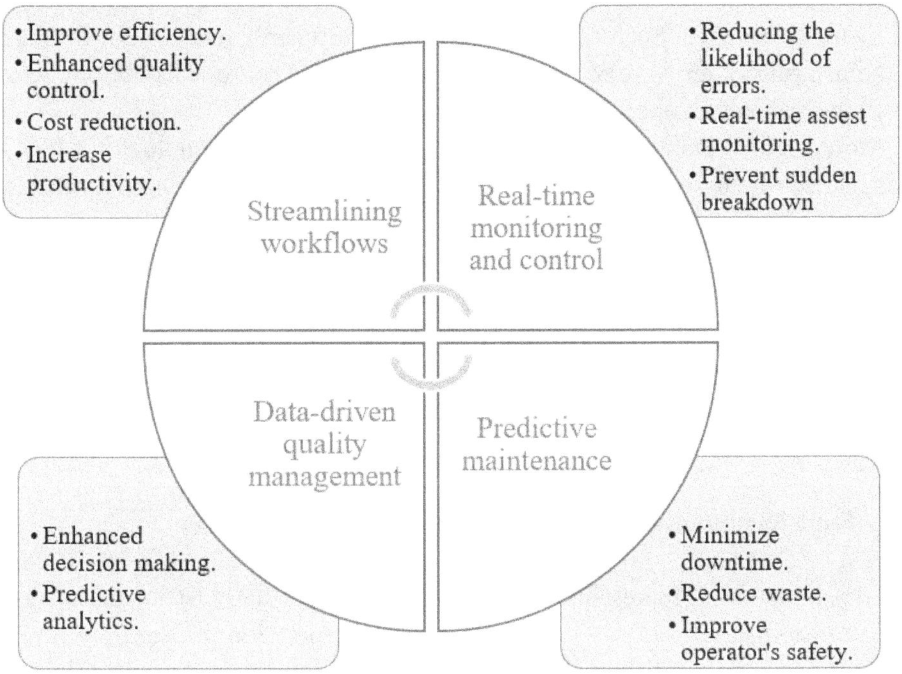

Source: Created by author(s)

The IoT is integral to the development of the manufacturing ecosystem, facilitating the real-time monitoring of production processes. It yields essential insights, allows for prompt adaptations to dynamic conditions, and promotes an automated response to contemporary challenges. Such real-time insight improves manufacturing by removing the necessity for manual reporting and significantly reducing the potential likelihood of errors. Additionally, real-time asset monitoring serves as an effective strategy for prolonging the operational lifespan of machinery. Advanced manufacturing facilities, equipped with costly machinery, can enhance equipment utilization through real-time condition assessments. For example, a state-of-the-art automotive manufacturing facility employs predictive maintenance techniques to assess the condition of its robotic arms, ensuring optimal performance and averting unforeseen malfunctions.

Predictive maintenance, on the other hand, is a forward-looking strategy that uses ML and data analytics to anticipate equipment failures before they occur, leveraging ML and data analytics (Goni et al., 2024). By continuously monitoring equipment conditions and analyzing data to detect patterns and irregularities, organizations can effectively time their maintenance activities to prevent failures. This approach not only extends the life of industrial assets but also minimizes operational disruptions and increases the efficiency of maintenance operations. The integration of hyperautomation facilitates the use of analytical tools that can identify and predict potential problems in advance. Such a proactive stance significantly reduces downtime, as manufacturing systems are equipped to analyze data and address disruptions before they adversely affect operations.

Moreover, hyperautomation facilitates a data-centric methodology for quality management by harnessing the capabilities of AI and ML to scrutinize extensive datasets and derive meaningful insights. This methodology empowers manufacturers to make well-informed decisions and refine their quality control mechanisms. By integrating AI, RPA, and IoT technologies, manufacturers can establish a cohesive ecosystem that improves and automates quality control operations. The adoption of these strategies can result in notable advancements in product quality and a decrease in defects and recalls. For example, AI-driven automated visual inspections can detect even minor deviations from established quality standards.

- **Transforming the manufacturing system**

Hyperautomation represents one of the novel concepts that bolster manufacturing autonomy (Kusiak, 2024). It encompasses the incorporation of data from diverse origins to develop a holistic understanding of manufacturing operations. This data undergoes real-time processing and analysis through the application of AI and ML techniques, facilitating the extraction of actionable insights. RPA is employed to streamline repetitive and rule-based activities within the manufacturing sector, including data entry, inventory oversight, and quality assurance. Moreover, it collaborates with human workers to enhance both the efficiency and precision of manufacturing processes. In addition, RPA bots can be programmed to automatically validate the data and facilitate predictive maintenance through the integration of sensors and AI algorithms to assess the condition of equipment. This forward-looking strategy allows manufacturers to detect potential problems prior to their development into more significant issues. Figure 10 shows the process hyperautomation works in the manufacturing industry, while the integration of several technologies is shown in Table 6.

Figure 10. Process of hyperautomation in manufacturing industry

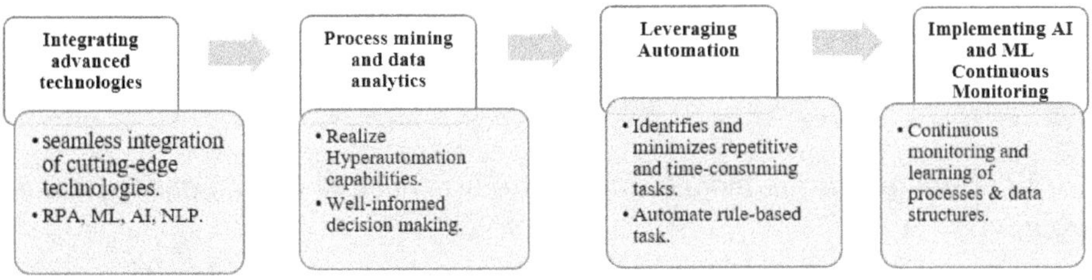

Source: Created by author(s)

Table 6. Methodologies to reshape manufacturing industry

SL.	Methodologies/Technologies	How it Works in Manufacturing Process
1	Technological Integration	• Incorporates AI, RPA, and IoT, creating a synergistic ecosystem. • Streamlines manufacturing and makes it adaptable to all businesses.
2	Robotic Process Automation (RPA)	• Identifies manual and repetitive tasks. • Ensures accuracy, efficiency, and reduce human intervention in manufacturing workflows.
3	AI-Powered Decision-Making	• Analyzes data and optimize resource allocation through data-driven and strategic decisions. • Empowers users with intelligent and robust decision-making.
4	IoT Connectivity and Real-Time Insights	• Enable real-time data monitoring in manufacturing processes. • Facilitate immediate responses to changing environments.
5	Predictive Analytics for Proactive Maintenance	• Applies analytical tools to identify & predict potential issues before they occur. • This proactive approach minimizes downtime and resolves the disruptions before they impact.
6	Continuous Monitoring and Adaptability	• Monitoring and learning of processes & data structures • Makes the required adjustments when needed.

Additionally, the advancements in hyperautomation are dependent on the digitization and modeling of the foundational processes (Kusiak, 2024). The concept of a digital twin plays a significant role in this context. However, the characteristics of the models differ from those found in conventional automation frameworks (Kusiak, 2024). In traditional automation, the models associated with digital twins range from physics-based to logic-based and data-driven approaches. Conversely, the digital twin models utilized in hyperautomation may integrate optimization techniques, process models (Kusiak, 2020), as well as data-driven and decision-making models (Kusiak, 2023). The integration of digital twins with predictive maintenance enables manufacturers to evaluate processes prior to their implementation and to strategize for the installation of new equipment. Hardware automation requires the provision of software to increase the economic value (Kusiak, 1990), which is not possible without enhancing manufacturing systems (Kusiak, 2024). Figure 11 shows the manufacturing models and digital twins of how the automation process in manufacturing converts into hyperautomation.

Figure 11. Manufacturing models and digital twins in automation and hyperautomation

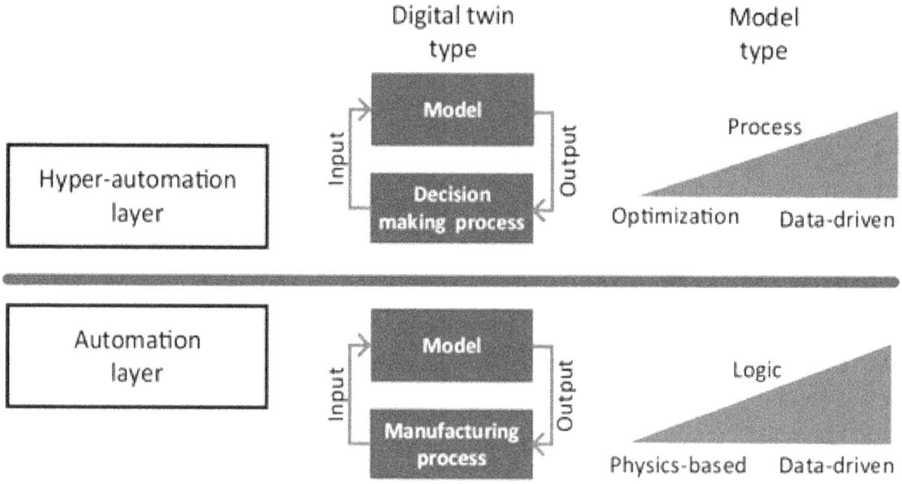

Source: Kusiak (2024)

- **Hyperautomation in improving quality control and assurance**

Hyperautomation is transforming quality control and assurance within manufacturing processes, tackling enduring challenges, and delivering unmatched accuracy and efficiency. By utilizing leading technologies, manufacturers are reengineering their quality management systems, leading to superior product quality, lower costs, and increased customer satisfaction. Enhancing quality control and assurance can be achieved through the implementation of AI-driven inspection, data-driven management, and the reduction of defects. Conventional manual inspection techniques demonstrate inconsistency and inefficiency in contemporary manufacturing settings. Human inspectors may experience fatigue, resulting in defect detection rates. Additionally, manual inspection procedures frequently lead to bottlenecks in rapid assembly lines and result in elevated labor expenses.

Thus, a data-driven methodology for quality management facilitates the analysis of extensive datasets to derive meaningful insights. This strategy empowers manufacturers to make well-informed decisions and refine their quality control processes, contributing to enhanced decision-making, predictive analytics, and real-time monitoring. The adoption of these strategies can result in substantial enhancements in product quality and a decrease in defects and recalls.

Hyperautomation in the Logistics Function

Hyperautomation is fundamentally transforming the logistics sector, prompting significant alterations in warehouse management, transportation, fleet operations, and so on. It affects all aspects of logistics, leading to increased operational efficiency, cost reduction, and enhanced decision-making. To maintain market position, it is imperative for companies to adopt innovations as the logistics environment progresses. To ascertain how these developments can be advantageous, it is essential to leverage the capabilities of hyperautomation in order to establish a position of leadership in the logistics revolution. Figure 12 shows the basic functions of logistics and the ways in which these functions can be hyperautomated.

Figure 12. Fundamental logistics processes to be hyperautomated

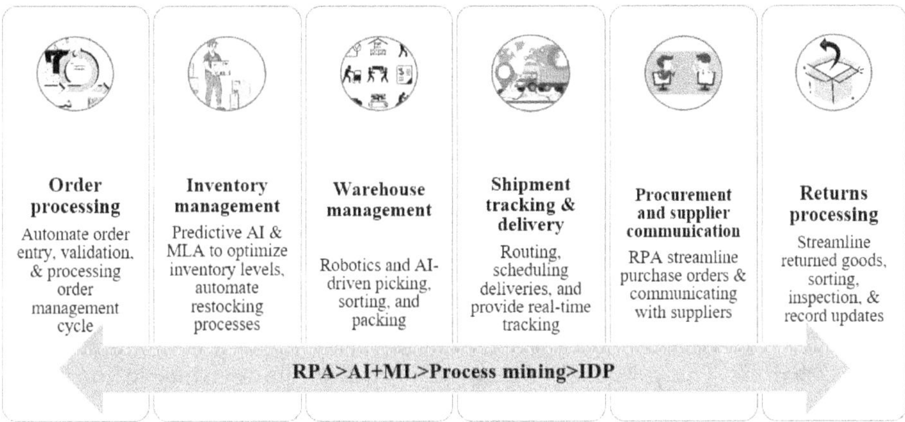

Source: Created by author(s)

Thus, hyperautomation ecosystem in logistics includes numerous functions and the core technologies enabling the synergy of technologies that transform logistics operations. It leverages next-generation technologies to make operations more resilient and agile. Logistics operations, including warehouse operations, transportation and fleet management, risk management, route optimization, and so on, are expected to be hyperautomated. The hyperautomation function in logistics management is summarized in Table 7.

- ***Intelligent warehouse operations:*** It employs computer vision for quality control and AI-driven inventory optimization to inspect products, thereby ensuring that they meet the requisite quality standards. One of the primary advantages of utilizing computer vision in quality control is its ability to conduct uninterrupted and unrelenting inspections on a 24/7 basis. In contrast to human inspectors, who may be susceptible to fatigue or a decline in focus, AI-driven vision systems are capable of continuous operation, enabling the real-time analysis of products to detect flaws that might otherwise be overlooked by human observers. This not only enhances safety but also generates significant savings in labor costs for organizations. Furthermore, AI-driven inventory optimization employs sophisticated data analysis techniques to predict future demand with remarkable accuracy, thereby streamlining the inventory audit process.
- ***Digital twins in warehousing:*** Digital twins have become an invaluable asset for enhancing warehouse operations. A digital twin of a warehouse serves as a precise digital replica of the physical warehouse environment, accurately reflecting its real-world attributes. This technology creates a secure platform for exploring various scenarios, thereby enabling thorough system analysis, optimization, and experimentation. The significance of digital twins in the context of warehousing is rooted in their ability to combine visualization and diagnostic functionalities with software applications. This integration allows warehouse managers to evaluate the effects of proposed modifications to warehouse layouts prior to their actual implementation.
- ***Transportation and fleet management:*** Hyperautomation is poised to revolutionize transportation and fleet management. The advent of autonomous vehicles (AVs) is poised to challenge conventional business practices, expenses, and economic frameworks across various modes of transport, including land, sea, and air. The principal advantage of AVs in the logistics sector is their substantial improvement in safety. The removal of human elements from the driving equation allows for the mitigation of human errors. These vehicles are equipped with an array of sensors and cameras, enabling them to navigate roadways with enhanced safety. Moreover, predictive maintenance of fleet optimization leverages data-driven insights to foresee potential vehicle issues before they occur. To implement it effectively, fleet operations managers require access to real-time, tailored telematics information for all classes of vehicles.
- ***Supply chain risk management (SCRM):*** SCRM is the strategic process by which organizations identify, evaluate, and mitigate risks present throughout their operations. In recent years, numerous companies have encountered substantial difficulties as a result of unforeseen vulnerabilities and disruptions.

This has led to a number of product recalls, with associated costs reaching hundreds of millions of dollars across a range of sectors. Hyperautomation in organizations applies a strategic approach and proactive mitigation in vulnerability analysis based on predictive analytics that led to managing risk.

- ***Scenario planning and simulation:*** Scenario planning enables organizations to strategically enhance supply chain (SC) resilience by preparing for significant disruptions. This approach offers a forward-looking perspective, promoting SC diversification through a "power of two" strategy to mitigate risks and integrate redundancy. By evaluating multiple scenarios, firms can assess alternatives, identify optimization opportunities, and align decisions with operational objectives such as cost efficiency, customer service, risk management, and sustainability. Implementing such simulations demands substantial computational resources, often facilitated by Software as a Service (SaaS) models. Sensitivity analysis further strengthens SC design by assessing scenario resilience against variable fluctuations. Collectively, these advanced methodologies in risk assessment and scenario planning allow organizations to develop robust and efficient SC networks capable of withstanding disruptions while maintaining performance.

Table 7. Hyperautomation function in logistics management

SL.	Logistics Operations Activities/Capabilities	Effective Hyperautomation Functions
1	Intelligent warehouse operations	• Computer vision for quality control. • AI-driven inventory optimization. • Automated packing & picking system (APPS).
2	Smart transportation and fleet operations	• Autonomous vehicles in logistics. • Predictive maintenance of fleet optimization. • Real-time route optimization. • Dynamic adjustment. • Better planning for improved efficiency.
3	SC risk assessment and mitigation	• Strategic approach. • Proactive mitigation. • Vulnerability analysis.
4	Digital twins in warehousing	• Virtual replica. • Enhanced tracking. • Risk-free optimization. • Agile response.
5	Scenario planning and simulation	• Strategic view. • Optimization. • Network diversification. • Sensitivity analysis.
6	Data-driven SC planning	• Advanced demand forecasting • Transform big data into smart predictions.

SWOT ANALYSIS OF HYPERAUTOMATION

Hyperautomation has emerged as a key concept that has bolstered manufacturing autonomy and SCM while focusing on extending automation beyond the traditional automation layer (Kusiak, 2024). Nevertheless, it has its weaknesses, challenges, and opportunities. In order to assess its shortcomings and highlight the prospects, a SWOT analysis is shown in Figure 13.

Strength and Benefits

The strengths and potentials of hyperautomation both in SCM and manufacturing are of utmost significance. As the transportation and logistics sector grows in complexity, businesses are progressively adopting it to enhance operational efficiency and achieve improved business outcomes. Hyperautomation facilitates process optimization, addresses narrow profit margins, and enhances visibility throughout the SC network. Companies can utilize AI-powered process models to refine workflows among various departments, human personnel, RPA bots, and other intelligent technologies to foster superior business results.

Thus, hyperautomation:

- Enhances collaboration among team members
- Brings a better return on investment (ROI)
- Reduces operational costs
- Improves data-driven decision-making
- Increases agility by providing quicker, richer, and precise insights
- Optimizes workflow allocation by ensuring repetitive tasks
- Improves customer experience

Weakness

Aside from offering potential advantages, hyperautomation also has its limitations. Inadequate data quality and insufficient technical expertise can obstruct automation initiatives. Thus, it is essential to invest in data management, data cleansing, and employee skill enhancement. So, establishment of data governance policies is vital for maintaining high-quality data. Additionally, investing in no-code automation solutions can minimize reliance on developers, thereby addressing skill shortages and conserving valuable resources that could be allocated more effectively. Moreover, the increasing variety of automation tools and platforms may complicate the selection process and integration of technologies. Therefore, conducting comprehensive market research and seeking advice from experts and IT partners can assist organizations in identifying and coordinating the most appropriate tools for their requirements.

Opportunities

While hyperautomation presents certain limitations and challenges, it offers opportunities to extend automation beyond tasks governed by clearly defined business rules, thereby enhancing value in SCM and manufacturing. However, it necessitates both scalability and readiness to embrace digital transformation. Organizations must engage technology specialists to collaborate on the ideation, implementation, and management of automation solutions. Furthermore, prioritizing the upskilling and reskilling of employees is essential to ensure they are well-acquainted with the automation tools and can effectively leverage new technological opportunities. Additionally, process mining plays a vital role in identifying current business processes and determining which should be optimized for maximum efficiency.

Figure 13. SWOT analysis

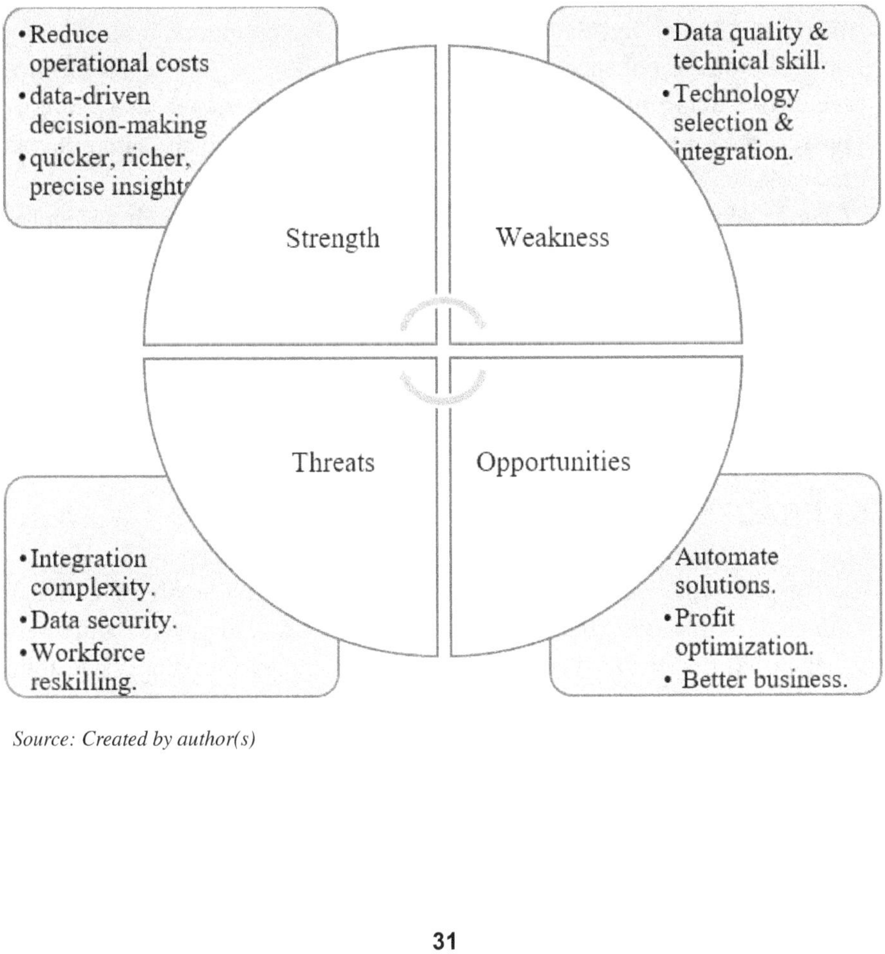

Source: Created by author(s)

Threats and Challenges

Despite the numerous benefits and opportunities, the challenges associated with the implementation of hyperautomation in the industry also pose some threats. The integration of technologies, including RPA, AI, ML, chatbots, poses significant challenges to their simultaneous application. Organizations need to carefully select technologies that can smoothly integrate with their existing infrastructure. As a result, they must either invest in training or hire professionals to gain the necessary skills. Some key challenges and considerations include:

- *Integration Complexity:* integration of various technologies and systems to realize hyperautomation can present significant complexities and challenges. Organizations must guarantee a smooth integration within their current infrastructure and processes to prevent disruptions and compatibility concerns.
- *Data Security and Privacy*: as organizations increasingly leverage advanced technologies and data-driven insights, they must prioritize the security and privacy of data. The processes of collecting, storing, and utilizing sensitive information must comply with stringent security protocols.
- *Workforce Reskilling*: the implementation of hyperautomation may compel organizations to enhance the skills of their workforce. This calls for investment in training and development initiatives to guarantee that employees possess the essential competencies to collaborate effectively with automated technologies.
- *Change Management*: the successful implementation of such an approach necessitates a transformation in organizational culture and effective change management strategies to secure the support of stakeholders and employees.
- *Scalability and Flexibility*: as the dynamics of businesses continue to change, organizations must ensure that their hyperautomation solutions possess the scalability and flexibility necessary to meet evolving business requirements.

BEST PRACTICES OF HYPERAUTOMATION

This chapter provided a comprehensive overview of the evolving concept of hyperautomation through a theoretical lens. The goal was to provide a theoretical framework for its implications for SCM, logistics, and manufacturing. Thus, it illustrates how hyperautomation is poised to revolutionize business processes, enhance SCM capabilities, and transform manufacturing and logistics in the 21st century. It also identifies the strengths, weaknesses, opportunities, and challenges associated with implementing hyperautomation. In doing so, this chapter contributes significantly to the theoretical discourse surrounding the concept and positions it as a new frontier in SCM and manufacturing.

Hyperautomation, which integrates technologies, has recently become a transformative force (Kaswan et al., 2025). The existing literature on hyperautomation indicates the need for a more comprehensive exploration of the topic. Haleem et al. (2021) explored the subject in depth, focusing in particular on the significant role of sensors in improving hyperautomation, while others highlighted its impact on business processes (Szelągowski & Berniak-Woźny, 2023). In addition, it can fulfill jobs rather than executing tasks (Lasso-Rodriguez & Winkler, 2020). This chapter synthesized the concept based on the contemporary trends enumerated in research papers, case studies, and online reports. As such, it not only illustrates a means of transformation but also demonstrates its impact on transforming service quality. It is imperative that business leaders actively engage with hyperautomation to maintain their competitive edge in an increasingly digital marketplace. This emerging technology is fundamentally changing the way organizations operate by enabling the optimization of internal processes that are typically performed manually. By automating repetitive tasks, streamlining workflows, and applying intelligent algorithms, hyperautomation enables companies to expand their capabilities, focus on strategic goals, and deliver superior value to their customers (George et al., 2023).

A key implementation of hyperautomation in SCM involves demand forecasting, where AI-driven algorithms process historical sales data, market trends, and external variables such as weather patterns to generate precise demand projections. Machine learning (ML) models enhance forecast accuracy by integrating real-time and historical datasets, enabling businesses to optimize inventory levels proactively. This data-driven approach reduces stockouts and overstocking, lowering holding costs and improving operational efficiency. Unlike traditional SCM methods that depend on error-prone manual processes—such as spreadsheet-based tracking and human intervention—hyperautomation leverages predictive analytics and intelligent automation to enhance decision-making. By adopting these advanced technologies, organizations can achieve cost optimization, streamline operations, and elevate customer satisfaction through responsive and data-informed supply chain strategies.

Therefore, the next step for managers is to focus on a specialized technology for SCM and logistics efficiency that provides a straightforward, low-effort approach to digitizing business processes. This tool should not only provide an objective assessment but also allow for optimal customization of the implementation strategy when selecting hyperautomation technology. This is especially important for the manufacturing industry, which typically operates with very limited resources and can't afford to make unsuccessful investments.

Hyperautomation in manufacturing focuses on automating and integrating multiple tools to improve and accelerate manufacturing operations. In this context, machines are using AI and ML in conjunction with IoT and robotics to develop highly automated and efficient manufacturing software solutions. Key elements of this approach include predictive maintenance, collaborative robots (cobots), supply chain optimization, RPA, digital twins, etc.

In addition, hyperautomation is instrumental in reducing operational costs by automating routine and repetitive tasks in logistics systems. In particular, RPA can autonomously manage functions such as order processing, invoice processing, and shipment tracking. This not only speeds up these processes but also significantly minimizes the potential for errors, resulting in cost savings. According to Deloitte (2020), organizations that adopt RPA can anticipate cost reductions of up to 30% in specific processes. By scrutinizing data from diverse sources, these technologies can pinpoint inefficiencies and propose measures to cut costs, such as optimizing logistics route planning or automating supplier negotiations. Furthermore, it promotes a more responsive SC capable of rapidly adjusting to fluctuations in demand or disruptions.

The analysis indicates that global SCM, logistics, and BPM can effectively utilize hyperautomation to enhance decision-making. This approach offers organizations the chance to embrace digital transformation in their operational practices, thereby creating a strong basis for future innovation (Kaswan et al., 2025). Accordingly, hyperautomation reflects the notion that what is currently disruptive will eventually stabilize tomorrow (Deloitte, 2020).

Hyperautomation Adoption Challenges and Mitigation Strategies

While hyperautomation offers significant efficiency and agility advantages, its implementation presents notable challenges. Resistance often stems from legacy systems and entrenched workflows, as employees may perceive automation as a threat to established roles (Beverungen et al., 2021). Mitigating this requires proactive strategies, including transparent communication, leadership involvement, and cross-functional collaboration. Early employee engagement can reduce apprehension and encourage adoption, while dedicated governance teams ensure alignment with organizational objectives. Financially, the substantial upfront costs—particularly for small and midsize enterprises—pose a barrier, despite potential long-term gains. A phased deployment approach or pilot programs can help validate benefits and mitigate risks before full-scale adoption. By balancing technological integration with change management, firms can navigate these challenges while maximizing hyperautomation's transformative potential.

Ethical challenges, particularly around algorithmic bias, decision opacity, and displacement of human judgment, also arise when hypoautomation is not carefully monitored, which can amplify biases and lead to unfair outcomes, especially in areas such as procurement or workforce management (Mittelstadt et al., 2016). Therefore, companies need to implement AI-driven, fairness-conscious models to ensure equitable outcomes. In addition, ethical review boards or AI ethics committees can provide oversight in sensitive decision-making areas, particularly hiring or vendor selection. Transparency protocols, such as explainable AI frameworks and user-centric dashboards, should be standardized to maintain accountability and trust (Wachter et al., 2017).

The adoption of hyperautomation in supply chain systems necessitates a fundamental workforce transformation. As rule-based, repetitive tasks become increasingly automated, this shift has simultaneously rendered some roles obsolete while generating new opportunities, including positions like automation strategists, RPA developers, and data governance specialists (Di Battista et al., 2023). This dynamic evolution highlights the critical importance of upskilling initiatives to maintain workforce adaptability and digital proficiency. Furthermore, employee psychological well-being, particularly concerns over job stability and diminished morale, must be addressed, as these factors can hinder both individual productivity and organizational resilience (Latif, et al., 2023). To mitigate such challenges, organizations should prioritize transparent communication and participatory change management approaches to cultivate trust and collaboration throughout the transition period (Ahmad et al., 2022).

Despite its capabilities, human insight cannot be excluded when adopting hyperautomation, as certain decisions involving contextual understanding, ethical reasoning, or emotional intelligence are best made by humans. Human oversight can ensure nuanced and responsible decisions in scenarios such as supplier conflict resolution and strategic sourcing decisions. Over-reliance on automation can also lead to blind spots, where anomalies go undetected due to system rigidity. In such cases, a balanced approach includes "human-in-the-loop" models, where automation supports human decision-making but does not replace it (Davenport & Rajeev, 2018).

The adoption of hyperautomation exhibits considerable variation across nations and sectors, influenced by economic, technological, and regulatory factors. Developed economics, including the United States, Germany, and Japan, demonstrate accelerated integration due to elevated labor expenses, robust technological frameworks, and conducive policy measures. Conversely, emerging markets such as India, Brazil, and Indonesia are leveraging hyperautomation as a strategic mechanism to bypass traditional developmental stages, enhancing operational efficiency and global market positioning—exemplified by India's Digital India campaign, which has spurred automation in logistics and public administration. Sectorally, industries like manufacturing, retail, and logistics lead in implementation, driven by the demand for operational efficiency in repetitive, high-volume tasks. In contrast, healthcare and education exhibit measured adoption, prioritizing ethical considerations and regulatory compliance alongside innovation. To facilitate broader adoption, particularly in developing regions, policymakers should implement fiscal incentives, skill development programs, and regulatory sandboxes to encourage experimentation. Collaborative initiatives between public and private entities can mitigate infrastructural and skill deficiencies by promoting localized research, technological literacy, and cost-effective solutions. Furthermore, international cooperation via industry consortia can enhance knowledge dissemination and standardization, enabling multinational corporations to deploy unified automation systems while adhering to regional legal frameworks (UNCTAD, 2021). Such coordinated efforts are critical for fostering equitable and sustainable automation advancements globally.

While automation can lead to more efficient use of resources and less waste through real-time analytics and predictive maintenance, it also raises significant environmental concerns. For example, edge computing devices not only consume more energy but also contribute to carbon emissions (Strubell et al., 2020). These concerns can be addressed while integrating green automation strategies by selecting energy-efficient devices, optimizing data center utilization through cloud-based platforms, and implementing edge computing to reduce transmission loads (Strubell et al., 2020). From a resiliency perspective, organizations should implement real-time monitoring, predictive analytics, and scenario planning tools to anticipate disruptions and dynamically adjust supply chain configuration.

Implications

This chapter extends its implications to SCM, business processes, and manufacturing, offering theoretical and practical insights. The analysis yields significant contributions to existing literature by enhancing comprehension of hyperautomation—its definition, operational mechanisms, and functional applications. Specifically, it examines its transformative effects on business operations, logistics, and production efficiency, thereby enriching the theoretical framework guiding industrial strategies. By elucidating hyperautomation's role in optimizing manufacturing processes, this chapter provides actionable insights for industry practitioners while advancing scholarly discourse on digital transformation in operational contexts. These findings underscore the technology's potential to redefine productivity and strategic decision-making.

A key contribution of this research lies in its conceptual framework, which delineates a phased approach for implementing hyperautomation strategies. This framework offers operations managers and manufacturers foundational guidance on adoption pathways, supported by empirical findings that clarify hyperautomation's structural dynamics. By bridging theoretical and practical dimensions, the study advances scholarly discourse on intelligent automation solutions while equipping industry practitioners with actionable insights for strategic deployment, thereby enriching both academic and applied perspectives on digital transformation in operational environments.

Third, following the conceptual mapping, this study primarily focused on providing manufacturers, practitioners, and managers with advanced intelligent tools and a holistic systems-oriented approach by detailing its functionality and workflow. The sequential phases of the hyperautomation workflow outlined in this study will deepen managers' understanding of various problems and processes and facilitate scalability and validation through the application of RPA and AI. As a result, the workflow illustrated in this study will clarify how it collectively creates value for future automation initiatives.

This study, subsequent to conceptual mapping, emphasizes equipping manufacturers, practitioners, and managers with sophisticated intelligent tools and a comprehensive systems-oriented framework by elucidating its operational mechanisms and workflow. The delineated sequential stages of the hyperautomation process enhance managerial comprehension of diverse challenges and procedures while promoting scalability and validation through the integration of RPA and AI. Consequently, the proposed workflow demonstrates its potential to generate value for forthcoming automation endeavors.

While hyperautomation remains an emerging concept, the findings of this chapter contribute to a more robust conceptual foundation for future research. By systematically examining key logistics functions and processes, this chapter expands the applicability of hyperautomation in logistics and SCM. Additionally, the analysis of hyperautomation's roles in logistics management enhances managerial strategic competencies in areas such as warehouse operations, fleet management, and planning simulations, offering actionable insights for industry practitioners.

The limited scholarly attention given to hyperautomation diminishes its theoretical rigor and real-world relevance, negatively impacting management and quality sciences. To address this gap, this chapter establishes clear definitions and frameworks, enhancing conceptual clarity in these disciplines. By delineating hyperautomation's principles and integrating systemic criteria, the chapter lays a critical foundation for future initiatives. Furthermore, this chapter seeks to facilitate the development of measurement tools to assess hyperautomation's impact within organizational and management sciences. In emphasizing transformative potential, the study highlights how hyperautomation can advance BPM, supply chain functions, and manufacturing operations toward innovative efficiencies.

CONCLUSION AND FUTURE RESEARCH DIRECTIONS

Hyperautomation enhances SCM and manufacturing agility, efficiency, and competitiveness amid growing market complexities. Future advancements in human augmentation and AI will enable near-autonomous operations, minimizing manual intervention. SCM will increasingly prioritize AI-driven strategic planning, innovation, decision-making, and customer relationship management. Consequently, the integration of advanced technologies will optimize operational performance and sustainability, ensuring the long-term viability of SCM and manufacturing systems.

This chapter examines the emerging paradigm of hyperautomation, seeking to conceptualize and theorize its framework through systematic analysis. It delineates strategic pathways, operational workflows, and functional mechanisms, while demonstrating how digital transformation will redefine SCM, logistics, manufacturing, and BPM. The findings position hyperautomation as a transformative catalyst, enabling organizations to enhance operational efficiency, agility, and competitive advantage. By integrating advanced technologies, firms can achieve significant benefits while strategically mitigating implementation challenges. As hyperautomation evolves, organizations must remain attuned to technological advancements to optimize its potential. Proactively addressing implications, challenges, and future trends will allow enterprises to thrive in an era increasingly shaped by cognitive automation and intelligent process optimization.

This chapter acknowledges several limitations and suggests directions for future research. The analysis is primarily based on a synthesis of academic literature, industry reports, online news, and working papers, which, while informative, necessitates further empirical validation. Although illustrative industry examples with performance metrics are included, more rigorous studies—particularly on hyperautomation's influence on logistical performance and capability factors (Hasan et al., 2024)—are needed to strengthen theoretical foundations in SCM and manufacturing. While the discussion targets academics and industry specialists, its technical nature does not preclude practical relevance; it offers actionable insights for executives by highlighting adoption challenges and proposing mitigation strategies. However, the current scarcity of scholarly research limits the generalizability and depth of findings, underscoring the need for expanded investigations in SCM. Future studies should employ empirical methodologies to validate conceptual frameworks, ensuring a more comprehensive understanding of hyperautomation's transformative potential in industrial and logistical contexts.

REFERENCES

Agbelusi, J., Ashi, T. A., & Chukwunweike, S. O. (2024). Breaking down silos: Enhancing supply chain efficiency through erp integration and automation. *International Research Journal of Modernization in Engineering Technology and Science*, *6*(9), 1935–1951. https://www.doi.org/10.56726/IRJMETS61691

Ahmad, T., Aakula, A., Ottori, M., & Saini, V. (2022). Developing A Strategic Roadmap For Digital Transformation. *Journal of Computational Intelligence and Robotics*, *2*(2), 2. https://tsbpublisher.org/jcir/article/view/64

Atluri, V., & Singla, A. Dahlström, P., Sukharevsky, A., Gaffey, B., Kaka, N., Lajous, T., Travasoni, A., & Vieira, B. (2024). *Beyond the hype: Capturing the potential of AI and gen AI in tech, media, and telecom*. McKinsey. https://www.mckinsey.com/industries/technology-media-and-telecommunications/our-insights/beyond-the-hype-capturing-the-potential-of-ai-and-gen-ai-in-tmt#/

Beverungen, D., Buijs, J. C. A. M., Becker, J., Di Ciccio, C., van der Aalst, W. M. P., Bartelheimer, C., vom Brocke, J., Comuzzi, M., Kraume, K., Leopold, H., Matzner, M., Mendling, J., Ogonek, N., Post, T., Resinas, M., Revoredo, K., del-Río-Ortega, A., La Rosa, M., Santoro, F. M., & Wolf, V. (2021). Seven paradoxes of business process management in a hyper-connected world. *Business & Information Systems Engineering*, *63*(2), 145–156. DOI: 10.1007/s12599-020-00646-z

Birkbeck, A., & Weston, P. (2024). Seeking ambidexterity through hyperautomation: What next for GBA logistics in their evolution from local labour entrepreneurs to global players in logistics. *Journal of Information Technology Teaching Cases*. https://doi.org/DOI: 10.1177/20438869241261074

Chen, Y.-C., & Hasan, M. K. (2023). Impacts of liner shipping connectivity and global competitiveness on logistics performance: The mediating role of the quality of port and infrastructure. *Transport*, *38*(2), 87–104. DOI: 10.3846/transport.2023.19372

Davenport, T. H., & Rajeev, R. (2018). *Artificial intelligence for the real world*. Boston Business Journal. https://www.bizjournals.com/boston/news/2018/01/09/hbr-artificial-intelligence-for-the-real-world.html

Deloitte. (2020). *Hyperautomation-The next frontier* (pp. 1–21). https://www2.deloitte.com/in/en/pages/technology-media-and-telecommunications/articles/hyperautomation-the-next-frontier.html

Di Battista, A., Grayling, S., Hasselaar, E., Leopold, T., Li, R., Rayner, M., & Zahidi, S. (2023). *Future of job report 2023*. World Economic Forum. https://www.weforum.org/publications/the-future-of-jobs-report-2023/

Fedosovsky, M. E., Uvarov, M. M., Aleksanin, S. A., Pyrkin, A. A., Colombo, A. W., & Prattichizzo, D. (2022). Sustainable Hyperautomation in High-Tech Manufacturing Industries: A Case of Linear Electromechanical Actuators. *IEEE Access : Practical Innovations, Open Solutions*, *10*, 98204–98219. DOI: 10.1109/ACCESS.2022.3205623

Frikha, R., & Hlali, A. (2023). The evolution of logistics management toward the digital transition. *International Journal of Commerce. Industry and Entrepreneurship Studies*, *3*(1), 66–75.

Gartner. (2019). *Top 10 strategic technology trends for 2020*. https://www.gartner.com/smarterwithgartner/gartner-top-10-strategic-technology-trends-for-2020

Gartner. (2021). *From automation to autonomy: The supply chain 2035 roadmap* (pp. 1–5). https://www.gartner.com/en/supply-chain/trends/supply-chain-automation

Gartner. (2022). *The top 8 supply chain technology trends* (pp. 1–7). https://www.gartner.com/en/supply-chain/trends/supply-chain-technology-trends

George, A. S., George, A. H., Baskar, T., & Sujatha, V. (2023). The rise of hyperautomation: A new frontier for business process automation. *Partners Universal International Research Journal*, *2*(4), 13–35.

Goni, K. M., Mohammed, A., Sundararajan, S., & Kassim, S. I. (2024). Proactive risk management in smart manufacturing: A comprehensive approach to risk assessment and mitigation. In *Artificial Intelligence Solutions for Cyber-Physical Systems*. Auerbach Publications.

Gunisity, S. R. (2024). Evolution of Automation to Hyperautomation: Leveraging RPA, AI ML, NLP for Optimal Operational Efficiency. *International Journal of Computer Trends and Technology - IJCTT*, *72*. https://doi.org//DOI: 10.14445/22312803

Haleem, A., Javaid, M., Singh, R. P., Rab, S., & Suman, R. (2021). Hyperautomation for the enhancement of automation in industries. *Sensors International*, *2*, 100124. DOI: 10.1016/j.sintl.2021.100124

Hasan, M. K., Lei, X., Hlali, A., & Bian, Z. (2024). Modelling capability factors of logistics industry based on ISM-MICMAC. *Heliyon*, *10*(22), e40539. DOI: 10.1016/j.heliyon.2024.e40539 PMID: 39641072

Hasan, M. K., Lei, X., Tang, W., Nishi, N. N., & Latif, Z. (2025). *Exploring logistics performance index (LPI) from global perspective: A study based on network analysis (NA)*. Operations Management Research., DOI: 10.1007/s12063-025-00550-3

Ilango, V. (2025). Challenges and future trends in the hyperautomation of sustainable agriculture. In Singh, S., Sood, V., Srivastav, A. L., & Ampatzidis, Y. (Eds.), *Hyperautomation in Precision Agriculture* (pp. 289–298). Academic Press., DOI: 10.1016/B978-0-443-24139-0.00024-2

Jiang, F., Wei, K. K., Ng, S.-P., Amin, M., Herjanto, H., & Liu, J. (2023). How blockchain technology hyperautomatically affects corporate performance by green supply chain? *Enterprise Information Systems, 17*(10), 2204305. DOI: 10.1080/17517575.2023.2204305

Kaswan, K. S., Dhatterwal, J. S., Malik, V., & Rajani. (2025). Hyper Automation 2.0 and Ecosystem Collaboration: Paradigm Shift in SCM. In A. Pandey & F. Al-Turjman (Eds.), *Transformation of Supply Chain Ecosystems* (pp. 281–301). Emerald Publishing Limited. https://doi.org/DOI: 10.1108/978-1-83549-246-820251017

Kumar, P. J. S., Petla, R. K., Elangovan, K., & Kuppusamy, P. G. (2022). Artificial Intelligence Revolution in Logistics and Supply Chain Management. In *Artificial Intelligent Techniques for Wireless Communication and Networking* (pp. 31–45). Wiley., DOI: 10.1002/9781119821809.ch3

Kusiak, A. (1990). Intelligent manufacturing systems. *The Journal of Technology Transfer, 15*(4), 49–51. DOI: 10.1007/bf02371524

Kusiak, A. (2020). Open manufacturing: A design-for-resilience approach. *International Journal of Production Research, 58*(15), 4647–4658. DOI: 10.1080/00207543.2020.1770894

Kusiak, A. (2023). Predictive models in digital manufacturing: Research, applications, and future outlook. *International Journal of Production Research, 61*(17), 6052–6062. DOI: 10.1080/00207543.2022.2122620

Kusiak, A. (2024). Hyper-automation in manufacturing industry. *Journal of Intelligent Manufacturing, 35*(1), 1–2. DOI: 10.1007/s10845-023-02265-3

Lasso-Rodriguez, G., & Winkler, K. (2020). Hyperautomation to fulfil jobs rather than executing tasks: The BPM manager robot vs human case. *Romanian Journal of Information Technology and Automatic Control, 30*(3), 7–22. DOI: 10.33436/v30i3y202001

Latif, Z., Riaz, A., Mahmood, S., & Hameed, R. M. (2023). An Exploration of Moral Identity's Role in Mitigating the Impact of Despotic Leadership on Organizational Culture and Organizational Agility in the Public Sector of Pakistan. *Foundation University Journal of Business & Economics, 8*(2), 142–168. DOI: 10.33897/fujbe.v8i2.816

Mathur, A., Dabas, A., & Sharma, N. (2022). Evolution From Industry 1.0 to Industry 5.0. *2022 4th International Conference on Advances in Computing, Communication Control and Networking (ICAC3N)*, 1390–1394. https://doi.org/DOI: 10.1109/ICAC3N56670.2022.10074274

Mittelstadt, B. D., Allo, P., Taddeo, M., Wachter, S., & Floridi, L. (2016). The ethics of algorithms: Mapping the debate. *Big Data & Society*, *3*(2), 1–21. DOI: 10.1177/2053951716679679

Mubarik, M. S., & Khan, S. A. (2024). Digital Supply Chain Transformation: Adoption and Approaches. In *The Theory, Methods and Application of Managing Digital Supply Chains* (pp. 107–120). Emerald Publishing Limited. https://doi.org/DOI: 10.1108/978-1-80455-968-020241007

Niedzielski, B., Buła, P., & Yang, M. (2024). Hyperautomation as a vital optimization tool in organizations: Cognitive approach with the use of Euler circles. *Journal of Electronic Business &amp. Digital Economics*, *3*(1), 61–73. DOI: 10.1108/JEBDE-02-2023-0004

Osman, A., Fowowe, O. O., Agboluaje, R., & Orekha, P. O. (2025). Integrating machine learning in business analytics consulting for proactive decision-making and innovation. *World Journal of Advanced Research and Reviews*, *25*(1), 1817–1836. DOI: 10.30574/wjarr.2025.25.1.0251

Srivastava, A., Pandey, P., Pandey, A., Gupta, A., Manglick, A., & Mahajan, N. (2025). Sustaining supply chain with automation and robotics. In Pandey, A., & Al-Turjman, F. (Eds.), *Transformation of Supply Chain Ecosystems* (pp. 173–188). Emerald Publishing Limited., DOI: 10.1108/978-1-83549-246-820251011

Stankov, S. P. (2024). DEVELOPMENT OF AUTOMATION IN THE DIRECTION OF HYPERAUTOMATION. *Annals of the Faculty of Engineering Hunedoara*, *22*(1), 179–184.

Strubell, E., Ganesh, A., & McCallum, A. (2020). Energy and Policy Considerations for Modern Deep Learning Research. *Proceedings of the AAAI Conference on Artificial Intelligence*, *34*(09), 09. Advance online publication. DOI: 10.1609/aaai.v34i09.7123

Surur, F. M., Mamo, A. A., Gebresilassie, B. G., Mekonen, K. A., Golda, A., Behera, R. K., & Kumar, K. (2025). *Unlocking the power of machine learning in big data: A scoping survey*. Data Science and Management., DOI: 10.1016/j.dsm.2025.02.004

Szelągowski, M., & Berniak-Woźny, J. (2023). The impact of hyperautomation on business processes in SMEs. *International Journal of Process Management and Benchmarking*, *13*(3), 384–400. DOI: 10.1504/IJPMB.2023.129646

UNCTAD. (2021). *Technology and innovation report 2021- catching technological waves: Innovation with equity*. https://unctad.org/publication/technology-and-innovation-report-2021

Wachter, S., Mittelstadt, B., & Floridi, L. (2017). Transparent, explainable, and accountable AI for robotics. *Science Robotics*, *2*(6), eaan6080. Advance online publication. DOI: 10.1126/scirobotics.aan6080 PMID: 33157874

KEY TERMS AND DEFINITIONS

Hyperautomation: An integration of advanced technologies like artificial intelligence (AI), machine learning (ML), Robotic Process Automation (RPA), and process mining to automate and optimize complex business processes end-to-end, enabling intelligent decision-making with minimal human intervention.

Robotic Process Automation (RPA): A technology that uses software robots or "bots" to automate repetitive, rule-based tasks by representing human interactions with digital systems, improving efficiency and reducing errors.

Machine Learning (ML): A subset of AI that enables systems to automatically learn and improve from experience by identifying patterns in data, without being explicitly programmed.

Generative AI (GenAI): A type of AI that creates new content—such as text, images, or code—by learning patterns from existing data and generating original, realistic outputs based on user prompts.

Intelligent Document Processing (IDP): An AI-driven technology that automates the extraction, classification, and processing of data from unstructured or semi-structured documents using ML, NLP, and computer vision to improve accuracy and efficiency.

Conversational User Experience (Conversational UX): An approach that enables natural, human-like interactions between users and digital systems (such as chatbots or voice assistants) to simplify tasks, provide assistance, and enhance engagement through dialogue.

Business Process Management (BPM): A systematic approach to designing, executing, monitoring, and optimizing an organization's workflows and processes to improve efficiency, agility, and performance.

Chapter 2
AI and IoT-Powered Smart Logistics:
Transforming Supply Chains for Efficiency and Sustainability

Md Mehedi Hasan Emon
https://orcid.org/0000-0002-6224-9552
American International University, Bangladesh

Most. Sharmin Ara Chowdhury
https://orcid.org/0009-0005-1050-8283
National University, Bangladesh

ABSTRACT

This chapter explores the transformative role of Artificial Intelligence (AI) and the Internet of Things (IoT) in revolutionizing logistics and supply chain management. It examines how the integration of these technologies enhances operational efficiency, end-to-end visibility, and sustainability. Key applications such as AI-powered demand forecasting, route optimization, and IoT-driven real-time monitoring are highlighted, demonstrating their capacity to reduce costs, improve decision-making, and minimize environmental impact. Furthermore, the chapter addresses the challenges associated with AI and IoT adoption, including data privacy, cybersecurity, and integration with legacy systems. Through industry case studies, the chapter illustrates the tangible benefits and real-world impact of smart logistics. Finally, it outlines future research directions and prospects for further advancements in these transformative technologies.

DOI: 10.4018/979-8-3373-2434-0.ch002

INTRODUCTION TO SMART LOGISTICS

Today's logistics is so much more than the traditional methods of goods transportation and storage. One may imagine now that Smart Logistics is something that is happening today because logistics is entering into a change from a paradigm that's truly different, part that is engendered by the rapid expansion of AI and IoT. Smart logistics is the use of digital technologies to facilitate exchange of real time data, intelligence automation, as well as prediction across supply chain networks. An operational upgrade leveraging AI and IoT technologies within logistics systems is not an operational upgrade but an innovation that engages strategic integration of AI and IoT technologies into logistics systems and ultimately leads to redefining efficiency, responsiveness and sustainability in supply chains. Smart logistics is important because it can give end to end visibility, optimizes the decision-making processes and agility in very complex supply chain ecosystems. Bolstering backwards nostalgic outraged nostalgia about things: living through 2020 forced us to be new. Instead, it is critical that companies undergo digital transformation, and smart logistics becomes the marker of competitive advantage. Through which intelligence and connectivity are embedded in logistics operations, firms anticipate the challenges, proactively respond to them and align operational changes to focus on wider environmental and social governance (ESG) goals. Scholastic debate on smart logistics focuses on the remark that smart logistics is not just a technological evolution but a strategic reorientation of the management of supply chain (Ding et al., 2021). IoT device deployment like smart sensors, RFID tags, GPS trackers are used for continuous monitoring of goods, assets and environmental conditions across the logistics network. At the same time, AI based analytics churns through the onslaught of data coming from these devices to deliver it in a form that is actionable for dynamic route optimization, predictive maintenance, real-time inventory management (Kang et al., 2024; Selvakumar et al., 2025). They also extend logistics capabilities towards integration of transportation services and are enhancing operational efficiency through reduced costs, waste, and carbon emissions that are in line with overall environmental, social, and economic sustainability goals of global supply chains.

First, the COVID 19 pandemic has further accelerated the need for smart logistics to reveal weaknesses within traditional logistics systems and emphasize the requirement for resilience and live balancing. The 2022 Global Supply Chain Survey shows that companies who already had invested in digital logistics infrastructures were able to be more agile in responding to supply chain disruptions (Modgil et al., 2022). According to Modgil et al. (2022), those that were using AI and IoT had a 20 percent faster recovery rate versus the conventional systems users. These empirical findings allow for backup of a paper at hand that reaffirms the important role played by smart logistics in ensuring that supply chains are resilient and responsive under unforeseen circumstances like in the present time. In addition, consumer expectations undergoing development are having a further impact on logistics systems. With the rapid development of the digital economy, customer requirement not only the speed of delivery but also short track master system being built through which the products are sourced, manufactured and delivered in a transparent and sustainable way (Sturgeon, 2021; Wu & Pi, 2023). By providing real time tracking and data driven transparency, smart logistics facilities companies to meet these expectations with their customers, thus building stronger, trust-based relationships with them. In terms of theory, smart logistics is in line with Resource Based View of a firm which asserts that differentiation through unique, elusive capabilities (real time analytics and adaptive logistics infrastructures) can be a source of a competitive advantage (Rodrigues et al., 2024). As such, AI and IoT integration into logistics becomes a strategic imperative for these firms to aim for differentiation through superior service quality, and operational excellence, and environmental stewardship. Yet the use of smart logistics as a concept is not without disadvantages. Barriers at the level of technology, such as high initial investment costs, data security concerns and interoperability of the different technological platforms still exist (Emon & Khan, 2025b; Senna et al., 2022).

Internet of Things (IoT) in Logistics

IoT cannot function without smart logistics, and this is where it includes the physical devices connected, and the systems talk from one to the other. Free flow of information between assets, goods and operators inside supply chains permits the direct interaction between IoT components and makes supply chains a living system where information is acquired, transmitted and analyzed constantly. In addition to many others, it can be used for real time tracking and condition monitoring, predictive maintenance and dynamic inventory management. Because logistics assets contain them, firms are enabled to reach the levels of visibility, responsiveness and control that were unthinkable until now.

Real-Time Tracking and Monitoring of Goods

Real time tracking is one of the most impressive uses of IoT in logistics. Critical parameters such as location, temperature, humidity, and shock exposure, are integrated into sensors in shipments, pallets or containers and provide continuous updates (Kavaliauskas et al., 2024). Logistics managers can track the movement of goods right from the start of the supply chain journey until the point when they are transported to the end customer, all from the comfort of an office desk through

GPS-enabled tracking gadgets, which frequently hook these gadgets into cloud platforms. Proactive interventions are possible in cases of route deviations, delays or environmental risks because of such visibility. Real time tracking is a profound idea. Real-time environmental monitoring is very important for industries producing perishable goods like pharmaceuticals or fresh produce as it can save them from spoilage by alerting operators to adverse conditions thereby predisposing them for immediate corrective actions (Costa et al., 2022). Real time detection also limits the risk of theft of the shipment as movement of shipment is instantly monitored. A 2023 survey by DHL shows that 25% fewer shipments are lost, and 30% more deliveries are received on time by companies who use IoT based tracking data (Jayaratne, 2024). In addition to operational efficiency, these also provide benefits in customer satisfaction. In the age of heavily demanding transparency from their customers, the ability to be transparent through real time shipment status builds trust and loyalty. Firms that use the IoT for tracking are better candidates to provide value-added services, for example, estimated time of arrival (ETA) updates and dynamic rerouting depending on customer preferences.

IoT-Enabled Predictive Maintenance in Transportation

More than monitoring what is shipped, IoT technologies have paved the way to predictive maintenance of goods at assets disposal. Maintenance has traditionally been reactive (in response to failure) or scheduled in periodic intervals for services that can be unproductive or can lead to failure that comes unannounced. However, IoT changes the paradigm by making vehicle health and performance parameters such as engine temperature, oil viscosity, brake pad wear and tire pressure, real time monitored (Visconti et al., 2025). In machine learning, we can closely analyze data streams (from connected sensors) which can help us predict when a component has a high risk of failure and hence schedule that component for maintenance. Therefore, predictive maintenance minimizes unplanned downtime, lowers repair costs and increases the operational life cycle of the fleet assets. Let's use UPS as an example, it now has predictive analytics incorporated into its fleet that has enabled 10 percent reduction in maintenance cost and 12 percent increase in vehicle uptime (Martyushev et al., 2023). Secondly, predatory maintenance improves driver safety and regulatory conscientiousness by guaranteeing that vehicles are in their best condition. Due to a growing level of competitive and regulated market environment, proactive monitoring of an asset's health provides tangible operational and strategic advantage.

Smart Warehouses and Inventory Management

IoT can change the face of the logistics industry, and the 'smart warehouse' is a good example. IoT enabled devices and systems to work together with other devices and systems in smart warehouses to automate how the inventory is managed resulting in dramatic efficiency and accuracy. Shelf, bin and storage units equipped with sensors continuously monitor stock levels and update inventory in enterprise resource planning (ERP) systems (Kocaoglu, 2024). In this context, weight sensors and RFID tags are very important. The system can autonomously trigger replenishment orders when the stock levels decrease below predetermined stock levels to prevent mixture stockouts as well as over stocking. By reducing carrying costs and improving working capital efficiency, this dynamic inventory management strategy is quite attractive. Stock picking, inventory audits, and goods movement are performed with minimal human intervention through coordinated use of Automated Guided Vehicles (AGVs), drones and robotic arms using IoT platforms (Vlachos et al., 2024). Rapid inventory counts in warehouses utilizing traditional manual audits would be time consuming and error prone when using Drones equipped with RFID scanners. It also helps speed up and improve order fulfillment by integrating IoT with warehouse management systems (WMS). Cirillo et al. (2024) provides the purpose of another landmark robotic example: Amazon's use of Kiva robots in its fulfillment centers to reduce order processing times by more than 50%. Also, warehousing operations can be environmentally less impacting through energy management systems enabled by IoT. Using real-time occupancy and environmental information, smart lighting, heating, ventilation, and air conditioning (HVAC) systems can adjust processes to saving huge amounts of energy and support firms in their sustainability practices.

ARTIFICIAL INTELLIGENCE (AI) IN LOGISTICS

AI supports the IoT by introducing cognitive abilities in logistics operations that allow data to be learned, patterns to be responded to, and decisions to be taken with limited human intervention. Logistics has not been the only thing that is being transformed into an intelligent, adaptive and sustainable function, much of it is being done by AI. From demand forecasting to risk management, from route optimization to warehouse automation, to its wide range of applications, this tool has broken down paradigms or even set new ones regarding efficiency and resilience for the end users.

AI-Powered Demand Forecasting and Route Optimization

Demand forecasting is one of the applications of AI in logistics that has caused quite an impact. Accuracy in demand forecasting is necessary for the optimal levels of inventory, customer satisfaction and reducing operational costs. While these traditional statistical forecasting methods are valuable, they tend to fail when retail markets become complex and very volatile. Whereas AI Driven models employ machine learning algorithms that analyze huge and diversified datasets like historical sales without market trends, seasonal fluctuations, promotional exercises, antisocial variables such as weather patterns and macroeconomic markers, to produce extremely exact forecasts (Hutton et al., 2022). Application of machine learning techniques including neural network and gradient boosting algorithm has shown to outperform the traditional models in modeling nonlinear relationship and dynamic shift in demand patterns (Wang et al., 2021). For instance, Amazon running AI based forecasting models to change its inventory decision in real-time is adjusted to consumer behavior signals and that has resulted in massive reduction in opportunities for stock outs and excess inventory and (Campbell et al., 2020). The ability to improve the forecast accuracy helps companies to more properly align the production schedules, more effectively use warehouse space, improve service levels, and create a more agile and cost-effective supply chain.

As part of route optimization, AI is also crucial in predicting. Powered by the AI algorithms, real time route optimization systems run through the massive volumes of the traffic data, the weather conditions, the time windows of delivery, the metrics of performance of the vehicles and the network of road to find the most efficient delivery routes. Dynamically re-routing vehicles in response to breaks like accidents or road closures are possible with these systems, and the deliveries are made in a timely fashion, and the fuel consumption lowered. Specifically, the environmental benefits of optimized route optimization driven by AI are very beneficial as a study by the El Moussaoui (2025) revealed that through optimized urban logistics routes carbon emissions of last mile deliveries can be reduced by 30%. Examples of successful deployment of AI-enabled ORION (On-Road Integrated Optimization and Navigation) system by companies such as UPS has resulted in savings of 100s of millions of miles of driving per year, meaning fuel savings into millions of dollars and significant reduction in carbon footprints (Hensher & Wei, 2024). This means that users of AI do not only get means that promote operational efficiency, but also an application that advances corporate sustainability goals in general.

Machine Learning Applications for Supply Chain Risk Management

Today's supply chains face diverse risks of supplier insolvencies, political instability, natural disasters, cyberattacks, and so on. More and more traditional approaches to risk management are reactive. Predictive and proactive risk management is the bassiest role that machine learning and, more generally, AI takes here. For example, machine learning models can be fed and analyzed with structured and unstructured data from many sources such as news feeds, social media, financial reports, shipment tracking systems, supplier databases to help identify emerging risks (Dangsawang & Nuchitprasitchai, 2024). These systems grow continually more capable of predicting, something firms can use to help anticipate disruptions and put into action mitigation strategies before the risks become real. For instance, during the COVID19 pandemic, such AI enabled risk assessment platforms facilitated companies such as IBM and Maersk to pre-emptively manage supply chain disruptions by streamlining health data of the global community, port closures and supply chain vulnerabilities (Crouhy et al., 2021; Emon, 2025). These companies used predictive analytics to forecast at risk suppliers, adjust inventory and change their transportation plans to keep their continuity undamaged despite great and unprecedented challenges. Additionally, AI enabled risk management tools can create various disruption scenarios and simulate them to determine possible impacts of different risk events and help the supply chain managers prepare for contingency plans. This kind of scenario analysis is important in building the supply chain resilience, which is now high on the list of top agenda items for supply chain managers due to the rising global uncertainties (Scholten et al., 2019).

AI-Driven Automation in Warehouse and Fulfillment Centers

AI has been adopted quite easily in fulfilling centers and warehouse operations. Picking, packing, sorting and inventory management have been within labor intensive process with high potential for inefficiency and errors against traditional warehouse processes. These operations were revolutionized by having AI coupled with computer vision and robotics technologies. A wide range of products can be accurately identified, grasped, and sorted by robotic picking systems guided by AI algorithms and computer vision (Liu et al., 2022). Machine learning enables these systems continually to improve their performance on tasks for new product types, as well as handling complex tasks with greater success. AI optimized AS/RS (Automated storage and retrieval system) that places and moves goods in the warehouse based on travel distance and maximizing of space utilization. Ocado is a company that has developed highly sophisticated AI powered fulfillment centers with centralized AI algorithms coordinating these swarms of robots performing picking and packing operations with fantastic efficiency (Choi et al., 2022; Emon & Khan, 2025a). With these centers processing thousands of orders an hour with only minor human intervention, the scalability and reliability of which AI driven warehouse automation, is shown. Aside from the efficiency gains, AI automated automation makes the workplace safer, saving human workers from engaging in physically demanding or hazardous jobs. In the light of an ongoing shortage of labor in the logistics sector, AI driven systems can merge human and enhance the ability to operate.

Intelligent Customer Service and Last-Mile Delivery Innovations

In its way, logistics business is greatly boosted by artificial intelligence thanks to the use of intelligent chatbots, virtual assistants and personalized delivery options. One aspect that AI can really contribute to is its ability to answer the queries of many customers pertaining to shipment status, delivery time, return policies etc. Natural language Processing (NLP) technologies allow these systems to understand and respond to the customer queries with a high level of contextual relevance improving the customer satisfaction at reduced operational cost. In delivery on the last mile, AI algorithms are used for the optimization of the delivery schedule, dynamic resource allocations, real time tracking and delivery windows for customers (Khan et al., 2024; Sorooshian et al., 2022). While somewhat in the earlier stages of deployment, some companies are experimenting with the use of AI driven autonomous delivery vehicles and drones to deliver goods, which would all but eliminate a need for contact in ultra efficient, highly efficient delivery models.

Integration of AI and IoT for Smart Logistics

When AI and IoT come together, it is at their most true potential, as a combination like Air and Water. Although their individual application would provide significant advantages in the areas of supply chain management, such synergistic effects of their integration result in intelligent, responsive, and extremely connected supply chain ecosystems. In this volatile global environment, this convergence brings operational efficiency as well as resilience, flexibility, and sustainability to the logistics networks.

Synergies Between AI and IoT for End-to-End Visibility

Supply chain operations that use an integration of AI and IoT provide real time, end to end visibility. Businesses currently rely on continual flows of real time data concerning goods' status, location and condition as they move through the supply chain (Y. Khan et al., 2022). Yet, having data is not enough without analytical skills to derive tangible intelligence from. That is where AI makes for an indispensable offering. IoT devices are raw data collected, and those AI algorithms interpret, contextualize, and analyze them to present the intelligence in a user-friendly format. For example, in cold chain logistics, IoT sensors in shipping containers monitor critical parameters like temperature, humidity and vibrations. When a temperature deviation occurs that impacts on the quality of perishable goods, AI systems can determine immediately if the product quality issue poses a risk, then ascertain the likelihood that. Product integrity will be compromised and whether corrective action is needed or disruption protocols, like rerouting shipments to alternate storage locations, should be initiated (Lorenc, 2023). This synergy between AI and IoT ensures that logistics managers are not responding to problems after they occur but have insights to help them proactively intervene. AI also helps in anomaly detection by discovering minuscule patterns that pair human operators could disregard, prior to issues like equipment malfunctions, route deviations or compliance infringement (Chowdhury et al., 2020). Thus, companies can obtain higher operation transparency, traceability, and customer trust, which are becoming more and more important in sectors such as the pharmaceutical industry, food logistics and high value manufacturing.

AI-Powered IoT Analytics for Predictive Supply Chain Decision-Making

Amongst providing visibility, AI and IoT integration puts new power within supply chains dependent on predictive analytics in ways that fundamentally change the game in terms of the decision-making. Typically, traditional supply chain management operates reactively once a disruption takes place. Nevertheless, AI driven predictive models based on historical and real time IoT sensor data predict future states of the supply chain characterized by equipment failures, rise in customer demand surge, supply shortages or transportation bottlenecks (Aljohani, 2023). For example, AI-IoT integration plays a key role in predictive maintenance in logistics. An AI model, when trained on noise sensors on machinery and vehicles, such as vibration levels, oil quality and temperature readings, can predict when the equipment is likely to fail, allowing maintenance to be conducted proactive, rather than on the breaking point. It not only reduces downtime, but maintenance costs also as well as reduces asset life cycles and continues logistics operations (de Almeida Pais et al., 2021).

In inventory management, the AI enhanced IoT systems can also predict stock levels using real sales data, the seasonal trends and external factors like weather or political events. For instance, AI algorithms can suggest ahead of time an upsurge in the demand of some goods related to forecasted storm or holiday, with the aim of changing the procurement and distribution plans (Chan & Wahab, 2024). This ability: to anticipate, prepares the firms to shift from reactive crisis management to strategic and data driven decision making that would make them more agile and resilient in the supply chain.

Intelligent Automation and Autonomous Logistics Operations

The connection of AI and IoT also pushes down the path of intelligent automation and eventually, the logistics sector becomes more autonomous. Real time IoT data streams and AI driven decision-making framework are heavily depending on for their autonomous vehicles, drones, robotic process automation systems to function correctly. For example, autonomous delivery drones use GPS, environmental sensor data, to navigate the complicated terrain, and AI algorithms change the flight paths according to the changes in weather or airspace restrictions (Bayomi & Fernandez, 2023). The AI-IoT systems handle fleets of autonomous robots such as these that do picking, packing and transporting tasks in warehouse environments with very little human intervention. Robots constantly interact with IoT enabled warehouse management systems (WMS) to assign tasks in an optimal manner, monitor operational status and prevent collision, thereby improving operation efficiency and safety (Emon & Khan, 2024; Plakantara et al., 2024). Additionally, these systems contain self-learning capabilities that let them continuously improve. As robots and autonomous vehicles are in operation, the generated operational data are fed into AI models that in turn improve navigation algorithms, allocation strategies for tasks and energy consumption patterns. With that feedback loop, this means that over time an optimized smarter and more efficient logistics ecosystem can self-optimize as we don't need to stay micromanaging this.

Enhancing Sustainability and Ethical Supply Chain Practices

In addition, the integration of AI and IoT plays an important part in the logistics agenda of sustainability. Through real time energy, consumption, emission and waste generation monitoring firms can identify inefficiencies and take corrective actions in order to minimize its environmental footprint (Huang & Mao, 2024). AI can be used to drive analytics over vehicle routing to find the most economical fuel usage, provide energy efficient practice guidance in the warehouse, and help with sourcing decisions in support of sustainability when provided answers to how close suppliers are performing against environmental benchmarks. Besides, the technology of AI-IoT systems also makes the supply chain more transparent, traceable, and hence, more ethical. Firms can also monitor labor practices across the supplier networks, ensure compliance with human rights standards, and ensure sustainable sourcing claims (Cao et al., 2024; T. Khan et al., 2024). When you combine AI, IoT and blockchain technology this further grows supply chain integrity in the form of immutability of product provenance and handling through fate.

CHALLENGES AND BARRIERS TO IMPLEMENTATION

There are critical challenges to widespread adoption of AI and IoT to logistics and supply chain management, despite the large amount of transformative potential these two offerings for logistics and supply chain management bring. It is both technical and economic and organizational and regulatory; in other words, the relationship between technological innovation and its practical realization is a complex one. Policymakers, industry leaders and academics searching for means to smooth the path onto smart logistics ecosystems must understand these barriers.

Data Privacy and Cybersecurity Concerns

The major obstacle encountered by integrating AI and IoT into logistics operations is security and data privacy threat from cybersecurity. The unlimited amount of data IoT devices generate in supply chains, while collecting operational, partner or customer sensitive information, is magnitudes higher. However, such an interconnected network without required safeguards remains favorable to the cybercriminals to exploit vulnerabilities for financial gain, corporate espionage, and disruption of services (Aslan et al., 2023). Since IoT networks and AI systems are critical to the security of our world, it requires a multi layered approach to securing the networks and systems from anyone who wishes to do harm. Although, all these protective measures lack specialized cybersecurity expertise and capabilities to be installed and maintained by many small and medium enterprises (SME) logistics firms (Chidukwani et al., 2022). Moreover, the combination of AI makes things even more complicated by the fact that machine learning models themselves can serve as potential target of adversarial attacks where the adversaries interfere with the input of the model to achieve the objective of damaging the performance of the model (Zhang et al., 2023). In addition to technical risks, companies are bound to protect personal data by data privacy regulations like the European Union's General Data Protection Regulation (GDPR) and national counterparts. An ounce of prevention, they say, is worth a pound of cure. Severe fines and the loss of reputation are some very serious things when data governance is not being taken seriously when deploying AI-IoT logistics. And even when companies collect data about their users' location, providing that data to federal agencies is more complicated.

Challenges integration with Legacy Systems

Adopting AI and IoT in logistics is also a problem given the other major challenge to its use: the integration of these cutting-edge technologies into the existing legacy systems. Taking as an example, many logistics companies, and even more so those with long operational histories, rely on an outdated IT infrastructure that never conceived of the data demanding and interrelated workload of modern AI and IoT platforms (Gohar & Nencioni, 2021). New technologies used to integrate into these legacy systems often mean expensive upgrades and development of complex and expensive middleware, and extensive system re-engineering. Legacy systems are also absent of necessary interoperability standards for data exchange without data silos and fragmented operations which go against the use cases of AI-IoT solutions (Carlos Ferreira et al., 2024). More harm to integration is resistance to change within organizations. Most logistics companies work in traditional corporate cultures focusing more on traditional practices than innovation. The process of taking new unfamiliar technologies is likely to elicit skepticism or fear of adoption from employees who are accustomed to legacy workflows, especially while they see these as a threat to job security or roles (Almatrodi et al., 2023). Taking together, the need for such integration is quite high, and therefore involves not only technical investments, but a high degree of change management effort in terms of training, leadership involvement and developing a digital first mindset.

Cost and Infrastructure Limitations

The main constraint in implementation has been the still high cost of AI and IoT technologies, which is a reverse onerous on SMEs that lack the finances of larger logistics companies. Initially integration of AI-IoT solutions requires big investments in hardware (e.g, integrating sensors, edge devices, robots), software (e.g., deploying AI platforms and data analytics tools) and basic infrastructure including extremely high internet connectivity, the cloud, and security precautions (Alahi et al., 2023). Additionally, the long-term costs of maintaining the system, updating the system, storing data, and keeping themselves compliant with cybersecurity are quite high. The return on investment (ROI) of smart logistics technologies is not obvious to firms operating on thin margins or in highly competitive markets therefore, discouraging adoption (Shee et al., 2021). Such disparities between regions enhance the challenge. This is especially the case in developing countries, where AI and IoT have yet to reach prime commercialization by virtue of the digital infrastructure; poor broadband connectivity, unreliable power supply, and lack of service provider cloud availability (Onyeji-Nwogu et al., 2020). The risk of developing a two-tier ecosystem coinciding with technologically advanced companies outpacing lagging competitors will get much worse if public agencies do not put in place targeted public-private efforts to bridge these gaps. These disparities are a policy makers' problem. To democratize access to smart logistics technologies (Sha et al., 2024), it is necessary to make strategic investments in national digital infrastructure, financial incentive to technology adoption and the development of the regulatory framework which enables innovation at high level of security and privacy.

Skills Gaps and Workforce Challenges

There is also a less explored but equally limiting hurdle to the use of AI and IoT in logistics and that is the skills gap within the existing workforce. These technologies can only be implemented with knowledge in technology such as data science, machine learning, cybersecurity, and systems integration. However, the current logistical workforce does not have the required digital skills which will support, manage and innovate on AI-IoT systems (Paśko et al., 2022). This isn't a skills gap that delays technology adoption…it is delay and it is also operational risk these systems can be mis understood / set up improperly and that leads to operational inefficiencies, security issues or compliance failures. To close the skills gap, reskilling programs, collaborations with academic institutions, on the job training in digital competencies are needed (Foroughi, 2021). Besides, a culture of lifelong learning and innovation needs to be fostered in the organization by organizational leadership, so that employees at all levels welcome technological change as an opportunity rather than a threat. Arguably, this transition in culture is just as challenging, if not more so, than the technical part of AI-IoT integration.

CASE STUDIES AND REAL-WORLD APPLICATIONS

AI and the IoT owe so much to the logistics sector which has merged them as an intersection point without much speculation and now shows plenty of proven stakes. Almost all the leading global corporations and sector-wide studies confirm that tangible benefits are realized by operational efficiency, sustainability and service quality promises via these technologies. Through analysis of the real world, we find out how the AI and IoT integration completely changes shipping framework from rigid and static structure to a dynamic, adaptable, and knowing structure.

The most well-known example is the logistics giant DHL, who spent large amounts developing IoT sensor network along with AI based analytical processing across its warehousing and transportation premises. Using IoT devices to cover assets such as forklifts, pallets and containers, DHL got an overall real time view of supply chain nodes (Ponis & Efthymiou, 2020). They are batteries of this kind which continuously pour their data regarding asset location, movement, temperature, and operational status. The mass amount of data that is given to computers to process what it takes to do this is referred to as AI algorithms, and these algorithms use this massive influx of data to provide predictive insight which can be used for proactive maintenance, routing, and even the allocation of resources. It is important to note that predictive maintenance with the help of AI has greatly reduced unplanned downtime, which amounted to 15% more utilization of fleet and 20% better computational efficiency of overall maintenance cost (Ntanis et al., 2025). As the case of Amazon further illustrates, this is a perfect example of transformations brought about by integration of AI and IoT technologies. Amazon also uses a sophisticated ecosystem of robotic systems powered by AI and smart shelving connected through IT. Amazon bought Kiva robots in 2012, enhanced them with AI capability and now Kiva robots use them to dynamically move shelves across the warehouse floor minimizing warehouse floor and order picking times (Ellithy et al., 2024). Real time inventory status is communicated between smart shelves embedded with IoT sensors and AI systems which can predict the stock shortages and automatically trigger the orders of re-stocking. Taken together, these innovations together reduce order handling by 40% and increase the accuracy of orders sharply (Ghobadian et al., 2020). Repeated examples of corporate success with AI and IoT integration are embarked on, and empirical evidence of their effectiveness also shows on a larger scale. D. Kumar et al. (2022) study looking at global logistics companies who had implemented AI and IoT integrated solutions found those companies (average 25–30% reduction in operation cost). Delivery accuracy increased by approximately 40% while customer satisfaction ratings also increased. It is important to note that these efficiency improvements came at the expense of measured environmental benefits – primarily, about 20 percent reduction in carbon associated with warehousing and transportation, since smart logistics plays a key role in corporate sustainability.

Compelling illustrations from the automotive logistics sector are also available. Incorporating of AI and IoT technologies into BMW Group's global logistics operations to improve inbound parts management and vehicle distribution (Ammar et al., 2022). BMW is using IoT sensors glued to shipping containers, and AI analytics platforms, to forecast on the African continent part shipments (from suppliers) across continents, to predict delays due to weather, customs clearance or transportation disruptions. The company thus can keep its hands on the controls with dynamic rerouting of shipments or adjustment of production schedules by avoiding highly expensive line stoppages. According to Nantee & Sureeyatanapas, (2021), adoption of these technologies has been estimated to have led to a 10% increase in supply chain responsiveness and a considerable drop in logistics-related production downtimes. JD Logistics, a part of China's largest commerce platform JD.com, is one of the most prominent examples of how AI and Internet of Things are changing the face of urban delivery networks in the field of last-mile logistics. Mohsen (2024) stated that JD has placed a fleet of autonomous delivery vehicles with AI navigation algorithms and IoT-based traffic sensors. These vehicles are automated vehicles that can analyze real time traffic, weather and customers who are available to optimize their own delivery routes. Specifically, the deployment of these smart vehicles has lowered the last mile delivery times Wesley by up to 30 percent and delivery costs (Abdelkader et al., 2021) in pilot cities like Beijing and Shanghai. Moreover, predictive analytics based on AI analytics has been integrated with a warehouse management system to forecast peak delivery period effectively, which encourages RD Logistics to align inventory stocking strategies of work force scheduling according to the demand changing. Cold chain logistics is just another important field where the integration of AI and IoT brought a lot of benefits. As temperature sensitive goods such as pharmaceuticals and perishable food items must be transported under strictly controlled environments, it has become necessary. For example, in the case of Pfizer's logistics operations, IoT enabled temperature sensors are placed in transportation containers with the use of AI based monitoring systems that always keep track of the shipment conditions (Poongodi et al., 2020). This is to avoid shipments to be rerouted should they detect any deviation from the prescribed temperature threshold, yet AI systems alert logistics coordinators automatically. The implementation of these technologies has diminished spoilage rates and concomitant financial losses significantly and has improved compliance with regulatory standard on transport of the sensitive goods. Similar changes have taken place in port operations. Among them is the Port of Rotterdam, Europe's largest airport, which has deployed the integration of AI and IoT under its 'Digital Twin' initiative. The port data, the implementation of which includes multiple thousands of IoT sensors distributed throughout the port and the maintenance of a real time digital replica of the port's infrastructure, operations and logistics flows. Using this data, AI models use it to optimize berth allocation, cargo handling as well as vessel traffic management. Due to such, vessel turnaround times have diminished, throughput capacity has increased without bodily extension, and environmental performance of the port is enhanced through curtailed need for vessel idling and related emanations (Sadiq et al., 2021). There are organizations utilizing AI and IoT in humanitarian logistics such as the World Food Programme (WFP) to improve disaster response efforts. In areas affected by natural disaster aftereffects, IoT/ AI enabled drones are deployed to assess damaging, uncover unreachable areas, and pinpoint the best routes for humanitarian aid distribution (Rejeb et al., 2021). Radically speeding up and surpassing the precision of aid distribution during crises in conflict-ridden regions was possible only after this integration proved the societal benefits of techno logical innovation beyond its commercial purposes. In fact, it is worth remembering that the integration of AI and IoT is not an easy task. Although pioneering adopters address various issues, including data interoperability, cybersecurity vulnerability, and capital costs of technological upgrades, the issues persist (Fernandez de Arroyabe et al., 2024).

FUTURE PROSPECTS AND RESEARCH DIRECTIONS

The current trajectory of AI and IoT for the logistics sector implies that a decade ahead will be manifested by increasing technological refinement and expanded incorporation within the supply chain operations. Nowadays, AI and IoT are not considered merely auxiliary technologies for supporting logistics for operations' efficiency, resilience, and sustainability, they have become the key pillars of logistics strategy. A complicated and dynamic manifestation is posed by emerging technological innovativeness, altering market anticipations and increasing authorities' attentiveness to transparency, as well as ethical behavior.

Another of the consequences of the trend that will be shaping the interface between AI and IoT in logistics is edge computing. Traditional cloud-based architecture provides high processing power and large storage capacity, whereas the ideas of scalability, flexibility, agility, easier management and availability of computing at a lower cost by leveraging an on-demand computing paradigm, have been accepted as advantages (Donta et al., 2023). However, there are challenges: real time analytics and decision making in such natural settings would require processing the data near its source – close to the network's periphery – that edge computing asserts will help to address. This feature is of great importance for applications of critical time in automated driving, dynamic warehouse control or predictive maintenance, among other things. To capitalize on the potential of the AI-IoT ecosystem towards logistics operations, research on scalable, energy efficient edge computing framework is widely required. At the same time, the use of blockchain technology is also part of a revolutionary change that improves the security, transparency and trust in the supply chains. As the blockchain used in cryptocurrencies is decentralized, immutable, and based on its own economy, blockchain creates robust solutions for goods tracking, provenance verification, and compliance with regulatory standard (Adamashvili et al., 2024). Thus, if we combine AI, IoT and blockchain technologies in logistics, supply chain transactions will be autonomous, self-executed, and would eliminate the administrative overhead and fraud risk by means of smart contracts. These represent, however, significant technical and organizational challenges, as sharing blocks and points across blockchain platforms remains challenging as well as consensus mechanisms are not very scalable. Therefore, future research must put the development of lightweight and bespoke for logistics blockchain protocols which can seamlessly work with AI and IoT infrastructures on a top priority list. The second is the application of digital twins or virtual replicas of physical supply chain entities that can be simulated, monitored and optimized. Digital twins generate logistics managers capacity to foresee disruptions, harness asset utilization, and run through alternative operational strategies in real time, without real world risk (Khan & Emon, 2025; Vashishth et al., 2025). Since digital twins are already starting to show large benefits on a very specific use case, their more comprehensive adoption will require an adherence to standardized modeling frameworks and protocols for data sharing among the different organizational boundaries. Approaches to these challenges will not be resolved if we continue to pursue supply chains that are made up of smart individuals but lack any sort of coordination.

However, despite technological progress, the most important gaps persist in the logistics industry to achieve equitable access to the benefits of AI and IoT for SMEs. However, such technologies entail high upfront investment costs, lack of technical expertise, and digitization of infrastructure (Marabelli et al., 2021). Future research needs to be done towards developing scalable, relatively low-cost AI and IoT solutions that best fit the constraints and operational realities specific to SMEs. Some possible promising ways to Democratize smart logistics are through public private partnership, open-source technology initiative, and modular technology architectures. The logistics industry is distributed over a technologically fragmented space dealing with varied sensors, communication protocols, data standards. As a result, without effective interoperability frameworks, the interoperability of AI and IoT solutions on multi-tier supply chains cannot be possible (Pfaff et al., 2023). According to future research in this context, universal standards and middleware solutions should be developed to synchronize data flow among heterogeneous devices and platforms from different vendors to provide plug and play capabilities.

CONCLUSION

While there has been a paradigm shift of logistics and supply chain management by integrating AI and IoT, it has every way to make long term impact in terms of efficiency in operational, resilience, and sustainability. This chapter and the forces its shows are not independent technological trends, but mutually reinforcing forces that, together, make possible the kind of intelligence, agility and end to end visibility that was not imaginable. AI-driven demand forecasting, route optimization, warehouse automation has been very helpful in increasing operational accuracy, reducing waste, cutting cost etc. With vast information already learnt from datasets and running in real time, logistics operations can identify issues to prevent these disruptions, use resources better, and provide services that match the dynamic market demands. IoT at the same time provides the necessary infrastructure for ongoing data generation, monitoring, and real time communication, which makes supply chain actors connected, informed and able to react immediately. Smart logistics ecosystems are the best example of how AI and IoT combined can bring up solutions of predictive analytics, autonomous decision making and adaptive systems. It indicates a clear and important shifting of logistics management mode from insecure, mechanized and manual toward cautious, information, data and extremely mechanized one. Industry case studies shared by the leaders of DHL and Amazon show how the strategic Application of AI and IoT technology resulted in huge operational improvements such as increased asset utilization, predictive maintenance, reduced carbon emissions as well as improved customer delivery of services. But such transformation is neither automatic nor easy. The barriers related to implementation such as the issues about data privacy, cybersecurity, the integration of the legacy system, and initial costs remain as analyzed in this paper. In addition, the barriers to the use of technology lead to an increase in the digital divide among small and medium sized companies in the logistics industry. To address these issues, both technological innovation and very sophisticated policymaking, industry collaboration, and investment in development of digital skills are required. AI and IoT logistics will be the future of AI and IoT once we advance in edge computing, blockchain integration, and billions of digital twin technologies. This innovation has shown to also augment supply chain transparency as well as efficiency and resilience. However, ethics are ridiculously important. Given that algorithms are increasingly dictating the decisions related to any movement good, worker practices, etc. transparency, accountability and fairness must be a foremost primacy to research and practice planners and policymakers must be undertaking too.

REFERENCES

Abdelkader, G., Elgazzar, K., & Khamis, A. (2021). Connected Vehicles: Technology Review, State of the Art, Challenges and Opportunities. *Sensors (Basel), 21*(22), 7712. DOI: 10.3390/s21227712 PMID: 34833782

Adamashvili, N., Zhizhilashvili, N., & Tricase, C. (2024). The Integration of the Internet of Things, Artificial Intelligence, and Blockchain Technology for Advancing the Wine Supply Chain. *Computers, 13*(3), 72. DOI: 10.3390/computers13030072

Alahi, M. E. E., Sukkuea, A., Tina, F. W., Nag, A., Kurdthongmee, W., Suwannarat, K., & Mukhopadhyay, S. C. (2023). Integration of IoT-Enabled Technologies and Artificial Intelligence (AI) for Smart City Scenario: Recent Advancements and Future Trends. *Sensors (Basel), 23*(11), 5206. DOI: 10.3390/s23115206 PMID: 37299934

Aljohani, A. (2023). Predictive analytics and machine learning for real-time supply chain risk mitigation and agility. *Sustainability, 15*(20), 15088.

Almatrodi, I., Li, F., & Alojail, M. (2023). Organizational Resistance to Automation Success: How Status Quo Bias Influences Organizational Resistance to an Automated Workflow System in a Public Organization. *Systems, 11*(4), 191. DOI: 10.3390/systems11040191

Ammar, M., Haleem, A., Javaid, M., Bahl, S., Garg, S. B., Shamoon, A., & Garg, J. (2022). Significant applications of smart materials and Internet of Things (IoT) in the automotive industry. *Materials Today: Proceedings, 68*, 1542–1549. DOI: 10.1016/j.matpr.2022.07.180

Aslan, Ö., Aktuğ, S. S., Ozkan-Okay, M., Yilmaz, A. A., & Akin, E. (2023). A Comprehensive Review of Cyber Security Vulnerabilities, Threats, Attacks, and Solutions. *Electronics (Basel), 12*(6), 1333. DOI: 10.3390/electronics12061333

Bayomi, N., & Fernandez, J. E. (2023). Eyes in the Sky: Drones Applications in the Built Environment under Climate Change Challenges. *Drones (Basel), 7*(10), 637. DOI: 10.3390/drones7100637

Campbell, C., Sands, S., Ferraro, C., Tsao, H.-Y. J., & Mavrommatis, A. (2020). From data to action: How marketers can leverage AI. *Business Horizons, 63*(2), 227–243.

Cao, Y., Lawson, B., & Pil, F. K. (2024). Social sustainability and human rights in global supply chains. *International Journal of Operations & Production Management, 44*(1), 370–390. DOI: 10.1108/IJOPM-10-2022-0670

Carlos Ferreira, J., Elvas, L. B., Correia, R., & Mascarenhas, M. (2024). Enhancing EHR Interoperability and Security through Distributed Ledger Technology: A Review. *Health Care, 12*(19), 1967. DOI: 10.3390/healthcare12191967 PMID: 39408147

Chan, H., & Wahab, M. I. M. (2024). A machine learning framework for predicting weather impact on retail sales. *Supply Chain Analytics, 5*, 100058. DOI: 10.1016/j.sca.2024.100058

Chidukwani, A., Zander, S., & Koutsakis, P. (2022). A Survey on the Cyber Security of Small-to-Medium Businesses: Challenges, Research Focus and Recommendations. *IEEE Access : Practical Innovations, Open Solutions, 10*, 85701–85719. DOI: 10.1109/ACCESS.2022.3197899

Choi, T., Kumar, S., Yue, X., & Chan, H. (2022). Disruptive Technologies and Operations Management in the Industry 4.0 Era and Beyond. *Production and Operations Management, 31*(1), 9–31. DOI: 10.1111/poms.13622

Chowdhury, A., Karmakar, G., Kamruzzaman, J., Jolfaei, A., & Das, R. (2020). Attacks on Self-Driving Cars and Their Countermeasures: A Survey. *IEEE Access : Practical Innovations, Open Solutions, 8*, 207308–207342. DOI: 10.1109/ACCESS.2020.3037705

Cirillo, V., Massimo, F. S., Rinaldini, M., Staccioli, J., & Virgillito, M. E. (2024). Monopoly Power upon the World of Work: A Workplace Analysis in the Logistics Segment Under Automation. *Review of Political Economy*, •••, 1–33. DOI: 10.1080/09538259.2024.2419611

Crouhy, M., Galai, D., & Wiener, Z. (2021). The Impact of Fintechs on Financial Intermediation: A Functional Approach. *The Journal of FinTech, 01*(01), 2031001. DOI: 10.1142/S270510992031001X

da Costa, T. P., Gillespie, J., Cama-Moncunill, X., Ward, S., Condell, J., Ramanathan, R., & Murphy, F. (2022). A Systematic Review of Real-Time Monitoring Technologies and Its Potential Application to Reduce Food Loss and Waste: Key Elements of Food Supply Chains and IoT Technologies. *Sustainability, 15*(1), 614. DOI: 10.3390/su15010614

Dangsawang, B., & Nuchitprasitchai, S. (2024). A machine learning approach for detecting customs fraud through unstructured data analysis in social media. *Decision Analytics Journal, 10*, 100408. DOI: 10.1016/j.dajour.2024.100408

de Almeida Pais, J. E., Raposo, H. D. N., Farinha, J. T., Cardoso, A. J. M., & Marques, P. A. (2021). Optimizing the Life Cycle of Physical Assets through an Integrated Life Cycle Assessment Method. *Energies, 14*(19), 6128. DOI: 10.3390/en14196128

Ding, Y., Jin, M., Li, S., & Feng, D. (2021). Smart logistics based on the internet of things technology: An overview. *International Journal of Logistics Research and Applications*, *24*(4), 323–345. DOI: 10.1080/13675567.2020.1757053

Donta, P. K., Murturi, I., Casamayor Pujol, V., Sedlak, B., & Dustdar, S. (2023). Exploring the Potential of Distributed Computing Continuum Systems. *Computers*, *12*(10), 198. DOI: 10.3390/computers12100198

El Moussaoui, A. E. (2025). Impact of logistics pooling on reduction of CO 2 emissions in last-mile logistics. *Management & Sustainability: An Arab Review*, *4*(2), 383–401. DOI: 10.1108/MSAR-04-2024-0023

Ellithy, K., Salah, M., Fahim, I. S., & Shalaby, R. (2024). AGV and Industry 4.0 in warehouses: A comprehensive analysis of existing literature and an innovative framework for flexible automation. *International Journal of Advanced Manufacturing Technology*, *134*(1–2), 15–38. DOI: 10.1007/s00170-024-14127-0

Emon, M. M. H. (2025). The Mediating Role of Supply Chain Responsiveness in the Relationship Between Key Supply Chain Drivers and Performance: Evidence from the FMCG Industry. *Brazilian Journal of Operations & Production Management*, *22*(1), 2580. DOI: 10.14488/BJOPM.2580.2025

Emon, M. M. H., & Khan, T. (2024). Unlocking Sustainability through Supply Chain Visibility: Insights from the Manufacturing Sector of Bangladesh. *Brazilian Journal of Operations & Production Management*, *21*(4), 2194. DOI: 10.14488/BJOPM.2194.2024

Emon, M. M. H., & Khan, T. (2025a). The mediating role of attitude towards the technology in shaping artificial intelligence usage among professionals. *Telematics and Informatics Reports*, *17*, 100188. DOI: 10.1016/j.teler.2025.100188

Emon, M. M. H., & Khan, T. (2025b). The transformative role of Industry 4.0 in supply chains: Exploring digital integration and innovation in the manufacturing enterprises. *Journal of Open Innovation*, *11*(2), 100516. DOI: 10.1016/j.joitmc.2025.100516

Fernandez de Arroyabe, I., Watson, T., & Phillips, I. (2024). Cybersecurity Maintenance in the Automotive Industry Challenges and Solutions: A Technology Adoption Approach. *Future Internet*, *16*(11), 395. DOI: 10.3390/fi16110395

Foroughi, A. (2021). Supply chain workforce training: Addressing the digital skills gap. *Higher Education. Skills and Work-Based Learning*, *11*(3), 683–696. DOI: 10.1108/HESWBL-07-2020-0159

Ghobadian, A., Talavera, I., Bhattacharya, A., Kumar, V., Garza-Reyes, J. A., & O'Regan, N. (2020). Examining legitimatisation of additive manufacturing in the interplay between innovation, lean manufacturing and sustainability. *International Journal of Production Economics, 219*, 457–468. DOI: 10.1016/j.ijpe.2018.06.001

Gohar, A., & Nencioni, G. (2021). The Role of 5G Technologies in a Smart City: The Case for Intelligent Transportation System. *Sustainability, 13*(9), 5188. DOI: 10.3390/su13095188

Hensher, D. A., & Wei, E. (2024). Energy and environmental costs in transitioning to zero and low emission trucks for the Australian truck Fleet: An industry perspective. *Transportation Research Part A, Policy and Practice, 185*, 104108. DOI: 10.1016/j.tra.2024.104108

Huang, R., & Mao, S. (2024). Carbon Footprint Management in Global Supply Chains: A Data-Driven Approach Utilizing Artificial Intelligence Algorithms. *IEEE Access : Practical Innovations, Open Solutions, 12*, 89957–89967. DOI: 10.1109/ACCESS.2024.3407839

Hutton, M., Corus, C., Dorsey, J., Minton, E., Roux, C., Blocker, C. P., & Zhang, J. Z. (2022). Getting real about consumer poverty: Deep processes for transformative action. *The Journal of Consumer Affairs, 56*(3), 1332–1355. DOI: 10.1111/joca.12479

Jayaratne, P. (2024). Technological Advancements and Cost Reduction in 3PL Sector. In *Transforming Logistics in a Developing Nation* (pp. 465–499). Springer Nature Singapore., DOI: 10.1007/978-981-97-7819-5_17

Kang, P. S., Wang, X., Son, J. Y., & Jat, M. (2024). *Service 4.0.* Springer Nature Switzerland., DOI: 10.1007/978-3-031-63875-6

Kavaliauskas, Ž., Šajev, I., Blažiūnas, G., Gecevičius, G., & Kazlauskas, S. (2024). Development and Investigation of a Smart Impact Detector for Monitoring the Shipment Transport Process. *Applied Sciences (Basel, Switzerland), 14*(16), 7102. DOI: 10.3390/app14167102

Khan, T., & Emon, M. M. H. (2025). Supply chain performance in the age of Industry 4.0: Evidence from manufacturing sector. *Brazilian Journal of Operations & Production Management, 22*(1), 2434. DOI: 10.14488/BJOPM.2434.2025

Khan, T., Emon, M. M. H., & Rahman, M. A. (2024a). A systematic review on exploring the influence of Industry 4.0 technologies to enhance supply chain visibility and operational efficiency. *Review of Business and Economics Studies, 12*(3), 6–27. DOI: 10.26794/2308-944X-2024-12-3-6-27

Khan, T., Emon, M. M. H., & Rahman, S. (2024b). Marketing Strategy Innovation via AI Adoption: A Study on Bangladeshi SMEs in the Context of Industry 5.0. *2024 6th International Conference on Sustainable Technologies for Industry 5.0 (STI)*, 1–6. https://doi.org/DOI: 10.1109/STI64222.2024.10951050

Khan, Y., Su'ud, M. B. M., Alam, M. M., & Ahmad, S. F., Ahmad (Ayassrah), A. Y. A. B., & Khan, N. (2022). Application of Internet of Things (IoT) in Sustainable Supply Chain Management. *Sustainability*, *15*(1), 694. DOI: 10.3390/su15010694

Kocaoglu, B. (2024). Enterprise Applications in Logistics. *Data Processing*, •••, 121–180. DOI: 10.1007/978-3-031-60290-0_5

Kumar, D., Kr Singh, R., Mishra, R., & Fosso Wamba, S. (2022). Applications of the internet of things for optimizing warehousing and logistics operations: A systematic literature review and future research directions. *Computers & Industrial Engineering*, *171*, 108455. DOI: 10.1016/j.cie.2022.108455

Liu, H., Zhou, L., Zhao, J., Wang, F., Yang, J., Liang, K., & Li, Z. (2022). Deep-Learning-Based Accurate Identification of Warehouse Goods for Robot Picking Operations. *Sustainability*, *14*(13), 7781. DOI: 10.3390/su14137781

Lorenc, A. (2023). How to Find Disruptions in Logistics Processes in the Cold Chain and Avoid Waste of Products? *Applied Sciences (Basel, Switzerland)*, *14*(1), 255. DOI: 10.3390/app14010255

Marabelli, M., Newell, S., & Handunge, V. (2021). The lifecycle of algorithmic decision-making systems: Organizational choices and ethical challenges. *The Journal of Strategic Information Systems*, *30*(3), 101683. DOI: 10.1016/j.jsis.2021.101683

Martyushev, N. V., Malozyomov, B. V., Kukartsev, V. V., Gozbenko, V. E., Konyukhov, V. Y., Mikhalev, A. S., Kukartsev, V. A., & Tynchenko, Y. A. (2023). Determination of the Reliability of Urban Electric Transport Running Autonomously through Diagnostic Parameters. *World Electric Vehicle Journal*, *14*(12), 334. DOI: 10.3390/wevj14120334

Modgil, S., Singh, R. K., & Hannibal, C. (2022). Artificial intelligence for supply chain resilience: Learning from Covid-19. *International Journal of Logistics Management*, *33*(4), 1246–1268.

Mohsen, B. M. (2024). AI-Driven Optimization of Urban Logistics in Smart Cities: Integrating Autonomous Vehicles and IoT for Efficient Delivery Systems. *Sustainability*, *16*(24), 11265. DOI: 10.3390/su162411265

Nantee, N., & Sureeyatanapas, P. (2021). The impact of Logistics 4.0 on corporate sustainability: A performance assessment of automated warehouse operations. *Benchmarking*, *28*(10), 2865–2895. DOI: 10.1108/BIJ-11-2020-0583

Ntanis, G., Aggelakakis, A., Boile, M., Tsaganos, L.-N., Papaefthimiou, K., Baroutsi, M., Chatzinikolaou, S., Paven, D., Vlascici, M., & Binchiciu, E. (2025). *Innovative Adaptation of Predictive Maintenance Familiarization Content to Address Contemporary Requirements in Transportation Sector.*, DOI: 10.1007/978-3-031-82818-8_15

Onyeji-Nwogu, I., Bazilian, M., & Moss, T. (2020). Big data and the electricity sector in African countries. *World Development Perspectives*, *17*, 100170. DOI: 10.1016/j.wdp.2020.100170

Paśko, Ł., Mądziel, M., Stadnicka, D., Dec, G., Carreras-Coch, A., Solé-Beteta, X., Pappa, L., Stylios, C., Mazzei, D., & Atzeni, D. (2022). Plan and Develop Advanced Knowledge and Skills for Future Industrial Employees in the Field of Artificial Intelligence, Internet of Things and Edge Computing. *Sustainability*, *14*(6), 3312. DOI: 10.3390/su14063312

Pfaff, Y. M., Birkel, H., & Hartmann, E. (2023). Supply chain governance in the context of industry 4.0: Investigating implications of real-life implementations from a multi-tier perspective. *International Journal of Production Economics*, *260*, 108862. DOI: 10.1016/j.ijpe.2023.108862

Plakantara, S. P., Karakitsiou, A., & Mantzou, T. (2024). *Managing Risks in Smart Warehouses from the Perspective of Industry 4.0* (pp. 1–47). https://doi.org/DOI: 10.1007/978-3-031-58919-5_1

Ponis, S. T., & Efthymiou, O. K. (2020). Cloud and IoT Applications in Material Handling Automation and Intralogistics. *Logistics (Basel)*, *4*(3), 22. DOI: 10.3390/logistics4030022

Poongodi, T., Lucia Agnesbeena, T., Janarthanan, S., & Balusamy, B. (2020). Accelerating data acquisition process in the pharmaceutical industry using Internet of Things. In *An Industrial IoT Approach for Pharmaceutical Industry Growth* (pp. 117–152). Elsevier., DOI: 10.1016/B978-0-12-821326-1.00005-X

Rejeb, A., Rejeb, K., Simske, S., & Treiblmaier, H. (2021). Humanitarian Drones: A Review and Research Agenda. *Internet of Things : Engineering Cyber Physical Human Systems*, *16*, 100434. DOI: 10.1016/j.iot.2021.100434

Sadiq, M., Ali, S. W., Terriche, Y., Mutarraf, M. U., Hassan, M. A., Hamid, K., Ali, Z., Sze, J. Y., Su, C.-L., & Guerrero, J. M. (2021). Future Greener Seaports: A Review of New Infrastructure, Challenges, and Energy Efficiency Measures. *IEEE Access : Practical Innovations, Open Solutions*, *9*, 75568–75587. DOI: 10.1109/ACCESS.2021.3081430

Scholten, K., Stevenson, M., & van Donk, D. P. (2019). Dealing with the unpredictable: Supply chain resilience. *International Journal of Operations & Production Management*, *40*(1), 1–10. DOI: 10.1108/IJOPM-01-2020-789

Selvakumar, P., Shanthi, M., Pitchiah, R., Sharma, M., Dahake, P. S., & T. C., M. (2025). *The Role of Artificial Intelligence in Business Model Innovation* (pp. 219–246). https://doi.org/DOI: 10.4018/979-8-3693-9571-4.ch009

Senna, P. P., Ferreira, L. M. D. F., Barros, A. C., Roca, J. B., & Magalhaes, V. (2022). Prioritizing barriers for the adoption of Industry 4.0 technologies. *Computers & Industrial Engineering*, *171*, 108428.

Sha, K., Taeihagh, A., & De Jong, M. (2024). Governing disruptive technologies for inclusive development in cities: A systematic literature review. *Technological Forecasting and Social Change*, *203*, 123382. DOI: 10.1016/j.techfore.2024.123382

Shee, H. K., Miah, S. J., & De Vass, T. (2021). Impact of smart logistics on smart city sustainable performance: An empirical investigation. *International Journal of Logistics Management*, *32*(3), 821–845. DOI: 10.1108/IJLM-07-2020-0282

Sorooshian, S., Khademi Sharifabad, S., Parsaee, M., & Afshari, A. R. (2022). Toward a Modern Last-Mile Delivery: Consequences and Obstacles of Intelligent Technology. *Applied System Innovation*, *5*(4), 82. DOI: 10.3390/asi5040082

Sturgeon, T. J. (2021). Upgrading strategies for the digital economy. *Global Strategy Journal*, *11*(1), 34–57. DOI: 10.1002/gsj.1364

Vashishth, T. K., Sharma, V., Sharma, K. K., Kumar, B., Chaudhary, S., & Panwar, R. (2025). Digital twins solutions for smart logistics and transportation. In *Digital Twins for Smart Cities and Villages* (pp. 353–376). Elsevier., DOI: 10.1016/B978-0-443-28884-5.00016-6

Vasiulis Ferreira Rodrigues, N., De Camargo Fiorini, P., Piato, É. L., Lopes de Sousa Jabbour, A. B., & Chiappetta Jabbour, C. J. (2024). Resources and capabilities for logistics 4.0 and sustainable value creation: A study of logistics service providers in an emerging market. *International Journal of Logistics Management*. Advance online publication. DOI: 10.1108/IJLM-11-2023-0471

Visconti, P., Rausa, G., Del-Valle-Soto, C., Velázquez, R., Cafagna, D., & De Fazio, R. (2025). Innovative Driver Monitoring Systems and On-Board-Vehicle Devices in a Smart-Road Scenario Based on the Internet of Vehicle Paradigm: A Literature and Commercial Solutions Overview. *Sensors (Basel)*, *25*(2), 562. DOI: 10.3390/s25020562 PMID: 39860930

Vlachos, I., Pascazzi, R. M., Ntotis, M., Spanaki, K., Despoudi, S., & Repoussis, P. (2024). Smart and flexible manufacturing systems using Autonomous Guided Vehicles (AGVs) and the Internet of Things (IoT). *International Journal of Production Research*, *62*(15), 5574–5595. DOI: 10.1080/00207543.2022.2136282

Wang, T., Hu, S., & Jiang, Y. (2021). Predicting shared-car use and examining non-linear effects using gradient boosting regression trees. *International Journal of Sustainable Transportation*, *15*(12), 893–907. DOI: 10.1080/15568318.2020.1827316

Wu, D., & Pi, Y. (2023). Digital technologies and product-service systems: A synergistic approach for manufacturing firms under a circular economy. *Journal of Digital Economy*, *2*, 37–49. DOI: 10.1016/j.jdec.2023.04.001

Zhang, J., Peng, S., Gao, Y., Zhang, Z., & Hong, Q. (2023). APMSA: Adversarial Perturbation Against Model Stealing Attacks. *IEEE Transactions on Information Forensics and Security*, *18*, 1667–1679. DOI: 10.1109/TIFS.2023.3246766

KEY TERMS AND DEFINITIONS

Artificial Intelligence (AI): A simulation process that puts human intelligence capabilities into machines enables them to perform human-like problem-solving and learning functions for decision operations.

Internet of Things (IoT): Physical devices linked by the internet transfer data among themselves to enable simultaneous observation and management operations.

Smart Logistics: Supply chains experience enhanced efficiency and visibility and sustainability through digital technologies including AI and IoT and other automated logistics instrumentation.

Predictive Analytics: Businesses utilize statistical algorithms combined with machine learning methods to examine historical data so they can predict future outcomes including demand predictions or potential disruptions.

Automation: The system performs automated tasks to boost operation efficiency and minimize human errors within logistics systems.

Real-Time Tracking: IoT sensors and GPS made it possible to monitor the good's location, condition and status along the full supply chain in real time.

Supply Chain Efficiency: The ability to improve the flow of goods, information and money through the supply chain, to reduce costs, delays and the use of resources.

Sustainability: The minimization of logistics and supply chain operations on their environmental impact by means of the optimization resources, the reduction of waste and carbon emissions.

Chapter 3

Smart Logistics Integrating AI, IoT, Blockchain, and Robotics for a Sustainable Future

Kirubhakaran Marisamy
https://orcid.org/0009-0003-2832-6379
Nehru Institute of Engineering and Technology, Coimbatore, India

Aarthi Selvakumar
https://orcid.org/0009-0006-9064-2091
Marwadi University, Rajkot, India

Balakrishnan Rajasekar
https://orcid.org/0009-0008-0932-7532
M.S. Ramaiah University of Applied Sciences, Bengaluru, India

Ravikumar Natarajan
https://orcid.org/0009-0009-3705-1681
Marwadi University, Rajkot, India

Anorgul Atajanova
https://orcid.org/0009-0000-5468-8187
Urgench State Pedagogical Institute, Urgench, Uzbekistan

Samariddin Makhmudov
https://orcid.org/0009-0008-2046-8889
Termez University of Economics and Service, Termez, Uzbekistan

ABSTRACT

The rapid integration of intelligent technologies is transforming global logistics, driving a shift from reactive processes to agile, information-driven systems. Intelligent Technologies for the Future of Logistics explores the impact of AI, IoT, Robotics, and Blockchain on supply chains, highlighting how these tools improve visibility, efficiency, and sustainability. The chapter evaluates each technology's core functions and their role in addressing logistics challenges like waste, opacity, and environmental harm. It also showcases real-world applications in transport logistics and emphasizes the synergy between technologies such as AI and blockchain. Despite notable benefits, barriers like high investment and workforce adaptation

DOI: 10.4018/979-8-3373-2434-0.ch003

are discussed. Drawing insights from logistics, IT, and environmental science, the chapter offers a multidisciplinary roadmap for creating resilient, green, and intelligent supply chains.

INTRODUCTION

The dynamic development of smart technologies has completely changed the world logistics. The reactive logistics processes based on traditional solutions are being swapped with dynamic and data-driven networks enabling flexible decision making and efficient operations. This shift is changing how goods are moved, used and managed through the global supply chains. Major accelerators of this revolution are Artificial Intelligence (AI), the Internet of Things (IoT), Robotics, and Blockchain. Their adoption in the logistics processes increases visibility, resource use, and general performance. These smart systems allow organizations to predict disruptions, computerize mundane jobs, and bring more visibility through the supply chain. The chapter is a critical analysis of how intelligent technologies are changing logistics and supply chain management (Anozie et al., 2024). It addresses theoretical backgrounds, examines the features of enabling technologies and discusses their synergistic effect on present-day logistics issues. Moreover, the chapter points out practical implementations and environmental consequences of digitalization in logistics. The goal is to offer not only scholarly along with practical knowledge on the development of logistics systems that are agile, resilient but also environmentally sustainable.

Overview of the Digital Transformation in Logistics

The increasing demand of speed, transparency and operational efficiency in the complicated global supply chains is executing the digital transformation of logistics. Digital technologies in the operations of logistics providers are becoming more integrated to keep them competitive and aligned to the expectations of the market, as manual processes and legacy systems are phased out. The key to this transition is the technologies of IoT, AI, big data analytics, blockchain, and automation (Ferreira & Reis, 2023). These tools allow monitoring the entire supply chain, predictive maintenance, automatic decision making and advanced communication. Logistics solutions that are data driven provide better performance and visibility than the old and paper-based systems. This transition does not only enhance operative performance but also contributes to sustainability, reducing waste and emissions, as well as resource usage. Digital technologies thus play a central role in the process of shifting the logistics to more intelligent, and eco-friendly patterns.

Importance of Intelligent Technologies in Modern Supply Chains

Smart technologies are important to increase the efficiency of contemporary supply chains, their responsiveness and resilience. The global logistics networks are becoming more complex and dynamic, the traditional way of doing things can no longer deliver on the speed, accuracy and sustainability demanded. AI, IoT, robotics, and blockchain technologies enable real-time visibility and provide data-driven decision making as well as automation across the logistics processes (Foster & Rhoden, 2020). These abilities tremendously enhance demand predictability, route design, inventory control and disruption reduction. In addition, smart systems help lower operational expenses, and environmental harm through wastes, emission, and resource productivity. They also build trust among stakeholders in that they can facilitate safe sharing of data and enhance traceability in supply chain operations. Overall, intelligent technologies are technological enablers, as well as strategic resources in the digital and sustainable supply chain transformation.

Objectives of the Chapter

- To analyze the role of AI, IoT, blockchain, and robotics in enhancing sustainability and efficiency in logistics.
- To evaluate real-world implementations of smart logistics technologies across road, maritime, and air transport.
- To identify barriers to green logistics adoption and propose actionable strategies for overcoming them.

FOUNDATIONS OF SMART LOGISTICS

Smart logistics is a revolutionary system of supply chain operations management through the use of the best advanced digital technologies for enhancing efficiency, visibility and responsiveness. It is based on key ideas from the field of logistics, computer science and systems engineering to develop an interconnected, intelligent logistics network. Essentially, smart logistics is characterized with the application of such cutting-edge technologies as IoT, AI, and big data, robotics and blockchain to logistics activities. Such an integration ensures real-time data harvesting, predictive analysis, auto decision-making and uninterrupted collaboration of stakeholders and operations (Madhura & Raghavendra, 2024).

Principles of Smart Logistics

Figure 1. Smart logistics framework

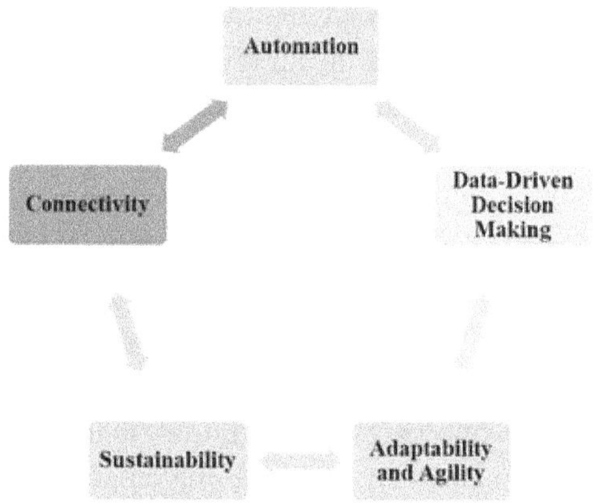

Figure 1 illustrates the interdependent components of smart logistics automation, data-driven decision making, adaptability, sustainability, and connectivity functioning in a continuous improvement cycle. The five capabilities that can be interrelated to make smart logistics systems are focused on increasing the operational efficiency and resilience. Connectivity means that every logistics object, including vehicles, containers, and warehouses, are interconnected and make it possible to monitor all of them in real-time and continuously. Automation is important as it helps to manage repetitive and time-consuming duties, such as inventory scans and package sorting with the help of AI-powered machines, thus decreasing the amount of manual work and inaccuracies. Data-driven decision making eliminates use of past assumptions and instead uses real-time data, analytics and intelligent algorithmic-based decisions to make sound and responsive logistics decisions. With adaptability and agility, the smart systems can promptly react to disruptions, spikes or drops in demand, or collapse of the supply chain, ensuring the continuity of operations (Ramesh et al., 2024). Finally, the sustainability is focused on by reducing carbon emissions, wastes, and increasing the optimality of the usage of resources with the help of the smart technologies implemented to encourage environmental responsibility.

Definition and the Scope of Smart Logistics

Smart logistics is the implementation of advanced digital technologies and intelligent systems to improve, automate and optimize logistics and supply chain activity. It requires the smooth integration of the tools like Internet of Things (IoT), Artificial Intelligence (AI), robotics, blockchain, and data analytics for the purposes of live monitoring, predictive analysis, and effective resource utilization. Smart logistics refers to a technology-based way of managing the movement, storage, and flow of products and information within the supply chain by intelligent systems, in order to enhance efficiency, visibility, agility and sustainability.

The field of smart logistics is versatile regarding the span of logistics functions and segments covered and aims at integrating the recent technologies to establish greater efficiency, visibility, and sustainability. Application of smart logistics in transportation management provides transportation tracking in real-time, dynamic routes optimization, and self-driving vehicles to deliver the goods. Warehousing is augmented through automated storage and retrieval systems, robotics and intelligent inventory management systems. The visibility of the supply chain can be reinforced through end-to-end traceability that is boosted by IoT sensors, GPS tracking, and blockchain technology. Regarding data analytics and forecasting, AI-based models enable accurate demand, risks, and strategic plans forecasting. The live delivery tracking, personalized notifications and faster order processing all of this improves the grade of customer service. And finally, but definitely not the least, smart logistics can also help in the sustainability endeavours by monitoring carbon emission, minimizing wastes and efficient use of logistics operations related energies.

Smart logistics does not belong to certain industries; rather, it can be used in all sectors like manufacturing, retail industry, e-commerce, healthcare, and transport (Kamble et al., 2025). Its wide range of coverage places it as a top driver of digital transformation in the global supply chains.

KEY THEORIES SUPPORTING INTELLIGENT LOGISTICS SYSTEMS

Smart logistics mechanism relies on a body of interdisciplinary theories that inform the convergence of technology, automation, and information-driven decision-making in the optimization of logistics mechanism. The systems theory explains logistics as an array of mutually supportive elements, e.g., transportation, inventory, and storage, which have to work together in unity. The view also allows the creation of interlinked intelligent logistics networks that will allow real-time communications, and coordination along the whole supply chain. The theory of Cyber-Physical

Systems (CPS) focuses on the idea of merging physical systems and digital cyber systems, leading to an IoT-enhanced logistics environment whereby sensors and other equipment connect to software to automatically monitor and control operations. The information theory highlights the importance of safe and effective data transfer and suggests applying blockchain and AI to keep the information safe, reduce delivery time, and make decisions regarding the supply chain. Philosophies such as Lean and Agile Logistics add the principles of wastes minimization and the ability to respond to changes, which are then materialized in the form of intelligent technologies that automate the work processes and can dynamically adapt to changes in demands or any supply chain disruption (Lee, 2019). The decision theory guides the application of AI and machine learning in generating the models that facilitate making the best decision-making in situations of uncertainty to enhance forecasting, routing, and risk-mitigation. Finally, the theory of sustainable development combines environmental objectives with logistics planning by favouring the adoption of smart technologies to minimise emissions and resource consumption, as well as facilitate cleaner operations. These theories when combined offer the intellectual basis of developing intelligent logistics systems which are efficient, adaptive and environmentally friendly.

TRADITIONAL VS. INTELLIGENT LOGISTICS: A COMPARATIVE ANALYSIS

The transformation from traditional to intelligent logistics is a significant shift in the running of the supply chains. Conventional logistics systems rely heavily on the manual systems, reactive and in pieces, intelligent logistics systems on the other hand rely on digital systems, proactive and interconnected (Ma et al., 2024). The differences between the two approaches are as discussed below Table 1

Table 1. Comparative analysis of traditional vs. intelligent logistics

Aspect	Traditional Logistics	Intelligent Logistics
Decision-Making	Based on historical data and human judgment	Data-driven, real-time, and AI-supported
Visibility	Limited end-to-end visibility	Full supply chain transparency using IoT and blockchain
Responsiveness	Reactive to problems and delays	Predictive and proactive through analytics and automation
Technology Use	Minimal or isolated systems	Integrated digital technologies (IoT, AI, robotics, etc.)

continued on following page

Table 1. Continued

Aspect	Traditional Logistics	Intelligent Logistics
Automation Level	Manual processes dominate	High degree of automation in warehousing, transport, and data
Data Handling	Siloed and often outdated	Centralized, real-time, and continuously updated
Customer Service	Slower delivery, limited tracking	Real-time tracking and enhanced customer communication
Sustainability	Higher energy use and emissions	Optimized for energy efficiency, emission control, and waste reduction
Scalability	Slower to adapt to change	Easily scalable and adaptive to demand fluctuations

Although the traditional logistics system has supported businesses for many decades, they fail to cope with the current speed and globalized market. Smart logistics, fuelled by smart technologies, provides the revolutionary upgrade: Agility improvement, lowing the cost and enhancing CX to align with sustainability efforts.

Key Intelligent Technologies in Logistics

Intelligent logistics uses modern technology for real-time tracking, data-driven decision making, automation, and supply chain visibility. Sensors linked to digital systems via IoT may monitor commodities, transportation, and equipment supply chains-wide. On-site data gathering improves inventory control and decreases delays (Mashayekhy et al., 2022). AI, machine learning, and predictive analytics estimate demand, system disruptions, and the best ways to improve operations. AI can process large volumes of data and find patterns that humans cannot, making decision-making simpler. Robotics and automation facilitate warehouse sorting, packaging, and logistics. Drones and driverless vehicles make delivery quicker, safer, and more familiar. Blockchain technology improves supply chain trust by permanently recording all transactions and movements in a ledger. These technologies build a connected, flexible, and environmentally friendly logistic ecosystem that meets market needs, cuts costs, and reduces environmental impact. They enable logistics companies to provide smarter, more efficient, and greener global supply networks.

Figure 2. Technological foundations of smart logistics

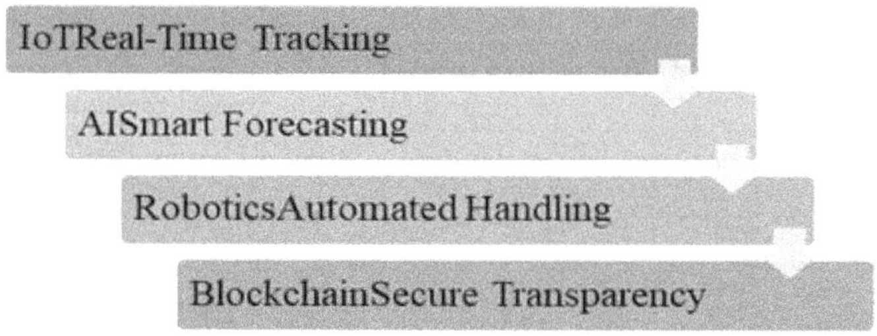

Figure 2 highlights the sequential integration of IoT for real-time tracking, AI for smart forecasting, robotics for automated handling, and blockchain for secure transparency in modern logistics systems.

IoT Real Time Tracking and Monitoring

Smart logistics allows monitoring and tracking commodities, assets and vehicles through the supply chain in real-time by the use of IoT. Sensors and GPS trackers are some of the IoT devices that collect and transmit data regarding the condition, location, and status of items and machinery. Using real-time information, logistics managers can optimize goods' transportation, anticipate delays and respond rapidly to obstructions. Cold chain logistics involves the use of IoT sensors that keep track of the perishable items' temperature and humidity. These sensors show that conditions are not ideal therefore actions can be taken before spoiling (Olufemi-Phillips et al., 2024). Maersk utilizes IoT sensors to track the shipping containers' position and state of affairs, like temperature, humidity, and shock levels, for ensuring product safety. Through monitoring the vehicles in real time, IoT helps in fleet management to optimize routes, reduce fuel consumption and guarantee scheduled deliveries. With visibility and data-informed decision-making, IoT optimizes operation, costs, and dependability of supply chain.

AI Forecasting and Decision-Making

AI enhances logistics as it has data analysis and machine learning algorithms whereby it pre-empts and decisions are made. AI systems are able to provide logistics firms with the capability to forecast demand as well as inventory management while improving route planning with such high volumes of data being obtained from historic patterns to live data. Businesses can ensure that they plan better, discard waste and improve service reliability with predictive capabilities. Top logistic firm in the world, DHL, uses AI, to predict demand in their supply chain. DHL applies machine learning algorithms to review past sales, season trends, and market conditions (Pal, 2023). They are in a better position to estimate demand and possess the right number of inventories at the right time, avoiding stockouts and surplus stocks.

The dynamic route optimization is a part of the AI-driven decision-making. AI algorithms optimize delivery truck routes using traffic, weather, and delivery windows. These sliced the delivery times, consumption of fuel, and their cost. UPS uses ORION (On-Road Integrated Optimization and Navigation), an artificial intelligence-based routing technology, to optimize daily delivery routes to save millions of miles and fuel. AI supports logistics enterprises in data-based decision-making, increasing the productivity level and enhancing customer service (Pasupuleti, 2025).

Robotics Automation in Locations and Movement

Robotic automation of handling and sorting of material and transport changes logistics. Warehouses, distribution centers, and transportation networks could hire robotics in order to improve efficiency, speed, and accuracy of the operations with the reduction of personnel and operating costs. Warehouses use Automated Guided Vehicles (AGVs) and robotic arms to convey, sort, and manage fragile or hazardous merchandises (Ramesh et al., 2024). The fulfilment centres of Amazon rely on robots such as Kiva (Amazon Robotics) to move items from the storage to packaging areas. Robots increase order fulfilment rate, improve inventory accuracy, and optimize warehouse space.

Autonomous delivery trucks and drones are also becoming more efficient when it comes to transportation. DHL has trialled autonomous vehicles that move freight long distances, while Alphabet's wing is experimenting with drone delivery for small products in urban areas in order to reduce time and cost of delivery. Logistics robots enhance efficiency, remove human error, and enhance scalability; therefore, supply chain management and transit become faster, safer and cheaper (DevOps Project Manager & Sharma, 2025).

Example

Logistics robots include automated Amazon warehouses. Kiva robots (now Amazon Robotics) move things through Amazon's massive warehouses. These robots autonomously pick up goods shelves and transport them to packers. Robotic automation speeds up order fulfilment, inventory management, and warehouse efficiency. Even DHL utilizes autonomous vehicles. Companies have tested self-driving trucks to transport goods long distances between warehouses and delivery points. Robots can streamline delivery routes, drive vehicles 24/7, cut transport costs, and boost efficiency by reducing human labour. Robots automate material handling and delivery, making the supply chain quicker, more precise, and cheaper.

Blockchain Data Security and Transparency

Blockchain technology changes logistics by securely, transparently, and immutably tracking transactions and objects throughout the supply chain. A distributed, tamper-proof digital ledger records all supply chain processes for visibility and data security. This boosts stakeholder trust since participants may access and check data in real time without intermediaries. Walmart and Nestlé use IBM's Food Trust Blockchain for logistics. This system lets stakeholders monitor food from farm to table. Blockchain can track food production, processing, and distribution throughout the supply chain for food safety. Transparency speeds product recall and authenticates source. Maersk automates shipping via blockchain. Trade Lens, a blockchain-based network created by Maersk and IBM, links shippers, port operators, and government authorities worldwide (Sun et al., 2023). This technology simplifies international trade by improving data security, eliminating bureaucracy, and providing a single source of truth. Blockchain improves logistics security, fraud reduction, and transparency, boosting global supply chain trust and efficiency.

Technology Integration and Synergy

Smart logistics incorporates technology in order to increase efficiency and agility of supply chains while enhancing sustainability. IoT, AI, blockchain, robots and big data analytics constitute a global system, which complement each other. To provide real-time data and automatic decision-makings, IoT and AI cooperate. AI uses data received from IoT devices to predict delays, optimize routes, and alter timetables.

Such blend allows working in a proactive logistics manner, not in reactive problem resolving .

Blockchain also leads to successful integration due to secure and transparent data transfer. Blockchain validates real-time IoT data-sets, eliminating fraud, and confidence of the stakeholders. This is recurring flow of data from IoT to AI and blockchain that offers intelligent self-optimizing supply chain. Robots provide further automation of the duties performed in the warehouse and in transport. Automated cars, drones, and robotic arms collaborates with AI to improve accuracy, efficiency, and work. These technologies create harmonious surroundings in which its part perfects others. The result is a brighter, faster, and transparent network of logistics that can adjust to the change of circumstances, meet the needs of customers, and contribute to the achievement of sustainability goals (Iqra University Pakistan & Zafar, 2024).

COMBINING AI, IOT, AND BLOCKCHAIN IN SMART LOGISTICS

Blockchain, AI, and IoT improve logistics. Combining these technologies allows real-time data collection, autonomous decision-making, safe, and transparent record-keeping, changing supply chains. The core connects goods, automobiles, and containers to digital systems via IoT. Supply chain IoT sensors track commodity location, condition, and movement in real time. Transportation container sensors may provide temperature, humidity, and shock data to centralized systems for processing. IoT devices generate massive amounts of data that AI analyzes (Ozdenizci Kose, 2020). AI can forecast demand changes, optimize routes, foresee disruptions, and make dynamic choices to increase operational efficiency using machine learning algorithms. IoT data may help AI schedule shipments in real time if traffic or weather is available. Blockchain protects, transparently stores, and immutably stores IoT sensor and AI data (Ahmad, 2025). The blockchain documents supply chain transactions to create a transparent path of goods from origin to destination. This boosts stakeholder trust, reduces fraud, and improves traceability, notably in food and medicines, where origins and quality are crucial.

Maersk Trade Lens monitors, analyzes, and stores supply chain data in real time using IoT, AI, and blockchain. This system gives manufacturers and customs authorities real-time information, boosting cooperation, efficiency, and accountability. Finally, AI, IoT, and blockchain create a seamless, intelligent supply chain system that records, analyzes, and securely distributes real-time data, improving efficiency, transparency, and strength.

Case Examples of Integrated Systems

The actual implementation of smart logistics technologies, including AI, IoT, blockchain, and robotics, have immensely contributed to increasing efficiency, transparency, and sustainability in different areas of transportation and the supply chain. In this section, we have provided some selected case studies to give an idea of how these technologies are used in practice, what quantifiable benefits they bring, and what innovations they involve in terms of logistics operations.

Walmart's Food Safety Blockchain: A Case of Smart Logistics Integration

Walmart together with IBM have come up with Food Trust Blockchain, which is an advanced technology aiming at improving the safety, traceability as well as transparency of food in its supply chain. It is an integrated system comprised of blockchain technology, IoT sensors, and AI analytics to solve food integrity, inventory optimization, and rapid response in the case of food safety incidents. The blockchain system is the central part of this effort as it enables Walmart to trace food items on the farm-to-shelf basis using a decentralized and secure ledger that is immutable. Each of the stakeholders such as growers, processors, distributors and retailers can have access to a common digital trail which captures the lifecycle of each product such as the harvesting events, shipping and storage among others. This inalterability provides that the data may not be modified without permission. Traceability is by far the greatest benefit, which allows Walmart to quickly locate and discontinue the use of contaminated products in its stores, which limits the health hazards to its customers (Bothra et al., 2021). IoT sensors are additional to this system, which measures temperature, humidity, and other environmental conditions of packaging, storage units, and transportation containers. Products that are perishable, such as dairy, meat, and produce need to have closely regulated environments to avoid spoilage. Such sensors are transmitting real-time information and it is observed that the data is analyzed and written in the blockchain. Once conditions fall outside of optimal ranges, notifications are delivered to interested parties, so that action may be taken immediately, rerouting deliveries or changing storage options.

The AI analytics then work on this data, assessing spoilage, predicting demand, and determining the optimal inventory level. Such changes in the environment that may go unnoticed by a human operator can be detected and rectified by AI. For instance, the system can forecast when products may be expired or if deliveries may be delayed due to weather conditions, enabling better stock rotation and less waste. Likewise, it serves as a support tool for automated restocking decisions to ensure optimum stock levels are maintained in stores without overstocking. This integration of blockchain, IoT, and AI has immensely improved the supply chain visibility and consumer confidence of Walmart. Scan a QR code, and one can trace the origin and handling of products, building the much-needed transparency during product recalls. The technology also enables Walmart to target these items first, preventing them from contaminating a huge number of other products. It has really made a huge impact. One of the trials involved Walmart tracing mangoes' origin in a matter of seconds, something that took days earlier (Han et al., 2021). Likewise, the case of contaminated lettuce was resolved in hours using blockchain-based data. With this enhancement, not only are food safety and customer trust strengthened, but they also contribute to sustainability by reducing waste and enhancing operational efficiency.

DHL's Smart Transportation and AI-Embraced Logistics

One of the giants globally for logistics and supply chains, DHL has ventured into the integration of systems including IoT, AI, robots and blockchain to enhance the company's logistics operations. This combined approach allows DHL to fulfil the growing demand for smarter solutions on the supply chain with more productive, reliable, and affordable services. Below are details of the ways DHL applying these technologies to facilitate logistics and transportation management. These are in packages, shipping containers, trucks and warehouses (Karulkar et al., 2024). Live, they monitor the location, condition, as well as movement of commodities in transit for DHL and its customers.

The goods are monitored by IoT sensors from warehouses to the point of delivery. A box that is in transit or out for delivery can be tracked by location, temperature, and humidity, which is important for sensitive goods such as medications or perishable food (Madupati, 2021). In turn, sensors can also track temperature, vibration, and shock while being transported. This ensures that commodities are treated with some standards and alerts in case something goes wrong. DHL leverages IoT to track pallets, forklifts, and containers, optimizing warehouse and transit operations. AI processes real-time data from IoT devices to enhance route optimization, predictive maintenance, and demand forecasting. By analyzing historical patterns, weather, and traffic data, AI helps DHL identify the most efficient delivery routes, reducing fuel consumption, delays, and delivery times. AI-driven predictive maintenance uses performance data and IoT sensor inputs to detect potential vehicle faults before breakdowns occur, minimizing downtime, lowering maintenance costs, and ensuring faster deliveries.

AI helps to optimize the inventory management and forecast demand. DHL can change its resources and inventory levels through the use of AI to forecast cargo volumes from customer data, delivery habits, and seasons (Mathur, 2024). DHL can meet the need in the presence of a variable demand without overstocking or under-stocking. DHL uses robots for precise and fast storage and sorting. Robotic arms, drones, and AGVs do repetitive activities with less human error and lower labour expenses. Warehouse management systems assist AGVs to move heavy products independently. It can properly scan, categorize, and sort things using robotic technology, which is crucial during busy seasons like holidays and product launches. DHL has also tested drones to deliver small products in distant or crowded metropolitan locations, reducing delivery truck use, costs, and last-mile delivery efficiency.

It uses blockchain technology to enhance data security, transparency, and traceability in its supply chain. This decentralized system records every transaction, avoiding tampering and fraud in food and pharmaceutical logistics. Products may be tracked internationally in real time, minimizing conflicts and increasing confidence. DHL is investigating smart contracts to automate payments and optimize operations. It improves supply chain data security, transparency, and traceability using blockchain. Tampering and fraud are prevented by the technology's immutable transaction records. Real-time monitoring promotes confidence among customers, suppliers, and authorities, particularly in sensitive industries like food and pharmaceuticals. DHL is investigating smart contracts to automate processes and speed up transactions with less mistakes and paperwork. By optimizing this hybrid method, the company delivers routed delivery, real-time tracking, predictive maintenance, and automated operations. These solutions meet current supply chain demands, improve customer experience, save operating costs, and promote sustainability. DHL develops innovative logistics technologies to improve global supply networks.

PRACTICAL APPLICATIONS OF SMART LOGISTICS TECHNOLOGIES

Industry uses for smart logistics technologies like IoT, AI, robots, and blockchain are extensive. IoT allows real-time cargo tracking and condition monitoring, ensuring perishable items are carried optimally. Fuel efficiency and fuel savings are improved with AI delivery route optimization (Pasupuleti, 2025). Robotics improve sorting and packing accuracy and speed in warehouses. Pharmaceutical and food businesses need blockchain for safe, transparent transaction records. These technologies boost operational efficiency, cost reduction, customer happiness, and sustainability, making them essential in contemporary supply chains and logistics.

Smart Logistics in Road, Maritime, and Air Transport

The integration of smart logistics technologies such as IoT, AI, blockchain, and robotics is revolutionizing the traditional transport sectors, namely road, maritime, and air transport. By leveraging these technologies, logistics operations in these transportation modes are becoming more efficient, transparent, secure, and environmentally sustainable (Tyagi, 2023). Below is a detailed exploration of how smart logistics is transforming each of these sectors.

Smart Logistics in Road Transport

Road transport plays a vital role in global logistics, handling the majority of the world's goods. Smart logistics technologies in road transport focus on improving fleet management, optimizing routes, and enhancing safety, efficiency, and sustainability. The Internet of Things (IoT) has given rise to the ability to embed sensors in vehicles (trucks, vans, etc.) and monitor activities associated with the movement of goods in real-time. More specifically, the use of sensors means logistics companies monitor the movement of goods, vehicle locations, and vehicle performance elements (speed, fuel consumption, temperature) and select the reference sites of interest (road/traffic/weather, vehicle operational performance) (Ullah & Havinga, 2023). Monitoring in lieu of delivery conditions will assist logistics companies to both ensure goods arrive on-time and also that it arrives in the right condition; for example, for temperature-sensitive goods.

For a smart truck example, the vehicle could have an array of sensors to monitor fuel levels, tire pressure and engine performance, which will send indicators back to a central system, allowing fleet managers to monitor the state of vehicle cargo in real-time. Fleet managers could take real-time decisions based on live performance metrics to increase operational performance of the fleet. AI could be a mechanism for route optimization based on data and analytics. In general, AI for data analysis can be deployed to better the fleet/carrier operations by improved productivity, fuel consumption, and consideration of existential factors related to routes traffic congestion, inclement weather, road closures, available distance on route total distance to delivery, etc (Vudugula, 2025). Further, AI will offer the ability to dynamically react and adjust its operations in real-time, optimizing not only delivery delays but also the fuel consumed based on the shortened antecedent delays. The result will be routes that are less costly and smaller carbon foot print by comparison.

Example: many delivery companies, such as UPS and FedEx, currently utilize AI algorithm legs to provide delivery optimizations for delivery routes, based on fuel consumption and time delays. For example, UPS employs a specific AI software called Orion Task Optimization software, with the goal to reduce 'left turns' for their drivers. The technology builds an optimal route for their drivers to decrease idle time and fuel consumption by accounting for recommendations based on real-time traffic and weather conditions.

The inception and use of autonomous trucks is one of the more significant innovations in smart road logistics. Companies such as Waymo and Simple are currently developing driverless trucks. The use of autonomous trucks will drastically change long-haul freight by lowering labour costs, increasing delivery efficiency, and improving road safety by eliminating human error. Additionally, it is becoming increasingly common to see robotic systems in warehouses load, unload, and sort packages. These robotic systems impact logistics by reducing the necessity for manual labour while increasing productivity and output. These include automated forklifts and delivery drones.

Blockchain is a more secure and transparent means by which road transport companies can represent movements of goods within the framework of a supply chain. Blockchain technology provides a decentralized ledger of all transactions and movements that cannot be tampered with or altered. Blockchain builds a history of the movement of the items in the supply chain from the time the package is loaded onto the truck, until the final delivery occurs (Alqarni et al., 2023). This is especially important when dealing with sensitive, or high-value goods that may require transparency from a compliance, fraud, or dispute resolution perspective.

Example: Road transport companies are beginning to use blockchain to represent shipments of pharmaceuticals in a secure and confidential manner. It helps track and verify whether or not the shipment complies with regulations and provides integrity in the supply chain.

Smart Logistics in Maritime Transport

Maritime transportation is an important aspect of international trade: over 80% of all international goods are transported by water. The maritime sector is implementing smart logistics systems and technologies to improve efficiency, reduce costs, and enhance environmental sustainability. IoT condition sensors are already widely used for port logistics applications, such as cargo monitoring, vessel performance, and environmental monitoring - including important aspects like temperature, humidity, vibrations, and fuel usage, and can help to ensure the safe and efficient transportation of goods. For instance, bulk cold chain logistics for perishables require logistics organizations to monitor the temperature and humidity continuously so that the goods are not spoiled (Alzate et al., 2024). Throughout the shipping process, vessels also use IoT condition sensors to monitor the condition of the vessel, engine performance, and fuel levels, while incorporating predictive maintenance to optimize fuel consumption, verify and prevent potential mechanical failures, and mitigate breakdown probabilities and impacts.

AI systems have emerged that can predict when a ship is required to undergo maintenance and also for equipment downtime maintenance in the maritime logistics supply chain. When equipment downtime occurs, it can result in additional costs to the shipper of goods. AI uses historical data and sensor readings to understand and predict statistical machinery failures, thereby allowing maritime transportation organizations to schedule maintenance more proactively. Predictive maintenance systems will reduce equipment damage costs and travel time of ships while maximizing operational uptime. AI is also essential in route planning it helps avoid busy shipping lanes, reduce fuel consumption, and increase efficiency of which ships are moving to their destination. By knowing the weather forecast, sea currents, and the historical data of traffic levels, AI can provide the optimal shipping routes, saving time and money.

Autonomous ships are beginning to look like one of the greatest innovations within maritime transport. Kongsberg and Wartsila are among the companies developing unmanned vessels that sail at sea with no human intervention, thanks to advanced AI and sensor systems. Autonomous ships are expected to reduce operational expenses since human crews are eliminated, increase safety while going from port to port where human errors could pose risks, while increasing the efficiency of ships as compared to vessels that are human operated. Also, they will communicate with ports and other vessels in real time to optimize travel times and avoid congestion in busy ports (Amifia et al., 2020).

Blockchain is becoming an increasingly common solution for tracking shipments and securing transaction records in maritime logistics. With blockchain, they are able to provide secure and immutable transactions for every step of the transportation phase, from customs clearance to vessel tracking. Although this improvement helps the transparency of records, it also enhances documentation and expectations to reduce fraud, documents required for shipping and administrative costs.

Smart Logistics in Air Transport

Air Transport is critical for high value and time sensitive goods; air transport is one of the fastest growing logistics areas. Smart Logistics technologies are currently being introduced in the aviation sector that improve speed, security, and sustainability, while managing the complexities of air cargo. As with road and maritime transport, IoT is used in air transport to track the location, condition, and performance of goods in addition to tracking the aircraft that is carrying them in real-time. Airlines and cargo operators are using IoT sensors to track temperature-sensitive goods, such as vaccines during transport to guarantee they are transported in their optimal conditions (Arnob & Majumdar, 2022). Real-time tracking would also provide the operators information to track the position of planes in the air as well as their engines performance, while allowing for forecasting for potential delays as well as weather, air traffic, or mechanical failures.

AI predictive maintenance is essential to ensuring aircraft are flight ready and in good condition prior to take off. Aircraft and its associated apparatus have sensors that collect information about its performance (engine temperature, duration of flight, load capacity, etc.). Subsequently, data interpretation is completed by AI algorithms that predict maintenance time and date based on these algorithms. Aircraft are less likely to experience mechanical failure, downtime before flights is reduced, and flight safety is more enhanced. Drones are increasingly being used for air cargo logistics, particularly for last-mile delivery in the urban environment. Drones can reduce delivery time and cost (also protect road congestion and minimise delivery times) all when providing reasonably priced deliveries for small packages in congested areas or very hard to reach areas. The likes of Amazon and FedEx are testing drone deliveries, so they can make deliveries faster than by road, all while helping reduce congestion and impact on the environments.

Blockchain is being used in air logistics as a secure, transparent cargo management solution in the air freight industry. Each step of the process when air transporting cargo can be tracked as blockchain guarantees that the air cargo has been documented at each stop and not subject to fraud. It is tamper-proof, and working with blockchain provides security for all transactions, tracking, and movements of cargo, which might include high-value items or sensitive items such as: health and pharmaceuticals, electronics, and luxury goods. Across a wide range of logistics operations, techniques to support the visual economy have arisen as a result of the rapid evolution of logistics practices in response to the unpredictable and linked environment in which businesses operate.

Smart logistics involving renewables, emissions tracking, electric vehicles, and journey planning may be experimental, but logistics 4.0 involving innovative collaborations and implementations has levelled the playing field for logistics firms globally in positively impacting the global agenda. Logistics and corporate sustainability are evolving with the green economy. Many logistics companies will witness massive tidal waves of green change every day, while others will view sustainable transformation and green logistics as a chance to grow. Environmentally critical green logistics may be one of the major changes to logistics (Barykin et al., 2023). Companies are under pressure from consumers and enterprises to adopt sustainable practices, affecting CSR and sourcing choices. Sustainable brand equity and customer loyalty help sustainable enterprises innovate.

SUSTAINABILITY AND GREEN LOGISTICS

Sustainability and green logistics focus on reducing the environmental impact of transportation, warehousing, and supply chain operations. These practices aim to minimize carbon emissions, reduce waste, and conserve energy by adopting eco-friendly technologies and renewable energy sources. Companies implement green logistics by optimizing routes, using electric or fuel-efficient vehicles, and embracing sustainable packaging. Beyond environmental benefits, sustainable logistics enhances corporate reputation, meets regulatory requirements, and reduces long-term operational costs. As climate change and resource depletion become urgent concerns, integrating sustainability into logistics is no longer optional but essential for responsible and future-ready supply chain management.

Conceptual Framework of Green Logistics

Advanced technologies, including AI, IoT, Electric Vehicles (EVs), and blockchain, have become the key part of the change to green logistics. Those technologies allow real-time monitoring, route optimization, energy efficient warehousing, and secure traceability of sustainable sourcing. The figure below shows a conceptual model summarizing the interaction between these technologies and the aspects of logistics to achieve environmental outcomes.

Figure 3. Framework for green logistics integration

Figure 3 outlines five key stages in sustainable logistics: Assessment, Planning, Technology Adoption, Monitoring, and Continuous Improvement. It visually represents a structured, iterative process to embed eco-friendly practices into supply chains. Each step is designed to promote emissions reduction, operational efficiency, and long-term sustainability.

Transportation Energy Efficiency

Transportation is a major carbon contributor in logistics. Firms are working to mitigate the environmental impacts on road, air, and shipping transportation by using energy-efficient vehicles and renewable fuel. Diesel trucks are at the beginning of a transformation into replacement electric, hybrid, and hydrogen vehicles. Tesla's Electric Semi Truck argues to reduce carbon emissions in long-haul freight transportation significantly. DHL and FedEx are also looking at electric delivery vehicles to decrease fuel consumption and pollution. In green logistics, using AI and IoT technology for route optimization is a key method (Singh, 2024). AI systems can analyze multiple inputs including, traffic patterns, weather, and congestion, to maximize fuel-efficient delivery routes. Reducing unnecessary kilometres travelled, and idle waiting time can reduce fuel consumption and emissions.

Example: UPS's ORION System optimizes delivery routes using AI reducing gallon fuel consumption by millions of gallons and reducing CO2 emissions on wasteful delivery routes. Energy use can be greatly reduced using sustainable storage methods as a key component of logistics operations. Green warehouses, for example, are using LED lighting, solar panels and energy management systems to cut back on energy use. Energy use can also be reduced by optimizing warehouse infrastructure, and using automation and robots.

Figure 4. Comparative annual CO_2 emissions - diesel vs. electric trucks

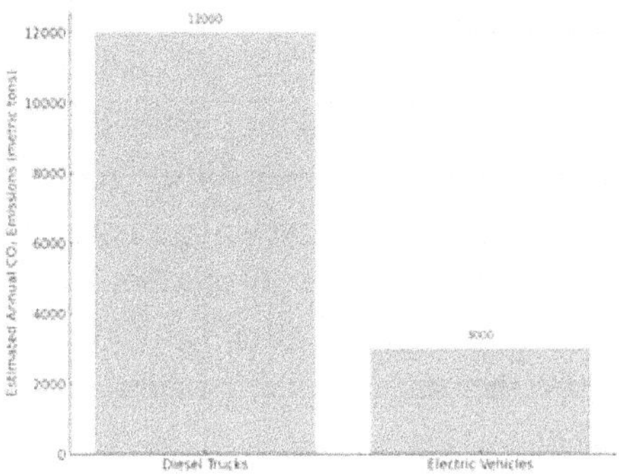

Figure 4 is comparing estimated CO_2 emissions between conventional diesel-powered trucks and electric delivery vehicles, illustrating the substantial reduction potential of EV adoption.

Figure 5. Impact of green technologies on supply chain emissions

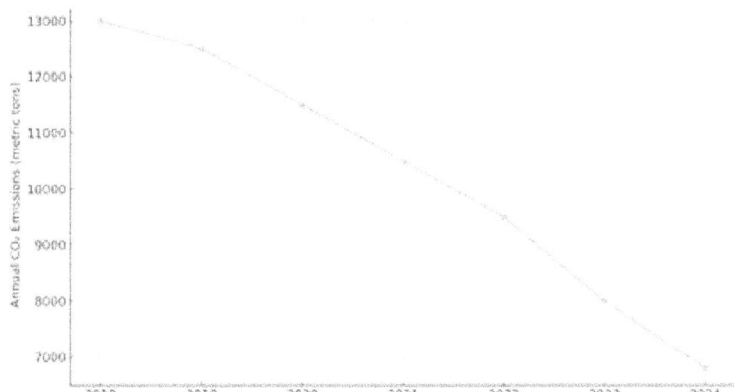

Figure 5 illustrates the annual decrease in CO_2 emissions from 2018 to 2024, highlighting the effectiveness of implementing green technologies in logistics.

Sustainable Supply Chain Partnership

Green logistics means coordination in the supply chain. Participating firms are able to share information, and align sustainability goals, applying less resource, preventing waste, and improving environmental performance in their supply chain. Coca-Cola has partnered with suppliers and vendors to reduce water, energy, and packaging waste throughout its transportation network while utilizing sustainable resources and working together on sustainable materials.

Circular Economy Models

A circular economy means the practice of reusing, refurbishing, and recycling minimizes waste. Reverse logistics activities that return, recycle, and reuse items and resources are helping logistics companies utilize the principles of a circular economy, reducing waste in the supply chain and minimizing the logistics environmental impact.

Example: IKEA's circular supply chain reuses old furniture through refurbishment and resale, reducing waste and helping the company meet its sustainability goals.

TECHNOLOGY INNOVATIONS LEADING GREEN LOGISTICS

Innovations like electric and driverless vehicles are critical in creating sustainable logistics. Electric vehicles eliminate fossil fuel consumption and pollution and trucks that drive themselves reduce fuel usage and improve transportation productivity. Blockchain technology provides greater visibility into the supply chain, allowing sustainability activities to be tracked throughout the entire chain while recording every transaction in an unalterable way. Blockchain tracing can authenticate sustainability of products and guarantee corporations' sustainability commitments (Tsymbal et al., 2023).

Example: Walmart and IBM are studying blockchain in their supply chains for sustainable seafood products and reducing the amount of food waste. An increase in smart cities with networked infrastructure is fostering green logistics. Smart traffic management, automated freight handling and warehouses contribute to reducing congestion and increases traffic flow. These technologies improve goods transportation by reducing congestion and traffic, thereby reducing energy used and emissions produced.

Challenges in Implementing Green Logistics

Green logistics is the way to achieve environmentally sustainable supply chains, but the transformation is fraught with a number of multifaceted issues. It is possible to divide these barriers into such broad categories as systemic, operational, and technological, each of which presents separate challenges to implementation. More insight on the nature of these challenges coupled with practical ways of dealing with them is crucial to any organization willing to adopt sustainable logistics operations.

Systemic Challenges

Complexity of regulatory frameworks is one of the main systemic issues of realization of green logistics. Ecological laws and sustainability standards are widely different among countries and regions, and multinational logistics companies are finding problems trying to adapt to them consistently. Such discrepancy in global standards usually impedes the efficient integration of green logistics operations. To address it, companies ought to promote the global cooperation in the field of sustainability policy-making and implement third-party compliance systems that help achieve compliance with a wide range of legal manuscripts. The other very big problem is the instability of the market incentives and policies. The sustainability of government subsidies, carbon pricing instruments, or environmental tax credits over the long term is uncertain in most jurisdictions, which makes it hard to justify investment in sustainable logistics. The corporations can overcome this risk through public-private partnerships and diversification of their investments strategically in various green technologies that have proved returns on investment.

Operational Challenges

In operational terms, the initial expense of switching to green technologies is still an important obstacle, especially in Small and Medium-Sized Businesses (SMEs). Electric fleets, solar-powered warehousing, and high-tech waste management systems are sustainable solutions that need considerable capital investments. This can be mitigated by a staged implementation plan that focuses on impact areas first and then backed up with some financial assistance in terms of grants or even leasing models. The issue of resistance to change in organizations is also a barrier to making headway as the employees and even those in decision-making positions may think that sustainable practices are invasive or that they are not necessary. Combating this, companies ought to invest in sound change management initiatives, training concerning the advantages of green logistics, and emphasize the monetary and reputation rewards of sustainable practices in the long term. Moreover, green logistics requires proper coordination of supply chain in order to succeed. In many cases, unlocked potential in sustainability initiatives is hampered by incompatible objectives or the insufficient visibility into the practices of supply chain members. Transparency and creating agreement on environmental goals can be improved by creating common Key Performance Indicators (KPIs) and using digital collaboration tools.

Technological Challenges

Technologically, most logistics systems have an infrastructure bottleneck, which restricts the implementation of green technology. Green transformation may be slowed down by the absence of electric vehicle charging points, renewable energy, and digital waste management systems. Investments in green field infrastructure should be done in stages and should be modular and scalable so that as new technologies and funds are available the infrastructure can be added to. Also, the process of green technologies integration with legacy systems may be technically complicated and resource-consuming. The usage of middleware platforms as well as API-based systems can facilitate this transition and facilitate interoperability. The other looming crisis is the digital divide in logistics institutions. Making smart green logistics a success depends on people who are able to manage and interpret AI, IoT, and blockchain system data. Firms need to fill this gap via upskilling initiatives, qualifications, and collaboration with academic organizations. Lastly, increasing the use of digital technologies creates cybersecurity and data privacy issues. Especially in the case of IoT and blockchain-powered systems, companies will have to implement multi-level cybersecurity measures and fully comply with data protection guidelines to prevent the loss of trust and operational integrity.

THE FUTURE OF GREEN LOGISTICS

Green logistics is not a passing trend; it's a response to logistics' environmental challenges. AI, IoT, robots and blockchain will play a key role in facilitating sustainable logistics operations in road, marine and air. For logistics companies, reducing their environmental impact and contributing to a sustainable future includes optimizing trip routes, number of trips taken, reducing waste, increasing energy efficiency, and alternating fuel use. As technology develops, and sustainability issues become more prevalent, green logistics will continue to play a vital role in the future of global supply chains (Ying, 2023).

Obstacles in Implementing Smart Logistics Technologies

While it brings a lot of change, smart logistics technology adoption faces critical barriers. In particular, there is high implementation cost for robotics and automated systems, especially for the so-called small and medium enterprises. Apart from this, the integration of these technologies with already in-use legacy systems is fraught with difficulties, including time-consuming processes, specialized skills, and occasionally halting ongoing operations for a while. The persistent skill gap also challenges adoption, since trained personnel capable of managing and maintaining these systems are in shortage. Data security is another concern; operating with large volumes of sensitive operational data puts them in the risk zone of cyberattacks. Regulatory compliance across different jurisdictions complicates matters, especially with cross-border operations where laws regarding data protection, environment, and safety differ. Resistance from within the organization also penalizes changes: Resisters fear job losses or doubt return on investment. Another talking point would be scale-up issues, where technology works well in a small environment but may have difficulties being effective in a larger and more complex one.

Strategies to Overcoming Barriers and the Future of Smart Logistics

To take advantage of the benefits from smart logistics technologies with AI, IoT, robotics and blockchain, companies will need to develop concrete strategies to deliver on addressing the environmental and economic barriers they currently face so they can create a sustained, agile and resilient future (Zhang et al., 2024).

Key Strategies for Successful Adoption

- **Workforce Development:** Training and upskilling to sustain the latent skills gap in relation to data analytics, robotics and AI Example: DHL leverages partnerships with institutions to develop employee capabilities in respect of automation and IA
- **Stepped Approach:** Implement smart technologies in stages, starting with areas of greatest impact, such as cost savings potential (e.g., route optimization, predictive maintenance, etc.) to build momentum. Example: UPS began with AI in their delivery models and gradually went to capacity with drones and autonomous vehicles.
- **Private/ Public Partnerships:** Think about partnerships with technology companies (cloud providers, infrastructure developers) and regulators to develop infrastructure and standards with reliability. Example: IBM and

Walmart's partnership to implement a blockchain improved their supply chain visibility and transparency.

- **Cybersecurity:** Safeguard the interconnected systems by deploying blockchain, encryption, and multi-layered protection of data to protect against compromises. Example: Maersk uses blockchain technology to protect and validate the integrity of data flowing through their logistics systems.
- **Sustainability:** Adopt technologies that will ameliorate the impact of freight logistics on the greenhouse emissions (i.e. electric vehicles and optimised travel routes with packaging technologies). Example: DHL's ambition to achieve carbon neutral logistics by 2050 using electric vehicles, and renewable-energy powered building facilities such as warehouses.
- **Blockchain for Transparency:** Using Blockchain to appropriately track and trace shipments will only strengthen the transparency of transactions associated with those shipments. Example: Maersk's Trade Lens initiative provides a tool for end-to-end shipment visibility (Aarthi et al., 2025).
- **Cloud & AI for Scalability:** Use cloud platforms and AI to scale your work flexibly and then optimize your rights as you make decisions in real time. Example: AWS provides platforms to use AI-driven analytics to enable global logistics to scale as needed.

The Future of Smart Logistics

Some of the emerging technologies of smart logistics will be laying the ground for promising solutions to the challenges faced today, with even more efficiencies waiting to be unlocked. Autonomous vehicles are predicted to change fundamentally the delivery operations, thereby cutting labour costs, mitigation safety risks, and perfecting delivery scheduling. FedEx and UPS are among the few industry leaders getting these solutions in the testing phase; hence, there will be a wider adoption of services in the near future. 5G Technology would provide a high speed, low latency communication required for real-time tracking, fleet management, and dynamic decision making. Businesses can hence respond faster and with more accuracy to customer needs and supply chain changes. Alongside, Edge computing is set to enhance responsiveness by localizing data processing at IoT endpoints in situations where such endpoints indicate vehicles or sensors with sporadic connectivity, thus ensuring smooth operations with minimal delay. Blockchain technology is expected to play a pivotal role in increasing transparency, reducing fraud, and streamlining cross-border logistics. It will simplify documentation, accelerate customs clearance, and improve regulatory compliance. Lastly, growing environmental awareness will push the logistics industry toward sustainable and green supply chains, prioritizing eco-friendly practices, emissions reduction, and resource efficiency in global operations.

CONCLUSION

The incredible and widespread effect of intelligent technologies on logistics and supply chain management is immeasurable. As discussed in this chapter, advances such as the IoT, AI, robotics, and blockchain are not only changing how goods are transported, stored, and tracked, but are also changing the platforms that decision-making and efficiency can rely on as part of global logistics systems. These technologies have the capability to empower logistics systems that are based on proactive, predictive, and information-based responses to these changes across supply and demand, customer expectations and environmental considerations over traditional, reactive logistics practices.

The intelligent technologies in the current era of logistics solve long-standing issues of the logistics sector. For example, IoT provides end-to-end visibility and the transmission of data from vehicles, containers and warehouse systems will support in the ongoing collection and transmission of data. This constant stream of data will provide a more accurate view of inventory, reduce waste, and support supply velocity. With the addition of AI to create valuable knowledge out of all of these data points, logistics companies can optimize routes, forecast demand, and automate maintenance. Blockchain adds another dimension of trust and security to the supply chain by ensuring that each transaction or movement is recorded, it is permanent. This may be especially useful in sectors with stringent regulatory and safety compliance such as food or pharmaceuticals that require full traceability.

Furthermore, the integration of these technologies creates a more informed and collaborative environment. The coordination of AI with IoT and blockchain will not only enhance and streamline operations, but it will enable accountability and transparency across the logistics chain. It will allow firms to respond to interruptions better like supply shocks, geo-political issues, or environmental emergencies because they are utilizing real-time intelligence and can put into place higher level of motion based on that intelligence. Sustainability is another important dimension operationalized through intelligent technologies. Smart logistics systems create greener operations by reducing waste, improving fuel use, and reducing carbon emissions. Technologies such as AI-based route optimizations and electric autonomous vehicles can help foster more environmentally responsible practices that can bring logistics in line with sustainability goals. Additionally, blockchain technology can provide traceable certification of green supply chains, with proof of ethical sourcing and certifications of carbon offsets.

While the advantages are many, the transition to completely intelligent means of logistics is not without challenges and expenses. Implementation costs, cybersecurity challenges, interoperability issues, need for a skilled workforce, transitioning operational logics and culture, and safely managing change are barriers an organization will face. It will require systematic change management, training, and requalification investment in the workforce, and long-term commitment to change in practices. In closing this chapter, we note that a multi-disciplinary approach is necessary to strategically navigate the digital and sustainable transition space in logistics. In the logistics domain, it takes collaboration across cyber scientists, environmental engineers, logistics professionals, government, and academia to realize the benefits of intelligent technologies. Logistics organizations must innovate, invest in human capital, and implement these technologies ethically and securely to create resilient, effective, and sustainable logistics networks.

The logistics of the future will chart the intelligent and sustainable logistics path. The intelligent technologies described in this chapter are designed to enhance productivity and competitiveness, but they will also support a vision of logistics that is transparent, accountable, and environmentally responsible. In the next decade, we can expect to see these smart systems emerge as the backbone of a more agile, adaptive, and sustainable future for the global supply chain landscape.

REFERENCES

Aarthi, S., Aravinthan, K., Ravikumar, R. N., Sivakumar, N., & Wanglen, S. (2025). Cryptography securing data in motion within Blockchain, internet of everything, and Federated Learning. In *Convergence of Blockchain, Internet of Everything, and Federated Learning for Security* (pp. 39–78). IGI Global.

Ahmad, N. R. (2025). Exploring the role of digital technologies in enhancing supply chain efficiency: A case study of E-commerce companies. *Indus Journal of Social Sciences, 3*(1), 226–237.

Alqarni, M. A., Alkatheiri, M. S., Chauhdary, S. H., & Saleem, S. (2023). Use of blockchain-based smart contracts in logistics and supply chains. *Electronics (Basel), 12*(6), 1340.

Alzate, P., Isaza, G. A., & Toro, E. M.. (2024). Operational efficiency and sustainability in smart ports: A comprehensive review. *Marine Systems Ocean Technology, 19*, 120–131. DOI: 10.1007/s40868-024-00142-z

Amifia, L. K., Riansyah, M. I., & Putra, P. D. (2020). Design of logistic transporter robot system. *Jurnal Ilmiah Teknik Elektro Komputer Dan Informatika, 6*(1), 19.

Anozie, U. C., Pieterson, K., Onyenahazi, O. B., Chukwuebuka, U. O., & Ekeocha, P. C. (2024). Integration of IoT technology in lean manufacturing for real-time supply chain optimization. *International Journal of Science and Research Archive, 12*(2), 1948–1957.

Arnob, A. M., & Majumdar, S. (2022). Resilient mobility and logistics systems for future: Bangladesh Perspective. *International Journal of Research and Innovation in Social, 06*(08), 186–193.

Barykin, S., Strimovskaya, A., Sergeev, S., Borisoglebskaya, L., Dedyukhina, N., Sklyarov, I., Sklyarova, J., & Saychenko, L. (2023). Smart city logistics on the basis of digital tools for ESG goals achievement. *Sustainability, 15*(6), 5507.

Bothra, P., Karmakar, R., Bhattacharya, S., & De, S. (2021). How can applications of blockchain and Artificial Intelligence improve performance of Internet of Things? –. *Survey (London, England).*

Ferreira, B., & Reis, J. (2023). A Systematic Literature Review on the Application of Automation in Logistics. *Logistics (Basel), 7*(4), 80. DOI: 10.3390/logistics7040080

Foster, M. N., & Rhoden, S. L. N. H. (2020). The integration of automation and artificial intelligence into the logistics sector. *Worldwide Hospitality and Tourism Themes*, *12*(1), 56–68.

Han, H., Liu, Z., Wang, X., & Li, S. (2021). Research of the relations among cloud computing, Internet of Things, big data, artificial intelligence, block chain and their application in maritime field. *Journal of Physics: Conference Series*, *1927*(1), 12026.

Kamble, S., Pandit, P., & Sansare, S. (2025). The economics of autonomous freight and logistics systems. *International Journal for Multidisciplinary Research*, *7*(2).

Karulkar, Y., Shah, A., & Naik, R. (2024). AI-powered business evolution. In *Advances in Business Information Systems and Analytics* (pp. 39–72). IGI Global.

Lee, I. (2019). The Internet of Things (IoT). In *Securing the Internet of Things* (pp. 1557–1574). IGI Global.

Ma, Z., Yang, X., Miao, R., & Yue, Y. (2024). Sustainable development of low-carbon supply chain economy based on the Internet of Things and environmental responsibility. *Economics - The Open-Access. Open-Assessment Journal*, *18*(1), 1–18. DOI: 10.1515/econ-2022-0099

Madhura, M., & Raghavendra, D. (2024). Leveraging IoT for smarter supply chain management and logistics: A comprehensive review and future perspectives. In *Futuristic Trends in IOT Volume 3 Book 8* (pp. 159–170). Iterative International Publishers, Selfypage Developers Pvt Ltd.

Madupati, B. (2021). Blockchain in day-to-day life: Transformative applications and implementation. *International Journal for Multidisciplinary Research*, *3*(1).

Mashayekhy, Y., Babaei, A., Yuan, X.-M., & Xue, A. (2022). Impact of internet of things (IoT) on inventory management: A literature survey. *Logistics (Basel)*, *6*(2), 33.

Mathur, T., & RV College of Engineering. (2024). reviewing optimization techniques in supply chains: AI and blockchain perspectives. International journal of scientific research in engineering and management, *08*(06), 1–5.

Olufemi-Phillips, A. Q., Ofodile Onyeka Chrisanctus and Toromade, A. S., Eyo-Udo, N. L., & Adewale, T. T. (2024). Optimizing FMCG supply chain management with IOT and cloud computing integration. *International Journal of Management & Entrepreneurship Research*, *6*(11), 3685–3722.

Ozdenizci Kose, B. (2020). Digital transformation of supply chains with mobile IoT. In *Advances in Business Information Systems and Analytics* (pp. 156–184). IGI Global.

Pal, K. (2023). Drivers of sustainable supply chain management using internet of things-based blockchain technology. In *Advances in Logistics, Operations, and Management Science* (pp. 171–201). IGI Global.

Pasupuleti, M. K. (2025). AI and IoT for the smart economy: Transforming manufacturing and service industries. In *AI and IoT in the Smart Economy: Revolutionizing Manufacturing and Services* (pp. 21–30). National Education Services.

Ramesh, K., Renjith, P. N., Balasubramani, S., Anto Bennet, M., Saritha, S., Pandey, D., & Kanike, U. K. (2024). Leveraging cutting-edge technologies and innovative strategies to optimize the IoT and AI integration in supply chain management. In *Utilization of AI Technology in Supply Chain Management* (pp. 159–173). IGI Global.

Sharma, V. (2025). Impact of automation on Retail Logistics: AI-powered solutions for efficient supply chains. *International journal of scientific research in engineering and management, 09*(02), 1–8.

Singh, G. (2024). Blockchain-based smart contracts. In *Advances in Computational Intelligence and Robotics* (pp. 183–203). IGI Global.

Sun, Y., Ma, A., Cui, X., & Gu, Y. (2023). Effective risk assessment and management with IoT in supply chains. *Frontiers in Management Science, 2*(5), 50–57.

Tsymbal, L., Natsvlishvili, T., & Verdenhofa, O. (2023). One Belt, One Road project: The impact of smart technologies on infrastructure and logistics. *Baltic Journal of Economic Studies, 9*(3), 214–221. DOI: 10.30525/2256-0742/2023-9-3-214-221

Tyagi, A. K. (2023). Blockchain and artificial intelligence for cyber security in the era of internet of things and industrial internet of things applications. In *Advances in Computational Intelligence and Robotics* (pp. 171–199). IGI Global.

Ullah, I., & Havinga, P. J. M. (2023). Governance of a Blockchain-Enabled IoT Ecosystem: A Variable Geometry Approach. *Sensors (Basel), 23*(22), 9031. DOI: 10.3390/s23229031 PMID: 38005419

Vudugula, S. (2025). Sustainable smart supply chains: A review of green technologies and their impact on logistics. *American Journal of Scholarly Research and Innovation, 4*(01), 1–32.

Ying, P. (2023). A study of enterprise warehouse management based on intelligent logistics. In *Advances in Social Science, Education and Humanities Research* (pp. 829–835). Atlantis Press SARL.

Zafar, F. (2024). Examining the effect of Internet of Things (IoT) adoption on supply chain performance. *South Asian Journal of Operations and Logistics, 3*(2), 282–294.

Zhang, F., Liao, Y., & Ding, Y. (2024). Development and application of smart logistics management service platform under big data technology. *Proceedings of the 4th International Conference on Economic Management and Big Data Applications.*

KEY TERMS AND DEFINITIONS

Smart Logistics: Integration of AI, IoT, robotics, and blockchain into logistics networks to enable dynamic, data-driven decision-making, real-time tracking, and automated operations, replacing reactive manual processes.

Artificial Intelligence (AI): Algorithms and machine learning systems that analyze logistics data to optimize routes, predict demand, automate warehouse operations, and enhance supply chain resilience through adaptive decision-making.

Internet of Things (IoT): Network of interconnected sensors (e.g., GPS, temperature monitors) embedded in vehicles, containers, and infrastructure to collect and transmit real-time data on location, conditions, and performance metrics.

Robotics: Autonomous machines (e.g., AGVs, drones, robotic arms) that automate physical tasks such as warehouse picking, parcel sorting, last-mile delivery, and inventory management to reduce labor costs and errors.

Blockchain: Decentralized ledger technology providing immutable, transparent records of transactions across supply chains, ensuring data integrity for provenance verification, smart contracts, and compliance.

Digital Supply Chain: End-to-end ecosystem where stakeholders (suppliers, carriers, retailers) share data via cloud platforms and APIs, enabling seamless coordination, predictive analytics, and real-time visibility.

Predictive Analytics: AI-driven analysis of historical and real-time data to forecast disruptions (e.g., port delays, demand surges), optimize inventory levels, and enable proactive resource allocation.

Sustainable Logistics: Eco-conscious practices leveraging digital technologies to minimize carbon emissions (e.g., route optimization), reduce waste (e.g., inventory precision), and promote circular economy models.

Supply Chain Resilience: Capability to anticipate, absorb, and recover from disruptions (e.g., geopolitical conflicts, natural disasters) using AI-driven risk modeling and IoT-enabled real-time monitoring.

Real-Time Visibility: Continuous tracking of goods across transport modes via IoT and blockchain, providing stakeholders with instant access to location, environmental conditions, and handling status.

Chapter 4

Real-Time Tracking Technologies' Effect on Supply Chain Transparency by Mediation of Smart Logistics Technologies in the Horn of Africa

Shashi Kant
https://orcid.org/0000-0003-4722-5736
Bule Hora University, Ethiopia

ABSTRACT

With an emphasis on the mediating function of smart logistics technologies (SLT), this study investigates the impact of real-time tracking technologies (RTT) on supply chain transparency in the Horn of Africa. The purpose of this study is to clarify how RTT might improve transparency through efficient integration with SLT in an area that has particular logistical problems and a changing technology environment. The study uses a mixed-methods technique to gather qualitative views from industry experts and quantitative data from logistics professionals. The results show that by providing real-time visibility into logistics processes, RTT greatly increases supply chain transparency. Additionally, SLT is recognized as an essential mediator that promotes improved stakeholder communication and data exchange. This study emphasizes how important it is to implement cutting-edge tracking and logistics technology in order to promote openness, establish credibility, and improve overall

DOI: 10.4018/979-8-3373-2434-0.ch004

operational performance.

INTRODUCTION

Considering the increasingly interconnected world of today, supply chain transparency has become more vital than ever. As global trade is likely to expand rapidly, it is essential to feed economic growth, especially in locations that include the Horn of Africa, that goods are efficiently carried from producers towards consumers. Because of its unique geopolitical climate along with economic opportunities, this region provides a great backdrop for studying the interaction among supply chain transparency and real-time monitoring technologies. This concept emerged primarily a result of the convergence of logistics management alongside information technology innovations, which have made traditional supply chains quicker to respond, dynamic, and adaptable to changing customer demands (Khan et al., 2023).

Global trends indicate a significant change towards the adoption of real -time monitoring technologies in supply chains, drawn by increased demand from consumers of transparency and efficiency. Regions such as North America and Western Europe have managed to integrate these technologies, supported by robust regulatory frameworks that promote digital innovation (Al-Khatib, 2023). For example, general rules for protecting data from the European Union (GDPR) provide an integrated approach to data confidentiality and strengthen trust in digital supply chain processes. These structures encourage businesses to embrace advanced technology and ensure compliance and protection of consumer rights. However, the horn of Africa is faced with unique challenges that hinder similar progress. Key obstacles include inadequate infrastructure, limited access to insufficient technology and financial resources (Khan et al., 2023). In Ethiopia, for example, despite government initiatives that modernize logistics, many companies are battling the lack of investment in outdated systems and digital tools. Furthermore, the various political landscapes in the region can lead to coherent regulatory policies, which further complicate the adoption of follow-up technologies. Real-world case studies can provide valuable information to overcome these obstacles. In Kenya, the implementation of a unique window electronic system streamlines the tariff process and demonstrates how digital tools can improve transparency and efficiency. This initiative demonstrates the potential benefits of technology that not only improves logistics, but also promotes trade and involves solid policy support (Ding et al., 2021). Systematic analysis of barriers is important for deepening discussion. These include technical limitations such as unreliable internet connectivity and high deployment costs, as well as cultural resistance to the introduction of new systems (Issaoui et al., 2019). Furthermore, the work capacity gap prevents effective implementation as it does not require sufficient training to use advanced follow-up technologies. The solution to these problems requires a multifaceted approach. Politicians should establish a regulatory environmental environment, while businesses should invest in employee training and improve infrastructure. By learning from global best practices and adapting them to local contexts, the Horn of Africa can enhance its supply chain transparency and operational efficiency, ultimately driving economic growth in the region.

The results of an empirical study, continuous tracking technology, such as GPS and RFID, improves visibility throughout the supply chain, allowing participants to keep a watch on product flow and respond swiftly when disturbances (Al-Khatib, 2023). Compared to research, improved monitoring ultimately results in fewer expenditures, more production, and happier consumers. Thankfully has been little study on how to incorporate sophisticated logistics technologies into this framework, such as data analytics, computerized processes, and Internet of Things devices, particularly throughout the Horn of Africa. Real-time tracking and smart logistics have proved difficult to implement in this area partly because of practical challenges that consist of political instability, shortage of infrastructure, as well as varying levels of technological penetration (Zelbst et al., 2019).

There are still unanswered questions about how to integrate these technologies to improve supply chain transparency in the Horn of Africa. Although previous research emphasizes the advantages of real-time tracking, it frequently overlooks the mediating function of smart logistics technology, which might enhance these benefits. By examining the complementary impacts of smart logistics and real-time monitoring technologies on supply chain transparency, this chapter seeks to close these gaps. This study will give future scholars and policymakers useful insights by doing a thorough examination of the existing environment (Al-Khatib, 2023). This study's main inquiry is: *"How can smart logistics technologies in the Horn of Africa mediate the effects of real-time tracking technology on supply chain transparency?"* It is imperative that this issue be answered since it not only clarifies the operational dynamics of supply chains in the area but also helps guide strategic policy choices meant to promote resilience and economic growth. This chapter seeks to establish a clear course for future research and policy formation by addressing practical issues and addressing the gaps in current knowledge, eventually assisting in the creation of a more transparent and effective supply chain ecosystem in the Horn of Africa.

BACKGROUND OF STUDY

One revolutionary strategy for increasing efficiency and transparency in supply chain management is the use of real-time tracking systems. The aforementioned technologies have the potential to greatly enhance supply chains throughout the Horn of

Africa, an area marked because it's strategic location and diverse economic activity. However, there are additionally significant barriers to successful implementation, which originate directly from sociopolitical dynamics along with infrastructure restrictions (Khan et al., 2023). Ethiopia shares a logistics business, who's the government has made significant investments in infrastructure for transport, offers a notable instance study. The nation continues to struggle with poor road systems and restricted access to contemporary communication technology in spite of these efforts. For example, according to a World Bank research, only around 30% of Ethiopia's rural roads are paved, making it more difficult to transport commodities in a dependable manner. This lack of infrastructure significantly reduces the efficacy of real-time tracking systems as irregular transportation routes might result in inaccurate cargo tracking and delivery delays (Khan et al., 2023).

World leaders in the field of logistics, such as DHL, Amazon, and Maersk, have successfully implemented supply chain transparency decisions that serve as a valuable thematic study in Africa (Pyra, 2024). For example, DHL used the Resilience 360 platform to provide real-time visibility into supply chain operations. This allows customers to proactively manage risks and dysfunctions. Using advanced analytics and data integration, DHL can increase transparency and make reasonable decisions based on actual information (Al-Khatib, 2023). This model illustrates how investment in technology leads to a more sustainable supply chain. In the same way, the use of Amazon complex monologies illustrates best practices in the transparency of the supply chain. The company uses a network of data and analysts of data to monitor reserves and optimization of delivery routes. This not only reduces operating costs, but also increases customer satisfaction thanks to appropriate timely delivery. Amazon's commitment to transparency supported by a robust regulatory framework establishes an organization's reference aimed at improving its logistics business (Shee et al., 2021). Maersk, a global leader in maritime and logistics, was also able to improve supply chain transparency through the Tradelelens platform, developed in collaboration with IBM. This blockchain-based decision will allow all stakeholders in the supply chain to access real data, improving cooperation and reducing inefficiency. Maersk demonstrates how technology can contribute to transparency and confidence among partners, providing a compelling example of the logistics sector in the Horn of Africa (Khatib, 2023).

The situation in the Horn of Africa is made more difficult by persistent political unrest and security issues. Fragmented supply chains that are challenging to oversee are the outcome of an unstable governance system. For instance, according to the UN, the incapacity to efficiently trace the flow of supplies frequently poses serious problems for humanitarian supply chains. This raises the possibility of resource loss and diversion in addition to decreasing accountability. The use of conventional logistics management techniques in these situations exacerbates transparency problems and emphasizes the pressing need for creative alternative. With its burgeoning digital scene, especially in Nairobi, which has emerged as a center for logistics innovation, the Horn of Africa makes a more promising argument. Better financial tracking and payment procedures inside supply chains have been made possible by the introduction of the M-Pesa mobile money system (Issaoui et al., 2019). Nevertheless, businesses continue to have difficulties integrating real-time tracking technologies with current logistical procedures in spite of these developments. Technology adoption by itself does not ensure success, as evidenced by a case study of a large Kenyan store that showed that although real-time tracking enhanced inventory management, a lack of thorough data integration across departments resulted in misalignment and inefficiencies (Ding et al., 2021).

The Horn of Africa has long struggled with issues that hinder supply chain transparency due to political instability, insufficient infrastructure and economic challenges. These factors have historically limited local capacity to establish effective commercial networks and reliable supply chains. However, the landscape changes with the advent of actual follow-up technologies, including RFID, GPS and IoT systems (Pyra, 2024). These innovations will increase visibility of transport goods, allowing stakeholders to effectively monitor shipments and improve global responsibility. The evolution of technology in this region has experienced progressive adoption of intelligent logistics technology and plays an important role in mediating the effectiveness of actual monitoring (Al-Khatib, 2023). Automated inventory management systems, data analytics, and integrated supply chain platforms are wider, but their implementation is uneven. Countries such as Kenya and Ethiopia are conducting comparative theme studies of regions that have implemented similar obstacles. For example, with investments in Kenya's digital infrastructure and partnerships with private organizations, Ethiopia is focusing on developing policies that will promote the adoption of technology and increase transparency in the national market. Despite these achievements, current issues are preserved. Progress is hampered by limited internet connectivity, lack of qualified personnel and resistance from traditional subjects in the supply chain. The summary table of key research in the literature review highlights its contribution to a political framework aimed at identifying trends in technology adoption, identifying gaps in full implementation strategies, and promoting supply chain transparency. These studies highlight the important need for a multifaceted approach, including stakeholder engagement, capacity building and regulatory support environments. Together, these efforts can use the possibilities of surveillance and intellectual logistics technology in real time to overcome existing obstacles (Khan et al., 2022).

These real-world examples highlight the many obstacles that the Horn of Africa has while using real-time tracking systems. A complicated environment need specialized implementation strategies due to differences in infrastructure, political stability, and technical preparedness (Shee et al., 2021). Additionally, nothing is known about the mediating function of smart logistics technologies, which leaves a knowledge vacuum regarding the efficient integration of these instruments to improve supply chain transparency (Akkaya & Kaya, 2019). This history lays the groundwork for the present study, which looks into these processes and offers a plan for getting over current obstacles to help the region's supply networks become more resilient.

STATEMENT OF PROBLEM

The disparity among the ideal condition of smooth, effective logistics and the actual circumstances that businesses and governments in the region experience today highlights the issue of inadequate supply chain transparency in the Horn of Africa (Osato Itohan Oriekhoe et al., 2024). The combination of smart logistics and real-time tracking technology should ideally result in an open and responsive supply chain ecosystem that improves accountability, cuts down on delays, and stimulates economic development. Empirical research, however, shows a paradoxical environment in which many firms find it difficult to successfully use these technologies. For example, whereas some research suggests that real-time tracking might enhance operational performance, other studies point to enduring problems such poor infrastructure, slow acceptance of new technologies, and organizational reluctance to change (Akkaya & Kaya, 2019).

Traveling in the Horn of Africa to increase supply chain transparency is the source of barriers that hinder the adoption of actual monologist. The main issues include infrastructure flaws, reliable internet access, and high initial costs associated with technology implementation (Khatib, 2023). In addition, a lack of awareness and understanding of stakeholders on the advantages of these technologies creates resistance to change, further complicating efforts to modernize supply chains. Business leaders and political decision -makers must recognize these obstacles to promote an environment conducive to technological adoption. Cybersecurity risks pose another significant concern in the digital logistics landscape. As supply chains become increasingly interconnected, the potential for cyber threats rises, exposing sensitive data and operational processes to malicious attacks (Helo & Shamsuzzoha, 2020). Organizations should prioritize robust cybersecurity measurements, including using encryption, achieving regular security audits, and implementing strict access controls. Additionally, investments in employee cybersecurity training allow employees to be equipped to recognize and respond to potential threats, ultimately ensuring the integrity of their supply chain operations. Labor training is crucial to facilitate the successful integration of tracking technologies into supply chains. Many African employees may not have the necessary digital skills for the effective operation of modern logistics systems (Al-Khatib, 2023). To address this gap, businesses and policymakers need to work together to develop comprehensive training programs that include both technical skills and change management strategies. These initiatives will enable employees to adapt to new technologies and increase overall operational efficiency. Furthermore, establishing partnerships between government, educational institutions and industry leaders can create a conveyor of qualified labor that meets the requirements of a digital logistics environment (Ding et al., 2021). ROG Africa can create trusted structures that support successful implementation of actual tracking technologies by managing recruitment barriers and determining cybersecurity priorities and investments in labor development. This overall approach not only increases supply chain transparency, but also stimulates economic growth and stability in the region (Shee et al., 2021).

These evidentiary inconsistencies highlight a number of holes that require attention. First, the literature currently available on the interaction among smart logistics technology and real-time tracking has theoretical gaps. Although both ideas have been studied independently, there aren't many thorough frameworks that combine the two technologies to evaluate how they affect supply chain transparency as a whole (Pyra, 2024). Second, there are still unanswered questions regarding the precise circumstances under which these technologies may be successfully applied in the distinct socioeconomic environment of the Horn of Africa. For instance, there hasn't been enough research done on how local government, cultural perspectives on technology, and workforce educational attainment relate to the adoption of new technologies (Astill et al., 2019). Examining the application of current models created in more stable and technologically sophisticated places to the Horn of Africa also reveals context gaps. There are conflicting findings on the efficacy of real-time tracking systems in this particular setting since the special difficulties of political instability, infrastructure deficiencies, and economic volatility have not been sufficiently taken into consideration in recent studies (Helo & Shamsuzzoha, 2020). The absence of the tools, training, and support networks required for companies to successfully implement and use new technologies also presents practical difficulties (Mann et al., 2018).

By offering a comprehensive examination of "*how smart logistics and real-time monitoring technologies may be used to improve supply chain transparency in the Horn of Africa*", this research seeks to close these gaps. This research will provide policymakers and business leaders with practical advice by creating a thorough framework that integrates theoretical insights, context-specific elements, and practical concerns. The results will offer a path for future researchers to investigate the intricacies of technology integration in demanding situations, in addition to theoretically advancing the literature on supply chain management. In the end, this study hopes to assist stakeholders in overcoming the real-world obstacles associated with putting these technologies into practice, promoting a more open and effective supply chain ecosystem in the Horn of Africa.

RELATED THEORIES

Resource-Based View: A variety of theoretical paradigms provide valuable insights into how immediate time tracking technologies impact supply chain transparency. The resource-based perspective (RBV), one fundamental viewpoint, preserves that a company's abilities and resources are important for attaining a competitive advantage. This idea emphasizes the need of introducing innovative technology, such as real-time tracking along with intelligent administrative tasks, into supply chains as valuable instruments for improving company efficiency and transparency. Organizations might boost their overall supply chain effectiveness by leveraging these advances to cultivate unique talents that will allow businesses to better respond to marketplace requirements including disruptions.

Technology Acceptance Model: A further significant concept is the technologies Acceptance Model (TAM), particularly looks at the way individuals acquire and use new technologies. TAM highlights the effects that perceived utility and ease of use have on technology adoption. It is critical to understand the factors that impact the widespread utilization of real-time monitoring systems around the Horn of Africa, in particular in contexts where technical literacy could vary substantially. This technique may be used to identify adoption barriers along with guide approaches for increasing user satisfaction and engagement regarding new technology (Pyra, 2024).

Diffusion of Innovations Theory: Everett Rogers Diffusion of Innovations Theory, whose investigates the reasons for, how, and how rapidly new ideas as well as technology spread throughout societies, is still relevant today. This theory, which emphasizes the significance of social buildings, means of communication, and associations with advantages in the diffusion process, can potentially be used to study the adoption patterns of smart logistics along with real-time monitoring technologies around the northwestern region of Africa. The findings of this study can shed some insight into the obstacles and promoters of technology integration throughout supply chains by examining the manner in which innovations are adopted locally (Al-Khatib, 2023).

EMPIRICAL LITERATURE REVIEW

Real-Time Tracking and Supply Chain Transparency

Over the past few decades, the empirical literature on real-time monitoring technologies and their impact on supply chain transparency has grown dramatically, exposing both the possible advantages and the difficulties of putting them into practice (Udeh et al., 2024). It has been demonstrated that real-time tracking technology, such as Internet of Things (IoT) devices, Radio Frequency Identification (RFID), and Global Positioning Systems (GPS), improve supply chain visibility. According to a research by (Jean, 2024), product visibility was greatly increased by integrating RFID technology into inventory management systems, which decreased stock outs and raised customer satisfaction. This result emphasizes how important real-time tracking is for enabling prompt information flow, which is necessary for supply chain decision-making to be successful (Khan et al., 2022).

Additional empirical study by (Zelbst et al., 2019) emphasized the connection among supply chain transparency and real-time monitoring, stressing that more visibility enables businesses to more efficiently trace the flow of commodities. Businesses using real-time monitoring systems reported a 30% increase in their capacity to follow items across the supply chain, according to their survey. Because stakeholders can instantly confirm the location and status of shipments, this improved traceability not only increases operational efficiency but also promotes responsibility among supply chain participants (Al-Khatib, 2023). Also, a study by (Akkaya & Kaya, 2019) examined how real-time tracking affected supply chain resilience and found that companies using these tools were better able to handle interruptions. According to the study, businesses were able to minimize the effect of unanticipated occurrences by making well-informed decisions more rapidly because to real-time data availability. Businesses with strong tracking capabilities, for example, were able to successfully reroute shipments and modify inventory levels during delays brought on by natural catastrophes or political unrest, proving a direct correlation among technology adoption and operational agility (Khan et al., 2023).

Empirical research, however, also emphasizes the difficulties in putting real-time tracking technology into practice. According to a survey by (Khan et al., 2023), a number of firms encounter major obstacles, including high implementation costs, a shortage of qualified staff, and employee reluctance to change. These difficulties may prevent tracking systems from reaching their full potential, which might result in inconsistent gains in openness.

H1: Real-Time Tracking Technologies has a significant effect on supply chain transparency

Real-Time Tracking and Smart Logistics Technologies

As businesses look to streamline their supply chain operations, the empirical research on how real-time tracking technologies affect smart logistics technology has become more and more pertinent. A more responsive and effective logistics infrastructure is made possible by real-time tracking technologies like GPS, RFID, and Internet of Things devices, which offer vital data that expands the capabilities of smart logistics systems (Issaoui et al., 2019). According to research by (Ding et al., 2021), route optimization and delivery accuracy are greatly increased when real-time tracking is included into logistics operations. According to their study, logistics companies that used GPS monitoring witnessed a significant drop in fuel use and a 25% reduction in delivery times, demonstrating how real-time data may improve transportation management efficiency. Additionally, a research by (Shee et al., 2021) investigated how smart logistics and real-time tracking technology may work together. The authors discovered that logistics operators may use predictive analytics through real-time data collecting, improving inventory control and demand forecasting. Businesses may eliminate excess inventory and enhance service levels by using real-time tracking to modify operations based on current demand signals. This potential was well demonstrated in a case study of an automotive supply chain, where operational efficiency was greatly increased by enabling just-in-time delivery procedures through real-time tracking (Akkaya & Kaya, 2019).

Also, (Osato Itohan Oriekhoe et al., 2024) empirical study emphasized the importance of real-time tracking in augmenting the automation capabilities of intelligent logistics systems. According to their findings, operational decision-making significantly improved for firms that combined automated technologies with real-time tracking. For example, the study demonstrated that automated inventory systems may reduce stockouts and overstock situations by 30% by using real-time tracking data to better effectively control stock levels. This illustrates how real-time tracking is a vital tool for logistics automation, facilitating smooth communication among different supply chain elements (Akkaya & Kaya, 2019). Nevertheless, the literature also points out difficulties in incorporating real-time tracking technology into frameworks for smart logistics. Although there are substantial potential advantages, many businesses struggle with data integration and system compatibility, according to a research by (Pyra, 2024). The efficacy of smart logistics systems may be harmed by fragmented information silos caused by a lack of defined processes. Also, (Astill et al., 2019) stressed that significant infrastructure and training investments are necessary for the effective deployment of these technologies, which may be prohibitive for smaller businesses and those located in poor nations.

H2: Real-Time Tracking Technologies has a significant effect on Smart Logistics Technologies

Smart Logistics Technologies and Supply Chain Transparency

Since organizations recognize the vital importance of increased accountability including visibility in their operations, the empirical research upon smart logistical technologies including their effects on the transparency of supply chains has developed in prominence (Helo & Shamsuzzoha, 2020). Intelligent algorithms (AI), big data analytics, and Network of Things, or IoT, products are just a few of the most recent innovations that comprise smart logistics and contribute to increased transparency in the logistics ecosystems. According to (Mann et al., 2018), the application and IoT in logistics allows for real-time data collection along with monitoring, considerably improving the visibility of products while they are transit. According to their findings, firms who use connected devices observed a 40% increase in tracking accuracy, providing stakeholders with a clearer picture overall cargo location along with status. Also, a research by (Udeh et al., 2024) looked at supply chain transparency and the use of big data analytics in smart logistics. The authors found that better decision-making and a deeper understanding of supply chain operations result from the capacity to evaluate enormous volumes of data from several sources. Businesses may monitor supplier performance, pinpoint bottlenecks, and improve demand forecasting by utilizing data. Because supply chain partners can obtain pertinent information instantly, this improved visibility not only improves operational efficiency but also builds confidence. The study specifically showed that companies with strong data analytics skills were able to increase total openness by 35%, which strengthened supply chain accountability and collaboration (Jean, 2024).

Also, research indicates that supply chain operations risks may be considerably reduced by integrating smart logistics solutions. AI-driven predictive analytics improves supply chain resilience by empowering businesses to foresee problems and proactively address them, according to research by (Khan et al., 2022). According to the survey, companies that used smart logistics solutions were better able to keep things transparent during emergencies because they could notify stakeholders in real time about changes in inventory levels or shipping delays. Since open communication is essential to preserving relationships amid interruptions, this capacity not only increases operational agility but also boosts stakeholder confidence (Jean, 2024). But the literature also points several obstacles that may stand in the way of using smart logistics technology to achieve transparency. Although there is a lot of room for greater openness, problems with data security and privacy might be major obstacles, according to a research by (Zelbst et al., 2019). Corporations typically hesitate to share sensitive information with partners out of fear of data breaches and abuse. Likewise, the complexity of connecting various technologies and systems may result in fragmented data, making it more challenging to gain an accurate supply-chain picture (Al-Khatib, 2023).

H3: Smart Logistics Technologies has a significant effect on supply chain transparency

Real-Time Tracking, Supply Chain Transparency, Smart Logistics

Empirical research has focused on how real-time tracking technologies, smart logistics technologies, and supply chain transparency interact, emphasizing how smart logistics mediates the use of real-time monitoring to increase transparency (Khan et al., 2023). GPS and RFID are examples of real-time tracking technology that offer vital information on the position and condition of cargo while it is in route (Khan et al., 2023). These technologies have the potential to greatly increase supply chain transparency when combined with smart logistics systems, which are distinguished by automated procedures, powerful analytics, and Internet of Things connection. According to research by (Issaoui et al., 2019), real-time tracking systems help businesses efficiently collect and use data, which is essential for making wise decisions in logistics operations. Also, a research by (Akkaya & Kaya, 2019) investigated how smart logistics technology mediated the connection among supply chain transparency and real-time tracking. According to the results, smart logistics solutions serve as a catalyst, converting unprocessed data from real-time tracking into insights that may be put to use. Businesses may track shipments, evaluate trends, predict demand, and manage inventory levels by utilizing big data analytics and IoT devices. This potential was well demonstrated in a case study involving a global retailer, where supply chain partners' information asymmetry was reduced by 50% as a result of the integration of smart logistics and real-time tracking technology (Khan et al., 2023). The increased transparency and data sharing encouraged cooperation and trust, which eventually increased the supply chain's efficacy (Ding et al., 2021).

In addition, empirical evidence from research conducted by (Shee et al., 2021) supports the notion that smart logistics mediates the relationship among real-time tracking and transparency by enhancing risk management capabilities. The study highlighted that organizations using smart logistics systems could better respond to disruptions by accessing real-time data on supply chain conditions. For instance, during unexpected delays, firms could quickly inform stakeholders and adjust their logistics plans accordingly. This proactive approach not only minimized the impact of disruptions but also reinforced transparency, as partners were kept informed of changes in real time (Osato Itohan Oriekhoe et al., 2024). Nevertheless, there are still obstacles in the way of completely reaping the rewards of this collaboration. According to a research by (Akkaya & Kaya, 2019), companies frequently encounter difficulties with data integration and system compatibility, even though combining real-time monitoring with smart logistics technology has several benefits. These difficulties may restrict the efficacy of transparency efforts and obstruct the flow of information. Additionally, worries about data security and privacy may discourage businesses from disclosing important information, so compromising the possibility of increased exposure.

> H4: Real-Time Tracking Technologies has a significant effect on supply chain transparency by mediation of Smart Logistics Technologies

CONCEPTUAL FRAMEWORK

Figure 1. Conceptual framework

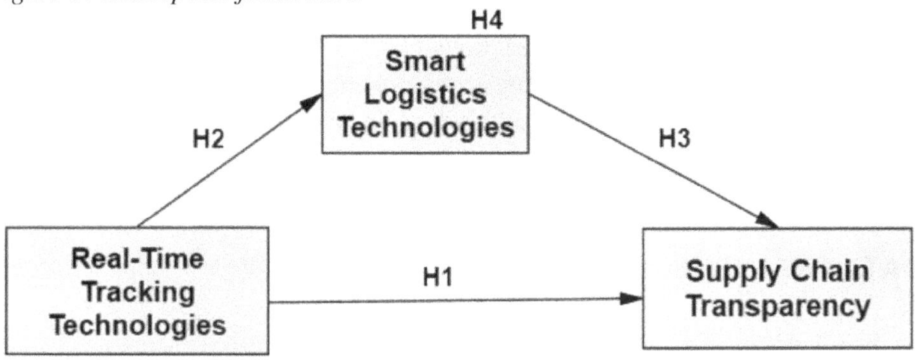

METHODOLOGY

In order to examine the impact of smart logistics and real-time tracking technology on supply chain transparency, this study used a quantitative research methodology. A stratified random sampling approach was used to choose a sample of 390 respondents, guaranteeing representation from a range of supply chain industrial sectors. In order to quantify variables pertaining to supply chain transparency, smart logistics technologies, and real-time tracking technologies, a structured questionnaire was created, combining existing scales from earlier research. Pre-testing and a thorough literature study were part of the scale creation process to guarantee the items' validity, reliability, and clarity. When the Kaiser-Meyer-Olkin (KMO) measure was calculated to determine whether the data was suitable for factor analysis, it produced a value over the permissible cutoff of 0.6, indicating a fair degree of sampling adequacy. The underlying component structure of the constructs was then discovered through the use of Principal Component Analysis with Varimax rotation in Exploratory component Analysis (EFA). The construct validity was confirmed by the EFA results, which showed unique factors relating to supply chain transparency, smart logistics technologies, and real-time tracking technologies. All factor loadings were over the suggested threshold of 0.4.

The proposed correlations among the components were then tested using structural equation modeling, or SEM. The SEM evaluation was carried out using AMOS software, which made it easy to assess the fit of the model and correlations across variables. The index of comparative fit (CFI), Tucker-Lewis index (TLI), and root mean square error of estimation (RMSEA) values were all within reasonable boundaries, suggesting that the simulation model fit the evidence well. In besides confirming what we had previously hypothesized links, our quantitative research provided more insight into how smart logistics equipment can facilitate supplier transparency using monitoring in real time.

All things considered, this strong methodological framework guaranteed the validity and dependability of the results, advancing our knowledge of the dynamics in the supply chain environment.

DATA ANALYSIS

Table 1. KMO and Bartlett's Test

Kaiser-Meyer-Olkin Measure of Sampling Adequacy.		**.850**
Bartlett's Test of Sphericity	Approx. Chi-Square	1419.738
	df	91
	Sig.	.000

The first row of Table 1 displays the outcomes of the Bartlett's Test of Sphericity and the KMO (Kaiser-Meyer-Olkin of Random Adequacy, two essential metrics for establishing if factor analysis of the collected data is appropriate. The KMO index score of 0.850 is greater than the suggested minimum threshold of 0.6, indicating a substantial degree of acceptable sampling. This shows that the variables are sufficiently connected to support the extraction of factors, suggesting that the data set is appropriate for factor analysis. Generally speaking, a KMO score in this range indicates that there are strong enough correlations among the components to identify underlying structures. Also, a significance level (p-value) of.000 and an estimated chi-square value of 1419.738 with 91 degrees of freedom were obtained using Bartlett's Test of Sphericity. The null hypothesis that the correlation matrix is an identity matrix—that is, that there are substantial correlations among the variables—is strongly rejected by this finding. This test's significance shows that factor analysis can provide insightful information about the data structure and that the variables employed in the study are in fact connected. When combined, the KMO and Bartlett's Test results offer a strong basis for moving forward with Exploratory Factor Analysis (EFA), demonstrating the dataset's resilience for additional investigation into the connections among supply chain transparency, smart logistics technologies, and real-time tracking technologies.

Table 2. Total Variance Explained

Component	**Initial Eigenvalues**			**Extraction Sums of Squared Loadings**			**Rotation Sums of Squared Loadings**		
	Total	% of Variance	Cumulative %	Total	% of Variance	Cumulative %	Total	% of Variance	Cumulative %
1	4.51	32.235	32.235	4.51	32.235	32.235	3.00	21.451	21.451
2	1.37	9.787	42.022	1.37	9.787	42.022	2.16	15.491	36.942
3	1.27	9.087	51.110	1.27	9.087	51.110	1.98	14.168	51.110

Extraction Method: Principal Component Analysis.

The findings of the Principal Component Analysis (PCA)-based Exploratory Factor Analysis (EFA) Total Variance Explained are summarized in Table 2. Prior to extraction, the baseline Eigenvalues show how much of the variation was explained by each component. The primary component is the most important factor influencing the dataset, with an Eigenvalue of 4.51 as well as accounting for 32.235% of the variance in its entirety. The first three elements constitute 51.110% of the overall variation, whereas the first two components account significantly 42.022%, implying that these three factors responsible for in excess of half of the amount of data variance. These results are further supported by the extraction sums of squared loadings, which show that the top three components remain significant after extraction. While the second and third components provide an extra 9.787% and 9.087% of the variation, respectively, the first component still accounts for 32.235%. A significant underlying structure among the variables is shown by the cumulative variance of 51.110%, which confirms the suitability of the components found. Also, upon rotation, the top three components explain 21.451%, 15.491%, and 14.168% of the variance, respectively, according to the rotation sums of squared loadings. Rotation attempts to give a clearer understanding of the component structure rather than maximize variance, therefore even though the total variance explained by the rotated factors is less than the extraction sums, this is normal. The findings show that although a number of factors influence the total variance, the first three are more important for comprehending the connections among the data. All things considered, these results lend credence to the idea that supply chain transparency, smart logistics technologies, and real-time tracking technologies are interrelated, with different factors affecting how they interact.

Confirmatory Principle Component

Confirmatory principle component examination is a sort of statistics used to verify the principle component arrangement of a group of directed proxies. Research can use CFA to assess hypotheses based on the underlying frame job and correlations among observable proxies. The investigation used CFA under table 3 to assess the hypothesis that there is a relationship among the proxies being guided and the latent notions that support them.

Table 3. Covariances

Covariance			Approxi	S.E.	C.R.	P	Hy.
Real-Time Tracking Technologies	<-->	Smart Logistics Technologies	.242	.021	8.231	***	H2
Smart Logistics Technologies	<-->	Supply chain transparency	.303	.032	7.692	***	H3
Real-Time Tracking Technologies	<-->	supply chain transparency	.254	.24	7.831	***	H1

The covariance's and statistical significance of the constructs of supply chain transparency, smart logistics technologies, and real-time tracking technologies are shown in Table 3. The direction and degree of the correlations among these variables are shown by the covariance's. Considering an estimated standard error (S.E.) around 0.021, the coefficient of variation between logistical planning and immediate time tracking devices is said to have the value 0.242. The critical ratio (C.R.) of 8.231 indicates that highly significant relationship ($p < 0.001$), exceeding the normative threshold of 1.96. This considerable association supports Hypothesis 2 (H2), implying which real-time data collection improves the performance of automated logistics systems. In addition, the causal relationship between supply chain transparency as well as smart logistics technology is 0.303, having a coefficient of estimation of 7.692 and a standard deviation equal 0.032. The connection is quantitatively substantial ($p < 0.001$), providing significant evidence for Hypothesis 3 (H3). The research conducted supports the premise that contemporary logistics technology enables increased responsibility and visibility by demonstrating that greater smart logistics abilities significantly boost supply chain integrity. The Pearson correlation coefficient between supply chain transparency as well as real-time tracking systems is found to have the value 0.254, resulting in a C.R. of 7.831 and a S.E. equal 0.24, and both statistically significant ($p < 0.001$). This conclusion confirms Hypothesis 1 (H1), which asserts because real-time tracking solutions directly increase supply chain transparency. When taken together, these covariance conclusions provide convincing empirical evidence for the link between logistical transparency, sophisticated logistics, as well as real-time tracking, emphasizing the important function that these developments provide in fostering a more efficient and successful supply chain.

Table 4. Validity concern

	CR	*AVE*	*MSV*	*MaxR(H)*	*RTT*	*SLT*	*SCT*
RTT	0.732	0.643	0.219	0.852	**0.654**		
SLT	0.758	0.657	0.132	0.763	0.171	**0.665**	
SCT	0.793	0.603	0.274	0.797	0.383	0.193	**0.684**

Note: RTT= **Real-Time Tracking Technologies**; SLT= **Smart Logistics Technologies**; SCT= **supply chain transparency**

The table 4 summarizes the reliability of indicators for the constructs being studied, notably real-time surveillance technologies (RTT), smart logistics techniques (SLT), along with supply chain transparency. The constructs are evaluated utilizing a combination of composite reliability (CR), the average variation extracted (AVE), Maximum Sharing Variance (MSV), while Maximum Reliability (MaxR(H). Three construct's CR values—RTT around 0.732, SLT around 0.758, as well as SCT at 0.793—exceed the allowable threshold around 0.7. Good internal consistency among the objects within each construct is shown by these values. Additionally acceptable are the AVE values, which quantify how much variation is captured by a construct in comparison to how much is caused by measurement error. With AVEs of 0.643, 0.657, and 0.603, respectively, RTT, SLT, and SCT all above the suggested minimum of 0.5. This implies that each concept accounts for a substantial amount of variation, hence confirming its validity. With RTT at 0.219, SLT at 0.132, and SCT at 0.274, the MSV values—which represent the greatest shared variation among constructs—are comparatively low. These values support discriminant validity by showing that there is little overlap among the notions. Also, with RTT at 0.852, SLT at 0.763, and SCT at 0.797, the MaxR(H) values—which evaluate the constructs' maximum reliability—are likewise good.

Mediating Role Examination

Figure 2. Structure equation model

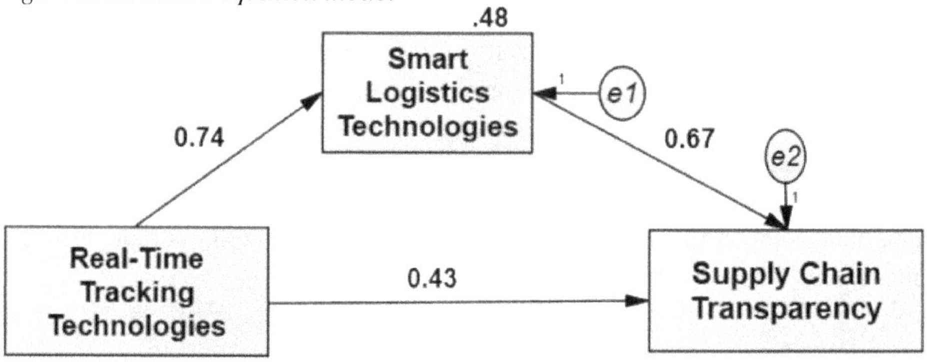

Model Fit Indices

Table 5. Indices for model fit

Sig.	Chi-Sq	RMR	Fitness Goodness	Fitness Confirmatory	TLI	RMSEA
0.004	1.954	.036	0.930	0.912	0.911	.028

The model fit indices obtained from the Structural Equation Modeling (SEM) study are shown in Table 5, offering a thorough assessment of the model's suitability for capturing the data. The model is statistically significant, with a significance level (Sig.) of 0.004, suggesting that the proposed correlations among the components are supported by the data.

When compared to the degrees of freedom, the comparatively low Chi-Square value of 1.954 lends credence to the idea that the model does a good job of fitting the data. A decent fit is also suggested by the reported Root Mean Square Residual (RMR) of 0.036, which is below the suggested cutoff of 0.05. Lower values show a better approximation among the observed and projected covariance. The Confirmatory Fit Index (CFI) and the Fitness Goodness Index (FGI) are two examples of goodness-of-fit indices that are stated to be 0.912 and 0.930, respectively. The model exhibits a robust fit within the data, indicating the sufficiency of the suggested links among the components, since both indices above the well recognized threshold of 0.90.

The model offers an excellent match by taking model complexity into consideration, as seen by the Tucker-Lewis Index (TLI), which is reported at 0.911, once more exceeding the 0.90 criterion. Finally, a tight fit of the model to the degrees of freedom is suggested by the Root Mean Square Error of Approximation (RMSEA), which is remarkably low at 0.028, much below the optimal threshold of 0.06.

Table 6. Regression examination

Relative			Approx.	S.E.	C.R.	P	Ass.
Real-Time Tracking Technologies	<-->	Smart Logistics Technologies	.864	.143	7.583	***	H2
			.328	.131	2.853	***	H3
Smart Logistics Technologies	<-->	supply chain transparency	.957	.192	7.958	***	H1

Table 6 summarizes the outcome of the regression analysis results for the linkages between chain of custody transparency (SCT), logistics optimization technologies (SLT), as well as real-time tracking technologies (RTT). The coefficients of regression reflect the relevance and strength associated with the hypothesized relationships. With a standard error (S.E.) about 0.143 as well as a critical ratio (C.R.) of 7.583, the causal relationship between smart logistics technologies and current monitoring technologies highly substantial, overall a regression coefficient about 0.864. This data ($p < 0.001$) strongly supports Hypothesis 2 (H2), indicating that the improving real-time tracking skills would likely lead to significant breakthroughs within smart logistics innovation. The interaction involving supply chain transparency with smart transportation technology appears considered significant ($p < 0.001$), yielding a correlation coefficient about 0.957, S.E. of 0.192, and C.R. of 7.958. The research presented here lends credence to Hypothesis 1 (H1), which implies that improved supply chain transparency is dependent on the effectiveness of smart logistics technology. Additionally, the link between chain of custody transparency as well as smart logistics technology proved statistically significant ($p < 0.001$), with a coefficient about 0.328, S.E. about 0.131, as well as C.R. of 2.853. In accordance to this study, smart logistics technology has a significant impact on the supply chain transparency, although not as much as immediate fashion tracking mechanisms.

Table 7. Mediating role effect

	Influence	Worth	Path Influence
Real-Time Tracking Technologies → Supply Chain Transparency	Direct Influence	.43	Direct influence stated
Real-Time Tracking Technologies → Smart Logistics Technologies → Supply Chain Transparency	Indirect Influence	.74*.67=.48	Indirect Influence Ensued
	Whole influence	.91	Partial mediation

The link among supply chain transparency (SCT) and real-time tracking technologies (RTT) is mediated by smart logistics technologies, as shown in Table 7. Real-time tracking is crucial for improving supply chain transparency, as seen by the large direct effect of RTT on SCT, which is measured at 0.43. This clear connection demonstrates how RTT promotes openness on its own, free from middlemen. On the other hand, it is determined that RTT's indirect impact on SCT through smart logistics technology is 0.48, which is equal to 0.74 times 0.67. According to this research, RTT impacts SCT through smart logistics technologies, strengthening the total impact of tracking technologies on transparency. The overall impact of RTT on SCT, both directly and indirectly, comes to 0.91 when all influences are taken into account. This overall influence shows a substantial correlation, with smart logistics technology mediating some of the effect. The fact that this link is referred to as "partial mediation" indicates that although smart logistics technologies help to improve the impact of RTT on SCT, there is still a considerable direct influence.

DISCUSSION

The study's conclusions highlight how important supply chain transparency (SCT), smart logistics technologies (SLT), and real-time tracking technologies (RTT) are to improving supply chain performance. The important connections found among these constructs demonstrate how RTT both directly and indirectly impacts SLT and contributes to SCT through SLT. Because of these two effects, companies that use RTT should anticipate significant gains in their logistical capabilities, which will increase supply chain transparency. Also, the statistical analyses—which include mediation effects and regression analyses—offer strong evidence in favor of the proposed correlations. The idea that improved tracking capabilities allow for more effective logistical operations is supported by the high regression coefficients, which show the beneficial impact of RTT on SLT. By indicating that investments in intelligent logistics are necessary to convert the advantages of RTT into improved supply chain visibility, the mediation analysis highlights the significance of SLT as a facilitator of transparency. The suggested framework's validity is further supported by the model fit indices, which show that the connections among RTT, SLT, and SCT are not only statistically significant but also practically applicable to businesses looking to enhance their supply chain dynamics.

African horns face important challenges to achieve supply chain transparency, following the historical context of political instability and infrastructure flaws. The region has begun using real follow-up technologies such as RFID, GPS and IoT systems, but the pathway for transparency remains complex. Around the world, regions such as Southeast Asia and certain regions in Europe can implement similar technologies, indicating the potential for improved visibility and efficiency of the supply chain. These examples highlight the importance of reliable political and normative frameworks that contribute to technology adoption and transparency. In the African horn, the political framework is often lagging behind technological achievements. Effective rules that encourage the adoption of intellectual logistics technologies are crucial for increasing transparency. Countries like Kenya have reached progress, integrating technologies into their national logistics strategies, while Ethiopia has focused on public procurement reforms which have priority for transparency. However, these executives should also be reinforced to support the large implementation of follow -up technologies. The economic consequences of adopting these technologies are important. Initial investments in real tracking systems can often outweigh these costs, although they can result in higher long-term profits, including reducing losses, improving efficiency, and increasing customer satisfaction. Nevertheless, organizations must also consider the cybersecurity risks associated with increasing digitalization. Implementing reliable cybersecurity measures, such as regular audits, employee training, and secure data management, is important to reduce these risks. Furthermore, work development strategies are important to support digital transformation of logistics. Training programs that improve digital skills among employees can encourage the adoption of new technologies and ensure that the workforce is ready to manage sophisticated systems. Collaboration between governments, educational institutions, and the private sector can create a skilled labor pool equipped to navigate the evolving landscape of digital logistics. By addressing these various dimensions—policy frameworks, financial considerations, cybersecurity, and workforce development—the Horn of Africa can leverage real-time tracking technologies to foster greater supply chain transparency and efficiency.

CONCLUSION

According to the results, RTT greatly improves SLT, which is essential for mediating the development of increased supply chain transparency. The significance of combining cutting-edge tracking and logistics technology to increase operational efficiency and visibility is shown by the strong statistical evidence for these linkages. According to the study, companies who invest in RTT may anticipate both immediate improvements to their logistical operations and increased transparency as a result of SLT's increased efficacy. This double effect emphasizes how strategically crucial it is to implement these technologies in the increasingly intricate and data-driven supply chain environment of today. Businesses may create a supply chain that is more responsive, transparent, and responsible by utilizing RTT and SLT. This will eventually improve decision-making and raise customer satisfaction. Additionally, the study's theoretical and practical implications are strengthened by the robust model fit indices, which validate the validity of the suggested framework. This study establishes the foundation for future research to examine other elements that could affect the connections among these structures as supply networks change. In conclusion, in order to improve supply chain transparency and generate competitive advantage in the market, the research recommends the strategic integration of real-time tracking and smart logistics technology.

MANAGERIAL IMPLICATIONS

The study's conclusions have a number of significant management ramifications for businesses looking to improve the efficiency of their supply chains. First and foremost, managers must give top priority to integrating cutting-edge tracking solutions into their logistics frameworks, as evidenced by the substantial positive correlation among real-time tracking technologies (RTT) and smart logistics technologies (SLT). Organizations may greatly enhance their logistics capabilities—which are crucial for managing the intricacies of contemporary supply chains—by implementing RTT. Additionally, SLT's mediating function in promoting supply chain transparency emphasizes how important it is for managers to spend money on intelligent logistics systems that promote operational visibility and data exchange. Improving openness facilitates improved decision-making and increased response to market fluctuations in addition to fostering trust among stakeholders. In order to deploy cutting-edge SLT solutions that make use of the data produced by RTT, managers had to think about forming strategic alliances with technology suppliers. The report also highlights the need of using technology in a comprehensive manner. In the end, managers may build a more flexible and transparent supply chain that improves customer satisfaction and competitive advantage by carefully coordinating RTT and SLT projects. The research's conclusions offer a road map for businesses looking to use technology as a major factor in supply chain operational excellence.

PRACTICAL IMPLICATIONS

The research presented here has substantial practical implications for firms aiming toward improving their supply chain procedures by integrating technology. The report suggests that logistics managers prioritize the use of real-time technology for tracking (RTT). Businesses may improve their responsiveness to disruptions and make faster choices by deploying RTT, which provides rapid visibility into their logistics operations. Prompt data access can results in improved customer service, faster lead times, and easier inventory management. Also, the paper underlines the value that smart logistics technology (SLT) has become for improving supply chain transparency. Enterprises should focus towards implementing SLT solutions which enable stakeholders to communicate together and share insights. The result might mean investing in innovations that enable fast exchange of data and communication, as well as fostering a climate of transparency and accountability throughout the supply chain. Organizations ought to think about creating comprehensive training programs for employees to make certain that they are equipped to use these developments effectively. Staff may maximize the benefits of RTT and SLT expenditures by becoming aware of how to use them to their full potential through interactive classes and ongoing support. Businesses may build agreements involving technology suppliers to stay up to date on the latest innovations in tracking as well as logistics solutions. Working engaging subject-matter experts may grant you with accessibility to cutting-edge techniques and instruments that boost operational performance along with sustainability.

THEORETICAL IMPLICATIONS

First, the established connections among supply chain transparency (SCT), smart logistics technologies (SLT), and real-time tracking technologies (RTT) add to the body of knowledge by offering empirical support for the integration of these concepts into a single framework. This study supports the idea that RTT may be used as a catalyst to improve SLT, which in turn promotes more supply chain transparency, in addition to being a stand-alone solution. Also, the discovery of SLT as a mediating variable provides a more sophisticated comprehension of the ways in which RTT affects SCT. This mediating function highlights the intricacy of supply chain dynamics by implying that technologies combine to create cumulative impacts rather than functioning alone. These revelations may open the door for other studies that examine additional possible moderators or mediators in comparable situations, broadening the theoretical discussion of supply chain technology adoption. The study also questions conventional wisdom that would have assumed that RTT's influence was just direct. By clarifying the indirect effects using SLT, this study invites researchers to look at technology's implications on supply chain outcomes from a more comprehensive angle. Richer theoretical frameworks that capture the interaction among different technology developments and supply chain performance measurements may result from this more comprehensive approach.

RECOMMENDATIONS

The study's conclusions allow for the formulation of a number of suggestions for businesses looking to integrate technology and enhance supply chain performance. First and foremost, businesses must give the implementation of real-time tracking technology (RTT) top priority. Businesses should invest in cutting-edge RTT systems that meet their unique supply chain requirements after carefully evaluating their present tracking capabilities. In addition to increasing visibility, this investment will enable better informed decision-making. Likewise, enterprises are urged to create along with apply smart logistics technologies (SLT) to supplement RTT. The following might include incorporating software systems which make it possible for smooth data exchange and collaboration across supply chain participants. Companies may enhance the entirety of their vendor networks and react more quickly to market changes by encouraging collaboration and openness. Development and training efforts should also be a priority. Employees must possess the appropriate abilities to efficiently use RTT and SLT. Organizations ought to make investments in extensive training courses the fact that prepares employees to use these advanced tools achieving successful operation. Occasional workshops as well as hands-on sessions may assist to increase user engagement while maintaining staff up to date on the newest technology breakthroughs. Organizations might also consider developing strategic partnerships alongside industry experts and technology providers. Working alongside outside partners can make it simpler to access innovative technologies and industry best practices for RTT and SLT deployment. This cooperation can also assist the supply chain foster an environment of innovation as well as continuous improvement. Subsequently it is recommended that firms monitor and review the effectiveness of their technical investments upon a regular basis. Corporations may assess the long-term influence of RTT and SLT by using key performance indicators (KPIs) for logistics transparency along with operational efficiency.

FUTURE DIRECTIONS

Upcoming research on supply chain management should build on this study's findings by tackling an extensive variety of critical issues. First, researchers may investigate the way sophisticated logistics technologies (SLT) as well as real-time tracking technologies (RTT) influence supply chain sustainability throughout the long haul. Understanding how these developments assist social and environmental goals will become increasingly important as firms place an increasing value upon sustainable practices. Another intriguing research topic is how business values and management influence the effective application of RTT and SLT. The next research might look into how different cultural traits influence the implementation and efficacy of these advances, thereby providing understanding of the organizational changes necessary to allow seamless integration of technology. Educational institutions should consider the consequences of emerging technologies such as artificial intelligence (AI) particularly the Internet of Things (IoT) on the RTT, SLT, along with supply chain transparency. Understanding how these innovative innovations could further advance tracking overall logistics operations will give us a better view of the coming decades of supply chain management. Additionally, comparative studies in different industries may assist understand how RTT as well as SLT implementation difference and what beneficial techniques emerge in diverse environments. This kind of study can help organizations tailor their computer strategy more effectively by identifying particular to a sector opportunities and challenges. Finally, looking toward the customer-centric aspects of supply chain transparency can reveal valuable information on how RTT and SLT affect client participation along with delight.

REFERENCES

Akkaya, M., & Kaya, H. (2019). Innovative and Smart Technologies in Logistics. *17th International Logistics and Supply Chain Congress (LMSCM), Istanbul, Turkey, January*, 97–105. https://www.researchgate.net/publication/338423597

Al-Khatib, A. W. (2023). Internet of things, big data analytics and operational performance: The mediating effect of supply chain visibility. *Journal of Manufacturing Technology Management*, *34*(1), 1–24. DOI: 10.1108/JMTM-08-2022-0310

Astill, J., Dara, R. A., Campbell, M., Farber, J. M., Fraser, E. D. G., Sharif, S., & Yada, R. Y. (2019). Transparency in food supply chains: A review of enabling technology solutions. *Trends in Food Science & Technology*, *91*(July), 240–247. DOI: 10.1016/j.tifs.2019.07.024

Ding, Y., Jin, M., Li, S., & Feng, D. (2021). Smart logistics based on the internet of things technology: An overview. *International Journal of Logistics Research and Applications*, *24*(4), 323–345. DOI: 10.1080/13675567.2020.1757053

Helo, P., & Shamsuzzoha, A. H. M. (2020). Real-time supply chain—A blockchain architecture for project deliveries. *Robotics and Computer-Integrated Manufacturing, 63*(November 2019), 101909. https://doi.org/DOI: 10.1016/j.rcim.2019.101909

Issaoui, Y., Khiat, A., Bahnasse, A., & Ouajji, H. (2019). Smart logistics : Study of the application of blockchain technology. *Procedia Computer Science, 160*(2018), 266–271. https://doi.org/DOI: 10.1016/j.procs.2019.09.467

Jean, G. (2024). Supply Chain Visibility and Transparency. ResearchGate. Available at:https://www.researchgate.net/publication/384335325_Supply_Chain_Visibility_and_Transparency/citation/download

Khan, M., Alshahrani, A. N., & Jacquemod, J. (2023). Digital Platforms and Supply Chain Traceability for Robust Information and Effective Inventory Management: The Mediating Role of Transparency. *Logistics (Basel)*, *7*(2). Advance online publication. DOI: 10.3390/logistics7020025

Khan, M., Parvaiz, G. S., Dedahanov, A. T., Abdurazzakov, O. S., & Rakhmonov, D. A. (2022). The Impact of Technologies of Traceability and Transparency in Supply Chains. *Sustainability (Switzerland)*, *14*(24). Advance online publication. DOI: 10.3390/su142416336

Mann, S., Potdar, V., Gajavilli, R. S., & Chandan, A. (2018). Blockchain technology for supply chain traceability, transparency and data provenance. *ACM International Conference Proceeding Series*, 22–25. https://doi.org/DOI: 10.1145/3301403.3301408

Oriekhoe, O. I., Oyeyemi, O. P., Bello, B. G., Omotoye, G. B., Daraojimba, A. I., & Adefemi, A. (2024). Blockchain in supply chain management: A review of efficiency, transparency, and innovation. *International Journal of Science and Research Archive, 11*(1), 173–181. DOI: 10.30574/ijsra.2024.11.1.0028

Pauzuolienė, J., Kavecke, I., & Pyra, M. (2024). Smart technologies integration and challenges in the context of logistics companies. *European Research Studies Journal*, 0(Special A), 999–1018. https://ideas.repec.org/a/ers/journl/vxxviiy2024ispecialap999-1018.html

Shee, H. K., Miah, S. J., & De Vass, T. (2021). Impact of smart logistics on smart city sustainable performance: An empirical investigation. *International Journal of Logistics Management, 32*(3), 821–845. DOI: 10.1108/IJLM-07-2020-0282

Udeh, E. O., Amajuoyi, P., Adeusi, K. B., & Scott, A. O. (2024). The role of IoT in boosting supply chain transparency and efficiency. *Magna Scientia Advanced Research and Reviews, 12*(1), 178–197. DOI: 10.30574/msarr.2024.11.1.0081

Zelbst, P. J., Green, K. W., Sower, V. E., & Bond, P. L. (2019). The impact of RFID, IIoT, and Blockchain technologies on supply chain transparency. *Journal of Manufacturing Technology Management, 31*(3), 441–457. DOI: 10.1108/JMTM-03-2019-0118

KEY TERMS AND DEFINITIONS

Real-Time Tracking Technologies (RTT): Digital systems (e.g., GPS, RFID, IoT sensors) enabling continuous monitoring of cargo location, condition, and movement across supply chains. In the Horn of Africa, RTT mitigates delays and enhances traceability but faces challenges like unreliable internet and infrastructure gaps, limiting real-time data accuracy in fragmented logistics networks.

Smart Logistics Technologies (SLT): Integrated digital solutions (e.g., AI analytics, automated inventory systems, blockchain platforms) that optimize logistics operations through data-driven decision-making. SLT transforms raw tracking data into actionable insights for warehousing, routing, and demand forecasting, acting as a critical mediator between RTT and supply chain transparency in resource-constrained regions.

Supply Chain Transparency (SCT): End-to-end visibility and accountability across sourcing, production, and distribution stages, facilitated by shared data among stakeholders. In the Horn of Africa, SCT reduces fraud (e.g., cargo diversion) and improves compliance but is hindered by political instability and legacy systems requiring RTT/SLT integration for progress.

Resource-Based View (RBV): Strategic theory asserting that competitive advantage stems from unique, valuable resources (e.g., RTT/SLT) controlled by a firm. RBV justifies investments in tracking and logistics technologies as "strategic assets" to build supply chain resilience and transparency in volatile economies like the Horn of Africa.

Technology Acceptance Model (TAM): Behavioral framework linking technology adoption to perceived usefulness and ease of use. TAM explains low RTT/SLT uptake in the Horn of Africa due to skills gaps and cultural resistance, underscoring the need for user-centric training and intuitive tool design.

Diffusion of Innovations Theory: Model analyzing how innovations spread through social systems via communication channels and stakeholder networks. This theory guides tailored RTT/SLT deployment in high-impact hubs (e.g., Kenyan ports) before regional scaling, addressing adoption barriers like literacy disparities.

Infrastructure Deficits: Gaps in physical/digital infrastructure (e.g., unpaved roads, low internet penetration) disrupting technology deployment. In Ethiopia, only 30% of rural roads are paved, compromising GPS reliability and exemplifying systemic hurdles to RTT/SLT implementation.

Cybersecurity Risks: Threats to data integrity from hacking or breaches, exacerbated by supply chain digitalization. Mitigation requires encryption, access controls, and audits modeled by platforms like DHL's Resilience360 to secure IoT-driven logistics in politically unstable regions.

Public-Private Partnerships (PPPs): Collaborative ventures between governments and firms funding infrastructure/logistics modernization. Kenya's "Single Window" e-system demonstrates PPP success, reducing customs delays through tech-driven process harmonization.

Tokenization: Representing physical assets (e.g., cargo, vessels) as blockchain-secured digital tokens. This enables decentralized finance (DeFi) applications like cargo-backed loans, accelerating capital access for SMEs in the Horn of Africa's shipping industry.

Chapter 5
Smart Logistics for a Sustainable Supply Chain Future

Parveen Sharma
https://orcid.org/0000-0002-7351-0525
Lovely Professional University, Phagwara, India

ABSTRACT

The fast growth of global supply chains has increased demand for ecologically sustainable, efficient, and intelligent logistics solutions. Because supply chains are constantly changing at a rapid pace, people now require logistics systems that are both sustainable and effective. This chapter examines how green logistics techniques, meant to cut down the environment's impact, can be combined with smart technology. This covers smart logistics, methods for industry sustainability, and how new technology helps achieve both types of goals. Besides, the chapter studies the changes ahead for the logistics industry, how performance is measured, and the difficulties of executing new changes. A growing number of studies give us useful directions on how to create smarter and greener supply chain systems everywhere.

INTRODUCTION TO THE INTEGRATION OF SMART TECHNOLOGIES FOR SUSTAINABILITY

The concepts articulated in the chapter title are effectively exemplified by the incorporation of sophisticated smart technologies, including Artificial Intelligence (AI), the Internet of Things (IoT), and Blockchain inside the logistics sector. These technologies are boosting operational capabilities while actively contributing to the overarching objective of developing sustainable logistics systems. This section

DOI: 10.4018/979-8-3373-2434-0.ch005

elucidates how digital innovations are transforming the logistics sector to address the increasing demands for environmental accountability and operational efficiency.

In recent years, the logistics sector has seen a significant upheaval. This transition is primarily motivated by the pressing necessity to enhance sustainability, augment responsiveness, and elevate efficiency throughout global supply networks. As enterprises and governmental entities increasingly prioritize sustainable and intelligent solutions, logistics has emerged as a crucial area for innovation and transformation.

There are two main themes that have become clear in this changing environment. The first one is intelligent or smart logistics, which uses computerized and data-driven methods to make logistics work more efficiently. The second type is environmental or “green” logistics, which tries to make sure that moving, storing, and distributing things has as little of an effect on the environment as possible. Not only do these two themes go together, they also go well with each other.

They paved the way for the supply chain's expansion in a new path where environmental sustainability and technology advancement coexist. This chapter lays the groundwork for a more thorough examination of how smart mobility technologies could transform and improve supply networks in the future when applied in accordance with environmental objectives. Logistics has become more intelligent through the use of IoT, AI, blockchain, robotics, and data analytics. This has improved operations management, increased visibility, and allowed for better decision-making (Ding et al., 2021; Song et al., 2020). The application of effective transportation, carbon emission management, and waste reduction reduces the adverse environmental effects of green logistics (Srivastava, 2007; Murphy & Poist, 2000). Because of globalisation and the growing complexity of supply chains, businesses must now incorporate eco-friendly practices with contemporary technologies. The core green goals of resource management and emission reduction depend on intelligent logistics solutions, which include real-time monitoring, future maintenance planning, and efficient use of available resources (Chung, 2021; Chen et al., 2024).

As consumers' awareness of climate change, legislation, and purchasing decisions increases, businesses are investing in smart and environmentally friendly logistics solutions. Min and Kim (2012) and Sarkis (2012). Integrating intelligent and ecologically sensitive logistics on a global scale has never been more crucial than it is right now. More and more groups are trying to address the existing logistical issues by making them more environmentally friendly and providing support to companies that care about the environment.

It is now evident that current logistics systems are shifting towards digital solutions in an attempt to reduce negative environmental consequences (Kamewor et al., 2024; Verbivska et al., 2023). According to Gruchmann (2018) and Shee et al. (2021), companies all over the world are utilising technology in the modern world to manage operations, improve service quality, and comply with regulatory obligations.

The purpose of this chapter is to demonstrate how technology and sustainability interact in the logistics sector.

To begin, the chapter discusses how various technologies are transforming logistical operations. Following that, it discusses several ways to eco-friendly logistics and how modern technologies might help them. Important obstacles in applying KPIs and performance criteria are discussed later, and we conclude by looking at the future of smart and green logistics. To ensure that students comprehend this issue thoroughly, the coursework makes extensive use of scientific knowledge. This chapter investigates how the integration of smart logistics technologies and green practices might serve as a foundation for developing future-ready, sustainable supply chains.

This chapter examines how the convergence of smart technologies and green logistics forms the foundation of new trends in sustainable supply chain operations. These trends correlate with the larger goals of smart logistics transformation, which are discussed in the previous chapter.

This research aims to establish a comprehensive framework for harmonizing smart technologies with sustainability objectives in global logistics. Specifically, it seeks to:

Purpose of the Chapter

This chapter aims to establish a comprehensive framework for harmonizing smart technologies with sustainability objectives in global logistics. Specifically, it seeks to:

Analyze Synergies: Investigate how AI, IoT, blockchain, and automation amplify circular economy principles—such as waste minimization, energy efficiency, and carbon neutrality—within supply chain operations.
Identify Implementation Pathways: Map scalable strategies for overcoming adoption barriers (e.g., legacy infrastructure, workforce gaps) while aligning technological deployment with UN Sustainable Development Goals.
Evaluate Dual Impact: Assess how integrated “green-tech” systems simultaneously enhance ecological resilience (e.g., emission reduction, resource conservation) and economic value (e.g., cost savings, investor attractiveness).
Propose Future-Ready Metrics: Develop performance indicators that quantify sustainability-tech convergence, moving beyond traditional efficiency benchmarks to measure regenerative outcomes.

EMERGING TECHNOLOGIES DRIVING SMART LOGISTICS

The emergence of intelligent, data-driven, and automated technologies is largely responsible for the current rapid and dynamic development of the logistics sector. The implementation of numerous cutting-edge digital technologies is enabling these developments and changing the way logistical activities are organised, tracked, and carried out.

Several major technologies Blockchain, robots, automation, artificial intelligence (AI), big data analytics, and the Internet of Things (IoT) are fundamental to this change. These technologies are no longer employed in isolation; rather, they are rapidly being combined to produce a powerful, interconnected ecosystem. This technical synergy is the foundation of what is now popularly referred to as "smart logistics."

Smart logistics is a modern logistics system that uses real-time data, intelligent algorithms, and automated procedures to improve the way commodities are carried, stored, and managed across the supply chain. By incorporating these technologies into day-to-day logistics activities, businesses may get greater visibility into their operations, make faster and more accurate choices, and respond more effectively to changing client needs and market situations.

The adoption of these technologies has a significant impact. Operational efficiency, supply chain agility, inventory visibility, and environmental sustainability are among the critical areas in which businesses can capitalize on significant improvements. The integration of these digital tools allows logistics providers to operate more responsibly and intelligently, whether through predictive analytics that predict demand, IoT sensors that monitor shipments in real time, or automation systems that minimize human error.

The integration of cutting-edge technologies is not just enhancing logistics—it is redefining it, creating a more responsive, transparent, and sustainable framework for global supply chain management.

In the Internet of Things (IoT), sensors are installed in warehouses, cars, and containers to facilitate data sharing with other network-connected equipment. This enables real-time tracking and observation, facilitating the creation of an intelligent environment (Song et al., 2020; Ben-Daya et al., 2019). In the transportation and warehousing sectors, IoT facilitates tracking, environmental monitoring, and efficiency enhancement. Artificial intelligence aids the logistics sector in demand forecasting, route optimisation for deliveries, inventory level planning, and customer service (Boute & Udenio, 2022; Chen et al., 2024). Blockchain Technology Data recording via blockchain is secure and executed in a decentralised fashion. By monitoring things and processes, the supply chain becomes more transparent and dependable (Hackius & Petersen, 2017; Tijan et al., 2019). It is mostly advantageous for the logistics of managing commodities requiring special attention, such as groceries and pharmaceuticals. Robotics aids packers, sorters, and pickers in executing their responsibilities with more efficiency. Drones and automated guided vehicles (AGVs) are being evaluated for their application in transporting goods within the facility and for final delivery. They provide swifter and more precise transportation while requiring minimal human assistance.

In order to help us make the right decisions, we can use big data to analyse the massive amounts of data that logistical systems collect. Predictive analytics has made it possible to predict delays, sudden spikes in demand, and equipment failures (Chung, 2021; De Vass et al., 2021). If you want better results, you need to use both of them at the same time. Chen et al. (2024) and Kasap (2025) state that the integration of robots into the logistics process yields benefits like real-time tracking, streamlined operations, lower risks, and energy savings—all of which are crucial elements of environmentally friendly and sustainable logistics systems. The list of the most significant smart technologies and their applications in the logistics sector is provided below.

Table 1. Key smart technologies and their applications in logistics

Technology	Primary Applications in Logistics	Key Benefits
IoT	Asset tracking, temperature monitoring, vehicle routing	Real-time visibility, reduced losses
AI	Route optimization, forecasting, scheduling	Predictive decisions, increased efficiency
Blockchain	Shipment traceability, smart contracts, secure records	Transparency, fraud prevention
Robotics	Warehouse automation, autonomous delivery	Speed, accuracy, reduced labor costs
Automation	Sorting, packing, conveyor systems	Streamlined processes, lower operational cost
Big Data Analytics	Demand planning, risk analysis, performance monitoring	Data-driven insights, proactive management

Digital logistics system improvements have become a top concern. As explained in the following sections, using these green technology and logistical approaches improves both the quality of work and the environmental friendliness of the process. These technologies not only automate and optimise logistics operations, but also set the framework for greener, more adaptable supply networks, which align with sustainability objectives.

SUSTAINABLE LOGISTICS PRACTICES AND GREEN SUPPLY CHAIN STRATEGIES

The logistics sector is currently experiencing a major transformation, largely driven by growing concerns about environmental sustainability. As global awareness of climate change and ecological degradation continues to rise, companies across the supply chain are feeling increasing pressure—from both customers and regulatory bodies—to adopt greener and more responsible practices in their logistics operations.

To meet these expectations, businesses are turning toward environmentally friendly logistics strategies that not only reduce their carbon footprint but also improve overall operational efficiency. These practices include optimizing transportation routes to reduce fuel consumption, using electric or low-emission vehicles, investing in energy-efficient warehouses, and adopting packaging solutions that generate less waste.

The goal is twofold: to minimize the negative environmental impact of logistics activities and, at the same time, ensure that customer demands for timely, affordable, and high-quality service are met. In today's competitive market, companies understand that being sustainable is no longer just an option—it has become a critical part of building long-term resilience and gaining customer trust.

By integrating green logistics into their business models, organizations are not only addressing environmental challenges but are also creating more durable and future-ready supply chains that align with global sustainability goals.

The use of warehouses account for a lot of energy and natural resources. Mainly, green warehouses include the use of energy-efficient lights, smart air conditioning and heating systems and environmentally safe construction materials (Martins et al., 2019). Thanks to automation, scanning items and moving them comes instantly which not only speeds up work but saves on power. Rainwater collection and solar power on the roof are being installed more often to make warehouse operations more independent (Gruchmann, 2018). When it comes to logistics, packaging is essential because of the environmental impact of using too much material and creating waste. As a result, many businesses are choosing materials that can be recycled or used again rather than plastic or cardboard. Also, using smart packaging like RFID or temperature tags aids in reducing wastes.

Reverse logistics is the term used to describe the practice of transporting goods backwards within the supply chain, for as through recycling, rubbish processing, or refunds. According to Jayarathna et al. (2023), we should utilise what we currently have instead of discarding it if we want a circular economy to take root. Reverse logistics can help a business remain sustainable, recover the value of its products, and cut down on the quantity of things that wind up in landfills.

A meaningful part of the logistic-related emissions is ecologically related to the transportation area of the supply-chain. Transportation is one of the primary spheres that should be enhanced considering the huge contribution of trucks, ships, airplanes, and delivery vehicles to greenhouse gas emissions. With the current worries about the environment and plans to ensure reduced emissions, most companies are getting busy making matters cleaner and smarter so as to make their carbon footprint narrow.

There are a number of measures that are being employed to address this problem. Companies are continually moving towards clean fuels like bio fuels, compressed natural gas (CNG) and electricity to fuel their fleet. More efficient consolidation of cargo is also taking place- smaller shipments are being pooled so that there are fewer journeys instead of making each trip, lessening the emissions made whilst saving costs as well.

Optimisation in routes has taken priority as well. Thanks to the GPS technology and the use of AI-powered logistics software, companies can now find the shortest and less structured way to navigate, which will save fuel and cut delivery time. Moreover, it has been observed that fleet electrification of transport is increasingly being seen, and what was not feasible due to the level of technology in the case of electric vans and trucks, now is a feasible option with the current advances in electric vehicles.

Nevertheless, approaches to climate action, particularly, the carbon offsetting and green freight projects, were used as a part of the toolkit of sustainability quite long ago, but the emphasis is gradually turning to the reduction of direct emission. Instead of merely paying to offset the emissions, the firms are now determined to reduce the sources of emissions by making active and irreversible changes in their operations (Benjaafar et al., 2012; Wang & Hui, 2020). This belongs to a wider trend in the logistics sector, the shift in compliance thinking to sustainability thinking.

The circular economy concept's primary goals are resource recovery and waste minimization. Green logistics enables material reuse, which benefits both the economy and the environment (Chen et al., 2022; Song, 2022). Smart logistics facilities now power their warehouses, technology centers, and delivery vehicles using solar, wind, or geothermal energy. As a result, logistics companies consume less fossil fuel and contribute to initiatives to reduce global greenhouse gas emissions (Islam et al., 2021). More firms are realizing that employing green logistics is no longer an option, but rather a requirement for success. The following discussion will illustrate how these ecologically favorable practices, along with digital advancement, result in logistics systems that are sustainable, eco-friendly, and poised for future success. Table 2 depicts common green logistics strategies and their effects on emissions/savings. These solutions form the environmental backbone of smart logistics systems, with the goal of reducing emissions while maintaining operating efficiency.

Table 2. Common green logistics practices and their impact on emissions/savings

Green Practice	Environmental Impact	Operational Benefit
Energy-efficient warehouses	Lower electricity consumption, reduced CO_2	Long-term cost savings, lower utility bills
Eco-friendly packaging	Reduced packaging waste and pollution	Better brand perception, reduced disposal costs
Reverse logistics	Minimized landfill, resource recovery	Reclaimed value, customer satisfaction
Route optimization	Lower fuel usage and emissions	Shorter delivery times, reduced transport costs
Use of EVs in transport	Zero tailpipe emissions	Lower fuel costs, noise reduction
Solar-powered facilities	Lower grid dependency and emissions	Predictable energy costs, incentives

INTEGRATION OF SMART TECHNOLOGIES FOR SUSTAINABILITY

Whereas superior technologies can be considered excellent means of attaining sustainability objectives, the use of technology is not the only form. Consideration must also be given to the use of green supply chain strategies by businesses and re-evaluation of conventional logistics methods which may perhaps not meet the current environmental expectations. The actual development of sustainable logistics can be solely a joint work of the innovative technologies and the change of mentality towards a more environmentally friendly, responsible decision making.

The supply chains that are both effective and green can be created by incorporating the principles of green logistics into the primary processes that include the optimization of resource utilization, minimization of waste, and decrease in emissions. With the assistance of the progressive digital technologies, the difference is even more prominent.

Blockchain, the Internet of Things (IoT), and Artificial Intelligence (AI) are now some of the most important technologies in this change. Blockchain makes the supply chain clear and easy to track, which helps businesses keep an eye on environmentally-friendly practices at every stage. IoT devices give you real-time information from cars, warehouses, and shipments, so you can precisely control how much energy you use and how much damage you do to the environment. At the same time, AI tools look at huge amounts of logistics data to guess how demand will change, make the best use of transportation plans, and make smart choices that cut down on waste.

Together, these technologies give logistics systems the power to not only adjust to market trends but also change with them, which will make transportation operations more environmentally friendly in the long run. Companies want to be both productive and good to the environment. Combining green strategies with smart technologies is showing to be a key way to get there.

AI FOR EMISSION REDUCTION AND OPTIMIZATION

AI has completely changed the logistics industry, especially when it comes to making processes more environmentally friendly. It has helped people make better choices by letting them optimise routes, match loads intelligently, and keep a tight grip on energy use. AI systems look at past travel information, delivery performance, and vehicle usage trends to find ways to save fuel and lower carbon emissions all along the logistics chain.

One of the best things about AI is that it can learn and change all the time. AI algorithms can suggest faster, greener options by looking at things like routes that aren't working well or transport delays that happen over and over again. AI is also very important for forecast maintenance, which is different from planning routes. AI systems can predict motor problems before they cause unexpected breakdowns by keeping an eye on how vehicles work in real time. Not only does this cut down on unneeded downtime, but it also makes the environment cleaner by cutting down on waste and emissions and extending the life of cars.

One of the best answers to the question of how AI can enhance business operations can be a consideration of the Data Information Knowledge Wisdom (DIKW) hierarchy. At its most basic form, AI will receive a massive quantity of raw data in the form of procedures and sensors. It then decodes this data into usable data. This information is then analysed to come up with knowledge that can be implemented. Finally, AI will enable us to stop merely knowing the data and utilize long-term, intelligent policies that will result in logistics working more efficiently in general (Tijan et al., 2019).

The application of AI in the manufacturing environment is advantageous in higher numbers. It has the potential to facilitate the more efficient use of room, schedule the time of equipment use, and monitor electricity consumption in real time. Artificial intelligence can save energy, too: robots and other automation devices can adjust their working model according to the demands and the workload patterns. Due to such planning, there is less loss, less downtime, and ample utilization of resources (Ferreira & Reis, 2021).

IOT FOR WASTE MONITORING AND ENERGY MANAGEMENT

Things that are real, like cars, trucks, office equipment, and pallets, are linked to the computers that run them by the Internet of Things (IoT). It's important to note this part of how things are changing. IoT lets you keep an eye on and track different business factors in real time by connecting sensors and communication devices. To name a few, these are pollution, temperature, humidity, and the way things are stored and moved. Things like fuel use, CO2 pollution, and even how much energy certain processes or pieces of equipment use can be sent and collected in real time by the IoT. One of the most important things it can do for moves is this. It's also possible for people who buy things to find out how those things or the ways they are made affect the world (Song et al., 2020; Ben-Daya et al., 2019). They can see it too, yes. People are more likely to be responsible and honest when the business setting is this open. In a lot of ways, using smart biological systems is like using the Internet of Things (IoT). Firms can keep an eye on performance, find issues, and fix them right away with IoT systems by setting up feedback loops that keep going. Things will get better over time because of this instead of just being changed once. It can quickly let the people who make decisions know if things like fumes or fuel use go over what is expected. Then these people can figure out what's wrong and fix it.

For the Internet of Things, this tech works great in shops too. Tech can change how it works based on what it needs right now thanks to smart systems and connected meters. Tool or light settings can be changed right away based on things like the weather outside or the number of people inside. Tools and lights that aren't being used can also be turned off. De Vass et al. (2021) say that these smart changes help save energy without making things less comfy or useful. In essence, IoT enables logistics operations to become more transparent, adaptive, and environmentally conscious, making it a key enabler of sustainable logistics practices in the digital age.

BLOCKCHAIN FOR TRANSPARENCY AND SUSTAINABLE SOURCING

Blockchain is becoming a strong way to make the supply chain more open and simple to follow. It's easier to keep track of everything going on in the supply chain because private records and sharing of specific details about each transaction or movement of goods are safe (Hackius and Petersen, 2017; Tijan et al., 2019). This includes where the goods come from and where they finally arrive. It tells you important things like where an item came from, how it was moved, and even how much pollution it caused while it was moving. Blockchain can be used to store real-time environmental data so that businesses can make a digital record that can't be changed. Businesses can see if their suppliers are following environmental rules and using eco-friendly materials with this level of openness. From getting the raw materials to making the goods and sending them out, this helps companies make sure that their whole supply chain is in line with their environmental goals.

Being this open is a big part of backing ethical ways to source goods.When blockchain is used, companies can be sure that things made on farms, mines, or factories didn't hurt the environment. A company that buys farm products can make sure that farmers don't do things like use too many chemicals or cut down too many trees. In the same way, blockchain can help show that minerals or metals were not obtained through unfair or damaging mining methods. In general, blockchain increases trust and responsibility by making it simple to see, track, and prove that eco-friendly methods are being used all along the supply chain. This helps businesses follow their rules about the environment and makes them look better to partners and customers who care about the environment.

SMART-GREEN INTEGRATION: REAL-WORLD CASE EXAMPLES

- Global Retailer (Example): To keep food from going bad during transport, a multinational store started using IoT to watch the cold chain and AI to plan the routes of its vehicles. The result was a 20% drop in energy use and 15% less waste produced during transport (Chung, 2021; Chen et al., 2024).
- The use of blockchain and AI by a third-party logistics provider helps in checking carbon emissions and enhancing how warehouses operate. They got approved for ISO 14001 and succeeded in lowering their energy usage in the warehouses by 25% (Kasap, 2025; Verbivska et al., 2023).
- The use of blockchain and AI by a third-party logistics provider helps in checking carbon emissions and enhancing how warehouses operate. They got approved for ISO 14001 and succeeded in lowering their energy usage in the warehouses by 25% (Kasap, 2025; Verbivska et al., 2023).

When smart tools and goals for sustainability work together, they change what modern logistics systems can do. These new ideas not only help the environment, but they also save money, make customers happy, and make sure that world standards arc mct. Thc selected cases demonstrate the tangible impact of integrating smart systems with green logistics principles, reinforcing the relevance of technology in achieving sustainability targets.

IMPLEMENTATION CHALLENGES AND BARRIERS

Plans that are smart and good for the environment are thought to save money, make things work better, and cut down on pollution by many. But putting these thoughts into action can be hard. Many businesses still find it hard to fully adopt these new ways of doing things, even though they have a lot of potential.

Tech problems are one of the biggest problems. Most of the time, you need to know a lot about new technologies like IoT, AI, and blockchain in order to add them to transportation systems that are already in place. You also need to be able to work with older systems. This could make it hard for small and medium-sized businesses to adopt if their staff doesn't have the right skills. Not having enough money is another big worry. Buying green transportation tools or smart technologies, like electric cars, buildings that use less energy, or data analytics platforms, can cost a lot at first. For small businesses that don't have a lot of cash on hand, prices like these can be the end of their business.

When people don't know the rules, things can also move more slowly. A lot of places are still changing their rules about the world and how to use technology properly. Business people can't trust their plans because of this. People who do business all over the world may also find it hard to understand laws that aren't clear or don't work the same way in every market and country. Even more trouble is that businesses don't want to make the change. You might have to make changes to your business if you want to break away from old ways of doing transportation. For instance, you may need to retrain workers, change the way work gets done, and break long-standing operational habits. If a group doesn't have good direction and a plan, they might not want to use green technologies or make the switch to them. To get around these problems and successfully adopt smart and sustainable logistics, everyone needs to work together. It means dealing with a number of different problems in different fields, including technical, financial, legal, and cultural ones. An intelligent and environmentally friendly logistics future can only be reached by companies that are open to change and have a plan for the whole future.

TECHNICAL AND INFRASTRUCTURE BARRIERS

Blockchain, AI, and the Internet of Things (IoT) are all technologies that have the potential to change logistics in big ways. However, they will only work if there is a reliable and safe digital system in place. These systems need constant data flow, real-time connectivity, and gadgets and platforms that can talk to each other without any problems. Even the most cutting edge tools can't work right without a stable digital network. Sadly, a lot of logistics networks are still using old, separate systems that don't work with each other. This makes it hard to share and combine data from different parts of the supply chain. This creates gaps that make it hard to make smart decisions and slow down operations (Ben-Daya et al., 2019; De Vass et al., 2021). It's hard to get a full and true picture of the logistics process when data is spread out in these kinds of settings.

IoT devices, which are needed for tracking and monitoring in real time, need strong, safe, and uninterrupted internet connections to work properly. In the same way, blockchain apps need a lot of computing power and advanced security measures to keep data safe and stop people from changing it. The execution process is harder to do and costs more because of these requirements. This makes things very hard for small and medium-sized businesses (SMEs). A lot of small businesses have trouble paying for the big investments needed to set up the digital infrastructure or get the computers that new technologies need. Smaller businesses with restricted funds may not be able to afford to keep their systems up to date, train employees, and keep digital security up to date (Tijan et al., 2019). Because of this, the digital gap still makes it hard for people, especially small and medium-sized businesses, to use smart technologies, even though they have clear benefits. To close this gap, we will need both new technologies and targeted help, like funds for infrastructure, cloud-based solutions that aren't too expensive, and training programs that all types of businesses can use to join the digital transformation of logistics.

- **Financial Constraints**

Companies do not invest heavily in smart technology because it is initially expensive to implement. Implementing Internet of Things (IoT) sensors, automation systems, electric vehicles, and artificial intelligence technologies often necessitates significant investment and long-term planning. Many organizations in developing industries may struggle to explain the amount to which their investments in artificial intelligence have benefited them (Islam et al., 2021; Ferreira & Reis, 2023). Furthermore, businesses face significant challenges in the absence of adequate environmental funding or government support (Sarkis, 2012; Kasap, 2025).

- **Policy and Regulatory Gaps**

There aren't always clear rules, which slows down progress when people want to use new technologies to make things better for the environment. There aren't clear rules about who owns data, how the law should treat Blockchain records, and how to track and report pollution. This is one of the biggest problems. It's hard for groups to know their jobs and follow the rules when there aren't any rules in place (Hackius & Petersen, 2017; Paskannaya & Shaban, 2019). It's hard to do things because of this legal confusion. When businesses want to use smart technologies like Blockchain or IoT to track pollution, they often can't figure out if their systems are legal or how to get ready for new rules that may be different in each area. Businesses find it even harder to do business across lines when there aren't any standards that everyone agrees on. This is because they have to follow a lot of different sets of rules that aren't always clear or consistent. A lot of laws that are meant to support sustainability focus on end goals, like lowering carbon emissions or making energy use more efficient. This makes things even more difficult to understand. But these rules don't always make it clear how to use smart transport tools to make that happen (Feng et al., 2022; Min & Kim, 2012). In this case, a policy might say that emissions need to go down, but it might not say whether AI-based route planning or Blockchain-based tracking systems are both good ways to do that.

Not being clear stops people from coming up with new ideas and makes it take longer for smart, green transport options to be used by more people. The government needs to make rules that are more clear and detailed to avoid these issues. The rules should cover not only the environmental impacts but also the digital tools and ways companies can use to make those impacts. It will be easier for businesses to follow the rules if the rules are made clear. This will make them more likely to spend money on smart technologies that last.

- **Organizational and Cultural Resistance**

Businesses may face opposition from their workforce while possessing technological and financial advantages. Research findings (Perotti et al., 2015; Nand et al., 2023) indicate that logistics departments have focused extensively on risk minimisation; yet, they lack the requisite technology and environmental understanding to effectively manage these changes. Verbivska et al. (2023) and Srivastava (2007) established that an organization's delayed progress and disjointed efforts may result from inertia, divided teams, and leadership lacking familiarity with smart logistics concepts. This was further evidenced by the organization's sluggish pace of progress.

- **Industry-Wise Gaps in Adoption**

Specific industries, like urban companies and manufacturing, are experiencing a swift transformation towards enhanced environmental awareness and intelligence. Moreover, certain sectors, especially maritime operations, agricultural supply chains, and heavy industry logistics, encounter challenges manifested as delays due to complexities, obsolete equipment, or substantial scale (Chung, 2021; Gruchmann, 2018).

For example, the automobile industry has taken significant steps toward adopting sustainable and intelligent logistics practices. Many automotive companies have invested in low-carbon manufacturing facilities, designed to reduce energy consumption and limit greenhouse gas emissions. In addition, AI-powered tools are now being used to improve supply chain forecasting, allowing manufacturers to better predict demand, manage inventory efficiently, and reduce unnecessary transportation—further cutting down on environmental impact.

However, despite these advances, certain challenges remain—especially in areas such as bulk shipping and last-mile delivery. These issues are particularly noticeable in rural or remote regions, where the lack of adequate digital infrastructure makes it difficult to fully implement smart logistics solutions (Martins et al., 2019; Gevaers et al., 2009). Limited access to reliable internet, insufficient transport networks, and the high cost of advanced technologies all contribute to these ongoing difficulties.

As a result, while the automotive sector is making meaningful progress in integrating green and intelligent logistics, achieving consistent sustainability across all geographical areas remains a work in progress. Bridging the infrastructure gap—especially in less developed regions—will be essential for scaling smart logistics solutions and ensuring that the benefits of innovation reach every part of the supply chain.

STRATEGIES FOR OVERCOMING BARRIERS

Particular sectors, including urban enterprises and manufacturing, are currently experiencing a rapid transition to a more environmentally conscious and intelligent state. Furthermore, delays are encountered in other industries, including maritime operations, agricultural supply lines, and heavy industry logistics, due to issues with complexity, outdated equipment, or large size (Chung, 2021; Gruchmann, 2018). For instance, the automotive sector has invested in low-carbon facilities and supply chain forecasting through the use of AI. Bulk shipping and last-mile logistics are still challenging in rural areas due to the absence of appropriate smart infrastructure (Martins et al., 2019; Gevaers et al., 2009).

Table 3. Challenge and possible strategy

Challenge	Possible Strategy
High tech cost	Government subsidies, green tax credits, leasing smart assets
Lack of digital skills	Training programs, partnerships with tech startups
Data and system fragmentation	Adoption of cloud-based, interoperable platforms

continued on following page

Table 3. Continued

Challenge	Possible Strategy
Policy uncertainty	Industry alliances for standards development
Organizational resistance	Top-down commitment, pilot projects, and sustainability champions

More people are using 5G due to joint projects between the public and private sectors, common logistics facilities and centers for cross-sector collaboration (Chen et al., 2024; Kamewor et al., 2024). By addressing these barriers holistically, organizations can accelerate the shift toward logistics systems that are both intelligent and ecologically responsible.

KEY PERFORMANCE INDICATORS (KPIS) FOR SMART AND GREEN LOGISTICS

Once we know what the main problems are and what could be done to fix them so that smart and green logistics can be used, the next important thing is to figure out how to directly measure how well they work. It is important to keep an eye on performance in any transportation system, but it's even more crucial when looking at smart and eco-friendly methods. If we don't have the right measuring tools, it's hard to show that these technologies are really helping, whether it's with the environment or with operations. The gap between innovation and results can be closed with accurate and useful success indicators. It's hard for logistics managers to justify investments if they can't easily measure results like lowered emissions, saved energy, faster delivery, or lower cost in smart technologies or green practices. A lack of reliable data may also create skepticism among stakeholders and hinder wider adoption.

Key Performance Indicators (KPIs) that are specific to their jobs are often used by transport managers to deal with this issue. These key performance indicators (KPIs) help you keep track of your work, find trouble spots, and make decisions based on facts. Many things can show you how safe and useful a system is, such as how much fuel is used per distance, how many deliveries are made on time, how much energy is used per warehouse unit, and how much carbon effect each package has. If you want to plan in a smart and green way, you need to keep track of your work. They can see how things are going with real-time KPIs. When they see how these relate to benchmarks, they can make changes to the system to make it work better. Firms that deal with logistics should be careful not to try out new technology just for the sake of trying something new. They should use it to change the business and the world in real, measured ways.

- **Metrics That Matter in Smart-Green Logistics**

It remains essential to monitor delivery costs, punctuality, and the volume of products managed. Currently, transportation businesses prioritise environmental considerations, including carbon emissions, fuel consumption, and trash production (Pajić et al., 2021; Chen et al., 2024). As logistics transitions to digitalisation, the critical performance indicators include real-time transparency, accurate projections, and AI-suggested delays. Due to their influence, manufacturing operations can enhance responsiveness and demonstrate greater environmental consideration (Gözaçan & Lafci, 2020; Ying et al., 2018). Table 4 presents a compilation of typical KPIs and their significance to technology-facilitated sustainability.

Table 4. Sample KPIs and their relevance to tech-enabled sustainability

KPI	Relevance	Supports Sustainability By
Carbon emissions per delivery	Tracks environmental impact of each shipment	Encourages route optimization and cleaner transport modes
Fuel consumption per km	Measures transport efficiency	Drives shift to electric or fuel-efficient vehicles
Order accuracy rate	Tracks fulfillment performance	Reduces returns and associated reverse logistics emissions
Energy consumption per warehouse	Measures warehouse efficiency	Promotes use of automation, solar panels, and smart lighting
Real-time tracking success rate	Measures IoT-based visibility	Enables proactive issue handling, reducing delays and waste
Inventory turnover ratio	Reflects supply-demand alignment	Reduces storage time, energy usage, and product spoilage
AI-based demand forecasting accuracy	Evaluates smart prediction tools	Minimizes overproduction and excess inventory
On-time delivery percentage	Measures reliability	Helps plan efficient routing and reduce idle time
Waste recycled vs. generated	Tracks green packaging and waste management	Supports circular economy efforts
% of green transport used	Tracks fleet sustainability	Encourages low-emission transport modes like EVs or rail

- **Benchmarking and Tracking Success**

By utilising industry standards in addition to their own dashboards, businesses are able to evaluate and evaluate their progress in the field of logistics. Artificial intelligence (AI) and data analytics tools allow for the immediate collection and display of information from sensors, logs, and ERP systems that are being acquired in real time (Ben-Daya et al., 2019; Song et al., 2020).

The corporation may routinely assess the CO2 emissions of each vehicle to determine compliance with industry norms and its historical performance (Islam et al., 2021). Similarly, blockchain can offer a method to document and safeguard transportation records, ensuring their integrity remains intact. This facilitates the monitoring of status (Tijan et al., 2019). Numerous firms depend on international standards like ISO 14001 or the GLEC framework, established by the Global Logistics Emissions Council, to align their KPIs with global environmental objectives (Sarkis, 2012; Kamewor et al., 2024). Intelligent KPIs inspire a business to develop further and also assist with their sustainability reporting, explaining to stakeholders their attitude toward the environment.

- **Future Directions**

The global logistics business will undergo a process of transformation as a result of future breakthroughs in sustainable technologies. In order to modify supply networks, a number of nations and sectors have already begun the process of formulating long-term goals that are comparable to Vision 2030. In the realm of logistics, the primary objectives of these concepts are to achieve zero emissions, eliminate waste, and totally automate digital activities. Businesses are being forced to alter their standard operating procedures in order to comply with newly enacted environmental regulations and to maintain their competitive edge in the digital market.

- **Forecasting the Future of Smart-Green Logistics**

During the next several years, AI will be used much more than it is now for decision-making in logistics. Supply chain optimisation in real time will occur due to advanced algorithms that respond well to changes in demand, different traffic levels and weather conditions. It is expected that last-mile delivery will require more unmanned vehicles and drones in the future, to make services faster and use less energy. Across the world, green standards are increasing in strictness. There is a good chance that governments and trade associations will place tighter rules on emissions, how much packaging is used and the use of non-renewable resources.

As people become more concerned about the environment and call for more responsibility, businesses are slowly switching to logistics methods that are better for the environment and last longer. Businesses are making the switch by using tools like digital records, environmental labels, and product tracking systems to make the whole supply chain more clear. Customers, regulators, and partners can all use these tools to see exactly how goods are sourced, transported, and handled. This makes the logistics process more open and accountable.

At the same time, there is a clear change in the way people think in all fields and among customers. Sustainable and low-waste practices are becoming more popular, which is changing how transportation operations are planned and run. Because people's tastes are changing, things like recycling packaging, reusing containers, and cutting down on wasteful resource use are no longer options; they're now important parts of planning logistics for everyday life.

From now on, logistics systems will focus more on circular ideas, which mean that items and materials will be used for as long as possible. The idea is to use energy and materials as efficiently as possible and produce as little waste as possible. Sustainability will be a big part of every part of the logistics process, from using biodegradable packaging to planning returnable transport routes to using digital tools to make the best use of goods.

This change is good for the environment and also meets changing laws and customer needs. In the end, it helps businesses build supply chains that are stronger, more resilient, and ready for the future.

By the net year, hyper-intelligent ecosystems will dominate logistics, featuring autonomous supply chains where AI agents negotiate contracts and reroute shipments around climate disruptions in real-time, alongside bio-digital fusion (e.g., engineered microbes breaking down IoT-tracked packaging waste) and quantum-powered circularity that instantaneously matches global waste streams to reuse opportunities. Simultaneously, decentralization will revolutionize networks through micro-logistics grids (hyperloop pods cutting last-mile emissions by 70%) and energy-positive infrastructure like solar-coated trucks powering grids during idle hours. Regulatory frameworks will evolve toward AI-driven carbon taxation levied based on route ecological sensitivity and mandatory algorithmic ESG audits using deep learning to certify ethical compliance. Yet existential challenges loom: e-waste tsunamis from obsolete IoT devices will require blockchain-tracked reuse programs, cyber-physical threats to autonomous fleets will demand quantum encryption, and workforce displacement necessitates global reskilling initiatives. To thrive, firms must build anticipatory governance (cross-industry AI ethics councils), invest in convergence talent (e.g., “Circular Systems Engineers”), and pioneer symbiotic business models like shipping companies leasing rooftop space for renewables to offset >120% of emissions. By 2050, logistics will transition from a cost center to an ecological restoration cnginc, measuring success in biodiversity net-gain per transaction through embedded carbon capture and real-time reforestation investments.

CONCLUSION

The key insights from the preceding discussion, highlighting how a unified approach to smart and green logistics can redefine sustainability in modern supply chains. This chapter points out that technology and ecology must share a strong relationship. Systems that are prepared for the future now need IoT devices, advanced forecasting made possible by AI and tracked by blockchain.

However, just technology alone is not enough. To be effective, environmental goals must be attached to it, should be implemented with care and should be tested using KPIs that really count. As we look ahead, we should have an approach that brings together using digital tools and caring about the environment. It's the only approach businesses have to handle matters like international trade, climate change and changes in customer standards and it's also the only means to stay ahead of the competition. It is possible for businesses to make their operations smart and green. In the future, it will play a major role in forming the next supply networks.

The accelerating expansion of global supply chains demands an urgent integration of green logistics practices and smart technologies to achieve ecologically sustainable, efficient, and resilient operations. This chapter demonstrates that combining environmental strategies, such as carbon footprint reduction and circular resource management with intelligent systems like IoT, AI, and blockchain enables real-time optimization of logistics networks while advancing UN Sustainable Development Goals. Key challenges include standardizing cross-industry protocols, aligning policy incentives, and reskilling workforces, yet the proven benefits underscore the transformative potential of this synergy. Emerging frontiers like autonomous electric fleets, bio-digital twins, and ethical AI governance highlight the trajectory toward a logistics paradigm where ecological stewardship and technological innovation drive collective resilience, necessitating collaborative action across academia, industry, and regulators to scale these solutions globally.

The integration of smart logistics technologies is pivotal for advancing sustainability and attracting transformative investments in modern supply chains. By leveraging real-time data analytics, IoT networks, and AI-driven optimization, organizations achieve unprecedented resource efficiency, reducing emissions through dynamic route planning and load consolidation while cutting operational costs via predictive maintenance and energy management. This dual benefit creates a compelling investment thesis: sustainable logistics infrastructure now delivers rapid returns on investment, with ESG-focused funds allocating substantially more capital to tech-enhanced green supply chains than traditional models. Crucially, smart systems enable circular economy transitions that align with global frameworks like the Paris Agreement and UN SDGs. Investors increasingly prioritize these measurable ecological and operational gains, recognizing that scalable smart logistics is not merely an operational upgrade but a strategic lever for long-term resilience, regulatory compliance, and market differentiation in an era of climate-conscious capitalism.

Smart logistics technologies serve as the backbone for ecological stewardship and investment innovation in global supply chains. By harnessing intelligent systems companies dramatically lower environmental footprints while boosting operational agility. This synergy transforms sustainability from a compliance cost into a value driver, attracting capital through demonstrable gains in energy efficiency, waste reduction, and carbon-neutral operations. For investors, the appeal lies in how these technologies future-proof supply chains against regulatory shifts and resource scarcity, creating competitive moats through ethical automation and closed-loop resource flows. As climate accountability reshapes markets, smart logistics emerges as the critical enabler for harmonizing planetary boundaries with economic growth, positioning early adopters at the forefront of both profit and purpose.

The fusion of green logistics methodologies and smart technological innovations represents not merely an operational evolution but a fundamental reimagining of global supply chains. As environmental imperatives intensify and market dynamics grow increasingly volatile, this dual approach emerges as the cornerstone for building resilient, responsible, and competitive logistics ecosystems. Organizations that pioneer this integration will not only mitigate ecological degradation but also unlock new value streams through enhanced efficiency, investor appeal, and regulatory alignment. Crucially, achieving this transformation demands unprecedented collaboration: policymakers must incentivize sustainable-tech adoption, industries must share data and best practices, and academia must bridge research with real-world implementation. The path forward is clear by uniting human ingenuity with intelligent systems, we can forge supply chains that harmonize planetary health with economic vitality, turning the twin challenges of sustainability and digital disruption into our greatest opportunity for enduring progress.

REFERENCES

Ben-Daya, M., Hassini, E., & Bahroun, Z. (2019). Internet of things and supply chain management: A literature review. *International Journal of Production Research, 57*(15-16), 4719–4742. DOI: 10.1080/00207543.2017.1402140

Benjaafar, S., Li, Y., & Daskin, M. (2012). Carbon footprint and the management of supply chains: Insights from simple models. *IEEE Transactions on Automation Science and Engineering*, *10*(1), 99–116. DOI: 10.1109/TASE.2012.2203304

Boute, R. N., & Udenio, M. (2022). AI in logistics and supply chain management. In *Global logistics and supply chain strategies for the 2020s: Vital skills for the next generation* (pp. 49–65). Springer., DOI: 10.1007/978-3-030-95764-3_3

Chen, A. P. S., Huang, Y. F., & Do, M. H. (2022). Exploring the challenges to adopt green initiatives to supply chain management for manufacturing industries. *Sustainability*, *14*(20), 13516. DOI: 10.3390/su142013516

Chen, W., Men, Y., Fuster, N., Osorio, C., & Juan, A. A. (2024). Artificial intelligence in logistics optimization with sustainable criteria: A review. *Sustainability*, *16*(21), 9145. DOI: 10.3390/su16219145

Chung, S. H. (2021). Applications of smart technologies in logistics and transport: A review. *Transportation Research Part E, Logistics and Transportation Review*, *153*, 102455. Advance online publication. DOI: 10.1016/j.tre.2021.102455

De Vass, T., Shee, H., & Miah, S. (2021). IoT in supply chain management: Opportunities and challenges for businesses in early industry 4.0 context. *Operations and Supply Chain Management*, *14*(2), 148–161. DOI: 10.31387/oscm0450293

Ding, Y., Jin, M., Li, S., & Feng, D. (2021). Smart logistics based on the internet of things technology: An overview. *International Journal of Logistics Research and Applications*, *24*(4), 323–345. DOI: 10.1080/13675567.2020.1757053

Feng, Y., Lai, K. H., & Zhu, Q. (2022). Green supply chain innovation: Emergence, adoption, and challenges. *International Journal of Production Economics*, *248*, 108497. DOI: 10.1016/j.ijpe.2022.108497

Ferreira, B., & Reis, J. (2023). A Systematic Literature Review on the Application of Automation in Logistics. *Logistics (Basel)*, *7*(4), 80. DOI: 10.3390/logistics7040080

Gevaers, R., Van de Voorde, E., & Vanelslander, T. (2009). Characteristics of innovations in last-mile logistics–using best practices, case studies and making the link with green and sustainable logistics. *Association for European Transport and contributors*, 1, 21.

Gözaçan, N., & Lafci, C. (2020). Evaluation of key performance indicators of logistics firms. *Logistics, Supply Chain. Sustainability and Global Challenges*, *11*(1), 24–32. DOI: 10.2478/jlst-2020-0002

Gruchmann, T. (2018). Advanced green logistics strategies and technologies. In *Operations, logistics and supply chain management* (pp. 663–686). Springer., DOI: 10.1007/978-3-319-92447-2_29

Hackius, N., & Petersen, M. (2017). Blockchain in logistics and supply chain: Trick or treat? In Digitalization in Supply Chain Management and Logistics (Vol. 23, pp. 3–18). *epubli GmbH*, https://doi.org/ DOI: 10.15480/882.1444

Islam, M. S., Moeinzadeh, S., Tseng, M. L., & Tan, K. (2021). A literature review on environmental concerns in logistics: Trends and future challenges. *International Journal of Logistics Research and Applications*, *24*(2), 126–151. DOI: 10.1080/13675567.2020.1732313

Jayarathna, C. P., Agdas, D., & Dawes, L. (2023). Exploring sustainable logistics practices toward a circular economy: A value creation perspective. *Business Strategy and the Environment*, *32*(1), 704–720. DOI: 10.1002/bse.3170

Kamewor, F. T., Kwateng, K. O., & Mensah, J. (2024). Green logistics practices: A bibliometric and systematic methodological review and future research opportunities. *Journal of Cleaner Production, 143735*. Advance online publication. DOI: 10.1016/j.jclepro.2024.143735

Kasap, A. (2025). Sustainable e-commerce: Examining green logistics and digitalization strategies. *Asya Studies*, *9*(31), 261–290. DOI: 10.31455/asya.1622024

Martins, V. W., Anholon, R., Quelhas, O. L., & Leal Filho, W. (2019). Sustainable practices in logistics systems: An overview of companies in Brazil. *Sustainability*, *11*(15), 4140. DOI: 10.3390/su11154140

Min, H., & Kim, I. (2012). Green supply chain research: Past, present, and future. *Logistics Research*, *4*, 39–47.

Murphy, P. R., & Poist, R. F. (2000). Green logistics strategies: An analysis of usage patterns. *Transportation Journal*, •••, 5–16.

Nand, A., Sohal, A., Fridman, I., Hussain, S., & Wallace, M. (2023). An exploratory study of organisational and industry drivers for the implementation of emerging technologies in logistics. *Industrial Management & Data Systems, 123*(5), 1418–1439. DOI: 10.1108/IMDS-08-2022-0467

Pajić, V., Radivojević, G., & Kilibarda, M. (2021). Influence of KPI of logistics processes on logistics costs. *International Journal for Traffic & Transport Engineering*, 11(4), https://doi.org/ (4).09DOI: 10.7708/ijtte2021.11

Sarkis, J. (2012). A boundaries and flows perspective of green supply chain management. *Supply Chain Management, 17*(2), 202–216. DOI: 10.1108/13598541211212924

Shee, H. K., Miah, S. J., & De Vass, T. (2021). Impact of smart logistics on smart city sustainable performance: An empirical investigation. *International Journal of Logistics Management, 32*(3), 821–845. DOI: 10.1108/IJLM-07-2020-0282

Song, H. (2022). Intelligent supply chain and tech-enabled supply chain finance. In *Smart Supply Chain Finance* (pp. 89–148). Springer., DOI: 10.1007/978-981-16-5997-3_3

Song, Y., Yu, F. R., Zhou, L., Yang, X., & He, Z. (2020). Applications of the Internet of Things (IoT) in smart logistics: A comprehensive survey. *IEEE Internet of Things Journal, 8*(6), 4250–4274. DOI: 10.1109/JIOT.2020.3034385

Srivastava, S. K. (2007). Green supply-chain management: A state-of-the-art literature review. *International Journal of Management Reviews, 9*(1), 53–80. DOI: 10.1111/j.1468-2370.2007.00202.x

Tijan, E., Aksentijević, S., Ivanić, K., & Jardas, M. (2019). Blockchain technology implementation in logistics. *Sustainability, 11*(4), 1185. DOI: 10.3390/su11041185

Verbivska, L., Zhygalkevych, Z., Fisun, Y., Chobitok, I., & Shvedkyi, V. (2023). Digital technologies as a tool of efficient logistics. *Revista de la Universidad del Zulia, 14*(39), 492–508. DOI: 10.46925//rdluz.39.28

Wang, L., & Hui, M. (2020). Research on joint emission reduction in supply chain based on carbon footprint of the product. *Journal of Cleaner Production, 263*, 121086. DOI: 10.1016/j.jclepro.2020.121086

Ying, F., Tookey, J., & Seadon, J. (2018). Measuring the invisible: A key performance indicator for managing construction logistics performance. *Benchmarking, 25*(6), 1921–1934. DOI: 10.1108/BIJ-11-2016-0176

KEY TERMS AND DEFINITIONS

Green Logistics: Environmentally optimized supply chain practices that systematically reduce ecological harm—from deploying electric fleets and optimizing warehouse energy use to implementing reverse logistics for product returns and recycling. This approach transforms traditional linear models into regenerative systems aligned with planetary boundaries.

Smart Technologies: Interconnected digital solutions—including AI algorithms for demand forecasting, IoT sensors for real-time cargo monitoring, and blockchain for transparent supplier verification—that enable autonomous decision-making. These technologies convert raw data into actionable sustainability insights, such as identifying emission hotspots across distribution networks.

Sustainability Integration: The strategic fusion of ecological targets with core business functions, ensuring every operational layer—from procurement to last-mile delivery—advances UN Sustainable Development Goals. This requires reengineering KPIs to reward carbon reduction alongside cost savings and embedding circularity into corporate governance structures.

Circular Economy: A production-consumption model that eliminates waste through intelligent design: predictive analytics extend product lifecycles, material passports enable component reuse, and digital platforms facilitate industrial symbiosis where one company's by-products become another's raw materials.

Supply Chain Resilience: Proactive adaptability to disruptions via machine learning-driven risk simulations and distributed ledger-enabled supplier networks. Resilience manifests as dynamic rerouting during climate events or rapid material substitution during shortages—all while maintaining carbon neutrality commitments.

ESG (Environmental, Social, Governance): A holistic evaluation framework where environmental metrics (Scope 3 emissions tracking), social equity (fair labor algorithms), and ethical oversight (AI-audited compliance) converge to attract impact investors and satisfy stakeholder capitalism demands.

Predictive Maintenance: Sensor-driven systems that anticipate machinery failures before they occur, using vibration analysis and thermal imaging to schedule repairs during low-energy periods. This prevents resource-intensive emergency fixes and extends equipment longevity by up to 40%.

Carbon Neutrality: Achieving net-zero emissions through multi-layered strategies: electrifying transport fleets, purchasing renewable energy credits, and deploying AI to optimize container utilization—thereby reducing empty runs and unnecessary fuel consumption across logistics corridors.

Technological Synergy: The exponential sustainability gains when combining technologies—e.g., blockchain verifies recycled content origins while IoT sensors monitor real-time energy usage—creating self-regulating systems where efficiency improvements automatically lower ecological footprints.

Performance Metrics: Advanced analytics measuring dual-capital outcomes: *natural capital* (carbon intensity per ton-mile, water saved through route optimization) and *economic capital* (ROI from sustainability tech investments, cost avoidance via waste reduction).

Chapter 6
Steering Sustainable Logistics Performance in the Large-Scale Retail Sector:
Towards an Integrated Approach Via the Balanced Scorecard

Naoual Bouhtati
Sidi Mohamed Ben Abdellah University, Fez, Morocco

Lhoussaine Alla
https://orcid.org/0000-0002-7238-1792
Sidi Mohamed Ben Abdellah University, Fez, Morocco

Aziz Hmioui
https://orcid.org/0000-0002-9032-4978
Sidi Mohamed Ben Abdellah University, Fez, Morocco

ABSTRACT

This chapter explores the use of Balanced Scorecards to manage sustainable logistics performance in the retail sector. It aims to integrate the issues of sustainability, digital transformation and crisis management. A literature review identifies four key dimensions (economic, social, environmental, governance) and mechanisms (digital technologies, circular economy, carbon footprint reduction, sustainable governance). The Logistics Balanced Scorecard (LBS) is proposed as a strategic tool for balancing priorities and fostering sustainable value creation. The results of the literature review highlight four main dimensions for steering sustainable logistics

DOI: 10.4018/979-8-3373-2434-0.ch006

performance: economic, social, environmental and governance. Key mechanisms include the integration of digital technologies, the adoption of circular business models, the reduction of the carbon footprint, and the implementation of sustainable governance policies. The corresponding KPIs measure cost efficiency, stakeholder satisfaction, reduction of CO_2 emissions, and transparency in sustainability reporting.

INTRODUCTION

The Large-Scale Retail Sector- also known as "Mass Retail", "Large-scale Retail", "Supermarket", "Superstores", "Large Retail Stores" or even "Mini-marts"- a pillar of the modern economy, is today facing logistical challenges of an unprecedented magnitude. The increasing complexity of supply chains, increased consumer demands for speed and personalization, and most importantly, the sustainability imperative are putting considerable pressure on businesses (Christopher, 2016). In this context, the management of overall supply chain performance (SCM) has become a major strategic issue, requiring an integrated and multidimensional approach (Mentzer et al., 2001), and particularly in the Large-Scale Retail Sector (Jaouad, 2017; SABIR, 2020).

The interest of this research lies in its timeliness and relevance to contemporary issues. Large-Scale Retail Sector companies are increasingly aware of the need to optimize their logistics performance economically, socially, and environmentally (Elkington, 1997). Digital transformation, with the rise of e-commerce and the use of technologies such as artificial intelligence and the Internet of Things, offers new opportunities to improve the efficiency and sustainability of supply chains, in particular in the Large-Scale Retail Sector. At the same time, crisis management, whether it is a pandemic, natural disaster or geopolitical disruption, has become an essential skill for ensuring the resilience of supply chains. Recent studies (Henrich et al., 2023) show that companies that invest in a sustainable and agile MGS perform better in the long term, both financially and in terms of reputation.

Despite the importance of the topic, several scientific gaps persist in the existing literature. On a theoretical level, traditional SCM models do not always take into account the complexity of large-scale retail supply chains, nor the specificities of sustainability and digital transformation issues (Heckmann et al., 2015). Methodological approaches are often limited to the financial aspects of performance, neglecting social and environmental dimensions (Hofmann, 2010). Empirically, the studies are often sectoral and do not allow to generalize the results to the whole of Large-Scale Retail Sector (Boyer & Verma, 2010).

This research aims to fill these gaps by exploring the management of sustainable logistics performance in Large-Scale Retail Sector. The purpose of this study is to analyse how companies in this sector can improve the integrated management of their supply chain, integrating the issues of sustainability, digital transformation and crisis management. The research problem can be formulated as follows: How can Large-Scale Retail Sector establishments improve the integrated management of their supply chain performance, by integrating sustainability issues, digital transformation and crisis management, and using balanced scorecards adapted to their specific context?

To answer this question, it proposes a mixed methodological approach combining a literature review and a prospective approach. Initially, our in-depth literature review will enable us to define the key concepts of the research and to present an overview of the mechanisms for promoting the sustainability of supply chains and the key indicators for managing them. Then, the prospective approach will enable us to draw up optimal scenarios for the strategic management of sustainable logistics performance in this sector.

Translated with DeepL.com (free version) the plan for this chapter is as follows: first, will present a State-of-the-Art Literature on Large-Scale Retail Sector performance management and balanced scorecards. In a second step, we will describe the methodological approach and the case studies carried out. In a third stage, will present the results of the analyses and the prospects for steering sustainable logistics performance in the sector.

THEORETICAL AND CONCEPTUAL FRAMING

Sustainable Retail Logistics

Sustainable logistics in the retail sector, at the intersection of supply chain management and sustainability imperatives, has been the subject of much recent research. This literature review aims to identify relevant and recent definitions by presenting their key dimensions. The definitions are summarized in table 1 below:

Table 1. A definitional approach to sustainable logistics in the retail sector

References	Definition
Khan et al. (2021)	"Sustainable logistics in large-scale distribution integrates social, environmental and economic dimensions into the management of logistical flows."
Mishra et al. (2023)	"An integrated logistics framework for mass distribution that promotes the circular economy while meeting the expectations of stakeholders."
Goel et al. (2025)	"A logistics framework designed to reduce the negative externalities of mass distribution while promoting circular practices."

Source: author's elaboration

Sustainable logistics in the retail sector is an integrated approach that aims to minimise environmental impact, optimise operational efficiency, promote social responsibility and integrate smart technologies, while ensuring economic viability and meeting stakeholder expectations. It encompasses reducing the carbon footprint, adopting ethical practices, promoting the circular economy and increasing cooperation between all players in the supply chain.

Translated with DeepL.com (free version) It follows that sustainable retail logistics can be defined as an integrated approach to supply chain management aimed at optimising logistical flows while reconciling environmental dimensions, economic, social and technological. It is based on eco-responsible and collaborative practices, such as reducing carbon emissions, the circular economy, data transparency, and minimising environmental impacts, while ensuring operational efficiency, Stakeholder satisfaction and compliance with global sustainability objectives. From the definitions listed above, it appear the holistic nature of sustainable logistics in mass distribution, which tends to integrate ecological imperatives harmoniously, economic and social while relying on technological innovations and collaborative practices to reconcile sustainability and logistics performance.

GM Sustainable Logistics Performance

The sustainable logistics performance of Large-Scale Retail Sector is measured through a set of indicators that assess the effectiveness, efficiency and impact of logistics activities on environmental, social and economic dimensions. It reflects the company's ability to achieve its strategic objectives while minimizing its ecological footprint and contributing to social welfare (Elkington, 1997; Golicic & Smith, 2013).

An exploration of recent work on the issue allows to draw a list of the main definitions of such performance (Table 2).

Table 2. A definitional approach to sustainable logistics performance in the retail sector

References	Definition
Kamewor et al. (2024)	"Sustainable performance in logistics involves optimized management of physical and information flows, allowing a reduction of negative externalities on the environment and society."
Gurtu et Johny (2021)	"Sustainable logistics performance is defined as the balance between operational efficiency, compliance with environmental standards and stakeholder satisfaction."
Wang et al. (2023)	"Logistics management based on the principles of sustainability, facilitating a transition to circular and resilient supply chains."

Source: author's elaboration

Sustainable logistics performance in the retail sector is an integrated approach that aims to balance economic efficiency, reduced environmental impact and social responsibility. It involves optimising physical and information flows, integrating sustainable practices into the supply chain, adopting green technologies, and taking into account stakeholder expectations, while facilitating the transition to circular and resilient supply chains.

From the table above, we can approach the notion of "Sustainable logistics performance in mass distribution" as the ability of companies in this sector to integrate economic, environmental and social principles into their logistic practices, to optimize physical and information flows while minimizing negative impacts on the environment and society. It is based on balanced management to reduce emissions, waste and costs while maintaining a high level of customer service, stakeholder satisfaction and competitiveness.

Logistics Forward Planning Dashboard

As part of this research, we have explored recent studies on the concept of a "Prospective Logistics Dashboard» (PLD) applied to sustainable logistics performance. The PLD, often adapted from the Balanced Scorecard (BSC), is distinguished by its integrative approach that focuses on indicators of economic, social and environmental sustainability. A summary of the most relevant definitions of the concept is given in Table 3 below:

Table 3. Recent FFB definitions

References	Definition
Weerapong & Singhdong (2024)	"The PLD is defined as an integrated tool to monitor and optimize logistics performance by balancing financial and non-financial dimensions, with a particular focus on environmental and social sustainability."
Singh et al. (2021)	"A Prospective Logistics Scorecard is a strategic approach to assessing sustainable logistics performance through indicators aligned with the organization's strategic objectives and societal expectations".
Hervani et al. (2022)	"Steering tool for assessing the resilience and sustainability of supply chains by combining financial, environmental and innovation indicators in a forward-looking framework".
Keivanpour (2022)	"The PLD is a method to integrate the principles of the Triple Bottom Line in logistics management, to ensure long-term sustainable performance through balanced indicators".
Qorri et al. (2018)	"A strategic approach to assess sustainable logistics performance by taking into account economic, ecological and social indicators through a balanced and integrated perspective".
Felsberger (2018)	"Analytical framework for translating strategic sustainability objectives into concrete operational actions in logistics management".
Pejić Bach et al. (2023)	"The Logistics Sustainability Scorecard is a decision-making tool combining financial and non-financial metrics, designed to optimize supply chain sustainability."
Pal et al. (2023)	"Tool for evaluating and monitoring logistics performance incorporating sustainability criteria, enabling continuous improvement in a competitive and responsible environment".
Xia et al. (2017)	"A sustainable logistics performance management framework based on the Balanced Scorecard, allowing operational actions to be aligned with sustainability objectives".
Lee & Wu (2014)	"The PLD is a conceptual framework for driving sustainable logistics performance by integrating environmental, social and economic dimensions into a holistic management system".

Source: Author's elaboration

The Prospective Logistics Scorecard (PLD) and associated tools are analytical and strategic frameworks designed to assess, monitor and optimise sustainable logistics performance. They integrate financial and non-financial dimensions, as well as economic, environmental and social indicators, in order to align operational actions with sustainability objectives. These tools aim to ensure long-term sustainable management, improve the resilience of supply chains and drive continuous improvement in a competitive and responsible environment.

The Logistics Forward Looking Dashboard (PLD) can be defined as an integrated and strategic framework, inspired by the Balanced Scorecard, designed to evaluate, pilot and optimize sustainable logistics performance. It is based on a balance between financial and non-financial indicators, while integrating environmental, social and economic dimensions. The PLD translates strategic sustainability objectives into concrete operational actions and aims to align logistics performance with sustainability imperatives such as Triple Bottom Line, supply chain resilience and innovation.

As a logistics performance management tool, the PLD is positioned as a strategic and holistic tool, essential to align logistics actions with sustainability objectives, while ensuring a competitive and resilient performance in a mass distribution context, by aligning the mechanisms and levers mobilized with the selected steering KPIs.

Theoretical Reference Framework for Research

After the conceptual framing of the research, we intend to carry out a literature review to identify a relevant state of the art. As a prerequisite, we propose to present the main theories to be mobilized to better understand, explain and model the management of sustainable logistics performance in the Large-Scale Retail Sector through forward-looking logistics dashboards.

After a thorough analysis of the theories which could serve as a basis for the analysis, finally selected the seven theories which consider to be most relevant (Table 4):

Table 4. Summary of theories that can be leveraged for the logistics outlook scorecard

Theory	Contributions for Research
Stakeholder theory (Freeman, 2010)	Identifies key stakeholders and prioritizes their expectations in a sustainable way (Zuro, 2024).
	Supports the creation of performance indicators aligned with stakeholders' social and environmental expectations (Siems et al., 2023).
	Promotes the management of conflicts between stakeholders through a balanced approach (Vegter et al., 2023).
	Strengthens social responsibility in supply chains (Vidal et al., 2023).
Resource and Skill Theory (RBV) (Penrose, 2009; Barney, 1991)	Identifies critical resources and skills to improve sustainable logistics performance (Gölgeci et al., 2019).
	Helps maximize the use of logistics assets for more sustainable practices (Kofar Kudu & Karia, 2024).
	Highlights the competitive advantage of intangible resources (e.g., know-how, technology) (Lee et al., 2024).
	Supports the integration of organizational skills into sustainable initiatives (Chen et al. 2021).

continued on following page

Table 4. Continued

Theory	Contributions for Research
Triple performance theory (TBL) (Elkington, 1997)	Integrates the economic, social and environmental dimensions in performance management tools (Bansal and Song, 2017).
	Promotes the development of balanced indicators to measure sustainable outcomes (Neri et al., 2021).
	Supports the transition to environmentally sound logistics practices (Govindan et al., 2020).
	Enables a more holistic view of sustainable logistics in Mass Retail (Sharma et al., 2021).
Value chain theory (Porter, 1985)	Identifies logistics activities with high sustainable impact in the value chain (Kwak et al., 2018).
	Helps to optimize flow management by reducing waste and maximizing added value (Budak, 2020).
	Supports the integration of sustainable practices into logistics processes (Baah et al. 2021).
	Enables alignment of logistics objectives with the overall business strategy (Xia et al., 2017).
Systems theory (von Bertalanffy, 1968)	Provides a global view of interactions between stakeholders and logistics processes (Kaur & Singh, 2019).
	Helps to understand the complex interdependencies in supply chains (Ivanov, 2022).
	Facilitates the identification of synergies between economic, social and environmental dimensions (Rebs et al., 2019).
	Supports the resilience of logistics systems to disruptions (Ivanov & Dolgui, 2021).
Theory of dynamic capabilities (Teece et al., 1997)	Facilitates companies' adaptation to rapid market changes and environmental constraints (Beske-Janssen et al., 2019).
	Encourages innovation in sustainable logistics practices (Birasnav et al., 2021).
	Builds capacity to integrate new technologies into supply chains (Chen et al., 2021).
	Promotes flexibility and agility in responding to stakeholder expectations (Hosseini et al., 2022).
Complexity theory (Simon, 1962; Anderson, 1999)	Helps manage the growing complexity of global supply chains (Ivanov, 2022).
	Allows modelling of dynamic and uncertain logistics systems (Alavi et al., 2021).
	Promotes robust decision-making in an uncertain environment (Birasnav et al., 2021).
	Supports resilience and adaptation of supply chains to disruptions (Ivanov & Dolgui, 2021).

Source: Author's elaboration

These theories allow a multidimensional and systemic approach that perfectly aligns with the objective of driving sustainable logistics performance through a prospective logistics dashboard such as the Balanced Scorecard. They cover strategic, operational and environmental aspects while taking into account stakeholder expectations.

The selected theories provide a solid basis for designing a forward-looking logistics dashboard that meets the specific requirements of the Large-Scale Retail Sector. By combining a systems approach, strategic alignment, resource and skills development, as well as multidimensional indicators. These theories effectively drive sustainable logistics performance while strengthening the competitiveness of companies. This theoretical and conceptual framework provides a solid basis for exploring the management of sustainable logistics performance in the retail sector. By combining a rigorous conceptual approach, an analysis of the state of the art and a mobilisation of relevant theories, this chapter aims to make a significant contribution to the understanding and improvement of the sustainable logistics performance of this sector. Future research should focus on the empirical validation of this framework and the development of tools and methods to help Large-Scale Retail Sector companies implement effective sustainable logistics practices.

METHODOLOGY

Methodological Outline

Considering the above problem, our methodological approach to selective thematic qualitative analysis is organized in two phases:

- ***Bibliometric request***: To carry out a review of relevant scientific literature on the prospective management of sustainable logistics performance in large-scale retail, we intend to use a sample of relevant references from bibliographic databases (Scopus).
- ***Qualitative analysis***: A more in-depth thematic analysis of the selected references (Miles and Huberman, 2003) will be carried out through content analysis (titles, abstracts and keywords), identification of emerging trends and their classification.

Selection Process

To implement such a methodological approach, we have adopted a rigorous reference selection process in accordance with the following Preferred Reporting Items for Systematic Reviews and Meta-Analyses (PRISMA):

Table 5. Reference selection process

Phase 1. Refined research equation	(TITLE-ABS-KEY ("logistics performance" OR "logistics efficiency" OR "logistics flexibility" OR "logistics agility" OR "logistics profitability" OR "logistics effectiveness" OR "logistics resilience" OR "performance management" OR "supply chain management" OR "SCM") AND TITLE-ABS-KEY ("digital age" OR "sustainability" OR "times of crisis" OR "forward-looking logistics" OR "flow management" OR "PKI logistics"))	8560
Phase 2. Initial database selection	Scopus	
Phase 3. Reference selection inclusion filters	-Filter by period: 10 years (2015 to 2024) -Filter by domain -Limited to business, management and accounting -Limited to social sciences -Limited to economics, econometrics and finance	4898
Phase 4. Reference selection exclusion filters	Limited to the article Limited to English	3 690
Phase 5. Reference selection scrubbing filters	Filtering by title and keywords Reading the abstracts Open access articles	1978
Phase 6. In-depth qualitative analysis	Most cited open access articles	50

Source: Author's elaboration

This rigorous reference selection process will help improve the quality of our systematic approach and make the analysis more relevant, transparent and rigorous to build a corpus of high-quality research on the development of forward-looking logistics dashboards for Mass Retail (Snyder, 2019; Rethlefsen & Page, 2022).

Analytical Sample

Based on the inclusion, exclusion and cleansing filters of our initial request on Bibliometrix, our sample of the chapter selected to conduct our in-depth literature review is composed of 50 references (Table 6).

Table 6. Most global cited documents (Bibliometrix)

Paper	Total Citations	TC per Year	Normalized TC
Lu H, 2024, Prod Plann Control	73	36,50	20,92
Chowdhury P, 2021, Transp Res Part E Logist Transp Rev	674	134,80	18,72
Ibn-Mohammed T, 2021, Resour Conserv Recycl	587	117,40	16,30
Genovese A, 2017, Omega	1007	111,89	15,29
Kalmykova Y, 2018, Resour Conserv Recycl	934	116,75	15,13
Rusch M, 2023, Bus Strategy Environ	165	55,00	14,88
Sahoo S, 2024, Electron Commer Res	51	25,50	14,62
Geissdoerfer M, 2018, J Clean Prod	802	100,25	12,99
Ngo Vm, 2024, Bus Strategy Environ	37	18,50	10,60
Khanra S, 2022, Bus Strategy Environ	220	55,00	10,36
Cannas Vg, 2024, Int J Prod Res	36	18,00	10,32
Dubey R, 2019, Technol Forecast Soc Change	502	71,71	9,37
Chandan A, 2023, Sustainability	91	30,33	8,21
Kouhizadeh M, 2018, Sustainability	470	58,75	7,61
Negri M, 2021, Bus Strategy Environ	274	54,80	7,61
Jabbour Cjc, 2016, J Clean Prod	544	54,40	7,47
Awasthi A, 2018, Int J Prod Econ	461	57,63	7,47
Kumar M, 2023, Bus Strategy Environ	80	26,67	7,22
Yang M, 2021, Technol Forecast Soc Change	259	51,80	7,19
Dubey R, 2024, Int J Prod Econ	25	12,50	7,17
Wiredu J, 2024, Bus Strategy Environ	25	12,50	7,17
Luthra S, 2020, Int J Prod Res	288	48,00	6,97
Park A, 2021, Sustainability	243	48,60	6,75
Badri Ahmadi H, 2017, Resour Conserv Recycl	441	49,00	6,70
Uda Sk, 2024, Uncertain Supply Chain Manag	22	11,00	6,31
De Mattos Nascimento Dl, 2024, Bus Strategy Environ	22	11,00	6,31
Riofrancos T, 2023, Global Environ Polit	69	23,00	6,22
Raman R, 2024, Discov Sustain	21	10,50	6,02
Mulligan C, 2024, Telecommun Policy	21	10,50	6,02
Burke H, 2023, Prod Plann Control	66	22,00	5,95
Khan Sa, 2022, Bus Strategy Environ	125	31,25	5,89
Dey Pk, 2020, Bus Strategy Environ	242	40,33	5,85
Wilhelm Mm, 2016, J Oper Manage	422	42,20	5,80

continued on following page

Table 6. Continued

Paper	Total Citations	TC per Year	Normalized TC
Gholipour A, 2024, Environ Dev Sustainability	20	10,00	5,73
Oyedijo A, 2024, Supply Chain Manage	20	10,00	5,73
Kayikci Y, 2024, Bus Strategy Environ	20	10,00	5,73
Zhang A, 2019, J Clean Prod	304	43,43	5,67
Gardner Ta, 2019, World Dev	297	42,43	5,54
Ribeiro Da Silva E, 2023, Resour Conserv Recycl	61	20,33	5,50
Zhang A, 2020, Resour Conserv Recycl	226	37,67	5,47
Chari A, 2022, Bus Strategy Environ	116	29,00	5,47
Kusi-Sarpong S, 2019, Int J Prod Res	292	41,71	5,45
Nasir Mha, 2017, Int J Prod Econ	355	39,44	5,39
Del Giudice M, 2020, Int J Logist Manage	222	37,00	5,37
Sgarbossa F, 2023, Int J Prod Econ	58	19,33	5,23
Ivanov D, 2018, Int J Prod Res	320	40,00	5,18
Yusuf Zfa, 2024, Uncertain Supply Chain Manag	18	9,00	5,16
Ali Mh, 2021, Technol Forecast Soc Change	182	36,40	5,05
Khan M, 2023, Bus Strategy Environ	56	18,67	5,05
Di Vaio A, 2020, Sustainability	206	34,33	4,98

Source: authors elaboration

State-of-the-Art and Modelling Sketch

Thematic Analysis of Mechanisms for the Prospective Promotion of Logistics Performance

Sustainable logistics performance in the Large-Scale Retail Sector is based on a combination of economic, social, environmental and governance mechanisms. The integration of these mechanisms into a comprehensive and coherent strategy enables companies to reconcile economic performance, social responsibility and environmental protection, while strengthening their resilience and attractiveness.

After systematic and integrated analysis of the documents relating to the references in the sample, it identified a battery of key mechanisms by dimensions for promoting sustainability of logistics performance in the Large Retail sector that is grouped into relevant thematic clusters (Table 7).

Table 7. Summary of key mechanisms for sustainable logistics performance

	Cluster	– Relevant Key-Mechanism
Economic dimension	**Technological and digital optimization**	– Cost optimization through circular economy and automation (Lu et al., 2024) – Reduction of waste through real-time data analysis (Lu et al., 2024) – Digitalization to improve economic resilience (Chowdhury et al., 2021) – Cost optimization through real-time data analysis for effective inventory management (Rusch et al., 2023)
	Circular business models	– Substitution of critical materials by circular alternatives (Ibn-Mohammed et al., 2021) – Economic models based on leasing/reuse (Genovese et al., 2017) – Recycling of waste as secondary resources (Kalmykova et al., 2018) – Circular economic models to maximize the value of resources (Geissdoerfer et al., 2018)
	Operational efficiency	– Supply chain flexibility in the face of crises (Chowdhury et al., 2021) – Economies of scale through inter-company synergies (Genovese et al., 2017) – Reduction of financial losses through digital product traceability (Rusch et al., 2023) – Proactive risk management to avoid costly disruptions (Ngo et al., 2024)
Social dimension	**Quality of life at work**	– Training of employees in circular technologies (Lu et al., 2024) – Protection of logistics workers (health/safety) (Chowdhury et al., 2021) – Improvement of working conditions in warehouses (Genovese et al., 2017) – Training employees in digital tools for improved productivity (Rusch et al., 2023)
	Equity and inclusion	– Inclusion of local communities in supply chains (Chowdhury et al., 2021) – Social equity in access to post-COVID resources (Ibn-Mohammed et al., 2021) – Supporting local SMEs for sustainable recovery (Ibn-Mohammed et al., 2021) – Inclusion of small producers through decentralized platforms (Sahoo et al., 2024)
	Community engagement	– Collaboration with stakeholders for sustainable jobs (Lu et al., 2024) – Consumer involvement in feedback loops (Genovese et al., 2017) – Consumer awareness of responsible purchasing (Kalmykova et al., 2018) – Creating green jobs in logistics (Kalmykova et al., 2018)
Environmental dimension	**Reduction of emissions**	– Reduction of carbon footprint through smart supply chains (Lu et al., 2024) – Optimizing transportation to reduce emissions (Chowdhury et al., 2021) – Reduced carbon footprint through AI-enabled logistics (Rusch et al., 2023) – Emission reduction through optimized logistics routes (Ngo et al., 2024)
	Resource management	– Closed-loop material reuse (Lu et al., 2024) – Packaging waste management (Chowdhury et al., 2021) – Recycling of end-of-life products (Ibn-Mohammed et al., 2021) – Reducing dependence on non-renewable resources (Ibn-Mohammed et al., 2021)
	Ecological innovation	– Eco-design of packaging (Genovese et al., 2017) – Use of renewable energies in logistics centres (Genovese et al., 2017) – Product life cycle analysis (Kalmykova et al., 2018) – Eco-design of products to facilitate their recycling (Geissdoerfer et al., 2018)
Governance dimension	**Strategic alignment**	– Alignment of CSR objectives with the corporate strategy (Lu et al., 2024) – Integration of CSR objectives in digital strategies (Rusch et al., 2023) – Alignment of corporate strategies with circular economy principles (Geissdoerfer et al., 2018) – Integration of green innovation criteria in strategic decisions (Khanra et al., 2022)
	Transparency and compliance	– Transparency through collaborative platforms (Chowdhury et al., 2021) – Regular audit of sustainable practices (Genovese et al., 2017) – Regulatory frameworks adapted to the circular economy (Kalmykova et al., 2018) – Implementation of transparent reporting systems for stakeholders (Rusch et al., 2023)
	Managerial innovation	– Management by means of circularity indicators (Lu et al., 2024) – Multi-stakeholder coordination for flow continuity (Chowdhury et al., 2021) – Public-private partnerships (Ibn-Mohammed et al., 2021) – Cross-sectoral collaboration for innovation (Kalmykova et al., 2018)

Source: Author's elaboration

This table structures the mechanisms identified in your source document according to the defined clusters, providing a solid basis for your literature review and the state of the art on piloting sustainable logistics performance.

The systematic analysis of key mechanisms, organized by dimensions (economic, social, environmental, governance) and thematic clusters, reveals convergent strategic orientations for the forward-looking management of sustainable logistics performance in Mass Retail.

- ***Economic Dimension:*** Sustainable economic performance is based on a triple trend. The Technology and Digital Optimization cluster highlights the importance of technologies (Industry 4.0, AI, Big Data) for cost optimization and efficiency (Lu et al., 2024; Rusch et al., 2023). The Circular Economic Models cluster highlights the transition to resource valuation and decoupling of economic growth from consumption of virgin materials (Ibn-Mohammed et al., 2021; Genovese et al., 2017). Finally, the Operational Efficiency cluster emphasizes agility, resilience to hazards (Chowdhury et al., 2021) and inter-company collaboration (Genovese et al., 2017) as performance and loss reduction levers.
- ***Social Dimension:*** The key social mechanisms revolve around the human and the ecosystem. The Quality of Work Life cluster focuses on protection (Chowdhury et al., 2021) and employee skills development in the face of technological and ecological change (Lu et al., 2024; Rusch et al., 2023). The Equity and Inclusion cluster reveals a trend towards broader integration of stakeholders, including local communities, SMEs and small producers, often through digital platforms (Chowdhury et al., 2021; Ibn-Mohammed et al., 2021; Sahoo et al., 2024). The Community Engagement cluster highlights the growing importance of collaboration (Lu et al., 2024) and consumer awareness (Kalmykova et al., 2018) to co-build sustainable value chains.
- ***Environmental Dimension:*** Environmental performance is driven by an integrated approach. The Emission Reduction cluster is focused on logistics and transport flow optimization, increasingly supported by AI and smart systems (Lu et al., 2024; Chowdhury et al., 2021; Rusch et al., 2023). The Resource Management cluster confirms the centrality of circular strategies: reuse, recycling, waste management (including packaging) and reduction of dependence on non-renewable resources (Lu et al., 2024; Chowdhury et al., 2021; Ibn-Mohammed et al., 2021) The Ecological Innovation cluster highlights the importance of eco-design (Genovese et al., 2017; Geissdoerfer et al., 2018), renewable energy adoption (Genovese et al., 2017) and life cycle analysis (Kalmykova et al., 2018) for proactive impact prevention.
- ***Governance dimension:*** Sustainability governance is evolving towards strategic and collaborative integration. The Strategic Alignment cluster emphasizes the anchoring of CSR objectives and circular economy principles at the heart of corporate strategy (Lu et al., 2024; Geissdoerfer et al., 2018; Khanra

et al., 2022). The Transparency and Compliance cluster reflects an increased requirement for traceability, audit and reporting, facilitated by collaborative platforms and framed by adapted regulations (Chowdhury et al. 2021; Genovese et al. 2017; Kalmykova et al. 2018; Rusch et al. 2023). Finally, the Managerial Innovation cluster highlights the development of new modes of steering (circularity indicators), multi-stakeholder coordination and partnerships (public-private, cross-sector) to innovate and deploy sustainable solutions (Lu et al., 2024; Chowdhury et al., 2021; Ibn-Mohammed et al., 2021; Kalmykova et al., 2018).

In summary, the forward-looking management of sustainable logistics performance in large retailers tends towards an integrated approach, where technological optimization and circular economy are major economic levers, inseparable from a broader social commitment (employees, communities, consumers) and proactive environmental management (emissions, resources, eco-innovation). The success of this transformation depends on strategic, transparent and collaborative governance.

Analysis of these mechanisms reveals a growing trend towards the holistic integration of sustainability dimensions into the logistics strategies of mass retailers, with particular emphasis on digitalization, circularity, multi-channel collaboration and indicator-based steering. These mechanisms converge towards a logistics performance paradigm where economic efficiency aligns harmoniously with social, environmental and responsible governance imperatives. This multidimensional approach, aligned with the concept of the Forward-looking Logistics Dashboard (PLD), allows a holistic understanding of the levers of action that promote efficient and sustainable logistics in the large-scale retail sector.

Analysis of key mechanisms reveals a multidimensional approach to sustainable logistics performance. At the economic level, the focus is on technological and digital optimization, circular business models and operational efficiency. The social dimension focuses on quality of life at work, equity and inclusion, as well as community engagement. In environmental matters, emission reduction, resource management and ecological innovation are priorities. Finally, governance focuses on strategic alignment, transparency and compliance, and managerial innovation. These groupings in thematic clusters underline a desire to integrate economic, social, environmental and governance aspects into the prospective steering of sustainable logistics performance.

These mechanisms provide a structured basis for integrating economic, environmental and social dimensions while leveraging innovation to enhance the efficiency and sustainability of logistics operations.

As a corollary to this observation, the question of adopting the same holistic approach in terms of understanding the management of the sustainability of the logistics chain in large-scale retailing, particularly through the definition of relevant KPIs, coherent and revealing of such complexity.

Thematic Analysis of the KPI for Prospective Management of Logistics Performance

The management of the sustainable logistics performance of Large-Scale Retail Sector is carried out through a set of key performance indicators (KPIs) that assess the effectiveness, efficiency and impact of logistics activities on environmental, social and economic dimensions (Elkington, 1997).

This approach reflects a set of strategies and practices implemented to optimize the supply chain while integrating environmental and social considerations. This approach aims to improve operational efficiency while reducing the ecological impact of logistics activities in the retail sector.

Sustainable logistics performance in the Large-Scale Retail Sector is based on a combination of economic, social, environmental and governance mechanisms. The integration of these mechanisms into a comprehensive and coherent strategy enables companies to reconcile economic performance, social responsibility and environmental protection, while strengthening their resilience and attractiveness.

Through our in-depth thematic analysis of the references that make up our sample, we were able to identify a battery of forward-looking KPIs for sustainable logistics performance in the Large-Scale Retail Sector, summarised in Table 8 below:

Table 8. Summary of key indicators for sustainable logistics performance

	Cluster	Quantitative Indicators	Qualitative Indicators	References
Economic dimension	**Operational efficiency and cost reduction**	**– Stock turnover rate (days). – Logistics cost as % of turnover.**	**– Flexibility of logistics processes. – Level of technology integration (IoT, AI).**	**(Gunasekaran et al., 2017; Carter & Rogers, 2008)**
	Sustainable financial performance	**– Green investment ROI. – Gross margin adjusted for sustainable costs.**	**– Strategic alignment with the SDGs. – Investor perception of sustainability.**	**(Eccles et al., 2014; Schaltegger & Wagner, 2011)**
Social dimension	**Stakeholder engagement and well-being**	– Turnover rate of logistics staff. – Number of CSN training hours/year.	– Employee satisfaction (surveys). – Involvement in local communities.	(Elkington, 1998; GRI, 2021)
	Societal impact	– Number of partnerships with local suppliers. – Accessibility rates for essential products.	– Recognition of social labels (e.g., fair trade). – Impact on economic inclusion.	(Carroll & Shabana, 2010; Porter & Kramer, 2011)

continued on following page

Table 8. Continued

	Cluster	Quantitative Indicators	Qualitative Indicators	References
Environmental dimension	**Resource management and circularity**	– Packaging recycling rate (%). – Energy consumption (kWh/ package). –	– Adoption of eco-design. – Maturity of the circular economy.	(Ellen MacArthur Foundation, 2015; Seuring & Müller, 2008)
	Reduced carbon footprint	– CO emissions/km driven. – Share of electric vehicles in fleet.	– Commitment to low-carbon initiatives. – Innovation in reverse logistics.	(Sarkis et al., 2011; IPCC, 2023)
Governance dimension	**Transparency and compliance**	– Number of CSR audits/year. – Rate of compliance with regulations (ex: REACH).	– Quality of CSR reports (GRI). – Ethical culture (internal assessments).	(Freeman et al., 2010; Jamali et al., 2017)
	Innovation and sustainable leadership	– R&D budget dedicated to sustainability (%). – Number of green patents filed.	– Long-term strategic vision. – Collaboration with sustainable startups.	(Hansen et al., 2009; Nidumolu et al., 2009)

Source: Author's elaboration

Table 8 presents the key indicators of sustainable logistics performance in Large-Scale Retail Sector, structured in economic (costs, ROI, sustainable revenues), social (employee/customer satisfaction, local inclusion, CSR) and environmental dimensions (CO2 emissions, recycling, energy consumption, clean technologies) and governance (certified standards, transparency, stakeholder engagement, sustainable policies). It provides an overview of measures to assess and improve performance by integrating sustainable development.

The analysis of the table presenting the key indicators (KPIs) of sustainable logistics performance for the GM sector, structured by dimensions and thematic clusters, reveals a multidimensional and prospective approach to management. Trends observed through quantitative and qualitative indicators underline a desire to integrate sustainability holistically into logistics operations.

- **Economic dimension:**
  - The cluster "***Operational efficiency and cost reduction***" highlights a classic orientation towards measurable optimization (inventory rotation, logistics cost in % of turnover). However, qualitative indicators (process flexibility, technology integration) suggest a trend towards agility and technological innovation as sustainable performance levers, going beyond mere cost reduction.
  - The "***Sustainable financial performance***" cluster transcends traditional finance. Quantitative KPIs (ROI of green investments, adjusted gross margin) aim to quantify the profitability of sustainable initiatives, while qualitative indicators (strategic alignment with SDGs, investor perception) assess the strategic integration and market acceptance of this sus-

tainable orientation. The trend is therefore towards financial and strategic valuation of sustainability.

- **Social dimension:**
  - The cluster "***Stakeholder engagement and well-being***" focuses on human capital and local anchoring. Quantitative indicators (turnover rate, CSR training hours) measure the stability and investment in CSR skills of staff. Qualitative aspects (employee satisfaction, community involvement) assess the internal social climate and interaction with the local ecosystem, indicating a tendency to consider employees and communities as essential stakeholders. These indicators help to structure an overall approach for the management of sustainable logistics performance in the large-scale retail sector. By adopting these KPIs, companies can not only improve their operational efficiency, but also meet the growing demands for environmental and social responsibility, while strengthening their long-term competitiveness.
  - The "***Societal impact***" cluster broadens the perspective. Quantitative KPIs (local partnerships, product accessibility) measure tangible contributions to the local economy and access to essential goods. Qualitative indicators (recognition of social labels, impact on inclusion) attest to external recognition and the effect on social equity, highlighting a trend towards broad and verifiable societal responsibility.
- **Environmental dimension:**
  - The cluster "***Resource management and circularity***" focuses on material and energy efficiency. Quantitative metrics (recycling rate, energy consumption) provide direct measures of impact. Qualitative indicators (adoption of eco-design, maturity of circular economy) assess the adoption of proactive and systemic strategies, indicating a trend towards prevention and circularity rather than simple end-of-life management.
  - The '***Reducing the carbon footprint***' cluster focuses specifically on climate. Quantitative KPIs (CO emissions/km, share of electric vehicles) directly measure the decarbonisation performance of transport. The qualitative aspects (engagement in low-carbon initiatives, innovation in reverse logistics) reflect strategic commitment and innovative capacity to reduce climate impact, showing a trend towards measurable and innovative climate action.
- **Governance dimension:**
  - The "***Transparency and compliance***" cluster ensures accountability. Quantitative indicators (number of CSR audits, compliance rate) measure the robustness of controls and compliance with regulations. Qualitative indicators (quality of CSR reports, ethical culture) assess

the communication and integration of values, suggesting a trend towards transparent and ethically based CSR governance.

- o The "***Innovation and sustainable leadership***" cluster positions the company as a player in change. Quantitative KPIs (sustainable R&D budget, green patents) measure the investment and results of sustainable innovation. Qualitative aspects (long-term strategic vision, collaboration with startups) assess prospective and partnership capacity, indicating a tendency to seek leadership through innovation and strategic vision in sustainability.

In conclusion, the proposed indicator framework reflects a sophisticated understanding of sustainable logistics performance. It balances quantitative measures of effectiveness, impact and compliance with qualitative assessments of strategy, culture, innovation and stakeholder engagement. The general trend is towards systemic integration of sustainability, driven by tangible evidence and clear policy directions, covering all economic, social, environmental and governance dimensions.

Outline of a Prospective Logistics Dashboard for Large-Scale Retail Sector

Integrating the key mechanisms and key performance indicators identified in a logistics scorecard (LBS) provides an operational framework for reconciling sustainability and performance in the retail sector.

- ***Key forward-looking mechanisms to promote logistics sustainability:***

The analysis of emerging trends in the key mechanisms reveals promising prospects for effective management of sustainable logistics performance in the retail sector, in particular through the implementation of a specifically adapted logistics dashboard (LBS), mainly via the following actions:

- **Holistic Integration of Sustainability Dimensions:** The TBLP makes it possible to move beyond a siloed vision by natively integrating the four dimensions (economic, social, environmental, governance) as interdependent strategic axes. The thematic clusters identified (Technological Optimisation, Circular Models, Quality of Working Life, Emissions Reduction, Strategic Alignment, etc.) can be used as a basis for defining strategic objectives within each TBLP perspective.

- **Translating Mechanisms into Action Levers and Prospective Indicators:** The strength of the TBLP lies in its ability to translate key mechanisms into measurable objectives and relevant performance indicators (KPIs).
  - → **Economic perspective:** Mechanisms such as 'cost optimisation through automation' (Lu et al., 2024) or 'waste recovery' (Kalmykova et al., 2018) will be translated into forward-looking KPIs such as the rate of warehouse automation, the ROI of green technology investments, or the revenue generated by recycled material flows.
  - → **Social perspective:** Mechanisms linked to 'employee training' (Lu et al., 2024; Rusch et al., 2023) or 'inclusion of local SMEs' (Ibn-Mohammed et al., 2021) can be monitored by KPIs such as the number of hours of green/digital skills training per employee, the job satisfaction rate, or the percentage of purchases made from local/social suppliers.
  - → **Environmental perspective:** Mechanisms such as 'reducing the carbon footprint through AI' (Rusch et al., 2023) or 'eco-design of packaging' (Genovese et al., 2017) will be translated into KPIs such as CO2 emissions per tonne-kilometre transported, the percentage of reusable/recyclable packaging, or the rate of use of renewable energy.
  - → **Governance perspective:** The mechanisms of 'strategic CSR alignment' (Lu et al., 2024; Geissdoerfer et al., 2018) or 'transparency via collaborative platforms' (Chowdhury et al., 2021) will be driven by KPIs such as the rate of integration of CSR objectives into managerial performance evaluations, the transparency score of the supply chain, or the number of public-private partnerships active for sustainability.
- **Forward-looking management and anticipation:** By focusing on the mechanisms identified as levers (e.g. technological investment, training, eco-design, partnerships), the TBLP adopts a resolutely forward-looking stance. It does not simply measure past results (lagging indicators), but actively monitors the factors that will determine future performance (leading indicators). This makes it possible to anticipate drift, adjust strategies in real time and proactively steer the transition towards more sustainable logistics.
- **Strategic Alignment and Cascade of Objectives:** The TBLP ensures consistency between the company's strategic vision of sustainability and its operational actions. It enables the general objectives defined at management level to be cascaded down to the various departments (logistics, purchasing, HR, marketing), ensuring that the key mechanisms are effectively implemented and contribute synergistically to overall performance.
- **Visualisation of Interdependencies and Trade-offs:** The multidimensional nature of the TBLP highlights interconnections, potential synergies (e.g. logistics optimisation reducing both costs and emissions) and any trade-offs

necessary between the different dimensions of performance (e.g. initial investment in clean technology vs. long-term benefits). It thus provides a factual basis for informed and balanced decision-making.

In conclusion, the use of a Logistics Balanced Scorecard (LBS), fed by the key mechanisms identified and structured around economic, social, environmental and governance dimensions, is a robust and relevant methodological approach. It provides the retail sector with the means to strategically and operationally steer its sustainable logistics performance, by transforming the trends identified into a coherent, measurable and forward-looking action plan.

- ***Key forward-looking mechanisms to promote logistics sustainability:***

The adoption of a Logistics Outlook Dashboard (TBLP), structured around the dimensions and clusters identified and mobilising the quantitative and qualitative key indicators discussed, offers significant prospects for an effective management of sustainable logistics performance in the Mass Retail sector. This TBLP transcends the simple retrospective measurement to become a true strategic navigation tool.

- **Holistic and Integrated Vision:**
  – The TBLP, by its multidimensional nature (Economic, Social, Environmental, Governance), imposes a systemic vision. It requires managers to consider the interdependencies between different facets of performance. For example, a decision to reduce logistics costs (economic - quantitative) through a change of supplier must be evaluated in the light of its potential impact on CO emissions (environmental - quantitative), working conditions at this supplier (Social - qualitative/quantitative via audits) and regulatory compliance (Governance - quantitative).
  – The combination of quantitative (measuring tangible results and effectiveness) and qualitative (assessing process maturity, culture, strategy and perception) indicators provides a deep and nuanced understanding. Numbers show what, qualitative aspects help to understand why and how to act prospectively.
- **Forward-looking and Strategic Management:**
  – The term "Forward-looking" is crucial. The TBLP is not just a report, but a future-oriented decision support tool. Indicators such as the "ROI of green investments", the "sustainable R&D budget", the "maturity of the circular economy" or the "long-term strategic vision" are intrinsically forward-looking and guide investments and strategic orientations.

– It aligns logistics operations with the company's overall strategic sustainability objectives (e.g., SDG alignment, carbon reduction targets). Regular monitoring of the TBLP's KPIs allows us to adjust tactical and operational actions to stay on track.

- **Performance Balance:**

  – The TBLP helps to manage tensions and seek synergies between different dimensions. It highlights that sustainable performance is not a zero-sum game. For example, investing in a fleet of electric vehicles (Environmental) may initially impact the logistics cost (Economic) but improve the brand image (Social/Governance - qualitative), reduce emissions (Environmental - quantitative) and potentially decrease long-term operational costs (fuel, maintenance - Economic). The TBLP makes these arbitrations and co-benefits visible.

- **Continuous Improvement and Innovation:**

  – By following qualitative indicators such as "process flexibility", "technology integration", "eco-design adoption" or "innovation in reverse logistics", the TBLP encourages continuous improvement that goes beyond incremental optimisation. It is driving the adoption of new technologies (IoT, AI) and innovative models (circular economy, reverse logistics).

  – The monitoring of indicators related to employee engagement (turnover, satisfaction, CSR training) and ethical culture (governance) highlights the importance of human and organizational capital as a lever for sustainable performance.

- **Communication and accountability:**

  – A well-constructed TBLP facilitates the communication of sustainable performance to internal stakeholders (management, employees) and external stakeholders (investors, clients, regulators). Indicators such as "quality of CSR reports" or "investor perception" directly reflect this dimension.

  – It strengthens accountability by providing both tangible (quantitative) and contextual (qualitative) evidence of logistics sustainability efforts and outcomes.

- **Conditions for success:**

  For this TBLP to be fully effective, several conditions must be met:

  – Data Quality and Availability: Ensure the reliable and regular collection of data for all indicators, including qualitative (through surveys, evaluations, audits).

  – Systems Integration: TBLP must be integrated into decision-making processes at all levels (strategic, tactical, operational).

  – Alignment and Ownership: TBLP objectives and indicators must be aligned with the overall strategy and understood/accepted by teams.

– Support Technology: Appropriate business intelligence tools are required to collect, analyze and visualize TBLP data in a user-friendly manner.

In short, the Logistics Outlook Dashboard, fed by a relevant and balanced set of quantitative and qualitative indicators such as those presented, is a powerful lever for the FMCG sector. It allows a shift from logistics management focused on costs and operational efficiency to strategic, integrated, and proactive management of sustainable logistics performance, which is Essential for long-term resilience and competitiveness in a changing economic and societal environment.

CONCLUSION AND PERSPECTIVES

The Large-Scale Retail Sector, a pillar of the modern economy, is facing a paradoxical challenge: to meet growing demand while reducing its environmental footprint and improving its social performance. Logistics, an essential link in this sector, is at the heart of this transformation. This chapter aims to develop a robust theoretical and conceptual framework for analyzing and improving the management of sustainable logistics performance in Large-Scale Retail Sector, based on an integrated approach via the balanced scorecard (Balanced Scorecard).

Sustainable retail logistics is defined as a set of activities to plan, execute and control the flow of goods, information and capital, integrating environmental dimensions, social and economic at all levels of the value chain, from raw material extraction to delivery to the final consumer. It goes beyond the simple reduction of negative externalities such as emissions, waste and nuisances, to aim at overall optimisation of flows, efficient management of resources and shared value creation for the company, society and the environment. This systemic approach involves close collaboration with all stakeholders, the adoption of innovative technologies and processes, and particular attention to consumer expectations in terms of social and environmental responsibility, to strengthen the competitiveness and resilience of the supply chain.

The sustainable logistics performance of Large-Scale Retail Sector is defined as the ability of a supply chain to achieve its economic objectives while minimizing its environmental impact and contributing positively to social well-being. It is measured through a set of multi-dimensional key performance indicators (KPIs) that assess the effectiveness, efficiency and impact of logistics activities on environmental (emissions, energy consumption, waste management), social (working conditions, community engagement, social responsibility) and economic (costs, profitability, level of service, customer satisfaction). This integrated approach aims to optimize processes, innovate in a sustainable way, engage stakeholders and ensure the long-term sustainability of the supply chain, Meeting regulatory and ethical requirements while maintaining competitiveness in the global marketplace.

The Forward-looking Logistics Dashboard (PLD) is a strategic lever for steering sustainable logistics performance in the Large-Scale Retail Sector. Using multi-dimensional key indicators, it balances economic, environmental and social priorities while promoting continuous improvement and sustainable value creation. This integrated approach is essential to meet current sustainability challenges, growing stakeholder expectations and the need for efficient and responsible logistics.

The PLD promotes a balanced, multi-dimensional approach that reduces costs, optimizes resources, improves traceability and strengthens resilience to logistical risks. It also promotes the transition to sustainable practices, meeting societal and environmental requirements while enhancing competitiveness. By aligning operational performance with sustainability principles, PLD becomes an essential long-term value creation lever, contributing to the achievement of the Sustainable Development Goals (SDGs).

The Prospective Logistics Dashboard (PLD) is a strategic tool for driving sustainable logistics performance in the Large-Scale Retail Sector. Structured around four key dimensions—environmental optimization, economic performance, social dimension and technological innovation—it integrates key mechanisms such as decarbonization, process automation, Partnership collaboration and predictive management.

The Prospective Logistics Dashboard (PLD) plays a central role in promoting sustainable logistics performance in the Large-Scale Retail Sector. By using a variety of key mechanisms and a multidimensional approach, it optimizes processes, reduces environmental impacts, improves collaboration and strengthens resilience. This strategic tool is an essential pillar to address today's sustainability challenges while creating significant competitive advantages.

The management of sustainable logistics performance in the large-scale retail sector, via the Logistics Prospective Dashboard (PLD), is based on a multidimensional approach integrating key economic, environmental and social indicators. Economic KPIs (total logistics cost, order cycle time, route optimization, warehouse fill rate) optimize resources and reduce costs. Environmental KPIs (CO emissions reduction, energy consumption, waste reduction, renewable energy adoption) support a transition to environmentally responsible practices. Social KPIs (customer satisfaction, compliance with social standards, return rate products, quality of service) ensure the consideration of stakeholders and strengthen the brand image.

In short, the PLD offers an integrated and balanced perspective, enabling continuous improvement of logistics performance while meeting regulatory and societal requirements. It acts as a strategic lever to align operational objectives with the principles of sustainable development, thus strengthening the competitiveness and resilience of Large-Scale Retail Sector businesses.

REFERENCES

Adetiloye, T. (2021). Collaboration planning of stakeholders for sustainable city logistics operations. *arXiv preprint arXiv:2107.14049.*

Ahi & Searcy. (2013). A comparative literature analysis of definitions for green and sustainable supply chain management. *Journal of Cleaner Production, 52*, 329–341.

Ahmadi, H. B., Kusi-Sarpong, S., & Rezaei, J. (2017). Assessing the social sustainability of supply chains using Best Worst Method. *Resources, Conservation and Recycling, 126*, 99–106.

Alavi, B., Tavana, M., & Mina, H. (2021). A dynamic decision support system for sustainable supplier selection in circular economy. *Sustainable Production and Consumption, 27*, 905–920.

Ali, M. H., Chung, L., Kumar, A., Zailani, S., & Tan, K. H. (2021). A sustainable Blockchain framework for the halal food supply chain: Lessons from Malaysia. *Technological Forecasting and Social Change, 170*, 120870.

Anderson, P. (1999). Perspective: Complexity theory and organization science. *Organization Science, 10*(3), 216–232.

Andronie, M., Lăzăroiu, G., tefănescu, R., U ă, C., & Dijmărescu, I. (2021). Sustainable, smart, and sensing technologies for cyber-physical manufacturing systems: A systematic literature review. *Sustainability, 13*(10), 5495.

Aranitou, V., Kostis, P. C., Manioudis, M., & Panagiotopoulou, M. (2024). Retailers and Sustainability: Navigating by the Star of Sustainable Retailing. In *The Economics of Retailing* (pp. 131-156). Palgrave Macmillan, Cham.

Awasthi, A., Govindan, K., & Gold, S. (2018). Multi-tier sustainable global supplier selection using a fuzzy AHP-VIKOR based approach. *International Journal of Production Economics, 195*, 106–117.

Baah, C., Amponsah, K. T., Issau, K., Ofori, D., Acquah, I. S. K., & Agyeman, D. O. (2021). Examining the interconnections between sustainable logistics practices, environmental reputation and financial performance: A mediation approach. *Vision (Basel), 25*(1), 47–64.

Bansal, P., & Song, H. C. (2017). Similar but not the same: Differentiating corporate sustainability from corporate responsibility. *The Academy of Management Annals, 11*(1), 105–149.

Barney, J. (1991). Firm Resources and Sustained Competitive Advantage. *Journal of Management*.

Barykin, S. E., Borisoglebskaya, L. N., Provotorov, V. V., Kapustina, I. V., Sergeev, S. M., De La Poza Plaza, E., & Saychenko, L. (2021). Sustainability of management decisions in a digital logistics network. *Sustainability*, *13*(16), 9289.

Bertalanffy, L. V. (1968). General systems theory as integrating factor in contemporary science. *Akten des XIV. Internationalen Kongresses für Philosophie*, *2*, 335–340.

Beske-Janssen, P., Schaltegger, S., & Liedke, S. (2019). Performance measurement in sustainable supply chain management: Linking research and practice. In *Handbook on the Sustainable Supply Chain* (pp. 331–356). Edward Elgar Publishing.

Birasnav, M., Chaudhary, R., Dunne, J. H., Bienstock, J., & Seaman, C. (2022). Green supply chain management: A theoretical framework and research directions. *Computers & Industrial Engineering*, *172*, 108441.

Budak, A. (2020). Sustainable reverse logistics optimization with triple bottom line approach: An integration of disassembly line balancing. *Journal of Cleaner Production*, *270*, 122475.

Burke, H., Zhang, A., & Wang, J. X. (2023). Integrating product design and supply chain management for a circular economy. *Production Planning and Control*, *34*(11), 1097–1113.

Cannas, V. G., Ciano, M. P., Saltalamacchia, M., & Secchi, R. (2024). Artificial intelligence in supply chain and operations management: A multiple case study research. *International Journal of Production Research*, *62*(9), 3333–3360.

Chandan, A., John, M., & Potdar, V. (2023). Achieving UN SDGs in food supply chain using blockchain technology. *Sustainability*, *15*(3), 2109.

Chari, A., Niedenzu, D., Despeisse, M., Machado, C. G., Azevedo, J. D., Boavida-Dias, R., & Johansson, B. (2022). Dynamic capabilities for circular manufacturing supply chains—Exploring the role of Industry 4.0 and resilience. *Business Strategy and the Environment*, *31*(5), 2500–2517.

Chen, D. Q., Preston, D. S., & Swink, M. (2021). How big data analytics affects supply chain decision-making: An empirical analysis. *Journal of the Association for Information Systems*, *22*(5), 1224–1244.

Chowdhury, P., Paul, S. K., Kaisar, S., & Moktadir, M. A. (2021). COVID-19 pandemic related supply chain studies: A systematic review. *Transportation Research Part E, Logistics and Transportation Review*, *148*, 102271. PMID: 33613082

Christopher, M. (2016). *Logistics and Supply Chain Management: Logistics & Supply Chain Management*. Pearson UK.

Da Silva, E. R., Lohmer, J., Rohla, M., & Angelis, J. (2023). Unleashing the circular economy in the electric vehicle battery supply chain: A case study on data sharing and blockchain potential. *Resources, Conservation and Recycling*, *193*, 106969.

De Mattos Nascimento, D. L., de Oliveira-Dias, D., Moyano-Fuentes, J., Maqueira Marín, J. M., & Garza-Reyes, J. A. (2024). Interrelationships between circular economy and Industry 4.0: A research agenda for sustainable supply chains. *Business Strategy and the Environment*, *33*(2), 575–596.

Del Giudice, M., Chierici, R., Mazzucchelli, A., & Fiano, F. (2021). Supply chain management in the era of circular economy: The moderating effect of big data. *International Journal of Logistics Management*, *32*(2), 337–356.

Dey, P. K., Malesios, C., De, D., Budhwar, P., Chowdhury, S., & Cheffi, W. (2022). Circular economy to enhance sustainability of small and medium sized enterprises. In *Supply chain sustainability in small and medium sized enterprises* (pp. 10–45). Routledge.

Di Vaio, A., Boccia, F., Landriani, L., & Palladino, R. (2020). Artificial intelligence in the agri-food system: Rethinking sustainable business models in the COVID-19 scenario. *Sustainability*, *12*(12), 4851.

Dubey, R., Bryde, D. J., Blome, C., Dwivedi, Y. K., Childe, S. J., & Foropon, C. (2024). Alliances and digital transformation are crucial for benefiting from dynamic supply chain capabilities during times of crisis: A multi-method study. *International Journal of Production Economics*, *269*, 109166.

Dubey, R., Gunasekaran, A., Childe, S. J., Papadopoulos, T., Luo, Z., Wamba, S. F., & Roubaud, D. (2019). Can big data and predictive analytics improve social and environmental sustainability? *Technological Forecasting and Social Change*, *144*, 534–545.

Dubey, R., Gunasekaran, A., Papadopoulos, T., Childe, S. J., Shibin, K. T., & Wamba, S. F. (2017). Sustainable supply chain management: Framework and further research directions. *Journal of Cleaner Production*, *142*, 1119–1130.

Elkington, J. (1997). The triple bottom line. *Environmental management: Readings and cases, 2*, 49-66.

Elkington, J. (1997). *The Triple Bottom Line of 21st Century Business*. Capstone.

Felsberger, A. (2018). *An overview of measurement approaches for evaluating the impact of the digital transformation on sustainable supply chain management* (Doctoral dissertation, Alpen-Adria-Universität Klagenfurt).

Freeman, R. E. (2010). *Strategic management: A stakeholder approach.* Cambridge university press.

Gardner, T. A., Benzie, M., Börner, J., Dawkins, E., Fick, S., Garrett, R., & Wolvekamp, P. (2019). Transparency and sustainability in global commodity supply chains. *World Development, 121*, 163–177. PMID: 31481824

Geissdoerfer, M., Morioka, S. N., de Carvalho, M. M., & Evans, S. (2018). Business models and supply chains for the circular economy. *Journal of Cleaner Production, 190*, 712–721.

Genovese, A., Acquaye, A. A., Figueroa, A., & Koh, S. L. (2017). Sustainable supply chain management and the transition towards a circular economy: Evidence and some applications. *Omega, 66*, 344–357.

Gholipour, A., Sadegheih, A., Mostafaeipour, A., & Fakhrzad, M. B. (2024). Designing an optimal multi-objective model for a sustainable closed-loop supply chain: A case study of pomegranate in Iran. *Environment, Development and Sustainability, 26*(2), 3993–4027. PMID: 36687734

Goel, R., Singla, J., & Kumar, S. (2025). The Digital Circular Economy: Advancing Sustainable Innovation through Technological Integration. In *Sustainability, Innovation, and Consumer Preference* (pp. 441-480). IGI Global Scientific Publishing.

Gölgeci, I., Gligor, D. M., Tatoglu, E., & Arda, O. A. (2019). A relational view of environmental performance: What role do environmental collaboration and cross-functional alignment play? *Journal of Business Research, 96*, 35–46.

Golicic, S. L., & Smith, C. D. (2013). A meta-analysis of environmentally sustainable supply chain management practices and firm performance. *The Journal of Supply Chain Management, 49*(2), 78–95.

Govindan, K., Khodaverdi, R., & Jafarian, A. (2013). A fuzzy multi criteria approach for measuring sustainability performance of a supplier based on triple bottom line approach. *Journal of Cleaner Production, 47*, 345–354.

Govindan, K., Rajeev, A., Padhi, S. S., & Pati, R. K. (2020). Supply chain sustainability and performance of firms: A meta-analysis of the literature. *Transportation Research Part E, Logistics and Transportation Review, 137*, 101923.

Gupta, A., & Singh, R. K. (2020). Managing operations by a logistics company for sustainable service quality: Indian perspective. *Management of Environmental Quality, 31*(5), 1309–1327.

Gurtu, A., & Johny, J. (2021). Supply chain risk management: Literature review. *Risks, 9*(1), 16.

Heckmann, I., Comes, T., & Nickel, S. (2015). A critical review on supply chain risk–Definition, measure and modeling. *Omega, 52*, 119–132.

Henrich, J., Li, J., Mazuera, C., & Perez, F. (2022). Future-proofing the supply chain. *McKinsey & Company*.

Hervani, A. A., Nandi, S., Helms, M. M., & Sarkis, J. (2022). A performance measurement framework for socially sustainable and resilient supply chains using environmental goods valuation methods. *Sustainable Production and Consumption, 30*, 31–52.

Hofmann, E. (2010). Linking corporate strategy and supply chain management. *International Journal of Physical Distribution & Logistics Management, 40*(4), 256–276.

Hosseini, Z. S., Flapper, S. D., & Pirayesh, M. (2022). Sustainable supplier selection and order allocation under demand, supplier availability and supplier grading uncertainties. *Computers & Industrial Engineering, 165*, 107811.

Ibn-Mohammed, T., Mustapha, K. B., Godsell, J., Adamu, Z., Babatunde, K. A., Akintade, D. D., & Koh, S. C. L. (2021). A critical analysis of the impacts of COVID-19 on the global economy and ecosystems and opportunities for circular economy strategies. *Resources, Conservation and Recycling, 164*, 105169. PMID: 32982059

Ivanov, D. (2018). Revealing interfaces of supply chain resilience and sustainability: A simulation study. *International Journal of Production Research, 56*(10), 3507–3523.

Ivanov, D. (2022). Viable supply chain model: Integrating agility, resilience and sustainability perspectives—lessons from and thinking beyond the COVID-19 pandemic. *Annals of Operations Research, 319*(1), 1411–1431. PMID: 32836614

Ivanov, D., & Dolgui, A. (2021). A digital supply chain twin for managing the disruption risks and resilience in the era of Industry 4.0. *Production Planning and Control, 32*(9), 775–788.

Jabbour, C. J. C., & de Sousa Jabbour, A. B. L. (2016). Green human resource management and green supply chain management: Linking two emerging agendas. *Journal of Cleaner Production, 112*, 1824–1833.

Jaouad, K. (2017). Développement des stratégies Supply chain par la mise en place des concepts Lean-Application dans le domaine industriel marocain de la transformation plastique.

Jiang, T., Wu, X., & Yin, Y. (2023). Logistics Efficiency Evaluation and Empirical Research under the New Retailing Model: The Way toward Sustainable Development. *Sustainability*, *15*(20), 15028.

Kalmykova, Y., Sadagopan, M., & Rosado, L. (2018). Circular economy–From review of theories and practices to development of implementation tools. *Resources, Conservation and Recycling*, *135*, 190–201.

Kamewor, F. T., Kwateng, K. O., & Mensah, J. (2024). Green logistics practices: A bibliometric and systematic methodological review and future research opportunities. *Journal of Cleaner Production*, •••, 143735.

Kaplan, R. S. (1996). *The balanced scorecard: translating strategy into action*. Harvard Business Review Press.

Kashem, M. A., Shamsuddoha, M., & Nasir, T. (2024). Digital-Era Resilience: Navigating Logistics and Supply Chain Operations after COVID-19. *Businesses*, *4*(1), 1–17.

Kaur, H., & Singh, S. P. (2019). Sustainable procurement and logistics for disaster resilient supply chain. *Annals of Operations Research*, *283*(1), 309–354.

Kayikci, Y., Gozacan-Chase, N., & Rejeb, A. (2024). Blockchain entrepreneurship roles for circular supply chain transition. *Business Strategy and the Environment*, *33*(2), 197–222.

Keivanpour, S. (2022). Sustainability balanced scorecard approach to Internet of Things enabled logistics systems. *Engineering Management Journal*, *34*(3), 450–474.

Khan, A., Chen, C. C., Suanpong, K., Ruangkanjanases, A., Kittikowit, S., & Chen, S. C. (2021). The impact of CSR on sustainable innovation ambidexterity: The mediating role of sustainable supply chain management and second-order social capital. *Sustainability*, *13*(21), 12160.

Khan, M., Ajmal, M. M., Jabeen, F., Talwar, S., & Dhir, A. (2023). Green supply chain management in manufacturing firms: A resource-based viewpoint. *Business Strategy and the Environment*, *32*(4), 1603–1618.

Khan, S. A., Mubarik, M. S., Kusi-Sarpong, S., Gupta, H., Zaman, S. I., & Mubarik, M. (2022). Blockchain technologies as enablers of supply chain mapping for sustainable supply chains. *Business Strategy and the Environment*, *31*(8), 3742–3756.

Khan, S. A. R., Godil, D. I., Jabbour, C. J. C., Shujaat, S., Razzaq, A., & Yu, Z. (2021). Green data analytics, blockchain technology for sustainable development, and sustainable supply chain practices: Evidence from small and medium enterprises. *Annals of Operations Research*, •••, 1–25.

Khanra, S., Kaur, P., Joseph, R. P., Malik, A., & Dhir, A. (2022). A resource-based view of green innovation as a strategic firm resource: Present status and future directions. *Business Strategy and the Environment*, *31*(4), 1395–1413.

Kicova, E., Rosnerova, Z., Ponisciakova, O., & Gajanova, L. (2023). Concept for the Customer Perspective of the Balanced Scorecard (BSC) System in Bus Transport Companies in the Slovak Republic. *Systems*, *11*(12), 575.

Kofar Kudu, U. B., & Karia, N. (2024). The effects of the factors affecting sustainability of Nigerian humanitarian logistics firms: The mediation effect of the leadership. *Global Business and Management Research*, •••, 16.

Kouhizadeh, M., & Sarkis, J. (2018). Blockchain practices, potentials, and perspectives in greening supply chains. *Sustainability*, *10*(10), 3652.

Kumar, M., Raut, R. D., Jagtap, S., & Choubey, V. K. (2023). Circular economy adoption challenges in the food supply chain for sustainable development. *Business Strategy and the Environment*, *32*(4), 1334–1356.

Kusi-Sarpong, S., Gupta, H., & Sarkis, J. (2019). A supply chain sustainability innovation framework and evaluation methodology. *International Journal of Production Research*, *57*(7), 1990–2008.

Kwak, D. W., Rodrigues, V. S., Mason, R., Pettit, S., & Beresford, A. (2018). Risk interaction identification in international supply chain logistics: Developing a holistic model. *International Journal of Operations & Production Management*, *38*(2), 372–389.

Lee, K. H., & Wu, Y. (2014). Integrating sustainability performance measurement into logistics and supply networks: A multi-methodological approach. *The British Accounting Review*, *46*(4), 361–378.

Lee, V. H., Foo, P. Y., Cham, T. H., Hew, T. S., Tan, G. W. H., & Ooi, K. B. (2024). Big data analytics capability in building supply chain resilience: The moderating effect of innovation-focused complementary assets. *Industrial Management & Data Systems*, *124*(3), 1203–1233.

López-Gálvez, F., Gómez, P. A., Artés, F., Artés-Hernández, F., & Aguayo, E. (2021). Interactions between microbial food safety and environmental sustainability in the fresh produce supply chain. *Foods*, *10*(7), 1655. PMID: 34359525

Lu, H., Zhao, G., & Liu, S. (2024). Integrating circular economy and Industry 4.0 for sustainable supply chain management: A dynamic capability view. *Production Planning and Control*, *35*(2), 170–186.

Luthra, S., Kumar, A., Zavadskas, E. K., Mangla, S. K., & Garza-Reyes, J. A. (2020). Industry 4.0 as an enabler of sustainability diffusion in supply chain: An analysis of influential strength of drivers in an emerging economy. *International Journal of Production Research*, *58*(5), 1505–1521.

Mentzer, J. T., DeWitt, W., Keebler, J. S., Min, S., Nix, N. W., Smith, C. D., & Zacharia, Z. G. (2001). Defining supply chain management. *Journal of Business Logistics*, *22*(2), 1–25.

Miles, M. B., & Huberman, A. M. (2003). *Analyse des données qualitatives*. De Boeck Supérieur.

Mishra, A., Dutta, P., Jayasankar, S., Jain, P., & Mathiyazhagan, K. (2023). A review of reverse logistics and closed-loop supply chains in the perspective of circular economy. *Benchmarking*, *30*(3), 975–1020.

Morcillo-Bellido, J., & Duran-Heras, A. (2020). Sustainability governance mechanisms in supply chains: An application in the retail sector. *Sustainability*, *12*(17), 6911.

Mulligan, C., Morsfield, S., & Cheikosman, E. (2024). Blockchain for sustainability: A systematic literature review for policy impact. *Telecommunications Policy*, *48*(2), 102676.

Nasir, M. H. A., Genovese, A., Acquaye, A. A., Koh, S. C. L., & Yamoah, F. (2017). Comparing linear and circular supply chains: A case study from the construction industry. *International Journal of Production Economics*, *183*, 443–457.

Negri, M., Cagno, E., Colicchia, C., & Sarkis, J. (2021). Integrating sustainability and resilience in the supply chain: A systematic literature review and a research agenda. *Business Strategy and the Environment*, *30*(7), 2858–2886.

Neri, A., Cagno, E., Lepri, M., & Trianni, A. (2021). A triple bottom line balanced set of key performance indicators to measure the sustainability performance of industrial supply chains. *Sustainable Production and Consumption*, *26*, 648–691.

Neri, A., Cagno, E., Lepri, M., & Trianni, A. (2021). A triple bottom line balanced set of key performance indicators to measure the sustainability performance of industrial supply chains. *Sustainable Production and Consumption*, *26*, 648–691.

Ngo, V. M., Quang, H. T., Hoang, T. G., & Binh, A. D. T. (2024). Sustainability-related supply chain risks and supply chain performances: The moderating effects of dynamic supply chain management practices. *Business Strategy and the Environment*, *33*(2), 839–857.

Oyedijo, A., Kusi-Sarpong, S., Mubarik, M. S., Khan, S. A., & Utulu, K. (2024). Multi-tier sustainable supply chain management: A case study of a global food retailer. *Supply Chain Management*, *29*(1), 68–97.

Pachar, N., Darbari, J. D., Govindan, K., & Jha, P. C. (2022). Sustainable performance measurement of Indian retail chain using two-stage network DEA. *Annals of Operations Research*, *315*(2), 1477–1515.

Pal, S. (2023). Integrating AI in sustainable supply chain management: A new paradigm for enhanced transparency and sustainability. *International Journal for Research in Applied Science and Engineering Technology*, *11*(6), 2979–2984.

Park, A., & Li, H. (2021). The Effect of Blockchain Technology on Supply Chain Sustainability Performances. *Sustainability*, *13*, 1726.

Pejić Bach, M., Klinčar, A., Aleksić, A., Rašić Jelavić, S., & Zeqiri, J. (2023). Supply chain management maturity and business performance: The balanced scorecard perspective. *Applied Sciences (Basel, Switzerland)*, *13*(4), 2065.

Pekkala, M. (2023). Sustainable supply chain management practices in retailing: Qualitative content analysis based on sustainability reports.

Penrose, E. T. (2009). *The Theory of the Growth of the Firm*. Oxford university press.

Porter, M. E. (1985). Technology and competitive advantage. *The Journal of Business Strategy*, *5*(3), 60–78.

Qorri, A., Mujkić, Z., & Kraslawski, A. (2018). A conceptual framework for measuring sustainability performance of supply chains. *Journal of Cleaner Production*, *189*, 570–584.

Quesado, P., Costa Oliveira, H., & Silva, R. (2025). Integrating sustainability goals into the balanced scorecard: A bibliometric analysis of the sustainability balanced scorecard. *Measuring Business Excellence*.

Raman, R., Lathabhai, H., Pattnaik, D., Kumar, C., & Nedungadi, P. (2024). Research contribution of bibliometric studies related to sustainable development goals and sustainability. *Discover Sustainability*, *5*(1), 7.

Rebs, T., Brandenburg, M., & Seuring, S. (2019). System dynamics modeling for sustainable supply chain management: A literature review and systems thinking approach. *Journal of Cleaner Production*, *208*, 1265–1280.

Rethlefsen, M. L., & Page, M. J. (2022). PRISMA 2020 and PRISMA-S: Common questions on tracking records and the flow diagram. *Journal of the Medical Library Association: JMLA*, *110*(2), 253. PMID: 35440907

Riofrancos, T. (2023). The security–sustainability nexus: Lithium onshoring in the Global North. *Global Environmental Politics*, *23*(1), 20–41.

Rusch, M., Schöggl, J. P., & Baumgartner, R. J. (2023). Application of digital technologies for sustainable product management in a circular economy: A review. *Business Strategy and the Environment*, *32*(3), 1159–1174.

Sabir, H. (2020). Pratiques de la grande distribution alimentaire et performance de la logistique urbaine: Revue de littérature. *Revue Internationale du Chercheur*, *1*(2).

Sahoo, S., Kumar, S., Sivarajah, U., Lim, W. M., Westland, J. C., & Kumar, A. (2024). Blockchain for sustainable supply chain management: Trends and ways forward. *Electronic Commerce Research*, *24*(3), 1563–1618.

Sánchez-Flores, R. B., Cruz-Sotelo, S. E., Ojeda-Benitez, S., & Ramírez-Barreto, M. E. (2020). Sustainable supply chain management—A literature review on emerging economies. *Sustainability*, *12*(17), 6972.

Sgarbossa, F., Arena, S., Tang, O., & Peron, M. (2023). Renewable hydrogen supply chains: A planning matrix and an agenda for future research. *International Journal of Production Economics*, *255*, 108674.

Sharma, N. K., Kumar, V., Verma, P., & Luthra, S. (2021). Sustainable reverse logistics practices and performance evaluation with fuzzy TOPSIS: A study on Indian retailers. *Cleaner Logistics and Supply Chain*, *1*, 100007.

Siems, E., Seuring, S., & Schilling, L. (2023). Stakeholder roles in sustainable supply chain management: A literature review. *Journal of Business Economics*, *93*(4), 747–775.

Simon, H. A. (1962). The Architecture of Complexity [Reprinted in: Herbert A. Simon, The Sciences of the Artificial, M.I.T Press, Cambridge, Massachusetts, 1969, pp. 84-118]. *Proceedings of the American Philosophical Society*, *106*, 467–482.

Singh, D., Lanka, K., & Gopal, P. R. C. (2021). Predicting Sustainable Supply Chain Performance Based on GRI Metrics and Multilayer Perceptron Neural Networks. *Emerging Frontiers in Operations and Supply Chain Management: Theory and Applications*, 159-180.

Snyder, H. (2019). Literature review as a research methodology: An overview and guidelines. *Journal of Business Research, 104*, 333–339.

Teece, D. J., Pisano, G., & Shuen, A. (1997). Dynamic capabilities and strategic management. *Strategic Management Journal, 18*(7), 509–533.

Tranfield, D., Denyer, D., & Smart, P. (2003). Towards a methodology for developing evidence-informed management knowledge by means of systematic review. *British Journal of Management, 14*(3), 207–222.

Tseng, M. L., Ha, H. M., Lim, M. K., Wu, K. J., & Iranmanesh, M. (2022). Sustainable supply chain management in stakeholders: Supporting from sustainable supply and process management in the healthcare industry in Vietnam. *International Journal of Logistics Research and Applications*, *25*(4-5), 364–383.

Uda, S., & Basrowi, B. (2024). Environmental education using SARITHA-Apps to enhance environmentally friendly supply chain efficiency and foster environmental knowledge towards sustainability. *Uncertain Supply Chain Management, 12*(1), 359–372.

Vegter, D., van Hillegersberg, J., & Olthaar, M. (2023). Performance measurement system for circular supply chain management. *Sustainable Production and Consumption*, *36*, 171–183.

Vidal, N. G., Spetic, W., Croom, S., & Marshall, D. (2023). Supply chain stakeholder pressure for the adoption of sustainable supply chain practices: Examining the roles of entrepreneurial and sustainability orientations. *Supply Chain Management*, *28*(3), 598–618.

Wang, Y., Yang, Y., Qin, Z., Yang, Y., & Li, J. (2023). A literature review on the application of digital technology in achieving green supply chain management. *Sustainability*, *15*(11), 8564.

Weerapong, P., & Singhdong, P. (2024). Assessment of sustainability in supply chain management: Literature study. *Social Science Innovation and Applied Management (SIAM).*

Wilhelm, M. M., Blome, C., Bhakoo, V., & Paulraj, A. (2016). Sustainability in multi-tier supply chains: Understanding the double agency role of the first-tier supplier. *Journal of Operations Management*, *41*, 42–60.

Wiredu, J., Yang, Q., Sampene, A. K., Gyamfi, B. A., & Asongu, S. A. (2024). The effect of green supply chain management practices on corporate environmental performance: Does supply chain competitive advantage matter? *Business Strategy and the Environment*, *33*(3), 2578–2599.

Xia, D., Yu, Q., Gao, Q., & Cheng, G. (2017). Sustainable technology selection decision-making model for enterprise in supply chain: Based on a modified strategic balanced scorecard. *Journal of Cleaner Production*, *141*, 1337–1348.

Xia, D., Yu, Q., Gao, Q., & Cheng, G. (2017). Sustainable technology selection decision-making model for enterprise in supply chain: Based on a modified strategic balanced scorecard. *Journal of Cleaner Production*, *141*, 1337–1348.

Yang, M., Fu, M., & Zhang, Z. (2021). The adoption of digital technologies in supply chains: Drivers, process and impact. *Technological Forecasting and Social Change*, *169*, 120795.

Yin, R. K. (2018). Case study research and applications.

Yusuf, Z., Yusuf, F., Nuryanto, U., & Basrowi, B. (2024). Assessing organizational commitment and organizational citizenship behavior in ensuring the smoothness of the supply chain for medical hospital needs towards a green hospital: Evidence from Indonesia. *Uncertain Supply Chain Management*, *12*(1), 181–194.

Zhang, A., Venkatesh, V. G., Liu, Y., Wan, M., Qu, T., & Huisingh, D. (2019). Barriers to smart waste management for a circular economy in China. *Journal of Cleaner Production*, *240*, 118198.

Zhang, A., Zhong, R. Y., Farooque, M., Kang, K., & Venkatesh, V. G. (2020). Blockchain-based life cycle assessment: An implementation framework and system architecture. *Resources, Conservation and Recycling*, *152*, 104512.

Zhang, H., Sun, X., Dong, K., Sui, L., Wang, M., & Hong, Q. (2022). Green Innovation in Regional Logistics: Level Evaluation and Spatial Analysis. *International Journal of Environmental Research and Public Health*, *20*(1), 735. PMID: 36613056

Zuro, Z. (2024, April). Stakeholder Theory And Corporate Sustainability: The Silent Stakeholder Problem. In *Economic and Social Development (Book of Proceedings), 110th International Scientific Conference on Economic and Social* (Vol. 5, p. 29).

KEY TERMS AND DEFINITIONS

Sustainable Retail Logistics: An integrated approach to supply chain management that optimizes logistical flows while balancing environmental, economic, social, and technological dimensions. It employs eco-responsible practices (e.g., carbon reduction, circular economy) and collaborative strategies to align operational efficiency with global sustainability goals.

Sustainable Logistics Performance: The measurable outcome reflecting a retail firm's ability to harmonize operational efficiency with reduced ecological footprints and social welfare contributions. Evaluated through triple-bottom-line indicators (economic, environmental, social).

Prospective Logistics Dashboard (PLD): A strategic tool adapted from the Balanced Scorecard (BSC) framework, designed to monitor and steer sustainable logistics performance. It integrates forward-looking indicators for resilience, digital maturity, and crisis preparedness.

Circular Economy in Logistics: A regenerative system prioritizing resource reuse, refurbishment, and recycling. In retail logistics, this manifests through: Reverse logistics networks, Packaging-as-a-service models, Waste-to-value supply chains

Stakeholder-Centric Logistics: An operational philosophy emphasizing satisfaction across all supply chain participants (suppliers, employees, customers, communities).

Resilience-by-Design: Preemptive structuring of supply chains to absorb disruptions (e.g., pandemics, geopolitical conflicts).

Chapter 7
Overcoming Hurdles:
Navigating Challenges in the Adoption of Smart Logistics

Md Mehedi Hasan Emon
https://orcid.org/0000-0002-6224-9552
American International University, Bangladesh

ABSTRACT

The integration of smart logistics technologies is revolutionizing supply chains by enhancing operational efficiency and promoting sustainability. However, the path to adoption is fraught with technological, financial, organizational, regulatory, and security challenges. This chapter critically examines these hurdles, offering strategic frameworks for overcoming them through targeted training, phased implementation, collaborative partnerships, robust business cases, and stringent cybersecurity measures. Drawing on empirical evidence and real-world case studies, it highlights the importance of leadership, organizational culture, and adaptive strategies. It also outlines future directions shaped by advancements such as autonomous systems and AI-driven logistics, emphasizing the need for interdisciplinary research and ethical governance. By addressing these complexities, the chapter aims to equip practitioners, researchers, and policymakers with actionable insights for fostering resilient and future-ready smart logistics ecosystems.

INTRODUCTION

Smart logistics represents a transformative development for worldwide supply chains since it brings enhanced operational effectiveness with improved sustainability and competitive abilities. Smart logistics implementation follows a complex route with multiple substantial barriers to overcome. The chapter performs a thorough

DOI: 10.4018/979-8-3373-2434-0.ch007

analytical review of business difficulties during smart logistics solution deployment to provide effective methods which resolve these problems. This section first identifies major implementation barriers of smart logistics by describing technical issues combined with financial limitations along with insufficient organizational support as well as legal complexities and security worries. This segment delivers a comprehensive investigation of these related issues that occur across organizational fields and industrial sectors. The chapter follows diagnostic evaluation of obstacles by introducing techniques for overcoming them. The implementation plan includes workforce training and development expenditure with phased and flexible strategies and strategic partnerships and compelling smart logistics business cases and robust data security execution. Multiple methods shaped from theoretical knowledge and practical experience deliver businesses systematic platforms to handle the obstacles of technical transition.

The chapter incorporates field cases alongside real industry data which demonstrates qualitative research for this topic. Prominent organizations used strategic vision combined with innovative techniques to succeed in adopting new systems for business advancement. The cases provide essential learning points which other organizations can adopt for implementing their smart logistics solutions. The closing scope evaluates upcoming patterns in logistics which includes automated transport systems along with AI supply chain efficiency improvements and expanding pressure to achieve environmentally friendly operations. Future research and industrial development need specific attention to follow the successful implementation of smart logistics through essential domains identified by this paper. The fundamental results obtained in this chapter lead to an acknowledgment that smart logistics adoption requires proper planning along with organizational focus and continuous adjustment. The chapter delivers practical knowledge about smart logistics transformation for both academics and industry professionals and policymakers who aim to build durable sustainable supply chains for forthcoming years.

IDENTIFYING CHALLENGES IN SMART LOGISTICS ADOPTION

Smart logistics possesses the ability to develop traditional supply chains into responsive connected networks which enable instant decisions alongside enhanced sustainability. Smart logistics' transition faces numerous substantial obstacles which frequently create complex relationships between them. Both academic and professional communities need to understand these challenges because they face them in their attempts to research the supply chain digital revolution and navigate unpredictable circumstances. The analysis investigates core barriers for using smart logistics systems by studying technical, financial, organizational, regulatory and security challenges.

Technological Barriers

Smart logistics systems face an important challenge because technological integration remains a major hindrance to their full deployment. Existing businesses that operated for a long-time count among those which still use outdated legacy systems developed before the digital era. Business application systems frequently lack modular design along with connectivity standards which makes it difficult to properly link them with emerging technology elements such as IoT devices, autonomous delivery systems blockchain platforms and artificial intelligence analytics (Bhuiyan et al., 2021; Gupta & Quamara, 2020). Current operational systems create major technological hurdles for businesses who aim to establish connected logistics systems. A warehouse management system powered by IoT needs real-time data exchanges with transportation management software, but data format mismatches and communication protocols differences and processing inability can trigger operational problems that result in system breakdowns (Affia & Aamer, 2022). Rapid technological advancement creates more complications for these existing operational problems. Organizations continuously battle to match speed with changing technology rates because new technologies appear faster than assessment and implementation processes. According to Cuervo-Cazurra & Li, (2021), Organizations located behind technological progress suffer from strategic disadvantages. In addition to experiencing both decreased operational effectiveness and weakened competitiveness. Urgent adoption of modern technologies can lead to separate systems because companies fail to identify how the new innovations should fit together in a connected smart logistics system.

Figure 1. Technological barriers to smart logistics integration

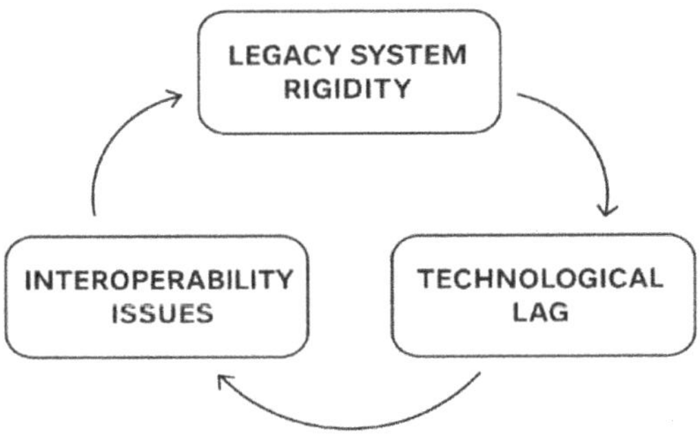

This conceptual figure shows how technological issues are interrelated, therefore limiting the smooth integration of smart logistics. As shown in Figure 1, there are three fundamental obstacles: Legacy System Rigidity, Interoperability Issues and Technological Lag. Visual representation of these elements is organized in the cyclic format with directional arrows, indicating the nature of their interdependence. The diagram is efficient in communicating the idea of how all these factors strengthen each other, overall hindering digital transformation of logistics systems.

Financial Constraints

The implementation of smart logistics faces major financial hurdles as a substantial factor. The use of smart logistics technology necessitates substantial financial expenditure. Large expenses go beyond hardware acquisitions of sensors robots and autonomous vehicles while additionally requiring software development capabilities to process large data volumes (Ding et al., 2021; Shee et al., 2021). After an initial equipment purchase comes a wide range of hidden costs for infrastructure developments and employee training along with cybersecurity investments and system maintenance operations. Businesses need to budget for continuous expenses relating to software licensing together with data storage networks security along with technical support. Mainstream expenses over time reduce available funds, especially in cases where intelligent logistics programs extend across multiple years with uncertain short-term financial outcomes. The process of obtaining adequate funds for substantial digital transformation poses challenging obstacles to small and medium enterprises. Multiple small and medium enterprises in logistics focus on maintaining operational survival since their historic profit margins remain thin (Naradda Gamage et al., 2020). Big companies need detailed explanations about smart logistics benefits because different investment proposals compete for funding resources. These explanations must use cost-benefit analyses along with predicted ROI returns.

Organizational Culture and Resistance to Change

The successful implementation of smart logistics faces major difficulties from organizational culture even though financial and technological resources exist. Leaders in organizational behavior literature have long noted worker concerns about unknown factors and work uncertainty and doubts about new technology performance which create change resistance (Zhu et al., 2023). Organizations within the logistics field show significant worry regarding emerging disruptive digital technologies which disturb their well-established operational patterns and command system. Workers who handle manual scheduling and inventory management as well as truck routing often view intelligent systems as invasive to their professional skills and job security. Without adequate proactive change management practices these negative reactions can surface as workers either fail to adopt the system actively or attack its implementation openly or quietly damage the initiative. Leading organizations effectively create readiness towards change through cultural development. Senior management failure to display commitment about new technology implementation reveals their ambivalence and causes intermediate managers and frontline staff to resist change implementation (Buchter, 2021). The standalone operational approach which maintains departments as separate units prevents cross-departmental integration between departments needed to operate smart logistics systems correctly. Organizations establishing innovative cultures need intentional approaches to make transparency a practice combined with continuous education and united technology vision. The process of creating cultural transformations is naturally difficult to achieve and time-consuming and needs ongoing leadership support combined with direct employee involvement and open communication channels for success.

Figure 2. Organizational resistance framework

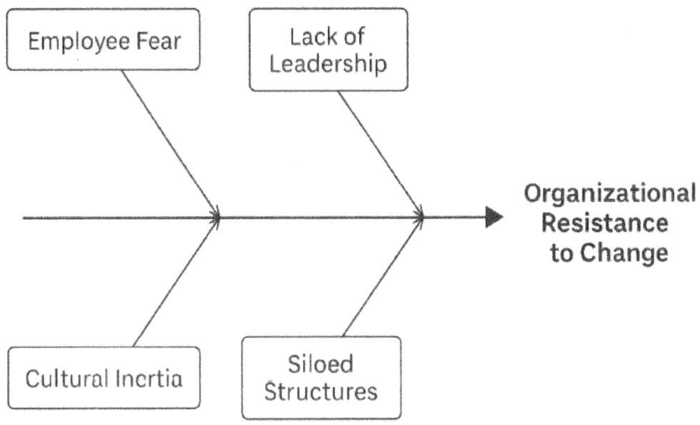

This fishbone model shows the underlying causes of resistance to change in the organization. Figure 2 is titled Organizational Resistance Framework; it has a horizontal arrow that is directed to the right, denoting the primary problem, which is organizational resistance to change. There are four major contributing factors that branch out diagonally of the central spine, which are Employee Fear, Lack of Leadership, Siloed Structures, and Cultural Inertia. All of these categories define one of the major internal obstacles that might impede the successful change initiative. The graphic presentation reinforces the main message about the necessity of specific interventions in every category to be able to control and diminish resistance in organizations.

Regulatory and Compliance Challenges

Smart logistics faces complex and flexible governance requirements which are not unified between different national governments. Multiple compliance obligations such as data protection under GDPR in Europe require management along with cybersecurity standards, vehicle automation regulations and international trade regulations by organizations (Andraško et al., 2021; Costantini et al., 2020; Landini, 2020). Nations as well as distinct regions within nations have inconsistent regulatory systems that control autonomous delivery drones and self-driving trucks. Businesses require compulsory authorization alongside safety compliance standards while adapting to potential restrictions which minimize their technological operational capabilities. These regulatory requirements slow down installation work while generating additional compliance expenses together with potential legal responsibilities. Global logistics operations encounter major difficulties when handling data privacy concerns alongside the challenges of international data transfer operations. Intelligent logistics systems base their operation on gathering massive amounts of sensitive information such as client data and shipping documentation and route optimization algorithms while storing and transmitting them. The regulations enforcing data protection impose strict obligations for every stage of data handling from acquisition all the way through to dissemination yet severe financial penalties exist for nonconformity. The absence of defined regulatory frameworks creates an unpredictable situation which makes development of multi-national logistics networks confusing for firms. The absence of precise regulatory standards in multiple jurisdictions results in increased compliance costs which makes intelligent logistics projects less attractive for robust investment.

Data Security and Privacy Concerns

The industry now faces rising cyberattacks because companies advance their logistical operations through digitization. According to Nag et al., (2024), the combination of IoT devices with cloud platforms and mobile services together with enterprise resource planning systems increases the surface for security threats. The combination of ransomware attacks with data breaches and denial-of-service assaults inflicts severe threats upon logistics operations by causing shipments delays in addition to financial damage and reputation damage as well as the risk of affecting national security sometimes. The 2017 NotPetya hack demonstrated how harmful linked logistics networks have become when Maersk faced substantial impacts on its global transportation operations (Sindiramutty et al., 2024). Data security together with confidentiality and data integrity throughout the logistics value chain remains vital to operational protection. Various organizations struggle to create broad cybersecurity safety measures that fit well with the advanced requirements of smart logistics systems. According to Khan et al., (2024), financial restrictions and inadequate cybersecurity know-how and quick-evolving attack methods make the situation harder. Data privacy concerns that customers have about their information mainly contribute to this issue. Companies requiring complete visibility into data collection practices alongside data usage and protection receive penalizes when they fail to satisfy these requirements and encounter both government actions and diminished customer loyalty. Most organizations struggle to fulfill their cybersecurity objectives despite building strong initial infrastructure and running regular vulnerability checks and increasing cyber awareness among staff members.

STRATEGIES FOR OVERCOMING CHALLENGES

Many complex implementation issues exist regarding smart logistics, but organizations possess the capability to overcome them. Organizations can make significant improvements in their capacity to develop intelligent logistics systems through strategic planned actions. Smart logistics implementation success requires full readiness in technology and dependent aspects on organizational agility and leadership commitment as well as active stakeholder engagement and established governance systems. With foundational strategies at hand this section deploys a meticulous evaluation of proven methods which conquer previously mentioned obstacles while offering a reference guide for smart logistics practitioners and policymakers

Investment in Training and Development

Smart logistics system implementation depends on human capital development with advanced technological proficiency skills. Advancements in technology fail to deliver their intended benefits without workforce preparation and acceptance towards change initiatives. According to Foroughi, (2021), Training programs that match employee learning needs combine technical abilities with strategic understanding about how digital technologies meet corporate objectives. The training curriculum should contain both technological competencies which include learning IoT platforms, big data analytics, autonomous systems and general abilities which include critical thinking, flexibility, and digital literacy. Training programs need to incorporate individualized approaches because customized educational strategies that understand the specific knowledge base and learning times of workers prove best for fostering genuine involvement in organizational activities (Giannakos et al., 2022; Khan et al., 2024). Organizations must develop a learning culture because it stands alongside technical training as their essential development tools. Modern professional learning opportunities enhance operational performance and reduce employee concerns about technological disruptions by spotlighting career potential in the developing digital logistics industry. Staff learning through certification programs with academic associations and seminars enables continuous educational development of workers who become agents of transformation over technology (Jain et al., 2021). The establishment of human capital development framework depends on leadership as its fundamental aspect. Training projects receive enhanced corporate backing from prominent leadership when the projects receive continuous endorsement which demonstrates their strategic importance. Organizational resilience improves together with creative potential when organizations invest in their human resources.

Phased Implementation Approaches

Smart logistics implementation represents a complex process carrying high safety risks combined with technical requirements and organizational adjustments and substantial financial needs. Implementation through phased deployment helps businesses stop these risks by letting them build their skills while making gradual procedure enhancements (Herm et al., 2023). The full-scale smart logistics transformation remains out of their reach, but businesses establish small pilot trails which demonstrate how this technology improves operations under regulatory conditions. Businesses utilize pilot programs to deploy new systems before expansion while they detect unknown challenges and require necessary system adjustments. The deployment of blockchain-based tracking systems starts in one warehouse before reaching extended implementation throughout the entire network. The method builds technical knowledge alongside organizational acceptance of new technology systems which leads to decreased resistance during widespread adoption. Through staged implementation organizations gain the ability to learn from observed experiences. The identification of real-world complexity and contextual variables becomes possible through systematic result evaluation and the collection of feedback at different project stages (Paparini et al., 2021). Repeated learning allows organizations to enhance their agility for effective changes toward adapting new technical environments and market needs. The implementation process of gradual adoption needs close supervision and detailed planning because of its complexity. Organizations require clear vital checkpoints containing evaluation standards and performance systems through which every step advances toward their fundamental strategic vision. Organizations need to guard against a problem where projects stall at the pilot level before advancing toward full implementation. Strong leadership commitment together with a clear long-term objective represents requirements that cannot be ignored.

Collaboration and Strategic Partnerships

The implementation of smart logistics technology requires essential coordination between parties and strategic alliances because of its complex nature. A single company lacks the full expertise to independently guide digital transformation because they lack all aspects of technological capabilities and infrastructure as well as regulatory insight. The establishment of collaborative relationships between technology providers and educational establishments and industrial collaboration groups along with public sector partners creates substantial access for businesses to information as well as innovation and resources (Ferraris et al., 2020; O'Dwyer et al., 2023). Companies that partner with technology suppliers can develop customized solutions which address specific constraints and needs of various organizations. Through academic partnerships companies gain access to new research opportunities and can use both innovative research and talent availability and objective technology evaluation services. Industry consortia operate as platforms that enable information sharing while creating common standards and resolving technical issues which assist companies through unknown technological risks. Moderating obstacles between public and private sectors becomes more effective through public-private partnerships (PPPs). The cooperation between private entities and government bodies helps obtain faster regulatory permits for autonomous logistics devices and takes part in constructing fundamental digital networks such as 5G and smart transportation routes (Monios & Bergqvist, 2020). Management of strategic collaborations must be handled very carefully. Well-built partnerships require teams to share aims while adopting structured management systems together with mutual trust alongside clear dispute resolution methods. Partnership management skills require development from organizations since cooperative relationships function as strategic resources not limited to transactional relationships.

Developing a Clear Business Case

The success of securing organizational endorsement for smart logistics projects depends on creating an effective business case. Jing et al., (2023) states that robust investments face resistance when returns are uncertain in competitive markets with tight profit margins. Business cases that want to succeed must prove more than simply innovation or modernization claims. The assessment should detail fundamental expense breakdowns together with strategic operation consequences alongside risk evaluation and accepted functionality gains of smart logistics adoption. Financial criteria such as ROI along with payback duration and TCO serve as essential determinants for decision making. Clear explanations of non-financial benefits that include increased customer pleasure, higher regulatory compliance and reduced environmental impact and brand reputation enhancement are necessary (Alatawi et al., 2023). Scenario analysis serves to strengthen the business case through performance evaluations of organization-level technology implementation at different market realities. Illuminating how other firms in the industry succeeded with tangible results from strategic logistics investment gives organizations a benchmark that strengthens their credibility. Each stakeholder group needs their specific business case modifications to tackle their goals and issues. The business case needs different viewpoints since executive leaders focus on strategic alignment and financial results, but operational supervisors need to demonstrate operational improvements and simplify processes. Creating a well-developed and complete business case creates better chances for receiving extensive organizational backing.

Emphasizing Robust Data Security Measures

Strong cybersecurity measures must be implemented across smart logistics operations because digital dangers have spread widely throughout society. The establishment of trust between consumers and partners and regulators demands verified national guarantees for protecting data while guaranteeing unaltered data quality and privacy and system access (Díaz-Rodríguez et al., 2023; Yele & Litoriya, 2024). The right step for organizations is to establish industry-standard cybersecurity practices at startups instead of trying to add security after their product launches. The essential technological security measures consist of end-to-end encryption supported by multi-factor authentication as well as the implementation of intrusion detection systems and network segmentation. Protective security mechanisms remain potent against new threats because of continuous vulnerability detection and penetration tests as well as security audits. The design process of systems and operational procedures requires active inclusion of essential data protection regulations like GDPR in the EU and CCPA in the US from the initial development phase. Every aspect of smart logistics system design needs to follow privacy-by-design standards that base data practices on minimization along with mandatory consent and system-wide transparency. The cybersecurity challenge exists as much from human and organizational factors as from technological issues. Every member of the organization must develop a cybersecurity culture which requires them to follow their security duties for information protection. The development of a complete security plan needs regular training alongside specific regulations and security best practices, leadership exemplification and consistent implementation. Nationwide logistics firms that make cybersecurity investments achieve dual advantages by reducing operational risks while building their position as secure partners throughout the global supply chains of modern trade.

Figure 3. Integrated smart logistics risk mitigation framework

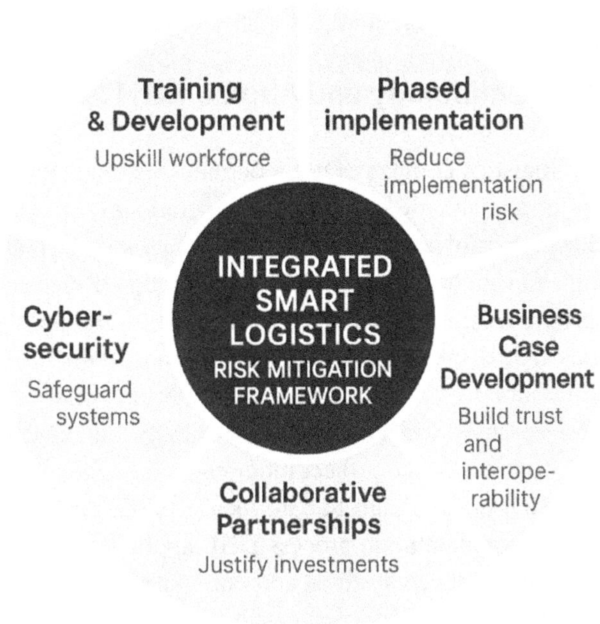

Figure 3 demonstrates a circular framework in which the five areas of strategic focus needed to reduce the risks of smart logistics are visually integrated. This hub is simply called Integrated Smart Logistics Risk Mitigation Framework with the five different segments surrounding it: Training & Development (Upskill workforce), Phased Implementation (Reduce implementation risk), Business Case Development (Build trust and interoperability), Collaborative Partnerships (Justify investments), and Cybersecurity (Safeguard systems). All of the annotated sections indicate the overall goal of the corresponding strategy, which allows making a comprehensive overview of the risk mitigation strategy.

CASE STUDIES AND EMPIRICAL EVIDENCE

Multiple sectors generate extensive practical data about both prospects and challenges that digital transformation initiatives face through their implementations of smart logistics technology. Examples from real life show that successful implementation requires more than technological innovation since it represents the convergence of strategic planning along with prepared organizations that work between sectors to develop their knowledge base continuously. Researchers and practitioners can benefit from analyzing case studies and empirical research in this part that describes the complex adoption process of smart logistics systems.

DHL: Wearable Technology and Augmented Reality in Logistics

As the leading logistics company DHL continues its innovation through intelligent technology implementations to improve operational efficiency worldwide. DHL achieved one major milestone by implementing augmented reality (AR) smart glasses that optimized warehouse order picking operations (Rejeb et al., 2021). The Vision Picking program through smart glasses provided warehouse personnel with visual instructions that displayed both the positions of items and optimal walk-throughs for the facility. Tests conducted for this project showed that efficiency during picking rose by 25% while new employee training and mistake rates showed reduction patterns. Success of the project required technological excellence of the devices together with well-designed human-focused implementation procedures. To ensure a smooth implementation process DHL applied extensive staff training together with constant feedback systems and cumulative deployment approaches (Shahin et al., 2024). The successful integration of intelligent logistical solutions depends on both technological advancement and ecological implementation of operational systems by employees. Successful digital transformation requires employee empowerment along with employee engagement because these elements function as essential facilitators (Cichosz et al., 2020).

Maersk and IBM: Blockchain for Global Trade Documentation

Maersk partnered with IBM to establish TradeLens as a blockchain-based platform which targets digitization and optimization of worldwide trade documentation (Aránguiz et al., 2021). The company identified problems with existing paper documentation systems which lacked transparency, so they searched for a solution to enhance supply chain information exchange with real-time security and clarity. The distributed ledger system of TradeLens creates protected shipping information which remains unmodifiable and assures its authenticity for authorized users. By eliminating paper-based document dependence TradeLens decreased expenses and processing speed because it enables instant data exchange between users. By 2021 TradeLens developed a network which incorporated more than 300 members spanning between ports and shipping lines and freight forwarders and customs agencies (Rukanova et al., 2023). Nonetheless, Maersk's expedition encountered obstacles. Potential users delayed their adoption of TradeLens because they worried about control over their data along with protectable confidential information and administrative rules. Such difficulties demanded thorough technical defenses along with precise work to build stakeholder trust and transparent platform management procedures and clear value exchange benefits (Zutshi et al., 2021). The partnership between Maersk and IBM demonstrates that ecosystem thinking combined with trust management and strategic communication enables advancement of smart logistics ideas after their pilot test period.

Empirical Studies: Leadership, Employee Engagement, and Incremental Implementation

Various organizational factors determine smart logistics adoption outcomes more strongly than the supposed power of technical machines. Several logistics companies demonstrate that leader-sponsored commitment drives successful digital transformation initiatives (Mohrman & Bartunek, 2023). The cultural foundation for innovation emerges through leadership support of smart technology alongside resource distribution and leadership by example in adapting to new systems. The entire study devoted its focus to understanding the fundamental role of worker participation. Organizations who invited their workers to participate from design until they resolved issues and acknowledged work received higher rates of technology acceptance coupled with performance improvements. The shift to transform resisted previous definitions as a primary barrier because employees connected the changes to their career development and organizational standards (Khaw et al., 2023). The implementation approach through gradual increases proved to be a topic that organizations kept returning to. The implementation method of phased rollouts allowed organizations to minimize operational risks by starting with achievable pilot projects then analyzing first project outcomes before enlarging their adoption (Skalli et al., 2024). The method enabled technological enhancements and organized a plan to build internal company confidence alongside momentum.

Additional Cases from Emerging Markets

Developing nations show increasing evidence of creative smart logistics projects which exist even with limited resources. Through its Cainiao Network division Alibaba applied big data analytics AI and IoT technologies to create a "smart logistics backbone" that spans the entire Chinese market as well as global areas (Liu, 2022). Thc Cainiao platform achieves major improvements in customer satisfaction by delivering real-time management of route optimization and delivery synchronization and warehouse administration. Multiple principles about successful enterprise development can be learned from Cainiao's operating performance. Multiple technologies work together instead of single advances to produce combined benefits in this successful implementation. Platform-based business models prove essential because they enable stakeholders to interact and share data at an extensive level. The case shows that flexible organizations which form strategic partnerships remain effective despite lacking the necessary market infrastructure in expanding markets. To boost its e-commerce operations Mercado Libre spent heavily developing an intelligent logistics network across Latin America. Despite challenging logistics situations across Latin America Mercado Libre enhances its service delivery and reduces delivery time by using automated fulfillment centers and AI inventory management along with local delivery partner alliances (Capobianco, 2023). Strategies in smart logistics emerge from resource limitations in developing economies through which organizations adopt flexible approaches and scalable operations and collaborative partnerships.

Lessons Learned and Future Research Directions

Multiple essential topics unite the ideas collected from case study research and empirical assessments. The implementation of technological innovation requires supporting organizational innovation measures. The creation of perpetual learning cultures combines with staff empowerment and direct association of technical projects to strategic objectives to achieve this result. Secondly, stakeholder management is essential. Smart logistics adoption requires equal attention to its technological aspects together with the human and social considerations which must be implemented throughout organizational domains and inter-organizational networks. The strategic mandate includes the essential elements of incrementalism and flexibility. Firms need to implement learning-oriented approaches which involve constant adaptation because smart logistics transformations bring unpredictable and complicated challenges. Several vital gaps remain despite the large quantity of existing empirical research. Future research must evaluate how smart logistics affects workforce operations throughout time, particularly regarding employee skills building along with job advancement patterns and union relations between workers. The comparison between different industries and geographical areas produces essential knowledge regarding which factors influence adoption outcomes. The field needs urgent attention on both ethical as well as environmental and social consequences of smart logistics technology because sustainability and equality issues have made this topic more significant (Ahmad et al., 2022; Shee et al., 2021).

IMPACT OF GEOPOLITICAL AND MACROECONOMIC FACTORS ON THE ADOPTION OF SMART LOGISTICS

The implementation of smart logistics, which is the incorporation of more recent digital innovations, including IoT, blockchain, AI, and automation, has disrupted supply chain management and activities across the globe. Nonetheless, in addition to technological preparedness and organizational desire, there are geopolitical and macroeconomic conditions that have immeasurable impacts on the speed, scale, and effectiveness of smart logistics adoption. These external forces are important to understand by the logistics companies with the view to developing flexible and resilient systems that can succeed in a world, which is becoming very uncertain.

Global Economic Volatility and Supply Chain Disruptions

Global economic volatility can be considered as one of the most influential macroeconomic factors affecting the adoption of smart logistics. The economic changes which are a result of inflation, currency volatility, and dynamic commodity prices have a direct impact on the capital and the appetite to invest in new technology implementations. As an example, smart logistics projects are regularly reduced or postponed in terms of expenditures on non-essential investments during economic downturns or recession (Wang, 2024). Economic upturns, on the other hand, allow more economic leeway to invest in state-of-the-art logistics technology. The COVID-19 pandemic provided a bleak example of how unexpected macroeconomic shocks break the supply chain and enhance the digital transformation. The crisis revealed the weakness of conventional logistics networks, including excessive reliance on individual suppliers, and absence of real time visibility, forcing businesses to embrace smart technologies capable of improving logistics networks. agility and responsiveness (Gumzej, 2021). Two-thirds of supply chain executives speed up their investment in digital logistics instruments after the pandemic to limit the effects of potential disruptions in the future (Khan et al., 2024). At the same time, supply chain disruptions caused by the pandemic (port congestion, labor shortages, etc.) signified the importance of end-to-end digitalization and automation of operations. IoT-based real-time tracking sensors and AI-based demand prediction technologies were among smart logistics technologies that played a pivotal role in dealing with unforeseeable changes in supply and demand (Adamashvili et al., 2024). These investments, however, depend on the general economic environment; a situation of continued inflationary pressures or an increase in the interest rates may hinder the financial ability of firms to maximize on such innovations.

Trade Restrictions and Regulatory Complexity

The international trade policy and regulatory environment have been found to significantly dictate the environment towards the adoption of smart logistics. Geopolitical tensions in recent years have led to a spiral of trade restrictions, tariffs, sanctions and export controls that make cross-border logistics operations more challenging. Such geopolitical tensions are affecting the adoption of smart logistics by increasing the cost of compliance and making it difficult to agree on data-sharing schemes that are critical to the integrated digital platforms. The application of blockchain and other distributed ledger technologies that are associated with higher levels of transparency and efficiency inevitably demands cross-border data transfers. The existence of multi-jurisdictional environment means that companies must address the dual challenge of addressing various regulatory demands and embracing smart logistics innovations to enhance competitiveness. Additionally, the regional trade agreements, like the Regional Comprehensive Economic Partnership (RCEP) and the African Continental Free Trade Area (AfCFTA), affect the smart logistics dynamics by making the custom clearance easier and prompting the alignment of the digital standards (Agwu, 2021). The logistics providers should be sensitive to these changing trade blocks to seize new opportunities in provision of technology-enabled logistics services.

Political Instability and Regional Tensions

Instability in politics such as civil unrest, conflicts and changes of administration pose major risks to logistics activities and investment plans. Smart logistics systems depend on continuous infrastructure, stable communication systems, and safe data environments, which may be jeopardized in politically volatile environments (Abdelkader et al., 2024; Shee et al., 2021). As another illustration, the current wars in Eastern Europe and the Middle East have also resulted in the disruption of supply routes, rising insurance premiums, and the need by companies to reship goods, sometimes at an increased expense of operation (Widdis, 2024). This kind of instability spills over to FDI and technology transfer deals that are important in adopting smart logistics in emerging markets (Baricako & Kedir, 2020; Jithin et al., 2024). The uncertainty surrounding the political environments of the various regions is causing investors to hesitate when it comes to investing in the application of advanced logistics technologies. Furthermore, when instability occurs, government interests in digital infrastructure investments might change towards impeding further developments. Additional levels of complexity are formed by regional geopolitical tension, i.e. territorial disputes in the South China Sea or tense relations between neighboring states. Such tensions can trigger governments to apply constraints on some technologies on the grounds of national security, especially in the logistics networks of critical infrastructure and data flows (Chang et al., 2020). These assessments of geopolitical risks should be part of smart logistics approaches used by businesses, such as diversification of supply origins and investment in flexible technology platforms. Geopolitical risk considerations should be part of the smart logistics approaches adopted by companies, such as diversification of supply sources or investment in flexible technology platforms.

Agile Strategies for Navigating Uncertainty

The complex interdependence of the macroeconomic and geopolitical factors implies that logistics companies will need to employ versatile, future-oriented strategies to achieve smart logistics. One of them is scenario planning, which allows organizations to predict different external trends, including trade policy changes, economic crises, and others, and develop response strategies that are not rigid. Simulating the possible future states helps the firms to allocate their resources better, set priorities related to technologies investments, and develop contingency capabilities. The risk mitigation frameworks are crucial as well. The frameworks have risk identification, assessment and management procedures that factor in geopolitical risks, regulatory changes and economic shocks. In addition, they should encourage public-private collaboration and interaction with policy makers to create conducive regulatory frameworks and promote cross border cooperation.

Influence on Investment and Compliance

The geopolitical and macroeconomic environment, the geopolitical and macroeconomic environment is very sensitive to investment decisions in smart logistics. Investors want to be sure about political and regulatory environment as well as economic sustainability before they invest money in high-cost technology initiatives. Uncertainties in politics raise the cost of capital and prolong the payback periods, and it becomes hard to determine the financial feasibility of smart logistics implementations. The complexity of compliance also increases as nations come up with a variety of data protection laws, cybersecurity regulations, and trade restrictions. Such complexity of regulations requires strong governance systems and flexible technology frameworks that can do dynamic monitoring of compliance. Compliance readiness is thus a key element that firms should carry out as part of their smart logistics strategies to prevent the imposition of penalties and reputational losses. Smart logistics adoption is not a simple technology project but an initiative that is strongly connected to overall geopolitical and macroeconomic conditions. The fluctuations in the economy, trade policy, political uncertainty, and complex regulations have a considerable influence on the path of the digital logistics revolution. Logistics companies will have to become nimble, risk-sensitive in their approach and will need to invest in elastic, regulatory-compliant technology stacks to move through these turbulent times. Subsequent studies ought to further investigate the play of dynamic geopolitical changes on the adoption of smart logistics, especially concerning the emerging markets and transnational data governance systems.

SOCIAL AND ENVIRONMENTAL RESPONSIBILITY IN SMART LOGISTICS

The new realities of the changing landscape of logistics are no longer guided by the solely dictates of speed, efficiency, or cost-effectiveness. As we live in a time of increased stakeholder awareness regarding environmental and social justice, the implementation of smart technologies in logistics should be complemented by the strong adherence to the idea of CSR. Being supported by the IoT, AI, blockchain, and other technologies, smart logistics offers not only possibilities to improve operations but also faces obligations to sustainable development and ethical governance. Supply chain digital transparency and real-time monitoring have pushed the emergence of a stronger visibility of supply chain activities that have in turn compelled logistics companies to proactively align their strategies with the larger objectives of environmental stewardship and social accountability. Carbon footprint of transportation and warehousing operations is one of the most urgent environmental issues in logistics. Optimization of routes and algorithms, telematics, and predictive analytics are components of smart logistics that may considerably decrease fuel use and greenhouse gas discharges. As an example, dynamic routing systems coupled with AI will be able to adjust to traffic limitations in real-time, thus reducing waiting time and redundant mileage. Moreover, automated warehouse systems and smart energy management systems can result in significant electricity consumption and cooling demand reductions. The environmental responsibility of smart logistics does not finish with efficiency improvements. A more comprehensive solution is switching to electrified or hydrogen-fueled vehicles, facility power rendered renewable, and the practices of the circular economy, such as the reverse logistics and reuse of assets. Another vital aspect of CSR in smart logistics schemes would be ethical sourcing and procurement practices. Globalization of the supply chains makes companies vulnerable to intricating webs of suppliers; many of whom are in jurisdictions with differing regulatory frameworks. Such components of smart logistics infrastructures as blockchain technology can make sourcing practices transparent and traceable so that a company can check whether labor laws, environmental regulations, and human rights standards are followed. Such traceability can assist logistics suppliers and their customers to show ethical responsibility, particularly in supply chains involving apparel, electronics and food where historical complexities of abuse within the supply chain have been rife.

The social responsibility perspective dictates that the employee welfare in logistics processes needs to be reevaluated under the umbrella of increased automation and digitalization. On the one hand, smart logistics systems have the potential to optimize operations, limit manual work, and create interesting job opportunities; on the other hand, there is the displacement of the workforce. A sustainable use of such technologies requires advanced workforce planning, investment in upskilling and reskilling initiatives, and the invention of new jobs that are in line with the changes in technology. Human capital should not be treated as a disposable resource, and it is important to consider it as the changing asset that needs to be developed on an ongoing basis. Furthermore, smart technologies would help improve safety in the workplace. As an example, wearable technology can track health data of the workers and warn managers when something is not working as it should be, thus preventing accidents and health-related emergencies in warehouses and distribution centers where the risk of such incidents is high. Socially responsible logistics is also comprised of community involvement and appropriate labor standards. The businesses that invest in local employment, pay into infrastructure building, and participate in community-based initiatives are likely to have a larger social license to operate. Logistics hubs especially occupy a large physical and economic footprint in the local communities, and it is thus valuable to the companies to alleviate any negative impact which may include noise pollution, congestion, or environmental deterioration. Logistics systems which are smart and incorporate environmental sensors along with a means to get the reaction of the community can assist firms to track and respond to these issues better. Notably, implementing smart logistics solutions with a focus on protecting the environment and society is not only an issue of ethical conformity but a question of competitiveness as well. The consumers, regulators and investors are showing preferences to those companies which exercise leadership in sustainability. The Environmental, Social and Governance (ESG) indicators are all part of the investment decision-making process nowadays and the logistics service providers that score highly on these indicators have a better chance of securing tie-ups and investments. Smart logistics should be envisioned not merely as the means of transforming operations, but also as the means of pursuing social and environmental agendas. Technology which enables smart logistics can be weaponized in a way that brings more transparency, reduces environmental damage, and encourages equal and equitable labor policies. Long-term survivability of logistics companies will be linked not only to their technological competency, but how well they incorporate ethical and sustainable practices as they continue to work within a digitally connected and socially conscious global community.

FUTURE DIRECTIONS

The upcoming smart logistics environment shows indications of becoming an intricate system with transformative characteristics and dynamic operations. Through autonomous delivery and AI analytical capabilities along with blockchain and green mobility initiatives innovative technologies are reshaping what is possible for logistics systems (Dong et al., 2021). New technologies provide improved capabilities yet create multiple challenges on multiple dimensions which include technical issues at the same time as ethical problems and regulatory obstacles and infrastructure needs. The efficient forward movement of smart logistics depends on understanding and tackling problems to ensure an efficient, fair and sustainable evolution.

Autonomous Delivery Systems and Operational Transformation

The development of autonomous delivery technology consisting of drones and self-driving vehicles together with robotic couriers leads to major industry disruptions in logistics. Drone delivery projects are underway at Amazon and FedEx as well as major car companies spend heavily developing autonomous vehicle technology for freight delivery (Graf & Anner, 2021). Self-governing system technology grants advantageous elements including cost reduction alongside more rapid deliveries along with dependable service quality particularly when addressing last-mile delivery complications.

The transformation toward autonomous systems brings multiple substantial hurdles to deal with. Several countries maintain different frameworks to regulate autonomous vehicle operations which exist in unclear states of development. Safety problems and cybersecurity risks with questions of public acceptability constitute major challenges. The incidents of autonomous car use created debates about liability responsibilities together with ethical frameworks that guide algorithm decision-making systems (Cunneen et al., 2020; Emon & Khan, 2025b). The solutions to these problems demand both better technologies alongside innovative regulation along with substantial governmental public policies.

AI-Driven Decision-Making and Ethical Complexities

The field of logistics strongly depends on artificial intelligence which enables optimized routing solutions and forecasts demand and sets dynamic prices and controls warehouse operations (Shi, 2022). By processing very large sets of data machine learning algorithms reveal previously unreachable information that leads to maximum operational effectiveness. Practicing greater dependence on artificial intelligence creates substantial problems about ethical conduct and governance systems. The need for understanding algorithmic bias together with transparency and accountability as well as explanations for AI-generated outputs has risen to greater importance (Hassija et al., 2024). The application of biased algorithms in logistics operations harms specific customer segments by showing preference to specific groups and leads operational systems to focus on price over sustainability and allow continued unfair labor practices to persist. Scientific research needs to undertake comprehensive analyses of the ethical consequences that AI brings to logistics systems. According to Díaz-Rodríguez et al., (2023), The development of robust AI governance frameworks requires combination of computer science technology and philosophy principles and business ethics expertise. Organizations need to distribute funds to develop "responsible AI" systems which combine technical excellence with social acceptance.

Carbon-Neutral Logistics and the Imperative of Sustainability

Smart logistics experiences a rapid growth in importance regarding sustainability. The transportation industry creates substantial carbon emissions while storage along with distribution operations from logistics form essential elements of this impact (Shee et al., 2021). More and more authorities, consumers and investors push logistics companies to establish carbon-neutral operation methods. Delivery trucks receive electrified power while warehouse facilities invest in renewable power generation systems and supply chain operations achieve better emission reduction (J. Wang et al., 2024). DHL and UPS are trying out electric delivery trucks together with urban micro-hubs as part of their efforts to decrease environmental impacts from final delivery operations. Multiple issues exist with the process of making carbon neutral logistics. The implementation of electricity-based transportation demands major investment in charging network development as well as changes to present vehicle service procedures. Effective environmental regulations must be established to thoroughly control the ecological impacts of battery manufacturing and disposal operations which prevent the movement of environmental damage ticks (Emon, 2025; John et al., 2024). Systemic thinking becomes essential to deal with the existing obstacles. Investigations into technical solutions backed by organizational and regulatory innovations and carbon pricing systems and circular economy models as well as cross-sector cooperation must happen to achieve system-wide decarbonization in logistics operations.

Interdisciplinary and Longitudinal Research Agendas

Advanced difficulties in smart logistics necessitate using comprehensive research methods because of their complexity. Information systems scholars along with organizational behavior researchers along with sustainability scientists should be part of designing digital infrastructure governance strategies and studying human adoption behavior while creating sustainability frameworks. The research also requires a long-term examination approach. Most academic investigations about smart logistics adoption today use temporary cross-sectional data while these study methods deliver static snapshots rather than dynamic process views. Longitudinal research provides complete awareness of organizational approaches during smart logistics adoption from exploration through pilot testing to expansion and institutional maintenance to ultimate reinvention when technological or environmental factors demand (Shee et al., 2021). Studying over time would help understand why originally superior digital technology systems gradually lose their effectiveness when organizations evolve their technical environments. Future research must focus on determining proper implementation methods of resilience and adaptation within smart logistics firm strategies.

Future Workforce and Skills Development

The main emphasis currently targets employment prospects in intelligent logistics systems. According to Mathew et al., (2023), the logistics industry faces major modifications to all job functions and required skills and working dynamics through automation and artificial intelligence. The workforce transition occurs through automation of basic manual work since it generates positions requiring advanced digital capabilities alongside analytical skills and systems thinking intelligence. The transformation demands organizations to evaluate workforce development strategies together with social equality programs and organizational change approaches. Organizations need to dedicate funding to both new emerging technologies and training initiatives which allow employees to succeed in advancing digitalized logistics environments (Cichosz et al., 2020; Emon & Khan, 2025a). The fundamental roles in creating supportive environments for workforce change are served by governmental authorities alongside academic facilities and business enterprises. Future research requires examination of work transformation in logistics through studying how technology adoption affects personnel welfare and their labor roles and social advancement patterns. Smart logistics systems gain functionality through worker participation methods which help combine technological goals with human requirements.

Building Resilient and Adaptive Smart Logistics Systems

Global logistics networks demonstrated their sensitivity to wide-reaching systemic disruptions when the COVID-19 pandemic happened. Conventionally used logistics systems exposed major weaknesses during supply disruptions and manpower shortages and rising demand thus expedited the adoption of intelligent technology (Dasaklis & Tsoulfas, 2024). Present-day designs of intelligent logistics systems need resilience to become a fundamental design requirement. Organizations need to build resilience through physical systems resilience together with workforce flexibility in addition to intercompany collaboration and the ability to plan for multiple possible future scenarios. According to Tariq, (2024), Businesses which implement predictive analytics together with digital twins and blockchain-based transparency platforms will gain enhanced oversight as well as enhanced adaptive response time toward disturbances. Future scientific research needs to approach the development of agile smart logistics systems to tackle uncertain market conditions. Researchers should investigate the relationship between efficiency and resilience and develop protocols to control dynamic risks that occur through digital logistics systems.

CONCLUSION

Smart logistics implements major changes to both operating methods and strategic supply chain management of present-day systems. Many substantial obstacles exist to obtain smart logistics alongside its extensive potential benefits. Organizations need to approach the main obstacles of technological constraints and budgetary restrictions and cultural resistance as well as legal confusion and cybersecurity threats with careful expertise. The identified challenges lack perseverance. Companies achieve quick implementation of smart logistics by intentionally developing human resources while deploying phased techniques for implementation and forming strategic alliances to develop clear business cases while implementing strict cybersecurity measures which reduce overall risks. Several practical studies and factual findings show that organizations need a complete adaptable method to succeed. DHL and Maersk demonstrate that technological adoption succeeds through company readiness combined with leader devotion and continuous learning culture. Organizations must work together across departments and between various organizations to handle the complex challenges during technological integration into existing logistical systems. Smart logistics development will be shaped by three main factors including the fast evolution of automated delivery systems combined with AI-based decision platforms and the requirement for emission-free logistics strategies. New developments in technology will bring about distinctive ethical challenges alongside regulatory and infrastructural problems that must be intentionally handled. Extended research collaborations across various disciplines along with long-term investigation methods present the key to obtaining essential complex knowledge needed for building sustainable enduring and equitable smart logistics network systems. The human aspect needs to stay at the core of every effort to transition into smart logistics systems. The implementation of new technologies should avoid any adverse impact on workforce enhancement and social inclusive programs. Future implementations should implement training combined with ethical administration and resilient company management to ensure smart logistics fuel benefit-sharing within the community. Smart logistics implementation stands as a fundamental and complex transformation required by enterprises to preserve their business sustainability while competing in the evolving digitalized world market. New technology development alone will not achieve success and require leaders who envision the future while making strategic decisions and remain committed to constant adjustments. These principles enable businesses to overcome their remaining adoption barriers while achieving the total transformative power of future smart logistics systems.

REFERENCES

Abdelkader, S., Amissah, J., Kinga, S., Mugerwa, G., Emmanuel, E., Mansour, D.-E. A., Bajaj, M., Blazek, V., & Prokop, L. (2024). Securing modern power systems: Implementing comprehensive strategies to enhance resilience and reliability against cyber-attacks. *Results in Engineering*, *23*, 102647. DOI: 10.1016/j.rineng.2024.102647

Adamashvili, N., Zhizhilashvili, N., & Tricase, C. (2024). The Integration of the Internet of Things, Artificial Intelligence, and Blockchain Technology for Advancing the Wine Supply Chain. *Computers*, *13*(3), 72. DOI: 10.3390/computers13030072

Affia, I., & Aamer, A. (2022). An internet of things-based smart warehouse infrastructure: Design and application. *Journal of Science and Technology Policy Management*, *13*(1), 90–109. DOI: 10.1108/JSTPM-08-2020-0117

Agwu, F. A. (2021). Globalization, Populism, Nationalism and the African Continental Free Trade Area. In *Foreign Policy in the Age of Globalization, Populism and Nationalism* (pp. 261–339). Springer Singapore. https://doi.org/DOI: 10.1007/978-981-16-3372-0_7

Ahmad, K., Maabreh, M., Ghaly, M., Khan, K., Qadir, J., & Al-Fuqaha, A. (2022). Developing future human-centered smart cities: Critical analysis of smart city security, Data management, and Ethical challenges. *Computer Science Review*, *43*, 100452. DOI: 10.1016/j.cosrev.2021.100452

Alatawi, I. A., Ntim, C. G., Zras, A., & Elmagrhi, M. H. (2023). CSR, financial and non-financial performance in the tourism sector: A systematic literature review and future research agenda. *International Review of Financial Analysis*, *89*, 102734. DOI: 10.1016/j.irfa.2023.102734

Andraško, J., Mesarčík, M., & Hamuľák, O. (2021). The regulatory intersections between artificial intelligence, data protection and cyber security: Challenges and opportunities for the EU legal framework. *AI & Society*, *36*(2), 623–636. DOI: 10.1007/s00146-020-01125-5

Aránguiz, M., Margheri, A., Xu, D., & Tran, B. (2021). International Trade Revolution with Smart Contracts. In *The Digital Transformation of Logistics* (pp. 169–184). Wiley., DOI: 10.1002/9781119646495.ch12

Baricako, J., & Kedir, A. M. (2020). *Disruptive Technology*. Foreign Direct Investment and Private Sector Development Polices in Africa., DOI: 10.1007/978-3-030-40647-9_11

Bhuiyan, M. N., Rahman, M. M., Billah, M. M., & Saha, D. (2021). Internet of Things (IoT): A Review of Its Enabling Technologies in Healthcare Applications, Standards Protocols, Security, and Market Opportunities. *IEEE Internet of Things Journal*, *8*(13), 10474–10498. DOI: 10.1109/JIOT.2021.3062630

Buchter, L. (2021). Escaping the Ellipsis of Diversity: Insider Activists' Use of Implementation Resources to Influence Organization Policy. *Administrative Science Quarterly*, *66*(2), 521–565. DOI: 10.1177/0001839220963633

Capobianco, J. P. (2023). The Keys to Successful Ventures in the Future. In *The New Era of Global Services: A Framework for Successful Enterprises in Business Services and IT* (pp. 33–148). Emerald Publishing Limited., DOI: 10.1108/978-1-83753-626-920231003

Chang, Y., Iakovou, E., & Shi, W. (2020). Blockchain in global supply chains and cross border trade: A critical synthesis of the state-of-the-art, challenges and opportunities. *International Journal of Production Research*, *58*(7), 2082–2099. DOI: 10.1080/00207543.2019.1651946

Cichosz, M., Wallenburg, C. M., & Knemeyer, A. M. (2020). Digital transformation at logistics service providers: Barriers, success factors and leading practices. *International Journal of Logistics Management*, *31*(2), 209–238. DOI: 10.1108/IJLM-08-2019-0229

Costantini, F., Thomopoulos, N., Steibel, F., Curl, A., Lugano, G., & Kováčiková, T. (2020). *Autonomous vehicles in a GDPR era: An international comparison* (pp. 191–213). https://doi.org/DOI: 10.1016/bs.atpp.2020.02.005

Cuervo-Cazurra, A., & Li, C. (2021). State ownership and internationalization: The advantage and disadvantage of stateness. *Journal of World Business*, *56*(1), 101112. DOI: 10.1016/j.jwb.2020.101112

Cunneen, M., Mullins, M., Murphy, F., Shannon, D., Furxhi, I., & Ryan, C. (2020). Autonomous Vehicles and Avoiding the Trolley (Dilemma): Vehicle Perception, Classification, and the Challenges of Framing Decision Ethics. *Cybernetics and Systems*, *51*(1), 59–80. DOI: 10.1080/01969722.2019.1660541

Dasaklis, T. K., & Tsoulfas, G. T. (2024). *The Future of Healthcare Supply Chains: Integrating Industry 4.0 Technologies for Improved Resilience and Sustainability* (pp. 533–551). https://doi.org/DOI: 10.1007/978-3-031-70292-1_25

Díaz-Rodríguez, N., Del Ser, J., Coeckelbergh, M., López de Prado, M., Herrera-Viedma, E., & Herrera, F. (2023). Connecting the dots in trustworthy Artificial Intelligence: From AI principles, ethics, and key requirements to responsible AI systems and regulation. *Information Fusion, 99*, 101896. DOI: 10.1016/j.inffus.2023.101896

Ding, Y., Jin, M., Li, S., & Feng, D. (2021). Smart logistics based on the internet of things technology: An overview. *International Journal of Logistics Research and Applications*, *24*(4), 323–345. DOI: 10.1080/13675567.2020.1757053

Dong, C., Akram, A., Andersson, D., Arnäs, P.-O., & Stefansson, G. (2021). The impact of emerging and disruptive technologies on freight transportation in the digital era: Current state and future trends. *International Journal of Logistics Management*, *32*(2), 386–412. DOI: 10.1108/IJLM-01-2020-0043

Emon, M. M. H. (2025). The Mediating Role of Supply Chain Responsiveness in the Relationship Between Key Supply Chain Drivers and Performance: Evidence from the FMCG Industry. *Brazilian Journal of Operations & Production Management*, *22*(1), 2580. DOI: 10.14488/BJOPM.2580.2025

Emon, M. M. H., & Khan, T. (2025a). The mediating role of attitude towards the technology in shaping artificial intelligence usage among professionals. *Telematics and Informatics Reports*, *17*, 100188. DOI: 10.1016/j.teler.2025.100188

Emon, M. M. H., & Khan, T. (2025b). The transformative role of Industry 4.0 in supply chains: Exploring digital integration and innovation in the manufacturing enterprises. *Journal of Open Innovation*, *11*(2), 100516. DOI: 10.1016/j.joitmc.2025.100516

Ferraris, A., Santoro, G., & Pellicelli, A. C. (2020). "Openness" of public governments in smart cities: Removing the barriers for innovation and entrepreneurship. *The International Entrepreneurship and Management Journal*, *16*(4), 1259–1280. DOI: 10.1007/s11365-020-00651-4

Foroughi, A. (2021). Supply chain workforce training: Addressing the digital skills gap. *Higher Education. Skills and Work-Based Learning*, *11*(3), 683–696. DOI: 10.1108/HESWBL-07-2020-0159

Giannakos, M. N., Mikalef, P., & Pappas, I. O. (2022). Systematic Literature Review of E-Learning Capabilities to Enhance Organizational Learning. *Information Systems Frontiers*, *24*(2), 619–635. DOI: 10.1007/s10796-020-10097-2 PMID: 33551669

Graf, L., & Anner, F. (2021). *Autonomous Vehicles as the Ultimate Efficiency Driver in Logistics.*, DOI: 10.1007/978-3-030-61093-7_15

Gumzej, R. (2021). *Intelligent Logistics Systems for Smart Cities and Communities.* Springer International Publishing., DOI: 10.1007/978-3-030-81203-4

Gupta, B. B., & Quamara, M. (2020). An overview of Internet of Things (IoT): Architectural aspects, challenges, and protocols. *Concurrency and Computation, 32*(21). Advance online publication. DOI: 10.1002/cpe.4946

Hassija, V., Chamola, V., Mahapatra, A., Singal, A., Goel, D., Huang, K., Scardapane, S., Spinelli, I., Mahmud, M., & Hussain, A. (2024). Interpreting Black-Box Models: A Review on Explainable Artificial Intelligence. *Cognitive Computation, 16*(1), 45–74. DOI: 10.1007/s12559-023-10179-8

Herm, L.-V., Janiesch, C., Helm, A., Imgrund, F., Hofmann, A., & Winkelmann, A. (2023). A framework for implementing robotic process automation projects. *Information Systems and e-Business Management, 21*(1), 1–35. DOI: 10.1007/s10257-022-00553-8

Jain, G., Sharma, N., & Shrivastava, A. (2021). Enhancing training effectiveness for organizations through blockchain-enabled training effectiveness measurement (BETEM). *Journal of Organizational Change Management, 34*(2), 439–461. DOI: 10.1108/JOCM-10-2020-0303

Jing, Z., Lu, S., Zhao, Y., & Zhou, J. (2023). Economic policy uncertainty, corporate investment decisions and stock price crash risk: Evidence from China. *Accounting and Finance, 63*(S1), 1477–1502. DOI: 10.1111/acfi.13077

Jithin, P., Arayankalam, J., Rajesh, S. P., & Tiwari, A. K. (2024). Decoding the digital leap: Exploring the role of global value chains in driving country-level digitalization. *Journal of Cleaner Production, 454*, 142208. DOI: 10.1016/j.jclepro.2024.142208

John, L., Patro, R., Padmakala, S., & Madhumala, R. B. (2024). *E-Mobility as a Service and Its Economic Impact.*, DOI: 10.4018/979-8-3693-2611-4.ch003

Khan, A., Jhanjhi, N., Abdulhabeb, G. A. A., Ray, S. K., Ghazanfar, M. A., & Humayun, M. (2024). *Securing IoT Devices Using Generative AI Techniques.*, DOI: 10.4018/979-8-3693-5415-5.ch007

Khan, T., Emon, M. M. H., & Nath, A. (2024). Quantifying the Effects of AI-Driven Inventory Management on Operational Efficiency in Online Retail. *2024 27th International Conference on Computer and Information Technology (ICCIT)*, 2092–2097. https://doi.org/DOI: 10.1109/ICCIT64611.2024.11021996

Khan, T., Emon, M. M. H., & Rahman, S. (2024). Marketing Strategy Innovation via AI Adoption: A Study on Bangladeshi SMEs in the Context of Industry 5.0. *2024 6th International Conference on Sustainable Technologies for Industry 5.0 (STI)*, 1–6. https://doi.org/DOI: 10.1109/STI64222.2024.10951050

Khaw, K. W., & Alnoor, A., AL-Abrrow, H., Tiberius, V., Ganesan, Y., & Atshan, N. A. (2023). Reactions towards organizational change: A systematic literature review. *Current Psychology (New Brunswick, N.J.)*, *42*(22), 19137–19160. DOI: 10.1007/s12144-022-03070-6 PMID: 35431526

Landini, S. (2020). *Ethical Issues*. Cybersecurity and Automated Vehicles., DOI: 10.1007/978-3-030-27386-6_14

Liu, J. (2022). *Development and Prospects of International Logistics in China Under the New Development Paradigm*., DOI: 10.1007/978-981-19-5833-5_10

Mathew, D., Brintha, N. C., & Jappes, J. T. W. (2023). *Artificial Intelligence Powered Automation for Industry 4.0* (pp. 1–28). https://doi.org/DOI: 10.1007/978-3-031-20443-2_1

Mohrman, S. A., & Bartunek, J. M. (2023). *How Can ODC Help Accomplish a Sustainable Future? A Joint Reflection* (pp. 1–26). https://doi.org/DOI: 10.1108/S0897-301620220000030003

Monios, J., & Bergqvist, R. (2020). Logistics and the networked society: A conceptual framework for smart network business models using electric autonomous vehicles (EAVs). *Technological Forecasting and Social Change*, *151*, 119824. DOI: 10.1016/j.techfore.2019.119824

Nag, A., Hassan, M. M., Das, A., Sinha, A., Chand, N., Kar, A., Sharma, V., & Alkhayyat, A. (2024). Exploring the applications and security threats of Internet of Thing in the cloud computing paradigm: A comprehensive study on the cloud of things. *Transactions on Emerging Telecommunications Technologies*, *35*(4). Advance online publication. DOI: 10.1002/ett.4897

Naradda Gamage, S. K., Ekanayake, E. M. S., Abeyrathne, G., Prasanna, R., Jayasundara, J., & Rajapakshe, P. S. K. (2020). A review of global challenges and survival strategies of small and medium enterprises (SMEs). *Economies*, *8*(4), 79.

O'Dwyer, M., Filieri, R., & O'Malley, L. (2023). Establishing successful university–industry collaborations: Barriers and enablers deconstructed. *The Journal of Technology Transfer*, *48*(3), 900–931. DOI: 10.1007/s10961-022-09932-2

Paparini, S., Papoutsi, C., Murdoch, J., Green, J., Petticrew, M., Greenhalgh, T., & Shaw, S. E. (2021). Evaluating complex interventions in context: Systematic, meta-narrative review of case study approaches. *BMC Medical Research Methodology*, *21*(1), 225. DOI: 10.1186/s12874-021-01418-3 PMID: 34689742

Rejeb, A., Keogh, J. G., Leong, G. K., & Treiblmaier, H. (2021). Potentials and challenges of augmented reality smart glasses in logistics and supply chain management: A systematic literature review. *International Journal of Production Research, 59*(12), 3747–3776. DOI: 10.1080/00207543.2021.1876942

Rukanova, B., van Engelenburg, S., Ubacht, J., Tan, Y.-H., Geurts, M., Sies, M., Molenhuis, M., Slegt, M., & van Dijk, D. (2023). Public value creation through voluntary business to government information sharing enabled by digital infrastructure innovations: A framework for analysis. *Government Information Quarterly, 40*(2), 101786. DOI: 10.1016/j.giq.2022.101786

Shahin, M., Maghanaki, M., Hosseinzadeh, A., & Chen, F. F. (2024). Improving operations through a lean AI paradigm: A view to an AI-aided lean manufacturing via versatile convolutional neural network. *International Journal of Advanced Manufacturing Technology, 133*(11–12), 5343–5419. DOI: 10.1007/s00170-024-13874-4

Shee, H. K., Miah, S. J., & De Vass, T. (2021). Impact of smart logistics on smart city sustainable performance: An empirical investigation. *International Journal of Logistics Management, 32*(3), 821–845. DOI: 10.1108/IJLM-07-2020-0282

Shi, J. (2022). Research on Optimization of Cross-Border e-Commerce Logistics Distribution Network in the Context of Artificial Intelligence. *Mobile Information Systems, 2022*, 1–11. DOI: 10.1155/2022/3022280

Sindiramutty, S. R., Jhanjhi, N. Z., Tan, C. E., Khan, N. A., Shah, B., & Manchuri, A. R. (2024). *Cybersecurity Measures for Logistics Industry.*, DOI: 10.4018/979-8-3693-3816-2.ch001

Skalli, D., Cherrafi, A., Charkaoui, A., Chiarini, A., Shokri, A., Antony, J., Garza-Reyes, J. A., & Foster, M. (2024). Integrating Lean Six Sigma and Industry 4.0: Developing a design science research-based LSS4.0 framework for operational excellence. *Production Planning and Control, •••*, 1–27. DOI: 10.1080/09537287.2024.2341698

Tariq, M. U. (2024). *Emerging Trends and Innovations in Blockchain-Digital Twin Integration for Green Investments.*, DOI: 10.4018/979-8-3693-1878-2.ch007

Wang, J., Guo, Q., & Sun, H. (2024). Planning approach for integrating charging stations and renewable energy sources in low-carbon logistics delivery. *Applied Energy, 372*, 123792. DOI: 10.1016/j.apenergy.2024.123792

Wang, R. (2024). Safeguarding Enterprise Prosperity: An In-depth Analysis of Financial Management Strategies. *Journal of the Knowledge Economy, 15*(4), 17676–17704. DOI: 10.1007/s13132-024-01752-z

Widdis, R. W. (2024). Back to the Future: Winnipeg's Reinvention from Borderland Trade and Transportation Gateway to Globalized Trade and Transportation Hub. *Journal of Borderlands Studies*, •••, 1–24. DOI: 10.1080/08865655.2024.2363198

Yele, S., & Litoriya, R. (2024). Blockchain-based secure dining: Enhancing safety, transparency, and traceability in food consumption environment. *Blockchain: Research and Applications*, *5*(2), 100187. DOI: 10.1016/j.bcra.2023.100187

Zhu, Y., Long, L., Liu, W., Shu, P., & Chen, S. (2023). How and when does authentic leadership reduce employee resistance to change? An explanation from uncertainty management theory. *Leadership and Organization Development Journal*, *44*(8), 969–993. DOI: 10.1108/LODJ-03-2023-0155

Zutshi, A., Grilo, A., & Nodehi, T. (2021). The value proposition of blockchain technologies and its impact on Digital Platforms. *Computers & Industrial Engineering*, *155*, 107187. DOI: 10.1016/j.cie.2021.107187

KEY TERMS AND DEFINITIONS

Smart Logistics: Currently organizations leverage IoT and AI along with blockchain and automation solutions to enhance efficiency and environmental sustainability along with transparency within their logistics systems.

Technology Adoption: New technologies get implemented into operational systems through a process that involves substantial cultural along with financial and strategic modification and usage by organizations or individuals.

Supply Chain Innovation: The establishment and implementation of new processes coupled with innovative technologies and business models to boost supply chain performance strength and sustainability.

Organizational Change: Organizations perform deliberate changes to their structures, processes or cultures to deal with internal or external pressures that support successful technology implementation.

Cybersecurity: Digital systems protection against unauthorized access and cyberattacks and breaches depends on employed practices along with technology implementation which is vital for interconnected logistics operations.

Sustainable Logistics: The systematic arrangement of logistics operations identifies environmental reduction measures and supports natural equilibrium maintenance alongside operational effectiveness needs.

Strategic Partnerships: Organizations from multiple sectors create collaborative agreements which enable knowledge sharing and resource collaboration for mutual objective attainment.

Regulatory Compliance: Governments along with industry organizations establish regulatory standards that companies must follow particularly in regions where data protection and transportation security and international logistics function.

Chapter 8
The Intersection of Smart Logistics Technologies and Financial Innovations

Nesrine Gafsi
https://orcid.org/0000-0003-3915-9396
Imam Mohammad Ibn Saud Islamic University, Saudi Arabia

ABSTRACT

Logistics acts as a company's bloodstream, organizing supply chains for production and distribution of goods and services to meet customer demands for the right quantity, cost, location, time, and product. Over time, logistics has evolved to encompass economic activities involving the movement of manufactured goods and capital. However, global transformation presents challenges for modern logistics due to growing demand, rapid urbanization, and increased operational costs, particularly under traditional methods. In response, smart logistics technologies like IoT, drones, LiDAR, blockchain, and AI have emerged alongside financial innovations such as cryptocurrencies and agile supply chain finance. This study explores whether key logistics firms should adopt these innovations. Results indicate that diversifying and integrating smart logistics technologies can provide a competitive edge. The findings emphasize the need for logistics management to proactively embrace smart technologies to boost corporate competitiveness.

INTRODUCTION

Smart logistics lies at the heart of enhancing the efficiency of cross-border trade in global supply chains. This chapter introduces the emergence and prospects of applying smart logistics technologies and related innovations in finance and business

DOI: 10.4018/979-8-3373-2434-0.ch008

models to help build smart logistics infrastructure, in order to achieve seamless interconnectivity in intermodal transportation of cross-border e-commerce. The rapid evolution of smart logistics technologies, which primarily refers to the Internet of Things, big data, artificial intelligence, blockchain, cloud computing, etc., has contributed to a surge and reconfiguration of cross-border e-commerce flows regionalizing products, shortening delivery times, and diminishing stocks-to-sales ratios, while also taking into consideration the fulfillment of personalized products. These technologies, backed by the emergence of new financial models and means, help deepen and broaden global production networks, which lead to upgrading our capacity for serving businesses, cities, and households.

The integration of smart logistics and fintech has emerged as a transformative force in global supply chains, particularly for cross-border e-commerce. Smart logistics technologies enable real-time tracking, predictive analytics, and automated decision-making, significantly reducing operational friction (Wang et al., 2016). Concurrently, fintech innovations such as blockchain-based payments, dynamic financing, and smart contracts streamline financial flows, allowing capital to align precisely with logistical milestones (Gomber et al., 2017). Research by Saberi et al. (2019) demonstrates that blockchain-enhanced supply chains can reduce documentation delays by 70%, while IoT-driven inventory systems minimize stockouts by 35% (Atzori et al., 2010). Despite these advances, critical gaps persist in understanding how these domains interoperate under regulatory heterogeneity, especially for small and medium enterprises (SMEs) navigating cross-border compliance. This chapter bridges these gaps by proposing unified frameworks for scalable, resilient, and sustainable logistics-finance ecosystems.

Furthermore, the rapid deployment of 5G networks and edge computing has accelerated real-time data processing for logistics operations, yet interoperability between legacy systems and AI-driven platforms remains fragmented. Cybersecurity vulnerabilities in integrated IoT-fintech ecosystems expose supply chains to systemic risks (Chen et al., 2024). These challenges underscore the urgency for standardized protocols that harmonize technical, financial, and regulatory dimensions across jurisdictions.

This chapter aims to examine the synergies between smart logistics technologies such as primarily the Internet of Things, big data, artificial intelligence, blockchain, and cloud computing and fintech innovations to optimize cross-border e-commerce supply chains, proposing frameworks for interconnected infrastructure that enables seamless intermodal transportation while quantifying impacts such as regionalized product flows, shortened delivery times, reduced inventory ratios, and enhanced mass customization capabilities, alongside assessing scalability for global production networks serving businesses, cities, and households; however, critical gaps persist in the literature, including the absence of integrated operational frameworks synchronizing financial and logistical systems in real-time, insufficient analysis of cross-border regulatory mechanics governing fintech-logistics convergence.

Object of the Chapter

- The chapter introduces the emergence and prospects of applying smart logistics technologies and related innovations in finance (fintech) and business models.
- It aims to show how these help build smart logistics infrastructure for seamless interconnectivity in intermodal transportation (especially for cross-border e-commerce).
- It highlights how these technologies and financial innovations lead to regionalizing products, shortening delivery times, reducing stocks-to-sales ratios, and fulfilling personalized products.
- Ultimately, it seeks to demonstrate how this integration deepens and broadens global production networks, enhancing service capacity for businesses, cities, and households.

OVERVIEW OF SMART LOGISTICS TECHNOLOGIES AND FINANCIAL INNOVATIONS

fintech innovations serve as critical enablers of sustainable finance, particularly through mobile banking and digital payment platforms that expand financial inclusion while reducing the carbon footprint of traditional banking infrastructure across the continent (Hlali & Gafsi, 2024). Thus, the intersection of smart logistics technologies and financial innovations discusses how the intelligent logistics technologies embracing the latest significant breakthroughs of Industry 4.0 may intersect with the up-to-date financial innovations at the present time and in the future. Let us clarify the key keywords employed there, i.e., smart finance and smart logistics. Unlike many researchers who emphasize the concept of an "intelligent investor" in finance, our research goes deep into the field of finance and considers more factors; for example, when and how a financial instrument or a financial market becomes "smart" enough. In parallel, as logistics employs an integrated business model, this book also encompasses such complicated networks, structures, or destinations in the physical and the cyber world, providing detailed and global coverage from moderation to postmodern portfolios that help smart investors. The economic effect of having an embedded perspective of smart logistics technology and finance may appear very promising conceptually; the impact and potential economic benefit associated with such integration are more complex due to the interdisciplinary research which is currently based largely on traditional finance and operations management (Helo & Thai, 2024).

Blockchain finance and the blockchain technology underneath are the best representatives of smart finance and smart logistics technologies, respectively, at the present time. Although the blockchain company vision may involve big business, small-to-medium-sized enterprises actually find that applying these new technologies is not that easy in two aspects. Blockchain's features, including transparency and decentralization, security and effectiveness, shed light on the essence of modern supply chains that involve many stakeholders, including venture capitalists and other business angels who provide the funding for small-medium enterprises' further development (Mustafa et al.2025).

In an era of rapid technological advancement and global interconnectedness, supply chains are undergoing profound transformations. Digital innovations such as artificial intelligence (AI), blockchain, the Internet of Things (IoT), and big data analytics enable real-time visibility, predictive decision-making, and automation throughout the supply chain. These developments drive efficiency, resilience, and customer responsiveness in volatile markets. Financial innovations including supply chain finance (SCF), dynamic discounting, and fintech-based solutions enhance liquidity, optimize working capital, and fortify supplier-buyer relationships by democratizing access to financing, especially for smaller firms. Recent studies (Hlali, 2023) focus on port infrastructure and logistics quality as key components of supply chain digital innovation in the Mediterranean context. The econometric analysis of 15 Mediterranean countries (2010–2018) founded that improvements in logistics quality and competence significantly influence port infrastructure development, while the structure of the economy (e.g., manufacturing value-add) also plays a moderate role. Earlier, (Hlali & Wanis, 2020), presented a descriptive model of container port logistics, highlighting the critical integration of physical, financial, and informational flows across the supply chain. Together, these digital and financial innovations combined with domain-specific insights to represent a paradigm shift enabling more intelligent, agile, and adaptive supply chains. For firms seeking to remain competitive and resilient amid global disruptions, harnessing both technological advances and innovative financing models, grounded in robust logistics infrastructure, is increasingly a strategic imperative.

THE DIGITIZATION OF GLOBAL SUPPLY CHAINS

While the digitization of supply chains is a recent phenomenon, it is also not yet a universal phenomenon. Such digitized supply chains enable the capture of vast streams of data across multiple entities and the use of this data to track value and inventory down the global supply chain to show that the owner of the money was the owner of the goods. This digitization is essential in enabling banks to play a greater role in such supply chains. Making supply chain activities and events "discrete" and thus unique and with a particular value is a requisite for the application of blockchain (Sallam et al.2023).

The evolution of software as a service to advanced analytics as a service is cutting the barriers to entry for companies of all sizes and allowing them to exploit the data to greater effect. These technologies may also be applied to supply chains to control not only the physical activities but also the funding of these activities (Frikha and Hlali 2023). Governments of countries are breaking down traditional sources of information risk and using big data to inform banks on the trustworthiness of borrowers. The combination of enhanced data and technological, policy, and institutional innovations is therefore important if banks are to play a greater role in the digitized smart supply chains many wish to see (Hardik, 2024).

- **Trends and Drivers in Supply Chain Digitization**

The beginning of digital transformation in logistics dates back to the late 20th century. It was first determined by step technologies in material handling equipment and simple control systems in warehouse equipment, allowing for automated guidance of forklifts and other handling machines. Gradually, more sophisticated automated systems were implemented in relevant software modules, such as warehouse management systems. Then, thanks to communication systems, they were united in a hierarchy of warehouse management software suites (Omol, 2024).

These solutions were oriented at optimizing daily operations, carrying out routine tasks, eliminating errors during the handover of material flow stages to the manual labor force, and managing inventories by updating their data upon new items and new cycles of activities. Hence, the primary objectives of the implemented complex of digital technologies lay in supporting full command and control over the material flow. Subsequently, the process of automation spread over transportation technologies with the aim of moving away from silo strategies in solving issues related to warehouse logistics, transportation, procurement, and production.

ROLE OF FINANCE IN SMART LOGISTICS

Finance is a critical force that drives companies to upgrade and modernize their logistics activities. Indeed, the escalating logistics operating and technology costs have retarded the development of some vital, emerging national economies. As a result, the conductivity of physical goods has become much more developed than their internet information in recent years. Consequently, the financial flows have surpassed those of physical goods in an increasing number of advanced national economies. Finance is expected to energize companies in establishing smart logistics technologies to reduce logistic operating costs, create lasting positive impacts on the associated economies, and possibly accelerate their growth (Islam et al.2024).

Smart logistics technologies are a subsumption of partial technologies designated for the efficient performance of logistics functions. That is, a smart logistics system conveys cutting-edge technologies in computing, material handling, transport/vehicle movement, and ergonomics, and/or physical facilities. Many realized smart logistics technologies can generate benefits in the reputational, safety, social, organizational, management, operational, information, service, monitoring, and quantitative aspects. They can change the operation levels of a logistics chain, a transportation network, a materials handling system, and warehouses or any device handling logistics, with many new implications. Their innovation can be viewed as emerging from Keeping Current, the third activity in the DIKW model (Lustenberger and Spychiger 2025).

- **Enabling and Optimizing Smart Logistics**

With the developing Internet of Things and big data analysis technologies, intelligent logistics has gradually entered people's sight, and its application field continues to expand. Smart logistics refers to the intelligent management technology that innovatively applies the Internet of Things, big data, cloud computing, and other technologies to facilitate close organization, efficient production, accurate packaging, rapid sorting, standard transportation, and flexible conveying, combining various types of reasonable logistics methods to achieve intelligent logistics through information, technology, and intelligence, which is supervised and managed by a highly integrated logistics information platform throughout the logistics process. The application of intelligent logistics in the financial field can quickly understand the operating status of the supply chain. The combination of multi-financial technology increases efficiency and reduces the cost of financing. Smart logistics is the application of the Internet of Things, cloud computing, and other technologies in traditional logistics, which can optimize business processes and improve operational efficiency on three levels. 1) The first level is the hardware level, which refers to the platform for classifying, tracking, and collecting data with sensors, thousands of eyes, barcode scanners, and RFID in the warehouses, containers, and vehicles. 2) The second level is the software level, including WMS that uses computer technology to replace manual management, reducing the cost of warehousing management and improving the response speed of the enterprise. MIS uses large-scale or joint machine decision-making to respond to dynamic changes in the business environment and supply chain management, as well as supply chain link management. 3) The third level is to upgrade intelligent applications, such as robots, unmanned devices, and QR codes, to optimize business processes (Sun et al.2022).

FINANCIAL TECHNOLOGIES (FINTECH) IN LOGISTICS

- Traditional banking services for smart transportation, logistics, and supply chain execution

Transportation, logistics, and supply chain processes generate large intercompany cash flows primarily within the transportation industry. In connection with cargo and transportation execution, financial institutions, being traditional intermediaries of logistics and transport companies, provide a relatively large number of traditional products and services for settlements, management of temporary free financial resources, and financial assistance. There are settlements for freight transportation, storage, and customs clearance, temporary resource management in swap deals, participation in repurchase agreements, financing trade in commodities and freight derivatives, and cash flow financing under freight transportation contracts. However, cash management of logistics and transportation companies, the formation of their own capital, and the redistribution of financial resources are not the core activities of these industry executives. Traditionally, in the LLP and TSL, the influence of the financial department on the financial results of the company is concealed. They provided only information about the movement of funds (Tiwari et al.2023).

APPLICATIONS OF FINTECH IN LOGISTICS

Following the rapid developments in computer, communication, and sensor technologies, logistics services worldwide have evolved dramatically. As with other service industries, the advancement in information technologies has effectively democratized access to global logistics and supply chain networks. The effects are far-reaching. Lower transaction costs and increased global specialization from more efficient handling of goods as they move around the world have helped countries improve economic welfare. In addition, logistics operations are major contributors to air pollution, road congestion, and noise pollution. The advances in logistics technology oftcn go hand in hand with the improvement of energy usage and waste disposal. While an increase in logistics activity would exacerbate the environmental challenges posed by the industry, further application of state-of-the-art technology could make the industry cleaner and more energy-efficient while still enjoying economic expansion. From the business processes led by technology, there seems to be a bigger focus on financially driven innovations in logistics technology in recent years (Goodarzi et al.2024). The Technology concepts that have been given specific finance-driven titles. The logistics process appears never to have seen such brand imagination, whereas potentially significant financial innovations are being created and embedded into logistics technologies. First, the cost of logistics operations. Automated trust calculation in blockchain and distributed ledger technology incurs an expensive cost in logistics. Predictive visa frameworks leverage blockchain technology to embed greater trust into transit visas, facilitating the export of goods by connecting financial smart contracts with border controls. The transportation payment systems aim to reduce financial barriers, promote good cash flow, and establish trading relationships between shipping parties across the supply chain. With digital payment services now on the increase, functioning on various platforms including alternative payment platforms and cryptocurrencies, we will see more logistics technologies applying these systems to curtail the cost of business transactions during logistics operations (Fareed et al., 2024).

DYNAMIC PRICING MODELS IN SMART LOGISTICS

In smart logistics practices, transportation prices dynamically respond to behavioral performance and real-time market variations. For instance, the parking of large transport vehicles may evidently benefit logistic transportation efficiency by reducing queuing time and congestion. This paper designs a dynamic approval time; late parking fee game model between a platform and heterogeneous drivers, leading to an optimal price policy. In short, our study determines how the game structure and the resulting input-output function shape key factors of the transport and closing policy. The real-time attainment status of vehicles determines the delay or denied utilization of busy parking places. We further estimate the equilibrium failure thresholds and the driver utilization rate under different pricing strategies and time-variant demand-supply conditions. Finally, the optimal transport and parking service policy found can not only effectively solve the dynamic empty-circle logistic problem but also alleviate the severe congestion and vehicular pollution problems currently associated with the urban allocation of large transport vehicles (Chen et al., 2024).

The billing policy of both logistic transportation and inventory management, as well as the dynamic commercial vehicle parking problem, is yet to be deeply researched. For the dynamic pricing justification analysis of the truck parking problem, an influential bottleneck issue closely related to the urban environment and the city's availability of comprehensive integrated corridors would be a lack of relatively ample empirical data. A policy study on traffic simulation systems and the marketing of integrated transportation hubs has already been conducted, assuming that the demand and provision of truck parking spaces will exist only if there are appropriate different types of customers willing to pay certain prices. The research results indicate that dynamic truck parking policies can help solve urban problems related to static truck parking pricing, such as traffic congestion peaks and underutilization of residual parking resources. Dynamic quality mapping and service selection for the Two-Sided Transportation Problem for urban areas with different levels of intelligent transport systems and smart logistics technology development have established a quantitative exploration framework, with the aim of solving the problem from both the physical service advertiser and the potential service consumer's perspectives over different planning stages. The mapping methodology addresses the travel time uncertainty and provision of personalized comfort service focus hypothesis. In lean results-driven logistics performance analyses of a complete day's data set, the average time impingement, average time cost, and variability of the total travel time service have been commonly valued as the intrinsic disadvantage concern of most carriers. The resource solo operator has, however, been excluded from the typical evaluation of the fairness of truck parking service. In a progressive battery performance optimization context, the role selection of battery switching service or gradual degradation service providers in smart parking lots can be considered. Some of the results give more attention to the impact of the meterage system and transport logistics risk management than the congestion pricing effects do. In the United States, there is low demand for parking technology evaluation, and this study is intended to estimate possible benefits. Although developed primarily for parking pricing, the tool can also be applied to both freight and passenger transportation pricing to assess the perceived burden and provide guidance on the implementation. (Kujawski & Nürnberg, 2023)

- Benefits and Challenges of Dynamic Pricing

The finance sector is at varying stages of digitization compared to the rest of the economy, with focus on customer-facing activities and back-office processes driven by expert systems. Nevertheless, when it comes to financial decisions, the most promising use cases for AI involve bulk-produced models that work at scale. AI's laboriousness, expensiveness, lack of singularity generalization, and dependence on data history limit its full sway over financial processes as we know them today. It includes dynamic pricing; however, the advantages of dynamic pricing on price-setting is not only compelling on the grounds of pricing but also what it teaches us about users' valuation. However, there are consequences for these perks (Williams, 2021).

Exploring the Pros and Cons Relative to Pricing Strategies. Dynamic pricing is about having your margins and eating them too. In marginal pricing, profits are 20-140% versus 5-15%. Dynamic pricing based on value could upturn income 20-40% and profit by as much as 50-100%. Dynamic pricing in traditional sectors such as hotels and airlines is more common than with buying ketchup at a supermarket, but let's also mention that fancy, dynamic pricing is also a go to, whenever such mechanisms can extract more from consumers. Their pricing efficiency is so high that it actually serves as a precursor to the well-known Coase theorem, which holds that the nature of the property right determines the set of potential solutions to problems related to the use of that property right (Ratanabanchuen et al.2024).

Dynamic pricing like other algorithm-based decisions uses data. They encompass much more than just the item purchased; they include previous purchases, location of purchases, usage of purchases, customer reaction to the product, weather, demand for the product and customer reaction to the pricing. At the heart of a decent dynamic pricing model lies converting pieces of data into "pull factors," the true worth of the item. The continuous evaluation of new events is required to filter out noise from useful signals (Seele et al.2021). No one truly understands these dynamic pricing laws, and they consequently fail in practice. Clients are agitated to see prices rising where the base line hasn't risen. The Federal Pamela may impose payment for inaccurate reports that will harm consumers' costs. Dynamic pricing optimization is a do-or-die exercise that forfeits sales volume rebates. Problems regarding availability, transparency, investor apprehensiveness, and legality might crop up while it's done. There is another potential fly in the ointment, which we shall confront at the end of this section: it is always tempting to mimic the models that yield outsized returns until they manifestly do not (Pautassi, 2024).

BLOCKCHAIN-BASED TRANSACTIONS IN LOGISTICS

- Transaction costs in logistics. Firms consider the costs they incur when they transact with other firms to buy and sell goods and/or services. These transaction costs are inclusive of the costs to locate a party suitable for a transaction, the needed information, and to negotiate and enter into a contract for a deal. In the field of logistics, transaction costs constitute the prominent portion of logistics costs. When trade is concerned, these transaction costs involve decorrelation, geographical dispersion, and problems of intermediation. Optimizing the logistics triangle that joins trade policy reform with the transport and logistics infrastructure should then be at the heart of the trade facilitation strategy. In this way, efficient logistics facilitate trade relations in services and investments (Agi & Jha, 2022).

- Blockchain technology in logistics transactions. Information asymmetry as well as transaction and decision-making delays and error risks can be solved through the use of blockchain technology. It integrates into a single management system the information and document flows that accompany a business process. Since blockchain technology creates a single environment for electronic document management in a deal, it leads to a substantial reduction in the costs of labor and time required to conduct logistic support for companies. This reduction becomes an important factor in controlling the transaction costs for partnerships and trade between companies across all manufacturing sectors. Upon transition to blockchain-driven single-document execution of a supply chain, transaction costs fall through an increase in contractual compliance from all shipment participants. A significant cost reduction can be achieved. This is achieved by minimizing the duration of administrative procedures (Javaid et al.2022).
- Key Features and Advantages of Blockchain in Logistics

At present, the trend of international smart logistics development is that a rapidly increasing number of reconstruction plans based on smart logistics share the resources of different enterprises through cooperation. This shift can: - reduce logistics costs, shorten the time of value realization, and provide customers with more bespoke services; - ensure the efficient and safe operation of the national economic system; - improve social and ecological benefits. Upgrading the logistics cooperation model by using blockchain can empower smart logistics financially. On the one hand, smart logistics is decentralized and contains multiple subjects position able in the supply chain, such as distribution lines, warehousing, transportation, customs and tax, online stores, and business banks. On the other hand, these can combine digital and real international logistics and create a “door-to-door” blockchain. By doing so, the real economy can be connected to digital finance to reduce logistics costs and realize an innovative breakthrough (Allioui et al., 2024).

In view of the core financial service model of blockchain in the actual economy, the main practical model of blockchain is to link the accounts of banks, commercial enterprises, and customs. In particular, an enterprise can pay a warehouse management fee or a handling fee, deducting and paying wages through blockchain, thus shortening the time the employer waits to receive the fee and realizing value returns. Banks can use the demand convenience and personal data to match the loans, improve the business operational supply chain, and reduce the risk. Customs can collect data in real time, optimize the declaration, and improve the financial process (Javaid et al.2022).

PREDICTIVE ANALYTICS IN LOGISTICS OPERATIONS

This chapter focuses on how the use of predictive algorithms is becoming more prevalent in various logistics operations. Working based on the concept of using data and mathematical algorithms to forecast unknown events, predictive analytics plays an important role in the improvement of responsiveness and automation in logistics operations. Data-driven logistics now relies on predictive analytics as a core success factor. This chapter reviews the state of the art in predictive analytics in various logistics operations, including demand forecasting, predictive inventory planning, predictive demand-driven supply chain risk management, machine failure condition monitoring, predictive operations and maintenance in logistics facilities, and predictive smart distribution of deliveries. The potential application of some existing predictive algorithms developed for relevant applications is studied and summarized. Following this, the future implications of this research on predictive analytics in logistics are outlined (Li et al.2024).

Forecasting events that are unknown is a process of using data and mathematical algorithms for predictive analytics. Utilizing some known event data, we build a mathematical model based on predictive analytics, take the model to apply to unknown further future event data and give reliable forecasts. There are numerous hurdles predicted events along with uncertainties, complex dynamics, unknown features, temporal constraints, and the fact that they must be resolved in real time. For solving these problems, tons of models are proposed according to different real-world applications, for modeling time series, for characterizing dynamic probabilistic transition, for page characteristics of sequence modeling, neural networks, etc. (Neu et al., 2022).

- *Use Cases and Benefits of Predictive Analytics*

This part explores the advantages and workings of sophisticated data analytics in logistics, such as prescriptive, predictive, and descriptive analysis. Even two fundamental descriptive questions, such as 'What was our standard turnaround time?' and 'How did it compare to that of our competitors?' require both historical and competitor datasets to answer with confidence. With predictive analytics, inventory can save money as its closing calculation is not only based on real transaction numbers but also on quantified expected demand and expected demand variability. The field of predictive supply chain analytics requires frequent performance data for predicting modes or services, and it is becoming more complex in reflection of the currently increasing number of data-driven demand and supply prediction approaches available. It is beneficial whenever a company is dealing with future delivery speed commitments, such as given offer commitment timeframes, financial forecasts, or as inventory operators with buffer sizing (Pasupuleti et al., 2024).

- *Case Studies in Finance-Driven Logistics Strategies*

The proposed finance-driven smart logistics strategies have been based on various aspects of review and models introduced, and applied to a real case of conglomerate companies. Longer examples and more complex systems are possible but require selection of appropriate models and methods for companies and for particular phases or steps. Additionally, of course, a clear definition of the links with capital market regulations and requirements is also important. However, the intent of this chapter is to clarify the achievability of practical results, by way of an illustrative simple example of company-leveraged supply chain finance. These short examples demonstrate in a very straightforward way the generalizations provided in this present chapter and show that companies can simply use the financial market to leverage their relationships with their immediate supply chain and leverage, by conjunction, the relationships among all members of their supply network (Gao et al.2024).

Here, without loss of generality, it is assumed that a supplier, a financial investor, a general, and a first-tier customer are direct parties to a finance-driven supply chain finance strategy. Consequently, the following remarks can be written with reference to the names of the parties. For a formal procedure in the supply chain finance process, generally the preexisting account receivables held by General Co. are appropriately sold at the liquidity discount rate set by the financial investors. This operation is proxy-based, using an audit of the resources within the abstract hierarchy, a check on the main history of customer payments, an internal analysis of the creditworthiness evolution of the parties involved in the sales contract, and with the set and regularization of customer payments, the possibility of intervening in the fulfillment of the sales contract by commercial intermediaries (Durach et al.2024).

- **Enhanced Efficiency and Cost Reduction**

Smart logistics technologies contribute to both cost reduction and efficiency improvement of logistics activities. RFID, WSN, and other similar technologies increase the precision and real-time grasp of logistics transportation and goods location. Algorithms and software systems can improve the utilization of logistics resources and workload distribution, optimize logistics business processes, and reduce transportation distance and time. Embedded sensors and communication devices in vehicles, transportation equipment, and goods can offer real-time monitoring, control, and management of vehicle working status, transportation safety, and quality assurance, as well as the quality of perishable and special items, and delays occurring from abnormal and dangerous events. With the help of cloud computing, multimedia technology applications, and high-speed Internet, supply chain partners can conduct efficient communication, cooperation, and relationships in wireless mode. These high-quality tools can provide strong support for both traditional and modern transportation/storage businesses such as freight transportation, material management, household moving, and e-commerce distribution (Sun et al.2022) (Prakash et al.2024).

Cost is the primary consideration in today's business competitive concerns. Transportation expenses account for 25-30 percent of national GDP. Smart logistics technologies can effectively reduce vehicle driving distance and loading rate, empty return of vehicles, oil consumption, adverse cargo selection, delivery mistakes, overtime spent, and customs clearance time, bringing the logistics start date forward and improving timely benefits. With the assistance of DSS, all these operational cost reductions and efficiency improvements will also be vastly increased. For example, a prospective good-oriented simulation optimization transportation routing scheduling system based on GIS has been utilized in a paper on post office delivery sortation systems. Their findings showed that 17 transport vehicles will be saved for every ten thousand pieces of a specific type of goods. It made the route optimization system help the enterprise reduce the OPEX to a minimal amount per piece and improve the service level simultaneously because it guarantees delivery before a specified time point. Therefore, the delivery process was optimized to increase the transport DC utilization rates as high as possible at a given cost, enhancing delivery efficiency and decreasing economic loss in different places (Mvelase & Ferrer, 2024).

IMPROVED DECISION-MAKING IN LOGISTICS OPERATIONS

Companies are increasing their capacity to make informed decisions by bringing together the most advanced artificial intelligence capabilities and a logistics-focused talent pool. They are using data lake technology to host transaction-ready data. They have adopted DataOps for agile data management and have built high-performance management dashboards that use machine learning and advanced diagnostics to support efficient decision-making. In marketing, the use of A/B testing has increased the efficacy of sales initiatives. Today's powerful decision-making tools can now be effectively applied to a broad array of business challenges. A business's logistics operations offer multiple opportunities for the efficient application of these new tools. It is well known that when logistics operations work in a coordinated and agile way, they can add a lot of value to what is a complex business. However, many firms remain sub-optimized because managers are waiting for data. It is widely noted that there is an ongoing drive to use blockchain technology to anchor end-to-end supply chains, providing continuity of data throughout the lifecycle of business transactions. Only by having the right data ready at the right time is it possible to monitor costs, head off logistical obstacles, and track business performance in real time (Pattanayak et al.2024).

- **Role of Financial Innovations in Decision-Making**

Today, the transformation of operating companies by introducing smart logistic systems is inconceivable without financing and investing significant resources in this transformation process. At the same time, financial innovations become a strategic decision in the provision of smart logistics and contribute to the companies' competitiveness under the conditions of the digital economy amid increasing financial scarcity of micro and macro components. The variety of financing and investing in smart logistics poses the need for the formation of a set of financial-institutional mechanisms focused on the market of financial services. Bearing in mind the problem of financial breakthroughs for operating companies, the issue of profitability and risk retention, with a significant focus on the welfare of business owners, the interaction of smart logistics technologies and the financial capacity of the current world is significant. The greater effectiveness of smart logistics implementation through stimulating financial innovation to a large extent may depend on the fleeting strategies of transformation, the promotion of internal resources, internal data, and the technology of business processes. Smart logistics have great potential to provide business benefits for companies operating in different areas and at different levels. By using smart logistics, they can optimize their processes and make both controlled and innovative decisions based on internal data technologies and external data flows. The choice of technological solutions in ensuring the process of direct knowledge is limited by the current financial capacity of the companies. In addition to current business growth, smart logistics will significantly increase business efficiency and require continuous testing of technology adapted to the changing needs of the company's activities. Funding and investing in smart logistics become events that follow the activities of managers, the timing of financial events, and the financial economy to ensure the integrity of the business. In the process of implementing smart logistics, business owners and managers are expected to have an increasing number of external activities by applying greater coordination complexity in the types of management relations and implementing the concept of capital cost (Raza et al., 2023).

SUSTAINABILITY AND GREEN LOGISTICS: ENVIRONMENTAL INTEGRATION THROUGH TECHNOLOGY AND FINANCE

The integration of sustainability principles into smart logistics and fintech represents a transformative evolution in global supply chains, driven by the urgent need to reconcile operational efficiency with ecological stewardship. This paradigm leverages IoT sensors for real-time emissions monitoring across transport modalities such as maritime, rail, and road freight, while blockchain technology creates immutable ledgers that record carbon footprints at each logistical node, enabling granular accountability and transparency (Gafsi & Louhichi, 2025; Sun et al., 2022). For instance, IoT-enabled devices track fuel consumption, idle times, and route inefficiencies, feeding data into AI algorithms that dynamically optimize delivery paths to avoid congestion and reduce greenhouse gas emissions by up to 20% (Chen et al., 2024). Concurrently, fintech innovations like tokenized carbon credits allow firms to trade verified emissions offsets transparently, incentivizing low-carbon practices through market mechanisms (Gafsi, 2025). Sustainability-linked loans further embed environmental KPIs into financial instruments, where interest rates adjust automatically based on real-time IoT metrics like fleet electrification rates or renewable energy usage in warehouses, thus aligning capital costs with ecological performance (Gafsi, 2025). Circular economy models are revolutionized through AI-driven reverse logistics systems that predict product return flows and optimize remanufacturing schedules, while smart contracts automate payments upon blockchain-verified recycling milestones, reducing waste and virgin material dependency (Sun et al., 2022). Policy-technology synergies are critical here: digital compliance platforms integrate ESG reporting standards across jurisdictions, automating submissions for regulations like the EU Carbon Border Adjustment Mechanism (CBAM) via unified data lakes that merge customs, tax, and emissions records (Hlali & Gafsi, 2024). Public-private partnerships (PPPs) amplify these advances, as seen in Kenya's Mombasa port initiative, where solar-powered smart warehouses and blockchain-enabled clearance systems cut processing times by 40% while slashing carbon output (Omol, 2024). Crucially, this sustainability integration regionalizes supply chains by prioritizing localized sourcing hubs—reducing transport distances and stocks-to-sales ratios through AI-demand forecasting—while offering consumers carbon-neutral last-mile delivery options, thus balancing efficiency, equity, and planetary boundaries (Gafsi & Louhichi, 2025; Saberi et al., 2019).

CONCLUSION

The integration of smart logistics and fintech represents a paradigm shift in global supply chain management, unlocking transformative efficiencies through synchronized data flows, automated decision-making, and secure transactional frameworks. While these innovations demonstrably enhance operational resilience and market responsiveness (Gafsi, 2025b), their full potential remains constrained by enduring challenges: regulatory misalignment across jurisdictions, systemic cybersecurity vulnerabilities, and unintended socioeconomic disparities in technology adoption (Gafsi, 2025). Future evolution demands collaborative stewardship. Embedding sustainability as a core architectural principle will further ensure that efficiency gains align with ecological stewardship and equitable growth (Gafsi & Louhichi, 2025; Gafsi, 2025). As these domains mature, their convergence promises to redefine supply chains as dynamic, self-regulating ecosystems where capital and goods fluidly traverse global networks.

The chapter analysis reveals that the integration of smart logistics and fintech fundamentally reconfigures global supply chains by synergizing physical and financial workflows into a unified digital ecosystem. Key findings demonstrate that:

- **Operational Efficiency**: IoT-driven tracking and blockchain-automated documentation eliminate traditional bottlenecks, reducing transit delays and administrative overhead.
- **Financial Fluidity**: Dynamic financing mechanisms enhance capital agility, enabling just-in-time liquidity for suppliers and carriers (Gafsi, 2025).
- **Regulatory Friction**: Jurisdictional disparities in data governance and digital compliance protocols emerge as primary barriers, particularly for SMEs engaging in cross-border trade.
- **Systemic Vulnerabilities**: Convergence amplifies cybersecurity risks, with IoT-fintech interfaces creating exploitable attack surfaces that demand zero-trust architectural frameworks.
- **Socioeconomic Impact**: Algorithmic bias in AI-driven demand forecasting perpetuates resource allocation imbalances, disproportionately affecting smaller enterprises in emerging markets (Gafsi, 2025).
- **Sustainability Synergies**: Embedded carbon ledger protocols within blockchain transactions enable granular emissions tracking, proving that environmental accountability can cocxist with cfficiency gains (Gafsi, 2025; Gafsi & Louhichi, 2025).

Furthermore, the study establishes a positive correlation between integrated technology deployment and sustainable outcomes, specifically, when environmental metrics are natively embedded in these systems, they enable measurable reductions in supply chain carbon footprints. These findings collectively underscore the necessity for harmonized standards that balance efficiency, security, and equity. These findings collectively affirm that successful integration hinges on tripartite collaboration among policymakers, technologists, and financial institutions, prioritizing interoperability, ethical AI, and inclusive design to transform supply chains into resilient, equitable networks.

REFERENCES

Agi, M. A. N., & Jha, A. K. (2022). Blockchain technology in the supply chain: An integrated theoretical perspective of organizational adoption. *International Journal of Production Economics*. Advance online publication. DOI: 10.1016/j.ijpe.2022.108458

Allioui, H., Allioui, A., & Mourdi, Y. (2024). *Maintaining effective logistics management during and after COVID-19 pandemic: survey on the importance of artificial intelligence to enhance recovery strategies*. OPSEARCH., DOI: 10.1007/s12597-023-00728-y

Atzori, L., Iera, A., & Morabito, G. (2010). The Internet of Things: A survey. *Computer Networks*, *54*(15), 2787–2805. DOI: 10.1016/j.comnet.2010.05.010

Chen, Q., Lei, Y., & Jasin, S. (2024). Real-time spatial–intertemporal pricing and relocation in a ride-hailing network: Near-optimal policies and the value of dynamic pricing. *Operations Research*. Advance online publication. DOI: 10.1287/opre.2022.2425

Chen, W., Men, Y., Fuster, N., Osorio, C., & Juan, A. A. (2024). Artificial Intelligence in Logistics Optimization with Sustainable Criteria: A Review. *Sustainability*, *16*(21), 9145. DOI: 10.3390/su16219145

Durach, C. F., Peers, Y., Wang, Y., & Repasky, T. (2024). Mitigating upstream disruptions: Effects of extended inventories in first-and second-tier suppliers. *Journal of Operations Management*, *70*(8), 1261–1285. DOI: 10.1002/joom.1332

Fareed, A. G., De Felice, F., Forcina, A., & Petrillo, A. (2024). Role and applications of advanced digital technologies in achieving sustainability in multimodal logistics operations: A systematic literature review. *Sustainable Futures : An Applied Journal of Technology, Environment and Society*. Advance online publication. DOI: 10.1016/j.sftr.2024.100278

Frikha, R., & Hlali, A. (2023). The evolution of logistics management toward the digital transition. International Journal of Commerce. *Industry and Entrepreneurship Studies*, *3*, 66–75.

Gafsi, N. (2025). Analysing the impact of renewable energy use, CO_2 emissions, oil production, and oil prices on sustainable economic growth: Evidence from Saudi Arabia using the ARDL approach. *Edelweiss Applied Science and Technology*, *9*(5), 2317–2326. DOI: 10.55214/25768484.v9i5.7465

Gafsi, N. (2025). Machine Learning Approaches to Credit Risk: Comparative Evidence from Participation and Conventional Banks in the UK. *Journal of Risk and Financial Management, 18*(7), 345. DOI: 10.3390/jrfm18070345

Gafsi, N. (2025). The Role of Customer and Market Orientation in Enhancing Islamic Insurance Performance: Evidence from Tunisia. *Journal of Ecohumanism, 4*(2), 2429. DOI: 10.62754/joe.v4i2.6636

Gafsi, N., & Louhichi, L. (2025). Role of green finance in sustainable energy transition and economic growth in MENA region. *Edelweiss Applied Science and Technology, 9*(6), 1704–1717. DOI: 10.55214/25768484.v9i6.8216

Gao, H., Kou, G., Liang, H., Zhang, H., Chao, X., Li, C. C., & Dong, Y. (2024). Machine learning in business and finance: A literature review and research opportunities. *Financial Innovation, 10*(1), 86. DOI: 10.1186/s40854-024-00629-z

Gomber, P., Koch, J.-A., & Siering, M. (2017). Digital Finance and FinTech: Current research and future research directions. *Journal of Business Economics, 87*(5), 537–580. DOI: 10.1007/s11573-017-0852-x

Goodarzi, A. H., Jabbarzadeh, A., Fahimnia, B., & Paquet, M. (2024). Evaluating the sustainability and resilience of an intermodal transport network leveraging consolidation strategies. *Transportation Research Part E, Logistics and Transportation Review, 188*, 103616. DOI: 10.1016/j.tre.2024.103616

Hardik, N. (2024). Digitalisation promotes adoption of soft information in SME credit evaluation: The case of Indian banks. *Digital Finance*. Advance online publication. DOI: 10.1007/s42521-023-00078-w PMID: 37362067

Helo, P., & Thai, V. V. (2024). Logistics 4.0–digital transformation with smart connected tracking and tracing devices. *International Journal of Production Economics*. Advance online publication. DOI: 10.1016/j.ijpe.2024.109336

Hlali, A. (2023). Impact of logistics and economic structure on seaport infrastructure: A case of Mediterranean countries. *Australian Journal of Maritime and Ocean Affairs, 16*(13). Advance online publication. DOI: 10.1080/18366503.2023.2217584

Hlali, A., & Gafsi, N. (2024). Analysis of Digitalization and Sustainable Development in Africa. *Perspectives on Global Development and Technology, 22*(5-6), 415–428. DOI: 10.1163/15691497-12341668

Hlali, A., & Wanis, A. (2020). Theoretical highlights in container port logistics systems. *Journal of Marine and Island Cultures, 9*(2). Advance online publication. DOI: 10.21463/jmic.2020.09.2.13

Islam, R., Ansari, M. E., Dewan, M. A., Sultana, S., & Rivin, M. A. H. (2024). Supply Chain Management Analysis and Design for a Variety of Economic Scenarios, Including Data and System Administration. *Journal of Software Engineering and Applications*, *17*(10), 770–785.

Javaid, M., Haleem, A., Singh, R. P., Suman, R., & Khan, S. (2022). A review of Blockchain Technology applications for financial services. *BenchCouncil Transactions on Benchmarks. Standards and Evaluations*, *2*(3), 100073. DOI: 10.1016/j.tbench.2022.100073

Kujawski, A., & Nürnberg, M. (2023). Analysis of the potential use of unmanned aerial vehicles and image processing methods to support road and parking space management in urban transport. *Sustainability*. Advance online publication. DOI: 10.3390/su15043285

Li, A., Zhuang, S., Yang, T., Lu, W., & Xu, J. (2024). Optimization of logistics cargo tracking and transportation efficiency based on data science deep learning models. *Applied and Computational Engineering*, *69*, 71–77. DOI: 10.54254/2755-2721/69/20241522

Lustenberger, M., & Spychiger, F. (2025). Blockchain in supply chains: An unfulfilled promise. *Supply Chain Management*. Advance online publication. DOI: 10.1108/SCM-03-2024-0192

Mustafa, G., Rafiq, W., Jhamat, N., Arshad, Z., & Rana, F. A. (2025). Blockchain-based governance models in e-government: A comprehensive framework for legal, technical, ethical and security considerations. *International Journal of Law and Management*, *67*(1), 37–55. DOI: 10.1108/IJLMA-08-2023-0172

Mvelase, L., & Ferrer, S. (2024). The economywide impact of bioethanol production in South Africa. *Energy Conversion and Management, X*. Advance online publication. DOI: 10.1016/j.ecmx.2024.100729

Neu, D. A., Lahann, J., & Fettke, P. (2022). A systematic literature review on state-of-the-art deep learning methods for process prediction. *Artificial Intelligence Review*. Advance online publication. DOI: 10.1007/s10462-021-09960-8

Omol, E. J. (2024). *Organizational digital transformation: from evolution to future trends*. Digital Transformation and Society.

Pasupuleti, V., Thuraka, B., Kodete, C. S., & Malisetty, S. (2024). Enhancing supply chain agility and sustainability through machine learning: Optimization techniques for logistics and inventory management. *Logistics (Basel)*. Advance online publication. DOI: 10.3390/logistics8030073

Pattanayak, S., Ramkumar, M., Goswami, M., & Rana, N. P. (2024). Blockchain technology and supply chain performance: The role of trust and relational capabilities. *International Journal of Production Economics*, *271*, 109198. DOI: 10.1016/j.ijpe.2024.109198

Pautassi, P. (2024). Algorithmic Pricing in the digital age.

Prakash, J., Murali, L., Manikandan, N., Nagaprasad, N., & Ramaswamy, K. (2024). RETRACTED ARTICLE: A vehicular network based intelligent transport system for smart cities using machine learning algorithms. *Scientific Reports*, *14*(1), 468. DOI: 10.1038/s41598-023-50906-7 PMID: 38172149

Ratanabanchuen, R., Saengchote, K., Nakavachara, V., Amonthumniyom, T., Parinyavuttichai, P., & Vinaibodee, P. (2024). The test of investors' behavioral bias through the price discovery process in cryptoasset exchange" Transactional-level evidence from Thailand. *arXiv preprint arXiv:2406.02878.*

Raza, Z., Woxenius, J., Vural, C. A., & Lind, M. (2023). Digital transformation of maritime logistics: Exploring trends in the liner shipping segment. *Computers in Industry*. Advance online publication. DOI: 10.1016/j.compind.2022.103811

Saberi, S., Kouhizadeh, M., Sarkis, J., & Shen, L. (2019). Blockchain technology and its relationships to sustainable supply chain management. *International Journal of Production Research*, *57*(7), 2117–2135. DOI: 10.1080/00207543.2018.1533261

Sallam, K., Mohamed, M., & Mohamed, A. W. (2023). Internet of Things (IoT) in supply chain management: Challenges, opportunities, and best practices. *Sustainable Machine Intelligence Journal*, *2*, 3–1. DOI: 10.61185/SMIJ.2023.22103

Seele, P., Dierksmeier, C., Hofstetter, R., & Schultz, M. D. (2021). Mapping the ethicality of algorithmic pricing: A review of dynamic and personalized pricing. *Journal of Business Ethics*, *170*, 697–719. DOI: 10.1007/s10551-019-04371-w

Sun, X., Yu, H., & Solvang, W. D. (2022). Towards the smart and sustainable transformation of Reverse Logistics 4.0: A conceptualization and research agenda. *Environmental Science and Pollution Research International*, *29*(46), 69275–69293. DOI: 10.1007/s11356-022-22473-3 PMID: 35972653

Sun, X., Yu, H., Solvang, W. D., Wang, Y., & Wang, K. (2022). The application of Industry 4.0 technologies in sustainable logistics: A systematic literature review (2012–2020) to explore future research opportunities. *Environmental Science and Pollution Research International*, •••, 1–32. DOI: 10.1007/s11356-021-17693-y PMID: 34893953

Tiwari, S., Sharma, P., Choi, T. M., & Lim, A. (2023). Blockchain and third-party logistics for global supply chain operations: Stakeholders' perspectives and decision roadmap. *Transportation Research Part E, Logistics and Transportation Review*, *170*, 103012. DOI: 10.1016/j.tre.2022.103012

Wang, S., Wan, J., Li, D., & Zhang, C. (2016). Implementing smart factory of Industrie 4.0: An outlook. *International Journal of Distributed Sensor Networks*, *12*(1), 1–10. DOI: 10.1155/2016/3159805

Williams, L. D. (2021). Concepts of Digital Economy and Industry 4.0 in Intelligent and information systems. *International Journal of Intelligent Networks*, https://doi.org/DOI: 10.1016/j.ijin.2021.09.002

KEY TERMS AND DEFINITIONS

Smart Logistics Technologies: Integrated digital solutions (e.g., IoT, AI, blockchain, predictive analytics) that automate and optimize supply chain operations through real-time data processing and decision-making. These technologies enhance efficiency by synchronizing warehousing, transportation, and inventory management, reducing operational friction and enabling responsive adjustments to market dynamics.

Financial Innovations (FinTech): Advanced financial tools such as blockchain-based payments, dynamic financing, and smart contracts that streamline capital flow within supply chains. By aligning financial transactions with logistical milestones (e.g., automated invoice settlements upon delivery confirmation), FinTech reduces liquidity gaps and democratizes access to funding, particularly for SMEs.

Cross-Border E-Commerce: Digital trade platforms facilitating international transactions, reliant on integrated smart logistics and FinTech for seamless customs clearance, real-time shipment tracking, and multi-currency payments.

Blockchain Technology: A decentralized digital ledger ensuring transparent, tamper-proof record-keeping across supply chains. In logistics, it enables secure asset tokenization, automates contractual compliance via smart contracts, and enhances traceability, reducing fraud risks and administrative costs while building stakeholder trust.

Internet of Things (IoT): Networked sensors embedded in cargo, vehicles, and infrastructure to monitor location, condition, and movement in real time. IoT data feeds predictive analytics engines, optimizing routes and inventory levels while enabling proactive risk management (e.g., temperature control for perishable goods).

Predictive Analytics: AI-driven analysis of historical and real-time data to forecast supply chain events like demand surges, machine failures, or delivery delays. Applied to logistics, it optimizes warehouse staffing, and enhances delivery accuracy through machine learning models.

Dynamic Pricing Models: Algorithmic price adjustments for logistics services based on real-time variables like fuel costs, demand fluctuations, and congestion levels. These models maximize asset utilization (e.g., reducing truck idle time) but raise ethical concerns around transparency and equitable access for smaller carriers.

Supply Chain Transparency: End-to-end visibility into product journeys enabled by synchronized data sharing among stakeholders. Technologies like blockchain and IoT create immutable audit trails, curbing counterfeit goods and ensuring compliance with sustainability protocols (e.g., carbon footprint tracking).

Intermodal Transportation: Coordinated use of multiple transport modes (e.g., ship-to-truck-to-rail) for single shipments, optimized through cloud-based platforms. Smart logistics integrate tracking and financial systems across modes, cutting transit times and costs while simplifying cross-border regulatory compliance.

Public-Private Partnerships (PPPs): Collaborative frameworks where governments and corporations co-invest in smart infrastructure (e.g., IoT-enabled ports or blockchain customs platforms). PPPs accelerate technology adoption in emerging markets, as demonstrated by Kenya's "Single Window" system reducing trade bottlenecks through shared data ecosystems.

Chapter 9
Blockchain for Logistics Transparency Securing the Supply Chain Through Decentralization

Asma Imran
https://orcid.org/0000-0002-0985-1755
COMSATS University Islamabad, Lahore, Pakistan

Munir Ahmad
https://orcid.org/0000-0003-4836-6151
Survey of Pakistan, Pakistan

ABSTRACT

This chapter examined the transformative role of blockchain technology in enhancing transparency and security within logistics and supply chain management. As global supply chains become increasingly complex and susceptible to issues such as fraud, data silos, and inefficiencies, blockchain offers a decentralized, tamper-proof ledger system that fosters trust, accountability, and real-time visibility across all stakeholders. The chapter explored how blockchain can mitigate long-standing logistical challenges by improving traceability, reducing counterfeiting, and optimizing coordination. Emphasizing both operational and ethical implications, it highlighted how blockchain adoption contributes to regulatory compliance, product authenticity, and sustainability.

DOI: 10.4018/979-8-3373-2434-0.ch009

INTRODUCTION

In recent times, blockchain technology has been making a big impact in many industries, improving both reliability and security. Because logistics involves many different suppliers, manufacturers, distributors, and retailers, blockchain provides a reliable and shared network that can help to improve how the supply chain functions. Blockchain's support for real-time tracking and proof of all activities encourages all stakeholders to work with trust and accountability, reducing risks from fraud, mistakes, and delays (Casino et al., 2019; Kshetri, 2018). The industry must deal with problems including a lack of clear information, separated data, fake products, and difficulty connecting different parties. Old-fashioned centralized systems regularly have issues with their information being manipulated, delays in sharing it, and a lack of traceability (Saberi et al., 2019). When global supply chains get more complicated, it is essential to have a solution that guarantees we can see our data and know it is safe along the full chain. Blockchain solves these issues by giving everyone who participates a single, verified record they can all use.

Being open and secure in the supply chain is necessary for smooth operations, winning customer trust, satisfying regulations, and supporting sustainability objectives. Adopting blockchain allows companies to fight fraud, keep products genuine, manage financial disclosures more easily, and perfect logistics systems, which lowers their expenses and puts them ahead of competitors. Being transparent about the origin of supplies also makes it easier to adhere to ethical standards and protect the environment, aligning a business with the latest global expectations.

This chapter examines how blockchain can help to improve both security and transparency in the logistics and supply chain sector. It aims to show the central principles of blockchain for logistics, review applications in practice, discuss problems faced, and explain possible patterns going forward. The chapter illustrates how decentralization can help ensure supply chain transparency and hand reliable information to stakeholders.

The chapter has been broken down into five main sections. The chapter starts with a simple explanation of blockchain and its important qualities for logistics. The next part of the discussion looks closely at current supply chain issues and how blockchain helps to solve them. The rest of the book looks at common difficulties that appear during development and implementation. Lastly, the chapter discusses future trends and areas where researchers might concentrate on blockchain in logistics transparency.

BLOCKCHAIN TECHNOLOGY

Blockchain technology is a significant innovation in how data and transactions are managed, shared, and verified. A blockchain is mainly a distributed ledger, a way to log transactions that is kept at the same time by individual participants called nodes (Crosby et al., 2016; Nakamoto, 2008). Unlike traditional databases, which a single authority controls, information is kept on blockchain by multiple servers all over the world (Tapscott & Tapscott, 2018).

Unlike classic data management, this approach does not count on a central trusted service to access data. In contrast, everyone connected to the blockchain network is responsible for updating and confirming it. Because every node has the whole blockchain, no single node can fail (Yli-Huumo et al., 2016). No matter which nodes are down or have been compromised, the network still works properly.

Every action or piece of information that joins the blockchain must first be added after the group of miners collectively verifies it in what is called consensus. These mechanisms, such as PoW and PoS, guarantee that the majority of miners or validators believe a transaction follows the blockchain's rules (Zheng et al., 2017). No one has to trust a single entity, because the network's majority must confirm each piece of data added to the ledger. The blockchain is stable network, and fraudulent or inaccurate information cannot be entered (Casino et al., 2019).

Transactions on the blockchain are put in blocks, and those blocks are linked together one after another by time. The previous block is always referenced in a hash in the new block, thus allowing them to be linked in sequence. As well as handling data well, it prevents others from revising or altering the ledger (Narayanan et al., 2016).

Decentralization and Security

In the centralized systems, data and control are given away from one main center. Despite being faster and easier to use, centralized databases are at risk from cyberattacks, bad decisions by employees, unintentional data loss, or system troubles (Kshetri, 2017; Zyskind et al., 2015).

On the other hand, blockchain's design allows all network members to share control. Only with agreement from more than one party, data can be updated or destroyed, making data tampering and fraud much less likely (Narayanan et al., 2016; Yli-Huumo et al., 2016). If an attacker tried to change a transaction, they would have to control a majority of the computers on the network, a situation considered both difficult and costly for large blockchains such as Bitcoin and Ethereum (Crosby et al., 2016; Mohanta et al., 2019).

All events in a blockchain are time-stamped, so anyone can see when each event took place, allowing a step-by-step and accurate review of all transactions. Because each block is linked with a hash, any changes to just one block would cause the hashes of every following block to fail, which would immediately attract the network's attention (Casino et al., 2019; Zheng et al., 2017).

With this, all transactions on the network are permanently recorded and help improve trust between users. In logistics, finance, and healthcare, where record authenticity is critical, blockchain helps ensure that companies are responsible and follow the rules (Saberi et al., 2019; Tian, 2016). With blockchain, any party can verify data for themselves, so you don't have to trust a single center to ensure it is correct (Tapscott & Tapscott, 2018). Overall, blockchain's architecture and powerful safety systems create a reliable way to keep and access data. With this new way of thinking, organizations can work together on one platform, trusting that their data is accurate, safe from attack, and not alterable.

Using blockchain, every action in the logistics process becomes clear and secure on a single, undisputable ledger. All those playing a role in transportation, such as raw material suppliers, manufacturing firms, shippers, customs staff, and retailers, can obtain verifiable information from one real source about their shipments (Francisco & Swanson, 2018; Hackius & Petersen, 2017). The moment a shipment leaves a factory; its details are added to the blockchain. Starting then, those in charge can use technology to keep an eye on the parcel's location, quality, and anticipated arrival date with no need for manual interventions.

Blockchain can address risks like fraud, theft, and counterfeiting. Blockchain record is stamped with time and cannot be changed, so faking the shipment is almost impossible without being noticed (Kouhizadeh & Sarkis, 2018). Because this approach increases trust within the network, it is vital in industries like pharmaceuticals, electronics, and luxury goods (Tian, 2016). Also, if tracking happens in real time, it becomes simpler to spot issues and react promptly, which boosts the supply chain's resilience and satisfies customers (Saberi et al., 2019).

Data Immutability and Compliance

What sets blockchain apart in logistics is its inability to be altered after it is built. As soon as something is stored on the blockchain, it takes the agreement of most of the network to change or remove it (Casino et al., 2019; Zheng et al., 2017). As a result, there is a reliable and traceable record of everything that occurs in the supply chain, important for handling both rules and quality (Saberi et al., 2019).

Firms can show the tracked history of their products using the unchanging nature of blockchain. By using blockchain, medicine transportation in the pharmaceutical industry can be monitored and any unauthorized changes can be detected, therefore helping to prevent fake medicine (Mettler, 2016; Tseng et al., 2018). In the food industry, permanent records let officials find and remove contaminated food, protect customers, and save companies from wasting money (Kamble et al., 2019; Tian, 2016).

With these automated trails, complying with international regulations is much easier and less costly than keeping and reviewing manual records (Galvez et al., 2018). Because the data is everlasting, it keeps companies responsible, lowers the risks of fraud, and increases the integrity of their supply chains (Francisco & Swanson, 2018; Kouhizadeh et al., 2021).

Smart Contracts for Workflow Automation

Besides making things transparent and easy to report, blockchain technology helps to set up smart contracts that automatically execute terms once conditions are met (Christidis & Devetsikiotis, 2016). Automating daily processes, reducing errors, and speeding up transactions can all be achieved with the use of smart contracts by logistics companies (Chang et al., 2019; Morkunas et al., 2019).

So, a smart contract can automatically pay the carrier once the delivery confirmation is added to the blockchain. Because manual checks are not necessary, business decisions are fast, and managing the process becomes simpler (Kshetri, 2014). Smart contracts are now being used in customs to analyze shipment documents and give the green light to release the goods after requirements are met.

Overseeing inventory is better as well, because smart contracts can watch stock levels, trigger a new order when an approved quantity is used, and prevent stockouts (Kamble et al., 2019). Automating these processes brings more trust and improvements to how work gets done, as all partners in the supply chain now benefit from secure enforcement of contracts (Saberi et al., 2019).

Types of Blockchains

Architecture for blockchain can be adjusted based on how best it should address a logistics scenario. Three main categories are public, private, and consortium blockchains, all of which have unique benefits when it comes to transparency, control, how many users they serve, and privacy (Casino et al., 2019; Zheng et al., 2017).

Public Blockchains

Everyone can join Ethereum and Bitcoin, which are public global blockchains accessible to all. Since these blockchains are decentralized, every participant is free to join, check, and confirm purchases and keep the ledger up to date. As a result, every exchange is easy for anyone to see, since any change must be agreed upon by the whole network (Guo & Yu, 2022; Narayanan et al., 2016).

Public blockchains run into certain problems when used in the logistics sector. Their openness means these systems can slow down during times of high trade volume, which might stop real-time operations such as logistics (Treiblmaier, 2018). Privacy is also an issue because all participants can see and access sensitive shipping or commercial data once it is uploaded to public blockchains (Yli-Huumo et al., 2016). Because of the limits to these systems, public blockchains are often used where trust is especially important and transaction numbers are not very high, like in verifying the beginning of supply chains or figuring out the origin of goods (Francisco & Swanson, 2018).

Private Blockchains

A private blockchain is controlled and run by one organization alone. Only participants who are authorized may participate in the network, process transactions, and view the ledger. As this framework hides data better and offers more control over it, companies using it are able to protect their private information and complete their important regulatory responsibilities (Zheng et al., 2017).

Because they concentrate governance, private blockchains can perform more transactions per second and process them faster than public blockchains (Li et al., 2018). But this also means centralization, since trusted execution environments rely on one single entity. Many times, private blockchains are used inside one firm or a secure network, such as for keeping inventory or managing private transportation services (Kamble et al., 2019).

Consortium Blockchains

Consortium blockchains are positioned in the middle between public and private types of architecture. Unlike the others, these blockchains are led by several teams of trustworthy organizations, instead of being directed by a sole entity. Because of this model, manufacturers, logistics providers, customs authorities, and retailers can all work on the same ledger with privacy controls in place (Peters & Panayi, 2016).

With the consortium model, partners manage to be transparent and open with organized data, but keep proprietary information securely out of reach. In addition, since consortium blockchains have limited network participants, they can perform more transactions faster than public blockchains (Wang et al., 2019).In the consortium blockchain, exchanging verified shipping data helps participants complete their trade documents more quickly, handle less paperwork, and avoid delays at ports and borders. Working together, businesses can show how consortium blockchains can make complicated logistics smooth and transparent.

TradeLens is considered a prime example of logistics using blockchain technology. With the help of a consortium blockchain, TradeLens creates a secure environment for shipping companies, ports, and customs to connect with freight forwarders and other stakeholders. However, TradeLens discontinued in 2023 due to insufficient global industry collaboration, which hindered its commercial viability despite developing a functional platform.

BLOCKCHAIN IN LOGISTICS

Complexity and Fragmentation in Supply Chains

Contemporary supply chains typically cover many different places, times, and laws. Such organizations use complex networks of suppliers, manufacturers, companies that handle shipping, customs officers, warehouses, distributors, and retailers, and every part of this network works separately. The usual approach for such participants is to enhance their business activities using custom Enterprise Resource Planning (ERP), Transportation Management Systems (TMS), or Warehouse Management Systems (WMS), which are not intended to communicate with one another. In turn, crucial data for goods in transit is spread across various systems, commonly causing issues with how data and messages are exchanged (Saberi et al., 2019).

Because of this division, information systems create separate spaces for information, with each stakeholder handling their knowledge. Having no unified, current look at transactions makes information across the supply chain incomplete, delayed, or differing. When leaving the manufacturer, a shipment's details can be filled out manually, sent by email, or uploaded into the database. Yet, updates sent to third-party logistics providers or customs officials might arrive too late, or the shipping paperwork they receive may not be matched. Some routine errors happen when data is labeled incorrectly, when proper customs forms are not included, or when there are duplicate entries. These mistakes appear often when using old systems or manual methods (Ellahi et al., 2023; Esmaeilian et al., 2020).

These flaws usually result in repeated delays and extra costs in operating the project. Should proper pre-arrival documentation be missing from a port authority, containers may be held for another check, resulting in delivery delays and extra charges. Similarly, a divided data system may lead business partners to debate whether freight was delivered or lost in transit. When there is no single source of information be trusted by all sides, resolving supply chain disputes takes longer and costs more money.

In 2017, Maersk Line, a big container shipping company, was disrupted by a cyberattack that stopped parts of its internal system, including cargo booking and tracking. After the attack, the company needed weeks to operate manually, and this showed just how prone centralized, divided IT systems in global supply chains are (Greenberg, 2018). The inability to instantly share and combine information between supply chain members is a major problem in such situations.

This way, fragmentation may be resolved with blockchain, which allows every licensed user to use a single shared, decentralized ledger. By keeping a record of all transactions instantly and confirming their accuracy by consensus and hash coding, blockchain significantly boosts the accuracy and openness of the supply chain's data. This means that teams don't need to reconcile or update each dataset by hand, and the only accurate numbers are visible to everyone, which keeps misunderstandings, delays, and arguments down (Treiblmaier, 2018).

Counterfeit Goods and Fraud Risks

The spread of fake goods is one of the biggest and most dangerous problems facing worldwide supply chains. The special danger with counterfeits is in the pharmaceutical, electronics, automotive, luxury fashion, and food industries, as fake or defective products can be extremely hazardous or even lethal (OECD & EUIPO, 2019). Revenue from global trade in counterfeit and pirated items stood at more than $500 billion in 2019, equaling 3.3% of world trade, according to the OECD. Fake products are dangerous for individuals' health and safety as well as for the economy. In places where regulations are less strict, for instance, it is easier for malicious goods such as fake drugs to enter the supply chain, causing treatment to fail, drug resistance to rise, and even death in some cases (WHO, 2023).

Because traditional supply chain systems store data centrally, keep documents manually, and are often disorganized, they include a high risk of fraud. With these systems, it is tough to see where products come from or confirm their true identity once they pass from one intermediary to another. As a product moves through different wholesalers and customs checkpoints, someone can make forgeries of any paperwork issued by the producer. When counterfeits get into the legal supply chain, it is very hard to find them if the packaging and labels look real.

During the COVID-19 pandemic, people's need for PPE and vaccines resulted in many counterfeit supplies being sold. According to Interpol, many fake masks, test kits, and medical devices were seized in countries all over the world, with many being advertised under fraudulent or misleading information. They not only put people's health at risk but also weakened trust in important supply chains in a time of emergency.

Countering these weaknesses, blockchain technology records every detail of a product's supply chain from the start to its final destination. Records of any transaction or event, including production, checking, shipping, or change in ownership, are stamped and protected by cryptography, making it almost impossible to change them afterward (Ellahi et al., 2023; Esmaeilian et al., 2020). Product papers for digital goods can now be made and tied to the secure blockchain identities of their physical counterparts. Such identities feature serial numbers, origin certificates, batch numbers, and other visible metadata that are always present for all authorized users in real time.

Compounds in the pharmaceutical industry, like Modum and MediLedger are testing blockchain solutions to confirm that drugs are authentic and have the correct storage temperatures during transport. Pharmacies and regulators can check within seconds on the blockchain whether a medicine has taken the proper route and conditions by simply scanning a QR code or an RFID tag (Ghadge et al., 2023). Furthermore, major luxury brands, including LVMH and De Beers, use blockchain, such as AURA and Tracr, to keep tabs on designer handbags and diamonds and curb the chances of fraud in costly markets (Tapscott & Tapscott, 2018).

In other words, using blockchain helps prevent fake products, gives all stakeholders the same information, and restores trust among partners. Using blockchain, people can confirm the truth about goods anytime, which benefits regulations, safety, and brand reputation in global markets.

Lack of End-to-End Traceability and Coordination

Currently, global supply chains cannot often track products constantly through every step of the process. With traditional logistics, it is difficult for companies to remain visible because of separate IT networks, manual methods, and poor cooperation among partners. Companies usually cannot watch their products at every moment or along the entire journey, but have to do so mostly at specific stops (Francisco & Swanson, 2018). Having complete trackability is especially important for industries like pharmaceuticals, food, and electronics, since the state and handling of products as they move can influence their safety, use, or usefulness.

An instance of this is in cold chain logistics, where temperature control for vaccines and fresh produce is limited. Failing to accurately check temperatures at all times may mean those items are no longer useful or have spoiled. An actual problem occurred when millions of COVID-19 vaccines were damaged by improper temperature controls, leading to a loss of money and negatively impacting public health efforts. If real-time environmental data and storage information are not available, it is almost impossible to determine whether and where a failure took place, so fixing problems is more difficult.

On top of that, problems with supply chain traceability become more severe due to the lack of synchronization between supply chain members. Many of the key individuals in an organization use systems that fail to connect efficiently. Therefore, data is not shared, important updates are put off, and frequently, information is not accurate or present. With global logistics spread out into many small parts, answering quickly to disruptions from port slowdown, extreme weather, or delays from suppliers is getting more difficult in today's environment (Choi et al., 2018; Yin et al., 2022). During the blockage of the Suez Canal, several businesses didn't get real-time updates, so they had difficulty sending goods and getting the inventory they needed, which resulted in lots of shipping delay issues and a shortage of products.

Using blockchain technology, organizations can now manage and check logistics data easily and quickly on a shared system that is open to all stakeholders. Using blockchain, the transfer of cargo from one party to another can be logged clearly, along with time information, geographic data, and current product condition (Saberi et al., 2019). A refrigerated container's temperature can be checked every 15 minutes using IoT devices and stored securely on a blockchain, making sure all rules about storing food are obeyed during transport. It gives more visibility and supports fast analysis of problems and quick action when deviations take place.

IBM created a food traceability system on the blockchain together with Walmart. Through blockchain, Walmart was able to clear up contamination issues in less than three seconds, when it once took six days (Yiannas, 2018). In addition, logistics companies like Maersk and FedEx implemented blockchain solutions to improve visibility, lower paper requirements, and allow partners in the supply chain to exchange data in real time.

To become more flexible, durable, and customer-aware, today's supply chains need complete traceability and coordinated communication. With its unified version of the truth and automated steps, blockchain takes a major step towards fixing known supply chain issues and leading a new era of smart and trusted supply chains.

Blockchain as a Transformative Solution

With blockchain, companies are finding solutions to the common supply chain issues that include dividing data, poor transparency, and gaps in trust between independent stakeholders. Blockchain provides a decentralized and protected record system that any involved party, from raw materials to retail, can update and access together. With blockchain, instead of a central admin, the ledger is a chain of links found on a network of different nodes. Since the events on the chain are securely linked and stamped with a time code, the history of blockchain can't be changed by a single actor; changes require approval from the majority of the network (Casino et al., 2019; Nakamoto, 2008).

Because recordkeeping cannot be changed and all transactions are visible, data tampering, fraud, and errors are reduced. To illustrate, documents important in supply chain processes, such as bills of lading, certificates of origin, and inspection reports, are commonly created manually or changed, which leads to problems in establishing a single data source that people can count on (Kshetri, 2018). On the other hand, any transaction done through blockchain can be checked and is permanent, so others can audit and confirm data on their own without an official authority.

An excellent example of using blockchain is Maersk's TradeLens, which tries to bring major shipping companies, port operators, customs officials, and freight forwarders onto one platform. With TradeLens, shipping data is updated instantly, helping every participant see how containers move and what happens in customs. Due to this transparency, documents are processed quickly, less paperwork is created, and disagreements between trading partners have decreased. All of this reduces costs and improves the efficiency of trading globally (Raja Santhi & Muthuswamy, 2022). Because of blockchain-enabled logistics supply, a port authority can immediately confirm the shipping line's manifest and inspection against the records on their system, making it unnecessary to repeat manual checks and speeding up clearance times.

Another example occurs in the pharmaceutical industry, using blockchain to address counterfeit drugs and protect both patients and a company's reputation. Data from the supply chain is recorded in MediLedger, a platform that uses blockchain to ensure all stages of drug distribution are secure and clear. By putting each drug batch on the blockchain, participants and regulators are able to confirm authenticity anytime throughout the supply process. It ensures compliance with laws and helps increase the trust of consumers (Ghadge et al., 2023).

Along with being transparent, the decentralization of blockchain contributes to the strength of supply chains. Having the ledger shared over multiple computers means the system usually survives cyberattacks, data loss, or errors that affect single centralized databases (Kouhizadeh et al., 2021). As a result, the network can run steadily even when some participants face interruptions or problems.

Authenticity and Provenance Verification

The ability to verify a product's origin from when it was produced to when it is sold is onc of the most powerful uses of blockchain technology for supply chains. In today's worldwide supply system, with goods being passed through much of the world, checking a product's history and real nature is a challenge that remains.

Fake products, fraud, and poor quality endanger people's lives most of all in food, pharmaceuticals, luxury goods, and electronics (Tian, 2016).

A record of every key occasion, from harvesting and processing to shipping and storage, is stored in a blockchain ledger that anyone authorized can see. Because the ledger is shared, both regulators and buyers can independently use it to verify that a product is genuine and comes from the correct supplier. Fast capability is necessary when safety or regulatory issues require quick attention.

An important use of blockchain can be seen in Walmart's effort to follow food through the supply chain with blockchain technology. Before Walmart started using blockchain, it could take up to several days to find the origin of unhealthy foods, which slowed down their responses during epidemics. With the adoption of blockchain, agricultural product traceability by Walmart is now performed in seconds, enabling fast associations with the affected farms and batches (Kamath, 2018). Because of swift pinpointing, accurate recalls help keep consumers healthy, cut down on wasted food, and save money for suppliers and retailers. At first, the project concentrated on leafy greens and is now also working with other perishable products.

The pharmaceutical sector is using blockchain to help identify and remove fake drugs, in addition to ensuring every product keeps its integrity as it moves through the supply chain. Taking false medications may result in treatment failing or becoming deadly for patients; for this, checking the medication origin must be done. Through platforms such as MediLedger, pharmaceutical businesses have a secure way to check and confirm how medicines are prepared, shipped, and handled. By connecting medical goods to digital information on the blockchain, users confirm that all medicines are legitimate and kept according to correct protocols, both for regulatory purposes and for public health reasons.

Due to blockchain, luxury products can now be traced to help block the sale of fake designer items. Firms like LVMH are now using blockchain platforms such as Aura Blockchain Consortium to make sure luxury products like watches, handbags, and jewelry are genuine (Saberi et al., 2019). Using the code on the box, users can check the products' background, which can strengthen confidence in the brand and help prevent fake items.

Real-Time Tracking and IoT Integration

Bringing blockchain technology and IoT together greatly increases their effectiveness and allows for instant, automated monitoring down the supply chain. With GPS trackers, RFID tags, temperature sensors, humidity monitors, and similar environmental sensors, IoT allows shipments to be constantly monitored, and all collected data is automatically stored on the blockchain. Because of this, manual and scattered data is replaced by a single, tamper-proof digital document that everyone on the team can see.

Shipments like vaccines, medicines, foods at risk of spoilage, and chemicals need round-the-clock environmental monitoring. Strict attention to the temperature is needed when storing and moving vaccines to prevent them from losing their effectiveness. Inside packaging, IoT sensors regularly monitor temperature and immediately inform if a certain level is exceeded. Due to the permanent recording of this data on blockchain, stakeholders are aware of any violation, know the place and time it happened, and keep unsafe items from getting to customers.

Companies can bring blockchain and IoT together, including shipping lines, ports, customs agencies, freight forwarders, and several others, to track global container shipments in or near real-time. GPS location, estimated arrival time, and the weather or conditions around the shipment can be regularly updated by IoT devices and then safely stored on the blockchain. Because of this visibility, goods can be cleared more smoothly, and less paperwork keeps containers from staying long in the port, cutting expenses for both parties.

As well as improving how operations run, integrating IoT and blockchain strengthens the supply chain's resistance to disruptions by allowing for quick action. Should the temperature on a seafood shipment rise too high, an alarm will be sent immediately, leading the shipper to reroute the products to a local cold storage or halt movement until everything has been checked. As a result, fewer products deteriorate, customers are better protected, and the brand's good name is maintained.

In addition, real-time trackers and the use of the Internet of Things in logistics show confirmation of proper handling and transport at every stage, which supports compliance with guidelines. Having this ability is very important for industries held to high quality standards, for example, the pharmaceutical and food safety organizations (Mourtzis et al., 2016).

Workflow Automation via Smart Contracts

With programmable automation, smart contracts are one of the main ways blockchain can help make supply chain operations more efficient. Essentially, smart contracts are computer code saved on a blockchain that will only enforce an agreement when certain requirements have been met. Having this ability means you don't need intermediaries or manual supervision, which used to cost more, increase risks, and add time.

Smart contracts in logistics and supply chain management make the automatic operation of necessary but repetitive tasks possible. You can see automation used in paying bills regularly. That is, a delivery transaction can trigger payment to the freight carrier the moment it is confirmed by a digital signature or an IoT system for delivery. Because of this system, most delays in payments and issues between buyers and sellers are prevented (Christidis & Devetsikiotis, 2016). As a consequence, carriers have better cash flow, and shippers benefit from being more efficient.

Customs clearance and following regulations are other important purposes of it. A smart contract can be set up by customs authorities to automatically look at shipment documentation, including certificates of origin, the classifications and charges needed, and any needed health or safety checks. As soon as regulations are met, the smart contract can order customs officials to release the goods, making travel through borders faster and clearing up the port's goods logjam (Saberi et al., 2019). Smart contracts enabled by blockchain have been tested at the Port of Rotterdam to help simplify customs, lower paperwork levels, and ease administrative problems (Notheisen et al., 2017).

Inventory management is supported by making use of smart contracts. IoT sensors and ERP systems can automatically activate the conditions for ordering more inventory thanks to smart contracts. Due to automation, stockouts are reduced, there is less risk of overstocking, and all operations in the warehouse are streamlined by connecting inventory movements to procurement.

Other than operating smartly, smart contracts also encourage greater openness and trust among those in the supply chain. Because of the blockchain, all parties can be sure that they're working with the same information and status in every contract. Common visibility keeps things from becoming controversial when automatic systems log and manage payments, released goods, and approvals (Mendling et al., 2018).

A good example is the Marco Polo Network on blockchain, which enables clients to automatically and securely settle payments, letters of credit, and financing by using smart contracts. Because these financial workflows are automatic, manual paperwork is less necessary, and international trade moves more quickly (Chang et al., 2020).

BLOCKCHAIN AND EMERGING TECHNOLOGIES

The intersection of blockchain with new technologies like Artificial Intelligence (AI), the Internet of Things (IoT), as well as cloud computing, is challenging the supply chains across the globe. The technologies supplement each other since they strengthen transparency, decentralization, automation, and traceability, which are the essential requirements of contemporary logistics. Specifically, this integration enhances the supply chain industry by eliminating such long-standing problems as fraud, not good visibility, counterfeit, and data silos. All of the technologies offer special advantages that, together with blockchain, can help build a more secure and efficient supply chain.

Blockchain and AI

Artificial Intelligence can easily crunch massive data sets of logistics information to find the shortest route, predict needs, and spot trends of efficiency loss or fraud. Nonetheless, the quality, reliability, and origin of input data are where blockchain can play an essential part, and AI algorithms heavily depend on these parameters.

An example is a multinational food distribution firm operating AI to forecast the risk of spoilage and the best way to deliver their routes, depending on the past projections and driving conditions. In case the blockchain is deployed to dictate each of the data points that enter the AI system (like the temperature records or a humidity factor in the course of transportation), blockchain guarantees the integrity of the data and eliminates ex-post control. It can boost the credibility of the predictive observations of the AI and enable data-driven, auditable, tamper-resistant automatic decision-making.

Moreover, AI might be utilized to improve blockchain technology and improve the fraudulent transaction detection to facilitate the supply chain prediction of challenges and suggest other suppliers in case of a crisis. Another example, analytics engines built on AI can discern deviations in the shipment route or invoice prices registered on the blockchain, to direct logistics companies in a timely manner to expose any danger.

Blockchain and IoT

The Internet of Things has transformed the world of logistics because it provides the possibility to track the goods, vehicles, and conditions in storage facilities in real-time. Sensors at every point in between, e.g., GPS trackers, RFID tags, and environmental sensors, generate a constant flow of information across the supply chain path. Nevertheless, security issues and the lack of transparency are common concerns when it comes to the accumulation of IoT data in a central location.

The sensitivity is less in the case of cold chain logistics, when the goods are transported over long distances and are temperature and humidity-sensitive, such as vaccines or dairy products, constant monitoring by IoT sensors is done. Connecting these IoT devices with a blockchain network has the benefit in the fact that each bit of data, say a temperature decrease during transport, is permanently and in real time recorded. In case the shipment is exposed to an unsafe temperature, smart contracts can be used to notify the stakeholders, and one can even make insurance claims automatically.

Such end-to-end insights are priceless in industries that require regulatory and quality tracing of materials like pharmaceuticals, fresh produce, and high-value electronics, as such information is necessary to document the handling history of the material. Blockchain promotes reliability among the entire chain of supply, as once the information is logged, it is impossible to use, delete, or mask it.

Blockchain and Cloud Computing

Cloud computing offers logistics corporations a high degree of flexibility, storage, and computational resources to facilitate large-scale operations. It allows access to common databases, data analysis dashboards, and electronic records at various locations. Nonetheless, the older cloud infrastructures are usually centralized, which poses security risks arising due to data ownership and unauthorized access, and system disruptions.

An international transportation company can adopt a cloud-based transportation management system (TMS) to monitor the transportation of its freight, handle the customs papers, and contract the shipping companies. The incorporation of blockchain into such a system will guarantee that the modification of any documents (such as a digital bill of lading, signing a document, or stamping customs clearance) is permanently embedded and can be verified throughout all nodes on the supply chain.

With another use case, access to logistics data stored in the cloud will be controlled by smart contracts that reside in a blockchain. As an example, a freight forwarder can be given the right to see the shipping status, whereas access to regulatory documents can be given to a customs officer only. Blockchain provides this access management in an obvious and unalterable way, whereas the cloud manages the information-intensive components of the storage and processing.

The combination of AI, IoT, cloud computing, and blockchain is not only related to the current technological trends; it means a strategic change in global logistics. Blockchain offers the base of trust that intelligence through AI, visibility through IoT, and scalability through cloud computing can build upon. Collectively, these technologies can solve the most essential pain points in supply chains: a shortage of transparency, data manipulation, delayed response time, and coordination failure. As logistics organizations make the transition to this integrated strategy, they may transition to more resilient, secure, and transparent operations, which are sine qua non attributes in a world of globalization, consumer curiosity about traceability, and the increasing complexity associated with supply chains.

CHALLENGES

Introduction of blockchain in the sphere of logistics is revolutionary. The barriers that nonetheless have to be resolved to obtain the full advantages of it are multi-dimensional, however. These are: technical constraints, legal and regulatory risks, customer, internal, or societal resistance. The discussion of each of the challenges, providing recommendations, is presented below and summarized in Table 1.

Technical Challenges

Scalability

One of the biggest technical hurdles for blockchain success in logistics is how easily it can be scaled. Ethereum and Bitcoin, two public blockchains, use proof-of-work algorithms to verify transactions, which takes significant computing power. As a consequence, the platform can handle fewer transactions per second, and the road network can be congested. In the field of logistics, thousands of activities, for example, notifying about shipments or making payments, take place each day among many participants worldwide, and these limitations may result in obstacles or delays. For instance, if all shipment and quality records are logged on a crowded blockchain, the process can stall the real-time tracking that is important in supply chains. Some people believe that new approaches such as rollups, sidechains, and proof-of-stake can help scale blockchain logistics, but these haven't found widespread use yet.

Energy Consumption

Energy efficiency is also a big issue. In proof-of-work systems, miners are required to do a lot of calculations that use a great deal of electricity. As the issue is getting more serious, logistics companies aiming to lower their carbon footprint need to start asking sustainability questions. The impact on the environment from these blockchains could largely erase the gains achieved with their operation. Eliminating mining in Ethereum 2.0 helped the network use much less energy. As a model, it helps design eco-friendly blockchain solutions that matter to the logistics sector, which always includes attention to the environment.

Interoperability with Legacy Systems

A majority of companies in logistics depend heavily on well-known systems like ERP, WMS, and TMS. It is both difficult and pricey to integrate blockchain platforms with different, often exclusive systems. The absence of standard protocols, APIs, or middleware in blockchain might turn blockchain solutions into separate and useless systems. Organizations might deal with challenges when they can't combine the records from their blockchain system with their company billing or inventory applications. Interoperability is achieved only when the industry works together to set technical standards and the format of exchanged data.

Data Storage Limitations

Data Storage Limitations also pose challenges, as blockchain is inherently inefficient for storing large datasets such as IoT sensor streams, high-resolution documentation, or multimedia evidence of delivery. A hybrid approach is advised; important metadata (e.g. timestamps, hashes) should be stored on-chain, and the actual data on off-chain storage (e.g. IPFS, decentralized clouding platforms). This maintains verifiability without overwhelming the blockchain.

System Integration and Complexity

Adoption can also get stifled by System Integration and Complexity. Most of the old ERP and logistics systems are unable to interface with decentralized networks. To make it easier, the development of modular plug-ins and APIs, detailed technical documentation, and an integration toolkit may be necessary.

Legal Challenges

Jurisdictional Ambiguity

Blockchain is global in operation, yet the law remains a nationally defined system, resulting in different applications and enforcement of blockchain records, digital identities, and smart contracts. This is legal fragmentation that places doubt in the minds of the logistics firms that are internationally established. One prescription entails aggressive regulation participation so as to have a co-production of blockchain governance structures and international law norms that would facilitate digital trade, as well as legal advice on local compliance in cross-jurisdictional contexts.

Data Privacy and Immutability Conflicts

The EU general data protection regulation privacy laws, which guarantee individuals' rights to have their data modified or removed, conflict with the nature of blockchain, where they should not be altered. This contradiction may be solved with the help of the selective on-chain / off-chain architecture when sensitive personal information is not stored on-chain but somewhere in editable databases, and only non-identifiable hashes or encrypted hints are present on the blockchain. This allows corrections or elimination of data without the loss of trust and audibility.

Smart Contract Legal Uncertainty

Smart contracts are not officially legally recognized and enforceable in most legal systems. This makes them less useful in logistic activities like automated payments or customs clearing. To combat this, firms should come up with a hybrid law system whereby the traditional legal contracts could be made to refer to and rely on smart contracts. Such composite models are enforceable in court and have the advantages of automation and transparency on-chain.

Regulatory Challenges

Lack of Standards

The blockchain environment is today defined by a variety of disparate protocols, data structures as well and governance patterns, which make implementations in various industries fragmented. These compromises in interoperability and adoption costs are high. One way through which organizations can counter this is by adopting emerging standards, such as ISO/TC 307, the World Economic Forum, and BiTA. Being a part of this also allows one to contribute towards establishing standards that are more suited to logistical specifications.

Institutional Readiness and Regulatory Resistance

The customs, ports, and transport regulators are usually non-digitally armed or educated to embrace blockchain solutions. They are reluctant to speed up the implementation ecosystem-wide. To solve this, logistics companies are advised to start the path of public-private pilot projects where the benefits of blockchain would be highlighted in certain territories, such as customs clearance or cargo authentication. Also, it is possible to upskill the stakeholders in the regulatory sector through training workshops and joint capacity-building programmes.

Societal and Organizational Challenges

Resistance to Change

Centralized systems have been used long time in many logistics organizations, and these organizations are reluctant to move to decentralized systems. Decisions may be held up by the worry that operations could be interrupted, high cost, and inability to appreciate ROI. Effective change management necessitates the involvement of stakeholders, effective communication of how the business will benefit, and whether the implementation will work with remaining workflows and priorities.

Complexity and Lack of Understanding

Blockchain is still a technology that is not easily understood by a non-expert. This is capable of sowing doubt or resistance between the employees and managers. One way to solve this divide is to remove blockchain complexity from the user interface, so it is to develop simple dashboards and mobile applications that ideally have an easy-to-use interface that shows the advantages, not blockchain lingo. Communication should be clear about the possible enhancements of traceability, accountability, and efficiency through blockchain. This is imperative in building trust.

Skill Gaps

Few professionals are available who are knowledgeable in blockchain and logistics processes. Implementation, integration, and maintenance of blockchain systems burdens in the absence of skilled personnels. Organizations are well advised to train their workforce by upskilling them using certification, academic collaborations, and intrinsic training centered around the use of blockchain in supply chain management and in the logistics industry.

Table 1. Summary of challenges

Category	Sub-Challenge	Description	Recommendation
Technical	Scalability	Blockchains struggle with high-volume, real-time logistics data.	Use Layer-2 solutions (sidechains, rollups) to increase transaction throughput.
	Interoperability	Diverse systems and platforms hinder seamless data sharing.	Deploy cross-chain protocols, blockchain-agnostic APIs, or middleware to enable integration.
	Data Storage Limitations	Blockchains are inefficient for storing large files or sensor logs.	Adopt a hybrid architecture: store hashes on-chain; use IPFS/cloud for off-chain data.
	Energy Consumption	High energy use in proof-of-work (PoW) blockchains raises sustainability issues.	Use energy-efficient consensus mechanisms like proof-of-stake (PoS) or delegated PoS; consider private blockchains.
	Data Integration	Difficulty in integrating blockchain with legacy logistics and ERP systems.	Implement APIs and connectors to bridge blockchain platforms with existing IT infrastructure.

continued on following page

Table 1. Continued

Category	Sub-Challenge	Description	Recommendation
Legal & Regulatory	Jurisdictional Ambiguity	Cross-border legal inconsistencies on blockchain use and recognition.	Engage with policymakers; co-develop regionally compatible blockchain frameworks.
	Data Privacy Conflicts	Blockchain immutability conflicts with data protection laws (e.g., GDPR).	Store sensitive data off-chain with on-chain hashes; use editable linked databases.
	Smart Contract Legal Uncertainty	Lack of recognition of smart contracts in courts/ legal systems.	Use hybrid legal agreements that incorporate and reference smart contracts.
Regulatory Standards	Lack of Industry Standards	No universal blockchain standards across supply chain sectors.	Align with ISO/TC 307, BiTA, and other standardization bodies; contribute to standards development.
	Institutional Readiness	Government and public agencies lack tools or skills to adopt blockchain.	Launch pilot projects with public-private partnerships; provide regulator training and capacity building.
Societal & Organizational	Resistance to Change	Organizations are hesitant to replace traditional systems.	Apply change management strategies; demonstrate ROI and align with existing processes.
	Complexity and Trust Gaps	Users often do not understand or trust blockchain technology.	Simplify user interfaces; communicate blockchain benefits clearly and in non-technical terms.
	Skills Shortage	Few professionals are trained in both blockchain and logistics.	Invest in upskilling through certifications, academic-industry programs, and continuous training.

CONCLUSION

As we move further ahead, blockchain will likely advance in step with related digital solutions such as IoT, AI, and advanced data tools. Blockchain, together with IoT devices, makes detailed, constant recording of supply chain data possible, which is automatically saved to the ledger. IoT sensors can keep an eye on the environment for perishable goods, staying safe and putting a smart contract into action if any issues appear. At the same time, AI can go through blockchain data to forecast changes in demand, optimize delivery paths, and spot risks, allowing supply chains to become more flexible and efficient.

Creating virtual replicas of supply chain assets and operations using blockchain is becoming popular, as they are updated with fresh data in real time. The use of digital twins makes it simpler for stakeholders to simulate events, spot inefficiencies, and handle upsets quickly with total accuracy and visibility. If a shipping container's digital twin is monitored through the blockchain, it can raise alerts regarding delays or regulatory issues throughout the supply chain very early on. Combining these two technologies can greatly improve how we forecast problems and handle disruptions.

Blockchain is growing, which means regulation outside of financial areas should also improve, improving support for its use in logistics worldwide. More and more authorities and policymakers are understanding that blockchain can be helpful for guaranteeing the integrity of supply chains, specifically in pharmaceuticals, food production, and manufacturing. Recognizing that the legal binding of the blockchain records will make things clearer and motivate investors. For instance, digital trade and recordkeeping steps taken by the European Union demonstrate how rules can help blockchain support secure and easy logistics between countries.

Besides this, greater use of smart contracts will facilitate automation across supply chains, making day-to-day work easier and raising its efficiency. With smart contracts, compliance is verified, payments are automated, reordering is set up, and conflicts can be sorted quickly, making the whole logistics process more efficient. To give an example, in the automotive industry, parts can be arranged for pickup and sent to assembly lines by smart contracts.

Strategic planning is required to fully take advantage of these opportunities. It is very important for companies from different industries to collaborate to build ecosystems where manufacturers, carriers, regulators, and customers can all operate together on blockchain. Together, these collaborative platforms support sharing, common guidelines, and joint leadership, resulting in more trust and less division. It's equally crucial to help supply chain professionals understand new technology, cybersecurity, and data analysis, as these areas are key for managing blockchain and AI-enabled systems. Endorsing standards that allow diverse blockchain networks to work well with main IT systems will help prevent them from becoming "blockchain silos." Efforts to increase the scalability and sustainability of blockchain should be largely led by industry consortia, standards bodies, and governments.

REFERENCES

Casino, F., Dasaklis, T. K., & Patsakis, C. (2019). A systematic literature review of blockchain-based applications: Current status, classification and open issues. In *Telematics and Informatics* (Vol. 36). https://doi.org/DOI: 10.1016/j.tele.2018.11.006

Chang, S. E., Chen, Y. C., & Lu, M. F. (2019). Supply chain re-engineering using blockchain technology: A case of smart contract based tracking process. *Technological Forecasting and Social Change, 144*. Advance online publication. DOI: 10.1016/j.techfore.2019.03.015

Chang, S. E., Luo, H. L., & Chen, Y. (2020). Blockchain-enabled trade finance innovation: A potential paradigm shift on using letter of credit. *Sustainability (Switzerland), 12*(1). Advance online publication. DOI: 10.3390/su1201018

Choi, T. M., Wallace, S. W., & Wang, Y. (2018). Big Data Analytics in Operations Management. *Production and Operations Management, 27*(10). Advance online publication. DOI: 10.1111/poms.12838

Christidis, K., & Devetsikiotis, M. (2016). Blockchains and Smart Contracts for the Internet of Things. In *IEEE Access* (Vol. 4). https://doi.org/DOI: 10.1109/ACCESS.2016.2566339

Crosby, M., Nachiappan, Pattanayak, P., Verma, S., & Kalyanaraman, V. (2016). Blockchain Technology - BEYOND BITCOIN. *Berkley Engineering*.

Ellahi, R. M., Wood, L. C., & Bekhit, A. E. D. A. (2023). Blockchain-Based Frameworks for Food Traceability: A Systematic Review. In *Foods* (Vol. 12, Issue 16). https://doi.org/DOI: 10.3390/foods12163026

Esmaeilian, B., Sarkis, J., Lewis, K., & Behdad, S. (2020). Blockchain for the future of sustainable supply chain management in Industry 4.0. *Resources, Conservation and Recycling, 163*. Advance online publication. DOI: 10.1016/j.resconrec.2020.105064

Francisco, K., & Swanson, D. (2018). The Supply Chain Has No Clothes: Technology Adoption of Blockchain for Supply Chain Transparency. *Logistics (Basel), 2*(1). Advance online publication. DOI: 10.3390/logistics2010002

Galvez, J. F., Mejuto, J. C., & Simal-Gandara, J. (2018). Future challenges on the use of blockchain for food traceability analysis. In *TrAC - Trends in Analytical Chemistry* (Vol. 107). https://doi.org/DOI: 10.1016/j.trac.2018.08.011

Ghadge, A., Bourlakis, M., Kamble, S., & Seuring, S. (2023). Blockchain implementation in pharmaceutical supply chains: A review and conceptual framework. In *International Journal of Production Research* (Vol. 61, Issue 19). https://doi.org/ DOI: 10.1080/00207543.2022.2125595

Greenberg, A. (2018). *The Untold Story of NotPetya, the Most Devastating Cyberattack in History*. Wired.

Guo, H., & Yu, X. (2022). A survey on blockchain technology and its security. *Blockchain: Research and Applications*, *3*(2). Advance online publication. DOI: 10.1016/j.bcra.2022.100067

Hackius, N., & Petersen, M. (2017). Blockchain in Logistics and Supply Chain: Trick or Treat? *Reinforced Plastics*, *9783745043*(April). Advance online publication. DOI: 10.15480/882.1444

Kamath, R. (2018). Food Traceability on Blockchain: Walmart's Pork and Mango Pilots with IBM. *The Journal of the British Blockchain Association*, *1*(1). Advance online publication. DOI: 10.31585/jbba-1-1-(10)2018

Kamble, S., Gunasekaran, A., & Arha, H. (2019). Understanding the Blockchain technology adoption in supply chains-Indian context. *International Journal of Production Research*, *57*(7). Advance online publication. DOI: 10.1080/00207543.2018.1518610

Kouhizadeh, M., Saberi, S., & Sarkis, J. (2021). Blockchain technology and the sustainable supply chain: Theoretically exploring adoption barriers. *International Journal of Production Economics*, *231*. Advance online publication. DOI: 10.1016/j.ijpe.2020.107831

Kouhizadeh, M., & Sarkis, J. (2018). Blockchain practices, potentials, and perspectives in greening supply chains. *Sustainability (Switzerland)*, *10*(10). Advance online publication. DOI: 10.3390/su10103652

Kshetri, N. (2014). The emerging role of Big Data in key development issues: Opportunities, challenges, and concerns. *Big Data & Society*, *1*(2). Advance online publication. DOI: 10.1177/2053951714564227

Kshetri, N. (2017). Can Blockchain Strengthen the Internet of Things? *IT Professional*, *19*(4). Advance online publication. DOI: 10.1109/MITP.2017.3051335

Kshetri, N. (2018). Blockchain's roles in meeting key supply chain management objectives. *International Journal of Information Management*, *39*, 80–89. DOI: 10.1016/j.ijinfomgt.2017.12.005

Li, Z., Wang, W. M., Liu, G., Liu, L., He, J., & Huang, G. Q. (2018). Toward open manufacturing a cross-enterprises knowledge and services exchange framework based on blockchain and edge computing. *Industrial Management & Data Systems, 118*(1). Advance online publication. DOI: 10.1108/IMDS-04-2017-0142

Mendling, J., Weber, I., Van Der Aalst, W., Vom Brocke, J., Cabanillas, C., Daniel, F., Debois, S., Di Ciccio, C., Dumas, M., Dustdar, S., Gal, A., García-Bañuelos, L., Governatori, G., Hull, R., La Rosa, M., Leopold, H., Leymann, F., Recker, J., Reichert, M., & Zhu, L. (2018). Blockchains for business process management - Challenges and opportunities. *ACM Transactions on Management Information Systems, 9*(1). Advance online publication. DOI: 10.1145/3183367

Mettler, M. (2016). Blockchain technology in healthcare: The revolution starts here. *2016 IEEE 18th International Conference on E-Health Networking, Applications and Services, Healthcom 2016*. https://doi.org/DOI: 10.1109/HealthCom.2016.7749510

Mohanta, B. K., Jena, D., Panda, S. S., & Sobhanayak, S. (2019). Blockchain technology: A survey on applications and security privacy Challenges. In *Internet of Things (Netherlands)* (Vol. 8). https://doi.org/DOI: 10.1016/j.iot.2019.100107

Morkunas, V. J., Paschen, J., & Boon, E. (2019). How blockchain technologies impact your business model. *Business Horizons, 62*(3). Advance online publication. DOI: 10.1016/j.bushor.2019.01.009

Mourtzis, D., Vlachou, E., & Milas, N. (2016). Industrial Big Data as a Result of IoT Adoption in Manufacturing. *Procedia CIRP, 55*. Advance online publication. DOI: 10.1016/j.procir.2016.07.038

Nakamoto, S. (2008). Bitcoin: A Peer-to-Peer Electronic Cash System | Satoshi Nakamoto Institute. *Bitcoin.Org*.

Narayanan, A., Bonneau, J., Felten, E., Miller, A., & Goldfeder, S. (2016). Bitcoin and Cryptocurrency Technologies: A Comprehensive Introduction. In *Bitcoin and Cryptocurrency Technologies: A Comprehensive Introduction*. Princeton University Press.

Notheisen, B., Hawlitschek, F., & Weinhardt, C. (2017). Breaking down the blockchain hype – Towards a blockchain market engineering approach. *ECIS 2017 Proceedings*.

OECD, & EUIPO. (2019). Trends in Trade in Counterfeit and Pirated Goods. *Illicit Trade*.

Peters, G. W., & Panayi, E. (2016). *Understanding modern banking ledgers through blockchain technologies: Future of transaction processing and smart contracts on the internet of money*. New Economic Windows., DOI: 10.1007/978-3-319-42448-4_13

Raja Santhi, A., & Muthuswamy, P. (2022). Influence of Blockchain Technology in Manufacturing Supply Chain and Logistics. In *Logistics* (Vol. 6, Issue 1). https://doi.org/DOI: 10.3390/logistics6010015

Saberi, S., Kouhizadeh, M., Sarkis, J., & Shen, L. (2019). Blockchain technology and its relationships to sustainable supply chain management. *International Journal of Production Research*, *57*(7). Advance online publication. DOI: 10.1080/00207543.2018.1533261

Tapscott, D., & Tapscott, A. (2018). Blockchain Revolution: How the Technology Behind Bitcoin and Other Cryptocurrencies Is Changing the World. In *Sage Publications, Inc.*

Tian, F. (2016). An agri-food supply chain traceability system for China based on RFID & blockchain technology. *2016 13th International Conference on Service Systems and Service Management, ICSSSM 2016*. https://doi.org/DOI: 10.1109/ICSSSM.2016.7538424

Treiblmaier, H. (2018). The impact of the blockchain on the supply chain: A theory-based research framework and a call for action. *Supply Chain Management*, *23*(6). Advance online publication. DOI: 10.1108/SCM-01-2018-0029

Tseng, J. H., Liao, Y. C., Chong, B., & Liao, S. W. (2018). Governance on the drug supply chain via gcoin blockchain. *International Journal of Environmental Research and Public Health*, *15*(6). Advance online publication. DOI: 10.3390/ijerph15061055 PMID: 29882861

Wang, Y., Han, J. H., & Beynon-Davies, P. (2019). Understanding blockchain technology for future supply chains: a systematic literature review and research agenda. In *Supply Chain Management* (Vol. 24, Issue 1). https://doi.org/DOI: 10.1108/SCM-03-2018-0148

WHO. (2023). Substandard and Falsified Medical Products. In *MCN: The American Journal of Maternal/Child* (Vol. 44, Issue 6).

Yiannas, F. (2018). A New Era of Food Transparency Powered by Blockchain. *Innovations: Technology, Governance, Globalization*, *12*(1–2). Advance online publication. DOI: 10.1162/inov_a_00266

Yin, Y., Chu, F., Dolgui, A., Cheng, T. C. E., & Zhou, M. C. (2022). Big data analytics in production and distribution management. In *International Journal of Production Research* (Vol. 60, Issue 22). https://doi.org/DOI: 10.1080/00207543.2022.2130589

Yli-Huumo, J., Ko, D., Choi, S., Park, S., & Smolander, K. (2016). Where is current research on Blockchain technology? - A systematic review. *PLoS One*, *11*(10). Advance online publication. DOI: 10.1371/journal.pone.0163477 PMID: 27695049

Zheng, Z., Xie, S., Dai, H., Chen, X., & Wang, H. (2017). An Overview of Blockchain Technology: Architecture, Consensus, and Future Trends. *Proceedings - 2017 IEEE 6th International Congress on Big Data, BigData Congress 2017*. https://doi.org/DOI: 10.1109/BigDataCongress.2017.85

Zyskind, G., Nathan, O., & Pentland, A. S. (2015). Decentralizing privacy: Using blockchain to protect personal data. *Proceedings - 2015 IEEE Security and Privacy Workshops. SPW, 2015*. Advance online publication. DOI: 10.1109/SPW.2015.27

KEY TERMS AND DEFINITIONS

Blockchain: A decentralized, distributed ledger technology that records transactions across multiple nodes, ensuring data immutability, transparency, and security through cryptographic hashing and consensus mechanisms.

Decentralization: The distribution of data control across a network of nodes, eliminating reliance on a central authority to reduce single points of failure and enhance system resilience.

Immutability: A core blockchain feature where once data is recorded, it cannot be altered or deleted without network-wide consensus, ensuring tamper-proof records for auditability.

Smart Contracts: Self-executing code stored on a blockchain that automates contractual obligations (e.g., payments, customs clearance) when predefined conditions are met, reducing manual intervention.

Consortium Blockchain: A semi-decentralized blockchain governed by a group of trusted organizations (e.g., manufacturers, logistics providers), balancing transparency with controlled access for supply chain collaboration.

Provenance Verification: The use of blockchain to authenticate a product's origin and journey (e.g., raw materials to retail), combating counterfeiting and ensuring regulatory compliance.

IoT Integration: Combining blockchain with IoT sensors (e.g., GPS, temperature monitors) to enable real-time, automated tracking of shipments and environmental conditions, with data immutably stored on-chain.

Traceability: End-to-end visibility of goods across the supply chain, facilitated by blockchain's unified ledger, allowing stakeholders to monitor location, status, and handling in real time.

Scalability Challenge: Technical limitations in blockchain networks (e.g., low transaction throughput in public blockchains) that hinder real-time logistics operations, addressed via Layer-2 solutions like sidechains.

Interoperability: The ability of blockchain systems to integrate with legacy logistics platforms (e.g., ERP, TMS) and other blockchains through standardized APIs, enabling seamless data exchange.

Chapter 10
Blockchain Adoption in Nigerian Port and Maritime Operations:
Impact on Shipment Tracking and Smart Bills of Lading

Nwoloziri Chinyeaka Nwokodi
https://orcid.org/0009-0006-3707-8057
Nigerian Defence Academy, Kaduna, Nigeria

Vijaya Kittu Manda
https://orcid.org/0000-0002-1680-8210
PBMEIT, India

ABSTRACT

The Ports and Maritime industry has long utilized technology interventions. This study examines the relationship between Blockchain technology and shipping operations in Nigerian ports. It evaluates Blockchain's role in the supply chain and its potential to improve information dissemination and efficiency. Two key roles of Blockchain technology are focused: Shipment Tracking and Smart Bills of Lading. The study used the survey method to collect data through questionnaires from a sample size of 120 respondents, including shipping company representatives and port workers in the commercial unit. The study finds a positive correlation between Blockchain technology and shipment tracking and between Blockchain technology and Smart Bills of Lading. It concludes that Blockchain technology is relevant in the Nigerian shipping industry for Shipment Tracking and Smart Bills of Lading. The study integrates various theories to explain adoption trends and supports findings. Government policy support and public-private collaboration can accelerate

DOI: 10.4018/979-8-3373-2434-0.ch010

Blockchain implementation in Nigerian ports.

INTRODUCTION

Traditional maritime ports are used chiefly as hubs for logistic operations. Modern ports are more than piers or harbors for the berthing of vessels. They are a comprehensive infrastructure and industry for shipping operations in the coastal and global maritime trades with complex network connections. Container ports now handle increased throughput and performance by investing in infrastructure development (Hlali, 2017). Technology can bring positive changes to port and maritime operations. It integrates scientific methods into practice, making these innovations beneficial to the industry (Jović et al., 2019). Scholars began interrogating how technological innovation eliminates obsolete operational methods in the shipping industry. They introduced new, more efficient, cost-effective, and time-saving approaches in the maritime industry (Kyaw, 2024). The sector involves information networks connecting various stakeholders (Jabbar & Bjørn, 2018). Figure 1 shows various stakeholders directly connected with the shipping and port operations. More specifically, seaport operations involve complex processes requiring numerous stakeholders' intervention (Hlali & Wanis, 2020) who exchange large volumes of data surrounded by the global supply chain network (Jović et al., 2019).

Most importantly, many rules and regulations govern the industry. They make transactions rigid, complex, and expensive financially and time-consuming. According to the World Bank, developing countries can boost maritime supply chain performance and resilience with digital tech (World Bank, 2021). The report highlighted that maritime transport is vital to the global economy yet remains vulnerable. Ships carry over 90% of all merchandise trade.

Figure 1. List of stakeholders directly connected with the shipping & port operations

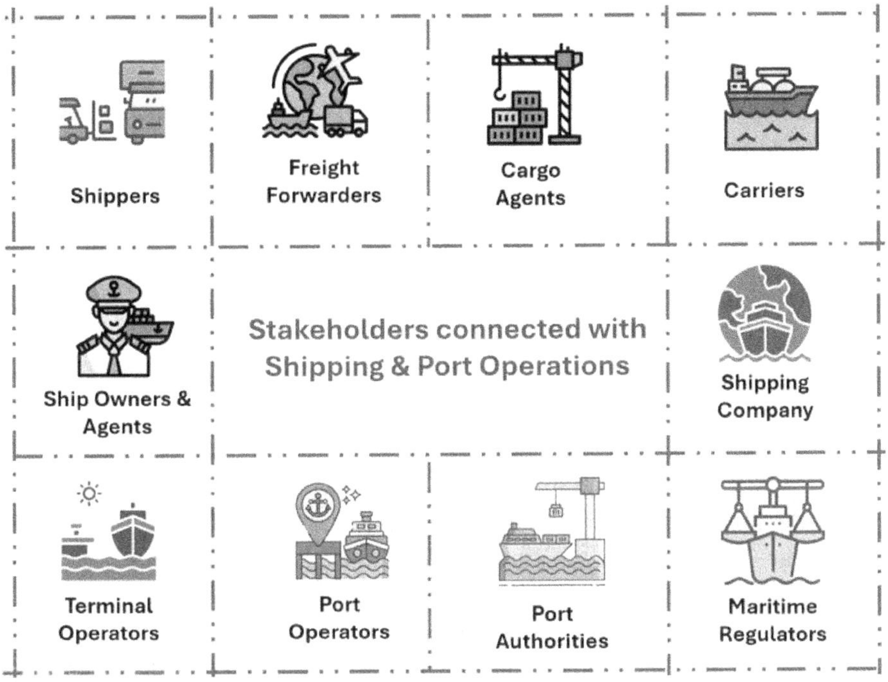

Source: Created by the Authors

Background

Blockchain technology's (BT) promise in shipping and port operations is widely studied (Filom & Vanhassel, 2020). However, empirical assessments often overstate technological determinism, neglecting the socio-institutional frictions characterizing adoption in low- and middle-income countries.. Various industries, such as banking, medicine, and logistics, adopted and began using the technology and showed acceptance of digital and decentralized ledgers. A "Block" records each transaction or a piece of data. A chain with a series of blocks is created, and newer blocks are appended at the end of the chain. BT is an innovation that preserves data integrity by preventing alterations. It ensures that data is recorded in immutable blocks across the chain. Once data is created as a digital ledger, it circulates to all systems in the chain as block data. The data thus becomes immutable. It is transparent and decentralized because it is visible to all operators in the global supply chain system. Technology is applied in data dissemination and information sharing. It quickly replaced manual and paper-based systems with streamlined digital processes in the shipping operations of the port industry. Some areas in the maritime industry that need improvement are shipment tracking, smart billing for lading, cargo tracking, and smart contracts (Filom & Vanhassel, 2020). This means more systematic operations, time-saving and money, reducing corrupt practices, and under declaration of items. Blockchain is essential for securely sharing knowledge and information. When applied to maritime logistics, it can significantly improve port documentation management (Ryzhkov, 2024) and support proficient and effective decisions (Pu & Lam, 2021).

Study Objects

Maritime supply chains suffer significantly from inefficiencies, a persistent lack of transparency, and highly complex networks involving multiple stakeholders. These challenges often lead to delays, increased operational costs, and difficulty tracking goods throughout the supply chain. Additionally, the fragmented nature of the industry and the varying regulatory standards across regions further complicate coordination and collaboration among stakeholders. As a result, there is a growing need for innovative solutions, such as digitalization and BT. Technology interventions are expected to help enhance visibility and streamline processes. They bring greater trust and efficiency across the maritime supply chain ecosystem.

While Blockchain adoption is growing globally, developing economies like Nigeria face unique barriers examined in this study. The study focuses on how Blockchain is used in Nigeria's port shipping operations supply chain. It also examines how technology can improve information sharing and make port operations more efficient. This study addresses a gap in the extant literature on BT in the Nigerian port industry. Few studies have explored how this digital technology can be applied in ports. In Nigeria, research is minimal. Hence, the study will fill this gap, and the findings will be relevant to the port authority's decision-making. Full adoption of Blockchain in financial transactions, shipment tracking, and bills of lading would reduce corruption and port delays. Accordingly, this chapter seeks to answer the following research questions:

1. To determine the significant relationship between blockchain technology and shipment tracking in Nigerian port industry operations.
2. Understanding the significant relationship between Blockchain technology and Smart Bill of Lading (SBL) in Nigerian ports industry shipping operations.

Hypothesis Development

Considering the need for study, the following hypothesis assumptions are postulated:

> $H0_1$: The relationship between Blockchain technology and shipment tracking is not statistically significant in the shipping operations of the Nigerian ports industry.
> $H0_2$: The relationship between Blockchain technology and Smart Bill of Lading (SBL) is not statistically significant in the shipping operations of the Nigerian ports industry.

Figure 2 illustrates the structural design of the study, showing the relationship between Blockchain and the shipping operations of Nigerian ports.

Figure 2. Relationship between blockchain and shipping operations of the Nigerian Ports Industry

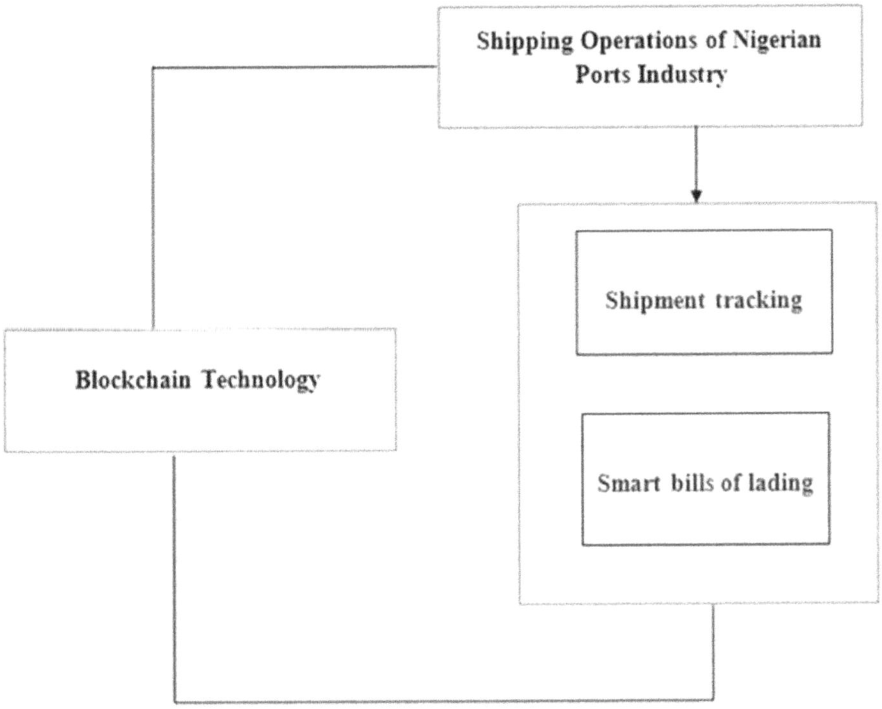

Source: Created by the Authors

LITERATURE REVIEW

Meta-analysis of datasets from research databases shows that studies between 2010 and 2020 focused on conceptual frameworks and early shipping applications with Blockchain. However, a shift toward empirical studies, smart contracts, and technology integration (with AI and IoT) was seen from 2021 onwards. This trend suggests that Blockchain research in this area has evolved from theoretical to applied form, and there is a strong focus on sustainability, efficiency, and decision-making frameworks.

Blockchain evolved over the years from being a peer-to-peer system with financial applications (Manda & Polisetty, 2018) to more diversified and more focused areas such as ecological (Anuradha Yadav et al., 2024) and advertising and marketing applications (Manda et al., 2024). Many organizations, such as hospitals, educational institutions, banking sectors, and logistics organizations, have already begun adopting and applying BT for information sharing and monitoring. BT is increasingly gaining the attention of various stakeholders in the maritime industry due to its relevance in shipping operations.

The Blockchain structure empowers users to generate value and authenticate digital data, fostering innovation in various business applications. However, this study delves explicitly into discussions regarding SBL and shipment tracking in the Nigerian ports industry's shipping operations. Shipment tracking refers to monitoring and tracing the movement of cargo or goods during the shipping process. Conventional tracking methods are frequently slow (Susanto & Kemaluddin, 2023). Blockchain technology, on the other hand, facilitates instant and remote access to data. Shipment tracking is pivotal in the shipping and logistics sector, furnishing stakeholders with crucial information about their goods during transit. It ensures shipping companies have real-time visibility, allowing them to accurately monitor the progress and location of shipments. In the event of issues, proactive measures can be taken to address and navigate potential delays. The primary goal is to trace all changes in the shipment and promptly notify relevant parties of any alterations (Susanto & Kemaluddin, 2023). A system based on Blockchain technology proves instrumental in tracking movements within the supply chain and validating these changes in real-time. Some studies focused on the data-sharing capabilities of the technology and how it can ease decision-making in the shipping industry (Gerakoudi-Ventouri, 2022). Recently, several studies have been conducted on implementing Blockchain in the maritime and shipping industry. Researchers explored the critical success factors and strategic considerations for Blockchain technology implementation in the maritime industry (X. Li et al., 2024). According to the study, the most important sub-criteria for Blockchain implementation in the maritime industry are:

1. Relative advantages
2. Internal leadership
3. Human resources capability
4. Scalability
5. Ease of use

It also presented a novel theoretical framework for critical success factors and strategic recommendations for marketing, skill enhancement, investment, and knowledge sharing. Few studies focused on the factors influencing Blockchain adoption in the maritime industry using Taiwan's technological and organizational environmental framework (Lin, 2024). The study concluded that knowledge absorption capability is the most crucial enabler, followed by perceived relative advantage and trading partner influence.

In contrast, perceived complexity does not significantly impact the intention to adopt Blockchain technology. On a similar subject, a study developed the relationship between Blockchain technology adoption in the maritime and shipping industry and its impact on maritime supply chain integration (Shin et al., 2024). The study adopted a comprehensive systematic review of pertinent studies and practical applications related to Blockchain in the maritime sector. In another instance, a research model based on process virtualization theory, inter-organizational trust, and institutional pressure was tested on 128 Taiwanese maritime-related firms. The study finds that market turbulence strengthens the positive effect of competence trust on Blockchain adoption in maritime. At the same time, coercive institutional pressure (regulatory or industry mandates) significantly impacts adoption (Lin, 2025).

Various studies focused on the Bill of Lading (BoL) as an important document in the shipping and freight chain. It serves basic purposes such as evidence of the contract of carriage, receipt of goods. The electronic bill of lading (eBL) was the first replacement for the paper BoL. The Digital Container Shipping Association (DCSA) published its new data and process standards in 2020 (Notteboom et al., 2021). However, technology has progressed faster. eBLs are replaced by a better form of technology called the Blockchain Smart Bill of Lading (SBL). It is a permanent record system that helps track transactions and assets in a business network. The Smart Bill of Lading is a modern version of the traditional BoL. It uses Blockchain to add digital security and improve its reliability. It is immutable, transparent, and unbreakable confidentiality, building deep trust in business while improving speed and cost-efficiency and reducing the risk of delay. The electronic format of bill of lading was challenging to use, but Blockchain has turned the clock and made the electronic bill of lading user-friendly.

Some studied real-time supply chains using Blockchain architecture for project deliveries (Helo & Shamsuzzoha, 2020). The architecture of the proposed portal system is connected to transport companies, tracking devices, consolidation points, and suppliers with Blockchain technology. The study concludes that real-time tracking and tracing are important in providing a unified view of global supply chains consisting of several parties. This illustrates the need to manage supply chains in multi-company project environments by adopting various tracking and tracing technologies. Blockchain technology proves its relevance in providing real-time information or data in a chain of immutable transactions.

Several studies have been conducted on Blockchain-based logistics and supply chain tracking systems (Dutta et al., 2020). The studies concluded that Blockchain-based tracking systems in the logistics industry play vital roles in supplier and customer relationships. It solves the trust problem and promotes customer satisfaction, especially the 24-hour delivery, which appeals to customers.

Some analyzed the concept of eBL technology for container shipping (Shi & Wang, 2021). The study addressed significant issues like the loss of paper BoL during circulation. It improved the structure and technology of eBL by adding Blockchain. The researchers then tested how well Blockchain fits with eBL. As a result, they created a new model for container shipping. This new model makes shipping data safer more stable, and offers better solutions for using eBL at container terminals.

Typical BoL issues are double-spending, duplicated documents, masqueraded information, and fraud and hacking threads related to the complexity of traditional format and fragmented supply chain activities. A multi-layer integrated IoT-Blockchain conceptual architecture was proposed to solve the traditional BoL issues (Irannezhad & Faroqi, 2023). The study formulated the tasks and functions of each IoT-Blockchain layer and illustrated how the proposed conceptual architecture can overcome several inefficiency and security issues in the status quo. The suggested conceptual framework aims to integrate IoT and Blockchain technologies with established port community systems' procedures to mitigate potential risks of issuing the BoL.

Tsiulin et al. (2020) examined and categorized the tendencies of Blockchain-based applications in the shipping industry and supply chain and their interrelations, including possible correlation of found categories with theoretical background and existing concepts (Tsiulin et al., 2020). The study explored whether Blockchain can be adopted into maritime shipping and port document workflow management. The study built a conceptual framework through a systematic project review carried along with scientific and grey literature. The findings revealed that the examined projects can be categorized into three primary conceptual domains: document workflow management, financial processes, and device connectivity. However, despite evident interconnections, none of the reviewed projects encompass all three areas simultaneously. Ideas related to the maritime document workflow garnered widespread support among the examined projects. Furthermore, these projects inadvertently align with goals previously established in scientific projects related to port management prior to the advent of Blockchain technology.

Some studies analyzed the issues regarding the transmission of a bill of lading and assessed the impact of Blockchain technology on the internal operations of a container terminal (Amico & Cigolini, 2024). The influence of Blockchain technology on the bill of lading lifecycle addresses critical aspects of terminal management, such as bolstering trust among stakeholders, improving security, and enhancing visibility. Unlike traditional Electronic Bills of Lading, Blockchain-based Bills offer superior privacy, security, trustworthiness, and flexibility.

The global maritime industry is an inter-organizational network with the players depending on and supporting each other. Trust is an important element in such partnerships and alliances. Ensuring fair and rational benefit distribution within maritime logistics alliances remains a critical challenge. A Blockchain-based smart contract can bring intelligent and automated benefit distribution within maritime logistics alliances. The smart contract is an automated system that enforces transparency, efficiency, and fairness in benefit distribution. Hence, Blockchain can be seen as a tool for enhancing alliance stability and trust (Qian et al., 2025).

Research Themes

Content analysis and qualitative assessment based on a literature review study on research publications helped the researchers understand major research themes. Table 1 lists the major research themes with a brief description of each.

Table 1. Research themes on "Blockchain in Shipping Operations"

Research Theme	Description
Shipment Tracking	Blockchain enables real-time cargo tracking, offering visibility across the entire shipping journey. It improves operational efficiency, reduces delays, and enhances stakeholder coordination by allowing secure, immutable updates on shipment status.
Smart Bill of Lading (SBL)	SBL is a Blockchain-based digital alternative to traditional paper bills of lading. It improves security, reduces delays, and eliminates issues like document falsification while enhancing trust and operational speed in shipping transactions.
Transparency & Trust	Blockchain's decentralized and tamper-proof nature fosters trust among parties in the maritime supply chain by ensuring data transparency and reducing corruption, fraud, and manipulation.

continued on following page

Table 1. Continued

Research Theme	Description
Process Efficiency & Cost Reduction	Automation via smart contracts and eliminating intermediaries reduce administrative burdens, processing times, and port and shipping operations costs. Blockchain also reduces transaction complexity.
Regulatory Compliance & Security	Blockchain helps ensure compliance with international shipping regulations by providing secure audit trails and immutable records, enhancing data integrity, and reducing legal or regulatory risks.

Source: Created by the Authors based on Content Analysis

Theoretical Underpinning

Guided by the New Technology Acceptance Theory (Iva, 2019) and the Technological-Organizational-Environmental (TOE) framework, this analysis interrogates the interaction between technological affordances, organizational readiness, and environmental contingencies in the context of blockchain adoption. New TechA Theory explains the willingness of organizations to embrace change. It allows for the easy adoption of newer and emerging technologies (Iva, 2019). It provides insights into why organizations would be more receptive than others concerning new technology. Emerging technologies are innovations under development or expected to be realized within five to ten years. They are breakthrough technologies and are poised to transform business and society significantly. These technologies can potentially disrupt existing industries by altering how industries work. They sometimes create new opportunities and applications in the process. Examples of such emerging technologies include Artificial Intelligence (AI), Blockchain, Internet of Things (IoT), Robotics, Autonomous Vehicles, Big Data, and Virtual Reality, each poised to revolutionize various sectors. These technologies are considered the leading technologies for digital transformation in logistics and ports (Notteboom et al., 2021). Besides, technologies benefit logistics and port operations in robotics, decision-making, process automation, and digitalization. Table 2 briefly describes the top theories connected to the topic.

Table 2. Theories connecting blockchain technology and shipping operations

Name of Theory	Brief Description
New Technology Acceptance Theory (New TechA Theory)	This theory explains the willingness of organizations to adopt new and emerging technologies. It explains why some organizations are more receptive to technological innovations like Blockchain, emphasizing perceived benefits, ease of use, and organizational readiness. The study in the document adopts this theory to analyze the adoption of Blockchain in Nigerian ports.
Diffusion of Innovation Theory	This theory describes how new technologies spread through societies or organizations over time. It categorizes adopters into innovators, early adopters, early majority, late majority, and laggards. The theory is relevant to Blockchain adoption in shipping, as it helps explain the varying rates at which ports and maritime stakeholders embrace the technology.
Transaction Cost Economics	This theory examines the costs associated with economic transactions, including search, negotiation, and enforcement costs. Blockchain reduces these costs by providing transparency, Immutability, and automation (e.g., smart contracts), making it highly applicable to shipping operations where multiple stakeholders interact.
Resource-Based View (RBV) Theory	RBV posits that firms gain competitive advantages by leveraging unique, valuable, and inimitable resources. Blockchain can be a strategic resource that enhances efficiency, trust, and collaboration in maritime supply chains. So, they align with RBV principles.
Principal-Agent Theory	This theory addresses conflicts of interest between principals (e.g., cargo owners) and agents (e.g., shipping companies). Blockchain mitigates these conflicts by ensuring transparency and reducing information asymmetry, bringing trust and accountability to shipping operations.
Technological-Organizational-Environmental (TOE) Framework	This framework identifies factors influencing technology adoption from three dimensions: technology, organization, and environment. In the maritime industry (as shown in Lin 2023's study), this theory helps assess readiness for Blockchain adoption by analyzing factors like relative advantage, leadership, and partner influence.
Process Virtualization Theory	This theory examines how and why specific physical processes can be efficiently digitized. Blockchain's ability to digitize and decentralize traditionally paper-heavy shipping processes (like bills of lading) aligns with this theory's principles.
Inter-Organizational Trust Theory	Trust is essential in supply chains involving multiple parties. This theory highlights how the immutability and transparency features of Blockchain can build trust among stakeholders in the shipping ecosystem (e.g., shippers, insurers, customs, and port authorities).
Institutional Theory	This theory examines how external pressures—such as regulatory demands or industry norms—drive organizations to adopt new technologies. The study mentions coercive institutional pressure (e.g., regulations or mandates), significantly influencing Blockchain adoption in the maritime sector, especially when compliance becomes a competitive or legal necessity.

Source: Compiled by the Authors based on Content Analysis

Research Gap

The literature review helped identify a research gap related to the limited exploration and application of Blockchain technology in the Nigerian port industry. There is a lack of localized, empirical research on the application and impact of Blockchain technology in the Nigerian port industry, particularly in improving shipping operations such as shipment tracking and Smart Bill of Lading. The study aims to fill this gap by providing insights into how Blockchain can be effectively implemented in Nigerian ports to enhance efficiency, transparency, and trust.

RESEARCH METHODOLOGY

The research methodology relies on a discrete event simulation model applied to a real-life scenario at the port of Livorno, Italy, focusing on berths, ship-to-shore cranes, and container storage yards. While this simulation was applied to Livorno, its findings on lead-time reduction are generalizable to Nigerian ports due to the similarities of the ports. Simulation outcomes indicate that Blockchain technology reduces the average container lead time in the terminal. The study collected data via a structured questionnaire to elicit responses from shippers and port operators on the impacts of the adoption of Blockchain technology on the efficiency of the Nigerian port industry shipping operations. The questionnaire was designed on a five-point Likert scale using Strongly Agree (SA), Agree (AG), Strongly Disagree (SD), Disagree (DA), and Unaware (UA), which were graded as 4, 3, 2, 1 and 0 respectively in the order of magnitude.

Given the lack of empirical studies on Blockchain in Nigerian ports, this study tests two hypotheses. The hypotheses are tested using the statistical tool of bivariate analysis. Bivariate analysis means analyzing the relationship between two value sets, X and Y (Sandilands, 2014). A bivariate Pearson Correlation analysis was adopted to test the hypotheses. The study population includes selected shipping companies in Onne, Port Harcourt, and Apapa ports and staff from port commercial units. The selected population was estimated at 1632 respondents as a more extensive study population provides more substantial and more reliable results because they have smaller margins of error and lower standards of deviation. The standard deviation quantifies the extent to which data values deviate from the mean. As a study's sample size increases, the error margin decreases. Larger sample sizes afford researchers better control over the risk of reporting false-negative or false-positive findings. A more significant number of samples results in increased precision of the study's outcomes. Based on the above population, the sample size for this study was determined using Cochran's formula, thus stated as in the equation (1):

n=

$$\frac{z^2 Npq}{N_e^2 + z^2 pq} \quad (1)$$

Where:

n = Sample size
N = Total Population
Z = Normal Distribution (Z = 1.96 for 95% confidence)
p = Proportion of population likely to be included in the sample (50% or 0.5 is assumed)
q = Proportion of population not likely to be included in the sample (50% or 0.5 is assumed)
e = Margin of error (0.05) at 95% confidence level

$$n = \frac{1.96^2 * 1632 * 0.5 * 0.5}{1632 * 0.04^2 + 1.96^2 * 0.5 * 0.5} \frac{267.32}{1.898} = 119.519$$

Therefore, the study's sample size (n) was 120.

RESULTS AND FINDINGS

Table 3 provides the Descriptive Analysis based on the respondents' responses as highlighted above.

Table 3. Descriptive analysis of blockchain technology

S/N	Question Items on Blockchain Technology	Mean	STD
1	Blockchain Technology has been fully adopted in Nigerian port industry shipping operations.	4.062	0.571
2	Transport logistics operational activities in the maritime industry use Blockchain Technology in information sharing and asset management.	3.981	0.757
3	Ports policies support modern technologies such as Blockchain Technology in operational activities such as Smart Bill of Lading and shipment tracking, amongst others.	4.552	0.634
4	Blockchain Technology has helped manage the falsification of information and the declaration of imported goods in the Nigerian port industry.	4.211	0.930

continued on following page

Table 3. Continued

S/N	Question Items on Blockchain Technology	Mean	STD
5	Information disseminated on Blockchain Technology has promoted trust and genuineness and reduced the time of custom examination in Nigerian ports	4.333	0.734
	Valid N listwise 120		

Source: Created by the Authors based on Statistical Analysis of the survey data

The results in Table 3 indicated that a more significant population of respondents concorded or agreed with the question items presented in the table, given the mean high scores of 4 points on average on a five-point scale. This could be rated on Blockchain Technology's significance in Nigerian ports industry shipping operations. Similarly, Table 4 provided the descriptive analysis based on the responses gathered from the respondents, as highlighted above.

Table 4. Descriptive analysis of shipment tracking

	Question Items on shipment tracking	Mean	STD
1	Our organization has adopted Blockchain technology in shipment tracking	4.848	0.373
2	Blockchain technology has helped manage emergencies and quick response in such situations	4.190	0.788
3	Blockchain technology on shipment tracking has helped in the satisfaction of clients through effective and efficient services that enhance our operational performances and port sustainability	4.352	0.570
4	Blockchain technology has promoted confidence among insurance companies and banking sectors, amongst others, in collaboration with shipping companies in providing services unbiased	4.281	0.608
5	The ports benefit from Blockchain technology in shipment tracking as it promotes efficiency in on-time berth allocation, cargo handling, and vessel turnaround time.	3.214	1.476
	Valid N listwise 120		

Source: Created by the Authors based on Statistical Analysis of the survey data

The results showed that most respondents agreed with the statements in the table, given the mean high scores of 4 points on average on a five-point scale. This could be regarded as the significance of Blockchain Technology shipment tracking in Nigerian ports industry shipping operations. Table 5 shows the descriptive analysis of the Smart Bill of Lading (SBL).

Table 5. Descriptive analysis of smart bill of lading (SBL)

	Question Items on Smart Bill of Lading	Mean	STD
1	Blockchain SBL has been fully adopted in shipping operations in the Nigerian port industry	3.533	1.872
2	The Ports, shipping companies, and clients have explored the benefits of Blockchain SBL over the traditional paper bill of lading	4.338	0.709
3	Blockchain SBL has overcome mutation and is under declaration familiar with the traditional paper bill of lading in Nigerian ports	4.295	0.823
4	SBL promotes confidence and enhances the speed of doing business in the Nigerian port industry	4.262	0.812
5	The ports, shipping companies, clients, and all concerns in the shipping activities rely so much on trusted Blockchain SBL as a vital document for shipping operations	4.757	0.556
	Valid N listwise 120		

Source: Created by the Authors based on Statistical Analysis of the survey data

The results showed that many respondents affirmed the question items presented in the table, given the mean high scores of 4 points on average on a five-point scale. This could be perceived as the significance of the Blockchain Smart Bill of Lading in Nigerian ports industry shipping operations. Table 6 shows the inferential statistical test results on the relationships between Blockchain technology, shipment tracking, Blockchain technology, and Smart Bill of Lading.

Table 6. Result of the impacts of blockchain technology on shipping operations of the Nigerian Ports Industry

Statistics	$H0_1$	$H0_2$
Pearson correlation	0.753**	0.804**
Sig(2-tailed)	.023	.014
N	120	120

**Correlation is significant at the 0.05 level (2-tailed)

Source: Created by the Authors based on Statistical Analysis

The results presented in Table 4 correspond to hypotheses $H0_1$ and $H0_2$. For $H0_1$, the r-value is 0.753, indicating a high positive correlation between the data set given at 75%. The p-value 0.023 < 0.050 shows that the relationship between Blockchain technology and shipment tracking is statistically significant at 95% confidence. Hence, the null hypothesis is rejected, and the alternate hypothesis is accepted. $H0_2$ examined the relationship between Blockchain technology and Smart Bill of Lading. The table results showed a strong positive association of 80.4% between Blockchain technology and SBL, which is also very significant given that p-value 0.014<0.050. Therefore, the null hypothesis is rejected, and the alternative is accepted at 95% confidence. Collectively, the results show strong stakeholder agreement (mean >4.0) on Blockchain's benefits, with significant correlations ($p<0.05$) for shipment tracking and Smart Bills of Lading.

DISCUSSION

Blockchain is a modern innovation that is adopted in many ports around the world today. With Blockchain technology in shipping transactions, the shipping industries have bolstered reliance and confidence in shipping operations. The study results show the efficacy of this new technology adoption in Nigerian ports and the shipping industry. The findings indicate strong correlations between Blockchain technology and shipment tracking, implying that shipments such as containers and vessels carrying such containers can be tracked and monitored by the transportation system from origin to destination. Ports and stakeholders benefit from these operations by gaining real-time shipment tracking. The ports derive benefits as they help prepare for the shipments' arrival regarding berth allocations and cargo handling gears, amongst others.

Blockchain in Port Operations

Research involving Game Theoretical Analysis on port adoption strategies shows that hybrid adoption methods that combine traditional and intelligent systems are most favorable as the network grows (K. Li et al., 2023). Network externality is a situation where the value increases with increased users. Studies confirm that ports with frequent delays gain more from partial smart tech adoption due to network effects. The good news is that Blockchain can integrate with legacy systems, thereby easing the transition.

The technology can help secure maritime communication (such as in maritime radio communication) and document workflow management systems (Ryzhkov, 2024). Ocean transportation is very time-consuming and requires advance payments. Certain types of businesses, such as Small and Medium Enterprises (SMEs), often have limited capital. They suffer from information asymmetry, excessive paperwork, and long financing cycles. Blockchain can help address pain points in logistics financing. It can help SMEs improve profitability by bringing trustworthy financing (Lu et al., 2024).

Port operations often do not have sufficient metrics for fuel-efficient routing, arrival punctuality, and just-in-time (JIT) compliance. When these metrics are captured, they can have the port has a shorter turnaround, which can result in less fuel consumption and, therefore, help in emission reduction efforts (J. Li et al., 2025; Nguyen et al., 2023). The immutability and traceability features help in the reliable recording of key performance indicators (KPIs) such as on-time arrivals and emissions data. Similarly, Smart contracts and Governance features enable automated incentive distribution (via tokens) to high-performing vessels. Finally, provenance can help in the transparent tracking of environmental contributions.

Smart Contracts and Bills of Lading

The positive correlation (r=0.80) between Blockchain and Smart Bills of Lading confirms its potential to reduce delays (H2). This aligns with global cases like Busan Port, suggesting scalability. Future research could explore hybrid AI/Blockchain models for emission tracking. Blockchain technology has a positive and highly significant relationship with the Smart Bill of Lading. This is one of the most significant benefits of adopting new technology in Nigerian ports. This Blockchain has curtailed the problems of delay emanating from inconsistencies in the Bill of Lading following the traditional approach in the industry. It has also voided the mutation challenge and the import cargo declaration. This technology has promoted transparency, originality, and confidence in dealing with clients and other participants in Nigeria's maritime transport trading industry. As a part of the implementation, it is important to assess the alignment between the country's Electronic Bill of Lading (E-B/L) Act and the Rotterdam Rules. This way, any legal gaps and practical barriers identified with the adoption can be addressed (Choi et al., 2025).

Theoretical Alignment of Study Findings

The study findings strongly align with various theories discussed in the Literature Review. For example, it connects with the New Technology Acceptance Theory (New TechA Theory). The high mean scores (e.g., 4.062 for Blockchain adoption) indicate that Nigerian ports and shipping companies are receptive to Blockchain technology due to its perceived benefits, such as efficiency and transparency. This reflects the theory's emphasis on organizational willingness to adopt emerging technologies. Similarly, the study findings connect with the Diffusion of Innovation Theory. The results show varying adoption and stakeholder agreement (e.g., mean scores ranging from 3.533 to 4.848). It resonates with this theory categorization of adopters (e.g., early adopters vs. laggards). The gradual uptake of Blockchain in Nigerian ports mirrors the diffusion process described in the theory.

The study findings connect with Transaction Cost Economics because it discusses reduced delays, falsification, and administrative burdens (e.g., a mean of 4.211 for managing falsification). Blockchain lowers transaction costs by automating processes (e.g., Smart Bills of Lading) and eliminating intermediaries. The strong correlation (r=0.804) between Blockchain and Smart Bills of Lading addresses information asymmetry, a key concern of Principal-Agent Theory. Blockchain's transparency ensures trust between principals (e.g., cargo owners) and agents (e.g., shipping companies), reducing conflicts of interest.

The study focuses on factors like port policies (mean 4.552) and stakeholder collaboration that align with this framework. It examines technological adoption through technological, organizational, and environmental lenses. For instance, regulatory support (environmental factor) and internal leadership (organizational factor) are critical to Blockchain's success in Nigerian ports. Thus, it connects well with the Technological-Organizational-Environmental (TOE) Framework.

The results highlight how Blockchain fosters stakeholder trust (e.g., mean 4.333 for promoting trust in customs). So, it reinforces the Inter-Organizational Trust Theory's premise that immutable, transparent systems enhance collaboration in multiparty supply chains. It reaffirms that Blockchain can improve customs clearance efficiency and reduce losses of perishable goods (L. Li & Zhou, 2025). The study's recommendation for government policy interventions to drive Blockchain adoption reflects Institutional Theory's emphasis on coercive pressures (e.g., regulations) as catalysts for technological change in industries like maritime logistics.

Application Scenarios and Impact Analysis

Nigerian Ports can benefit from various application scenarios/use cases arising out of Blockchain adoption. The first and most prominent of them all is cargo tracking. Blockchain-based tracking systems can provide real-time updates on cargo movement, reducing transit times and increasing visibility. The second biggest application is supply chain management. Blockchain can improve transparency and accountability throughout the supply chain. So, it is a efficient dispute resolution and payment processing. Third is document management. Digitalization of shipping documents, such as bills of lading and certificates of origin, can reduce paperwork and increase efficiency. Finally, customs clearance happen quickly. Blockchain-based systems can streamline customs clearance processes, reducing clearance times and costs.

With regard to impact analysis, there will be increased efficiency. Reduced paperwork, automation, and streamlined processes can lead to faster cargo clearance and reduced transit times. Then, there is improved security. Tamper-proof and secure data storage can reduce the risk of fraud and cyber attacks. There will be enhanced transparency. Real-time visibility into supply chain operations can enable better decision-making and reduce disputes. Eventually, there will be cost savings. There will be reduced paperwork, increased efficiency, and streamlined processes can lead to cost savings for port operators, shipping lines, and logistics providers.

These will potentially benefits Nigerian Maritime Logistics with increased competitiveness, economic growth, and job creation. By using blockchain technology, Nigerian ports can potentially enhance their logistics operations, increase efficiency, and reduce costs, ultimately contributing to economic growth and development.

Sustainability and Emissions

Blockchain systems can reduce port emissions by minimizing or eliminating unnecessary work. Stakeholders implementing it can improve transportation demand, social welfare, and profits. These connect well with the theory of low-carbon port construction, which can help stakeholders (Government, port authority, and shipping company) to move towards low-carbon transportation modes using governance strategy, investment, and pricing decisions (Z. Li et al., 2024). So, investment in technology enhances consumer surplus and social welfare in the maritime supply chain by reducing perishable goods loss (L. Li & Zhou, 2025).

CHALLENGES AND LIMITATIONS

Implementing new technology comes with resistance to change, especially when the industry involves labor and the working class. Port staff would generally see technology as a threat to their job security. Similarly, stakeholders fear the cost and effort required to transition to the new technology. Governments can use the Public Private Partnership (PPP) model to encourage private parties to join the project. The end users of the technology would be new to the usage of the software or applications. Hence, training programs must be designed and arranged at regular intervals to prepare them and align them with the new changes the technology brings in. It would be even better if they were involved in the design process. Regulators generally fear uncertainty arising from adopting new technology, especially if the technology know-how is unavailable or sourced locally. Regulatory support is key for a smooth transition to the new technology. Hence, white papers and consultation papers should be released. The adoption due dates should be gradual and phased, with milestones in the journey. Similarly, regulatory and legal hurdles, if any, need to be examined at all adoption process phases and addressed in a time-bound manner.

CONCLUSION

The study finds that Nigerian ports and shipping industries adopted the theory of new technology acceptance by adopting and implementing Blockchain technology in shipping operations, especially in shipment tracking and smart billing of lading. This study confirms Blockchain's relevance in Nigerian shipping for shipment tracking and Smart Bills of Lading. The study recommends collaboration between port authorities and shipping companies to implement Blockchain in the Nigerian ports industry's shipping operations. Port authorities should pilot Blockchain-based Smart Bills of Lading at Apapa Port, leveraging lessons from Busan's Chain Portal. The Government should encourage the industry through policy implementations to aid the adoption of new technologies relevant to the shipping industry's seamless operations.

Blockchain can facilitate data-driven decision-making in port operations. So it can improve efficiency and reduce operational costs. However, there is a need to evaluate costs against network benefits before choosing a full/hybrid adoption to promote the adoption of Blockchain technology in port operations (K. Li et al., 2023). Similarly, there is a need to create awareness of network effects to drive smart tech uptake. Sufficient studies have looked at using AI-driven predictive maintenance of shipyards in Maintenance, Repair, and Overhaul (MRO) services (Chava & Dharmavaram, 2025). However, the need of the hour is to have a technology integration of Blockchain with Machine Learning (ML) to speed optimization in fuel use, emissions, and scheduling. Hybrid models integrating Blockchain with AI involving external data, such as weather data, are required. Similarly, on-chain verification of emission reports for audits in the maritime industry is still evolving (J. Li et al., 2025).

Considering that technologies are evolving, the development of regulatory frameworks and their acceptance by regulators need further investigation. For example, the studies can investigate compliance with international maritime standards. Case studies or pilot projects are needed to test Blockchain implementation. This can be done with select Nigerian ports, and then assessments regarding feasibility, challenges, and benefits can be evaluated. Future studies can examine potential cybersecurity risks associated with Blockchain adoption in maritime operations and develop strategies to mitigate them. Comparative analysis can be undertaken regarding the adoption in Nigerian ports with other ports globally. The analysis can help identify the best practices and areas for improvement. Developing user-centric models and applications that consider the needs and perspectives of various stakeholders is vital. Blockchain will surely have an impact on small-scale operators. However, the quantification of the effects of adoption on small-scale shipping operators and port workers, ensuring inclusive benefits, has yet to be studied.

REFERENCES

Amico, C., & Cigolini, R. (2024). Improving port supply chain through blockchain-based bills of lading: A quantitative approach and a case study. *Maritime Economics & Logistics*, *26*(1), 74–104. DOI: 10.1057/s41278-023-00256-y

Chava, Shri. V. K., & Dharmavaram, V. G. (2025). Al-Driven Predictive Maintenance in Shipyards: Enhancing Project Management Efficiency and Operational Cost Reduction through Statistical, Data-Driven Strategies for MRO Services. *Journal of Information Systems Engineering & Management*, *10*(12s), 63–75. DOI: 10.52783/jisem.v10i12s.1707

Choi, S.-B., Ahn, Y.-H., Ma, J.-H., & Dar, Q. F. (2025). Blockchain-Based Revision of Korea's E-Bill of Lading Act in Line with Rotterdam Rules. *Journal of Korea Trade*, *29*(1), 25–51. DOI: 10.35611/jkt.2025.29.1.25

Durán, C., Yazdi, A. K., Derpich, I., & Tan, Y. (2024). Leveraging Blockchain for Maritime Port Supply Chain Management through Multi-criteria Decision Making. *Mathematics*, *12*(10), 1511. DOI: 10.3390/math12101511

Dutta, P., Choi, T.-M., Somani, S., & Butala, R. (2020). Blockchain technology in supply chain operations: Applications, challenges and research opportunities. *Transportation Research Part E, Logistics and Transportation Review*, *142*, 102067. DOI: 10.1016/j.tre.2020.102067 PMID: 33013183

Filom, S., & Vanhassel, E. (2020). *Blockchain application for shipping industry documents*. 19. https://www.researchgate.net/profile/Siyavash-Filom/publication/343417519_Blockchain_application_for_shipping_industry_documents/links/5f29365aa6fdcccc43a8abe2/Blockchain-application-for-shipping-industry-documents.pdf

Gerakoudi-Ventouri, K. (2022). Review of studies of blockchain technology effects on the shipping industry. *Journal of Shipping and Trade*, *7*(1), 2. DOI: 10.1186/s41072-021-00105-2

Helo, P., & Shamsuzzoha, A. H. M. (2020). Real-time supply chain—A blockchain architecture for project deliveries. *Robotics and Computer-integrated Manufacturing*, *63*, 101909. DOI: 10.1016/j.rcim.2019.101909

Hlali, A. (2017). Efficiency of the 26 major container ports in 2015: Comparative analysis with different models. International Journal of Economics & Strategies. *Management of Business*, (10), 15–20.

Hlali, A., & Wanis, A. (2020). Theoretical highlights in container port logistics systems. *Journal of Marine and Island Cultures*, *9*(2). Advance online publication. DOI: 10.21463/jmic.2020.09.2.13

Irannezhad, E., & Faroqi, H. (2023). Addressing some of bill of lading issues using the Internet of Things and blockchain technologies: A digitalized conceptual framework. *Maritime Policy & Management*, *50*(4), 428–446. DOI: 10.1080/03088839.2021.1930223

Iva, B. (2019, December 16). *N*ew TechA Theory—New Technology Acceptance Theory. https://www.linkedin.com/pulse/new-techa-theory-technology-acceptance-iva-blazecki/

Jabbar, K., & Bjørn, P. (2018). Infrastructural Grind: Introducing Blockchain Technology in the Shipping Domain. *Proceedings of the 2018 ACM Conference on Supporting Groupwork*, 297–308. https://doi.org/DOI: 10.1145/3148330.3148345

Jović, M., Filipović, M., Tijan, E., & Jardas, M. (2019). A Review of Blockchain Technology Implementation in Shipping Industry. *Pomorstvo*, *33*(2), 140–148. DOI: 10.31217/p.33.2.3

Kyaw, A. Y. (2024). Application of Advanced Technology on Transport Ships as a Technological Revolution in the Maritime Industry. *Maritime Park Journal of Maritime Technology and Society*, 1–7. https://doi.org/DOI: 10.62012/mp.v3i2.35384

Li, J., Han, D., Weng, T.-H., Wu, H., Li, K.-C., & Castiglione, A. (2025). A secure data storage and sharing scheme for port supply chain based on Blockchain and Dynamic searchable encryption. *Computer Standards & Interfaces*, *91*, 103887. DOI: 10.1016/j.csi.2024.103887

Li, K., Gharehgozli, A., & Lee, J.-Y. (2023). Smart technologies and port operations: Optimal adoption strategy with network externality consideration. *Computers & Industrial Engineering*, *184*, 109557. DOI: 10.1016/j.cie.2023.109557

Li, L., & Zhou, J. (2025). Blockchain Effects and Investment Strategies in the Maritime Supply Chain Under Perishable Goods Loss. *Systems*, *13*(3), 196. DOI: 10.3390/systems13030196

Li, X., Zhou, Y., & Yuen, K. F. (2024). Blockchain implementation in the maritime industry: Critical success factors and strategy formulation. *Maritime Policy & Management*, *51*(2), 304–322. DOI: 10.1080/03088839.2022.2119614

Li, Z., Wang, L., Wang, G., Xin, X., Chen, K., & Zhang, T. (2024). Investment and subsidy strategy for low-carbon port operation with blockchain adoption. *Ocean and Coastal Management*, *248*, 106966. DOI: 10.1016/j.ocecoaman.2023.106966

Lin, H.-F. (2024). Blockchain adoption in the maritime industry: Empirical evidence from the technological-organizational-environmental framework. *Maritime Policy & Management*, *51*(7), 1474–1496. DOI: 10.1080/03088839.2023.2175063

Lin, H.-F. (2025). Examining the determinants of Blockchain technology-enabled maritime supply chain system adoption intention: Does market turbulence play a moderating role? *Marine Policy*, *174*, 106616. DOI: 10.1016/j.marpol.2025.106616

Lu, B., Lu, H., & Wang, H. (2024). Design and value analysis of the blockchain-based port logistics financial platform. *Maritime Policy & Management*, *51*(6), 1037–1061. DOI: 10.1080/03088839.2023.2205870

Manda, V. K., & Polisetty, A. (2018). Status Check on Blockchain Implementations in India. SSRN *Electronic Journal*. https://doi.org/DOI: 10.2139/ssrn.3265654

Manda, V. K., Sagi, S., & Yadav, A. (2024). Blockchain in Advertising and Marketing: Revolutionizing the Industry Through Transparency and Trust. In Tarnanidis, T. K., & Sklavounos, N. (Eds.), (pp. 89–112). Advances in Marketing, Customer Relationship Management, and E-Services. IGI Global., DOI: 10.4018/979-8-3693-2754-8.ch005

Nguyen, S., Leman, A., Xiao, Z., Fu, X., Zhang, X., Wei, X., Zhang, W., Li, N., Zhang, W., & Qin, Z. (2023). Blockchain-Powered Incentive System for JIT Arrival Operations and Decarbonization in Maritime Shipping. *Sustainability*, *15*(22), 15686. DOI: 10.3390/su152215686

Notteboom, T., Pallis, A., & Rodrigue, J.-P. (2021). *Port Economics, Management and Policy* (1st ed.). Routledge., DOI: 10.4324/9780429318184

Pu, S., & Lam, J. S. L. (2021). Blockchain adoptions in the maritime industry: A conceptual framework. *Maritime Policy & Management*, *48*(6), 777–794. DOI: 10.1080/03088839.2020.1825855

Qian, X., Shen, L., Wang, Y., Lin, J., Jin, Z., Ge, Y.-E., & George Haddad, S. S. (2025). Stability analysis of maritime logistics alliance based on Blockchain. *Transport Policy*, *163*, 219–231. DOI: 10.1016/j.tranpol.2024.12.025

Ryzhkov, Y. (2024). Maritime Radio Communication: Language Challenges and How to handle them. *Humanities Science Current Issues*, *2*(82), 392–395. DOI: 10.24919/2308-4863/82-2-55

Sandilands, D. (2014). Bivariate Analysis. In Michalos, A. C. (Ed.), *Encyclopedia of Quality of Life and Well-Being Research* (pp. 416–418). Springer Netherlands., DOI: 10.1007/978-94-007-0753-5_222

Shi, H., & Wang, X. (2021). Research on Electronic Bill of Lading of Container Shipping Based on Blockchain Technology. *Journal of Physics: Conference Series, 2029*(1), 012123. DOI: 10.1088/1742-6596/2029/1/012123

Shin, S., Wang, Y., Pettit, S., & Abouarghoub, W. (2024). Blockchain application in maritime supply chain: A systematic literature review and conceptual framework. *Maritime Policy & Management, 51*(6), 1062–1095. DOI: 10.1080/03088839.2023.2234896

Susanto, H., & Kemaluddin, N. (2023). Innovative Blockchain-Based Tracking Systems, A Technology Acceptance for Cross-Border Runners During and Post-Pandemic. *Sustainability, 15*(8), 6519. DOI: 10.3390/su15086519

Tarnanidis, T., Papathanasiou, J., Ismyrlis, V., & Kittu Manda, V. (Eds.). (2024). *Multiple-Criteria Decision-Making (MCDM) Techniques and Statistics in Marketing*. IGI Global., DOI: 10.4018/979-8-3693-9122-8

Tsiulin, S., Reinau, K. H., Hilmola, O.-P., Goryaev, N., & Karam, A. (2020). Blockchain-based applications in shipping and port management: A literature review towards defining key conceptual frameworks. *Review of International Business and Strategy, 30*(2), 201–224. DOI: 10.1108/RIBS-04-2019-0051

World Bank. (2021). *Accelerating Digitalization Across the Maritime Supply Chain*. https://www.worldbank.org/en/topic/transport/publication/accelerating-digitalization-across-the-maritime-supply-chain

Yadav, Anuradha, Shivani, Shivani, Manda, Vijaya Kittu, & Sangwan, Vikramaditya, & Demkiv, A. (2024). Blockchain technology for ecological and environmental applications. *Ecological Questions, 35*(4), 1–20. DOI: 10.12775/EQ.2024.050

KEY TERMS AND DEFINITIONS

Blockchain Technology (BT): A decentralized, immutable digital ledger that records transactions across multiple nodes. In maritime logistics, BT enables secure data sharing, reduces fraud, and automates processes via smart contracts.

Smart Bill of Lading (SBL): A blockchain-based digital version of the traditional bill of lading. SBL serves as a tamper-proof record of cargo receipt, contract of carriage, and ownership title, reducing documentation delays and fraud risks.

Shipment Tracking: Real-time monitoring of cargo movement using BT. Provides end-to-end supply chain visibility by recording location, condition, and handling events on an immutable ledger, enabling proactive issue resolution.

Port Community System (PCS): Integrated digital platforms connecting stakeholders (shippers, carriers, customs). BT enhances PCS by adding decentralized security, real-time data sync, and automated compliance checks.

New Technology Acceptance Theory (New TechA): Framework explaining organizational willingness to adopt innovations. Predicts BT adoption based on perceived benefits (efficiency, cost reduction) and institutional readiness.

Process Virtualization Theory: Examines digitization of physical workflows. Explains how BT virtualizes paper-based maritime processes (e.g., bills of lading, customs clearance) while preserving legal validity.

Network Externality: Phenomenon where BT's value increases as more stakeholders join the network. Critical for ports where collaboration amplifies efficiency gains (e.g., shared shipment tracking).

Hybrid Adoption Model: Strategy combining BT with legacy systems. Mitigates transition risks in ports with limited digital infrastructure (e.g., partial BT integration for SBL while retaining manual backups).

Coercive Institutional Pressure: Regulatory mandates driving BT adoption (e.g., government policies requiring digital bills of lading). Overcomes resistance in bureaucratic port environments.

Chapter 11
Blockchain Technology and Smart Contract in Supply Chain: Issues in Maritime Sector

Arbia Hlali
https://orcid.org/0000-0002-1850-4579
Taibah University, Saudi Arabia

Naser Abdel Raheem Al Ali
https://orcid.org/0000-0002-6884-3835
Russian University of Transport, Russia

Mohammad Kamrul Hasan
https://orcid.org/0000-0003-3866-0090
Tongling University, China

Chinyeaka Nwokodi Nwoloziri
https://orcid.org/0009-0006-3707-8057
Nigerian Defence Academy, Kaduna, Nigeria

Radwan Eskhita
https://orcid.org/0000-0001-8286-5435
Lucerne University of Applied Sciences, Switzerland

ABSTRACT

The maritime industry faces significant challenges, including inefficiencies, fraud, and a lack of transparency in the supply chain. Companies like Maersk are exploring blockchain technology and smart contracts to address these issues through secure

DOI: 10.4018/979-8-3373-2434-0.ch011

and automated transactions. This chapter examines the transformative potential of blockchain technology and smart contracts within the maritime transport sector, aiming to provide a comprehensive overview of their current applications and future possibilities in the maritime supply chain. The chapter concludes that the adoption of these technologies is not without challenges, including regulatory hurdles, integration issues, and the need for standardization. By analyzing both the benefits and obstacles associated with blockchain and smart contracts, this study aims to elucidate their role in the transformation of the maritime sector.

INTRODUCTION

Frikha and Hlali (2023) examined the transformative impact of digitalization on logistics management, emphasizing how the digital transition serves as a pivotal factor in modernizing supply chains and enhancing operational efficiency. Their study highlighted the integration of advanced technologies, such as blockchain and automation, as crucial for addressing traditional challenges, including delays, inefficiencies, and limited transparency in stakeholder interactions. This aligns seamlessly with the application of blockchain and smart contracts in maritime logistics, where digital solutions play a critical role in streamlining operations, ensuring data accuracy, and fostering secure, real-time collaboration. Blockchain's decentralized ledger and the automated execution of smart contracts.

Blockchain technology has emerged as a transformative force across various industries, providing innovative solutions to longstanding challenges in supply chain management. In the maritime sector, which is characterized by complex logistics, multiple stakeholders, and a global scope, the adoption of blockchain and smart contracts offers an opportunity to enhance efficiency, transparency, and security. In recent years, the efficiency of major container ports has garnered significant attention within the maritime sector, especially as global trade continues to grow. Hlali (2017) conducted a detailed analysis of the operational efficiency of 26 major container ports in 2015, utilizing various models to assess their performance. This study highlighted how crucial port efficiency is for enhancing cargo handling, minimizing turnaround times, and optimizing logistical operations. The findings indicate that ports that adopt innovative strategies and leverage new technologies consistently outperform their peers. This underscores the importance of ongoing improvement in port management practices to meet the evolving demands of international trade.

As the maritime industry evolves, blockchain technology emerges as a game-changer for enhancing port efficiency. By facilitating real-time data sharing and promoting transparency across supply chains, blockchain can effectively address many of the inefficiencies identified in traditional port operations. The use of smart contracts takes this a step further, automating transactions and streamlining processes, which helps to reduce delays and build trust among stakeholders. As more ports begin to implement blockchain solutions, they can tackle challenges such as documentation errors and fraud more effectively. This integration of port efficiency with blockchain technology not only sets the stage for improved operational performance but also heralds a new era of innovation in the maritime sector, where efficiency and technological advancement go hand in hand.

The maritime supply chain is characterized by complex interactions among shipping companies, port authorities, customs agencies, freight forwarders, and end customers. Each participant plays a vital role in ensuring the seamless flow of goods across international borders. However, this complexity frequently results in inefficiencies, delays, and heightened costs. According to the World Economic Forum (2018), inefficiencies in the maritime supply chain can account for as much as 20% of shipping costs, underscoring the necessity for innovative solutions.

Blockchain technology has the potential to modernize operations by providing real-time visibility into the movement of goods and automating processes through smart contracts. This technology fosters trust among stakeholders by ensuring that all parties have access to the same information, thereby reducing disputes and enhancing collaboration (Kouhizadeh & Sarkis, 2018).

Despite the promise of blockchain and smart contracts, significant hurdles remain. Technical challenges related to scalability and interoperability, coupled with regulatory uncertainties and industry resistance, pose barriers to widespread adoption.

Technological progress is a crucial factor in industrial and economic development (UNCTAD, 2018). The invention of machinery facilitated the mechanization of production, while the discovery of electricity promoted mass production. Additionally, the advent of the Internet has enabled the coordination of various stages of production from remote locations within the global industry. This has resulted in the fragmentation of production and the emergence of global value chains (World Trade Organization, 2019). Hlali and Wanis (2020) offer valuable insights into container port logistics systems, emphasizing the necessity for technological innovations to optimize operations and enhance efficiency. Their study underscores the importance of integrating advanced solutions to tackle challenges such as resource management, operational delays, and coordination among stakeholders.

Blockchain, as a pillar of digital transformation, acts as a catalyst for improving port infrastructure quality within logistics systems, particularly by addressing regional inefficiencies. The integration of digital tools with physical infrastructure also enhances resilience, for instance, AI-powered predictive maintenance systems utilize blockchain-verified sensor data from quay walls and cranes to anticipate and prevent failures. Moreover, blockchain helps standardize logistics data across critical nodes, improving coordination and transparency. (Hlali, 2023) highlights how underfunded infrastructure remains a challenge in many service-based economies. These advancements underline the interdependence between digital systems and infrastructure quality: real-time data streams allow for precise asset management, while tamper-proof audit trails built on blockchain foster trust and secure private investments in initiatives such as dredging operations and cold-chain logistics upgrades.

Blockchain technology has a significant impact on various sectors of the economy. The automation of processes through smart contracts can simplify administrative procedures, reduce costs, facilitate claims for reimbursement, and manage multinational insurance contracts (Mohamed et al., 2024). The pilot projects tested in the marine insurance sector are particularly relevant to international trade. Additionally, blockchain is just beginning to penetrate the e-commerce landscape, potentially revitalizing it and influencing existing business models.

Blockchain could serve as the future infrastructure for the service sector, leveraging its automation capabilities to enhance the use of smart contracts. In the service sector, blockchain may have a similar transformative effect as robotics has had on the manufacturing industry. The primary impact of blockchain will be a reduction in costs (Gerakoudi-Ventouri, 2022).

Historically, Bitcoin, described in the study of Nakamoto (2009), was the first blockchain model that served as a ledger for the exchange of cryptocurrency. In blockchain technology, there is no need for trusted third parties such as banks to keep track of, authenticate, and validate all transactions (Om et al., 2021). In the case of Bitcoin and more generally first-generation blockchains, transactions are exchanges of simple values, such as cryptocurrencies, between participants of the network. Each member of the network has a copy of the blockchain that can be thus considered as the digital record of transactions. Transactions are listed there and grouped by “packages” called blocks.

The blockchain was used in several fields, such as the food industry (Kamble et al. 2020), health (Kuo et al. 2017). In similar context, (Dong et al., 2023) analyze how the adoption of traceability technologies like blockchain can significantly improve performance in food supply chain networks. Their study finds that increased visibility not only enhances operational efficiency but also promotes consumer trust and supplier coordination. In addition, blochchain used in the protection of personal data (Politou et al., para. 2018). Also, Zafar et al. (2022) review the key challenges in integrating blockchain with IoT, such as scalability, latency, data volume, and energy consumption. They also suggest hybrid consensus mechanisms and edge computing as promising solutions to improve real-world applicability.

In the context of port logistics and supply chains, blockchain technology has emerged as a transformative tool for enhancing operational efficiency, transparency, and trust among diverse stakeholders. Queiroz et al. (2019) emphasize that blockchain enables real-time, tamper-proof data sharing between shipping companies, port authorities, customs agencies, and logistics providers, thereby significantly reducing administrative delays, paperwork burdens, and the risk of fraud. Lambourdière and Corbin (2020) further demonstrate that blockchain can optimize container tracking, cargo documentation, and vessel scheduling, especially in complex and congested port environments where coordination is critical. The integration of smart contracts enables automated execution of key logistics processes based on verified conditions, minimizing human intervention and potential disputes. Collectively, these advancements position blockchain as a foundational technology for building more resilient, transparent, and digitally connected port logistics ecosystems.

Currently, there are a number of studies where blockchain technology has been used in the maritime industry, particularly shipping and port management (Rodrigue, 2020; Tsiulin, 2020). Blockchain technology has several benefits that can improve maritime transport (Jović et al., 2020).The objective of this chapter is to develop the vision of the use of blockchain and smart contracts in the legal system, since these tools must be used as a means to ensure equality of conditions and benefits to the parties intervening. Therefore, it is necessary to highlight several advantages that revolve around the execution, protection of personal data, defense of consumer rights, right of withdrawal, interpretation, probative value, elements, and solution of controversies as a consequence of the use of smart contracts or smart legal contracts. This, with the aim of having a comprehensive view of the application of blockchain in maritime transport. Also, the chapter aims to provide a comprehensive overview of the current state and future potential of blockchain technology and smart contracts in the maritime supply chain. So, to accomplish the paper, it is organized as follows: Section two describes the general roles of blockchain and smart contracts. Section three represents the role of blockchain and smart contracts in supply chain management. Section four studies the roles of blockchain and smart contracts in the maritime sector. Section five describes the challenges and issues in implementing blockchain and smart contracts in the sixth section. Section six represents some case studies, Section seven discusses the future trends and developments.

CHAPTER OBECTIVES AND STRUCTURE

This chapter aims to explore the integration of blockchain technology within the maritime industry, focusing on its potential to address key challenges and enhance operational efficiency. The objectives include examining the impact of blockchain on supply chain management, identifying integration strategies, and analyzing existing network infrastructures in ports and vessels. The chapter is systematically structured to provide a comprehensive analysis, beginning with an overview of blockchain applications and followed by an exploration of integration techniques and challenges.

It concludes with a discussion on future directions and recommendations for the successful adoption of blockchain in maritime operations.

PRINCIPLES OF BLOCKCHAIN OPERATION

It is not the intention here to restate what many reports and books have already detailed regarding the functioning of blockchain technology. The aim is, on the one hand, to recall the essential principles behind the technological system referred to by this term, and above all, on the other hand, to focus on aspects that are rarely discussed or mentioned outside expert and specialist communities.

In this regard, it is important to clarify that blockchains can be considered specific cases of distributed ledgers, and for this reason, a conflation is often made between what can be called blockchain technology and Distributed Ledger Technology (DLT). Since the notion of a ledger is crucial in post-trade activities, the interest in blockchains becomes clear for those reflecting on the architecture of the financial system and potential ways to improve it.

Distributed ledgers allow users of an electronic network to record and manage data related to the functioning of the network. The information managed by this shared ledger may vary depending on the system's design but typically includes various transactional data: exchange prices of securities or physical assets, their virtual identifiers, etc. This information is distributed among users, who can then use it to process their transfers without relying, in a distributed model, on a central trusted validation system.

The functioning of a distributed ledger such as a blockchain involves the following elements:

- A peer-to-peer (P2P) network that is either public or fully/partially private
- A distributed database serving as a "ledger" in which all transactions and other relevant information for network members are recorded
- A set of cryptographic tools and methods ensuring the security of the network—particularly against any attack or attempt to corrupt the distributed ledger—and the integrity of exchanges among its members
- A consensus algorithm governing the updating and evolution of the ledger, enabling the automation of the transaction validation process between network members through a set of rules
- An incentive mechanism embedded in the network's operating protocol, necessary to compensate active network participants—namely, those who ensure the proper functioning and security of the network, particularly and especially when the network is completely open

THE ROLES OF BLOCKCHAIN AND SMART CONTRACTS

The Role of Blockchain and Smart Contracts in Achieving Economic Profit

Blockchain technology and smart contracts are revolutionizing various industries by enhancing operational efficiency, reducing costs, and creating new business models. Their application can lead to significant economic benefits for organizations by streamlining processes, improving transparency, and minimizing fraud.

- **Enhancing Operational Efficiency**

One of the primary ways that blockchain and smart contracts contribute to economic profit is by enhancing operational efficiency. Traditional supply chains are often hindered by inefficiencies stemming from manual processes, excessive paperwork, and a lack of real-time data. Blockchain offers a decentralized ledger that enables all parties in the supply chain to access the same information simultaneously. This transparency minimizes the time spent on reconciliations and disputes, resulting in faster transaction cycles and reduced operational costs. For example, companies such as Maersk and IBM have implemented blockchain solutions to optimize shipping processes, leading to decreased shipping times and costs.

- **Reducing Transaction Costs**

Smart contracts automate the execution of agreements based on predefined conditions. This automation eliminates the need for intermediaries, such as lawyers or brokers, reducing transaction costs. For example, in the insurance industry, smart contracts can automatically trigger payouts when certain conditions are met, eliminating lengthy claims processes and associated administrative costs. By reducing the reliance on intermediaries, businesses can retain a larger portion of their revenue, directly contributing to economic profit.

- **Improving Transparency and Trust**

Blockchain's inherent transparency fosters trust among stakeholders. In industries such as the food supply chain, where traceability is crucial, blockchain enables consumers to verify the origin and journey of products. This transparency can enhance brand loyalty and justify premium pricing, ultimately leading to increased sales and economic profit. Companies that adopt blockchain for traceability can differentiate themselves in the market, attracting conscientious consumers who are willing to pay more for verified products.

- **Minimizing Fraud and Errors**

Fraud and errors can significantly affect a company's bottom line. The immutable ledger of blockchain ensures that once a transaction is recorded, it cannot be altered or deleted. This feature reduces the risk of fraud and discrepancies in financial reporting. For instance, in the banking sector, blockchain can facilitate secure transactions and diminish the likelihood of fraudulent activities, thereby safeguarding revenue streams and enhancing profitability.

- **Facilitating New Business Models**

Blockchain and smart contracts facilitate the development of innovative business models that can generate economic profit. For example, decentralized finance (DeFi) platforms utilize blockchain technology to provide financial services without relying on traditional intermediaries, thereby creating new revenue streams. Furthermore, the tokenization of assets enables companies to raise capital through Initial Coin Offerings (ICOs) or Security Token Offerings (STOs), granting access to a wider investor base and potentially enhancing profitability.

The integration of blockchain technology and smart contracts into business operations offers numerous opportunities for generating economic profit. By enhancing operational efficiency, reducing transaction costs, improving transparency, minimizing fraud, and facilitating new business models, organizations can leverage these technologies to boost profitability. As industries increasingly adopt blockchain solutions, those who embrace this innovation are likely to gain a competitive advantage and achieve substantial economic benefits.

THE ROLE OF BLOCKCHAIN AND SMART CONTRACTS IN SUPPLY CHAIN MANAGEMENT

Blockchain technology and smart contracts are revolutionizing supply chain management by enhancing transparency, efficiency, and security. By providing a decentralized and immutable ledger, blockchain allows all stakeholders to access real-time information about transactions, significantly improving visibility and traceability (Kshetri, 2018). This is particularly crucial in industries like food and pharmaceuticals, where the ability to track products from origin to consumer ensures safety and compliance. Additionally, the streamlined processes enabled by blockchain reduce the reliance on intermediaries, thereby lowering transaction costs and minimizing delays. Smart contracts further enhance this transformation by automating the execution of agreements based on predefined conditions. This automation not only accelerates processes, such as payment upon delivery, but also reduces administrative burdens and the potential for errors or fraud (Tapscott & Tapscott, 2016). Moreover, smart contracts can include compliance checks that ensure adherence to regulations, adding an extra layer of security and trust among stakeholders. As these technologies continue to gain traction, they promise to create more resilient and responsive supply chains, ultimately driving economic profit and fostering collaboration among all parties involved. The integration of blockchain and smart contracts is paving the way for a more efficient and transparent supply chain ecosystem, setting the stage for significant advancements in how goods are produced, tracked, and delivered (Mougayar, 2016; IBM, 2020).

THE ROLE OF BLOCKCHAIN AND SMART CONTRACTS IN THE MARITIME SECTOR

Blockchain technology and smart contracts are set to significantly enhance the maritime sector by improving transparency, efficiency, and security in shipping and logistics. The maritime industry is characterized by complex global supply chains, and blockchain provides a decentralized and immutable ledger that allows all parties involved—such as shipping companies, port authorities, customs officials, and freight forwarders—to access real-time information about shipments. This increased visibility facilitates better tracking of cargo, reduces the risk of theft or loss, and ensures compliance with regulations (Kshetri, 2018).

Additionally, the maritime sector frequently depends on various intermediaries for documentation and transaction processing, which can result in delays and increased costs. By leveraging blockchain technology, companies can streamline these processes, reducing their reliance on intermediaries and consequently lowering transaction costs. Smart contracts further enhance this efficiency by automating critical processes, such as executing agreements for cargo delivery and facilitating payment upon arrival. This automation minimizes administrative burdens and decreases the potential for errors or fraud (Tapscott & Tapscott, 2016).

Moreover, smart contracts can incorporate compliance checks and initiate actions based on specific conditions, ensuring that all parties adhere to maritime regulations and standards. This functionality adds an additional layer of security and trust among stakeholders, which is essential in an industry where regulatory compliance is critical. As blockchain technology and smart contracts continue to gain traction in the maritime sector, they promise to foster a more efficient, transparent, and secure shipping ecosystem, ultimately enhancing operational performance and generating economic benefits for all participants involved (Mougayar, 2016; IBM, 2020).

- **Blockchain Technology in the Maritime Sector**

Blockchain technology is defined as a decentralized digital ledger that records transactions across multiple computers in a manner that ensures the security and transparency of data (Nakamoto, 2008). Each block in the chain contains a list of transactions, a timestamp, and a cryptographic hash of the previous block, creating a secure and tamper-proof record. This structure ensures that once data is recorded, it cannot be altered without the consensus of the network participants.

- **Benefits of Blockchain in Maritime Logistics:**
- **Real-time Tracking**: Blockchain enables real-time tracking of shipments, providing stakeholders with visibility into the status of goods throughout the supply chain. For instance, the use of IoT devices in conjunction with blockchain can provide continuous updates on the location and condition of cargo, allowing for proactive decision-making. This capability is crucial in mitigating risks such as theft, damage, or spoilage (Kouhizadeh & Sarkis, 2018).
- **Document Management**: The technology can streamline documentation processes, reducing paperwork and the risk of errors associated with traditional methods. Smart contracts can automate compliance checks and documentation verification, significantly speeding up processes like customs clearance. The digitization of documents also minimizes the risk of loss or damage, which is common with paper-based systems (Bumblauskas et al., 2020).
- **Enhanced Security**: With its cryptographic features, blockchain can enhance the security of sensitive data, protecting it from unauthorized access. The decentralized nature of blockchain means that there is no single point of failure, making it more resilient to cyberattacks. Furthermore, the transparency of blockchain allows stakeholders to audit transactions easily, increasing accountability (Wang et al., 2019).
- **Cost Reduction**: By reducing the need for intermediaries, minimizing disputes, and enhancing operational efficiencies, blockchain can lead to significant cost savings in maritime logistics.

Several companies have begun to harness the potential of blockchain in maritime logistics. For instance, Maersk and IBM have collaborated to develop TradeLens, a blockchain-based platform that facilitates secure and efficient information sharing among supply chain participants. TradeLens has onboarded numerous stakeholders, including port operators and customs authorities, to create a collaborative ecosystem (IBM, 2020). The Table 1 summarize the main studies, their use cases, benefits, and challenges in the maritime industry using blockchain technology.

Table 1. Benefits and challenges of blockchain technology in maritime industry

Reference	Use Cases	Benefits	Challenges
Kumar et al. (2019)	Rice supply chain	Ensures food safety, improves traceability, reduces fraud	Implementation complexity, scalability
Korpela et al. (2017)	Digital Supply Chain (DSC)	Enhances data security, improves B2B operations	Cross-platform compatibility, resource constraints
Jensen et al. (2019)	TradeLens for maritime logistics	Transparency, real-time tracking, efficient collaboration	High energy consumption, privacy issues
Irannezhad et al. (2020)	Logistics and transportation	Improved coordination, secure data exchange	Regulatory hurdles, adoption cost
Tijan et al. (2019)	Decentralized data storage	Cost reduction, paperless operations	High initial investment, scalability concerns
PU and Lam (2020)	Maritime finance, insurance	Fraud prevention, enhanced transparency	Complex regulatory compliance
Loklindt et al. (2020)	Data exchange in shipping	Reduces transaction costs, improves global trade	Interoperability issues, lack of standards
Peronja et al. (2020)	Freight cost analysis	Reduces operational costs, improves environmental impact	Complex cost-benefit analysis, resistance to change
Czachorowski et al. (2019)	Maritime systems	Improves supply chain visibility, anti-cybercrime measures	Technological limitations, infrastructure requirements
Ripple (2020)	Ship finance transactions	Secures transactions, mitigates fraud risks	Scalability, privacy concerns

- **Smart Contracts: Definition and Functionality**

Smart contracts are self-executing contracts with the terms of the agreement directly written into code (Szabo, 1997). They operate on blockchain platforms, automatically executing actions when predetermined conditions are met. This automation reduces the need for intermediaries and streamlines processes, resulting in cost savings and increased efficiency. The Key Features of Smart Contracts are:

- **Automation**: Smart contracts can automate various processes within the supply chain, such as payment processing and cargo release. For example, a smart contract could automatically release payment to a shipping company once the cargo is delivered and verified by the receiving party. This reduces the time spent on manual checks and accelerates the payment cycle, improving cash flow for businesses (Kouhizadeh & Sarkis, 2018).

- **Transparency**: All stakeholders have access to the same information, which reduces the potential for disputes and enhances trust. The immutable nature of blockchain ensures that once a smart contract is executed, it cannot be altered, providing a clear record of all transactions. This transparency is particularly beneficial in complex supply chains where multiple parties are involved (Bumblauskas et al., 2020).
- **Efficiency**: By eliminating manual processes and reducing the need for intermediaries, smart contracts can significantly speed up transactions. The implementation of smart contracts can reduce transaction times from days to mere minutes, as transactions are automatically executed once predefined conditions are met. This efficiency can lead to faster delivery times, reduced operational costs, and improved customer satisfaction. For instance, Casino et al. (2019) highlight that blockchain-based smart contracts in supply chains can automate validation and settlement processes, significantly accelerating operations and minimizing human error.
- **Dispute Resolution**: Smart contracts can help minimize disputes by providing transparent and immutable records of transactions. In the event of a disagreement, the terms of the smart contract serve as a clear reference point. This capability can significantly reduce legal costs and the time spent resolving disputes (Wang et al., 2019).

The integration of smart contracts into maritime logistics holds great promise, yet challenges remain in terms of legal recognition and standardization. Many jurisdictions have not yet established clear legal frameworks for smart contracts, which can create uncertainty for stakeholders.

CHALLENGES AND ISSUES IN IMPLEMENTING BLOCKCHAIN AND SMART CONTRACTS

Despite the potential benefits, several challenges hinder the widespread implementation of blockchain and smart contracts in the maritime sector:

- **Technical Challenges**: Issues such as scalability and interoperability between different blockchain platforms can impede adoption. The maritime industry comprises various stakeholders, each potentially using different systems, making seamless integration difficult. For example, the Ethereum blockchain, while popular for smart contracts, faces scalability issues during periods of high demand, which could delay transactions (Kouhizadeh & Sarkis, 2018).

- **Regulatory and Legal Issues**: The lack of clear regulatory frameworks surrounding blockchain and smart contracts raises concerns about their legal validity and enforceability. Many countries have yet to establish laws that recognize smart contracts, creating uncertainty for stakeholders. Furthermore, differing regulations across jurisdictions can complicate international shipping operations. The challenge lies in creating harmonized regulations that can facilitate global trade while ensuring compliance with local laws (Bumblauskas et al., 2020).
- The UNCTAD (2017) mentioned that the main difficulty is in setting up an electronic alternative to traditional paper documents is related to reproduction in a secure electronic environment, while ensuring that electronic documents or data messages have the same legal value as paper documents. Therefore, the implement of the new transport contract regime linked the new Merchant Navy Code to the relevant provisions of the Rotterdam Rules as example. It created a modern and uniform maritime transport law. A major reform relating to the regime of the maritime transport contract by enshrining the electronic transport document alongside the transport document, freedom of contract under the volume contract.
- Deploying blockchain at scale necessitates a regulatory framework that acknowledges the legal validity of transactions conducted via blockchains, specifies the applicable laws and responsibilities, and regulates how data can be accessed and utilized. The most critical issue is the legal status of transactions managed by blockchains. Legislation must recognize the validity of electronic signatures, electronic documents, and electronic transactions, particularly those managed by blockchains. In 2017, the United Nations Commission on International Trade Law (UNCITRAL) adopted the Model Law on Electronic Transferable Records, and several governments are currently working on legislation to recognize transactions managed by blockchains. However, much remains to be accomplished (Pejovic & Lee, 2022). This is particularly problematic in the case of permissionless blockchains, although technical solutions can often be identified for permissioned blockchains.
- The legal issues surrounding data privacy and the right to be forgotten in certain legislations can pose significant challenges. The principles underlying the right to be forgotten appear, at first glance, to be incompatible with the immutable nature of blockchain technology. However, some observers argue that both concepts ultimately serve the same purpose: to empower individuals with greater control over their personal data, albeit through different mechanisms. Additionally, two legal developments could facilitate the inte-

gration of blockchain technology: the codification of law, which seeks to render legal texts machine-readable to streamline the conversion of contractual obligations into digital contract code (smart contracts), and the establishment of a global legal business identification system (Jean et al., 2018). Given the profound impact that blockchain technology could have on global trade, it is crucial to comprehend the legal implications of this technological advancement in order to develop collective solutions within the maritime industry. Therefore, addressing the legal concerns associated with its deployment should be a priority.

- To facilitate the large-scale deployment of this technology, it is crucial to establish a comprehensive ecosystem modeled after the governance framework of the Internet. This ecosystem should unite businesses, civil society organizations, software developers, academics, governments, and intergovernmental organizations in various contexts to address standardization, legal, and policy issues. While blockchain has the potential to enhance international trade, effective commerce necessitates intelligent solutions and standardization, which can only be achieved through collaborative efforts (Reza et al., 2022; Mohd et al., 2022).
- **Resistance to Change**: The maritime sector is traditionally conservative, and many stakeholders may be reluctant to adopt new technologies due to the perceived risks and costs associated with implementation. A survey conducted by the International Maritime Organization in 2021 found that 60% of maritime executives identified resistance to change as a significant barrier to the adoption of innovative technologies. This resistance can arise from a lack of understanding of blockchain technology, concerns regarding the initial investment, and the fear of disrupting existing workflows.
- **Data Privacy and Security Concerns**: While blockchain technology provides enhanced security, the sharing of sensitive information on a public ledger raises significant privacy concerns. Stakeholders must strike a balance between transparency and the necessity of protecting proprietary data. Solutions such as permissioned blockchains, which restrict access to authorized participants, can help mitigate these concerns (Kouhizadeh & Sarkis, 2018). Furthermore, there is a pressing need for robust cybersecurity measures to safeguard blockchain networks against potential threats.

CASE STUDIES

The introduction of blockchain technology in maritime transport is becoming essential (Rodriguez, 2015). This innovative technology has already been applied across various sectors related to the maritime and transport industry. Consequently, blockchain has the potential to enhance all businesses associated with maritime activities, particularly in shipbuilding, vessel operations, container traffic, logistics, and seaport activities.

According to Savin (2020), blockchain technology has recently gained traction in the shipping industry. In 2017, the maritime giant Maersk partnered with IBM to enhance its blockchain solutions aimed at facilitating digital international trade. Furthermore, several industry stakeholders have initiated their own projects or joined industry consortiums to leverage blockchain technology (Bajpai, 2017). For instance, T-Mining is a project associated with the Port of Antwerp, while TradeLens is a side project of Maersk (Safety4sea, 2018).

- **TradeLens**: Developed by Maersk and IBM, TradeLens is a blockchain platform that connects various stakeholders in the supply chain, enabling real-time tracking and secure information sharing. The platform has demonstrated significant improvements in efficiency and transparency, with over 175 organizations participating, including port operators, shipping lines, and customs authorities. TradeLens has reduced the time required for documentation processes by up to 40%, resulting in faster clearance times and lower operational costs (IBM, 2020).
- **Port of Rotterdam**: The Port of Rotterdam has launched a blockchain pilot project aimed at enhancing the efficiency of its logistics processes. This initiative focuses on improving data sharing among port authorities, shipping companies, and customs, leading to reduced delays and increased operational efficiency. The pilot has demonstrated a 30% reduction in processing times for customs documentation, highlighting the potential of blockchain technology to streamline port operations (Port of Rotterdam, 2021).
- **Walmart and IBM**: Walmart has partnered with IBM to utilize blockchain technology to enhance food safety within its supply chain. By implementing a blockchain solution, Walmart can trace the origin of food products in seconds, significantly improving its ability to address food safety concerns. This initiative has resulted in a 50% reduction in the time needed to trace the source of food products, thereby enhancing food safety and minimizing the risk of contamination (Walmart, 2019).
- **A Case of MAERSK**

The costs associated with bureaucratic procedures are estimated to account for between fifteen and fifty percent of the total expenses related to the physical transportation of goods (Dobrovnik et al., 2018). In an effort to address these inefficiencies and digitize all paper records, IBM and Maersk partnered in 2015 to implement blockchain technology in their operations, thereby connecting all intermediaries within the ecosystem on a single platform. This global system is designed to prevent unauthorized manipulation, digitize the flow of commerce, and enable real-time tracking of shipments from end to end. This collaboration allows for the tracking of millions of container shipments each year and facilitates interactions between distributors and customs authorities along designated trade routes (Sadouskaya, 2017). For instance, a shipment of refrigerated products from Kenya to the port of Rotterdam requires permissions and approvals from approximately thirty intermediaries, who must interact with one another more than two hundred times.

In addition, documents such as shipping permits can be susceptible to fraud (Hackius & Petersen, 2017). This case examined how the application of blockchain technology could enhance trust and security in the flow of digitized documents while increasing the efficiency of the global supply chain (Sadouskaya, 2017). Shipping from the port of Mombasa requires the approval of three different agencies, which authorize the export and the signing of six documents that detail the product's origin, quality, chemical treatments, and customs duties (Sadouskaya, 2017).

All actions and data related to documents and products are shared on the platform instantly and in real time, particularly information regarding the exact location of goods, their current position within the supply chain, the distributor in possession of them, and the next step in their transport. It is crucial that perishable products are not delayed, as this could result in significant waste. This system has the potential to significantly reduce delays and fraud, saving millions of dollars annually. According to the World Economic Forum, reducing barriers within the international supply chain could increase global GDP by nearly five percent and total trade volume by fifteen percent (World Economic Forum, 2013). Blockchain holds the key to achieving this, and Maersk is already aware of its potential.

In January 2018, IBM and Maersk announced their intention to create a platform that integrates digital services based on blockchain technology. This initiative aims to unify the industry by providing a more efficient and secure method for conducting international trade. The platform was tested by customers interested in developing a more effective trading process. The goal of the IBM-Maersk collaboration is to transform the current state of international transactions into a more organized and simplified future model. Currently, the existing system suffers from inconsistent information across borders, leading to blind spots at critical points in commerce. Additionally, it faces challenges such as complex communication, reliance on paper documentation, and time-consuming manual processes. Risk assessments often lack sufficient information, customs processes are frequently vulnerable to fraud, and the administrative costs associated with handling a shipment are nearly equivalent to the transportation costs themselves.

The objective pursued by IBM-Maersk is to transition to a digitized model that is efficient, secure, and centralized for the entire supply chain. This model ensures that the identity of each participant is verified, and the information they upload is immutable. Additionally, it allows for the use of digital documents, which facilitate improved risk assessment. By eliminating administrative tasks associated with handling paper, the model reduces the need for intervention from each party, streamlining the process to include only what is strictly necessary at any given moment.

The information managed within the supply chain through TradeLens is communicated to all relevant parties and stored with a strong emphasis on privacy and security. Access is restricted to only those individuals authorized for specific operations, and measures are in place to mitigate any potential issues (Ganne & Patel, 2019). To date, the TradeLens platform has facilitated the digitization of several commercial processes within the supply chain, including concept testing and proof of value in production environments. This has occurred either as part of the platform's offerings or through third parties leveraging its capabilities. The participation encompasses various processes, such as document handling in commerce, open account transactions, issuance of maritime transport insurance, bills of lading, shipping instructions, generation of advance shipping notice documents, and customs clearance, among others (Ganne & Patel, 2019). Several companies and authorities, including DuPont, Dow Chemical, Tetra Pak, and the Port of Houston, were among the initial participants in testing the platform. Additionally, the initiative has involved the Port of Rotterdam Community Port System, the Netherlands Customs Administration, and the U.S. Customs and Border Protection, among others.

The TradeLens environment comprises several organizations, including ports, terminal operators, and transit operators. Notable members include two-thirds of the largest shipping lines globally, as well as authorities, customs agencies, suppliers, and banks (Ganne & Patel, 2019). The Maersk and IBM TradeLens platform has garnered significant media attention. New organizations, such as CargoX, provide neutral solutions for companies of all sizes, enabling carriers, freight forwarders, and logistics companies to leverage the most reliable commercial networks facilitated by blockchain technology. Leading ports and terminals, which play a critical role in the global supply chain, are also embracing the integration of blockchain into their operations. For instance, the Port of Veracruz in Mexico is launching a blockchain project aimed at enhancing cargo transport security, and it is not alone in this initiative. Maersk has not only secured the cooperation of initial users but has also gained the commitment of numerous maritime gateways worldwide to utilize the platform. This platform will provide real-time access to shipping data and documents, including IoT and sensor data. While this solution has received substantial support, other leading operators, port terminals, and supply chain specialists have also indicated their readiness to challenge the status quo.

In November 2018, news emerged about a consortium formed to develop a platform based on blockchain technology, which includes companies such as COSCO, CMA-CGM, DP World, and PSA International, known as the Global Shipping Business Network (GSBN). This coalition of influential shipping leaders has created a product designed to compete with the TradeLens service, potentially presenting the first serious challenge to Maersk and IBM's dominance in the blockchain space. Inspired by the partnership between Maersk and IBM, several other established players in the shipping industry and trade-related organizations are exploring their own blockchain solutions. For instance, South Korea has established a government-backed shipping and logistics consortium focused on developing and testing blockchain solutions to strengthen its national shipping industry. In a manner similar to the IBM-Maersk solution, the objective of this project is to securely share data among all participants while significantly reducing the extensive amount of administrative paperwork. The consortium comprises 15 members, including the shipping giant Hyundai Merchant Marine (HMM), Samsung SDM, IBM Korea, the Ministry of Oceans and Fisheries, and the Busan Port Authority (Kang, 2017; Zeng, 2017). Furthermore, in September 2017, HMM announced a successful pilot voyage to test blockchain technology in collaboration with other consortium members, with a second test scheduled for October. In Japan, a comparable consortium has been established to develop and test a blockchain-enabled data-sharing platform among major shipping companies, including Mitsui OSK Lines (MOL), Nippon Yusen Kaisha (NYK Line), and Kawasaki Kisen Kaisha (K Line), along with other trade-related companies in Japan (Hadhi, 2017). Another initiative was recently established in Singapore, where shipping company Pacific International Lines, port operator PSA International, and IBM Singapore signed a memorandum of understanding (MoU) to collaboratively develop blockchain-based network solutions aimed at reducing fraud and documentation errors (Tan, 2017). A shared objective among these previous initiatives is the digitization of the bill of lading. Although digital versions of the bill of lading have been available for many years, they have not achieved widespread success.

These case studies highlight the potential benefits of blockchain technology in maritime logistics while also showcasing the challenges encountered during implementation. They offer valuable insights into the practical applications of blockchain and the collaborative efforts necessary for successful adoption.

- **Blockchain issues from ports and government authorities**

Blockchain technology has also garnered the interest of government agencies. The Danish Maritime Authority is currently working to digitize its entire ship registration process and has recently launched a project focused on utilizing blockchain. Additionally, various port authorities in Northern Europe have begun developing their own blockchain management platforms (Alper, 2017). These initiatives include the ports of Rotterdam and Antwerp, which are respectively the largest and second-largest ports in Europe. The port of Antwerp, in collaboration with the logistics technology startup T-mining, is working to eliminate physical paperwork and enhance operational efficiency (Tan, 2017). Furthermore, the Malaysia Institute of Supply Chain Innovation (MISI), in partnership with Shanghai Jiaotong University, has initiated a joint research project aimed at developing a blockchain solution to improve the Less-than-Container-Load (LCL) market in China, an area characterized by fragmentation, low levels of information sharing, and frequent delays. MISI identifies three advantages that blockchain technology may offer to the LCL market: it fosters trust among participants by enhancing the flow of information; it eliminates intermediaries, thereby reducing both costs and processing time; and it accelerates transactions by ensuring that all necessary information and trade documents are accessible to all participants (Tan, 2017).

FUTURE TRENDS AND DEVELOPEMENTS

The future of blockchain in the maritime sector is promising, with several trends emerging:

- **Integration with Emerging Technologies**: The integration of blockchain technology with the Internet of Things (IoT) and artificial intelligence (AI) can significantly enhance efficiency in maritime logistics. For instance, IoT devices can deliver real-time data on cargo conditions, which can be securely recorded on the blockchain to ensure transparency. This synergy can facilitate predictive analytics, enabling stakeholders to anticipate potential issues before they occur. Additionally, AI algorithms can analyze the data collected from blockchain and IoT systems to optimize shipping routes and reduce costs (Kouhizadeh & Sarkis, 2018).
- **Global Regulatory Developments**: As blockchain technology matures, it is likely that regulatory frameworks will evolve to accommodate its use. This evolution could lead to greater legal recognition of smart contracts and clearer guidelines for their implementation. The European Union has already initiated discussions on blockchain regulations, which may pave the way for broader adoption (European Commission, 2021). Collaborative efforts

among regulatory bodies, industry stakeholders, and technology providers will be essential in creating a conducive environment for innovation.

- **Increased Collaboration**: Stakeholders in the maritime supply chain are expected to collaborate more closely to develop standardized practices for blockchain implementation, facilitating smoother integration. Industry consortia are actively working to establish standards that promote interoperability among various blockchain solutions. Collaborative initiatives can foster trust among stakeholders and accelerate the adoption of blockchain technology.

Blockchain technology and smart contracts have the potential to revolutionize the maritime supply chain by improving efficiency, transparency, and security. However, challenges related to technical implementation, regulatory frameworks, and industry resistance must be addressed to fully realize these benefits. By examining successful case studies and emerging trends, the maritime sector can progress toward a more sustainable and efficient future through the integration of blockchain technology. Tan & Saraniemi (2023) highlight that **trust** is central to blockchain-enabled marketing. Their research identifies blockchain as a tool not just for operational transparency, but as a strategic asset in shaping consumer perceptions and loyalty. They advocate for future research into how blockchain redefines value co-creation and relationship marketing.

By fostering collaboration among stakeholders, investing in technology, and advocating for supportive regulatory frameworks, the maritime industry can fully harness the potential of blockchain and smart contracts. As the sector continues to evolve, adopting these technologies will be essential in addressing the pressing challenges of inefficiency, fraud, and environmental sustainability.

CONCLUSION

The modern supply chain is characterized by its complexity, involving numerous stakeholders and vast amounts of information exchanged daily, which presents challenges such as process transparency, collaboration among stakeholders, and strategic alignment within the chain. While IT tools have enhanced supply chain efficiency, resilience, and effectiveness, they also introduce issues related to data security, centralization, and the speed of exchanges. The emergence of blockchain technology, initially designed for Bitcoin mining (Nakamot, 2009), has disrupted traditional financial systems, which were based on hierarchical structures (wang et al., 2019). This decentralized and shared technology is now being explored for its potential applications in supply chain management, raising questions regarding its benefits and challenges (Wang et al., 2019; Queiroz and Fosso Wamba, 2019; Upadhyay, 2020). Blockchain offers enhanced transparency by allowing all participants to access immutable records, thereby increasing trust and accountability throughout the supply chain. It also fosters improved collaboration by providing a shared platform for data exchange, leading to better alignment and coordination among stakeholders. Furthermore, blockchain enhances data security by reducing risks associated with centralized data management and facilitates real-time information sharing, enabling quicker decision-making and responsiveness to market changes. However, the integration of blockchain into supply chain management presents several challenges, including scalability issues as transaction volumes rise, interoperability concerns between different blockchain systems, regulatory compliance questions, and cultural resistance among stakeholders who may be hesitant to adopt new technologies. Thus, while the impact of blockchain technology on supply chain management is profound, offering significant opportunities, addressing these challenges is crucial for realizing its full potential and transforming supply chain operations effectively.

The dematerialization of maritime transport documents presents significant economic benefits. It enhances the efficiency of goods transportation and improves the competitiveness of companies in the maritime sector by saving time and reducing costs. Moreover, solutions for dematerialization and secure electronic transactions, along with emerging disruptive technologies such as blockchain, offer innovative and sustainable approaches for the electronic management of negotiable transport documents.

On a legal level, the dematerialization of documents disrupts the legal system concerning the formation of contracts for maritime transport. Transport law, already frequently challenged by common law, now faces additional challenges from electronic commerce and requires adaptation to the current e-commerce landscape of the global trading system. This situation represents a significant upheaval in property law, the law of obligations, intellectual property law, and the law of evidence.

In conclusion, this study underscores the transformative potential of blockchain technology and smart contracts in enhancing security and trust in maritime transactions. The capability of blockchain to certify and validate operations at the transaction level provides a robust solution for combating fraud and minimizing waste in goods transport. However, the research also identifies significant gaps, particularly in the legal regulations and procedural frameworks necessary to support these technologies within the maritime sector. The study reveals that while blockchain technology offers promising solutions, the lack of a comprehensive legal framework presents a substantial barrier to its widespread adoption. Therefore, there is an urgent need for the development of well-defined legal regulations to govern the use of blockchain and smart contracts, ensuring their effective integration into maritime operations. Addressing these legal challenges is essential for unlocking the full benefits of blockchain technology, ultimately leading to more secure, efficient, and trustworthy practices in the maritime and shipping industries.

REFERENCES

Bumblauskas, D., Bumblauskas, J., & Mardirosian, M. (2020). Blockchain in Logistics and Supply Chain Management: A Review of the Literature. *Logistics (Basel), 4*(3), 18. DOI: 10.3390/logistics4030018

Casino, F., Dasaklis, T. K., & Patsakis, C. (2019). A systematic literature review of blockchain-based applications: Current status, classification and open issues. *Telematics and Informatics, 36*, 55–81. DOI: 10.1016/j.tele.2018.11.006

Czachorowski, K., Brezočnik, M., & Trkman, P. (2019). The role of blockchain technology in improving maritime systems and reducing cybercrime. *Maritime Policy & Management, 46*(8), 1024–1039. DOI: 10.1080/03088839.2019.1644318

Dobrovnik, M., Herold, D., Fürst, E., & Kummer, S. (2018). Blockchain for and in Logistics: What to Adopt and Where to Start. Logistics, 2, 18. Consultado en https://www.mdpi.com/2305-6290/2/3/18

Dong, L., Jiang, P., & Xu, F. (2023). Impact of traceability technology adoption in food supply chain networks. *Management Science, 69*(3), 1518–1535.

Frikha, R., & Hlali, A. (2023). The Evolution Of Logistics Management Toward The Digital Transition. International Journal of Commerce. *Industry and Entrepreneurship Studies, 3*, 66–75.

Ganne, E., & Patel, D. (2019). Blockchain & DLT in trade: A Reality Check. Obtenido de World Trade Organization: https://www.wto.org

Gerakoudi-Ventouri, K. (2022). Review of studies of blockchain technology effects on the shipping industry. J. shipp. trd. 7, (2) https://doi.org/DOI: 10.1186/s41072-021-00105-2

Hackius, N., & Petersen, M. (2017). Blockchain in logistics and supply chain: trick or treat? Digitalization in Supply Chain Management and Logistics (pp. 3-18). Consultado en https://tore.tuhh.de/bitstream/11420/1447/1/petersen_hackius_blockchain_in_scm_and_logistics_hicl_2017.pdf

Hadhi, A. (2017). MOL, NYK and K Line to develop trade data sharing platform using blockchain. Lloyd's List. Available at: https://lloydslist.maritimeintelligence.informa.com/LL111092/MOL-NYK-and-K-Line-to-develop-trade-data-sharing-platform-using-blockchain

Hlali, A. (2017). Efficiency of the 26 major container ports in 2015: Comparative analysis with different models. International Journal of Economics & Strategies. *Management of Business*, (10), 15–20.

Hlali, A. (2023). Impact of logistics and economic structure on seaport infrastructure: A case of Mediterranean countries. *Australian Journal of Maritime and Ocean Affairs*, *16*(2), 175–185. DOI: 10.1080/18366503.2023.2217584

Hlali, A., Ablanedo-Rosas, J. H., & Ruiz-Torres, A. J. (2023). Operational efficiency of major cargo seaports in some developing regions: Results from a bootstrap DEA. International Journal of Shipping and Transport Logistics, 16(3/4), 1 290-319. https://doi.org/DOI: 10.1504/IJSTL.2023.129874

Hlali, A., & Wanis, A. (2020).. . *Theoretical Highlights in Container Port Logistics Systems Journal of Marine and Island Cultures*, *9*(2), 181–191. DOI: 10.21463/jmic.2020.09.2.13

IBM. (2020). *Blockchain for business: A practical guide*. Retrieved from IBM.

IBM. (2020). *TradeLens: A Blockchain-based Shipping Solution*. Retrieved from IBM.

Irannezhad, E., Mahmud, K., & Islam, T. (2020). Blockchain technology in logistics and transportation: Challenges and opportunities. *Journal of Transportation and Logistics*, *8*(2), 123–135. DOI: 10.1016/j.tra.2019.11.007

Jensen, T., Hedman, J., & Henningsson, S. (2019). How TradeLens delivers business value with blockchain technology. *MIS Quarterly Executive*, *18*(4), 221–243.

Jović, M., Tijan, E., Žgaljić, D., & Aksentijević, S. (2020). Improving Maritime Transport Sustainability Using Blockchain-Based Information Exchange. *Sustainability*, *12*(21), 8866. DOI: 10.3390/su12218866

Kamble, S. S., Gunasekaran, A., & Sharma, R. (2020). Modeling the blockchain enabled traceability in agriculture supply chain. International Journal of Information Management, 52, 101967. Elsevier. https://doi.org/DOI: 10.1016/j.ijinfomgt.2019.05.023

Kang, T.-J. (2017). HMM completes pilot blockchain voyage with reefer-laden boxship. Lloyd's List. Available at: https://lloydslist.maritimeintelligence.informa.com/LL111275/HMM-completes-pilot-blockchain-voyage-with-reefer-laden-boxship

Korpela, K., Hallikas, J., & Dahlberg, T. (2017). Digital supply chain transformation toward blockchain integration. *Supply Chain Management*, *22*(3), 251–264. DOI: 10.1108/SCM-02-2016-0046

Kouhizadeh, M., & Sarkis, J. (2018). Blockchain and the Circular Economy: A New Paradigm for Sustainable Supply Chain Management. *Resources, Conservation and Recycling*, *135*, 1–6. DOI: 10.1016/j.resconrec.2018.02.014

Kshetri, N. (2018). Blockchain's roles in strengthening cybersecurity and protecting privacy. *Journal of International Management*, *24*(3), 251–263.

Kumar, A., Shukla, S., & Dwivedi, Y. K. (2019). A comprehensive framework for adopting blockchain in supply chains. *Journal of Cleaner Production*, *231*, 271–282. DOI: 10.1016/j.jclepro.2019.05.273

Lambourdiere, E., & Corbin, E. (2020). Blockchain and maritime supply-chain performance: dynamic capabilities perspective. Worldwide Hospitality and Tourism Themes, 12(1), pp. 24-34. Emerald Publishing Limited. https://doi.org/DOI: 10.1108/whatt-10-2019-0069

Loklindt, C., Moeller, C., & Kinra, A. (2020). How blockchain enables sustainable supply chain innovation: Insights from container shipping. *International Journal of Physical Distribution & Logistics Management*, *50*(5), 602–625. DOI: 10.1108/IJPDLM-03-2020-0104

Mohamed B. F., Yussuf A., Haithem M., Syed A. S., Omar A. M., Sandy T., Xavier B., Raouf Abozariba, M. I., Adel A. (2024). A survey on blockchain technology in the maritime industry: Challenges and future perspectives, 157(1), 618-637. https://doi.org/DOI: 10.1016/j.future.2024.03.046

Mohd, J., Abid, H., Ravi, P. S., Rajiv, S., & Shahbaz, K. (2022). A review of Blockchain Technology applications for financial services. BenchCouncil Transactions on Benchmarks. *Standards and Evaluations.*, *2*(3). Advance online publication. DOI: 10.1016/j.tbench.2022.100073

Mougayar, W. (2016). *The Business Blockchain: Promise, Practice, and the Application of the Next Internet Internet Internet.* Wiley.

Nakamoto, S. (2008). Bitcoin: A Peer-to-Peer Electronic Cash System. Retrieved from Bitcoin.org.

Nakamoto, S. (2009). Bitcoin open source implementation of P2P currency, P2P Foundation, https://p2pfoundation.ning.com/forum/topics/bitcoin-open-source

Om P, Bashir A, Vinay T, Surendra S, (2021). Key management for blockchain technology. 7(1), 76-80. https://doi.org/DOI: 10.1016/j.icte.2019.08.002

Pejovic, C., & Lee, U. (2022). UNCITRAL Model Law on Electronic Transferable Records as a Potential Legal Regime for the Use of Electronic Bills of Lading. European Transport Law, 57(1), 13-32. Available @ https://kyushu-u.elsevierpure .com/en/publications

Peronja, I., Gračan, D., & Hlača, B. (2020). Blockchain technologies for freight cost optimization in maritime trade. *Maritime Economics & Logistics*, *22*(3), 453–472. DOI: 10.1057/s41278-020-00152-x

Politou, E., Alepis, E., & Patsakis, C. (2018). *Forgetting personal data and revoking consent under the GDPR: Challenges and proposed solutions. Journal of Cybersecurity, 4(1)*. Academic., DOI: 10.1093/cybsec/tyy001

Queiroz, M. M., & Fosso Wamba, S. (2019). Blockchain adoption challenges in supply chain: An empirical investigation of the main drivers in India and the USA. *International Journal of Information Management*, *46*, 70–82.

Queiroz, M. M., Telles, R., & Bonilla, S. H. (2019). Blockchain and supply chain management integration: a systematic review of the literature. Supply Chain Management: An International Journal, 25(2), pp. 241-254. Emerald Publishing Limited. https://doi.org/DOI: 10.1108/scm-03-2018-0143

Reza, T., Pejvak, O., Vahid, S., Pankaj, C. P., & Rana, M. (2022). Block by block: A blockchain-based peer-to-peer business transaction for international trade. *Technological Forecasting and Social Change*, *180*(1). Advance online publication. DOI: 10.1016/j.techfore.2022.121714

Ripple. (2020). Blockchain in ship finance: Leveraging Ripple's technology for secure transactions. Ripple Case Studies.

Rodrique, J.-P. (2020). Routledge, New York, 456 pages, ISBN 978-0-367-36463-2.

Safety4sea (2018). Port of Antwerp works on blockchain pilot project – SAFETY4SEA. Available at: https://safety4sea.com/port-of-antwerp-works-on-blockchain -pilot-project/

Savin, A. (2020). Blockchain, Digital Transformation and the Law: What Can We Learn from the Recent Deals? University of San Francisco Maritime Law Journal, 31(2), 107-113. https://heinonline.org/HOL/Page?collection=journals&handle= hein.journals/usfm31&id=2&men_tab=srchresults

Tan, T. M., & Saraniemi, S. (2023). Trust in blockchain-enabled exchanges: Future directions in blockchain marketing. *Journal of the Academy of Marketing Science*, *51*(4), 914–939.

Tan, W. Z. (2017). Antwerp to use blockchain technology in container handling operations. Lloyd's List. Available at: https://lloydslist.maritimeintelligence.informa.com/LL108882/Antwerp-to-use-blockchain-technology-in-container-handling-operations

Tan, W. Z. (2017). PIL and PSA jump on the blockchain bandwagon with IBM. Lloyd's List. Available at: https://lloydslist.maritimeintelligence.informa.com/LL110930/PIL-and-PSA-jump-on-the-blockchain-bandwagon-with-IBM

Tijan, E., Aksentijević, S., Ivančić, L., & Jardas, M. (2019). Blockchain technology implementation in logistics. *Sustainability*, *11*(4), 1185. DOI: 10.3390/su11041185

Tsiulin, S., Reinau, K. H., Hilmola, O.-P., Goryaev, N., & Karam, A. (2020). Blockchain-based applications in shipping and port management: A literature review towards defining key conceptual frameworks. *Rev. Int. Bus. Strateg.*, *30*, 201–224.

UNCTAD. (2017). Report on maritime transport available at https://unctad.org/system/files/official-document/rmt2017_en.pdf

Upadhyay, N. (2020). Demystifying blockchain: A critical analysis of challenges, applications and opportunities. *International Journal of Information Management*, *54*, 102120.

Walmart. (2019). Walmart and IBM: Food Safety and Traceability. Retrieved from Walmart.

Wang, Y., Gunasekaran, A., Ngai, E. W. T., & Papadopoulos, T. (2019). Big Data in Logistics and Supply Chain Management: Antecedents and Consequences. *Transportation Research Part E, Logistics and Transportation Review*, *99*, 212–228. DOI: 10.1016/j.tre.2016.01.013

Wang, Y., Han, J. H., & Beynon-Davies, P. (2019). Understanding blockchain technology for future supply chains: A systematic literature review and research agenda. *Supply Chain Management*, *24*(1), 62–84.

Wang, Y., Singgih, M., Wang, J. et Rit, M. (2019). Making sense of blockchain technology: How will it transform supply chains?. International Journal of Production Economics, 211: 221– 236. 241. https://doi.org/DOI: 10.1016/j.ijpe.2019.02.002

Zafar, S., Bhatti, K. M., Shabbir, M., Hashmat, F., & Akbar, A. H. (2022). Integration of blockchain and Internet of Things: Challenges and solutions. *Annales des Télécommunications*, •••, 1–20.

Zeng, X. (2017). HMM completes first blockchain pilot voyage. Fairplay IHS Markit. Available at: https://fairplay.ihs.com/container/article/4291331/hmm-completes-first-blockchain-pilot-voyage

KEY TERMS AND DEFINITIONS

Blockchain Technology: Blockchain technology represents a paradigm shift in data management by establishing a decentralized, immutable digital ledger that records transactions across a distributed network of nodes. In maritime logistics, this architecture eliminates single points of failure and enables tamper-proof verification of cargo movements, customs documentation, and financial settlements.

Smart Contracts: Smart contracts are self-executing digital agreements where contractual terms (e.g., payment triggers, penalty clauses) are encoded into programmable logic deployed on blockchain platforms. In maritime operations, they autonomously execute actions when predefined conditions are met.

Distributed Ledger Technology (DLT): Distributed Ledger Technology (DLT) encompasses blockchain and other architectures (e.g., Hashgraph) that synchronize databases across decentralized networks without central oversight. DLT's application in maritime logistics enables multi-stakeholder data sharing real-time records of vessel schedules or container statuses.

Consensus Algorithm: Consensus algorithms are protocols governing how network participants validate transactions and update the ledger. Maritime blockchain networks typically employ *Practical Byzantine Fault Tolerance (PBFT)* or *Proof-of-Authority (PoA)*, where designated validators (e.g., port authorities, major carriers) approve transactions within seconds. Unlike energy-intensive models like Bitcoin's Proof-of-Work, PoA minimizes computational overhead while maintaining trust among permissioned stakeholders. TradeLens uses a hybrid consensus model where customs agencies validate shipping documents, reducing clearance times from days to hours while ensuring regulatory compliance.

Peer-to-Peer (P2P) Network: A Peer-to-Peer (P2P) network architecture decentralizes data exchange by enabling direct communication between nodes (e.g., vessels, terminals, logistics providers) without routing through central servers. In maritime contexts, P2P enhances resilience: during cyberattacks on port management systems, vessels can continue sharing navigational data via blockchain-secured P2P channels.

TradeLens: TradeLens is a blockchain-based platform co-developed by Maersk and IBM to digitize global trade documentation. It integrates data from over 600 maritime stakeholders onto a unified ledger, replacing paper-based processes with automated digital workflows. When a vessel departs Singapore, TradeLens triggers smart contracts that simultaneously notify Rotterdam's terminal operators, update cargo insurance records, and initiate letters of credit.

Automated Bill of Lading (B/L): The Automated Bill of Lading (B/L) digitizes traditional paper bills using blockchain and smart contracts to dynamically manage cargo ownership rights. Upon container loading at origin ports, a digital B/L is minted as an NFT on blockchain. As the shipment progresses, IoT sensors detect location milestones (e.g., passing through Malacca Strait), triggering automatic ownership transfers to the next stakeholder. At discharge, the smart contract verifies biometric receiver authentication and releases payment.

Predictive Port Maintenance: Predictive Port Maintenance integrates blockchain-verified IoT data with AI analytics to forecast infrastructure failures before they disrupt operations. Crane strain sensors at the Port of Antwerp, for example, stream real-time load metrics to a blockchain ledger, where AI models detect abnormal patterns indicating imminent failures. Maintenance crews receive automated work orders via smart contracts, enabling repairs during off-peak hours.

Decentralized Finance (DeFi) in Shipping: Decentralized Finance (DeFi) replaces traditional banking intermediaries with blockchain-based protocols for maritime financing. Platforms like *ShipFinance DAO* tokenize vessel ownership, allowing fractional investment via security tokens, while smart contracts manage loan disbursement against cargo collateral.

Chapter 12
Green Logistics Strategies:
Advancing Sustainability Through Smart and Digital Innovations

Tahsina Khan
https://orcid.org/0000-0001-8032-3376
Bangladesh University of Professionals, Bangladesh

ABSTRACT

This chapter explores the evolving field of green logistics, focusing on the integration of smart and digital innovations to advance sustainability. It examines key strategies for reducing environmental impact, including sustainable transportation methods, energy-efficient warehousing, and waste reduction through circular economy approaches. The role of the Internet of Things (IoT) in enhancing logistics efficiency through real-time tracking, predictive analytics, and AI-driven demand forecasting is highlighted. Additionally, the chapter discusses the transformative potential of digital innovations such as blockchain, cloud-based platforms, and big data analytics in optimizing resource usage and ensuring sustainability. Through case studies and best practices, the chapter illustrates how these strategies are being implemented across industries, while addressing challenges and future directions for advancing green logistics.

INTRODUCTION

The logistics industry currently functions as a sustainability pioneer of supply networks that has manage two types of performance, namely, operational performance and environmental accountability. The current chapter discusses the green

DOI: 10.4018/979-8-3373-2434-0.ch012

logistics practices in detail with the emphasis on smart technology and digital tools as the keys to achieving sustainability objectives. The chapter describes in detail procedures that enable the joint adoption of sustainable measures by logistic companies without sacrificing superiority in the marketplace. Second part of the chapter initiates an introductory discussion that identifies fundamentals of green logistics and its key ideas. In this section sustainability has been found to be an essential element in today's supply chains which makes green logistics very important for today's company formula over other considerations. The last one of the three parts of the present chapter consists of three essential parts to Sustainable Transportation Methods and Energy-Efficient Warehousing and Distribution and Waste Reduction and Circular Economy Approaches. Section 4 considers how IoT technology acts as an instrument for sustainability transformation through time-sensitive provision of data-guided operations' decisions. The section explores three practical cases of digital intelligence supporting sustainability goals with Smart Sensors as well as IoT-Enabled Analytics and AI-Driven forecasting systems' analysis.

Section five of this chapter discusses different digital tools that modernize and maintain the practices of logistics. Here the authors address three different sub-parts of their studies that aimed to make transparency more transparent with the help of blockchain technology and proceed with the description of cloud-based optimization platforms and explanations on how big data paves the way for sustaining driven choices. The sixth part of this Chapter includes case studies and best practices that feature the application of successful green logistics strategy deployment. The given case examples integrate theoretical academic knowledge with implementation examples that provide actual insight to readers. This part will assess the obstruction that prevents further adoption of the green logistics solutions by considering the issues of technical restraint and monetary problems and impediments that hinder the process. Upcoming things in technology and self-sufficient supply chains with hyper-connected logistics networks are presented by the author as pioneering fields of research. The author ends the chapter by stating in Section 8 that digital innovation is both the activation and the fundamental driving force for sustainable changes in the industry of logistics. From this section, the author clarifies how environmentally requirements and the possibilities that technology offers affect one another in furthering understanding of how the integrated sustainable supply chain's futures will take shape.

UNDERSTANDING GREEN LOGISTICS

The application of green logistics involves a broad range of approaches associated with practices and technology advancement to reduce the ecological impact along the whole supply chains. The niche known as green logistics has emerged as a carbon emission reduction system, but continued to develop and currently comprises the field of the great scope that adopted energy efficiency, waste reduction and resources preservation and full environmental protection principles (Nikseresht et al., 2024). A complete rethinking process of commodity production and shipment to its storage and distribution adopts sustainability concepts in all the operation facets. The green logistics system as demonstrated is compatible with triple bottom line thinking because it stipulates simultaneous delivery of environmental balance, social prosperity and economic returns. The current modern organizations now understand that sustainable logistics strategies hold with them several competitive advantages as compared to being financial loads to the organizations. The green logistics delivers four important benefits: strengthened the recognition of brands, increased customer retention rates as well as cost reduction and superior positions in future controlled worldwide markets (Sekarini & Selvabaskar, 2024). If organizations incorporate the green logistics principles into strategic planning, they make a critical move that has replaced the stand-alone charity moves with full integration of organizational value-based practices.

There are many consolidating stimuli that have promoted the adoption of green logistics. It is consumer environmental awareness, together with strict regulations and deterioration of effects from the climate, that drives logistics businesses to modify traditional models of operation. The current digital technologies such as IoT, AI and blockchains offer organization a fine ability to trace the operations in supply chains effectively and accurately (Vijaykumar et al., 2024). Green logistics (GL) functions via extensive methods of optimization rather than based on the individual measures of environmental character. Sustainability needs are present throughout the supply chain network at levels of deciding the location of facilities, choosing the means of transportation, planning inventory, packaging and handling in reverse logistics (Khan et al., 2024; Liu et al., 2021). The implementation of the route optimization practice, which aims at saving fuel, results in the reduction of operational costs, and produces significant greenhouse reduction. This association is revealed as operating efficiency gets associated with environmental responsibility via investments in accommodation that prefers energy-efficient buildings and environmentally sound sources of power for logistics centers. Additional focus on the life cycle thinking is one of the critical features of the green logistics systems. The traditional logistics system used to give much emphasis to fast cost reduction that used to be its main concern while disregarding the future ecological issues predicted upon the depletion of resources and waste production and pollution. Green logistics (GL) applies a cradle-to-cradle strategy that prioritizes on the acquisition of sustainable materials and creation of returnable and recyclable packaging and end-of-life products handling through closed-loop supply channels (Mishra et al., 2023). The wide-ranging business model acknowledges the fact that logistics operations have environmental impacts other than pollution caused by transportation, so all the supply chain players must come up with a single response.

Green approaches to logistics are implemented by organizations to varying degrees and it is determined by business-to-business and geographical location. Green logistics principles selected and applied to any given business are determined by the business development levels as well as the regulatory systems, infrastructural standards, and the regional sustainability views (Vienažindienė et al., 2021). European companies are aiming for electric vehicles with carbon-neutral warehouses but coming into the picture are emerging market enterprises which deploy the resources to optimize load factors via consolidation of ships with some biofuel usage as an interim solution. The variances of wants across regions justify why some environmental and economical practices need to be developed (Hlali, 2023). The importance of green logistics continues to grow while its practical realization encounters a plethora of important barriers. Major initial costs in finances and parallel technical complexity and resistance to changes in operational aspects and feeble measures of sustainability still stall progress (Nnabuife et al., 2025). To establish a good environment for green innovation various stakeholders including corporations, politicians and academics among the consumers overcoming prevailing impediments must come together. The fusion of the green subsidies with carbon and emissions trading systems is a catalyst to motivate companies to invest in sustainable technology and a collaborative supply chain standard allows companies to function better together.

Today, green logistics analysis considers social sustainability issues such as standards of the workforce in logistics activities and the impacts of the community from logistics facilities as well as responsible commodity purchasing criteria (Emon & Khan, 2024; Hoang et al., 2025). The united way of viewing sustainability serves to demonstrate that authentic sustainability acknowledges the environmental concerns and integrates the elements of economic and social considerations into one unified system. Green logistics is one of the cores developing branches of contemporary supply chain operations. Practice goes beyond bare minimum environmental directives to become a strategic necessity to develop innovative methods and improve sustainability and resilience in a business. Green logistics tenets will come into increased focus in the supply chain operations since the evolution of technologies and social needs change. The disciplines of sustainable supply chain management are likely to further develop with better digital technologies as well as improved sustainability measurements and improved supply chain system wide collaboration to a sustainable international economy.

STRATEGIES FOR REDUCING ENVIRONMENTAL IMPACT

The logistics industry, as an industry with only the basic needs of transport and energy resources for the operations, supported the principal spoilers of the environment for years. Awareness of environmental sustainability has triggered the sector to develop programs that minimize its negative impacts on the environment and maintain or enhance its operational performance. The development of green logistics is synonymous with the introduction of new sustainable methods in shipping with storage and waste management. The analysis reveals essential procedures that are to aid in the alleviation of environmental impacts in logistics through sustainable transport systems, energy efficient storage and elimination of waste from the model of the circular economy.

Sustainable Transportation Methods

Experts in logistics identify transportation to be the most environmentally degrading component that releases the greatest emissions that lead to global greenhouse gases. Transport development with a sustainable aspect has significantly accelerated within the last few years. In this regard, the use of electric vehicles (EVs) is a highly effective approach to reducing pollution around the environment. Once implemented, electric vehicles in last mile operations show reduced carbon emission as compared to old internal combustion engines vehicles (Dadashzada et al., 2024). These environmentally friendly cars have several operating cost advantages-they use less fuel, and they don't have to be maintained as much.

The logistics industry has been transformed into autonomous delivery mechanisms that use AI and IoT technology have entered the market. The established systems are driving performance optimizers and superior routing methods that deliver lower fuel consumption with minimal traffic jams and chopping the unnecessary waiting hours (Dimri et al., 2024; Hlali & Wanis, 2020). Autonomous trucks in conjunction with drones fitted with AI modify their routes in real times to consider the traffic flows, delivery emergencies, and external weather conditions thus improving operational effectiveness while limiting the impact of the environment. The fuel-efficient and effortless communication between vehicles initiated by the IoT sensor networks create reduced overall emissions.

The use of alternative fuels like biofuels with hydrogen, natural gas in conjunction with electric and autonomous cars is the point for reducing emissions in the case of transportation. The renewable biofuels from wastes and algae can replace the traditional diesel and gasoline systems as they are low emission but with performance not lost (Emon, 2023; Thanigaivel et al., 2022). Freight operation over long-distance using hydrogen powered vehicles is viable as its utilization only releases water vapor in its exhaust. The linking of rail lines with sea transport and road highways, that is, the multimodal transport, brings significant sustainability improvements. According to Centobelli et al., (2020), Environmental sustainability is improved for enterprises when they shift to using rail and maritime freight as opposed to using road transport. These sustainable transport modes of electric vehicles as well as autonomous vehicles and the alternative fuels/multimodal transport are an ecosystem in the fight against climate change due to the global implication.

Energy-Efficient Warehousing and Distribution

A crucial element of green logistics is the emphasis on energy-efficient storage and delivery. Warehouses, as essential components of supply chains, need significant energy, especially for illumination, heating, cooling, and mechanical operation. Thus, reducing energy usage in warehouse operations is essential for sustainability initiatives. The integration of solar energy systems into warehouse facilities is one of the most successful strategies in this context. Solar panels affixed to warehouse roofs may provide renewable energy for lighting, heating, and electric vehicle charging stations, therefore reducing dependence on grid electricity and decreasing the facility's total carbon emissions (Amin Mirjalili et al., 2023). Moreover, sophisticated insulation solutions may significantly enhance the energy efficiency of warehouse structures by lowering heat loss or gain, hence diminishing the need for energy-intensive heating or cooling systems. This not only reduces energy usage but also enhances the working environment inside the facility by ensuring more steady interior temperatures. Another advancement in enhancing energy efficiency in warehouses is the implementation of intelligent lighting systems. These systems use motion sensors, daylight sensors, and intelligent controllers to autonomously modify lighting settings according to occupancy and the availability of natural light, leading to substantial energy savings. Simultaneously, automation technologies include robotic picking systems, automated guided vehicles (AGVs), and intelligent conveyor belts enhance operational efficiency and decrease energy usage. These solutions enhance processes, reduce downtime, and improve energy consumption in material handling (Hasan et al., 2024; Oyekanlu et al., 2020). Consequently, energy-efficient warehouses are both more sustainable and economically advantageous over time, making them appeal to logistics operators aiming to reconcile environmental and financial factors.

Waste Reduction and Circular Economy Approaches

One of the significant green logistics strategies is the shift from the organized, linear, conventional supply chains, which are targeting "take-make-dispose "policy to a far more sustainable circular economy concept. Among methods utilized by the circular economy in minimizing waste and consumption of resources and in extending the life of products and substances are recycling, remanufacturing and reuse. Reverse logistics plays an important essential role in the circular economy that seeks to eliminate waste in the supply chain. This thing saves the objects from being disposed in garbage cans by returning the objects for renovation or recycling (Emon & Khan, 2025d; Mishra et al., 2023). Therefore, there are so many companies who already consider the end-of-life facet when creating the designs and make disassembly, reuse, recycle easy. A part of the practices in the logistics sphere to measure the environmental impacts of goods during the entire life-cycle is LCA (Emon, 2025; Su et al., 2020), starting from raw material extraction to end of life disposal. LCA can be applied by companies to point out what areas could be improved to reduce impact on the environment, to make the logistics more efficient, and reengineer the products to be more sustainable. The waste on packages is one of the biggest aspects of the environmental degradation in logistics where the model of a circular economy is being implemented more and more. Today, various companies end up paying the price for biodegradable, recyclable or reusable sustainable packaging material. With the move of the business to the concept of bulk shipments, even to reusable containers, packaging is being stripped off the backs of products factory packed to titanic eliminations strips, as well.

ROLE OF IOT IN GREEN LOGISTICS

As a disruptive technology, the Internet of Things (IoT) is rapidly acknowledged as a solution to alleviate supply chain's environmental impact. Therefore, the Internet of Things (IoT) allows for the collection of data in real time, the more sophisticated predictive analytics, and informed decision making to minimize the consumption of resources, carbon cmissions and operational inefficiencies in logistics. Combining IoT with sustainable methods of logistics allows better visibility, better fleet management, and smarter inventory systems that help minimize the environmental impact of logistical operations. In this section, this work explores the key roles of IoT in improving sustainability in the logistics area such as smart sensors for real time monitoring, predictive analytics for route and fleet checks and AI for demand prediction.

Smart Sensors for Real-Time Tracking and Monitoring

Real time tracking and monitoring is the fundamental part of IoT in logistics and smart sensors play its key role. The sensors are combined into trucks, equipment, and commodities and create a continuous flow of data that managers can monitor and manage many operating factors. As this visibility is in real time the efficiency of logistical operations and their environmental footprint can be improved. In the transportation industry, smart sensors do the monitoring of all essential variables such as vehicle emissions, fuel consumption and the driving behaviors (Emon et al., 2025; Haghshenas et al., 2024). However, organization can 'pinpoint' wasteful driving behaviors such as long extended idling and abrupt acceleration that increase fuel usage and emissions using this data. Using this real time data companies may be able to take remedial measures like changing driving behavior or optimizing route. Directly, they may signal to drivers when fuel economy is insufficient, such as to change one's speed or reduce idle time, to facilitate emissions reductions.

In addition to transportation, increasingly, the use of smart sensors for monitoring temperature sensitive products increases. Temperature regulation is needed for companies operating in sectors where the commodities are perishable, such as food or medicines. Such temperature sensors are enabled with IoT to oversee and keep controls on temperature conditions in transit and storage and guarantee that items are within set temperature ranges. Apart from decreasing spoilage and waste, this improves energy efficiency in refrigeration systems, thus reducing energy consumption due to temperature regulation (Chen et al., 2024). In addition, IoT sensors are not only automobiles and commodities. Additionally, they enter the logistics facilities and warehouses to manage energy consumption of equipment, heating, ventilation, air conditioning (HVAC), lighting, and material handling equipment. In this instance, collecting information on equipment efficiency can help firms identify what they can do to reduce energy use and enhance the overall sustainability of a warehouse operation (Ali et al., 2023). Thus, smart sensors act as vital intermediaries to get real time tracking and monitoring and that data is required to minimize the environment impact by enhancing energy efficiency, removing waste and optimizing logistical process.

IoT-Enabled Predictive Analytics for Route and Fleet Optimization

An example of the disruptive use of the IoT is the use of predictive analytics based on the IoT for sustainable logistics. With respect to extensive real time and historical data, predictive analytics algorithms can forecast traffic conditions, optimize delivery routes, and so on, to enhance the fleet management tactics. These qualities are of great advantage to logistics companies who are looking for ways of reducing consumption of fuel, emissions and running expenses. Route optimization is one of the main uses of IoT enabled predictive analytics. Algorithms may accommodate IoT data on patterns of traffic, conditions of roads, weather, and routes can dynamically change routes to minimize fuel consumption and delivery durations. It may also suggest other routes during peak time or re-distributed cars to avoid congested zones for more fluid and efficient transportation (Jacobsen, 2023). Excluding fuel usage, this method helps in reducing air pollution as well as congestion in metropolitan cities. Fleet efficiency heavily relies on the use of fleet IoT enabled predictive maintenance. Fleet management normally uses conventional methods, which are usually based on planned maintenance but with superfluous downtime or postponements of solving equipment problems. Predictive maintenance systems such as IoT sensors assess the status of the vehicle components (engine, brakes and tires) to detect possible problems before the breakdowns. Unforeseen maintenance is taken out, emergency repairs reduced, and vehicles work at peak performance, thereby cutting emissions and effects to operations (Alrajhi et al., 2023; Emon & Khan, 2025a). Along with this, the assessment of driver performance is an important part of enhancing the fleet operations with using the data generated by IoT. Fleet managers can monitor velocity, braking patterns and acceleration and may sense and correct wasteful driving habits. Some ways of decreasing fuel usage and thereby malpractice emissions are by instructing drivers to use more fuel-efficient means of driving. The joint enhancement of sustainability and cost efficiency of logistics operations is achieved by these enhancements. This results in robust tools for route and fleet optimization that allow logistics companies to greatly minimize the environmental impact and economical costs attributed to their business.

AI-Driven Demand Forecasting to Minimize Excess Inventory

It is inventory management, a very important domain where Internet of Things (IoT) and artificial intelligence (AI) come together to enhance the sustainability of logistics. Inventory excess incurs high storage and warehousing expenses, runs up energy bills to maintain inventory, and leaves a trail of items that have grown obsolete or wasted. This difficulty is overcome by AI enhanced demand forecasting, leveraging the data generated from IoT, that's synchronized with the actual demand trends and terms, that then feed compatible production and logistics operations. Demand forecasting with AI brings in industry trends and environmental variables, demands previous sales data to forecast future demand accurately. This, in turn, enables logistics companies to supervise stocks and thus avoid overproduction and spare stocks (Frontoni et al., 2020). By aligning with real demand, companies may decrease waste, lower energy requirements in warehouses and the carbon footprint of overproduction and surplus inventory storage. Also, AI meta cestodes may use real-time data from IoT devices to enhance their accuracy. Sales data, inventory levels and consumer preferences can increase the accuracy of demand forecasts, which in turn would help real time supply chain operations to adjust as the market changes (Emon & Khan, 2025b; Tadayonrad & Ndiaye, 2023). Such a dynamic inventory management practice offsets warehousing and transportation's environmental impacts by preventing over inventory of items that require enormous resources for storage, handling and shipment. The use of AI driven demand forecasting models enables the organization to match supply with real demand thus reducing waste, reducing energy consumption and making the logistics ecosystem more sustainable.

DIGITAL INNOVATIONS FOR SUSTAINABLE LOGISTICS

Digital technology is swiftly incorporated in the logistics sector with significant potential to enhance operational sustainability. Blockchain technology, cloud-based logistics platforms, big data analytics among others have created innovations in green logistics operational efficiency albeit bringing certain gains associated with green logistics such as better resource management, emission reduction and supply chain transparency. This section explores how the use of digital technologies can enable better realization of sustainable logistics practices by increasing transparency and traceability, improve resource utilization and facilitate judicious decision making based on data.

Blockchain for Enhanced Transparency and Traceability

The logistics industry is investing a lot of attention to blockchain technology as it can help provide transparency, traceability, and trust in the delivery process on a chain. It provides Blockchain technology to give a decentralized, unalterable database to the recording of transaction that all the participants to the chain have genuine time information. Given the importance of substantiated sustainability assertions in green logistics, this characteristic is particularly useful. Blockchain based on sustainability allows for the monitoring and validation of sustainability such as ecological delivery, ethical source of materials, and ecofriendly manufacturing techniques. But the record of each stage in a product's life cycle (raw material acquisition, through manufacture and delivery) is safe, transparent and verifiable using blockchain (Emon & Khan, 2025c; Matenga & Mpofu, 2023; Ruiz-Torres et al., 2022). It ensures that sustainability assertions are both verifiable and credible and makes consumption of such assertions by consumers, regulators and other stakeholders more trustful as to whether the organizations comply with environmental regulations as they are authentically doing.

The blockchain environment encourages cooperative environmental activities among supply chain stakeholders owing to its decentralized nature. First, supply networks are inherently information asymmetric, in which one side will hide or alter an important fact. Blockchain deals with this problem by giving us a single repository of the truth with complete transparency of it. By increasing trust, Blockchain will enable more efficient cooperation on sustainability initiatives such as pollution reduction, energy efficiency improvement and promotion of circular economy activities (Rehman Khan et al., 2022). Furthermore, the ability for blockchain to record all transactions in an immutable way means that all sustainability-related information, which for example might be CO2 emissions and waste management parameters, can be tracked and verified based on a transaction trail, throughout the entire supply chain. In this way, blockchain increases operational efficiency and is enabled to have green logistics organizations drive and sustain adoption of such practices to support the compound work objectives of green logistics.

Cloud-Based Logistics Platforms for Resource Optimization

The advent of cloud computing has become a crucial ingredient of modern logistics, where such cloud computing provides diverse means to manage data, resources, and interdigital communication of supply chain stakeholders. Cloud based logistics solution, deliver data storage in cloud which helps in the seamless integration of many players into the supply chain such as suppliers, transit carriers, and retailers. It centralizes operations, streamlines operation, eliminates duplication of effort, and improves efficiency in general. The use of cloud-based technologies highly improves sustainability by maximizing warehouse space use. Real time insight into inventory level and demand variation is being offered for logistics companies to optimize space usage and reduce the requirement of additional storage facility. The environment is mitigatcd from environmentally dangerous development and operation of new warehouses helping organizations achieve their sustainable goals (Hlali & Gafsi, 2024). Cloud platforms can offer consolidated load or fewer transportation trips to get goods movement to decrease the quantity. These technologies facilitate the combination of shipments by using real time data of orders, destinations and suitable capacity, leading to reduction in the number of trucks on the road, reduction in fuel consumption and less emission (Mishra et al., 2024).

Additionally, the use of cloud-based logistics solutions makes it easy to optimize resources through increased communication among the stakeholders. Real-time notification of product availability, delivery timeline, or any other possible interruptions are delivered by cloud solutions thus reducing the unnecessary delays and improving efficiency on a whole. Finally, both reduced operating costs and decreased environmental impact are achieved through optimization of superfluous transit, waste, energy consumption, and other logistics operational characteristics. Therefore, the application of cloud-based logistics systems fosters the advancement of the overarching objectives of sustainable logistics through a more efficient, able to do and resource management, considerably reducing carbon footprint.

Role of Big Data in Sustainability-Driven Decision-Making

Sustainability oriented logistics decision making depends essentially on the use of big data analytics. The extensive data that is generated by IoT devices, sensors, and other digital systems may be used by logistics companies to create shifts from reactive to predictive, and prescriptive decision-making models. Logistics managers can better make more informed and proactive choices to reduce environmental impact through the analysis of extensive datasets such as fuel consumption, emissions, changes of meteorological trends, disruptions of supply chain, and demand of consumers. Network reconfiguration modeling is a primary use of big data in green logistics. Structural change influences the supply chain topology through data analytics technologies and hence may need evaluation of the possible environmental effects of the different supply chain topologies using data analytic technologies before any alterations are made (Ivanov & Dolgui, 2021; Khan et al., 2025). Businesses can then consider many different scenarios which will give the most equilibrium between operational efficiency and environmental sustainability.

Big data analytics facilitate predictive maintenance, a vital aspect of sustainability. By using data from IoT sensors placed in transportation fleets and warehouse machines, logistics companies can forecast maintenance needs and avoid avoidable breakdowns or equipment failure (Alshdadi et al., 2025). This minimizes waste, avoids the environmental impacts of malfunctioning equipment and ensures that vehicles and machines are operating at their peak efficiency which, in turn, reduces energy consumption and emission. Additionally, by performing big data analytics, logistical organizations can improve their demand forecasting to better align their supply chain operations with real demand of real consumers. The examination of past sales data, in addition to external factors such as market trends and seasonality may serve to optimize the production, transportation and inventory management of the companies to reduce risk of over production, excess inventory and resource wastage. As a result, logistics companies require big data analytics for making sustainable and data-based decisions which are environmentally innocuous and improve operational efficiency.

CASE STUDIES AND BEST PRACTICES IN GREEN LOGISTICS

The urgent need for sustainable practices has been recognized by many enterprises as an environmental and economic necessity to reduce expenses in the interest of all stakeholders involved in processes along the logistics chain. Many industries have included green logistics techniques in their operations through operations that reduce environmental issues and ultimately increase operational efficiency and earn money. This section includes many significant case studies, all of which provide evidence of how firms from numerous sectors have successfully completed their green logistics program. The examples presented in this work offer insight into the effectiveness of the methods, the technology, and the practices of providing support for sustainability in logistics operations.

DHL's GoGreen Program: A Commitment to Carbon Efficiency

The GoGreen initiative is an initiative undertaken by DHL, a world giant in the logistics and express services, who have been on the frontline in the incorporation of sustainability in its operations. During DHL worldwide supply chain operations, GoGreen is used for initiation in 2008 to reduce the influence on the environment by limiting carbon emissions. The initiative has a holistic approach that indicates green transportation, eco-friendly storage and alternative climate neutral shipping. The underlying principle of GoGreen is carbon efficient mobility. The company has put a lot into various sustainable means of transport such as biofuels, electric vehicles (EVs) and hybrid trucks. It has a global fleet of over 5,000 electric cars and hence; it has one of the biggest fleets of the logistics sectors EVs (Malladi et al., 2022). As CO2 emissions are becoming an issue in metropolitan areas, this fleet is important in alleviating the same. In fact, DHL has formed partnerships with the manufacturers of biofuel to allow the introduction of sustainable fuels to its fleet with the purport to reduce their carbon footprint to such an extent (Al-Mohannadi et al., 2024). Since it is committed to sustainable storage, DHL has employed energy efficient solutions across the world in the company's facilities. Some such technologies are solar panels, energy efficient lighting system, and exquisite heating and cooling. This climate neutral shipping project by DHL allows the customers to offset the carbon emission of their packet delivery and to raise awareness of the environmental impact of the operations by the company. By 2020 DHL offset more than 33M Mt CO2 which corresponds to its energy saving and carbon offset programs (Stanford et al., 2023). The GoGreen initiative shows that a logistical colossus can make use of environmental benevolence as well as operational success. Thus, DHL has decreased its carbon footprints, setting an example in front of other logistics firms to follow their suits, in the same lines of sustainability in shipping, storage, and client solutions. From the exposure, the program offers information about the possibility of long-lasting economic gains in the forms of reduced fuel cost, increased brand image and increased loyalty of consumers which can be a competitive advantage in the fast-moving market (Kumar, 2020).

Maersk's Investment in Biofuel-Powered Vessels: Leading the Way in Maritime Sustainability

The preeminent global container shipping company, Maersk, has gone ahead to reduce its environmental impact by investing in biofuel powered boats. Traditionally, maritime transport has been a big contributor of emissions from the logistics sector when measured in terms of global carbon emissions. Invests in sustainable marine logistics technology and thus established itself as a pioneer in tackling these problems. It was in 2020 when it completed the first test for a vessel running on a biofuel mix of Maersk, a step forward to the company's objective of becoming carbon neutral by 2050 (Mandegari et al., 2023). These experiments use biofuels of different types, including algae and waste oils, which means that what's generated is a more environmentally harmless product than most of what would ordinarily be used in marine fuels. The program has become a part of Maersk's overall plan to reduce emissions of its fleet, where we are now developing low carbon shipping routes, with energy efficient ship designs and integration in operation of renewable energy sources, such as wind power, for propulsion. The innovations in the maritime sector, however, are inherent in Maersk's focus on biofuel powered boats. Although the shipping industry is notoriously difficult to decarbonize, Maersk's investment in biofuels is a ground-breaking attempt at significant emissions reductions. Furthermore, the company's dedication to sustainability is beyond its fleet. Sadiq et al., (2021) also reports that Maersk has also looked to minimize its carbon footprint in the shipping company's docks and warehouses with the use of energy efficient technology like LED lighting and automation. The examples from Maersk show that the sustainability in logistics, especially in marine shipping, is possible and vital for an enduring success. Maersk meanwhile is helping to accelerate the trend for greener supply chains by providing capital for biofuels and other forms of sustainable developed technologies.

Amazon's Shipment Zero Initiative: Achieving Net-Zero Carbon Emissions by 2030

Amazon, one of the leading e-commerce and logistics companies globally, wants to make 50 percent of shipments become net zero carbon emission by 2030 using its Shipment Zero initiative (K.V. et al., 2025). According to the corporation, its logistics activities (shipped and packaged), represent a very big piece in its total carbon footprint. Therefore, to reach this ambitious goal, Amazon has been incorporating sustainable supply chain logistics solutions. The use of electric delivery vehicles is a fundamental element of Amazon's sustainable logistics strategy. Amazon has started deploying electric vehicles (EVs) for package delivery in the metropolitan areas in collaboration with firms like Rivian. The distribution of millions of products every day requires a chunk of the carbon out of Amazon's global delivery network, and electric vehicles are a key component in its plan for doing just that. By substituting conventional gasoline powered delivery vans with electric cars, Amazon may reduce greenhouse gas emissions 160 times as much as business travel, making up a larger portion of the greenhouse gas footprint than business travel itself (Bronner et al., 2021). Machine learning based logistics optimization is one of Amazon's approach's major components. So, Amazon is using AI to reduce the energy used and expenses spent on delivering and storing goods. Because Amazon foresees demand, harmonizes delivery routes, and improves truckers' efficiency, it able to reduce the number of cars on the road and decrease the fuel use. Secondly, Amazon is so dedicated to their eco-friendly packaging that they invented different package means which would reduce package size and weight and use recyclable package materials. A great example of the integration of machine intelligence and electric vehicles to combat e-commerce shipping industry's emissions is Amazon's Shipment Zero. When it comes to supply chain transparency, Amazon is dedicated to maintaining sustainable practices by getting consumers to know specifics about the carbon impact of their purchases. Amazon is taking the lead to progressive sustainability practices in other e-commerce enterprises by setting lofty sustainability objectives.

Key Takeaways: Green Logistics as a Path to Profitability

Green logistics techniques however while requiring a great amount of investment offer long term economic, regulatory and reputational advantages as case studies of DHL, Maersk and Amazon illustrate. By becoming sustainable, from beginning to finish, organizations in their supply chains experience reduced costs from increased efficiency including less fuel use, lower energy costs, and fewer interruptions. There is a symbiotic relationship between the companies that undertake sustainability activities and the customers they serve; increased customer loyalty and a stronger company reputation are necessary in an age when customers make sustainability a priority. Moreover, the examples show the relevancy of innovation to the achievement of sustainability in logistics. To achieve the same, companies make use of the newest technology like electric cars, biofuels, machine learning, and blockchain to widen their supply chains and diminish their ecological impact. These case studies demonstrate the efficacy of green logistics in being a corporate social responsibility measure but more than that it is also a strategic need although it may confer competitive advantages in the rapidly evolving global market. Companies which invest in green logistics will be strategically positioned to meet the regulatory and environmentally conscious customers' demands in the future, which will offer a more sustainable and resilient future.

CHALLENGES AND FUTURE DIRECTIONS IN GREEN LOGISTICS

Increasingly, green logistics has played a crucial role as part of the sustainable supply chain management by implications that are ecological and operational. Nonetheless, despite its clear benefits, several substantial obstacles impede the widespread implementation of green logistics. The problems are largely related to the existence of such serious financial obstacles, infrastructural constraints and organizational resistance, especially among small (SMEs). In particular, whereas a lot of the policy intervention required to facilitate the transition to sustainable logistics is fundamental, such policies need to be equitable to technical and social issues. Thus, the future sustainable logistics will be shaped by prospective development like autonomous supply chain, Hyperloop mobility, and renewable energy-based logistics hubs etc. While this, these, will also be improved, they need to be resolved ethically, such as data privacy, algorithmic bias, equitable access a green technology, if not, then this will have no fair, or inclusive ending.

Barriers to the Adoption of Green Logistics

The major obstacles to implementing green logistics technology are its substantial absence of high level of green intermediary costs in the initial investment. Large initial capital expenditure is required to acquire and keep electric vehicle (EV) fleets. As high financial burden remains significant challenge despite potential long-term savings from decrease in fuel consumption and maintenance costs above initial expenditures especially for small and medium sized enterprises that in many cases do have enough cash or financial alternatives (Bakhtiari et al., 2020). Additionally, it is another big challenge caused by green logistics infrastructure constraints related to charging networks for electric vehicles. Although there are still many locations where a robust charging infrastructure to support widespread adoption of electric cars is still lacking, there is a need to have one for the masses. Logistics organizations are hampered in their capacity to convert their fleets to use electric options because their current electric vehicles are unable to use more sustainable logistics practices (Kin et al., 2021), because there is a lack of infrastructure to charge electric trucks and vans.

Infrastructural constraints are one of the factors, while interoperability issues between different digital platforms make green logistics a more difficult move. With increasing computerization and networked logistics networks, lack of standardization in data format, platform, and communication protocol could lead to inefficiency and increased operating expenses. Customization of the amalgamation of many systems to monitor pollutants, measure fuel use and oversee supply schedules may involve much time and cost expenditure (Firoozi et al., 2024). These interoperability issues stand to potentially keep logistics companies from embracing green tech if the expense is greater than that anticipated with the savings. Organizational inertia is yet another impediment to the implementation of green logistics on the broad side. Many of these enterprises, for example, those who are already established with business operations as well as with conventional logistical frameworks, may be reluctant to change. To facilitate the transition to green logistics, technical improvements, the revision of the business culture, leadership endorsement and staff education are needed. It may be difficult for organizations to invest in new technology, even if it provides no immediate benefits, and current staff probably do not have the right expertise when implementing green logistics procedures. Because of the reluctance to change and a lack of understanding of the potential advantages of sustainability, there is a substantial obstacle to widespread the wide implementation of green logistics solutions (Leung et al., 2023). In addition, the SMEs' inadequate understanding of sustainable solutions creates an additional obstacle to it. Nowadays, many small and medium size enterprises do not have the capacity and knowledge to assess and implement green logistics initiatives efficiently. In the case that these firms do not have clear regulatory incentives or public pressure, they can be more likely to delay or even avoid adopting the sustainable measures (Zhou et al., 2023). However, to resolve this problem, providers of SMEs with support in expertise, resources, and financial aid must be given sufficient support to enable shift from more unsustainable logistics to more sustainable logistics.

Policy Interventions to Accelerate Green Logistics

Gaining insights into these obstacles is essential to overcome them and speed up the implementation of green logistics through policy interventions. Enacting rules that promote the use of sustainable logistics techniques may help governments and regulatory agencies in fostering a conducive environment. By acting as carbon pricing, this may internalize the environmental costs associated with logistical operations, stimulating technological carbon reduction by offending corporations for increased expenses. Such a well-structured carbon pricing mechanism, both at the carbon tax and cap and trade systems level, would enable carbon pricing to encourage adoption of cleaner technologies and practices in logistical operations such as electric vehicles and renewable energy sources (Eslamipoor & Sepehriyar, 2024). In equal importance are subsidies for green technology to reduce the hefty initial costs of shifting to a more sustainable logistics. Tax concessions, grants and low interest loans may enhance the affordability of green technology to enterprises, particularly for small and medium sized enterprises that may have difficulties making early expenditure. Focusing governments can be provided with assistance for the development of green infrastructure such as electric car charging stations and renewable energy-powered logistics hubs (Jain et al., 2025). Both are vital policy actions: establishment of uniform sustainability reporting systems. Through these frameworks, the logistics sector becomes transparent where organizations can have their environmental consequences monitored, quantified, and reported on a regular basis. The company will be accountable and customers, investors and other stakeholders will be able to work with educated choices on the sustainability of their company logistics partners with standardized reporting. It is expected that governments can encourage the general use of green logistics techniques and encourage enterprises to reach environmental bottoms (Baah et al., 2020).

Emerging Trends in Green Logistics

Future trends to become nascent and impact the realm of green logistics were anticipated. The autonomous supply chain example provides increased productivity and more reduced environmental impacts on the proposal of self-driving trucks, drones, and automated warehouse systems. In terms of route efficiency and fuel use, autonomous cars could reduce emissions in the last addition of city transport, but at the same time drones make the final mile delivery possible with low emissions. This will diminish dependence on human labor and thus reduce energy consumption and increase operational efficiency (Silva et al., 2022). A hyperloop transportation would be a disruptive mode of sustainable logistics. Systems in which hyperloop move cargo at relatively high speeds, using magnetic levitation and low-pressure tube for reducing transportation emissions. By the time you are reading this post, this technology may have come a long way toward becoming a more efficient alternative to the trucks and trains used in conventional transportation of long-distance freight (Dong et al., 2021). The integration of such hyperloop technologies might serve to reduce time sensitivity and help alleviate a more sustainable form of delivery, for commodities with a time requirement. In addition, in the promotion of sustainable logistics, the establishment of renewable energy fueled logistics hubs is expected to be key. Solar, wind, and other renewable energy sources are employed by these hubs to power warehouse operations to minimize the carbon footprint of logistical operations. By decentralizing energy production and its absorption into logistical operations, organizations are completely able to get rid of their usage of fossil fuels and obtaining the path of net zero emissions (Ferdaus et al., 2024).

Ethical Considerations in Green Logistics

The ethical relevance of digital technology and sustainability in logistics firms cannot be ignored as they continue to evolve into more digital ways and act having in mind the principles of sustainability. To ensure an inclusive and just transition to green logistics, special considerations of data privacy, algorithmic biases, fair access to green technology among others are necessary. A logistics firm stockpiles a lot of data on consumer activities, transit routes and some environmental effects, worsening the problem of data privacy. Using data rights is important and essential to protect people's privacy rights and to increase public confidence in new technologies. Additionally, social and environmental consequences of the wider impact of algorithms, such as route optimization algorithms, may not be considered. Algorithms must be made transparent, just, and equitable, and should not ruin certain populations or stakeholders (Bogina et al., 2022). Finally, the denouement is finally, fair access to green technology becomes a major ethical issue. It is imperative that such green logistics technologies as the use of electric cars and renewable energy powered infrastructure does not afford green logistics to SMEs, rural regions and developing nations. Sustainability policies would also need more use of inclusiveness and equality of all enterprises, to ensure widespread benefits of greener logistics shift to enterprises (Tsang et al., 2023).

CONCLUSION

The sustainability effort in the field of logistics has seen considerable advancement, in the recent past, due to the urgent need to minimize the impacts on the environment without compromising efficiency of the operations. Green logistics strategies, which include a vast variety of approaches aimed at decreasing the ecological footprint of logistics operations, have become undeniably important with businesses trying on the one hand to follow the environmental path and, on the other hand, to meet the demand of consumers for more sustainable practices. The development of digital technologies and smart technologies has been a breakthrough in a quest to make green logistics a norm in the industry, giving solutions to both environmental challenges and increasing the efficiency of the logistics sector. The core of green logistics lies in the focus on decreasing the impact on the environment and the use of such methods as sustainable means of transport, warehouse efficiency in terms of energy spending, as well as the development of circular economy. Sustainable modes of transport as well as the use of alternative fuels such as electricity has made logistic companies less reliant on fossil fuels and minimizing the emission of greenhouse gases. What's more, energy efficient warehousing and distribution tactics, accomplished with state-of-the-art designs of buildings and renewable energy sources, have substantially reduced energy expenditure in logistics activities. The implementation of the principles of circular economy: waste minimization and reuse of resources has also become an important aspect of the reduction of the total environmental 'footprint' of supply chains.

A transformative role of the Internet of Things (IoT), in green logistics, has come to the fore. With the use of smart sensors, IoT-enabled technologies enable real-time tracking and monitoring of goods, assets, and transportation fleets. With the help of this data, the logistics managers get a glimpse of the performance of the supply chain and thus can optimize the routes; make vehicles more fuel efficient and increase the time spent driving and reduce idle times. Predictive analytics which were made possible due to the use of the IoT systems in future have revolutionized fleet management as logistic companies have been able to project demand more accordingly and adapt routes and schedules for delivery while cutting down on fuel consumption. Likewise, demand forecasting based on AI has helped to limit the superfluous inventory, which minimizes waste and its environmental expenses. The digital innovations, especially block chain, cloud-based logistics platforms and big data analytics have also been necessary tools for sustainability of logistics. The blockchain technology increases transparency and traceability through supply chains, so that sustainability assertions can be tested and ethical sourcing techniques are implemented. Through cloud computing, data management will be centralized and collaboration and resource allocation within the supply chain is optimized in the logistics companies. Big data analytics gives predictive insights to the managers of the logistic industry to assist them to make informed, sustainability-based decisions such as fuel consumption optimization, processes in supply chain optimization among others.

Many case studies and best practices of the industry giants, such as GoGreen program from DHL, investment of Maersk into biofuel operated ships, and Amazon's Shipment Zero, demonstrate the successful implementation of green logistics strategies into the global supply chains. Such companies prove that even though the up-front expenses on green technologies may be high, the long-term pay-off in terms of the environment and the economy, as well as reputation, considerably exceeds the price. What is more, such examples highlight the vital role of innovation and technological progress as the engine of sustainability in logistics, which allows us to conclude that the digitalization of companies' operations can help them not only implement sustainability initiatives but also improve the efficiency of operation and customer satisfaction. Nevertheless, with the positive developments taking place in green logistics, there are those issues that remain unresolved. -Investment costs associated with adopting sustainable technologies are still very high upfront; infrastructural limitations; and organizational inertia. SMEs and smaller businesses usually experience challenges in accessing the financial resources and capital to invest in green logistics solutions. But with the help of policy interventions like carbon pricing, subsiding green technologies, and development of standardized sustainability reporting frameworks, these problems can be remitted. Also, the future of green logistics can be predicted with the help of upcoming trends, namely autonomous supply chains, hyperloop transportation systems, and logistics hubs, powered by renewable energy sources. Such advances hold the prospect of continued improvement in the environmental impact of logistics operations while at the same time making logistics efficiency and cost savings a reality. However, as the logistics industry adopts digital and technological changes, the ethics behind these developments need to be put into consideration. Privacy issues relating to data, algorithmic biases, and just access to green technologies need to be considered to ensure that a transition to sustainable logistics is inclusive and just. Through preemptive measures in dealing with these ethical challenges, the logistics sector can come up with a fairer and transparent system where all parties, that is, businesses, consumers, and communities, stand to benefit.

REFERENCES

Al-Mohannadi, A. A., Ertogral, K., & Erkoc, M. (2024). Alternative Fuels in Sustainable Logistics—Applications, Challenges, and Solutions. *Sustainability*, *16*(19), 8484. DOI: 10.3390/su16198484

Ali, S. S., Kaur, R., & Khan, S. (2023). Evaluating sustainability initiatives in warehouse for measuring sustainability performance: An emerging economy perspective. *Annals of Operations Research*, *324*(1–2), 461–500. DOI: 10.1007/s10479-021-04454-w

Alrajhi, A., Roy, K., Qingge, L., & Kribs, J. (2023). Detection of Road Condition Defects Using Multiple Sensors and IoT Technology: A Review. *IEEE Open Journal of Intelligent Transportation Systems*, *4*, 372–392. DOI: 10.1109/OJITS.2023.3237480

Alshdadi, A. A., Almazroi, A. A., & Ayub, N. (2025). IoT-driven load forecasting with machine learning for logistics planning. *Internet of Things : Engineering Cyber Physical Human Systems*, *29*, 101441. DOI: 10.1016/j.iot.2024.101441

Amin Mirjalili, S. M., Aslani, A., & Zahedi, R. (2023). Towards sustainable commercial-office buildings: Harnessing the power of solar panels, electric vehicles, and smart charging for enhanced energy efficiency and environmental responsibility. *Case Studies in Thermal Engineering*, *52*, 103696. DOI: 10.1016/j.csite.2023.103696

Baah, C., Jin, Z., & Tang, L. (2020). Organizational and regulatory stakeholder pressures friends or foes to green logistics practices and financial performance: Investigating corporate reputation as a missing link. *Journal of Cleaner Production*, *247*, 119125. DOI: 10.1016/j.jclepro.2019.119125

Bakhtiari, S., Breunig, R., Magnani, L., & Zhang, J. (2020). Financial Constraints and Small and Medium Enterprises: A Review*. *The Economic Record*, *96*(315), 506–523. DOI: 10.1111/1475-4932.12560

Bogina, V., Hartman, A., Kuflik, T., & Shulner-Tal, A. (2022). Educating Software and AI Stakeholders About Algorithmic Fairness, Accountability, Transparency and Ethics. *International Journal of Artificial Intelligence in Education*, *32*(3), 808–833. DOI: 10.1007/s40593-021-00248-0

Bronner, W., Gebauer, H., Lamprecht, C., & Wortmann, F. (2021). Sustainable AIoT: How Artificial Intelligence and the Internet of Things Affect Profit, People, and Planet. In *Connected Business* (pp. 137–154). Springer International Publishing., DOI: 10.1007/978-3-030-76897-3_8

Centobelli, P., Cerchione, R., & Esposito, E., & Shashi. (2020). Evaluating environmental sustainability strategies in freight transport and logistics industry. *Business Strategy and the Environment*, *29*(3), 1563–1574. DOI: 10.1002/bse.2453

Chen, Y., Zhang, X., Ji, J., & Zhang, C. (2024). Cold chain transportation energy conservation and emission reduction based on phase change materials under dual-carbon background: A review. *Journal of Energy Storage*, *86*, 111258. DOI: 10.1016/j.est.2024.111258

Dadashzada, I., Garza-Reyes, J. A., Roy Ghatak, R., & Gonzalez-Aleu, F. (2024). An investigation into the major barriers to the adoption of electric vehicles in last-mile deliveries for sustainable transport. *International Journal of Logistics Management*. Advance online publication. DOI: 10.1108/IJLM-01-2024-0007

Dimri, S. C., Indu, R., Bajaj, M., Rathore, R. S., Blazek, V., Dutta, A. K., & Alsubai, S. (2024). Modeling of traffic at a road crossing and optimization of waiting time of the vehicles. *Alexandria Engineering Journal*, *98*, 114–129. DOI: 10.1016/j.aej.2024.04.050

Dong, C., Akram, A., Andersson, D., Arnäs, P.-O., & Stefansson, G. (2021). The impact of emerging and disruptive technologies on freight transportation in the digital era: Current state and future trends. *International Journal of Logistics Management*, *32*(2), 386–412. DOI: 10.1108/IJLM-01-2020-0043

Emon, M. M. H. (2023). A Systematic Review of the Causes and Consequences of Price Hikes in Bangladesh. *Review of Business and Economics Studies*, *11*(2), 49–58. DOI: 10.26794/2308-944X-2023-11-2-49-58

Emon, M. M. H. (2025). The Mediating Role of Supply Chain Responsiveness in the Relationship Between Key Supply Chain Drivers and Performance: Evidence from the FMCG Industry. *Brazilian Journal of Operations & Production Management*, *22*(1), 2580. DOI: 10.14488/BJOPM.2580.2025

Emon, M. M. H., & Khan, T. (2024). A Systematic Literature Review on Sustainability Integration and Marketing Intelligence in the Era of Artificial Intelligence. *Review of Business and Economics Studies*, *12*(4), 6–28. DOI: 10.26794/2308-944X-2024-12-4-6-28

Emon, M. M. H., & Khan, T. (2025a). The mediating role of attitude towards the technology in shaping artificial intelligence usage among professionals. *Telematics and Informatics Reports*, *17*, 100188. DOI: 10.1016/j.teler.2025.100188

Emon, M. M. H., & Khan, T. (2025b). The transformative role of Industry 4.0 in supply chains: Exploring digital integration and innovation in the manufacturing enterprises. *Journal of Open Innovation*, *11*(2), 100516. DOI: 10.1016/j.joitmc.2025.100516

Emon, M. M. H., & Khan, T. (2025c). The Role of Traditional Media in Crisis Amplification: How Mainstream Media Magnifies Fake News and Ethical Dilemmas in Supply Chain Crises. In *Mass Media and Impact of Fake News on Supply Chains* (pp. 59–90). IGI Global., DOI: 10.4018/979-8-3373-2175-2.ch003

Emon, M. M. H., & Khan, T. (2025d). The Rise of Circular Supply Chains: Recycling and Closed-Loop Systems Could Mitigate Inflationary Pressures. In *Supply Chain Disruptions and Impact on Global Inflation* (pp. 195–226). IGI Global., DOI: 10.4018/979-8-3373-1982-7.ch008

Emon, M. M. H., Khan, T., Rahman, M. A., Hamid, A. B. A., & Yaakub, N. I. (2025). GreenTech Revolution: Navigating Challenges and Seizing Opportunities. In *AI and Green Technology Applications in Society* (pp. 63–90). IGI Global Scientific Publishing. https://doi.org/DOI: 10.4018/979-8-3693-9879-1.ch003

Eslamipoor, R., & Sepehriyar, A. (2024). Promoting green supply chain under carbon tax, carbon cap and carbon trading policies. *Business Strategy and the Environment*, *33*(5), 4901–4912. DOI: 10.1002/bse.3721

Ferdaus, M. M., Dam, T., Anavatti, S., & Das, S. (2024). Digital technologies for a net-zero energy future: A comprehensive review. *Renewable & Sustainable Energy Reviews*, *202*, 114681. DOI: 10.1016/j.rser.2024.114681

Firoozi, A. A., Tshambane, M., Firoozi, A. A., & Sheikh, S. M. (2024). Strategic load management: Enhancing eco-efficiency in mining operations through automated technologies. *Results in Engineering*, *24*, 102890. DOI: 10.1016/j.rineng.2024.102890

Frontoni, E., Marinelli, F., Rosetti, R., & Zingaretti, P. (2020). Optimal stock control and procurement by reusing of obsolescences in manufacturing. *Computers & Industrial Engineering*, *148*, 106697. DOI: 10.1016/j.cie.2020.106697

Haghshenas, S. S., Astarita, V., Haghshenas, S. S., & Guido, G. (2024). Artificial Intelligence-Powered Driver Behavior Analysis for Fuel Consumption Optimization: A Pathway to Greener Roads. *2024 10th International Conference on Control, Decision and Information Technologies (CoDIT)*, 116–122. https://doi.org/DOI: 10.1109/CoDIT62066.2024.10708512

Hasan, M. K., Lei, X., Hlali, A., & Bian, Z. (2024). Modelling capability factors of logistics industry based on ISM-MICMAC. *Heliyon*, *10*(22), e40539. DOI: 10.1016/j.heliyon.2024.e40539 PMID: 39641072

Hlali, A. (2023). Impact of logistics and economic structure on seaport infrastructure: A case of Mediterranean countries. *Australian Journal of Maritime and Ocean Affairs*, *16*(2), 175–185. DOI: 10.1080/18366503.2023.2217584

Hlali, A., & Gafsi, N. (2024). Analysis of Digitalization and Sustainable Development in Africa. *Perspectives on Global Development and Technology*, *22*(5–6), 415–428. DOI: 10.1163/15691497-12341668

Hlali, A., & Wanis, A. (2020). Theoretical highlights in container port logistics systems. *Journal of Marine and Island Cultures*, *9*(2). Advance online publication. DOI: 10.21463/jmic.2020.09.2.13

Hoang, T.-H., Tran, T.-T., Huynh, L. N. T., Vo, D. K., Huynh, B. G., Tran, T. M. T., & Le Nguyen, N. D. (2025). Advances and barriers in promoting green logistics 4.0 from a multi-stakeholder perspective–a systematic review. *Environment Systems & Decisions*, *45*(2), 14. DOI: 10.1007/s10669-025-10006-5

Ivanov, D., & Dolgui, A. (2021). A digital supply chain twin for managing the disruption risks and resilience in the era of Industry 4.0. *Production Planning and Control*, *32*(9), 775–788. DOI: 10.1080/09537287.2020.1768450

Jacobsen, M. (2023). Mediating Infrastructural Discipline: Established Practices and Changing Structures of Dar es Salaam's Transport Sector. *Urban Forum*, *34*(4), 481–500. https://doi.org/DOI: 10.1007/s12132-022-09477-5

Jain, P., Tandon, A., & Bansal, R. C. (2025). *Integration of Renewable Energy Sources (RES) into Electric Vehicle (EV) Charging Infrastructure: State-of-the-Art Review* (pp. 171–214). https://doi.org/DOI: 10.1007/978-981-96-0361-9_9

Khan, T., Emon, M. M. H., & Nath, A. (2024). Quantifying the Effects of AI-Driven Inventory Management on Operational Efficiency in Online Retail. *2024 27th International Conference on Computer and Information Technology (ICCIT)*, 2092–2097. https://doi.org/DOI: 10.1109/ICCIT64611.2024.11021996

Khan, T., Emon, M. M. H., Rahman, M. A., Hamid, A. B. A., & Yaakub, N. I. (2025). Bridging the Gap: Realizing GreenTech Potential. In *AI and Green Technology Applications in Society* (pp. 91–122). IGI Global Scientific Publishing. https://doi.org/DOI: 10.4018/979-8-3693-9879-1.ch004

Kin, B., Hopman, M., & Quak, H. (2021). Different Charging Strategies for Electric Vehicle Fleets in Urban Freight Transport. *Sustainability*, *13*(23), 13080. DOI: 10.3390/su132313080

Kumar, V. (2020). Global implications of cause-related loyalty marketing. *International Marketing Review*, *37*(4), 747–772. DOI: 10.1108/IMR-06-2019-0160

K.V. T., Rattan, P., & Nair, R. R. (2025). Greening the Click-Environmental Initiatives in Global E-Commerce Marketing. In *Green Marketing Perspectives* (pp. 261–272). Emerald Publishing Limited. https://doi.org/DOI: 10.1108/978-1-83608-772-420251021

Leung, T. C. H., Guan, J., & Lau, Y.-Y. (2023). Exploring environmental sustainability and green management practices: Evidence from logistics service providers. *Sustainability Accounting. Management and Policy Journal*, *14*(3), 461–489. DOI: 10.1108/SAMPJ-03-2022-0133

Liu, A., Zhu, Q., Xu, L., Lu, Q., & Fan, Y. (2021). Sustainable supply chain management for perishable products in emerging markets: An integrated location-inventory-routing model. *Transportation Research Part E, Logistics and Transportation Review*, *150*, 102319. DOI: 10.1016/j.tre.2021.102319

Malladi, S. S., Christensen, J. M., Ramírez, D., Larsen, A., & Pacino, D. (2022). Stochastic fleet mix optimization: Evaluating electromobility in urban logistics. *Transportation Research Part E, Logistics and Transportation Review*, *158*, 102554. DOI: 10.1016/j.tre.2021.102554

Mandegari, M., Ebadian, M., van Dyk, S., & Saddler, J. (John). (2023). Decarbonizing British Columbia's (BC's) marine sector by using low carbon intensive (CI) biofuels. *Biofuels, Bioproducts & Biorefining*, *17*(4), 1101–1114. DOI: 10.1002/bbb.2495

Matenga, A., & Mpofu, K. (2023). Blockchain-based Product Lifecycle Management using Supply Chain Management for Railcar Remanufacturing. *Procedia CIRP*, *116*, 486–491. DOI: 10.1016/j.procir.2023.02.082

Mishra, A., Dutta, P., & Gottipalli, N. (2024). An optimization model for the downstream supply chain network, considering consolidated warehouses and the selection of transportation mode. *International Journal of Productivity and Performance Management*, *73*(3), 912–942. DOI: 10.1108/IJPPM-05-2022-0231

Mishra, A., Dutta, P., Jayasankar, S., Jain, P., & Mathiyazhagan, K. (2023). A review of reverse logistics and closed-loop supply chains in the perspective of circular economy. *Benchmarking*, *30*(3), 975–1020.

Nikseresht, A., Golmohammadi, D., & Zandieh, M. (2024). Sustainable green logistics and remanufacturing: A bibliometric analysis and future research directions. *International Journal of Logistics Management*, *35*(3), 755–803. DOI: 10.1108/IJLM-03-2023-0085

Nnabuife, S. G., Hamzat, A. K., Whidborne, J., Kuang, B., & Jenkins, K. W. (2025). Integration of renewable energy sources in tandem with electrolysis: A technology review for green hydrogen production. *International Journal of Hydrogen Energy, 107*, 218–240. DOI: 10.1016/j.ijhydene.2024.06.342

Oyekanlu, E. A., Smith, A. C., Thomas, W. P., Mulroy, G., Hitesh, D., Ramsey, M., Kuhn, D. J., Mcghinnis, J. D., Buonavita, S. C., Looper, N. A., Ng, M., Ng'oma, A., Liu, W., Mcbride, P. G., Shultz, M. G., Cerasi, C., & Sun, D. (2020). A Review of Recent Advances in Automated Guided Vehicle Technologies: Integration Challenges and Research Areas for 5G-Based Smart Manufacturing Applications. *IEEE Access : Practical Innovations, Open Solutions, 8*, 202312–202353. DOI: 10.1109/ACCESS.2020.3035729

Rehman Khan, S. A., Yu, Z., Sarwat, S., Godil, D. I., Amin, S., & Shujaat, S. (2022). The role of block chain technology in circular economy practices to improve organisational performance. *International Journal of Logistics Research and Applications, 25*(4–5), 605–622. DOI: 10.1080/13675567.2021.1872512

Ruiz-Torres, A. J., Mahmoodi, F., Ohmori, S., & Hlali, A. (2022). Suppliers portfolio and returner incentive decisions in closed-loop remanufacturing systems under multiple stochastic scenarios. *International Journal of Sustainable Engineering, 15*(1), 208–225. DOI: 10.1080/19397038.2022.2110330

Sadiq, M., Ali, S. W., Terriche, Y., Mutarraf, M. U., Hassan, M. A., Hamid, K., Ali, Z., Sze, J. Y., Su, C.-L., & Guerrero, J. M. (2021). Future Greener Seaports: A Review of New Infrastructure, Challenges, and Energy Efficiency Measures. *IEEE Access : Practical Innovations, Open Solutions, 9*, 75568–75587. DOI: 10.1109/ACCESS.2021.3081430

Sekarini, S., & Selvabaskar, S. (2024). *AI-Powered Branding*., DOI: 10.4018/979-8-3693-7122-0.ch002

Silva, Ó., Cordera, R., González-González, E., & Nogués, S. (2022). Environmental impacts of autonomous vehicles: A review of the scientific literature. *The Science of the Total Environment, 830*, 154615. DOI: 10.1016/j.scitotenv.2022.154615 PMID: 35307440

Stanford, V. I., Buc, L., Houck, A., & Jost, E. (2023). *Using Pricing as a Tool to Achieve Carbon Neutrality*. Implications for the United States Postal Service., DOI: 10.1007/978-3-031-25362-1_16

Su, Y., Duan, H., Wang, Z., Song, G., Kang, P., & Chen, D. (2020). Characterizing the environmental impact of packaging materials for express delivery via life cycle assessment. *Journal of Cleaner Production*, *274*, 122961. DOI: 10.1016/j.jclepro.2020.122961

Tadayonrad, Y., & Ndiaye, A. B. (2023). A new key performance indicator model for demand forecasting in inventory management considering supply chain reliability and seasonality. *Supply Chain Analytics*, *3*, 100026. DOI: 10.1016/j.sca.2023.100026

Thanigaivel, S., Priya, A. K., Dutta, K., Rajendran, S., & Vasseghian, Y. (2022). Engineering strategies and opportunities of next generation biofuel from microalgae: A perspective review on the potential bioenergy feedstock. *Fuel*, *312*, 122827. DOI: 10.1016/j.fuel.2021.122827

Tsang, Y. P., Fan, Y., & Feng, Z. P. (2023). Bridging the gap: Building environmental, social and governance capabilities in small and medium logistics companies. *Journal of Environmental Management*, *338*, 117758. DOI: 10.1016/j.jenvman.2023.117758 PMID: 36996566

Vienažindienė, M., Tamulienė, V., & Zaleckienė, J. (2021). Green Logistics Practices Seeking Development of Sustainability: Evidence from Lithuanian Transportation and Logistics Companies. *Energies*, *14*(22), 7500. DOI: 10.3390/en14227500

Vijaykumar, V., Mercy, P., Lucia Agnes Beena, T., Leena, H. M., & Savarimuthu, C. (2024). Convergence of IoT, Artificial Intelligence and Blockchain Approaches for Supply Chain Management. In *Blockchain, IoT, and AI Technologies for Supply Chain Management* (pp. 45–89). Apress. https://doi.org/DOI: 10.1007/979-8-8688-0315-4_2

Zhou, P., Song, F. M., & Huang, X. (2023). Environmental regulations and firms' green innovations: Transforming pressure into incentives. *International Review of Financial Analysis*, *86*, 102504. DOI: 10.1016/j.irfa.2023.102504

KEY TERMS AND DEFINITIONS

Green Logistics: Integration of sustainable practices across supply chain operations to minimize environmental impact while maintaining operational efficiency and economic viability.

Operational Performance: Metrics evaluating efficiency, cost-effectiveness, and reliability of logistics activities (e.g., delivery times, inventory turnover).

Environmental Accountability: Responsibility for ecological impacts of logistics operations, including carbon emissions, resource use, and waste generation.

Sustainable Transportation Methods: Strategies to reduce transport emissions through electric vehicles, route optimization, and alternative fuels.

Energy-Efficient Warehousing: Facilities designed with renewable energy, smart lighting, and HVAC systems to minimize energy consumption.

Circular Economy Approaches: Systems prioritizing reuse/recycling of materials via returnable packaging and closed-loop supply chains.

IoT Technology: Network of interconnected sensors providing real-time data for emissions tracking, fleet monitoring, and resource optimization.

AI-Driven Forecasting: Predictive analytics using artificial intelligence to optimize inventory and reduce waste through improved demand planning.

Blockchain Transparency: Immutable ledger technology enabling traceability of sustainable practices across supply chains.

Chapter 13
Green Logistics 5.0: An Examination of Innovation Driven by Sustainability Using Foundation Models in Logistics

Ankit Garg
https://orcid.org/0000-0003-4558-8074
Ajay Kumar Garg Institute of Management, India

Ruchika Nayyar
Amity Business School, Amity University, Noida, India

Surabhi Singh
https://orcid.org/0000-0002-8565-7348
G.L. Bajaj Institute of Management and Research, India

Himanshu Sharma
https://orcid.org/0009-0009-7905-1145
Ajay Kumar Garg Institute of Management, India

Rahul Singhal
https://orcid.org/0000-0002-2672-8521
Ajay Kumar Garg Institute of Management, India

ABSTRACT

This chapter investigates how foundation models might be incorporated into Logistics 5.0 to support a green strategy that fosters sustainability and long-term financial viability. Through the use of foundation models, the study seeks to improve social responsibility, guarantee sustainable innovation, and organize the environmental framework of the logistics sector. The company ideology, products, processes, and

DOI: 10.4018/979-8-3373-2434-0.ch013

business models are all included in the multi-layered approach, which emphasizes sustainability-oriented innovation (SOI) as a need rather than just a tactic. According to the results, artificial intelligence—in particular, foundation models can achieve social, economic, and governance goals while optimizing a range of logistical processes, such as route planning, packaging reduction, and warehouse management.

INTRODUCTION

Since logistics contributes significantly to environmental deterioration, finding creative, sustainable solutions is crucial. It is more important than ever to strike a balance between sustainability and efficiency as supply networks grow more intricate and international. The adoption of foundation models, which use machine learning techniques, artificial intelligence, and predictive analytics to optimize logistics processes while lowering their environmental effect, is one viable alternative. The incorporation of FMs into Logistics 5.0 is consistent with the industry 5.0 paradigm, which emphasizes intelligent, sustainable, and human-centric systems. To create a more environmentally friendly logistics environment, this study investigates how FMs might improve warehouse productivity, reduce packaging waste, and optimize shipping routes. Organizations may greatly reduce waste generation, increase the accuracy of demand forecasting, and reduce their carbon footprint by utilizing these cutting-edge AI-driven models. This will ultimately promote a more accountable and resource efficient supply chain.

Beyond just improving the environment, the use of FMs in logistics also increases operational effectiveness, reduces expenses, and boosts customer happiness. The study emphasizes a multifaceted strategy that combines business models, operational procedures, product development, and corporate philosophy to emphasize the vital role that sustainability-oriented innovation (SOI) plays in logistics. In order to provide a more effective and responsible supply chain, FMs help businesses at the operational level minimize energy use, recommend environmentally friendly recycling practices, and produce predictive insights for product returns. To cut down on needless fuel use and emissions, AI-powered route optimization algorithms, for example, can dynamically modify transportation schedules based on real-time traffic data, meteorological conditions, and fuel efficiency metrics. In a similar vein, companies can reduce overproduction and excessive storage costs by using machine learning-based demand forecasting models to match production and inventory management with real market demand. By lowering inefficiencies and encouraging a circular economy, these enhancements not only support sustainability but also increase the supply chains' overall resilience.

FMs have several benefits in logistics, but there are drawbacks to their widespread use. Large investments in workforce development, infrastructure, and digital transformation plans are necessary for the integration of these technologies. The high upfront expenses of deploying AI-driven logistics systems may be a barrier for many businesses, especially small and medium-sized organizations (SMEs). Additionally, regulatory compliance adds another level of complexity because businesses must comply with varied environmental and data privacy rules in different locations. Additionally, it is challenging to create a cohesive framework for FM adoption due to the dispersed structure of global supply chains and the absence of standardization in logistical procedures. As businesses need to guarantee smooth communication between diverse logistics technologies, such as enterprise resource planning (ERP) systems, warehouse management systems (WMS), and transportation management systems (TMS), interoperability of disparate digital systems continues to be a major challenge. This paper looks at these issues and possible solutions, providing information on how companies can successfully incorporate FMs into their logistical processes while maintaining cost effectiveness and regulatory compliance. The convergence of cutting-edge technologies like blockchain, digital twins, and the Industrial Internet of Things (IIoT) is one of the main factors facilitating the adoption of FM in logistics. These technologies have the potential to completely transform logistics by improving sustainability, transparency, and teamwork when paired with FMs. For example, blockchain technology can offer a decentralized, unchangeable record for tracing shipments, confirming the legitimacy of products, and guaranteeing ethical sourcing methods. Businesses may increase supply chain visibility, decrease fraud, and improve traceability by combining blockchain technology with AI-driven predictive analytics. This builds stakeholder confidence. Businesses can model and optimize warehouse layouts, transportation routes, and inventory management methods with the help of digital twins, which provide real-time virtual reproductions of physical logistics assets. This improves resource utilization and enables better decision-making. Logistics operators can maintain ideal conditions for perishable commodities while reducing energy usage by using real-time data on variables like temperature, humidity, and vehicle performance via IIoT-enabled smart sensors and linked devices.

Although there are many advantages to these technological developments, putting them into practice calls for a methodical strategy that takes into account both technical and human considerations. The ability of businesses to invest in workforce training, cultivatc an innovative culture, and handle possible job displacement issues will determine how well FM adoption in logistics goes. Businesses must create reskilling and upskilling programs to give staff members the digital skills they need to collaborate with intelligent systems as AI-driven automation replaces human operations. Additionally, companies must give ethical issues first priority when using AI models, making sure that algorithms used for decision-making are open, objective, and consistent with sustainability objectives. In order to ensure a seamless transition to FM-powered logistics, this study examines the function of organizational change management, emphasizing the necessity of leadership dedication, staff involvement, and ongoing learning programs.

Figure 1. Optimizing logistics for sustainability

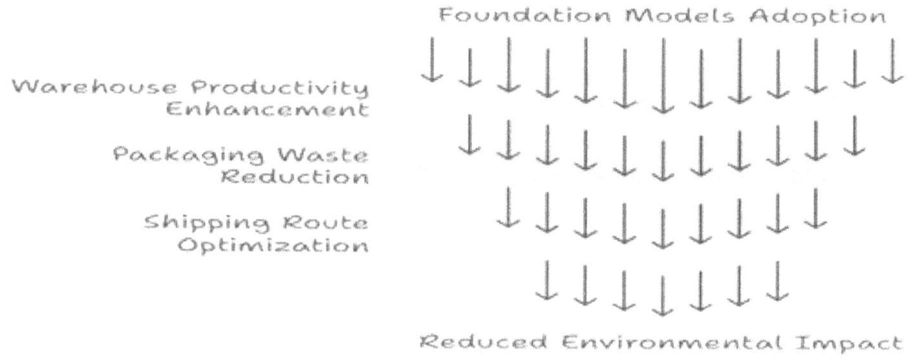

The long-term economic feasibility of these models is another crucial factor in the adoption of FM in logistics. Businesses may see a significant return on investment (ROI) despite the very high initial costs. Through increased productivity, decreased fuel consumption, cheaper inventory holding costs, and optimum asset use, AI-driven logistics solutions can result in significant cost savings. Furthermore, by satisfying the growing customer demand for ecologically friendly goods and services, businesses who adopt sustainability-focused logistics techniques stand to benefit from a competitive edge. The economic argument for FM adoption is being strengthened by the introduction of incentives by governments and regulatory agencies for companies who adopt green logistical strategies. With a thorough examination of cost-benefit trade-offs and the long-term viability of AI-driven supply chain models, this study looks at the financial effects of incorporating FMs into logistics operations.

FMs have enormous potential to revolutionize the logistics sector, and it is impossible to overestimate their contribution to sustainability. Businesses may increase overall supply chain resilience, decrease environmental impact, and increase efficiency by integrating AI-driven analytics, predictive modeling, and intelligent decision-making tools into logistics operations. To achieve broad FM adoption, however, technological, financial, and regulatory obstacles must be overcome while maintaining human-centric concerns at the forefront of digital transformation initiatives. In order to shape a sustainable and innovative future, cooperation between industry stakeholders, technology suppliers, and legislators will be essential as logistics businesses manage these difficulties.

In summary, the logistics industry has undergone a paradigm shift with the integration of FMs into L5.0, providing a strategic approach to efficiency, sustainability, and long-term company success. Notwithstanding the current obstacles, adopting FM is not only desirable but also necessary for the future of sustainable logistics because the advantages greatly exceed the disadvantages. By utilizing cutting-edge technologies like blockchain, digital twins, and IIoT, logistics companies can establish a supply chain ecosystem that is more open, cooperative, and ecologically conscious. In order to guarantee a seamless transition to AI-powered, sustainability-driven logistics, the study highlights the necessity of a comprehensive strategy that takes into account technological, economic, and societal factors. Adoption of FMs will be essential to promoting innovation, enhancing operational resilience, and propelling the logistics sector's long-term success as the industry develops.

Research Objective

The main objectives of this research are to fill in the information voids regarding foundation models (FMs) and acknowledge the increasing significance of logistics in contemporary operational environments. Knowing in advance how cultured technologies like FMs function in logistics is becoming very important as industries continue to place a priority on efficiency and sustainability. By focusing on examining how Logistics 5.0 (L5.0) will be successfully integrated to promote sustainable logistics practices, this study aims to provide a thorough conceptual framework that is in line with sustainability-oriented innovation. The main aim of this research is to demonstrate the revolutionary potential of advanced logistics technologies, including automation, artificial intelligence (AI), and intelligent decision-making systems, in decreasing environmental impact and improving operational efficiency by analyzing critically, assessing, and clarifying the core ideas of L5.0.

Figure 2. Revolutionizing logistics 5.0

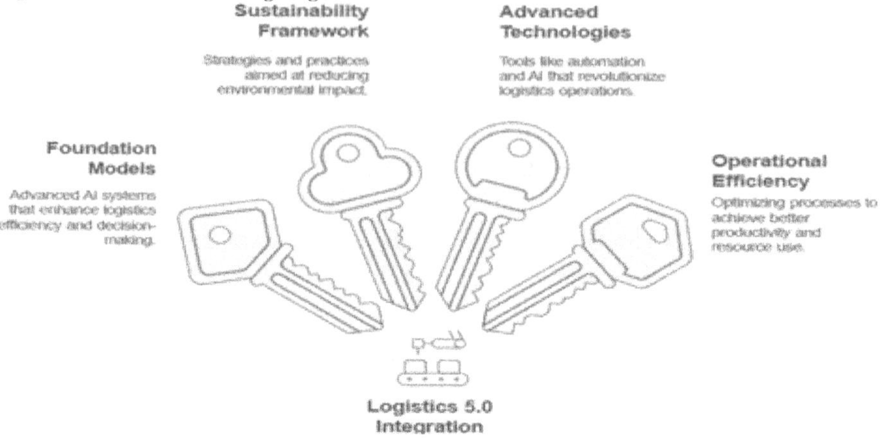

This is how the cutting-edge technologies help to improve supply chain transparency, optimize transportation routes, and help to reduce resource waste, which is a very critical component of our study. Effective Traditional logistics systems help in supply chain operations, but sometimes they can't meet the growing demand for sustainability in the face of changing consumer expectations and environmental requirements. The incorporation of L5.0 offers the potential to bridge this gap and assist businesses in transitioning to more data-driven, sustainable logistics operations. Which is driven by AI-driven FMs. Conceptual framework will be offered thoroughly, the study prepares organizations to comprehend and apply sustainability-focused logistics solutions. This study also provides useful insights on how companies can reduce carbon emissions, simplify inventory control, and the ideas of the circular economy to be adopted. With the help of case studies, data-driven insights, and real-world implementation scenarios, to verify its applicability beyond theoretical investigation, the proposed conceptual model will undergo empirical testing.

Strategic guidance which was useful is offered by them, conceptual models need to be empirically tested to ensure that they remain viable in real-world corporate settings. Though the main objective of this study is to investigate how FMs can be useful for companies to meet sustainability goals, adhere to environmental laws, maximum utilization of resources, and boost overall operational efficiency. Such Companies those who are using Logistics 5.0 technologies are examined in the empirical portion of the study, which helps to determine their experiences, difficulties, and leads to sustainable practices after being put into practices. Through the promotion of sustainable logistics methods, decision-making processes can be improved, and increased supply chain resilience, the study evaluates the precise ways in which FMs contribute directly to the production of value business. The waste can be decreased by businesses by anticipating demand changes and minimizing overproduction and wasteful inventory stockpiling by using AI-powered predictive analytics. If the energy use is minimized, resources allocated effectively and guaranteeing that products are carried and kept in the most environmentally friendly way possible, automated logistics systems can lead to improvement of warehouse operations. Parallel to this, routes of delivery can be modified dynamically by AI-driven route optimization systems in response to current traffic and patterns of weather, reducing emissions and fuel consumption. Those Businesses who incorporate these technologies helps them to improve cost effectiveness, competitiveness, and sustainability performance are more concerned in those markets where more environmental factors are focused.

This case examine how policies and frameworks affect the adoption of sustainable logistics practices and companies make sure that environmental regulations are followed with the help of FMs. Regulatory agencies are globally enforcing more stringent sustainability standards, plans to reduce waste, carbon footprint tracking, and green supply chain requirements. If we come to conclusion, companies need to adjust by incorporating smart compliance solutions. Because of their ability to analyze big information and generate actionable insights, FMs are crucial in assisting businesses in overcoming these regulatory barriers. Many Businesses uses sustainability data, pinpoint opportunities for development, and proactive action is taken to conform for changing environmental regulations by utilizing automated monitoring and reporting systems.

This study also highlight that how supply chain networks work together more effectively with the help of FMs. Coordination of sustainability initiatives by stakeholders is hampered by the segmented data that plague traditional logistical operations. However it is sad that the company may improve supply chain visibility and enable smooth information exchange between manufacturers, suppliers, and distribution partners by utilizing cloud-based logistics solutions and AI-powered analytics. The operational efficiency will be enhanced and uniformity will be maintained during implementation of sustainability efforts throughout supply chain as there are two benefits of this openness.

The paper also ensures that integrating FMs and L5.0 into logistics operations presents certain difficulties. Instead advantages of these technologies, organizations frequently handles obstacles like high upfront costs, difficult technological integration, and difficulties with worker adaption. There will be difficulty for small and medium-sized businesses (SMEs) to meet the infrastructure and budgetary requirements of implementing AI-driven logistics solutions. There are some strategic ways for removing these barrier are examined in this study, like investing in workforce training initiatives, adopting technology gradually, and using technology for working with suppliers to provide scalable and affordable solutions.

Suggested framework is practically tested, the study offers empirical proof of its viability and efficacy, telling how companies can successfully integrate FMs and L5.0 to achieve (SDG) sustainable goals. With the help of actual case studies, the case let identifies that businesses have effectively incorporated AI-driven logistics solutions and focus on the observable advantages, such as lower costs, less environmental impact, and better supply chain performance. Many of the businesses wishing to start their own sustainable transformation journeys so that they can get greatly benefitted from these case studies, as this shows practical insights into best business practices, typical problems, and tried-and-true solutions.

While ending this study brings worthy best insights for both scholarly research and real-world business applications, directly adding to the larger conversation on the nexus of technology, sustainability, and logistics. Businesses must use cutting-edge technologies that allow them to function more ethically and effectively in a time when sustainability is vital for long-term survival rather than only a competitive advantage. The conclusion of this research bolds necessary FMs will be in deciding the direction of logistics in the future and provide a path way for businesses looking to be highly competitive while supporting global sustainability goals.

This research bridges the gap between theory and practice, making it an essential tool for companies, legislators, and business executives seeking to promote sustainability through Logistics 5.0. The incorporation of AI-powered foundation models signifies a paradigm shift in logistics operations, changing how companies handle environmental responsibility, supply chain management, and decision-making. The research's findings will be vital in helping firms move toward a future where logistics is not just effective but also resilient, ethical, and sustainable as sectors continue to change in response to changes in regulations and technology.

METHODOLOGY

A strong, flexible, and ecologically sustainable logistical framework is created by this study by combining state-of-the-art foundation model (FM) solutions with best practices for sustainability-oriented innovation. The framework of logistics 5.0 presents the prospects which are thoroughly analyzed using a multi-layered methodology, guaranteeing a full comprehension of its function in contemporary supply chain management. The methodology consists of three interrelated parts: in-depth interviews with key academic and industry stakeholders, a thorough literature review, and the development of a coherent functional and technical framework aimed at supporting the successful deployment of FM-driven solutions. The wide picture of the trends, difficulties, and possibilities in logistics innovation has been offered, this study offers insightful information on the industry. Together, the interviews of the experts help to create a more subtle knowledge of the industry, especially after analyzing the viewpoints of both large international fifth-party logistics (5PL) companies and smaller Italian third-party logistics (3PL) suppliers. The gap has been bridged with the help of realization aid between theoretical models and practical implementations, guaranteeing that the framework has been suggested that it is based on viability. The framework can also be refined by validating initial use cases through real-world business implementations, which results in the creation of a systematic, structured model with tools and procedures to ease the shift to L5.0 solutions. The efficiency can be improved by utilizing foundation models, resilience, and environmental responsibility in the logistics industry. research promotes sustainable logistics practices by fusing theoretical investigation with empirical confirmation. The conclusion of this study presents a comprehensive method for fusing state-of-the-art technology with environmentally friendly logistics practices, giving business and academic stakeholders hands-on practices for negotiating the changing landscape of Logistics 5.0.

We have used a systematic research technique to check the efficacy of sustainability-driven innovation. The research explores the complex relationship between innovation and sustainability programs, finding important drivers and barriers that affect their implementation. It does this by applying the "5W+1H" paradigm, which addresses why, what, who, when, where, and how. With the help of this method's organized analysis, every facet of innovation focused on sustainability is carefully considered in the framework of Logistics 5.0 (L5.0). The Ishikawa cause-effect analysis model, also referred to as the fishbone diagram, is used in the study to classify the difficulties in putting the L5.0 framework into practice. The four main dimensions of these issues are methods, materials, personnel, and machines. The viability and efficacy of incorporating L5.0 principles into logistics operations are significantly influenced by each of these variables. To make sure that the shift to L5.0 complies with legal requirements and industry standards, the "methods" category looks at the tactics, guidelines, and best practices needed to promote sustainability. "Materials" emphasizes the significance of minimizing environmental effects through the concepts of the circular economy by concentrating on the sustainable sourcing, production, and disposal of logistics-related materials. The book Manpower covers workforce-related subjects like the need for skill development, training, and change management strategies to speed up the implementation of L5.0 procedures and technology. Last but not least, "machines" refers to the automation systems and technological advances that make L5.0 deployment possible. For example, robotics can help with supply chain operations, intelligent logistics networks can make logistics more efficient, and AI-powered decision-making tools can help make smart choices.

Table 1. Difference between traditional and FM-driven systems

Dimension	Traditional Logistics	FM-Driven Logistics (Logistics 5.0)
Demand Forecasting	Based on historical sales or manual inputs	AI-driven predictive analytics using real-time & big data
Inventory Management	Fixed reorder levels and buffers	Dynamic optimization through real-time FM insights
Warehouse Optimization	Manual layout planning, often inefficient	FM-simulated layout planning using heatmaps, IoT, and smart sensors
Route Planning	Fixed routes, static traffic considerations	Real-time adaptive routing using AI and traffic/ weather data
Energy Efficiency	Reactive adjustments, high energy waste	Proactive FM control of lighting, temperature, and operations
Sustainability Metrics	Tracked manually, sometimes irregular	Automated carbon tracking, packaging analysis, and emissions logs
Decision-Making	Human intuition-based	Assisted by explainable AI and data-driven decisions
Reverse Logistics	Manual returns & resale classification	FM-predicted return trends and optimal reuse pathways

This study provides a thorough look at how innovation may help sustainability in logistics while methodically finding and solving potential problems by combining various analytical aspects. To ensure that the suggested results are both conceptually sound and applicable in actual logistical situations, this methodical approach plays a crucial role in bridging the gap between theoretical study and practical implementation. This research shows a major turning point in the creation and use of the L5.0 model, pushing forward both industry and scholarly understanding. With the help of the alignment of sustainability-focused innovation with foundational models (FMs), the research aims to improve logistics companies' capacity to attain long-term success therefore reducing their environmental impact. Data-driven insights can be used by businesses to optimize supply chain efficiency, forecast demand variations, and reduce waste through wise resource allocation by integrating FMs into logistics operations. The dedication of industry toward sustainability is further strengthened by the cooperation between FMs and L5.0 technologies, which can make it easier to implement energy-efficient transportation strategies, real-time tracking systems, and predictive analytics.

CASE EXAMPLE 1: AI-OPTIMIZED ROUTING AT DHL

Context:

DHL deployed AI-enhanced route optimization across its European last-mile delivery network. The solution, powered in part through a foundation-model methodology, combined traffic, weather, and fuel information.

Impact:

- Fuel usage decreased by 14%
- CO_2 emissions decreased by 18%
- Delivery delays decreased by 9%
- Customer satisfaction increased due to better ETAs

CASE EXAMPLE 2: SIMULATED EXAMPLE – MID-SIZED 3PL PROVIDER LEVERAGES FM FOR WAREHOUSE OPTIMIZATION

Scenario:

A medium-sized third-party logistics provider (with 5 warehouses) used FM-driven warehouse layout simulation and demand forecasting.

Results (within 6 months):

- 25% decrease in warehouse picking time
- Energy consumption reduced by 12% through AI-driven environmental control
- Inventory holding costs reduced by 22%
- Stockouts decreased by 30% through better forecasting

The outcome of the research highlights the significance of a well-rounded strategy that blends academic understanding with practical business expertise to ensure that creative sustainability tactics are both successful and expandable. By implementing this, it can offer useful advice to companies, decision-makers, and scholars who are willing to create and apply next-generation logistics solutions that support international sustainability objectives. Changes in the logistics industry to meet new environmental, technological, and financial concerns emphasizes the need for constant innovation and adaptability. At last, our studies add to the larger conversation on sustainable logistics by providing a strong framework for merging state-of-the-art technology with ecologically proactive methods, in that way influencing the direction of the sector.

RESULTS OF THE REVIEW

After analyzing recent scholarly studies on sustainability-oriented innovation (SOI), their effects on logistics and the function of foundation models (FMs) are found in this area. It interprets how SOI functions internally in businesses and how Industry 5.0 might lead to a more sustainable logistical environment. This title is linked to SOI with Adams et al. (2016), which offers a framework that highlights the necessity of intentional organizational changes in business models, processes, and products to meet sustainability objectives. In the view of traditional innovation, social, economic, and environmental goals are integrated in SOI, necessitating a multidisciplinary and systemic approach. Although the research by Kneipp et al. (2023) highlights how SOI improves business models, Aka (2019) examines how process-oriented it is and stresses how crucial manager-stakeholder interactions are Furthermore, Miranda et al. (2023) discusses about open innovation as an important instrument for promoting SOI, especially through knowledge integration and external cooperation. If we focus on another important element of this study, FMs whose development from specialized models to general-purpose assistants is described in research by Li et al. (2024). Though Awais et al. (2023) focus on issues with analysis, benchmarking, real-world comprehension, biases, and interpretability, Yang and Lin's (2020) studies offer conceptual tools for comprehending the decision-making breadth of FMs. Even with these problems, FMs have a lot of potential to make the supply chain more open, help people make better decisions, and make the logistics process more efficient. As per Hanumantu (2024), Industry 5.0 is a transition towards supply chains that are both technology-driven and human-centric, incorporating automation, artificial intelligence, the Internet of Things, and data analytics. Rising Interest in green logistics techniques, like eco-friendly shipping and warehousing, which supplements more general sustainability aims, is highlighted by research by Trstenjak et al. (2023). This research indicates that there is still a deficiency of knowledge about Industry 5.0, which demands for educational programs to prioritize this Unlike previous industry revolutions, L5.0 focuses on how people and machines can work together. This means that programs to increase the size and skills of the workforce are needed.

Decision support system, Frederico (2021) suggests a model for implementing L5.0 that considers variables like payback period, investment expenses, and compliance with green logistics guidelines. As per findings, such as that done by Villar et al. (2023), artificial intelligence (AI), big data, and the Internet of Things (IoT) are a necessary part for supply chain optimization, environmental impact reduction, and efficiency gains.

The Multiple aspects like entrepreneurial and digitalization of logistics innovation are also explored, with analyzing the relationship with the help of study between entrepreneurial orientation, sustainability intentions, and the moderating influence of digitalization. And Thanasi-Boçe et al. (2023) shows insights towars sustainable entrepreneurship in North Macedonia, Khodor et al. (2024) look into the ways in which digitalization and dynamic capacities clash the formation of sustainable businesses. Moreover the researcher, Makhloufi (2024) finds how big data analytics affects absorptive ability and green entrepreneurship.

In order to maintain L5.0, the study discusses the integration of FMs into logistics, forecasting how the collaboration can increase warehouse layouts, minimize packaging waste, and optimize routes. With the help of bridging gap the theoretical insights with practical applications, the research contributes to advancing sustainable logistics practices and supporting the transition towards a more efficient, eco-friendly supply chain.

LOGISTICS 5.0 AND SUSTAINABILITY-ORIENTED INNOVATIONS (SOIS)

The word Sustainability-oriented innovations (SOI) redefine traditional trade-offs and incorporate sustainable principles into business strategy with the motive to increase firm value while also advancing societal and environmental well-being. The three level of sustainability orientation can be used to categorize these developments, each of them which shows a varying level of dedication to sustainability. To ensure that businesses meet market expectations without changing materially and their core operations, the level first of innovation, sustainability-related innovations, concentrating on creating goods or services that address particular client wants while including some characteristics of sustainability. The technology of Nike's Flyknit, which decrease waste and increases manufacturing efficiency, is the second example of innovations that are focused on sustainability. Level three explains incorporates sustainability concepts into the creation process of new products or services (Kopnina et al., 2023). All these innovations actively integrate social and environmental factors into design and production processes, surpassing customer-driven demands. And at last level, sustainability-driven innovations make sustainability at top priority and use initiative taking research and development to address urgent environmental issues. A good example of illustration is Patagonia's efforts, though the consistently makes investments in ethical sourcing, circular economy tactics, and sustainable materials to reduce its environmental effect (Albareda & Hajikhani, 2019). SDG driven innovations has been developed for those who are at lower levels of sustainability orientation, are not only reactive; rather, they show a long-term strategic commitment for promoting systemic change in industries. Profitability can be maintained in Businesses while gaining a competitive advantage, strengthening brand loyalty, and supporting more simple sustainability goals by using SOI into practice. The development can be seen that how companies are changing their role in tackling global sustainability issues, supporting the idea that environmental responsibility and economic success are harmonizes factors that influence simultaneous business practices rather than hostile ones.

Figure 3. Sustainability Oriented Innovations (SOI)

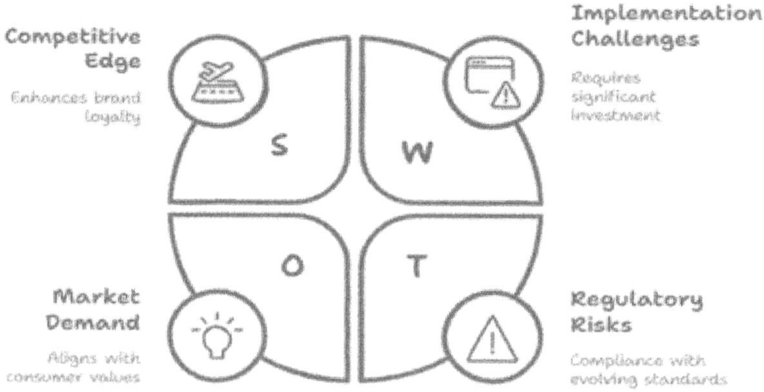

Anciently many businesses have depended on manual internal innovation processes. The dynamic (changing) nature of modern corporate environments has taken a shift toward cutting-edge technologies like artificial intelligence (AI), According to (Adams et al., 2016; Idrees et al., 2023; Yang & Lin, 2020; Zhou et al., 2015). Such practices might greatly help organizations in collaboratively building SOIs. Businesses must strategically manage and distribute their resources to successfully implement SOIs (Carnes et al., 2017). It is important for industry 5.0 to know what factors are most important and which stages of innovation process are best for putting them inti action critical (Aka, 2019a, b). The research for future is necessary to know the level of integration, and its impact on sustainability performance, and the barriers to collaborate in the development of SOIs (Biclesanu et al., 2021).

The innovative work of Miranda et al. (2023) is enlarge and enhanced in this publication by embrace insights from sustainability-oriented innovation research and practical experience. This framework is proposed to serves as a helpful roadmap for companies attempting to align their creative ideas with sustainability objectives. By scrutinizing the role of promotion in innovating sustainability, this study shows that how sustainable operations promote knowledge sharing and enable businesses to advanced their outside expertise. By reviewing carefully "5 W's" (why, what, who, when, and where) and "1 H" (how) of SOI, a thorough conceptual framework is build. The essential components identified throughout this investigation.

ENABLING GREEN LOGISTICS THROUGH FMS

Foundation models (FMs) are sophisticated artificial intelligence models with a great degree of flexibility that are intended for large-scale, general-purpose applications (Kolides et al., 2023). In contrast to task-specific models, FMs can execute a wide range of tasks because they are trained on large datasets with a large number of parameters. Because of their versatility, they can be tailored for specific purposes in a variety of fields. Language models that can produce text that is human-like, image models that can categorize, alter, or produce images, and multimodal models that combine and analyze many data sources, including text and images, are a few examples (Myers et al., 2024). These models are called "foundational" because, like a foundation supporting a building, they provide the fundamental structure for creating more specialized AI applications (Waqas et al., 2023).

Logistics 5.0 and Foundation Models' Function

The next stage of logistics development is called Logistics 5.0 (L5.0), which integrates cutting-edge technology like robotics, artificial intelligence (AI), digital twins, and Industrial IoT (IIoT) with a focus on sustainability. L5.0 aims to improve environmental responsibility, adaptability, and operational efficiency. Logistics managers may make well-informed, multi-criteria decisions about investments, green initiatives, and strategic priorities with the help of AI-powered decision support systems (Skitsko, 2023). AI-driven optimization can help with a variety of logistics tasks, including transportation, warehouse management, inventory control, packaging, and reverse logistics. By streamlining operations throughout the logistics lifecycle, from predictive demand forecasting and sustainable transportation planning to energy-efficient warehouse design, foundation models (FMs) facilitate this shift.

By improving demand forecasting, automating repetitive processes, and streamlining supply chain operations, FMs contribute significantly to inventory control and management (Villar et al., 2023). These models provide precise demand projections, lessen overstocking, and enhance inventory planning by examining past sales data, inventory levels, and market trends. A more efficient and economical supply chain is ensured by FMs' assistance in optimizing purchase choices and manufacturing schedules (Villacis et al., 2024).

Figure 4. Optimizing logistics with foundational model

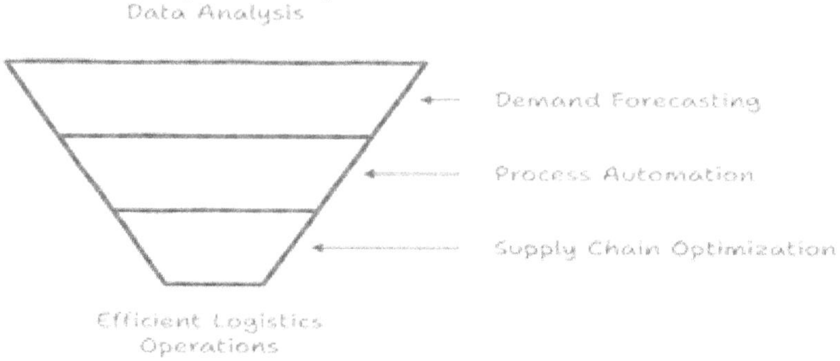

FMs examine product dimensions and recommend material-efficient designs that minimize waste and guarantee protection in packaging optimization (Camilleri et al., 2023). In order to optimize packaging solutions according to particular transportation requirements, they also use predictive analytics to evaluate past transport damage data. Additionally, by assessing the environmental impact of various packaging solutions, FMs help choose sustainable materials and promote greener logistics methods.

Warehouse optimization is yet another important area where FMs offer significant advantages. Many warehouses have underused space as a result of poorly planned layouts. To maximize product placement, minimize operator walking lengths, and save energy, FMs examine picking patterns, storage needs, and product dimensions (Torchio, 2023). In order to determine the most effective configurations and increase overall operational efficiency, these models also replicate various warehouse layouts and traffic patterns. By predicting demand, modifying temperature control, and optimizing lighting based on occupancy and daylight availability, FMs also improve energy efficiency.

By forecasting demand variations and optimizing staging arrangements, FMs increase efficiency in staging operations, where products are sorted and consolidated prior to shipping (Richards & Grinsted, 2024). With AI-powered vision systems that identify flaws before to shipment, they support quality control, optimize personnel based on workload analysis, and allow real-time alterations to staging areas to guarantee high-demand items remain accessible. In order to suggest the best loading sequences and delivery routes for outbound logistics, FMs examine traffic patterns, meteorological conditions, and delivery priorities. This increases productivity and minimizes delays.

By examining delivery locations, traffic patterns, and environmental considerations, FMs offer improved route optimization for transportation management and operations in order to reduce emissions and fuel consumption (Zhang et al., 2024).

Additionally, they streamline delivery to cut down on travel time and promote the use of environmentally friendly modes of transportation like rail and electric cars (Dattero-Snell, 2023). Predictive analytics facilitates autonomous logistics operations, such as automated warehouses and self-driving cars, foresee interruptions, and improve inventory management. In order to help enterprises take proactive steps to reduce risks, FMs also automate document processing, derive insights from shipping records and invoices, and anticipate any interruptions (Zekhnini et al., 2024).

FMs assist in forecasting return rates based on consumer behavior and product trends in reverse logistics, which handles the processing of returned items. This allows for more effective planning and processing of returned goods (Appolloni et al., 2022). By evaluating the quality of returned goods and suggesting refurbishment or other uses instead of disposal, these models help to reduce waste and their negative effects on the environment. By examining the composition of waste and determining the best recycling techniques, FMs also assist responsible waste management and encourage sustainable practices in logistical operations.

Logistics companies can attain notable enhancements in cost-effectiveness, sustainability, and operational efficiency by incorporating FMs into L5.0. These AI-powered models improve overall supply chain resilience, optimize resource allocation, and facilitate data-driven decision-making. The use of FMs in a variety of logistics tasks, such as inventory control and reverse logistics, shows how revolutionary they can be in creating a more effective and sustainable logistics environment.

The Foundation Models' Revolutionary Effect on Logistics

The high energy consumption of lighting, ventilation, and cooling systems, the excessive packaging waste that raises transportation costs and landfill usage, and the emissions from delivery trucks that contribute to environmental pollution are just a few of the inefficiencies that traditional logistics operations face. By maximizing energy efficiency, decreasing packaging waste, and enhancing transportation routes, foundation models (FMs) provide a game-changing approach (Oloruntobi et al., 2023). To make logistics more effective and ecologically conscious, they also improve warehouse layouts, forecast product returns, and suggest sustainable recycling techniques.

FMs can be used for a number of tasks, such as route planning, image identification, and text-based analysis. Their advantages include improved reverse logistics, energy efficiency, sustainable transportation, and better warehouse layout. Logistics companies may increase customer happiness, cut expenses, improve operational efficiency, and obtain a competitive edge by utilizing these AI-driven models.

Nevertheless, there are difficulties in putting FMs into practice (Myers et al., 2024). The challenges of incorporating FMs into logistics are highlighted by these barriers, which are grouped according to the 4 Ms of the Ishikawa framework: Machines, Manpower, Materials, and Methods (Nicoletti, 2012). The causal links between these obstacles to attaining a green Logistics 5.0 (L5.0) are graphically depicted in Figure 2. Notwithstanding these challenges, FMs represent a significant and promising development in the logistics sector because to the chances for creativity and cooperation presented by L5.0.

FUTURE DIRECTIONS

Further studies ought to examine how sophisticated foundation models (FMs), such deep learning and neural networks, might improve sustainability and streamline logistical processes. An ecosystem for logistics that is more transparent, connected, and sustainable may result from integrating FMs with cutting-edge technologies like blockchain and Industrial IoT (IIoT), as the logistics industry grows more intricate and data-driven. By increasing real-time tracking, improving decision-making, and decreasing inefficiencies, these technologies have the potential to completely transform supply chain management while also minimizing their negative effects on the environment. Furthermore, by combining blockchain technology with FMs, logistics operations can become more secure and traceable, guaranteeing ethical sourcing, adherence to sustainability standards, and a lower chance of fraud. Similarly, IIoT integration can make predictive maintenance possible, minimize downtime, and optimize energy use, all of which help make logistics networks more environmentally friendly and effective. Even if technological innovations have a lot of promise, it's crucial to take into account how they may affect society. The use of FMs in logistics may cause major changes in the composition of the workforce, possibly replacing old occupations with new ones that call for highly skilled technical competencies.

To guarantee an equitable and smooth transition, studies should therefore also concentrate on the socioeconomic effects of FM adoption, addressing issues with workforce training, reskilling initiatives, and the digital divide. By assessing the wider effects of these technologies, future research can shed light on how companies, legislators, and educators might work together to create plans that strike a balance between creativity and duty. In the end, exploring how FMs, blockchain, and IIoT intersect in the logistics sector will not only further sustainability initiatives but also contribute to the development of a robust, flexible, and morally motivated sector that can successfully navigate upcoming obstacles while promoting both economic expansion and environmental stewardship.

FMs have some drawbacks despite their potential. Their efficacy relies on having access to thorough, high-quality data, which can be difficult in logistical settings where data might be erroneous or lacking. For small and medium-sized businesses, implementing FMs often means making significant investments in infrastructure and worker training. Furthermore, if these models are not created with justice and fairness in mind, there is a chance that they will reinforce prejudices. Maintaining the effectiveness of FM systems requires regular updates and maintenance, and proactive measures to retrain and upskill employees are necessary to reduce job displacement.

In conclusion, even if FMs have the potential to transform logistics and promote sustainability, resolving their issues is essential to guaranteeing their ethical and responsible application. To fully realize their advantages for a more sustainable and successful logistics sector, a transparent, well-regulated strategy that places a high priority on equity, inclusivity, and ongoing development is required.

CHALLENGES AND FACTORS TO TAKE INTO ACCOUNT WHEN APPLYING FOUNDATION MODELS (FMS) IN LOGISTICS

The application of foundation models (FMs) in logistics and sustainability poses a number of difficulties, notwithstanding its revolutionary potential. These issues must be properly handled to guarantee their responsible and efficient use. The following list of five main points highlights the main disadvantages of FMs in logistics, along with possible solutions.

Figure 5. Navigation FM challenges in logistics

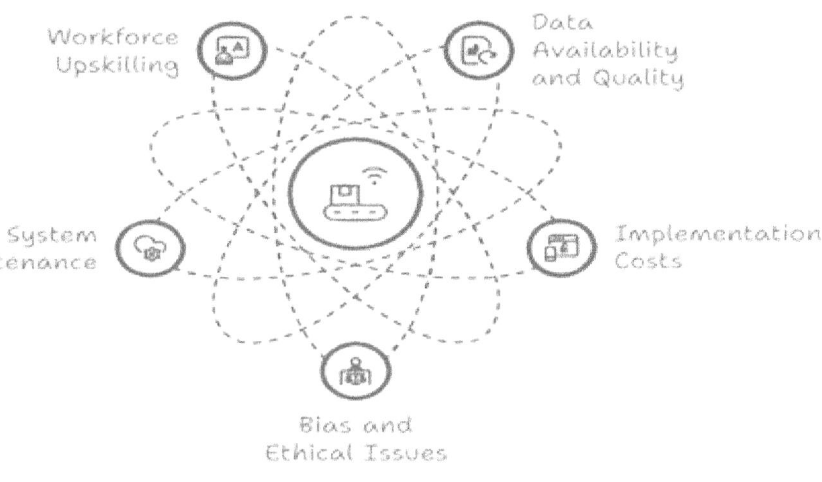

Issues with Data Availability and Quality

For efficient operations, FMs mostly depend on having access to thorough, high-quality data. But data gaps, mistakes, and inconsistencies are typical in real-world logistical settings. The use of disparate data management systems by numerous stakeholders in supply chains frequently results in fragmented and insufficient information. Furthermore, inaccurate FMs might result from biased or out-of-date data, which can affect decision-making. Investing in strong data gathering and management systems that guarantee real-time, high-quality data flows is necessary for organizations to lessen this problem. By combining blockchain technology, Internet of Things (IoT) sensors, and sophisticated data validation methods, data accuracy and dependability can be increased. Furthermore, establishing uniform data-sharing guidelines throughout the logistics sector can improve FMs' efficacy by guaranteeing a dependable and consistent data infrastructure.

- **For small and medium-sized businesses (SMEs), high implementation costs are a concern.**

Significant expenditures in software development, processing power, and infrastructure are needed to implement FMs in logistics operations. While large firms might have the financial means to implement AI-driven systems, small and medium-sized businesses (SMEs) may find the implementation costs to be a significant obstacle. In addition to hardware and software purchases, businesses typically need to budget for ongoing system upgrades and employee training. Cloud-based AI solutions that eliminate the need for costly on-premise technology can be investigated by businesses to make FMs more accessible. SMEs can also benefit from government incentives and public-private collaborations when implementing AI-driven logistics solutions. Companies may also choose to incorporate AI in stages, beginning with small-scale trial projects and progressively increasing its integration as they develop their operational and financial capabilities.

Bias Potential and Ethical Issues

The possibility of bias reinforcement is one of the main dangers of FMs, especially if the models are not created with inclusivity and justice in mind. Systems that use artificial intelligence (AI) to make decisions are educated on past data, which may include biases in supplier selection, resource allocation, or recruiting procedures. These prejudices can result in discriminatory effects in logistics operations, such as unfair pricing practices, special treatment for particular suppliers, or skewed workforce management choices, if they are not addressed. Businesses need to give openness and accountability a priority when developing FM in order to overcome these ethical issues. Using representative and varied datasets, identifying biases through frequent audits, and putting fairness-focused AI governance frameworks into practice are all part of this. Adopting explainable AI (XAI) solutions can also assist organizations in comprehending the decision-making process, guaranteeing the impartiality and ethics of AI-driven logistical operations.

Updating and Maintaining Systems

For FMs to continue to be effective, especially in the rapidly evolving logistics environment, they need regular updates and maintenance. Outdated AI models may generate suggestions that are erroneous or inappropriate as supply chain dynamics change as a result of market trends, regulatory changes, or unanticipated disruptions (governance conflicts, pandemics, etc.). Furthermore, FM-based logistics systems are susceptible to cyberattacks or inefficiency if they are not regularly monitored and adjusted.

Establishing a proactive maintenance approach that include regular system updates, ongoing model training with fresh data, and frequent performance reviews is essential for ensuring long-term efficiency. FMs may stay up to date with the most recent advancements in the business by automating updates and scalability with the use of cloud-based AI models. In order to keep an eye on system performance and make sure logistics procedures continue to run smoothly, companies need also set up specialized AI oversight teams.

The Need for Employee Upskilling Due to Workforce Displacement

Concerns of job displacement arise from the incorporation of AI-driven FMs into logistical operations, as automation and intelligent decision-making systems supplant conventional positions. FMs have the potential to greatly increase operational efficiency, but if they are widely used, the need for administrative and human labor in logistics networks may decline. Employees must be retrained and upskilled in order to adapt to the changing labor market, which calls for proactive measures.

Businesses should launch reskilling initiatives that give staff members the abilities they need to collaborate with AI-driven technology in order to reduce job displacement. Programs that teach data analytics, digital supply chain management, and AI literacy can assist employees in moving into new positions that support FM-driven automation. Businesses might also promote a human-AI collaboration model in which workers use AI insights to improve their decision-making skills rather than having automation completely replace them.

An Appropriate Method for Adopting FM

Notwithstanding the enormous potential that FMs have to revolutionize logistics and promote sustainability, resolving these issues is essential to guaranteeing their proper and moral application. Prioritizing equity, inclusivity, and ongoing progress requires an open, well-regulated strategy from organizations. Businesses can fully utilize the benefits of FMs while minimizing their dangers by concentrating on data quality, lowering implementation costs, addressing ethical issues, guaranteeing routine system maintenance, and investing in staff upskilling. A well-rounded approach that takes human aspects and technology into account will open the door to a logistics industry that is more inclusive, efficient, and sustainable.

RESULTS

This paper uses a variety of strategies to successfully accomplish its two research objectives (ROs). By tackling RO1, it creates a thorough functional and technological framework for Logistics 5.0 (L5.0), elucidating its essential components and creating a common vocabulary and concept. The framework analyzes obstacles, indicates areas for optimization, and describes key areas for FM deployment. L5.0 is important for businesses and logistics companies that want to strike a balance between sustainability, flexibility, cost effectiveness, and service quality. L5.0, a dynamic, data-driven model, is a reference system that is updated continually and can integrate many data sources for both short- and long-term planning. Depending on the particular use case, real-time or post-hoc updates may be required for monitoring, operational execution, or planning.

Figure 6. Optimizing logistics with FM technologies

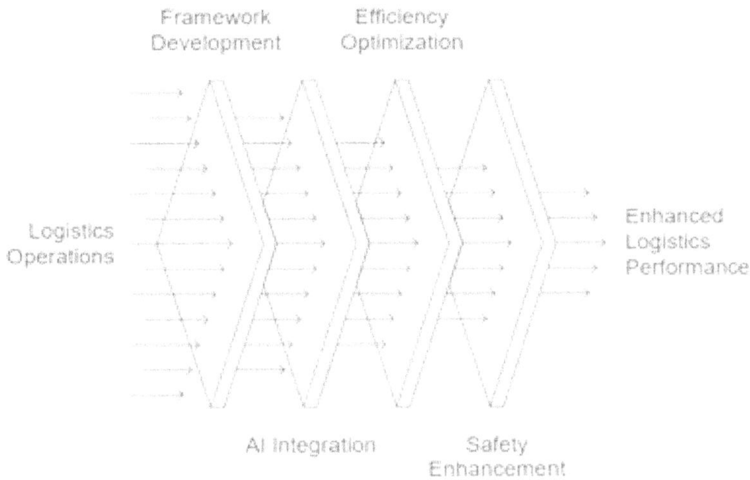

This study makes a contribution to RO2 by providing a technological framework for the implementation of FM in logistics. By optimizing warehouse layouts, space use, and route planning through algorithmic analysis and predictive modeling, AI and FMs greatly increase operational efficiency. These models provide better transportation route optimization, automated design development for effective storage, and demand forecasting. AI-driven FMs in operational logistics streamline worker task allocations, offer real-time monitoring to enhance supply chain visibility and responsiveness, and enable predictive analytics for inventory management. Automated guided vehicles (AGVs) and autonomous mobile robots (AMRs) are two other FM-powered devices that increase transportation efficiency. AI-driven sorting and packing systems further increase logistics process accuracy.

Through anomaly detection, predictive maintenance, and improved monitoring and control systems, FMs contribute to logistics safety and reliability in addition to efficiency improvements. Organizations can attain notable cost savings, enhanced decision-making, and increased flexibility in a logistics environment that is becoming more intricate and competitive by incorporating FM technology into their operations.

CONCLUSION

By combining the green approach with Logistics 5.0 (L5.0), businesses may improve operational efficiency and reap major environmental advantages. This is a critical step in attaining sustainable innovation and entrepreneurship. A more profitable and sustainable logistics sector is created when sustainability concepts are integrated with logistics operations, which emphasizes the necessity for companies to implement technologically advanced and environmentally friendly tactics. Businesses may optimize resource use, lower carbon footprints, and support global environmental goals by integrating sustainability into logistics. This will also ensure that their operations meet changing social and regulatory standards. In order to achieve environmental sustainability goals, this article integrates important business components such as corporate philosophy, product development, operational procedures, and business models. It emphasizes that in the current global environment, sustainability is now a business need for companies looking to remain viable over the long term, not just a strategic benefit. The study highlights the Sustainability-Oriented Innovation (SOI) methodology's ability to produce observable environmental, social, and economic advantages. Supply chain management and logistics are becoming more responsible and future-ready thanks in large part to SOI, which is redefining company strategies. By enhancing warehouse layouts, reducing packaging waste, and optimizing transportation routes, artificial intelligence—in particular, foundation models, or FMs—plays a crucial role in promoting green logistics. Through data-driven decision-making, operational redundancy, and sustainability-driven innovation, these AI-powered models not only improve logistical efficiency but also advance larger social, economic, and governance goals. Notwithstanding their benefits, the report notes the difficulties in integrating FMs in logistics, including the high upfront expenditures, the need for regulatory compliance, and the difficulties in technical integration. In order to properly use the promise of foundation models for sustainable operations, businesses must overcome the considerable obstacles posed by the intricacy of incorporating AI into conventional logistics frameworks. Strategic planning, stakeholder participation, and ongoing AI technology improvements are necessary to meet these difficulties and guarantee smooth implementation and long-term success. This study adds significant value by putting forth a framework that serves as a useful instrument for accomplishing Environmental, Social, and Governance (ESG) goals in addition to facilitating the adoption of L5.0 and FMs. In a market that is becoming more and more focused on sustainability, companies may preserve their competitiveness while generating value that goes beyond profitability by integrating ESG concepts into their logistics strategies. By providing a defined path for companies to move toward more sustainable and effective logistics systems, the framework this study presents emphasizes the significance of fusing technical innovation with green logistics. Given the increasing demand on businesses to implement sustainable practices from investors, consumers, and regulatory agencies, this study emphasizes how important it is to use AI-driven logistics solutions to satisfy ESG targets while boosting overall operational resilience. Finally, by bridging the gap between technology, business strategy, and sustainability, this study offers a forward-looking viewpoint on how foundation models and Logistics 5.0 will influence the development of sustainable logistics. In order to redefine contemporary supply chains and forward the global sustainability agenda, the research emphasizes the transformative potential of artificial intelligence, logistics, and sustainability-oriented innovation.

REFERENCES

Adams, R., Jeanrenaud, S., Bessant, J., Denyer, D., & Overy, P. (2016). Sustainability-oriented innovation: A systematic review. *International Journal of Management Reviews*, *18*(2), 180–205. DOI: 10.1111/ijmr.12076

Aka, B. (2019a). Understanding sustainability-oriented innovation: A process perspective. *Journal of Cleaner Production, 235*, 1220 1228 .https://doi.org/DOI: 10.1016/j.jclepro.2019.02.271

Aka, K. G. (2019b). Actor-network theory to understand, track and succeed in a sustainable innovation development process. *Journal of Cleaner Production*, *225*, 524–540. DOI: 10.1016/j.jclepro.2019.04.148

Albareda, L., & Hajikhani, A. (2019). Innovation for sustainability: Literature review and bibliometric analysis. In *Innovation for sustainability: Business transformations towards a better world* (pp. 35–57). Palgrave., DOI: 10.1007/978-3-319-97385-2_3

Appolloni, A., Jabbour, C. J. C., D'Adamo, I., Gastaldi, M., & Settembre-Blundo, D. (2022). Green recovery in the mature manufacturing industry: The role of the green-circular premium and sustainability certification in innovative efforts. *Ecological Economics*, *193*, 107311. DOI: 10.1016/j.ecolecon.2021.107311

Atiku, S. O., Jeremiah, A., Semente, E., & Boateng, F. (2024). *Eco-innovation and sustainable development in Industry 5.0*. IGI Global., DOI: 10.4018/979-8-3693-2219-2

Awais, M., Naseer, M., Khan, S., Anwer, R. M., Cholakkal, H., Shah, M., Yang, M. H., & Khan, F. S. (2023). Foundational models defining a new era in vision: A survey and outlook. *arXiv preprint arXiv:2307.13721*, 1–40.

Biclesanu, I., Anagnoste, S., Branga, O., & Savastano, M. (2021). Digital entrepreneurship: Public perception of barriers, drivers, and future. *Administrative Sciences*, *11*(4), 125. DOI: 10.3390/admsci11040125

Camilleri, T., Farrugia, P., & Refalo, P. (2023). A multi-user-centred design approach framework to develop aesthetically pleasing and sustainable OTCP packaging. *Packaging Technology & Science*, *36*(10), 873–887. DOI: 10.1002/pts.2763

Carnes, C. M., Chirico, F., Hitt, M. A., Huh, D. W., & Pisano, V. (2017). Resource orchestration for innovation: Structuring and bundling resources in growth- and maturity-stage firms. *Long Range Planning*, *50*(4), 472–486. DOI: 10.1016/j.lrp.2016.07.003

Coza, H. (2024). Architectural approaches in the production process of logistics spaces. In *Theories and practices for sustainable urban logistics* (pp. 215–233). IGI Global., DOI: 10.4018/979-8-3693-1447-0.ch011

Dattero-Snell, D. (2023). *Appraisal of electric vehicle retrofit for transport decarbonization within agriculture: Whole system approach* (Doctoral dissertation, Cardiff University).

Dwivedi, Y. K., Hughes, L., Ismagilova, E., Aarts, G., Coombs, C., Crick, T., & Williams, M. D. (2021). Artificial intelligence (AI): Multidisciplinary perspectives on emerging challenges, opportunities, and agenda for research, practice, and policy. *International Journal of Information Management*, *57*, 101994. DOI: 10.1016/j.ijinfomgt.2019.08.002

Ermini, C., Visintin, F., & Boffelli, A. (2024). Understanding supply chain orchestration mechanisms to achieve sustainability-oriented innovation in the textile and fashion industry. *Sustainable Production and Consumption*, *49*, 415–430. DOI: 10.1016/j.spc.2024.07.008

Frederico, G. F. (2021). From supply chain 4.0 to supply chain 5.0: Findings from a systematic literature review and research directions. *Logistics (Basel)*, *5*(3), 49. DOI: 10.3390/logistics5030049

Hanumantu, D. (2024). Logistics 5.0: The next evolution of logistics systems. *International Journal of Physical Distribution & Logistics Management*, *54*(1), 34–48.

Idrees, H., Xu, J., & Andrianarivo Andriandafiarisoa Ralison, N. A. (2023). Green entrepreneurial orientation and knowledge creation process as enablers of green innovation performance: The moderating role of resource orchestration capability. *European Journal of Innovation Management*. Advance online publication. DOI: 10.1108/EJIM-02-2023-0143

Inigo, E. A., & Albareda, L. (2016). Understanding sustainable innovation as a complex adaptive system: A systemic approach to the firm. *Journal of Cleaner Production*, *126*, 1–20. DOI: 10.1016/j.jclepro.2016.02.043

Khan, S., Singh, R., Sta, J. C., Santos, G., & Ferreira, L. P. (2022). Modelling of determinants of logistics 4.0 adoption: Insights from developing countries. *Machines (Basel)*, *10*(12), 1242. DOI: 10.3390/machines10121242

Kneipp, J. M., Gomes, C. M., Zaluski, F. C., Pontelli, G. E., & Favarin, R. R. (2023). The relationship between adopting sustainability-oriented innovation practices and the business models of Brazilian industrial companies. *International Journal of Environment and Sustainable Development, 22*(3), 349–367. DOI: 10.1504/IJESD.2023.132090

Kopnina, H., Padfield, R., & Mylan, J. (2023). Strategic change for sustainability. In *Sustainable Business* (pp. 148–164). Routledge., DOI: 10.4324/9781003266150-10

Lasswell, H. D. (1932). The triple-appeal principle: A contribution of psychoanalysis to political and social science. *American Journal of Sociology, 37*(4), 523–538. DOI: 10.1086/215791

Lazzaris, J., Carvalho, A. M., & Carvalho, M. S. (2022). Supply chain quality management and industry 5.0: A literature review and analysis. *2022 IEEE International Conference on Industrial Engineering and Engineering Management (IEEM)*, 285–289. https://doi.org/DOI: 10.1109/IEEM55944.2022.9989770

Torchio, F. (2023). Survey on automated systems for smart warehouses (Doctoral dissertation, Politecnico di Torino). https://doi.org/DOI: 10.6092/polito/amsphd/2023/001

Trstenjak, M., Mustapić, M., Gregurić, P., & Opetuk, T. (2023). Use of green Industry 5.0 technologies in logistics activities. *Tehnički glasnik, 17*(3), 471–477. https://doi.org/DOI: 10.31803/tg-20230518185836

Villacis, M. Y., Merlo, O. T., Rivero, D. P., & Towfek, S. K. (2024). Optimizing sustainable inventory management using an improved big data analytics approach. *Journal of Intelligent Systems and Internet of Things, 11*(1), 55–64. DOI: 10.54216/JISIoT.110106

Villar, A., Paladini, S., & Buckley, O. (2023). Towards Supply Chain 5.0: Redesigning supply chains as resilient, sustainable, and human-centric systems in a post-pandemic world. *Operations Research Forum, 4*(3), 60. Springer International Publishing. https://doi.org/DOI: 10.1007/s43069-023-00234-3

Waqas, A., Bui, M. M., Glassy, E. F., El Naqa, I., Borkowski, P., Borkowski, A. A., & Rasool, G. (2023). Revolutionizing digital pathology with the power of generative artificial intelligence and foundation models. *Laboratory Investigation, 100255*(11), 100255. DOI: 10.1016/j.labinv.2023.100255 PMID: 37757969

Yang, Z., & Lin, Y. (2020). The effects of supply chain collaboration on green innovation performance: An interpretive structural modeling analysis. *Sustainable Production and Consumption, 23*, 1–10. DOI: 10.1016/j.spc.2020.03.010

Zaid, O., Arif, J., & Jawab, F. (2024). Human-centric supply chain management towards Industry 5.0. In *2024 IEEE 15th International Colloquium on Logistics and Supply Chain Management (LOGISTIQUA)* (pp. 1–7). IEEE. https://doi.org/DOI: 10.1109/LOGISTIQUA61063.2024.10571421

Zekhnini, K., Benabdellah, A. C., Bag, S., & Gupta, S. (2024). Supply chain 5.0 digitalization: An integrated approach for risk assessment. *Management Decision*. Advance online publication. DOI: 10.1108/MD-12-2023-2329

Zhang, X., Chen, H., Hao, Y., & Yuan, X. (2024). A low-carbon route optimization method for cold chain logistics considering traffic status in China. *Computers & Industrial Engineering, 110304*. Advance online publication. DOI: 10.1016/j.cie.2024.110304

Zhou, K., Liu, T., & Zhou, L. (2015). Industry 4.0: Towards future industrial opportunities and challenges. *2015 12th International Conference on Fuzzy Systems and Knowledge Discovery (FSKD)* (pp. 2147–2152). IEEE. https://doi.org/DOI: 10.1109/FSKD.2015.7382284

KEY TERMS AND DEFINITIONS

Foundation Models (FMs): Large-scale AI systems trained on diverse datasets to perform multiple logistics tasks without task-specific training. They enable adaptive decision-making for sustainability goals through predictive analytics and automation.

Logistics 5.0 (L5.0): Integration of AI, IoT, robotics, and human-centric design in supply chains. Focuses on sustainability, resilience, and real-time optimization, moving beyond automation to collaborative human-machine ecosystems.

Sustainability-Oriented Innovation (SOI): Strategic integration of environmental/social goals into business models, processes, and products. Classified into three levels: sustainability-related (eco-features added to existing offerings), sustainability-focused (sustainability as a core design principle), and sustainability-driven (proactive R&D to solve environmental crises).

Circular Economy Logistics: Systems designed for reuse, refurbishment, and recycling. FMs optimize reverse logistics by predicting return rates and identifying reuse pathways to minimize waste.

Digital Twins: Virtual replicas of physical logistics assets (e.g., warehouses, fleets) that simulate real-world conditions. Enable predictive optimization of layouts, energy use, and traffic flow.

Industrial IoT (IIoT): Network of interconnected sensors monitoring variables like temperature, humidity, and vehicle performance. Provides real-time data for FMs to optimize perishable goods handling and energy consumption.

Explainable AI (XAI): Transparent AI systems that provide interpretable decision logic. Critical for ethical FM deployment in logistics, ensuring fairness in route planning or resource allocation.

Human-AI Collaboration: Operational model where FMs augment (not replace) human workers. Requires upskilling programs for roles like AI-augmented inventory analysts or sustainability coordinators.

ESG Integration: Embedding Environmental, Social, and Governance metrics into logistics decisions. FMs automate carbon tracking, ethical sourcing verification, and regulatory compliance reporting.

Chapter 14
Optimizing Reverse Logistics in Retail Sector

Nimit Sharma
https://orcid.org/0009-0001-0305-9978
REVA University, India

Vijaya Kittu Manda
https://orcid.org/0000-0002-1680-8210
PBMEIT, India

A. Shivasharana
https://orcid.org/0000-0002-0743-4480
REVA University, India

Majeed Mohammed
https://orcid.org/0000-0001-9804-5335
Tamale University, Ghana

ABSTRACT

Reverse Logistics (RL) has become a critical challenge in supply chain management, especially for retail and e-commerce. With online shopping growth, product returns have increased due to sizing issues, quality concerns, and unmet customer expectations. This study analyzes return causes in online apparel shopping and proposes cost optimization strategies. Our findings show that understanding return drivers—fit issues, quality mismatches, and delivery delays—helps businesses reduce returns and enhance customer satisfaction. The research emphasizes adopting AI, blockchain, and IoT technologies to improve reverse logistics efficiency. Recommendations include implementing centralized return centers, automating supply chains, and educating customers to minimize costs. The study highlights RL's role in sustainability through recycling, refurbishment, and waste reduction

DOI: 10.4018/979-8-3373-2434-0.ch014

practices. This research provides valuable insights for students, academics, and industry professionals seeking to address RL challenges and enhance supply chain sustainability in the apparel industry and beyond.

INTRODUCTION

Reverse Logistics (RL) is the extension of Supply Chain Systems and Closed-Loop Systems. They assist in the return of products or materials (Camilleri, 2025). The RL approach affirms that end-of-life products are effectively gathered and re-absorbed into the production cycle. RL works in the opposite way as a traditional supply chain. So, the products flow from the point of consumption (final destination) back to the origin for reclamation, refurbishment, or disposal (Mishra et al., 2023). It creates a circular flow of materials rather than a linear path to disposal. RL comes into the picture when a customer who received a product is unsatisfied and applies for returns. Some key factors driving reverse logistics growth are (Aryee & Adaku, 2024; Vintimilla Alvarez & Alarcón Valero, 2025):

1. Expansion in e-commerce markets
2. Tightened environmental regulations and legislation
3. Focus on Corporate Social Responsibility
4. Increased focus on sustainability and circular economy (CE)
5. Increased technological integration
6. Increased competitiveness and opportunities
7. Opportunity to improve organizational reputation, competitiveness, and brand image (Attia, 2025)

RL also has applications in industries beyond e-commerce, such as seafood (Trung et al., 2024), photovoltaic systems (Spellmeier et al., 2025), and military supply chains (Melchers, 2024). RL is also a vital link in the supply chain of the secondhand market (Shahrjerdi, 2024).

Background

Product returns are a growing problem and have financial and environmental impacts (Frei et al., 2020). The fashion sector often has high return rates. Understanding the reasons for apparel returns is crucial for retailers to improve product quality, enhance customer satisfaction, and optimize return policies, ultimately reducing costs (thereby improving profits) and increasing brand loyalty (Stöcker et al., 2021). Figure 1 gives a glimpse of various reasons for apparel return.

Figure 1. Reasons for apparel returns in online shopping

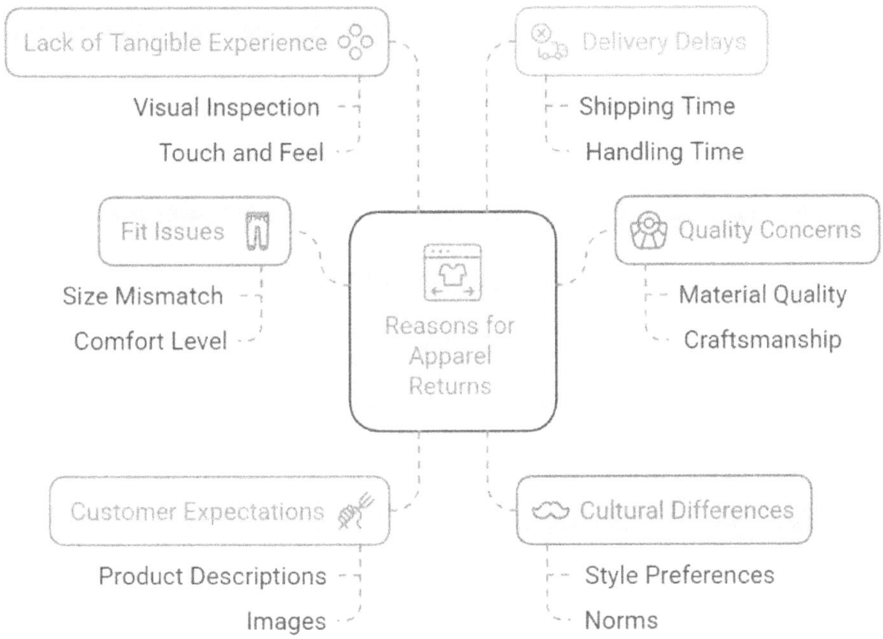

A brief discussion of the reasons follows:

1. **Issues related to fit**: Research indicates that a significant proportion of returns arises from items not fitting as expected. A key reason is inconsistent brand-sizing standards and a need for a tactile online shopping experience (Kong, 2024). Incorrect sizing information leads to customers ordering the wrong size, or the variation of the sizing standards in different brands causes confusion and leads to returns. The fabric stretch, cut, and design may also lead to a garment's failure to meet customer expectations even after ordering the correct size.
2. **Issues related to quality**: The customer's thought of returning an already ordered product will be influenced by several quality-related factors. It includes material quality, durability, and overall product performance. Discrepancies between the product received and the customer's expectations regarding quality and appearance contribute to return rates. For instance, customers report dissatisfaction when the product does not match the online representation, leading to a higher likelihood of returns (Kaushik et al., 2022).

3. **Issues related to customer expectations**: Misalignment with customer expectations and preferences plays a significant role in apparel return rates. Smartphone screens can distort the appearance of the products in online images. There may be a color variance in the apparel image and customer expectations. Highly edited or unrealistic images create unrealistic expectations among the customer. Social media influencers sometimes promote unrealistic product performance and appearance (Bozzi et al., 2022).
4. **Cultural difference**: Cultural differences also play a vital role in varying expectations regarding return policies and influencing customer expectations regarding return policies. In individualistic cultures like the USA, consumers may prioritize their self-satisfaction and hence are not much bothered about the returns they make. In countries like Indonesia, where the collective approach is common, people feel more hesitant to return the products due to fear of negative judgment (Putra et al., 2024).
5. **Lack of tangible experience:** The absence of physical product interaction, like the product's touch and feel, presents a significant challenge to the consumers. This inability results in discrepancies between actual and perceived product attributes, contributing to post-purchase dissatisfaction (Shaban et al., 2024). There is an increased perceived product risk because of this, which leads to consumer anxiety and potential dissatisfaction. This return reason connects well with disconfirmation theory and cognitive dissonance theory (Wang et al., 2023).
6. **Delay in receiving the product**: With the rapidly changing and trend-driven nature of the fashion industry, consumers often anticipate the apparel promptly. Delayed shipments make consumers feel the product needs to update their evolving fashion preferences. So, technology interventions such as using big data are happening to shorten the delivery time, leading to an era of anticipatory shipping (Weingarten & Spinler, 2021).

Need for Study

Despite being a vital link in direct logistics optimization, reverse logistics is often neglected (Fani et al., 2025). There has been a rapid growth of e-commerce and increasing return rates. However, businesses must develop structured and efficient reverse logistics strategies to minimize costs and enhance customer experience. Hence, understanding why products are returned is important for companies. This information can help them make informed decisions. There can be reduced unnecessary returns, improved product design, and optimized inventory management. Further, by analyzing returned goods data, the companies can get insights into consumer behavior and purchasing patterns. So, the efforts put into this activity fetch multiple returns. This information can help businesses to refine marketing strategies. They can adjust pricing models and improve their product quality. It is known that there is a rising focus on sustainability and circular economy principles in recent times. There is an urgent need to study the role and contributions of the reverse logistics sector. In particular, the focus can be on waste reduction, resource recovery, and compliance with environmental regulations. By integrating advanced technologies such as Artificial Intelligence (AI), Blockchain, and IoT, businesses can enhance traceability and efficiency in reverse logistics. This study explores challenges, opportunities, best practices, and optimization strategies that can be adopted. It emphasizes the apparel and e-commerce sectors, where return rates are among the highest.

Chapter Structure

The chapter begins with the "Introduction" section, which introduces the concept of reverse logistics and the need to take up the study. The "Literature Review" section shows the publication trends, research themes, and theories involved. The following section deals with reverse logistics in online apparel shopping, explaining the journey of the goods, types of returns, advantages, and challenges involved. The "Strategies for Optimization" section deals with strategies that can be incorporated. Sections on sustainable and circular economy (CE) aspects and the use of AI and Digital Technologies are included due to their recent increased importance. A section carrying success stories and case studies of companies that benefited from real-life implementation of reverse logistics is included. Practical and managerial implications and future research considerations are shared. Conclusion comments are given at the end.

LITERATURE REVIEW

A literature review is conducted to identify significant research themes on reverse logistics. Publication data for the last twenty years (2005 to 2025) from three leading databases – Scopus, Web of Science, and Dimensions.ai is collected. Filters are applied to screen the results to fit the RL concept. Content and thematic analysis are performed. Table 2 explains the filters applied to narrow down the data. Figure 2 shows increasing scholarly publications trends.

Table 1. Search filters are applied to databases/indexes using the term "reverse logistics."

Search Database/Index	Search Filter Applied
Dimensions.ai	Title and abstract
Scopus	Article title, Abstract, Keywords
Web of Science	Search for the term in Title, Topic, Abstract, and Keyword Plus

Figure 2. Increasing publications trend on the topic of "reverse logistics."

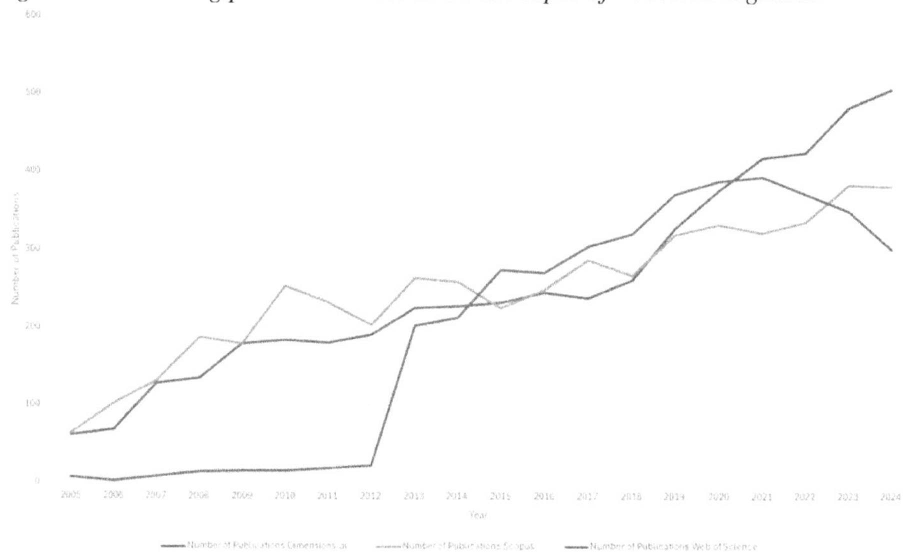

Major Research Themes

Studying research themes helps researchers identify emerging trends, gaps, and key focus areas. It ensures that their work contributes to advancing knowledge and addresses relevant challenges. Examining research themes in reverse logistics allows for identifying sustainable practices and cost-effective return strategies. It specifies innovative approaches to managing returned goods and improving supply chain efficiency and environmental impact. Table 3 summarizes the themes and the scope of each theme.

Table 2. Research themes on reverse logistics

Research Theme	Scope
Returns Management	• Handling customer returns efficiently to minimize costs and maximize value recovery. • Includes product recalls, damaged goods, and customer dissatisfaction.
Remanufacturing & Refurbishment	• Restoring returned or used products to a like-new condition for resale. • Reduces waste and enhances sustainability.
Recycling & Waste Management	• Processing returned products to recover materials for reuse. • Ensures proper disposal of non-recoverable goods.
Regulatory Compliance & Legal Considerations	• Studying regulatory frameworks, compliance challenges, and legal implications of product returns. • Adhering to environmental laws and industry regulations regarding waste disposal and recycling. • Compliance with extended producer responsibility (EPR) policies.
Supply Chain Efficiency & Cost Reduction	• Assessing the financial implications of efficient vs. inefficient reverse logistics operations. • Optimizing reverse logistics to reduce costs while maintaining efficiency. • Includes warehouse management, transportation, and handling of returned goods.
Technology & Digitalization	• Using Warehouse Management Systems (WMS), AI, Blockchain, and the IoT for better tracking and decision-making. • Algorithm development for logistics network optimization and data-driven decision-making • Enhancing visibility and automation in reverse logistics processes.
Customer Satisfaction & Service Quality	• Ensuring smooth returns and replacements to build trust and brand loyalty. • Improving customer experience through faster processing and refund policies.
Product Life Cycle & Sustainability	• Designing products for easier disassembly, reuse, and recycling, keeping in mind the environmental impact • Reducing carbon footprint • Focus on circular economy principles to extend the product lifespan.
Collaboration & Partnerships	• Engaging with suppliers, logistics partners, and third-party service providers to improve efficiency (Anon et al., 2024). • Shared responsibility for returns, refurbishments, and waste management.
Data Analytics & Performance Measurement	• Using Big Data and analytics to optimize reverse logistics. • Identifying trends, predicting returns, and improving overall efficiency.

Major Research Theories

Theories provide a foundational framework to explain, predict, and guide research, ensuring a systematic approach to knowledge development. Because reverse logistics is still an evolving topic, having a theoretical underpinning helps understand key drivers, decision-making processes, and sustainability impacts in reverse logistics.

Reverse logistics concepts can be discussed from the perspective of various theories (V. Sharma et al., 2021). A partial list of theories and a brief description of the theories are presented in Table 4.

Table 3. Research theories on reverse logistics

Name of Theory	Brief Description
Resource-Based View (RBV)	RBV helps firms understand how to leverage internal resources to optimize reverse logistics (Bentamar et al., 2021).
Transaction Cost Theory (TCT) and Relational Exchange Theory (RET)	TCT examines the cost-effectiveness of in-house vs. outsourced reverse logistics processes and examines how interfirm transactional and relational assets drive firm performance (FP) in digitally integrated supply chains (Patil et al., 2024).
Closed-Loop Supply Chain (CLSC) Theory	CLSC helps study how forward and reverse logistics integrate for better sustainability (Mishra et al., 2023).
Game Theory (GT)	GT helps analyze strategic interactions between retailers, manufacturers, and logistics providers in reverse logistics (Hosseini-Motlagh et al., 2023).
Queuing Theory (QT)	QT can be used in queuing models to optimize processing times for returns and remanufacturing and implement fourth-party logistics systems (Hong et al., 2021).
Theories on Network Flow (NFT)	Network flow explains how reverse logistics networks can be optimized for efficiency and cost savings (Dabo & Hosseinian-Far, 2023).
Lean & Agile Supply Chain Theories (LASCT)	LASCT helps understand how lean and agile principles can improve reverse logistics performance (V. Sharma et al., 2021).
Stakeholder Theory (ST)	ST examines the roles of different stakeholders in reverse logistics optimization (Pushpamali et al., 2021).
Diffusion of Innovation Theory (DIT)	DIT helps study the adoption of new technologies (AI, blockchain, IoT) in reverse logistics (Mwanyota, 2021).
Sociotechnical Systems Theory (SST)	SST helps analyze how human and technical factors influence the efficiency of reverse logistics operations (Loske et al., 2021).

REVERSE LOGISTICS IN ONLINE APPAREL SHOPPING

Researchers conducted several surveys to better understand consumer behavior, especially in the context of product returns. Reducing product damage and order inaccuracies significantly decreases the need for RL. Together, these two reasons account for 43% of returns. Leading Reverse logistics market players actively invest in introducing advanced technologies and systems to optimize backward logistics processes. By focusing on operations such as product handling, returns management, and warehousing, these companies aim to streamline the return process. The rise in online shopping has brought a culture where customers frequently return clothing after trials if it does not meet their expectations. The customers feel it easy to ask for many pieces in different colors, of which he/she holds only one piece and returns the rest. A strong reverse logistics system is necessary to manage such voluminous returns (Li & Li, 2015). The amount of reverse logistics is around 8 to 10% of the product's value, making it a significant factor. Return rates in apparel are much higher when compared to other sorts of online shopping returns (N. Sharma et al., 2024a).

RL in the Apparel Market Segment

At least 30% of all online products are returned compared to 8.89% in brick-and-mortar stores. Around 49% of retailers offer free return shipping. 27% of shoppers would purchase an item that costs more than $1,000 if offered free returns, compared to 10% who would purchase otherwise. The Apparel market segment of e-commerce is a sector of online retailing that focuses on selling clothing and fashion accessories through digital channels (Bazaki & Wanick, 2023). These E-commerce channels provide consumers with a convenient and accessible way to purchase a wide range of apparel products, including dresses, shirts, pants, shoes, and accessories like handbags, jewelry, and hats. The e-commerce apparel market has experienced significant growth in recent years. Factors driving the industry trends are the increasing popularity of online shopping, the rise of direct-to-home consumer brands, and the COVID-19 pandemic (Momoko Sakaguchi & Eiji Aoki, 2022). Lockdowns during COVID gave people more time at home, leading to an increased focus on comfortable and casual clothing, showing changing consumer preferences (Ivascu et al., 2022), especially among women (Gogoi et al., 2021). The most common reasons for purchasing apparel online are better discounts, ease of exchange, refund, and return, more selection options, and many more (Parul Kakade et al., 2024). Competition amongst retailers forces them to facilitate hassle-free return facilities to attract and retain customers. E-commerce companies recognize this importance and offer convenient return processes to enhance customer satisfaction and build trust (Jeyalakshmi & Sagarika, 2024). Thus, it helps meet customer expectations and also helps gain a competitive advantage (Stevenson & Rieck, 2024). The statistics are clear on this:

1. 92% of consumers will repurchase something if returns are easy.
2. 79% of consumers want free return shipping.
3. 67% of shoppers check the returns page before making a purchase.
4. 62% of shoppers are more likely to shop online if they can return an item in-store.

Journey of the Product to the End-Consumer

Once the product reaches the customer, the unboxing creates an initial impression. The more sophisticatedly a product is handled and presented, the more positive the incline towards the brand/product. A well-crafted unboxing can evoke positive emotions, enhancing satisfaction and fostering repeat business (Newton, 2023). The product is then compared to the one viewed online after going through the fabric feel, stitch, and overall craftsmanship. Sometimes, the customer finds it unsatisfactory upon initially opening the packaging. Despite this dissatisfaction, the consumer proceeds to try on the item, resulting in the degradation or loss of original packaging materials, paper, and pins. This action diminishes the product's perceived value, and the increase in product returns complicates recouping the original sale price. In such a case, the company/retailer has to meticulously evaluate the product for any signs of wear and tear, damage, or defects, such as a broken zipper, detached logo button, or missing accessories. It has to restore the garment to an acceptable condition before reintroducing the item into the market. It involves positioning the product within a secondary market where reselling can create new revenue streams for the companies. This revenue generation contributes to the growth of the secondary market as companies recognize the potential value by implementing reselling strategies and investing in the required infrastructure and processes.

Role of Reverse Logistics in Modern Supply Chain Management

Unlike the brick-and-mortar stores in the physical market, there is no option for an online retailer to put a board like "No returns." The exponential growth in online apparel sales has led to a corresponding increase in product returns, which raises questions about sustainability and the cost of managing these returns. The commercial revolution that has come up in recent years shows the fast-growing stage of online sales recently (N. Sharma et al., 2024b). Companies can utilize reverse logistics to increase sales, grow their market share, and lower manufacturing costs.

Returns and Their Treatment

Figure 3 gives a glimpse of various types of returns. A brief description of each of the types of returns follows.

Figure 3. Types of returns

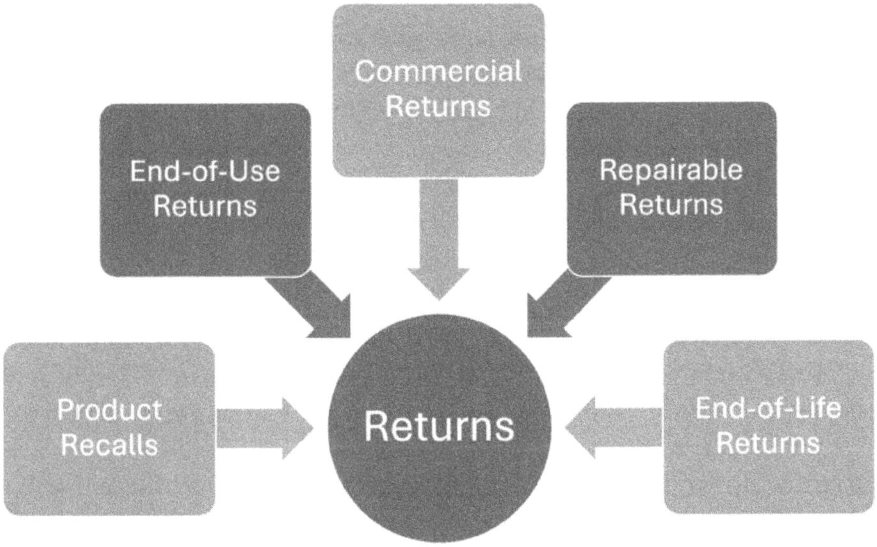

1. **End-of-life returns**: End-of-life returns in the apparel industry encompass garments returned to retailers or manufacturers after their intended use has expired. These returns often result from wear and tear, outdated fashion trends, quality issues, or lenient return policies. Implementing strategies to extend the life span of garments, such as repair services, garment care instructions, and educating the customer about sustainable fashion practices and responsible consumption, can be the solution for such returns. Circular Economy (CE) integration helps clothing not end up in landfills but turn into raw material for manufacturing, though there are challenges (Khanna et al., 2025). These returns concepts apply to civil construction waste management (Lopes et al., 2022) and the construction materials industry. The limited uptake of reprocessed construction materials undermines the efficiency of diverting demolition waste from landfills. There is an urgent need to develop markets, improve material accessibility, and strengthen regulatory support to enhance reverse logistics outcomes (Tennakoon et al., 2025).
2. **End-of-use returns**: End-of-use apparel refers to garments that have reached their end of functional life due to wear and tear, quality issues, or fashion obsolescence. Such challenges can be addressed by extending the life span of

garments through efficient recycling, adopting a circular business model, and implementing policies to promote sustainable practices in the fashion industry.

3. **Recalls**: The top recall items are clothing, textiles, and fashion items (Kumar, 2022). A 'recall' means calling back items from the market that have already been sold. It can be due to found defects after sale, like manufacturing errors, safety hazards (such as choking hazards, loose buttons, or chemical contamination), or non-compliance with safety standards or regulations. Implementing stringent quality control measures, communicating recalls clearly to the customer, establishing efficient reverse logistics channels, and implementing systems to track products throughout the supply chain can solve this issue.
4. **Commercial returns**: Commercial returns refer to products returned due to defective products, incorrect orders, and unsatisfactory orders. Companies can address these issues by improving quality control and accurate order fulfillment by ensuring correct shipping of the products and focusing on customer satisfaction initiatives.
5. **Repairable returns**: Repairable returns consist of apparel with minor flaws that some basic repairs can mend. Such issues can be handled by extending warranties, take-back programs, and offering online tutorials and workshops on basic garment repairs.

Advantages of Reverse Logistics

Potential Cost Savings: Organizations should establish dedicated by-product handling and management infrastructure to optimize costs and environmental impact. They need to conduct a comprehensive evaluation of by-product disposal options. Even incineration of rejected or used products can yield recoverable energy, contributing to corporate social responsibility initiatives. Minimizing direct disposal helps because product components are often valuable raw materials for other industries. Adopting more sustainable materials for manufacturing and packaging can help avoid product waste. RL can help collect empty packaging for potential reuse. Researchers proposed frameworks for structured decision-making in this regard. Mixed integer linear programming can minimize transport and fixed opening costs in a reverse logistics network (El Boudali et al., 2022). RL helps electronics manufacturers to deal with safe disposal practices when handling e-waste. They allow post-consumption sorting and disassembling of product components (Singh et al., 2025).

- **Enhancing Customer Satisfaction**: Efficient handling of returns can enhance customer loyalty and satisfaction.
- **Data insights:** Analysing return data can offer a valuable understanding of customer liking, product performance, and supply chain inefficiencies, if any.

- **Sustainability:** By implementing effective reverse logistics practices, apparel companies can reduce their environmental impact and improve their sustainability reputation.
- **Consumer Insights from returned goods**: Companies can analyze returned goods data to understand consumer behavior and response towards the product bought. Companies that take necessary actions based on the insights benefit from improved customer satisfaction and cost savings.
- **New revenue streams**: Reselling the product after refurbishing is an opportunity to create another source of income. If done responsively, the product that was once discarded as worthless by the customer can fetch revenue for the companies.

Challenges in Reverse Logistics

Reverse Logistics is a complex process and often comes with several operational challenges (Onyeka & Chikwendu, 2025), especially for apparel reverse logistics. Multicriteria decision-making (MCDM) tools such as the Fuzzy Analytical Hierarchy Process (FAHP) can help rank and prioritize the barriers (such as external barriers, organizational barriers, and social barriers) (Putri et al., 2024). Similarly, Enterprises can use multiple criteria group decision-making (MCGDM) approaches, such as the weighted aggregated sum product assessment (WASPAS) method, to choose the best reverse logistics supplier (Rong & Wan, 2025). Some challenges include:

1. **Revisiting Agreements**: Various stakeholders in RL sign agreements with each other. These contractual acts are often aimed at legally sharing the responsibility of product lifecycle but might not be CE-efficient. Therefore, sectoral agreements may need to be revised to incorporate circular economy (CE) requirements (Leal et al., 2025).
2. **High Return rates**: Apparel has a higher return rate when compared to other products due to factors like wrong fit, size, and color preferences, leading to increased handling and transportation costs.
3. **Seasonality**: Fast and ever-changing fashion adds to reverse logistics. To avoid this, delaying the delivery can create a challenge of the product becoming obsolete. Fashion trends and seasonal fluctuations impact the value and marketability of returned items.
4. **Limited reuse and recycling options**: Many apparel items are difficult to recycle as many fabrics are mixed fibers. Separating each fiber and recycling the product is not cost-efficient.

5. **Policy support:** Governments are pushing companies to have a strong RL system. Like any other industry, companies implementing RL need to ensure that they always comply with government policies. Firms that adhere to environmental regulations experience better sustainability outcomes (Kalubanga & Mbekeka, 2024).
6. **Cost of running an RL**: Reverse logistics systems are expensive (Camilleri, 2025). Small businesses struggle to afford these systems. Companies must spend money to collect used products. They also pay workers to sort and process returned items. Sometimes, these costs are higher than the benefits. This happens when few people want to buy recycled materials. A strong market for recovered materials is needed to make reverse logistics profitable.

STRATEGIES FOR OPTIMIZATION

Studies show that developing and implementing the correct and successful reverse logistics strategy is a managerial challenge. It involves using managerial skills and knowledge to improve the supply chain's operational efficiency. Theories such as resource-based views (RBV) acknowledge this by highlighting the identification and categorization of resources and capabilities of a firm (Thornton, 2025). Several strategies are applied in reverse logistics (Jeyalakshmi & Sagarika, 2024). They include:

1. Creating return rules
2. Optimization transportation
3. Improving product design
4. Putting take-back programs in place
5. Making use of technology
6. Educating workers
7. Cooperating with partners
8. Taking measures that impact the environment
9. Encouraging Circular Economy
10. Involving customers

Companies must build green marketing strategies to effectively communicate and educate customers and employees (Stoica, 2021).

To address the challenges and capitalize on the opportunities, apparel companies can implement various strategies:

1. **Centralized return centers**: Consolidating return processing in centralized facilities can improve efficiency and cost management.

2. **Technology adoption**: Automation, Data Analytics, and modern disruption technologies such as Artificial Intelligence (AI) can streamline operations and optimize decision-making. Technologies such as RFIDs, Blockchain, and the Internet of Things (IoT) offer real-time tracking of goods.
3. **Product design**: Incorporating design elements that facilitate disassembly and recycling can improve the end-of-life management of apparel products.
4. **Customer education**: Clear product information and sizing guides can reduce return rates.
5. **Reverse logistics partnerships**: Collaborating with logistics providers specializing in reverse logistics can enhance operational efficiency.

Identification of Cost Drivers in Apparel Returns

Figure 4 shows the need to understand and identify the various cost drivers in one return handled by the company.

Figure 4. Cost drivers in apparel returns

Source: Author

Strategy: If the customer maintains less than 5% total annual return. The next two deliveries will be free. There can be a free prime membership for less than 2% returns.

Return Incentives: These are monetary or other tools to incentivize the end-user of a reusable asset to return it, which can go through another reuse cycle. Returns should be incentivized and facilitated for the end-consumer to keep the reusable asset in the loop for multiple use cycles and make reuse more sustainable. These transaction costs can be avoided by offering alternative return incentives. It can be vouchers, discounts on future purchases, or depositing funds onto a card.

Collection Point: The point where a consumer can return reusable assets. It indicates the start of the reverse logistics. When collection points allow different kinds of reusable assets (e.g., containers, cups, bottles, amongst others) from various brands, they are called universal collection points.

Standards: A standard or norm is a recognized agreement on specifications or criteria of a product or process. Standards can be formally (e.g., ISO norms) or informally established (e.g., organically grown within a company)

Repair: The repairing of damaged or worn textiles significantly reduces the necessity for returns, replacements, and, ultimately, disposal. Integrating innovative technologies into repair processes, including robotics and artificial intelligence, in routine repairs such as stitching and patching enhances efficiency and quality. It further contributes to a more sustainable and efficient reverse supply chain.

Discard, Recycle, or Remanufacturing: Remanufacturing constitutes a closed-loop supply chain wherein components are designed for cyclic rebuilding and reuse. Commonly employed in the automotive, aviation, and heavy equipment industries, remanufacturing offers significant cost reductions compared to virgin material production. This circular approach yields triple benefits for supply chains by curtailing expenses, minimizing resource consumption, and diverting waste from landfills.

Implementing centralized return centers for apparel: A central point for returns or a centralized return center leads to significant cost savings. Centralized return centers reduce transportation costs, efficiently utilize warehouse space, and handle expenses, allowing for better resource allocation and potential cost savings. Processing and handling products increase efficiency, leading to quicker turnaround times for refunds and exchanges (Leng, 2023). However, few studies suggest decentralizing specific operations to reduce carbon footprint while maintaining service levels and lead times (Fani et al., 2025).

Companies are increasingly adopting green warehousing strategies that are human and environmentally friendly (Majeed et al., 2025). However, traditional warehouses require layout redesign in bi-directional logistics contexts (Vintimilla Alvarez & Alarcón Valero, 2025). Redesigning is also required to integrate with energy-efficient storage systems and other modern technology based on CE principles (H. Rashid, 2019). Also, these systems facilitate better information sharing, such as valuable data on return rates, reasons for returns, and product performance. Such information can sync with a digital Warehouse Management System (WMS). Double verification of physical goods and documents and enhancing communication with suppliers and consumers will help reduce potential roundtrips (Putri et al., 2024). This data helps e-commerce apparel retailers to identify trends, improve product quality and optimize inventory management improving customer satisfaction (Wang & Jotikasthira, 2024).

Use of Supply Chain Automation in Apparel Reverse Logistics: Augmented robotic automation for warehouse operations with the help of AI can help manage inventory through real-time analytics. The textiles and fashion industry is an early adopter of Digital Product Passsport. Using DPP helps in efficient returns and repairs, optimizing refurbishment and recycling, and counterfeit prevention (Colucciello, 2025).

Core Strategies for Optimizing Apparel Reverse Logistics

Discount coupons: Gifting discount coupons or compensation on the next purchase if the good is not returned will not only help the reverse logistics to be minimized but also lead to increased sale

Detailed product description and customer review and feedback section: Analytic systems on e-commerce platforms increase impulsive buying amongst consumers. Discounts and other promotions hurry the customer to buy. Sometimes, this makes consumers perceive an incorrect product quality image, leading to heightened uncertainty about the product. Most portals have a liberal return policy that makes the impulsive customer buy but eventually return the items. So, a careful balance between the two is required (N. Rashid et al., 2025). The product description page should be detailed and accurate. The page can include customer input, influencing the customer's decision-making before purchasing the product. The section on customer feedback in the online portal that accurately mentions customer feedback can makc dccision-making more transparent.

Virtual Try-ons: The digital versions of in-store trial rooms are virtual try-ons. These solutions necessitate a high degree of customer immersion and active participation. These solutions allow the customer to try on fashion products virtually with the help of AR and VR technologies in real time. Virtual reality will help the customer upload his photo online and then check how the fashion product looks on him by us making the customer's avatar or mannequin (For example- Spectacles based on facial topography). Augmented reality will help the user to know in real-time, by using his camera, how the product looks on her. The customer can mix and match various combinations to analyze what suits her better. It can also help the customer with further purchase suggestions based on her selected product. Virtual try-ons and virtual face recognitions consumers use can effectively bridge the gap between online and offline shopping. These solutions can adhere to many reverse returns at the pre-purchase stage itself.

Foundation models and Generative AI: AI can significantly reduce product return processes within the fashion industry. By leveraging foundation models and generative AI, retailers can enhance decision-making around return policies, inventory management, and customer experience. Predictive analytics can identify potential return items, allowing for proactive measures to reduce returns. Further, by analyzing the return data, retailers can gain valuable insights into product performance, customer preferences, and areas for product improvement. AI can analyze customer feedback, such as comments like "Great Fit" and "Fun Colour" of a particular shirt style, and generate images of similar shirts that the customer would like to purchase. This capability facilitates optimized inventory management by aligning production with precise customer demand (Harreis et al., 2023).

Chatbots: AI-enabled chatbots can facilitate a more precise understanding of a customer's requirements. In addition to size and color, the customer can specify the desired costume shape, enabling a higher degree of customization in apparel. It will give the apparel a more customized look. Chatbots are highly enabled to promptly and accurately address customer inquiries, facilitate customers' shopping experience, and optimize customer service within the online retail apparel business. A significant advancement in chatbots is open AI-powered chatbots. These chatbots are designed to deliver product information and personalized recommendations based on customer preferences and customer history. AI-powered chatbots can efficiently handle customer inquiries related to returns, providing real-time support and reducing return processing time. Chatbots can help customers in numerous languages.

Styling Recommendations: The model size and the apparel size worn by the model should be clearly and completely stated to avoid ambiguity. The dressing style recommendations will also help the consumers to dress up, unlike the model shown, as frequently customers try to compare themselves with the model shown in the image.

Showrooming: Showrooming of a product means displaying the product in the stores where a customer visits in person and experiences the color, design, fitting of the garment, and the quality of the fabric, buttons, zip, or accessories used on it. The product can be bought online from the specific website once the customer is satisfied with the garment's experience. Such showrooms are called "Immersive Retailing" or "Experience Stores" (Mishra et al., 2023). They simplify decision-making for the customer. Such showrooms can serve as effective brand marketing by various companies. Once customers finalize their selections, the products can be delivered to them. This approach can significantly reduce product returns as customers can assess items first-hand before committing to a purchase. It also reduces the physical ledger making for daily transactions. It can be called a new business model wherein the customer's in-store experiences are with the retailers who act as advisors.

Create Reason codes: Creating codes for every reason, like a change of mind, wrong size, minor wear and tear while shipping, and many more, are programmed into the returns management system. This makes it simpler to process and monitor the returns.

Minor wear and tear: Occasionally, when wearing new apparel, issues may arise, such as a button popping out, a stitch opening up, or a zipper malfunctioning. Alternatively, the cloth gets crumbled or dirty. The product can be washed, repaired, and repacked to appear new for such minor damage. It has the potential to be resold in the market at a discounted price, and the customer will get the following free shipping cost as an incentive. The key is to analyze how much a customer would be willing to pay for the product in this condition after determining the cost of repackaging. Conducting comprehensive market research can help you reach the most granular levels.

Handling unauthorized apparel returns: It has been experienced that sometimes the customer intentionally practices return of the product after using it. Such unauthorized returns should be handled wisely as this dramatically impacts customer relationships. It is a courtesy to receive used products, but such favors, if done several times, may exponentially affect the company's sales. Retailers are sometimes allowed to return the goods after usage to show their customer loyalty and hope for the same brand loyalty from the customer.

Other Practical Recommendations

1. **Cost Optimization Techniques for Apparel Returns:** Apparel wear simulation allows consumers to visualize how the product will fit and look in different body movements and postures (Doyeon Kong, 2024). Formulating returns management strategies plays a critical role in cost optimization. The returns management components should align with the overall business goals.
2. **Technology as a consumer communication tool:** Online user-friendly platforms that enable a smooth return process, from generating return labels to tracking shipments, can simplify the return process. Explicit and easy-to-understand return policies should be encouraged to reduce unnecessary returns.

3. **Design for disassembly and remanufacturing:** Adopting modular designs and prioritizing recyclable and biodegradable materials will not only facilitate easy disassembly of apparel by allowing the reuse of a component in some other product but also streamline the end-of-life processes of the same and minimize the environmental impact. High-quality, reusable packaging materials like zip-lock packs can simplify the return process and reduce packaging waste. European Union actively promotes reusable primary packaging to enhance sustainability in agri-food supply chains. While food traceability is well-established, packaging traceability remains lacking. Hence, researchers proposed a flexible Data Architecture Framework (DAF). The ultimate objective is establishing closed-loop networks for a more sustainable agri-food supply chain, reducing waste and raw material consumption, and ensuring economic and environmental sustainability in the food industry (Bartolotti et al., 2025).
4. **Offering Rewards or Discounts for returned garments:** Some companies impose restrictions through return fees and short return window periods. Others, such as Dress the Population and Triumph, have turned innovative and introduced keep rewards for not returning a product. "Keep Discounts" and "Keep Donations" have a significant positive impact on customers' intrinsic attributions (Horsthemke & Böhm, 2025). Product take-back programs such as offering rewards and discounts for returned garments enable the company to gain greater control over the returned goods, allowing efficient processing and disposition. Effective take-back programs can Optimize the process can be facilitated by logistics networks, including transportation, warehousing, and apparel recycling operations.
5. **Creation of Platforms for Resale or Donation:** Establishing online marketplaces can facilitate customers reselling, renting, or donating apparel. Thus, the usage and product lifespan expands, reducing pressure to produce new quantities. Additionally, offering clothing rental subscription models can minimize product ownership and the associated waste. Fashion brands can derive three benefits from entering such a secondhand market: Firstly, they can have complete control over the brand image and shape and manage the brand in the minds of consumers throughout the entire consumer journey. Secondly, they can build a deeper relationship with the consumers by capturing valuable insights by reconnecting with consumers at the end of the garment's life- when the consumers are now sellers. Thirdly, they can expand into new consumer segments by attracting consumers unwilling or unable to afford new high-end apparel. Such consumers may become brand loyalists in secondhand purchases (Gandhi et al., 2024).

6. **Try before buying model:** Retailers have increasingly adopted 'try before you buy' models to reduce return rates and enhance customer satisfaction. It is a retail strategy wherein the consumer tries the product physically in brick-and-mortar stores before committing to a purchase. Consumers can try in-store items and purchase them online with home delivery or store pick-up. Apparel and other items can also be sent to consumers' homes, allowing them to try them on at their convenience.

SUSTAINABILITY AND CIRCULAR ECONOMY (CE) APPROACHES

Reverse logistics promotes sustainability by reducing waste, reusing materials, and recycling, making it an effective strategy to reach sustainability goals (Gupta & Mukherjee, 2025). Manufacturing firms using RL reported improved operational, social, and environmental performance, though only negligible improvement is seen in economic performance (Opoku & Li, 2025). Managers of organizations understand that commitment and dedication towards RL are required to strengthen their firm's competitive performance (Attia, 2025). Integrating Additive Manufacturing (AM) with reverse logistics can help create more circular supply chains (Balloni et al., 2025). AM supports material recycling and product repair, which are essential components of reverse logistics. Alongside remanufacturing (Ji-Hyland et al., 2025), RL is a key enabler of Circular Economy Practices (CEP) (Onyeka & Chikwendu, 2025). It carries a definition in ISO 59004:2024 standard focusing on Circular Economy (CE). Reverse logistics is the "process of managing, collecting and moving products from their current location after the "end of use" to recover or retain value through proper handling (ISO, 2025). Recycling requires product disassembly. Reverse logistics comes into the picture to collect products from end users. This collection process involves using energy, water, chemicals, production, and distribution capacity.

To achieve circularity, there is a need to integrate reverse logistics into supply chain operations (Kandasamy et al., 2025). Manufacturers understand this. So, they see reverse logistics as a strategic building block of CE. This changed view helps them in achieving greater sustainability (Wenig & Hamann, 2025). Different industries will allocate different priorities to executing reverse logistics supply chain management. The whole process involves various decision-making tools. Some modern decision-management tools include Fuzzy VIKOR and Fuzzy TOPSIS. These tools help determine the order of priority using mathematical and statistical approaches. Hence, they are regarded as scientific. Consider the example of a study conducted on the logistic aspects of the Indonesian palm oil industry. The study has put reuse and repair as the first two priority preferences per Fuzzy VIKOR. At the same time, it is the reverse (the priority is to repair, and the second priority is to reuse), according to Fuzzy TOPSIS. The third to fifth priorities are the same: Refurbishment, Recycling, and Remanufacturing for both methods (Nugroho et al., 2025). From financial aspects, Reverse logistics financing and CLSC financing strategies demonstrated moderate levels of circularity alignment (Zambujal-Oliveira et al., 2025). Studies show insufficient sustainable reverse logistics service quality (SRLSQ) theoretical frameworks (Dabees et al., 2023). Table 5 shows reverse logistics connects well with the United Nations Sustainable Development Goals (UN SDG, 2025).

Table 5. Reverse logistics and UN SDGs

UN SDG	Brief Description
SDG 12: Responsible Consumption and Production	Reverse logistics supports sustainable production and consumption. It reduces waste, recycles materials, and promotes circular economy principles. It ensures that products are reused, refurbished, or properly disposed of instead of being sent to landfills.
SDG 13: Climate Action	RL helps optimize logistics and minimize unnecessary transportation. So, it helps reduce carbon and green greenhouse gas (GHG) emissions and supports climate action efforts positively impacting the environment (Opoku & Li, 2025).
SDG 9: Industry, Innovation, and Infrastructure	RL integrates well with digital technologies such as AI, blockchain, and IoT. They improve efficiency, reduce costs, and optimize supply chains, aligning with sustainable industrialization.
SDG 11: Sustainable Cities and Communities	RL helps in proper waste management. Efficient RL contributes to reducing urban waste and pollution. They help in ensuring cities become sustainable.
SDG 8: Decent Work and Economic Growth	RL can create new business and job opportunities. As an emerging concept, many opportunities worldwide exist in the refurbishment, recycling, and resale industries. Thus, they help in contributing to economic growth while promoting sustainability.
SDG 14 & SDG 15: Life Below Water & Life on Land	By reducing waste and improper disposal of products (like electronics and apparel), RL helps prevent land and ocean pollution, preserving ecosystems.

ARTIFICIAL INTELLIGENCE AND DIGITAL TECHNOLOGIES FOR REVERSE LOGISTICS

The logistics sector has always embraced newer technologies to drive efficiency. Process automation first studies all the steps and processes involved in the company. It then gives specific recommendations to the company. The recommendations can help the company reduce costs and improve delivery times. Technologies are helping develop custom logistics services that meet the requirements of various business classes. So, customized forward and reverse logistics solutions can be built for SMEs, e-commerce companies, and exporters. Artificial Intelligence (AI) (Bhowmik et al., 2024; Wilson et al., 2022), Blockchain (Wu, 2022), and IoT (Rahmanifar, 2025) are among the top technologies that are helping the logistics sector. The system uses all these data to predict the return rate and probability. It studies data and can give results about which products are likely to be returned by the customer. Deep learning can process the images of returned items to identify defects. It can predict the potential incorrect sizing of the product. It also helps in improving quality control. It identifies and categorizes customers based on their return behavior. So, it allows targeted marketing and flexible return policies. Hence, AI methods can connect with other departments of the organization and allow the teams to work as a single unified team from an external point of view.

Reinforcement Learning (RL) is a popular method in AI. It helps in making decisions based on the results provided by deep learning. It can be used to determine optimal inventory levels for returned items. This decision is arrived at based on the demand and return rates. It minimizes stock out and overstock of inventory. RL can learn from existing data by looking into the patterns. It can suggest the best pricing strategies for returned items to maximize revenue and minimize losses. It also optimizes resource allocation for handling returned items and reducing transportation costs.

AI and Decision Science-based Information Systems (DSIS) can help connectivity between forward and reverse logistics and integrate them with green industry environments. Such systems require timely and accurate information captured from IoT and other sensor technologies for mapping and modeling (Nimmagadda et al., 2025). Future research should focus on the cross-sector applicability of AI-driven strategies, real-time implementation challenges, and integrating ethical considerations and privacy concerns into AI frameworks (Fariba, 2025). AI adoption in RL has challenges, such as higher initial investment costs, data security concerns, and workforce skill gaps (Trung et al., 2024).

CONCLUSION

Smart logistics are driving a fundamental transformation in supply chain systems. Reverse Logistics (RL) are playing a crucial role in it. This evolution includes monitoring environmental and social factors at each process stage. The changes encourage consumers to buy only the needed items (clothes) and use them for their optimum lifespan. So, the change is promoting a circular economy. Informative content about fabric care, styling, and sizing is now helping customers make decisions. Customers can maximize their purchases and reduce unnecessary returns. At the same time, businesses are adopting advanced technologies like AI. Automation is helping them to streamline reverse logistics processes, enhance efficiency, and minimize environmental impact. So, companies can reduce waste by integrating sustainability and circular economy principles. They also get an opportunity to create new revenue streams through refurbishment and resale of returned products. The future of reverse logistics lies in the seamless integration of forward and reverse supply chains. Stakeholders get data-driven insights when technologies are used and integrated. Collaborative partnerships streamline the processes. As the global market evolves, businesses will increasingly prioritize sustainability. Customer satisfaction will gain importance, and companies that achieve this will gain a competitive edge. It ensures long-term success in an increasingly eco-conscious world.

REFERENCES

Anon, S. Y., Amin, S. H., & Baki, F. (2024). Third-Party Reverse Logistics Selection: A Literature Review. *Logistics (Basel)*, *8*(2), 35. DOI: 10.3390/logistics8020035

Aryee, R., & Adaku, E. (2024). A review of current trends and future directions in reverse logistics research. *Flexible Services and Manufacturing Journal*, *36*(2), 379–408. DOI: 10.1007/s10696-023-09493-y

Attia, A. (2025). The effect of commitment to sustainable supply chain management and reverse logistics on performance in context of UAE food industry. *Sustainable Futures : An Applied Journal of Technology, Environment and Society*, *9*, 100442. DOI: 10.1016/j.sftr.2025.100442

Balloni, A., Monferdini, L., & Bottani, E. (2025). The Impact of Additive Manufacturing on Supply Chain Management: Trends, Challenges and Future Directions. *Procedia Computer Science*, *253*, 2961–2970. DOI: 10.1016/j.procs.2025.02.020

Bartolotti, G., Guidani, B., Ronzoni, M., Manzini, R., & Accorsi, R. (2025). Data architecture framework for reverse logistics management in reusable food packaging networks. *Procedia Computer Science*, *253*, 1343–1351. DOI: 10.1016/j.procs.2025.01.196

Bazaki, E., & Wanick, V. (Eds.). (2023). *Reinventing Fashion Retailing: Digitalising, Gamifying, Entrepreneuring*. Springer International Publishing., DOI: 10.1007/978-3-031-11185-3

Bentamar, A., Taj, K., & Ourahou, O. (2021). Resource-Based Approaches: A Framework for Analyzing Competitiveness in the Context of Reverse Logistics. *European Scientific Journal ESJ*, *17*(19). Advance online publication. DOI: 10.19044/esj.2021.v17n19p194

Bhowmik, O., Chowdhury, S., Ashik, J. H., Mahmud, G. I., Khan, M. M., & Hossain, N. U. I. (2024). Application of artificial intelligence in reverse logistics: A bibliometric and network analysis. *Supply Chain Analytics*, *7*, 100076. DOI: 10.1016/j.sca.2024.100076

Bozzi, C., Neves, M., & Mont'Alvão, C. (2022). Fashion E-Tail and the Impact of Returns: Mapping Processes and the Consumer Journey towards More Sustainable Practices. *Sustainability*, *14*(9), 5328. DOI: 10.3390/su14095328

Camilleri, M. A. (2025). Cocreating Value Through Open Circular Innovation Strategies: A Results-Driven Work Plan and Future Research Avenues. *Business Strategy and the Environment*, bse.4216. https://doi.org/DOI: 10.1002/bse.4216

Colucciello, A. (2025). *Drivers and Barriers to the implementation of the Digital Product Passport* [Master's Thesis in Sustainability Transition Management, University of Bologna]. https://amslaurea.unibo.it/id/eprint/34334/1/TesiMagistrale_Albino_Colucciello.pdf

Dabees, A., Barakat, M., Elbarky, S. S., & Lisec, A. (2023). A Framework for Adopting a Sustainable Reverse Logistics Service Quality for Reverse Logistics Service Providers: A Systematic Literature Review. *Sustainability*, *15*(3), 1755. DOI: 10.3390/su15031755

Dabo, A.-A. A., & Hosseinian-Far, A. (2023). An Integrated Methodology for Enhancing Reverse Logistics Flows and Networks in Industry 5.0. *Logistics (Basel)*, *7*(4), 97. DOI: 10.3390/logistics7040097

El Boudali, J., Qbadou, M., & Mansouri, K. (2022). Designing of the reverse logistics network for returnable packaging. *2022 14th International Colloquium of Logistics and Supply Chain Management (LOGISTIQUA)*, 1–6. https://doi.org/DOI: 10.1109/LOGISTIQUA55056.2022.9938079

Fani, V., Bucci, I., Bandinelli, R., & Da Silva, E. R. (2025). Sustainable reverse logistics network design using simulation: Insights from the fashion industry. *Cleaner Logistics and Supply Chain*, *14*, 100201. DOI: 10.1016/j.clscn.2024.100201

Fariba, S. (2025). A Review of Advances in Retail Product Return Management: The Role of AI and Digital Technologies in Enhancing Sustainability. *Marketing in Service of Nature and Humanity, 36*, 806–823. https://www.researchgate.net/profile/Bente-Fatema-3/publication/389051849

Frei, R., Jack, L., & Brown, S. (2020). Product returns: A growing problem for business, society and environment. *International Journal of Operations & Production Management*, *40*(10), 1613–1621. DOI: 10.1108/IJOPM-02-2020-0083

Gandhi, S., Strohmer, M. F., Lakner, M., Hickerson, T., & He, S. (2024). Strong supply chains through resilient operations: Five principles for leaders to win in a volatile world. Wiley.

Gogoi, N., Saikia, D., & Neog, P. (2021). Influence of Covid-19 Pandemic on Clothing Interests of Working Women. *International Journal of Current Microbiology and Applied Sciences*, *10*(01), 509–516. DOI: 10.20546/ijcmas.2021.1001.062

Gupta, S., & Mukherjee, S. K. (2025). Advancing AYUSH Exports Through Sustainability and Ethical Practices: A Path to Global Leadership. https://doi.org/DOI: 10.5281/ZENODO.14929371

Harreis, H., Koullias, T., Roberts, R., & Te, K. (2023, March 8). Generative AI: Unlocking the future of fashion. https://www.mckinsey.com/industries/retail/our-insights/generative-ai-unlocking-the-future-of-fashion

Hong, W., Xu, Z., Liu, W., Wu, L., & Pu, X. (2021). Queuing theory-based optimization research on the multi-objective transportation problem of fourth party logistics. *Proceedings of the Institution of Mechanical Engineers. Part B, Journal of Engineering Manufacture*, *235*(8), 1327–1337. DOI: 10.1177/0954405420969266

Horsthemke, J., & Böhm, E. (2025). Different Keep Rewards in Product Return Management. *Marketing in Service of Nature and Humanity, 36*, 837–840. https://www.researchgate.net/profile/Bente-Fatema-3/publication/389051849

Hosseini-Motlagh, S.-M., Johari, M., Nematollahi, M., & Pazari, P. (2023). Reverse supply chain management with dual channel and collection disruptions: Supply chain coordination and game theory approaches. *Annals of Operations Research, 324*(1–2), 215–248. DOI: 10.1007/s10479-022-04909-8

ISO. (2025). *Reverse Logistics*. 3.5.14 Reverse Logistics - International Standards Organization. https://www.iso.org/obp/ui/en/#iso:std:iso:59004:ed-1:v1:en

Ivascu, L., Domil, A. E., Artene, A. E., Bogdan, O., Burcă, V., & Pavel, C. (2022). Psychological and Behavior Changes of Consumer Preferences During COVID-19 Pandemic Times: An Application of GLM Regression Model. *Frontiers in Psychology*, *13*, 879368. DOI: 10.3389/fpsyg.2022.879368 PMID: 35572289

Jeyalakshmi, R., & Sagarika, V. (2024). A Study on Reverse Logistics in Customer Satisfaction through Sustainable Supply Chain. *IJMRSET, 7*(12). https://www.researchgate.net/profile/Jeyalakshmi-R/publication/388916839

Ji-Hyland, C., White, D., & Khavdarov, R. (2025). The impact of circular economy practices on sustainable logistics performance. *International Journal of Logistics Research and Applications*, 1–27. https://doi.org/DOI: 10.1080/13675567.2025.2465579

Kakade, P., Patil, N., Shete, A., Roy, A., & Kalyani, Y. (2024). Digital Apparel Try-Ons: A Technological Odyssey into the World of Virtual Dressing Rooms and Consumer Engagement. [IRJAEM]. *International Research Journal on Advanced Engineering and Management*, *2*(02), 12–19. DOI: 10.47392/IRJAEM.2024.0003

Kalubanga, M., & Mbekeka, W. (2024). Compliance with government and firm's own policy, reverse logistics practices and firm environmental performance. *International Journal of Productivity and Performance Management*, *73*(5), 1427–1478. DOI: 10.1108/IJPPM-09-2022-0463

Kandasamy, J., K E K, V., Ethirajan, M., & Murali, N. (2025). *Circular Supply Chain Management: A Sustainability Approach*. Springer Nature Switzerland. https://doi.org/DOI: 10.1007/978-3-031-81750-2

Kaushik, V., Kumar, A., Gupta, H., & Dixit, G. (2022). Modelling and prioritizing the factors for online apparel return using BWM approach. *Electronic Commerce Research*, *22*(3), 843–873. DOI: 10.1007/s10660-020-09406-3

Khanna, K., Kuik, S., & Ban, J. (2025). Circular Supply Chain Management: Bridging Business Innovation and Sustainability Through Best Practices. *Circular Economy*, *3*(1). Advance online publication. DOI: 10.55845/VLHS2148

Kong, D. (2024). 4D Golf Apparel Wear Simulation for Improved Online Shopping Experience. *Conference: Bridging the Divide*, https://doi.org/DOI: 10.31274/itaa.17382

Kong, D. (2024, January 24). 4D Golf Apparel Wear Simulation for Improved Online Shopping Experience. *Bridging the Divide*. Bridging the Divide. https://doi.org/DOI: 10.31274/itaa.17382

Kumar, V. (2022). Product Recalls in European Textile and Clothing Sector—A Macro Analysis of Risks and Geographical Patterns. *Stats*, *5*(4), 1044–1061. DOI: 10.3390/stats5040062

Leal, T. L. M. D. C., Araújo, J. C. G. D., & Rodrigues, L. B. (2025). Avaliação dos acordos setoriais de logística reversa como mecanismos de promoção da economia circular. *Brazilian Journal of Production Engineering*, *11*(1), 192–212. DOI: 10.47456/bjpe.v11i1.46051

Leng, C. (2023). Information sharing in supply chain based on products return and game theory. In Batista, P., & Zhang, Y. (Eds.), *Second International Conference on Applied Statistics, Computational Mathematics, and Software Engineering (ASCMSE 2023)* (p. 81). SPIE. https://doi.org/DOI: 10.1117/12.2692080

Li, G., & Li, W. (2015). The Analysis of Return Reverse Logistics Management Strategy Based on B2C Electronic Commerce. *Proceedings of the 2015 International Conference on Economics, Social Science, Arts, Education and Management Engineering*. 2015 International Conference on Economics, Social Science, Arts, Education and Management Engineering, Xi'an, China. https://doi.org/DOI: 10.2991/essaeme-15.2015.162

Loske, D., Klumpp, M., Keil, M., & Neukirchen, T. (2021). Logistics Work, Ergonomics and Social Sustainability: Empirical Musculoskeletal System Strain Assessment in Retail Intralogistics. *Logistics (Basel)*, *5*(4), 89. DOI: 10.3390/logistics5040089

Majeed, M., Gideon, A., & Tijani, A. (2025). Green Warehousing Practices for Firms. In M. Majeed, K. Agarwal, & A. Tijani, *Green Supply Chain Management* (1st ed., pp. 133–152). Apple Academic Press. https://doi.org/DOI: 10.1201/9781003560845-8

Melchers, S. J. (2024). Military Supply Chain: Analysis Designing an Information Sharing System for Enhancing Efficiency in Military Supply Chain Operations [Master Thesis, Eindhoven University of Technology]. https://pure.tue.nl/ws/portalfiles/portal/351901285/Master_Thesis_Stijn_Melchers.pdf

Mishra, A., Dutta, P., Jayasankar, S., Jain, P., & Mathiyazhagan, K. (2023). A review of reverse logistics and closed-loop supply chains in the perspective of circular economy. *Benchmarking*, *30*(3), 975–1020. DOI: 10.1108/BIJ-11-2021-0669

Mwanyota, J. L. (2021). Reverse Logistics, Process Innovation, Operational Performance and Competitive Advantage of Manufacturing Firms in Kenya [Thesis, University of Nairobi]. https://erepository.uonbi.ac.ke/handle/11295/155696

Newton, E. (2023). Packaging Has an Undeniably Powerful Impact on Customer Experience. https://parcelindustry.com/article-6208-Packaging-Has-an-Undeniably-Powerful-Impact-on-Customer-Experience.html

Nimmagadda, S. L., Wood, L. C., Namugenyi, C., Mani, N., Singh, A., & Vishnu, T. (2025). Information System Guided Reverse Logistics – Managing the Green Industry Environments. *Pre-ICIS Workshop Proceedings 2024*. https://aisel.aisnet.org/sprouts_proceedings_siggreen_2024/7/

Nugroho, B. Y., Shariff, S. R., Fathurahman, H., & Haris, M. H. (2025). Determining Priority Factors for Executing of Reverse Logistics in Palm Oil Industry of Indonesia. *Journal of Ecohumanism*, *4*(2). Advance online publication. DOI: 10.62754/joe.v4i2.6382

Onyeka, N. C., & Chikwendu, O. C. (2025). Circular economy strategies in industrial engineering: From theory to practice. *International Journal of Multidisciplinary Research and Growth Evaluation*, *6*(1), 1773–1782.

Opoku, R. K., & Li, X. (2025). Sustainable management practices, operational and sustainable performance in manufacturing contexts: Empirical evidence from a developing economy. *Journal of Responsible Production and Consumption*, *2*(1), 48–82. DOI: 10.1108/JRPC-07-2024-0035

Patil, K., Garg, V., Gabaldon, J., Patil, H., Niranjan, S., & Hawkins, T. (2024). Firm performance in digitally integrated supply chains: A combined perspective of transaction cost economics and relational exchange theory. *Journal of Enterprise Information Management*, *37*(2), 381–413. DOI: 10.1108/JEIM-09-2022-0335

Pushpamali, N., Agdas, D., Rose, T. M., & Yigitcanlar, T. (2021). Stakeholder perception of reverse logistics practices on supply chain performance. *Business Strategy and the Environment*, *30*(1), 60–70. DOI: 10.1002/bse.2609

Putra, A. R., Kopot, C., & Zhao, L. (2024). *Cultural Differences in Apparel Product Return Behavior: An Exploratory Study of Indonesia and USA E-Commerce Consumers. Bridging the Divide*. Bridging the Divide., DOI: 10.31274/itaa.17473

Putri, A. R., Tusadiah, W., Rizaldy, W., & Alfaridi, N. (2024). Analysis of Barrier Reverse Logistics Practices in Courier Companies in Indonesia. *Advances in Transportation and Logistics Research*. GROSTLOG 2024. https://proceedings.itltrisakti.ac.id/index.php/ATLR/article/download/691/731

Rahmanifar, G. (2025). Green vehicle routing and logistics optimization: IoT-driven solutions for modern urban challenges [Dipartimento Di Ingegneria Civile, Edile E Ambientale]. https://tesidottorato.depositolegale.it/handle/20.500.14242/188585

Rashid, H. (2019). Integrating Circular Economy Principles in Logistics to Drive Sustainable Warehousing Practices. *IJIRMPS*, *7*(5), 1–9.

Rashid, N., Imtiaz, A., Ali, J., & Sorooshian, S. (2025). Mitigating The Impact of Purchase Uncertainty on Reverse Supply Chain Through Impulsive Consumer Buying with Moderation of Lenient Return Policies. *Cleaner Logistics and Supply Chain*, *14*, 100207. DOI: 10.1016/j.clscn.2025.100207

Rong, Y., & Wan, G. (2025). An Integrated Fermatean Fuzzy Group Decision Method based on Sugeno-Weber Operators for the Selection of Reverse Logistics Supplier. *Computer and Decision Making: An International Journal*, *2*, 508–529. DOI: 10.59543/comdem.v2i.10537

Sakaguchi, M., & Aoki, E. (2022). Study on the comparison of consumer impression of e-commerce and real stores in the fashion tech era, and the effectiveness of VR utilization. In *Lecture notes in networks and systems* (Vol. 497, pp. 528–537). Springer., DOI: 10.1007/978-3-031-08812-4_51

Shaban, A., Saraeva, A., Rose, S., & Clark, M. (2024). The invisible hand of touch: Testing a tactile sensation-choice satisfaction model in online shopping. *Journal of Sensory Studies*, *39*(1), e12897. DOI: 10.1111/joss.12897

Shahrjerdi, R. (2024). Rethinking the Secondhand Supply Chain: A Technological and Sustainable Approach. *Advances in Industrial Engineering, Online First*. https://doi.org/DOI: 10.22059/aie.2024.380818.1904

Sharma, N., Saraswat, C., Sharma, J., Mittal, M. L., & Keprate, A. (2024a). Multi-Objective Optimization for Economic and Environmental Sustainability in Apparel E-commerce Reverse Logistics. *International Journal of Mathematical. Engineering and Management Sciences*, *9*(1), 111–128. DOI: 10.33889/IJMEMS.2024.9.1.00

Sharma, N., Saraswat, C., Sharma, J., Mittal, M. L., & Keprate, A. (2024b). Multi-Objective Optimization for Economic and Environmental Sustainability in Apparel E-commerce Reverse Logistics. *International Journal of Mathematical. Engineering and Management Sciences*, *9*(1), 111–128. DOI: 10.33889/IJMEMS.2024.9.1.006

Sharma, V., Raut, R. D., Mangla, S. K., Narkhede, B. E., Luthra, S., & Gokhale, R. (2021). A systematic literature review to integrate lean, agile, resilient, green, and sustainable paradigms in the supply chain management. *Business Strategy and the Environment*, *30*(2), 1191–1212. DOI: 10.1002/bse.2679

Singh, A., Goel, A., Chauhan, A., & Singh, S. K. (2025). Sustainability of electronic product manufacturing through e-waste management and reverse logistics. *Sustainable Futures : An Applied Journal of Technology, Environment and Society*, *9*, 100490. DOI: 10.1016/j.sftr.2025.100490

Spellmeier, J. P., Rosa, C. B., Rigo, P. D., Mello, M. F., & Hoss, M. (2025). Design of a Business Model for Competitive End-of-Life Performance of Photovoltaic Systems in Brazil. *Renewable Energy*, *122755*. Advance online publication. DOI: 10.1016/j.renene.2025.122755

Stevenson, A. B., & Rieck, J. (2024). Investigating Returns Management across E-Commerce Sectors and Countries: Trends, Perspectives, and Future Research. *Logistics (Basel)*, *8*(3), 82. DOI: 10.3390/logistics8030082

Stöcker, B., Baier, D., & Brand, B. M. (2021). New insights in online fashion retail returns from a customers' perspective and their dynamics. *Journal of Business Economics*, *91*(8), 1149–1187. DOI: 10.1007/s11573-021-01032-1

Stoica, M. (2021). Green Marketing Communication Strategies: An Integrative Literature Review. *The Annals of the University of Oradea. Economic Sciences*, *30*(30 (1)), 388–396. DOI: 10.47535/1991AUOES30(1)043

Tennakoon, G. A., Rameezdeen, R., & Chileshe, N. (2025). Understanding the Limited Uptake of Reprocessed Construction Materials: A Pro-Environmental Behaviour Perspective. *Sustainable Development*, sd.3400. https://doi.org/DOI: 10.1002/sd.3400

Thornton, M. (2025). *Management Strategies and Processes for Improving Product Returns* [Doctoral Study, Walden University]. https://www.proquest.com/openview/3d9098519ccb2be1cd0ea0198a306901/1

Trung, C. T., Xuan, T. P. T., & Thanh, H. T. (2024). *Application of Artificial Intelligence in Reverse Logistics: A Case Study of Seafood Enterprises in The Mekong Delta*. 9. https://www.researchgate.net/profile/Chuyen-Tran-Trung-2/publication/388860284

UN SDG. (2025). The 17 Goals—Sustainable Development. https://sdgs.un.org/goals

Vintimilla Alvarez, P., & Alarcón Valero, F. (2025). A framework for facility layout problem characterization in a bi-directional logistics context. *Journal of Industrial Engineering and Management, 18*(1), 130. DOI: 10.3926/jiem.8573

Wang, Y., & Jotikasthira, N. (2024). A Quantitative Study of The Impact of Supply Chain Management on Customer Satisfaction. *Frontiers in Business, Economics and Management, 12*(3), 3. Advance online publication. DOI: 10.54097/vteg6mls

Wang, Y., Yu, B., & Chen, J. (2023). Factors affecting customer intention to return in online shopping: The roles of expectation disconfirmation and post-purchase dissonance. *Electronic Commerce Research*. Advance online publication. DOI: 10.1007/s10660-023-09769-3

Weingarten, J., & Spinler, S. (2021). Shortening Delivery Times by Predicting Customers' Online Purchases: A Case Study in the Fashion Industry. *Information Systems Management, 38*(4), 287–308. DOI: 10.1080/10580530.2020.1814459

Wenig, C., & Hamann, J. (2025). Increasing Supply Chain Resilience with Reverse Logistics: Hypotheses for a Value Model. *Industry 4.0 Science, 41*(1), 34–40.

Wilson, M., Paschen, J., & Pitt, L. (2022). The circular economy meets artificial intelligence (AI): Understanding the opportunities of AI for reverse logistics. *Management of Environmental Quality, 33*(1), 9–25. DOI: 10.1108/MEQ-10-2020-0222

Wu, J. (2022). Sustainable development of green reverse logistics based on blockchain. *Energy Reports, 8*, 11547–11553. DOI: 10.1016/j.egyr.2022.08.219 PMID: 36089958

Zambujal-Oliveira, J., Franco, A., & Fernandes, B. (2025). Aligning Financing Strategies With Circular Business Principles: A Multicriteria Decision Framework. *Business Strategy and the Environment*, bse.4199. https://doi.org/DOI: 10.1002/bse.4199

KEY TERMS AND DEFINITIONS

Reverse Logistics: The process of managing the return of products (moving goods) from the point of consumption (end customer) back to the origin (manufacturer or supplier) for purposes such as return, reclamation, refurbishment, recycling, or disposal.

Supply Chain: The network of organizations, people, activities, information, and resources involved in producing the product or service and delivering (moving) it from supplier to customer.

Logistics: The detailed planning, coordination, execution, and implementation of complex operations involving the movement of goods, services, and information from one place to another, usually from the point of origin to the point of consumption.

Artificial Intelligence (AI): The simulation of human intelligence in machines programmed to think, learn, reason, and make decisions, often used to optimize processes and solve complex problems. In Reverse Logistics, AI can predict the customer's probability of return or optimize the logistics network.

Big Data: Enormous and complex datasets that require advanced techniques to store, process, and analyze for insights. The analysis can reveal patterns, trends, and associations computationally, especially relating to human behavior and interactions.

Machine Learning: A subset of AI that uses algorithms and statistical models to enable computer systems to improve their performance on a task through experience and data analysis. ML makes predictions or decisions without explicit programming.

Sustainability: The practice of meeting current needs without compromising the ability of future generations to meet their own needs. It often involves responsible use of resources, minimizing environmental impact, and bringing about social and economic balance.

Circular Economy: An economic model that aims to minimize waste and maximize resource efficiency by promoting reuse, recycling, and regeneration of materials.

E-Commerce: The buying and selling goods and services online through digital platforms.

Retail: The sale of goods or services directly to consumers, typically through stores, online platforms, or other distribution channels.

Chapter 15
Advanced Transportation Technologies for Next-Generation Logistics

Sitesh Kumar Singh
https://orcid.org/0000-0002-7108-0808
College of Engineering, National University of Science and Technology, Oman

Jaishri Gothania
https://orcid.org/0000-0002-2656-642X
Lingaya's Vidyapeeth University, India

Rituraj Jain
https://orcid.org/0000-0002-5532-1245
Marwadi University, India

ABSTRACT

The chapter will focus on the disruptive aspects of using AI, IoT, Robotics, and Blockchain in transportation today. With the world facing increasing supply chain challenges caused by urbanism, climate change, and technological disruption, smart logistics are providing avenues of increasing efficiency, resilience, and sustainability. It gives a conceptual summary, discusses its applications in road, maritime, and air transport, and is supplemented with case studies. The main themes identified are intermodal integration, digitalization of the supply chain, and significant barriers to implementation, which are cost, cybersecurity, and regulatory problems. Future enablers and emerging technologies such as digital twins, edge AI, and 6G can therefore be identified. The chapter ends with strategic recommendations to policymakers, industry leaders, and researchers by giving a stepwise process by which the digital transformation of logistics in the 21st century can be examined.

DOI: 10.4018/979-8-3373-2434-0.ch015

INTRODUCTION TO SMART LOGISTICS AND TRANSPORTATION

Logistics and transportation are experiencing a radical digitalization due to the active adaptation to the new requirements of world trade, urbanization, and sustainability. Logistics operations have long been typical of siloed systems, manual procedures, reactive administration, but are starting to adopt intelligent technologies to gain real-time observability, data-driven decision-making, and automation. This pivot to what is being dubbed as smart logistics merely indicates a new normal a scenario where interconnected, adaptive, and autonomous systems are transforming the flow of goods and services through road, maritime, air, and rail transport systems (Kurniadi, 2025).

The gist of this evolution is the meeting of disruptive technologies the Internet of Things (IoT), Artificial Intelligence (AI), Robotics, and Blockchain. Altogether, these inventions can help to end-to-end optimize the logistics improving its efficiency, reliability, sustainability, and responsiveness to customers (Mohammad et al., 2024). This section establishes the main concepts that support the idea of smart logistics and presents the concept of the digital transformation of transport systems in this framework.

- **Defining Smart Logistics and Intelligent Transportation**

Smart logistics can be defined as the use of high technologies and data analysis to facilitate and optimize logistics processes. It includes goods and assets in real-time tracking, predictive fleet maintenance of transports, warehouse automation, digital coordination of supply chains, and customer-friendly delivery concepts. This practice does not only focus on operational efficiency but also tries to focus on flexibility and resilience of the supply chains (Rodrigue, 2020).

Intelligent Transportation Systems (ITS) is a branch of smart logistics that aims at increasing the performance and connectivity of transport infrastructure and services. ITS uses digital sensors, AI algorithms, and communication technologies to control the traffic streams, provide safety, and decrease environmental implications. As an example, ITS is becoming more useful in urban freight logistics to limit congestion and carbon emissions (McKinnon, 2018).

Digital supply chains, in their turn, extend the concept to the upstream and downstream operations that bring suppliers, manufacturers, distributors, and retailers together on the shared digital platforms and data ecosystems (Kurniadi, 2025).

- **Evolution of Logistics in the Digital Era**

Logistics has long been a specialist area, facilitating trade and economic growth, however, until globalization and the digital economy, its purpose has changed. The initial developments in use of logistics were dependent on paperwork, human prudence and physical facility. The digitization came in the late 20th century with the introduction of Enterprise Resource Planning (ERP) systems barcode tracking. Nevertheless, those systems were still quite fragmented and reactive (Rodrigue, 2020).

The Fourth Industrial Revolution (Industry 4.0) was the breaking point. The technologies including IoT, cyber-physical systems, cloud computing, and AI started to converge and promise interconnected, intelligent, and autonomous systems (Mohammad et al., 2024). Logistics operators started to invest into the platforms offering real-time visibility into the supply chain, predictive analytics and automated decision making, ushering in the era of smart logistics.

The evolution is not technological but also includes new consumer habits and the development of e-commerce and global shocks like the COVID-19 pandemic that made the importance of resilient and agile supply chains (Kurniadi, 2025). This has led to the fact that digitalization of logistics is no longer an optional innovation, but a strategic necessity.

- **Key Drivers for Smart Logistics Transformation**

The following are some of the reasons why the use of smart logistics as modelled in Figure 1 and discussed below is being accelerated:

- **Globalization and Trade Expansion:** Greater international trade requires regionally coordinated, real-time logistics activities (Rodrigue, 2020).
- **Growth of E-commerce:** The development of online shopping has created the problem of last-mile delivery and the necessity to interact with clients in real-time (McKinnon, 2018).
- **Environmental Regulations:** There is pressure on Governments and industries to cut emissions, which has led to an interest in electric vehicles, route optimization and low-carbon logistics (McKinnon, 2018).
- **Urbanization:** Smart city programs are set to alleviate gridlocks and enhance mobility, which provides an alliance between smart logistics and city planning (Kurniadi, 2025).
- **Supply Chain Disruptions:** Pandemics, geopolitical instability, climate change demonstrates the brutcncss of conventional logistics and highlight the importance of flexibility and transparency (Mohammad et al., 2024)

Figure 1. Key drivers for smart logistics transformation

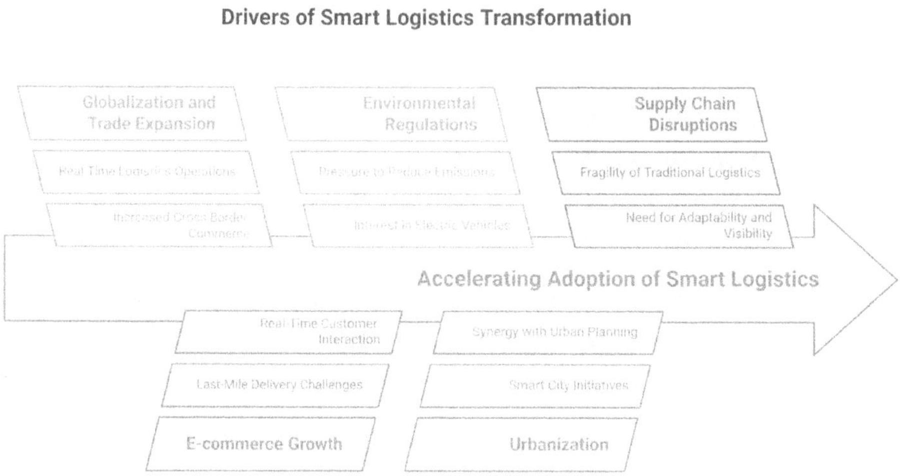

These changes are not happening in vacuum. Rather, they are all connected in a network of global drivers, technological enablers, integrative frames and feedback mechanisms, which constitute the whole that is the smart logistics ecosystem.

To integrate these dimensions, Figure 2 shows a graphic abstract model that demonstrates how emerging technology, policy framework, and global pressures integrate influences on the development of smart logistics and intelligent transportation systems.

Figure 2. Conceptual model for smart logistics transformation

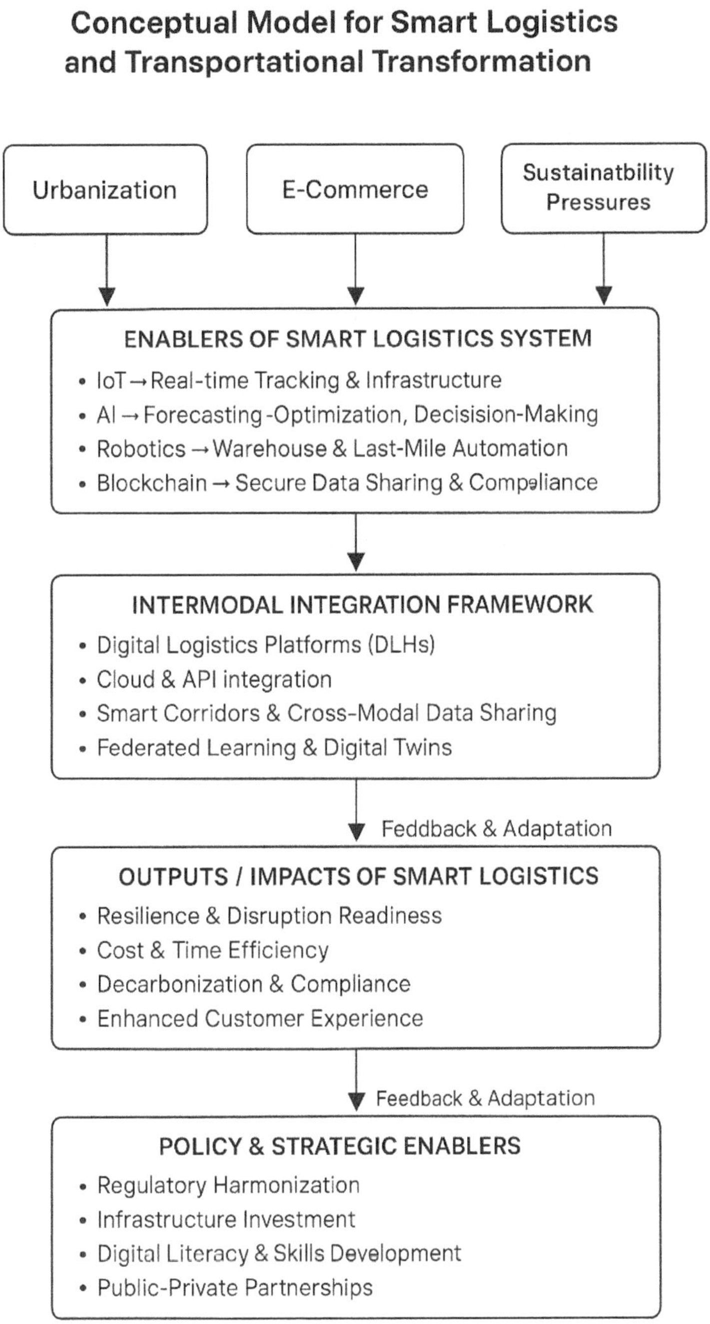

The framework represents the conceptual relationship between the global drivers (e.g., urbanization, e-commerce, and sustainability), technological enablers (e.g., IoT, AI, robotics, blockchain), and seamless twenty-first century integration to obtain resiliency, efficiency, and policy-oriented smart logistics ecosystems.

- **Technological Foundations of Smart Logistics**

To appreciate smart logistics, it is important to comprehend the contribution of each of the core technologies as shown in Figure 3 and discussed below:

- The IoT can track and monitor the goods, vehicles and infrastructure in real-time. Cargo, containers, and vehicles have sensors that produce data about the location, condition, temperature, and delays (Rodrigue, 2020).
- Machine Learning and AI can assist in predictive analytics and demand forecasting, as well as route optimization, enabling operators to create dynamical adjustments according to the changing situations (Jain et al., 2023).
- Warehouse automation (such as autonomous guided vehicles or robotic picking arms) is driven by robotics, which is also venturing into last-mile delivery, using drones and self-driving delivery bots (Kurniadi, 2025).
- Blockchain can guarantee integrity and trust in data, making it suitable to use in decentralized systems to support logistics documentation, contract execution, and cargo origins (Mohammad et al., 2024)

Figure 3. Technological foundations of smart logistics

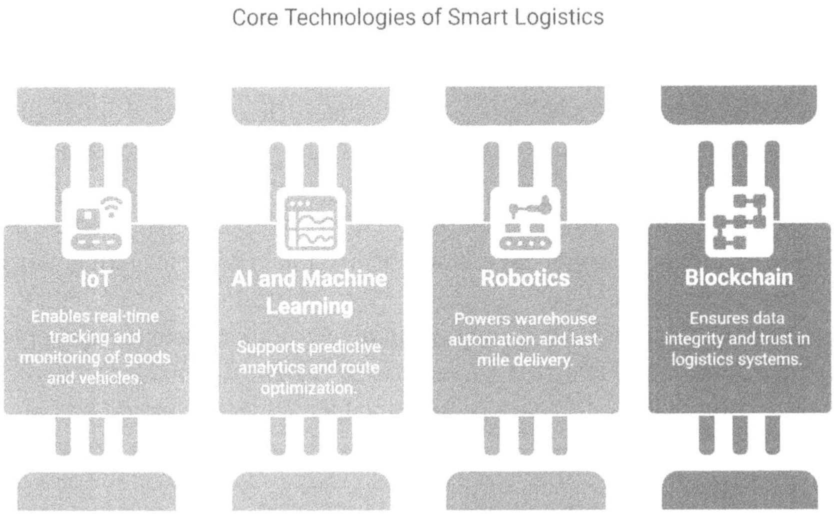

These technologies don't operate on an isolation basis. Their combination, e.g., to use IoT data in AI-based predictions or to logistics events on a blockchain ledger opens the potential of smart logistics to the fullest.

SMART LOGISTICS IN THE CONTEXT OF SUSTAINABILITY

Smart logistics is important to the realization of sustainability objectives besides efficiency and cost reduction. Such technologies as AI and IoT can optimize fuel use by improving routes, anticipate maintenance to minimize vehicle off-roads, and make a modal shift towards cleaner transportation means (McKinnon, 2018).

The blockchain can facilitate the green logistics certification system by tracking the carbon footprint, and robotics can minimize the energy consumption in warehouses by performing accurate automation. In this regard, smart logistics is taking its position in accordance with the global agendas, including the UN Sustainable Development Goals (SDGs) and Net Zero Emissions targets (Kurniadi, 2025).

The scholarly value of smart logistics is that it belongs to multiple disciplines, including engineering and computer science in addition to supply chain management and policy studies. To the practitioners, the concept offers a guide to technology investment and digital strategy. To policy makers, it shows the regulatory and infrastructural changes that need to be made to accommodate innovation.

The chapter attempts to fill these gaps by providing conceptual understanding, technological information, and evidence-based discussion that could be used in making informed decisions in any sector.

To substantiate the applicability of smart technologies, (Jain et al., 2023) present the extensive survey of AI applications in civil engineering logistics and transport and highlight how real-time data analytics and autonomous systems are significant towards improving the efficiency and sustainability of operations within smart cities. This is exactly in line with the premise behind this chapter technology-enabled logistics transformation.

The presented section has provided an initial idea of the conceptual and practical basis of smart logistics, laying the groundwork to explore the enabled technologies, real-world cases, intermodal integration, implementation challenges, and research opportunities in the next sections in greater detail (Rodrigue, 2020; Kurniadi, 2025).

KEY TECHNOLOGIES DRIVING SMART LOGISTICS

The rapid embrace of the emerging technologies providing capabilities to make operations data-driven, predictive, and self-governing is transforming the overall logistics industry across the globe. The Internet of Things (IoT), Artificial Intelligence (AI), Robotics and Blockchain are among the most transformative of them. These technologies can be used on their own to optimize logistics processes, but their real potential is in convergence to form an integrated ecosystem of smart logistics. Hence, table 2 describes the strategy for integration of smart logistics ecosystem. Each technology is thoroughly analyzed in this section, including the description of their functionalities and application in a specific sector, as well as their synergetic interaction as part of smart transportation systems.

- **Internet of Things (IoT): Creating a Hyperconnected Logistics Environment**

Conceptual Overview

The Internet of Things (IoT) in logistics refers to the use of a variety of physical objects including vehicles, containers, pallets, and equipment that have sensors and software to transmit data in real-time. Architecture allows logistics operators to have a more efficient overview of the movement of goods throughout the supply chain (Fatorachian et al., 2025).

Applications in Smart Transportation

The IoT-enabled systems facilitate the entire supply chain visibility with the provision of comprehensive details about the location, condition and status of the shipments. Figure 4 and the following represent some of the core applications:

Figure 4. Applications of IoT enabled system in smart transportation

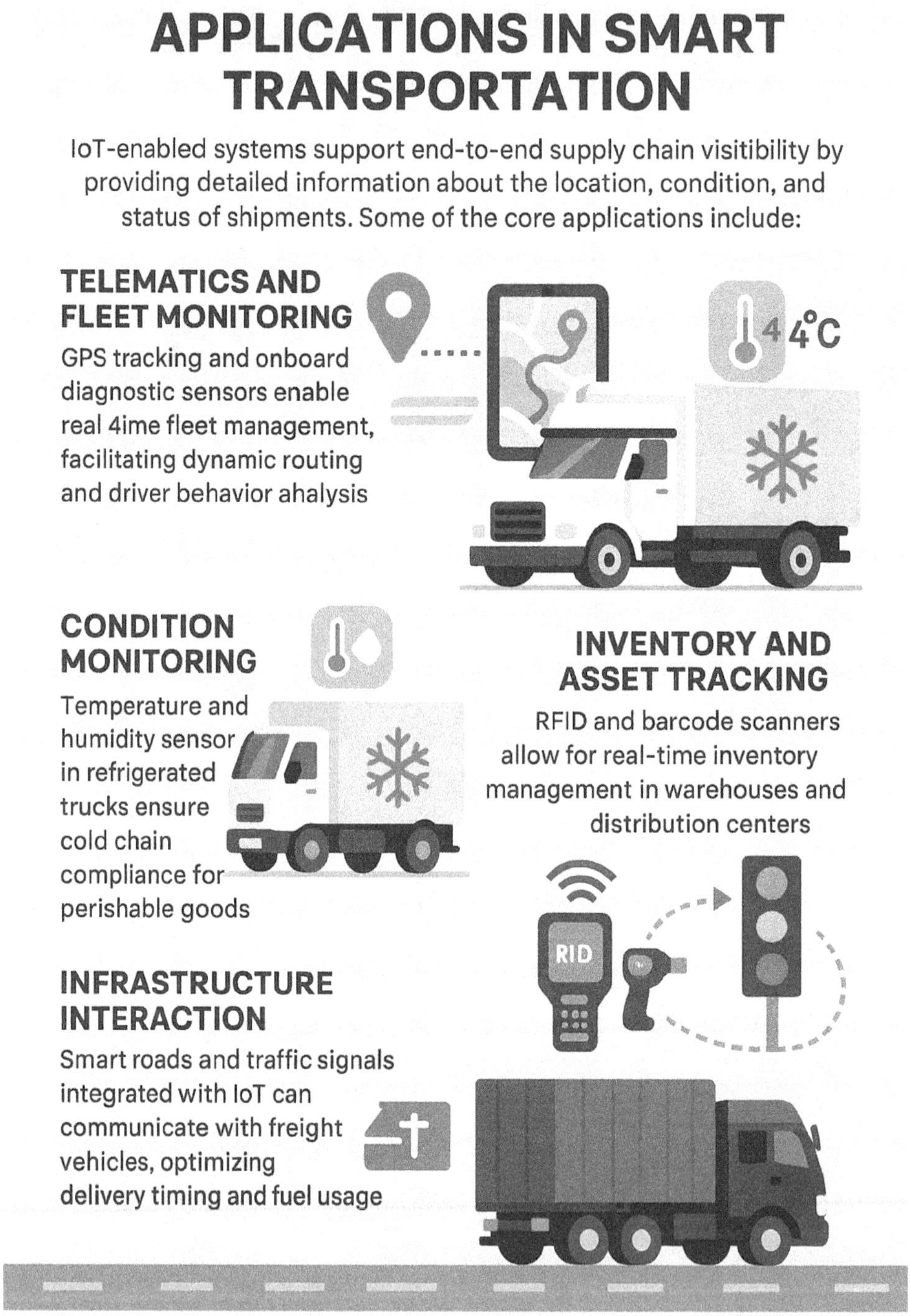

- Telematics and Fleet Monitoring: Onboard diagnostic sensors and GPS tracking allow real time fleet control, which can be used to do dynamic routing or study driver behavior.
- Condition Monitoring: Refrigerated trucks can have temperature and humidity sensors to make sure that the cold chain is maintained in case of perishable goods.
- Inventory and Asset Tracking: RFID and barcodes scanners can be used to manage inventory in real-time at warehouses and distribution centers.
- Infrastructure Interaction: IoT can be connected to smart roads and traffic lights to interact with the freight vehicles to determine the best time to deliver goods and how to optimize fuel consumption.

With more complex supply chains, IoT becomes a critical driver of predictive maintenance, dynamic routing, and smart warehousing. This leads to cost reduction, higher service levels and responsiveness to the disruption.

- **Artificial Intelligence (AI): Strengthening Adaptive and Predictive Logistics**

Theoretical Foundations

AI in logistics means the use of an algorithm that tried to repeat the human brainwork, especially in learning, perception, and decision-making. Machine learning (ML), a sub-branch of AI, allows models to be trained on historic data and tune into novel circumstances, whereas deep learning supports the manipulation of unstructured data like pictures and sound.

Logistics-Specific Functions

The use of AI leads to considerable improvement in the resilience and efficiency of logistics networks by the following description and representation with Figure 5:

Figure 5. Logistics specific functions of AI

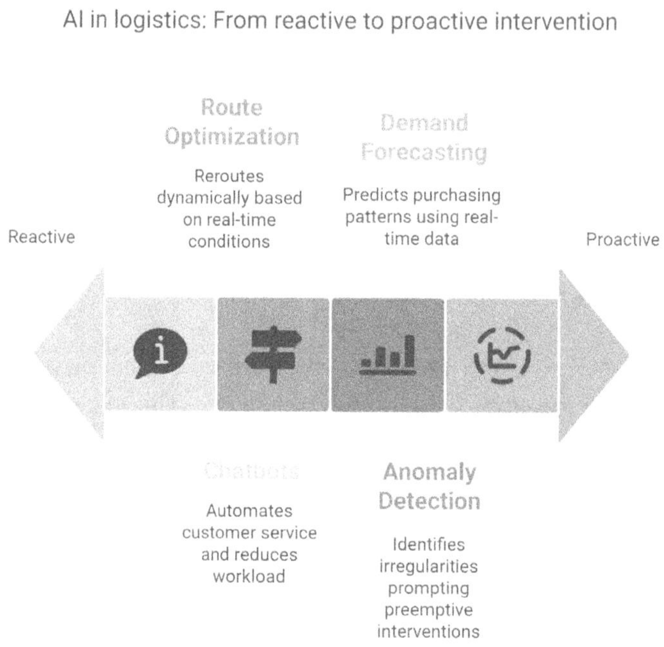

- **Demand Forecasting:** AI algorithms forecast the buying behavior based on the sales data in real-time along with social media and environmental sensor data.
- **Optimized Routes:** AI-powered logistics solutions optimize routes dynamically depending on traffic, weather, and customer availability.
- **Anomaly Detection:** Machine learning will be able to detect abnormalities in the pattern of shipments or the functioning of equipment triggering corrective actions in advance.
- **Chatbots and Virtual Assistants:** Customer service automation helps logistics firms reduce human workload and improve response times.

According to Awasthi, (2024), AI has been instrumental in reducing turnaround time and improving asset utilization in supply chain hubs in Southeast Asia, particularly when integrated with sensor-based tracking and forecasting models.

- **Robotics: Automating the Physical Layer of Logistics**

Definition and Scope

Areas of robotics in logistics are many and encompass Autonomous Mobile Robots (AMRs), robotic arms, aerial drones, and Automated Guided Vehicles (AGVs). Such robots can handle inventory, pick items, package them, deliver them, and load/unload cargo without human supervision (Tubis & Rohman, 2023).

Deployment Across Logistics Functions

- **Warehouse Automation:** Robotic picking arms combined with vision systems and AI algorithms can sort through thousands of items an hour, as well as outperform humans in terms of efficiency, all with the same level of accuracy.
- **Sorting Systems:** AMRs dynamically sort through isles in the warehouse with the help of LiDAR, SLAM (Simultaneous Localization and Mapping) and path optimization algorithms.
- **Last-Mile Delivery:** Delivery drones and autonomous ground robots have been developed in Urban logistics that can navigate sidewalks and deliver parcels within less than 30 minutes.
- **Port Automation:** Robotic cranes and autonomous vehicles have already made the transfer of containers aboard to warehouse happen smoothly in smart maritime terminals.

Another example is DHL that has introduced collaborative robots ("cobots") to assist human employees in repetitive and ergonomically demanding duties, which yielded a decrease in injuries and an increase in productivity (Sainath, 2024).

- **Blockchain: Securing and Streamlining the Logistics Ledger**

Technology Overview

Blockchain is a distributed digital registry which in a secure and immutable manner stores transactions on a distributed system of nodes. Each information is categorized into "blocks" which are timestamped and linked to the previous block via cryptographic hashes, thus making the data almost impossible to modify.

Applications in Smart Supply Chains

Blockchain results in transparency and a new degree of belief in logistics by:

- **Real-time Document Verification:** Smart contracts can verify documents in real time and trigger customs clearance, payment release and cargo transfer at the occurrence of some pre-programmed conditions.
- **Provenance and Compliance:** Technology can help a business track the source of the goods and ethical sourcing which is a legal requirement in food, pharmaceutical and clothing supply chains.
- **Dispute Resolution:** An immutable record of transaction can help resolve fast disputes regarding spoiled goods, missed delivery, or misinterpretation.

Most recently, in 2021 the Port of Antwerp launched a logistics platform on blockchain to digitalize the documentation of hazardous goods and improve the co-ordination of the freight forwarders, customs, and shipping lines (Wang et al., 2021).

- **Technological Convergence: Toward a Holistic Smart Logistics Ecosystem**

The Need for Integration

Even though each of the technologies has a distinct set of advantages, through the conjunction of the implementation of all of them, a logistics network can become not only efficient but also smart, adaptive and sustainable. AI, IoT, robotics and blockchain combination enables:

- **Proactive Supply Chains:** IoT sensors alert on the actual condition of the shipment in real-time; AI estimates the risks and anticipates the delays; blockchain stores the transaction record in an unsafe place; and robots make versatile decisions and act on them on the ground.
- **Automated Decision-Making:** The systems determine in real-time warehousing operations, shipping routes and resource choice using a mix of on-device sensor information and historical examples.
- **Green Logistics:** AI can plan the most efficient routes to reduce carbon emissions; blockchain can be applied to trace the sustainability credentials and IoT can assist to encourage fuel economy by facilitating predictive maintenance.

EMERGING INNOVATIONS

This convergence is already truly remarkable with the introduction of Edge AI, digital twins, 5G/6G connectivity likely to make it even more significant. To take one example, logistics networks can be disrupted, and recovery scenarios can be simulated in real time in digital replicas of the networks (digital twins), and real time control of autonomous vehicles and robots is ensured via low latency communications enabled by 5G (Qiu et al., 2023).

Strategic and Policy Considerations

The implementation of smart logistics technologies is a multi-stakeholder, long-term planning, and investment coordination. The important factors to consider are:

- **Standardization and Interoperability:** The scalability of deployment depends on ensuring compatibility of devices, platforms and protocols.
- **Cybersecurity and Data Privacy:** With the number of devices accessing the network, there are more ways to breach it. There should be strong encryption, access and audit mechanisms.
- **Policy Frameworks:** Policy makers must encourage the use of smart logistics by offering subsidies, innovation zones and friendly policies.

Skills and Inclusion: Reskilling initiatives and digital literacy drives are necessary to ensure that the workforce is equipped to deal with the technological changes.

The propose is that effective smart transport schemes should incorporate linked urban planning, predictive modelling and participatory policy formulation processes that are inclusive of regional infra-structure and economic realities (Singh and Saraswat, 2019).

CASE STUDIES ACROSS TRANSPORT MODES

The adoption of intelligent logistics technologies has assumed various forms based on the modes of transport due to operation limitations and market and regulatory environments. In this section, evidence-based analysis of practical case studies of road, maritime, and air transport is given, and then cross-modal integration is explained. With the emphasis placed on practical demonstrations, the section explains how Artificial Intelligence (AI), Internet of Things (IoT), Robotics, and Blockchain have ceased being theoretical concepts and became the pursuers of efficiency, resilience, and sustainability in global logistics.

- **Road Transport: AI-Powered Optimization and Traffic Intelligence**

Urban Freight Routing in Barcelona

A convincing example of AI implementation into urban logistics is the Smart Urban Freight project by Barcelona, named Ciutat Intelligent. The city implemented a platform that uses real-time traffic information, AI-powered predictive routes, and smart loading zones. The system examined vehicle traffic patterns, curb side availability and delivery times to determine dynamically the delivery slots of commercial vehicles.

This artificial intelligence-based system lowered the average delivery time by 20 percent and illegal parking and idling emissions were also greatly reduced. It has shown the potential of using AI in combination with geospatial and temporal data to resolve the issue of urban congestion and improve routing and last-mile delivery performance (Kamargianni et al., 2016).

India's FASTag System and Predictive Tolling

The introduction of FASTag an RFID based toll collection system in India has been updated by using machine learning algorithms to anticipate congestion at toll booths and divert logistics fleet through alternate paths as shown in Figure 6. AI models can offer the best travel routes based on past records of vehicle flow, road congestion, and condition indicators.

Figure 6. India's FASTag system and predictive tolling

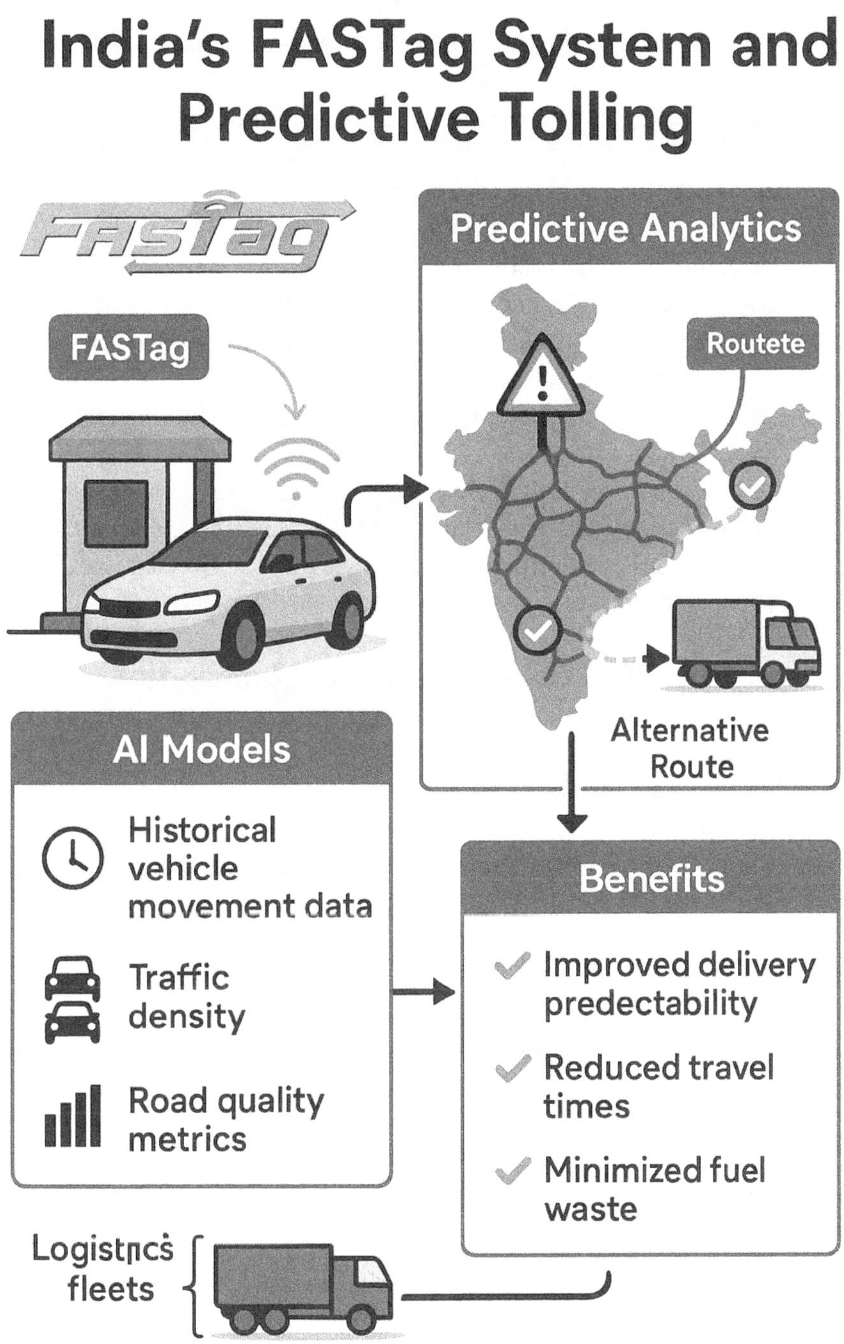

This has enhanced the predictability of delivery, decreased travel time, as well as minimized fuel waste along the national freight corridors (Pandey & P, 2025). The convergence of predictive analytics and electronic tolling is an example of how even the conventional highway infrastructure can be turned into smart logistics networks.

- **Maritime Transport: Blockchain and IoT in Port Ecosystems**

TradeLens and the Port of Rotterdam

Rotterdam, among the most active ports in Europe, has agreed to use the TradeLens blockchain network, a joint initiative by IBM and Maersk, to digitalize shipping paperwork. The site gave port authorities, customs agents and logistics suppliers real-time access to shipment information. This saved 40 percent in document handling time and increased transparency throughout the container handling process (Hofmann et al., 2019).

Bill of landing, letters of credit, and customs declarations are some of the documents that are now automatically validated and transmitted through smart contracts. This blockchain implementation decreased the time loss because of mismanagement of documents and enhanced the trust between the stakeholders.

IoT Sensors in Smart Containers (Port of Singapore)

The smart containers, which are enabled by the internet of things (IoT), are implemented by the Maritime and Port Authority of Singapore (MPA) to monitor the status of smart containers in real-time, including location, temperature, and humidity. The control tower at the port combines information provided by container sensors, terminal equipment, and weather monitoring systems to determine the schedule of the vessels in real-time.

The IoT systems have assisted in decreasing the port dwell time by 15 percent, improving the security of cargo, and berth crane allocation. Pham (2023) opined that the developments play a critical role in aiding the Singapore government vision of making the country a global logistics hub by the Tuas Mega Port project, which is fully automated and AI-driven by 2040.

Port-Centric Logistics and Data Exchange

Such ports as Antwerp and Hamburg have already created Port Community Systems (PCS) based on the combination of blockchain and IoT to exchange information with shippers, freight forwarders, and customs authorities. Such platforms enable predictive analytics to handle cargo flows during extraordinary occasions or outbursts to guarantee resilience and continuity in maritime logistics (Ahmad et al., 2021).

- **Air Transport: Robotics and AI in Cargo Handling**

DHL's Robotic Cargo Sorting in Leipzig

The European Air Hub in Leipzig, operated by DHL, is a reference point in air cargo processes integration of robotics. The sorting of the parcel is done using robotic arms that have vision systems and object recognition using AI. Such robots are capable of processing Parcel up to 6,000 parcels an hour with an accuracy of 99.8 percent (Boorová et al., 2024).

AI finds applications in sorting anomalous consignments, monitoring volumetric variations, and adjusting the velocity of conveyors in real-time. This has seen them lose dependence on seasonal workers and brought about consistency in their throughput during peak periods.

Predictive Scheduling at Heathrow Airport

London Heathrow Airport applies predictive analytics powered by AI to schedule air freight slots. The AI system predicts possible delays by examining historical data, weather predictions, and aircraft turnaround time and preemptively reschedules cargo handling operations.

This forecasting method has also enhanced aircraft turnaround rates, increased coordination with ground logistics suppliers and reduced airside congestion (Du Plessis et al., 2025).

Drone-Based Inventory in Airport Warehouses

Scandinavian airports have tested drone inventory management systems of spare parts and cargo warehouses. Drones with RFID scanners and SLAM navigation do automated stock audits, eliminating the use of scaffolding or manual inventory counting.

Such systems, as Tubis et al. (2021) observe, can not only enhance safety but also speed up stock verification cycle up to 60%, which is a clear value case of robotic automation in vertical logistics processes.

- **Cross-Modal Integration and Smart Corridor Case Studies**

The European TEN-T Corridors

One of the examples of smart intermodal integration is the Trans-European Transport Network (TEN-T). On such corridors as the North SeaBaltic, nations have introduced integrated digital solutions in the form of rail, road, and inland waterways. The systems incorporate IoT devices to track container movements, AI to anticipate intermodal delays and blockchain to enable cross-border custom clearances. This model has saved 25% of transshipment time between modes and enhanced cross-jurisdictional coordination (Bottcher, 2006).

China-Europe Freight Trains

Another interesting cross-modal logistics example is the China-Europe Railway Express (CR Express). CR Express combines GPS tracking, cloud platforms, and delay prediction algorithms based on AI to operate cargo across a variety of regulatory environments in rail, road, and port nodes.

By 2021, more than 13,000 trains have linked Chinese industrial zones to European markets, cutting the transit time by half, in comparison with 40 days (sea) to less than 20 days. IoT sensors with just-in-time logistics allow tracking the inventory turnover in the automotive and electronics industries in a more efficient way.

INTERMODAL INTEGRATION AND SMART SUPPLY CHAINS

The development of intelligent logistics does not only require the implementation of high-tech but also their harmonization over the various means of transport road, rail, air, and maritime depicted in Figure 7. This intermodal integration proves to be critical in developing resilient, efficient, and adaptive supply chains that may dynamically adjust to real-time demands, disruptions, and environmental situations. This part discusses the notion of intermodal integration in the context of smart logistics, evaluates the contributions of digital platforms and data interoperability, and estimates the major challenges and enablers regarding technical, organizational, and policy aspects.

Figure 7. Concept of intermodal integration of smart logistics and smart supply chain system

Understanding Intermodal Integration in Smart Logistics

Intermodal logistics means the synchronized transfer of cargo with more than one carrier mode within the framework of one logistics. Intermodal transport has traditionally suffered coordination inefficiencies, owing to fragmented infrastructure, incompatible IT systems as well as institutional silos (Vural et al., 2020). Smart intermodal logistics, in contrast, uses digital technologies to coordinate planning, execution and monitoring across these modes in real time.

The platforms and protocols used in the heart of smart intermodal integration include:

- System to system data exchange (fleet management, terminal operations, customs, etc.)
- Together scheduling and routing
- Cargo visibility and traceability between nodes
- Interfaces and interoperable standards

Such features allow logistics operators to reduce the costs, handover delays and increase service reliability throughout the supply chain.

ROLE OF DIGITAL PLATFORMS AND DATA INTEROPERABILITY

Digital Logistics Hubs

Digital platforms can act as the hubs of integrated logistics. As an example, Digital Logistics Hubs (DLHs) are interfaces where different stakeholders can interact on a common platform and information is shared between carriers, shippers, port operators, and regulators. These portals usually are:

- Shipment tracking real time dashboards
- Capacity forecasting predictive algorithms
- Transaction automation using Smart contracts
- System interoperability through API based interfaces

An example of such an approach is the International Data Spaces (IDS) project initiated by the Fraunhofer Institute, which creates standardized, secure data-sharing spaces between logistics partners in Europe (Bates, 2025).

Cloud Integration and API Gateways

The intermodal operations of today could not be possible without cloud computing and open APIs that facilitate the communication of legacy transport management systems (TMS), warehouse management systems (WMS), and enterprise resource planning (ERP) systems to talk to each other.

An example of such a model successfully is the Port of Hamburg, where API-based integration has enabled shipping lines, rail operators, and customs agents to coordinate activities on a shared digital surface, minimizing idle time and maximizing port-throughput capacity (Notteboom, 2016).

CASE STUDY: CROSS-PLATFORM INTEGRATION IN INDIAN FREIGHT CORRIDORS

The Dedicated Freight Corridors (DFC) of India like the Eastern DFC and Western DFC are an emerging paradigm of intelligent intermodal integration. The DFCs, intended to divert freight volume back to the railroad, will have the aid of a Logistics Data Bank (LDB) system wherein the container movement information, enabled by RFID and GPS,will be integrated with data within ports, inland container depots and road carriers.

Singh and Bansal (2016) showed the synthesis of multimodal traffic data analysis (vehicle volume, travel time, cargo types, etc.) to aid in the optimization of corridor planning and enhance terminals synchronization. Their research emphasized the necessity of a common data schema and joint governance model to reap the maximum benefit of integration.

Emerging Innovations in Intermodal Coordination

Digital Twins for Corridor Simulation

Digital twins: in real time, digital copies of logistics infrastructure are being introduced to simulate and optimize intermodal transport flows. As another example, Siemens Mobility has created a digital twin of intermodal hubs that models the behavior of trucks, trains, and cranes in different demand and disruption conditions (Thürer et al., 2022).

Federated Learning in Supply Chains

Federated learning can solve the privacy issue of data: AI models can be trained on decentralized data without raw data being transferred. It is particularly useful in intermodal settings where data must be secured but needs to be utilized to optimize it (Tahir & Tariq, 2024).

AI-Based Resilience Modelling

Resilience modeling has recently been backed up by AI algorithms, which have proven capable of predicting disruptions, analyzing alternate routing and mode-switching scenarios, and finding optimal solutions. They are connected in real time with weather data, geopolitical warnings and port congestion indices to enable dynamism in changing environments.

FUTURE DIRECTIONS AND RECOMMENDATIONS

To become truly integrated, intermodal ecosystems, smart logistics require the following recommendations, which are visualized in Figure 8 as evolution of smart logistics over stages of ecosystem integration:

1. **Develop Open Standards:** Technical barriers between industries will be broken by adopting industry-wide open APIs, ontologies, and communication protocols that will facilitate a much easier exchange of data.
2. **Encourage Cooperation:** Governments ought to provide data sharing and co-investment incentives in common digital infrastructure.
3. **Develop Digital Capabilities:** There is a need to have capacity building programs that would assist SMEs and government agencies to embrace and experience the positive impacts of intermodal integration.
4. **Intermodal Governance:** Cross-sector and cross-border coordinating organizations ought to be formalized to harmonize standards, data procedures, and conflict resolutions techniques.
5. **Pilot Innovation Zones:** Smart logistics sandboxes or zones may be places where it is possible to safely test new technologies, regulatory methods, and business models.

Figure 8. Future directions and recommendations for smart logistics

CHALLENGES AND BARRIERS TO ADOPTION

Although the potential of smart logistics technologies is huge, their implementation in global supply chains is not homogeneous. Extra-large multinational logistics companies have already started Artificial Intelligence (AI), the Internet of Things (IoT), Robotics, and Blockchain; nevertheless, the way towards general implementation is still hidden with numerous technical, economic, organizational, and policy-related challenges. Such difficulties not only hinder innovation but also have the potential to embed inefficiencies in logistics systems that are already strained by global shocks, climate imperatives and growing consumer demands. The given section profoundly discusses the complex barriers to the implementation of smart logistics technologies based on modern literature and supported by case facts.

Financial Constraints and Return on Investment (ROI) Uncertainty

Among the obstacles that have received the most mentions is the fact that implementing smart logistics solutions necessitates a large capital investment. Robotic warehouses, IoT-connected fleets, or blockchain-powered logistics ledgers all require massive initial investments, not just in hardware and software but also in integrating those systems with existing ones and training workers to use them (Shee et al., 2021). In the case of many firms, especially small and medium enterprises (SMEs), such investments are tough to entertain unless they have apparent and imminent payoffs.

Besides, ROI in intelligent logistics is difficult to calculate because of such intangibles as customer experience improvement, risk avoidance, and sustainability influence, which do not always appear on financial sheets immediately. Logistics companies with their margins as they are less likely to implement long-term technology planning unless it is combined with either obvious fiscal benefit or governmental support scheme.

Case Insight: According to a survey of logistics SMEs in Southeast Asia in 2021, not more than 30 percent had adopted real-time fleet tracking systems because of cost issues, although they were aware of the operational advantages (Archer et al., 2008).

Legacy Infrastructure and System Incompatibility

One of the basic barriers to the introduction of technology is a fractured and aged infrastructure on which many current logistics structures are built. These inherited systems between manual customs procedures to paper-based inventory monitoring frequently do not possess the interoperability to openly combine with the current computerized advances (Şerbetçioğlu & Oflaç, 2024).

Moreover, the lack of homogeneity of the platforms applied in the transport modes and regions results in a quilt of incompatible systems. As an example, a port can have an IoT-based tracking and predictive analytics, but the inland transportation system can use an analog scheduling model, making real-time visibility useless.

Technical Challenge: The combination of IoT sensor data and blockchain-based verification systems would benefit greatly from standardized APIs and data formats capabilities, which are not reliably available throughout the spectrum of logistics operators or public agencies.

Workforce Resistance and Skills Gap

The most formidable obstacle is most commonly the human aspect of digital transformation. The logistics industry is labor-intensive by tradition, and the shift towards automation and digital coordination causes labor issues related to the fear of job loss, the obsolescence of skills, and role ambiguity.

The employees and lower-level managers in most instances are resistant to new technologies; this is caused by unfamiliarity, absence of training or threats as they perceive them to job security. Also, the skills gap regarding data analytics, cyber-security, AI programming, and robotic systems maintenance is particularly acute and prevents the implementation of technology (Karp et al., 2024).

In their survey of traffic system improvement in Indore, Singh and Prabhakar (2017) also noted that even rudimentary data collecting systems had a difficult time being accepted without capacity-building and outreach efforts to stakeholders. Their evidence highlights the necessity of participatory methods of implementing smart logistics infrastructure.

Cybersecurity and Data Privacy Risks

The more digitized and interconnected logistics operations are, the more exposed they are to cyber threats. Connected gadgets, self-driving cars, and management systems based on the cloud create various points of vulnerability to cyberattacks. In the case of breaches, supply chain failures, information leakage, or even physical damage may occur in case systems managing transport assets get compromised (Cheung et al., 2021).

Although Blockchain is frequently mentioned regarding its security properties, it is not resistant to smart contract bugs, sybil attacks, or the theft of private keys. In the same way, AI models can also be vulnerable to data poisoning and model manipulation.

Risk Example: In 2022 a global freight operator was hit by a ransomware group and IoT-connected warehouse systems were down several days, costing the company millions of dollars in revenue and damaged reputation.

Regulatory and Policy Fragmentation

One of the most significant non-technological obstacles is the unavailability of harmonious regulatory frameworks to facilitate the implementation of emerging technologies in logistics. Transport policies in most nations continue to rely on the old definitions of infrastructure and services and cannot cover autonomous vehicles, digital platforms, or decentralized data systems (Paiva et al., 2021).

Summary of Barriers and Mitigation Strategies

Table 1 talks of the overview of the obstacles and countermeasures of the adoption of smart logistics system.

Table 1. Barriers and mitigation strategies for smart logistics

Barrier Category	Key Challenges	Potential Mitigations
Financial	High upfront costs, uncertain ROI	Public funding, tax incentives, cost-sharing models
Technical	Legacy systems, data interoperability issues	API standardization, cloud-native platforms, phased integration
Workforce	Skills gap, resistance to change	Upskilling programs, change management frameworks
Cybersecurity	System vulnerabilities, data privacy concerns	Cyber hygiene protocols, regulatory compliance, blockchain safeguards
Regulatory	Policy lag, legal uncertainty, international inconsistency	Policy reform, cross-border cooperation, digital regulation updates
Organizational	Leadership inertia, misaligned incentives	Culture transformation, innovation hubs, performance-linked KPIs
Environmental and Social	Emissions from digital infrastructure, automation displacement, inequity	Sustainability scoring, inclusive planning, targeted investments

FUTURE DIRECTIONS AND POLICY IMPLICATIONS

With the ongoing transformation of logistics systems towards digitalization and automation, there is an urgent need to examine where this is heading and to develop prospective policies that will embraces technological developments but meet the social, economic and ecological needs and requirements. Already, the combination of Artificial Intelligence (AI), Internet of Things (IoT), Robotics, and Blockchain has created the basis of smart logistics, but the subsequent round of innovations featuring digital twins, edge AI, and 6G connectivity is likely to push the envelope of supply chain intelligence, agility, and resilience.

The section will look at future trends, how these trends will affect policymaking and strategy, and future direction and strategic recommendations on how to create inclusive, sustainable, and flexible logistics ecosystems.

EMERGING TECHNOLOGIES SHAPING THE FUTURE OF LOGISTICS

Figure 9. Emerging technologies for smart logistics

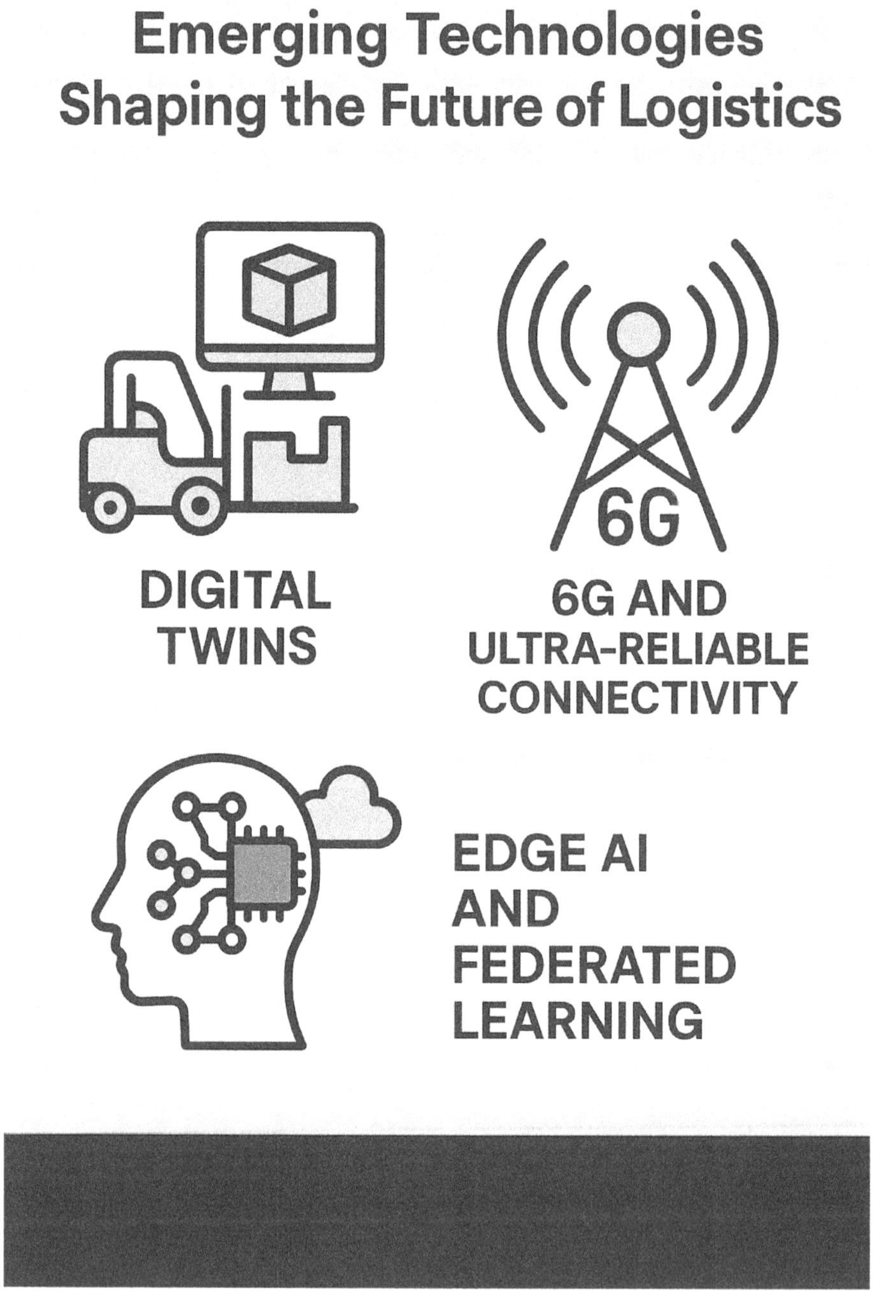

Digital Twins

Digital twin: Digital twin is a real time virtual model of physical logistics systems that can simulate the behavior of operation in various situations as shown in Figure 9. Digital twins (which are made possible with sensors are IoT, AI, and cloud computing) can help logistics planners simulate such disruptions (e.g. port congestion, supply delays), as well as test upstream response strategies to disruptions (Attaran & Celik, 2023).

Edge AI and Federated Learning

Edge AI means the execution of artificial intelligence models locally on a distributed set of devices (e.g., Internet of Things connected sensors, drones) instead of a centralized location in the cloud; see figure 8. This eliminates latency, makes data more private, and enables more rapid decision making in logistics where timing matters.

By extension, federated learning will also allow various stakeholders in logistics to train AI models together without exchanging sensitive data. Technology is especially applicable in cases of intermodal systems, where data ownership, security, and heterogeneity are critical factors (Li et al., 2023).

6G and Ultra-Reliable Connectivity

Whereas the implementation and deployment of the 5G is still ongoing in many parts of the world, the 6G vision has slipped into ultra-reliable low-latency communication (URLLC), far-reaching IoT integration, and AI-native networking architectures as explained in figure 8. In the case of logistics this would permit:

- Real-time addressing of autonomous vehicles
- Centimeter-level precision in tracking cargo in real time
- Fluid transfer of data on multimodal platforms

STRATEGIC TRENDS IN SUPPLY CHAIN EVOLUTION

Decentralization and Platformization

Supply chains are shifting away not only in their processes of single-point illustration but also toward ecosystems that are platform-based and the multi-player interaction (suppliers, shippers, regulators, consumers) access mutual reserves of digital infrastructures. This is reflected in outfits like Cainiao, the Alibaba platform, and Amazon Supply Chain Hub.

Expect modular and plug-and-play supply chains which can be set up or reconfigured largely according to demand shocks, geopolitical discontinuities, or eco-discontinuities, in future.

Resilience Through Redundancy and Intelligence

The pandemic, blockage of the Suez Canal and recent bouts of geopolitical tension have underscored the weaknesses of hyper-efficient but fragile supply chains. Alternatively, Singh et al. (2025) states that resilience is going to be a part of the strategic logic applied by logistics businesses that will demand ethical thinking ahead and technological flexibility to address risks without breaking the continuity line.

Sustainability as a Core Performance Metric

Sustainability is no longer a reporting activity it is a business strategy. Efforts to optimize routes, electrify fleets, and build carbon tracking platforms already qualify as green logistics, and they will come to be included in logistics KPIs.

The creation of carbon accounting blockchains and automated emissions certification will give sustainability assertions quality following and visibility (Batwa & Norrman, 2021).

STRATEGIC RECOMMENDATIONS FOR STAKEHOLDERS

Table 2 talked about strategic recommendations towards the different kinds of stakeholders at smart logistic systems.

Table 2. Strategic recommendations for stakeholders to integrate smart logistics

Stakeholder	Recommendations
Policymakers	Develop adaptive regulations, fund digital infrastructure, promote open standards
Industry Leaders	Invest in digital twins, platform interoperability, and AI-driven resilience models
Academia	Advance interdisciplinary research on ethical, technical, and policy dimensions
SMEs	Join shared digital platforms, access government incentives, prioritize cybersecurity
Tech Providers	Focus on modular, scalable, and secure solutions for diverse logistics settings

SHAPING A DIGITAL AND INCLUSIVE LOGISTICS FUTURE

The future of any smart logistics is not about secluded innovations; rather it is about the system change. With the changing environment in logistics because of new technologies, such as digital twins, federated AI, and 6G, those interested in this sphere must demonstrate forethought and cooperate to make the best of it.

The advances in ethics, policy and engineering will characterize the next epoch of mobility (Singh et al., 2025). The unintelligent, but also unethical, non-inclusive, and unsustainable logistics systems will not form the core of strong economies and liveable cities.

CONCLUSION

The digitalization of logistics and transportation is evolving more and more quickly because of the appearance of such technological solutions as Artificial Intelligence (AI), Internet of Things (IoT), Robotics, Blockchain, Digital Twins, 6G, and Edge AI. This chapter took a very critical look at these technologies, their cross-modal implementation, systemic challenges and policy issues. The association of AI, IoT, Robotics, and Blockchain has turned out to be very tender as the findings of key demonstrations show that it is creating logistics out of a reactionary, manual process to a smart, automated, and networked system. Such technologies allow real-time tracking, predictive maintenance, dynamic routing, last mile automation as well as secure data sharing, which together improve operation agility, transparency and responsiveness to customers. Nevertheless, they are not balanced in their application in the transport road, maritime, and air components because of the imbalance in infrastructure, administrative capability, and stakeholder interactions. The key opportunity on the horizon is intermodal integration of rail, road, air, and sea logistics, whose weaknesses are old systems, data silos, and fragmented regulations. Other scalable adoption obstacles that the chapter observes are capital-intensive, unclear returns on investment, opposition by the workforce, labor gap, cybersecurity threats, and insufficient regulatory policies. The above barriers show that a holistic change involving more than just adoption of technology is important, which should be made through cultures, organizations and policies. According to Singh & Gupta (2021), it refers to such precedents as PRT in the cities of India, emphasizing that technical feasibility and institutional preparedness should come hand in hand to enable sustainable, inclusive, and efficient logistics ecosystems to thrive in increasingly urbanized and demanding nexuses.

This section provides recommendations on how to develop smart logistics strategically, to guide policymakers, the industry leaders as well as researchers. At the policymaking level, the focus is to come up with the smart logistics country strategies that are consistent with the urban transport, climate, and economic strategies. They are advised that they need to embrace new rules that are adaptive, particularly those that already exist on the way AI, autonomous vehicles, blockchain, and many other things are already being governed in the cases with cryptocurrency. Financial incentives and training of small and medium enterprises (SMEs) to support their digitalization and development of open data protocols through academic-industry partnership are essential. The authors recommend that the leaders in the industry should invest in making platforms more interoperable with open, modular and vendor-neutral systems and develop robust supply chains with redundancy and predictive processes. It is also necessary to focus on cybersecurity by protecting IoT networks, auditing, as well as training employees. Sustainability must be part of logistics key performance indicators (KPIs) based on emissions and waste reduction being certified on blockchain. In the case of researchers and innovators, the idea is to create human-cantered AI that will consider ergonomics, transparency, and trust of the workers. To test the innovations in smart logistics, it is advised to perform real-world pilot projects in the city testbeds environment and living labs. It is also important to address the urban-rural gap by using such technologies as drones, mobile warehouses, and decentralization of smart logistics to provide equal access to smart logistics opportunities. Finally, it is suggested to conduct solid research on the ethical and legal aspects of smart logistics, especially, data ownership and privacy, surveillance, and the effects of automation on society. Collectively, these recommendations are meant to build an inclusive, safe, and sustainable smart logistics ecosystem.

REFERENCES

Abayadeera, M. R. (2024). Digital Twin Technology: A Comprehensive Review. *International Journal of Scientific Research and Engineering Trends*, *10*(4), 1485–1504. DOI: 10.61137/ijsret.vol.10.issue4.199

Ahmad, R. W., Hasan, H., Jayaraman, R., Salah, K., & Omar, M. (2021). Blockchain applications and architectures for port operations and logistics management. *Research in Transportation Business & Management*, *41*, 100620. DOI: 10.1016/j.rtbm.2021.100620

Archer, N., Wang, S., & Kang, C. (2008). Barriers to the adoption of online supply chain solutions in small and medium enterprises. *Supply Chain Management*, *13*(1), 73–82. DOI: 10.1108/13598540810850337

Attaran, M., & Celik, B. G. (2023). Digital Twin: Benefits, use cases, challenges, and opportunities. *Decision Analytics Journal*, *6*, 100165. DOI: 10.1016/j.dajour.2023.100165

Awasthi, S. (2024). Artificial intelligence in supply chain management. *Journal of Student Research*, *13*(1). Advance online publication. DOI: 10.47611/jsrhs.v13i1.5996

Bates, L. (2025, January 20). *How data spaces can impact the future of mobility and logistics - Factual Consulting*. Factual Consulting. https://factual-consulting.com/data-spaces-impact-future-mobility-logistics

Batwa, A., & Norrman, A. (2021). Blockchain Technology and Trust in Supply Chain Management: A Literature Review and Research agenda. *Operations and Supply Chain Management an International Journal*, 203–220. https://doi.org/DOI: 10.31387/oscm0450297

Boorová, B., Mijušković, V., Aćimović, S., & Đurđić, D. (2024). Application of Artificial intelligence in Logistics 4.0: DHL case study analysis. *Ekonomika Preduzeca*, *72*(5–6), 292–304. DOI: 10.5937/ekopre2406292b

Bottcher, B. (2006). The Trans-European Transport Network (TEN-T): history, progress and financing. *Communications - Scientific Letters of the University of Zilina*, *8*(1), 51–54. https://doi.org/DOI: 10.26552/com.c.2006.1.51-54

Cheung, K., Bell, M. G., & Bhattacharjya, J. (2021). Cybersecurity in logistics and supply chain management: An overview and future research directions. *Transportation Research Part E, Logistics and Transportation Review*, *146*, 102217. DOI: 10.1016/j.tre.2020.102217

Du Plessis, M. J., Gerber, R., Goedhals-Gerber, L. L., & Van Eeden, J. (2025). Shaping the future of freight logistics: Use cases of artificial intelligence. *Sustainability, 17*(4), 1355. DOI: 10.3390/su17041355

Fatorachian, H., Kazemi, H., & Pawar, K. (2025). Enhancing smart city logistics through IoT-Enabled Predictive Analytics: A digital twin and cybernetic feedback approach. *Smart Cities, 8*(2), 56. DOI: 10.3390/smartcities8020056

Hofmann, E., Strewe, U. M., & Bosia, N. (2017). Supply chain finance and blockchain technology. In *SpringerBriefs in finance*. https://doi.org/DOI: 10.1007/978-3-319-62371-9

Jain, R., Singh, S. K., Palaniappan, D., & Parmar, K.. (2023). Data-Driven Civil Engineering: Applications of Artificial Intelligence, Machine Learning, and Deep Learning. *Turkish Journal of Engineering, 9*(2), 354–377. DOI: 10.31127/tuje.1581564

Kamargianni, M., Li, W., Matyas, M., & Schäfer, A. (2016). A critical review of new mobility services for urban transport. *Transportation Research Procedia, 14*, 3294–3303. DOI: 10.1016/j.trpro.2016.05.277

Karp, V., Burko, I., Murenets, I., Polynyak, V., & Krysovatyy, I. (2024). Enhancing competitive advantage through digital innovation and organisational culture in the logistics sector. *Salud Ciencia Y Tecnología - Serie De Conferencias, 3*. https://doi.org/DOI: 10.56294/sctconf2024.1165

Kurniadi, W. (2025). Digital transformation in the transportation and logistics industry. *Siber Journal of Transportation and Logistics, 3*(1), 1–6. DOI: 10.38035/sjtl.v3i1.429

Li, Q., Cui, Y., Song, T., & Zheng, L. (2023). Federated Multiagent Actor–Critic Learning Task offloading in Intelligent Logistics. *IEEE Internet of Things Journal, 10*(13), 11696–11707. DOI: 10.1109/jiot.2023.3244783

Mohammad, A. S., Khanfar, I. A., Oraini, B. A., Vasudevan, A., Suleiman, I. M., & Fei, Z. (2024). Predictive analytics on artificial intelligence in supply chain optimization. *Data & Metadata, 3*, 395. DOI: 10.56294/dm2024395

Notteboom, T. (2016). The adaptive capacity of container ports in an era of mega vessels: The case of upstream seaports Antwerp and Hamburg. *Journal of Transport Geography, 54*, 295–309. DOI: 10.1016/j.jtrangeo.2016.06.002

Paiva, S., Ahad, M., Tripathi, G., Feroz, N., & Casalino, G. (2021). Enabling Technologies for urban smart mobility: Recent trends, opportunities and challenges. *Sensors (Basel), 21*(6), 2143. DOI: 10.3390/s21062143 PMID: 33803903

Pandey, S. C., & P, V. K. (2025). Adaptive AI-Driven Toll Management: Enhancing traffic flow and sustainability through Real-Time prediction, allocation, and task optimization. *Future Transportation*, *5*(1), 21. DOI: 10.3390/futuretransp5010021

Pham, T. Y. (2023). A smart port development: Systematic literature and bibliometric analysis. *The Asian Journal of Shipping and Logistics*, *39*(3), 57–62. DOI: 10.1016/j.ajsl.2023.06.005

Qiu, F., Chen, M., Wang, L., Ying, Y., & Tang, T. (2023). The architecture evolution of intelligent factory logistics digital twin from planning, implement to operation. *Advances in Mechanical Engineering*, *15*(9). Advance online publication. DOI: 10.1177/16878132231198339

Rodrigue, J. (2020). The geography of transport systems. In *Routledge eBooks*. https://doi.org/DOI: 10.4324/9780429346323

Sainath, K. L. (2024). Robots in Logistics: Apprehension of current status and future trends in Indian warehouses. In *Lecture notes in electrical engineering* (pp. 201–211). https://doi.org/DOI: 10.1007/978-981-97-8031-0_21

Şerbetçioğlu, C., & Oflaç, B. S. (2024). Emerging Trends in Supply Chain Resilience: A Systematic Literature review. *Markets Globalization & Development Review*, *9*(4). Advance online publication. DOI: 10.23860/mgdr-2024-09-04-04

Shee, H. K., Miah, S. J., & De Vass, T. (2021). Impact of smart logistics on smart city sustainable performance: An empirical investigation. *International Journal of Logistics Management*, *32*(3), 821–845. DOI: 10.1108/ijlm-07-2020-0282

Singh, S. K., & Bansal, A. (2016). Multimodal Interpretation and Analysis of Traffic Survey Data. *International Journal of Innovative Research in Science, Engineering and Technology*, *5*(5), 7040–7048. https://www.ijirset.com/upload/2016/may/59_Multimodal.pdf

Singh, S. K., & Gupta, T. (2021). Critical Analysis and Feasibility of PRT for Gurgaon City. *International Journal of Scientific Research in Science, Engineering and Technology*, *8*(1), 83–86. DOI: 10.32628/IJSRSET21812

Singh, S. K., Jain, R., Palaniappan, D., & Parmar, K.. (2025). Future of Mobility: Potential Challenges and Ethical Considerations. In *AIoT for Smart Transportation: Transforming the Future of Mobility*. IET Publishers., DOI: 10.1049/PBTR047E_ch12

Singh, S. K., & Prabhakar, K. (2017). Statistical Analysis of Traffic of Rotary Intersection. *International Journal of Engineering Sciences & Research Technology*, *6*(2), 327–334. DOI: 10.5281/zenodo.290268

Singh, S. K., & Saraswat, A. (2019). Design service volume, capacity, level of service calculation and forecasting for a semi-urban city. *Revue d'Intelligence Artificielle, 33*(2), 139–143. DOI: 10.18280/ria.330209

Tahir, B., & Tariq, M. (2024). Federated learning for Supply Chain Management 5.0. In *Federated Learning for Multimedia Data Processing and Security in Industry 5.0* (pp. 181–201). https://doi.org/DOI: 10.1049/pbpc066e_ch9

Thürer, M., Li, S. S., & Qu, T. (2022). Digital Twin Architecture for Production Logistics: The Critical role of Programmable Logic Controllers (PLCS). *Procedia Computer Science, 200*, 710–717. DOI: 10.1016/j.procs.2022.01.269

Tubis, A. A., & Rohman, J. (2023). Intelligent Warehouse in Industry 4.0—Systematic Literature review. *Sensors (Basel), 23*(8), 4105. DOI: 10.3390/s23084105 PMID: 37112446

Tubis, A. A., Ryczyński, J., & Żurek, A. (2021). Risk assessment for the use of drones in warehouse operations in the first phase of introducing the service to the market. *Sensors (Basel), 21*(20), 6713. DOI: 10.3390/s21206713 PMID: 34695924

Vural, C. A., Roso, V., Halldórsson, Á., Ståhle, G., & Yaruta, M. (2020). Can digitalization mitigate barriers to intermodal transport? An exploratory study. *Research in Transportation Business & Management, 37*, 100525. DOI: 10.1016/j.rtbm.2020.100525

Wang, J., Liu, J., Wang, F., & Yue, X. (2021). Blockchain technology for port logistics capability: Exclusive or sharing. *Transportation Research Part B: Methodological, 149*, 347–392. DOI: 10.1016/j.trb.2021.05.010

KEY TERMS AND DEFINITIONS

Smart Logistics: Integration of advanced technologies (IoT, AI, robotics) and data analytics to optimize logistics processes, enabling real-time tracking, predictive maintenance, warehouse automation, and resilient supply chain coordination.

Intelligent Transportation Systems (ITS): Digital infrastructure using sensors, AI, and communication technologies to enhance transport efficiency, safety, and sustainability by managing traffic flow, reducing congestion, and minimizing emissions.

Digital Supply Chains: Networked ecosystems connecting suppliers, manufacturers, distributors, and retailers via shared digital platforms for seamless data exchange and operational coordination.

Internet of Things (IoT): Network of sensor-equipped physical assets (vehicles, containers, infrastructure) transmitting real-time data on location, condition, and status to optimize tracking, routing, and maintenance.

Artificial Intelligence (AI): Algorithms simulating human cognition to perform logistics functions like demand forecasting, route optimization, anomaly detection, and customer service automation.

Robotics: Autonomous systems (e.g., AMRs, drones, robotic arms) automating physical tasks such as warehouse picking, sorting, last-mile delivery, and port operations.

Blockchain: Decentralized ledger technology ensuring data integrity for secure logistics documentation, contract execution, and transparent cargo provenance tracking.

Predictive Maintenance: AI-driven analysis of IoT sensor data to anticipate equipment failures, reducing downtime and optimizing fleet/asset utilization.

Last-Mile Delivery: Final logistics phase involving parcel transport to end-consumers, optimized via drones, autonomous robots, or dynamic routing algorithms to address e-commerce demands.

Autonomous Guided Vehicles (AGVs): Self-navigating robots using LiDAR/SLAM technology for material transport in warehouses or ports, enhancing efficiency and safety.

Compilation of References

Aarthi, S., Aravinthan, K., Ravikumar, R. N., Sivakumar, N., & Wanglen, S. (2025). Cryptography securing data in motion within Blockchain, internet of everything, and Federated Learning. In *Convergence of Blockchain, Internet of Everything, and Federated Learning for Security* (pp. 39–78). IGI Global.

Abayadeera, M. R. (2024). Digital Twin Technology: A Comprehensive Review. *International Journal of Scientific Research and Engineering Trends*, *10*(4), 1485–1504. DOI: 10.61137/ijsret.vol.10.issue4.199

Abdelkader, G., Elgazzar, K., & Khamis, A. (2021). Connected Vehicles: Technology Review, State of the Art, Challenges and Opportunities. *Sensors (Basel)*, *21*(22), 7712. DOI: 10.3390/s21227712 PMID: 34833782

Abdelkader, S., Amissah, J., Kinga, S., Mugerwa, G., Emmanuel, E., Mansour, D.-E. A., Bajaj, M., Blazek, V., & Prokop, L. (2024). Securing modern power systems: Implementing comprehensive strategies to enhance resilience and reliability against cyber-attacks. *Results in Engineering*, *23*, 102647. DOI: 10.1016/j.rineng.2024.102647

Adamashvili, N., Zhizhilashvili, N., & Tricase, C. (2024). The Integration of the Internet of Things, Artificial Intelligence, and Blockchain Technology for Advancing the Wine Supply Chain. *Computers*, *13*(3), 72. DOI: 10.3390/computers13030072

Adams, R., Jeanrenaud, S., Bessant, J., Denyer, D., & Overy, P. (2016). Sustainability-oriented innovation: A systematic review. *International Journal of Management Reviews*, *18*(2), 180–205. DOI: 10.1111/ijmr.12076

Adetiloye, T. (2021). Collaboration planning of stakeholders for sustainable city logistics operations. *arXiv preprint arXiv:2107.14049.*

Affia, I., & Aamer, A. (2022). An internet of things-based smart warehouse infrastructure: Design and application. *Journal of Science and Technology Policy Management*, *13*(1), 90–109. DOI: 10.1108/JSTPM-08-2020-0117

Agbelusi, J., Ashi, T. A., & Chukwunweike, S. O. (2024). Breaking down silos: Enhancing supply chain efficiency through erp integration and automation. *International Research Journal of Modernization in Engineering Technology and Science*, *6*(9), 1935–1951. https://www.doi.org/10.56726/IRJMETS61691

Agi, M. A. N., & Jha, A. K. (2022). Blockchain technology in the supply chain: An integrated theoretical perspective of organizational adoption. *International Journal of Production Economics*. Advance online publication. DOI: 10.1016/j.ijpe.2022.108458

Agwu, F. A. (2021). Globalization, Populism, Nationalism and the African Continental Free Trade Area. In *Foreign Policy in the Age of Globalization, Populism and Nationalism* (pp. 261–339). Springer Singapore. https://doi.org/DOI: 10.1007/978-981-16-3372-0_7

Ahi & Searcy. (2013). A comparative literature analysis of definitions for green and sustainable supply chain management. *Journal of Cleaner Production*, *52*, 329–341.

Ahmadi, H. B., Kusi-Sarpong, S., & Rezaei, J. (2017). Assessing the social sustainability of supply chains using Best Worst Method. *Resources, Conservation and Recycling*, *126*, 99–106.

Ahmad, K., Maabreh, M., Ghaly, M., Khan, K., Qadir, J., & Al-Fuqaha, A. (2022). Developing future human-centered smart cities: Critical analysis of smart city security, Data management, and Ethical challenges. *Computer Science Review*, *43*, 100452. DOI: 10.1016/j.cosrev.2021.100452

Ahmad, N. R. (2025). Exploring the role of digital technologies in enhancing supply chain efficiency: A case study of E-commerce companies. *Indus Journal of Social Sciences*, *3*(1), 226–237.

Ahmad, R. W., Hasan, H., Jayaraman, R., Salah, K., & Omar, M. (2021). Blockchain applications and architectures for port operations and logistics management. *Research in Transportation Business & Management*, *41*, 100620. DOI: 10.1016/j.rtbm.2021.100620

Ahmad, T., Aakula, A., Ottori, M., & Saini, V. (2022). Developing A Strategic Roadmap For Digital Transformation. *Journal of Computational Intelligence and Robotics*, *2*(2), 2. https://tsbpublisher.org/jcir/article/view/64

Aka, B. (2019a). Understanding sustainability-oriented innovation: A process perspective. *Journal of Cleaner Production, 235*, 1220 1228 .https://doi.org/DOI: 10.1016/j.jclepro.2019.02.271

Aka, K. G. (2019b). Actor-network theory to understand, track and succeed in a sustainable innovation development process. *Journal of Cleaner Production*, *225*, 524–540. DOI: 10.1016/j.jclepro.2019.04.148

Akkaya, M., & Kaya, H. (2019). Innovative and Smart Technologies in Logistics. *17th International Logistics and Supply Chain Congress (LMSCM), Istanbul, Turkey, January*, 97–105. https://www.researchgate.net/publication/338423597

Alahi, M. E. E., Sukkuea, A., Tina, F. W., Nag, A., Kurdthongmee, W., Suwannarat, K., & Mukhopadhyay, S. C. (2023). Integration of IoT-Enabled Technologies and Artificial Intelligence (AI) for Smart City Scenario: Recent Advancements and Future Trends. *Sensors (Basel)*, *23*(11), 5206. DOI: 10.3390/s23115206 PMID: 37299934

Alatawi, I. A., Ntim, C. G., Zras, A., & Elmagrhi, M. H. (2023). CSR, financial and non-financial performance in the tourism sector: A systematic literature review and future research agenda. *International Review of Financial Analysis*, *89*, 102734. DOI: 10.1016/j.irfa.2023.102734

Alavi, B., Tavana, M., & Mina, H. (2021). A dynamic decision support system for sustainable supplier selection in circular economy. *Sustainable Production and Consumption*, *27*, 905–920.

Albareda, L., & Hajikhani, A. (2019). Innovation for sustainability: Literature review and bibliometric analysis. In *Innovation for sustainability: Business transformations towards a better world* (pp. 35–57). Palgrave., DOI: 10.1007/978-3-319-97385-2_3

Ali, M. H., Chung, L., Kumar, A., Zailani, S., & Tan, K. H. (2021). A sustainable Blockchain framework for the halal food supply chain: Lessons from Malaysia. *Technological Forecasting and Social Change*, *170*, 120870.

Ali, S. S., Kaur, R., & Khan, S. (2023). Evaluating sustainability initiatives in warehouse for measuring sustainability performance: An emerging economy perspective. *Annals of Operations Research*, *324*(1–2), 461–500. DOI: 10.1007/s10479-021-04454-w

Aljohani, A. (2023). Predictive analytics and machine learning for real-time supply chain risk mitigation and agility. *Sustainability*, *15*(20), 15088.

Al-Khatib, A. W. (2023). Internet of things, big data analytics and operational performance: The mediating effect of supply chain visibility. *Journal of Manufacturing Technology Management*, *34*(1), 1–24. DOI: 10.1108/JMTM-08-2022-0310

Allioui, H., Allioui, A., & Mourdi, Y. (2024). *Maintaining effective logistics management during and after COVID-19 pandemic: survey on the importance of artificial intelligence to enhance recovery strategies.* OPSEARCH., DOI: 10.1007/s12597-023-00728-y

Almatrodi, I., Li, F., & Alojail, M. (2023). Organizational Resistance to Automation Success: How Status Quo Bias Influences Organizational Resistance to an Automated Workflow System in a Public Organization. *Systems*, *11*(4), 191. DOI: 10.3390/systems11040191

Al-Mohannadi, A. A., Ertogral, K., & Erkoc, M. (2024). Alternative Fuels in Sustainable Logistics—Applications, Challenges, and Solutions. *Sustainability*, *16*(19), 8484. DOI: 10.3390/su16198484

Alqarni, M. A., Alkatheiri, M. S., Chauhdary, S. H., & Saleem, S. (2023). Use of blockchain-based smart contracts in logistics and supply chains. *Electronics (Basel)*, *12*(6), 1340.

Alrajhi, A., Roy, K., Qingge, L., & Kribs, J. (2023). Detection of Road Condition Defects Using Multiple Sensors and IoT Technology: A Review. *IEEE Open Journal of Intelligent Transportation Systems*, *4*, 372–392. DOI: 10.1109/OJITS.2023.3237480

Alshdadi, A. A., Almazroi, A. A., & Ayub, N. (2025). IoT-driven load forecasting with machine learning for logistics planning. *Internet of Things : Engineering Cyber Physical Human Systems*, *29*, 101441. DOI: 10.1016/j.iot.2024.101441

Alzate, P., Isaza, G. A., & Toro, E. M.. (2024). Operational efficiency and sustainability in smart ports: A comprehensive review. *Marine Systems Ocean Technology*, *19*, 120–131. DOI: 10.1007/s40868-024-00142-z

Amico, C., & Cigolini, R. (2024). Improving port supply chain through blockchain-based bills of lading: A quantitative approach and a case study. *Maritime Economics & Logistics*, *26*(1), 74–104. DOI: 10.1057/s41278-023-00256-y

Amifia, L. K., Riansyah, M. I., & Putra, P. D. (2020). Design of logistic transporter robot system. *Jurnal Ilmiah Teknik Elektro Komputer Dan Informatika*, *6*(1), 19.

Amin Mirjalili, S. M., Aslani, A., & Zahedi, R. (2023). Towards sustainable commercial-office buildings: Harnessing the power of solar panels, electric vehicles, and smart charging for enhanced energy efficiency and environmental responsibility. *Case Studies in Thermal Engineering*, *52*, 103696. DOI: 10.1016/j.csite.2023.103696

Ammar, M., Haleem, A., Javaid, M., Bahl, S., Garg, S. B., Shamoon, A., & Garg, J. (2022). Significant applications of smart materials and Internet of Things (IoT) in the automotive industry. *Materials Today: Proceedings*, *68*, 1542–1549. DOI: 10.1016/j.matpr.2022.07.180

Anderson, P. (1999). Perspective: Complexity theory and organization science. *Organization Science*, *10*(3), 216–232.

Andraško, J., Mesarčík, M., & Hamuľák, O. (2021). The regulatory intersections between artificial intelligence, data protection and cyber security: Challenges and opportunities for the EU legal framework. *AI & Society*, *36*(2), 623–636. DOI: 10.1007/s00146-020-01125-5

Andronie, M., Lăzăroiu, G., tefănescu, R., U ă, C., & Dijmărescu, I. (2021). Sustainable, smart, and sensing technologies for cyber-physical manufacturing systems: A systematic literature review. *Sustainability*, *13*(10), 5495.

Anon, S. Y., Amin, S. H., & Baki, F. (2024). Third-Party Reverse Logistics Selection: A Literature Review. *Logistics (Basel)*, *8*(2), 35. DOI: 10.3390/logistics8020035

Anozie, U. C., Pieterson, K., Onyenahazi, O. B., Chukwuebuka, U. O., & Ekeocha, P. C. (2024). Integration of IoT technology in lean manufacturing for real-time supply chain optimization. *International Journal of Science and Research Archive*, *12*(2), 1948–1957.

Appolloni, A., Jabbour, C. J. C., D'Adamo, I., Gastaldi, M., & Settembre-Blundo, D. (2022). Green recovery in the mature manufacturing industry: The role of the green-circular premium and sustainability certification in innovative efforts. *Ecological Economics*, *193*, 107311. DOI: 10.1016/j.ecolecon.2021.107311

Aránguiz, M., Margheri, A., Xu, D., & Tran, B. (2021). International Trade Revolution with Smart Contracts. In *The Digital Transformation of Logistics* (pp. 169–184). Wiley., DOI: 10.1002/9781119646495.ch12

Aranitou, V., Kostis, P. C., Manioudis, M., & Panagiotopoulou, M. (2024). Retailers and Sustainability: Navigating by the Star of Sustainable Retailing. In *The Economics of Retailing* (pp. 131-156). Palgrave Macmillan, Cham.

Archer, N., Wang, S., & Kang, C. (2008). Barriers to the adoption of online supply chain solutions in small and medium enterprises. *Supply Chain Management*, *13*(1), 73–82. DOI: 10.1108/13598540810850337

Arnob, A. M., & Majumdar, S. (2022). Resilient mobility and logistics systems for future: Bangladesh Perspective. *International Journal of Research and Innovation in Social*, *06*(08), 186–193.

Aryee, R., & Adaku, E. (2024). A review of current trends and future directions in reverse logistics research. *Flexible Services and Manufacturing Journal*, *36*(2), 379–408. DOI: 10.1007/s10696-023-09493-y

Aslan, Ö., Aktuğ, S. S., Ozkan-Okay, M., Yilmaz, A. A., & Akin, E. (2023). A Comprehensive Review of Cyber Security Vulnerabilities, Threats, Attacks, and Solutions. *Electronics (Basel)*, *12*(6), 1333. DOI: 10.3390/electronics12061333

Astill, J., Dara, R. A., Campbell, M., Farber, J. M., Fraser, E. D. G., Sharif, S., & Yada, R. Y. (2019). Transparency in food supply chains: A review of enabling technology solutions. *Trends in Food Science & Technology*, *91*(July), 240–247. DOI: 10.1016/j.tifs.2019.07.024

Atiku, S. O., Jeremiah, A., Semente, E., & Boateng, F. (2024). *Eco-innovation and sustainable development in Industry 5.0*. IGI Global., DOI: 10.4018/979-8-3693-2219-2

Atluri, V., & Singla, A. Dahlström, P., Sukharevsky, A., Gaffey, B., Kaka, N., Lajous, T., Travasoni, A., & Vieira, B. (2024). *Beyond the hype: Capturing the potential of AI and gen AI in tech, media, and telecom*. McKinsey. https://www.mckinsey.com/industries/technology-media-and-telecommunications/our-insights/beyond-the-hype-capturing-the-potential-of-ai-and-gen-ai-in-tmt#/

Attaran, M., & Celik, B. G. (2023). Digital Twin: Benefits, use cases, challenges, and opportunities. *Decision Analytics Journal*, *6*, 100165. DOI: 10.1016/j.dajour.2023.100165

Attia, A. (2025). The effect of commitment to sustainable supply chain management and reverse logistics on performance in context of UAE food industry. *Sustainable Futures : An Applied Journal of Technology, Environment and Society*, *9*, 100442. DOI: 10.1016/j.sftr.2025.100442

Atzori, L., Iera, A., & Morabito, G. (2010). The Internet of Things: A survey. *Computer Networks*, *54*(15), 2787–2805. DOI: 10.1016/j.comnet.2010.05.010

Awais, M., Naseer, M., Khan, S., Anwer, R. M., Cholakkal, H., Shah, M., Yang, M. H., & Khan, F. S. (2023). Foundational models defining a new era in vision: A survey and outlook. *arXiv preprint arXiv:2307.13721*, 1–40.

Awasthi, A., Govindan, K., & Gold, S. (2018). Multi-tier sustainable global supplier selection using a fuzzy AHP-VIKOR based approach. *International Journal of Production Economics*, *195*, 106–117.

Awasthi, S. (2024). Artificial intelligence in supply chain management. *Journal of Student Research*, *13*(1). Advance online publication. DOI: 10.47611/jsrhs.v13i1.5996

Baah, C., Amponsah, K. T., Issau, K., Ofori, D., Acquah, I. S. K., & Agyeman, D. O. (2021). Examining the interconnections between sustainable logistics practices, environmental reputation and financial performance: A mediation approach. *Vision (Basel)*, *25*(1), 47–64.

Baah, C., Jin, Z., & Tang, L. (2020). Organizational and regulatory stakeholder pressures friends or foes to green logistics practices and financial performance: Investigating corporate reputation as a missing link. *Journal of Cleaner Production*, *247*, 119125. DOI: 10.1016/j.jclepro.2019.119125

Bakhtiari, S., Breunig, R., Magnani, L., & Zhang, J. (2020). Financial Constraints and Small and Medium Enterprises: A Review*. *The Economic Record*, *96*(315), 506–523. DOI: 10.1111/1475-4932.12560

Balloni, A., Monferdini, L., & Bottani, E. (2025). The Impact of Additive Manufacturing on Supply Chain Management: Trends, Challenges and Future Directions. *Procedia Computer Science*, *253*, 2961–2970. DOI: 10.1016/j.procs.2025.02.020

Bansal, P., & Song, H. C. (2017). Similar but not the same: Differentiating corporate sustainability from corporate responsibility. *The Academy of Management Annals*, *11*(1), 105–149.

Baricako, J., & Kedir, A. M. (2020). *Disruptive Technology*. Foreign Direct Investment and Private Sector Development Polices in Africa., DOI: 10.1007/978-3-030-40647-9_11

Barney, J. (1991). Firm Resources and Sustained Competitive Advantage. *Journal of Management*.

Bartolotti, G., Guidani, B., Ronzoni, M., Manzini, R., & Accorsi, R. (2025). Data architecture framework for reverse logistics management in reusable food packaging networks. *Procedia Computer Science*, *253*, 1343–1351. DOI: 10.1016/j.procs.2025.01.196

Barykin, S. E., Borisoglebskaya, L. N., Provotorov, V. V., Kapustina, I. V., Sergeev, S. M., De La Poza Plaza, E., & Saychenko, L. (2021). Sustainability of management decisions in a digital logistics network. *Sustainability*, *13*(16), 9289.

Barykin, S., Strimovskaya, A., Sergeev, S., Borisoglebskaya, L., Dedyukhina, N., Sklyarov, I., Sklyarova, J., & Saychenko, L. (2023). Smart city logistics on the basis of digital tools for ESG goals achievement. *Sustainability*, *15*(6), 5507.

Bates, L. (2025, January 20). *How data spaces can impact the future of mobility and logistics - Factual Consulting*. Factual Consulting. https://factual-consulting.com/data-spaces-impact-future-mobility-logistics

Batwa, A., & Norrman, A. (2021). Blockchain Technology and Trust in Supply Chain Management: A Literature Review and Research agenda. *Operations and Supply Chain Management an International Journal*, 203–220. https://doi.org/DOI: 10.31387/oscm0450297

Bayomi, N., & Fernandez, J. E. (2023). Eyes in the Sky: Drones Applications in the Built Environment under Climate Change Challenges. *Drones (Basel)*, *7*(10), 637. DOI: 10.3390/drones7100637

Bazaki, E., & Wanick, V. (Eds.). (2023). *Reinventing Fashion Retailing: Digitalising, Gamifying, Entrepreneuring*. Springer International Publishing., DOI: 10.1007/978-3-031-11185-3

Ben-Daya, M., Hassini, E., & Bahroun, Z. (2019). Internet of things and supply chain management: A literature review. *International Journal of Production Research*, *57*(15-16), 4719–4742. DOI: 10.1080/00207543.2017.1402140

Benjaafar, S., Li, Y., & Daskin, M. (2012). Carbon footprint and the management of supply chains: Insights from simple models. *IEEE Transactions on Automation Science and Engineering*, *10*(1), 99–116. DOI: 10.1109/TASE.2012.2203304

Bentamar, A., Taj, K., & Ourahou, O. (2021). Resource-Based Approaches: A Framework for Analyzing Competitiveness in the Context of Reverse Logistics. *European Scientific Journal ESJ*, *17*(19). Advance online publication. DOI: 10.19044/esj.2021.v17n19p194

Bertalanffy, L. V. (1968). General systems theory as integrating factor in contemporary science. *Akten des XIV. Internationalen Kongresses für Philosophie*, *2*, 335–340.

Beske-Janssen, P., Schaltegger, S., & Liedke, S. (2019). Performance measurement in sustainable supply chain management: Linking research and practice. In *Handbook on the Sustainable Supply Chain* (pp. 331–356). Edward Elgar Publishing.

Beverungen, D., Buijs, J. C. A. M., Becker, J., Di Ciccio, C., van der Aalst, W. M. P., Bartelheimer, C., vom Brocke, J., Comuzzi, M., Kraume, K., Leopold, H., Matzner, M., Mendling, J., Ogonek, N., Post, T., Resinas, M., Revoredo, K., del-Río-Ortega, A., La Rosa, M., Santoro, F. M., & Wolf, V. (2021). Seven paradoxes of business process management in a hyper-connected world. *Business & Information Systems Engineering*, *63*(2), 145–156. DOI: 10.1007/s12599-020-00646-z

Bhowmik, O., Chowdhury, S., Ashik, J. H., Mahmud, G. I., Khan, M. M., & Hossain, N. U. I. (2024). Application of artificial intelligence in reverse logistics: A bibliometric and network analysis. *Supply Chain Analytics*, *7*, 100076. DOI: 10.1016/j.sca.2024.100076

Bhuiyan, M. N., Rahman, M. M., Billah, M. M., & Saha, D. (2021). Internet of Things (IoT): A Review of Its Enabling Technologies in Healthcare Applications, Standards Protocols, Security, and Market Opportunities. *IEEE Internet of Things Journal, 8*(13), 10474–10498. DOI: 10.1109/JIOT.2021.3062630

Biclesanu, I., Anagnoste, S., Branga, O., & Savastano, M. (2021). Digital entrepreneurship: Public perception of barriers, drivers, and future. *Administrative Sciences, 11*(4), 125. DOI: 10.3390/admsci11040125

Birasnav, M., Chaudhary, R., Dunne, J. H., Bienstock, J., & Seaman, C. (2022). Green supply chain management: A theoretical framework and research directions. *Computers & Industrial Engineering, 172*, 108441.

Birkbeck, A., & Weston, P. (2024). Seeking ambidexterity through hyperautomation: What next for GBA logistics in their evolution from local labour entrepreneurs to global players in logistics. *Journal of Information Technology Teaching Cases.* https://doi.org/DOI: 10.1177/20438869241261074

Bogina, V., Hartman, A., Kuflik, T., & Shulner-Tal, A. (2022). Educating Software and AI Stakeholders About Algorithmic Fairness, Accountability, Transparency and Ethics. *International Journal of Artificial Intelligence in Education, 32*(3), 808–833. DOI: 10.1007/s40593-021-00248-0

Boorová, B., Mijušković, V., Aćimović, S., & Đurđić, D. (2024). Application of Artificial intelligence in Logistics 4.0: DHL case study analysis. *Ekonomika Preduzeca, 72*(5–6), 292–304. DOI: 10.5937/ekopre2406292b

Bothra, P., Karmakar, R., Bhattacharya, S., & De, S. (2021). How can applications of blockchain and Artificial Intelligence improve performance of Internet of Things*?*
. Survey (London, England).

Bottcher, B. (2006). The Trans-European Transport Network (TEN-T): history, progress and financing. *Communications - Scientific Letters of the University of Zilina, 8*(1), 51–54. https://doi.org/DOI: 10.26552/com.c.2006.1.51-54

Boute, R. N., & Udenio, M. (2022). AI in logistics and supply chain management. In *Global logistics and supply chain strategies for the 2020s: Vital skills for the next generation* (pp. 49–65). Springer., DOI: 10.1007/978-3-030-95764-3_3

Bozzi, C., Neves, M., & Mont'Alvão, C. (2022). Fashion E-Tail and the Impact of Returns: Mapping Processes and the Consumer Journey towards More Sustainable Practices. *Sustainability, 14*(9), 5328. DOI: 10.3390/su14095328

Bronner, W., Gebauer, H., Lamprecht, C., & Wortmann, F. (2021). Sustainable AIoT: How Artificial Intelligence and the Internet of Things Affect Profit, People, and Planet. In *Connected Business* (pp. 137–154). Springer International Publishing., DOI: 10.1007/978-3-030-76897-3_8

Buchter, L. (2021). Escaping the Ellipsis of Diversity: Insider Activists' Use of Implementation Resources to Influence Organization Policy. *Administrative Science Quarterly*, *66*(2), 521–565. DOI: 10.1177/0001839220963633

Budak, A. (2020). Sustainable reverse logistics optimization with triple bottom line approach: An integration of disassembly line balancing. *Journal of Cleaner Production*, *270*, 122475.

Bumblauskas, D., Bumblauskas, J., & Mardirosian, M. (2020). Blockchain in Logistics and Supply Chain Management: A Review of the Literature. *Logistics (Basel)*, *4*(3), 18. DOI: 10.3390/logistics4030018

Burke, H., Zhang, A., & Wang, J. X. (2023). Integrating product design and supply chain management for a circular economy. *Production Planning and Control*, *34*(11), 1097–1113.

Camilleri, M. A. (2025). Cocreating Value Through Open Circular Innovation Strategies: A Results-Driven Work Plan and Future Research Avenues. *Business Strategy and the Environment*, bse.4216. https://doi.org/DOI: 10.1002/bse.4216

Camilleri, T., Farrugia, P., & Refalo, P. (2023). A multi-user-centred design approach framework to develop aesthetically pleasing and sustainable OTCP packaging. *Packaging Technology & Science*, *36*(10), 873–887. DOI: 10.1002/pts.2763

Campbell, C., Sands, S., Ferraro, C., Tsao, H.-Y. J., & Mavrommatis, A. (2020). From data to action: How marketers can leverage AI. *Business Horizons*, *63*(2), 227–243.

Cannas, V. G., Ciano, M. P., Saltalamacchia, M., & Secchi, R. (2024). Artificial intelligence in supply chain and operations management: A multiple case study research. *International Journal of Production Research*, *62*(9), 3333–3360.

Cao, Y., Lawson, B., & Pil, F. K. (2024). Social sustainability and human rights in global supply chains. *International Journal of Operations & Production Management*, *44*(1), 370–390. DOI: 10.1108/IJOPM-10-2022-0670

Capobianco, J. P. (2023). The Keys to Successful Ventures in the Future. In *The New Era of Global Services: A Framework for Successful Enterprises in Business Services and IT* (pp. 33–148). Emerald Publishing Limited., DOI: 10.1108/978-1-83753-626-920231003

Carlos Ferreira, J., Elvas, L. B., Correia, R., & Mascarenhas, M. (2024). Enhancing EHR Interoperability and Security through Distributed Ledger Technology: A Review. *Health Care*, *12*(19), 1967. DOI: 10.3390/healthcare12191967 PMID: 39408147

Carnes, C. M., Chirico, F., Hitt, M. A., Huh, D. W., & Pisano, V. (2017). Resource orchestration for innovation: Structuring and bundling resources in growth- and maturity-stage firms. *Long Range Planning*, *50*(4), 472–486. DOI: 10.1016/j.lrp.2016.07.003

Casino, F., Dasaklis, T. K., & Patsakis, C. (2019). A systematic literature review of blockchain-based applications: Current status, classification and open issues. In *Telematics and Informatics* (Vol. 36). https://doi.org/DOI: 10.1016/j.tele.2018.11.006

Centobelli, P., Cerchione, R., & Esposito, E., & Shashi. (2020). Evaluating environmental sustainability strategies in freight transport and logistics industry. *Business Strategy and the Environment*, *29*(3), 1563–1574. DOI: 10.1002/bse.2453

Chandan, A., John, M., & Potdar, V. (2023). Achieving UN SDGs in food supply chain using blockchain technology. *Sustainability*, *15*(3), 2109.

Chang, S. E., Chen, Y. C., & Lu, M. F. (2019). Supply chain re-engineering using blockchain technology: A case of smart contract based tracking process. *Technological Forecasting and Social Change*, *144*. Advance online publication. DOI: 10.1016/j.techfore.2019.03.015

Chang, S. E., Luo, H. L., & Chen, Y. (2020). Blockchain-enabled trade finance innovation: A potential paradigm shift on using letter of credit. *Sustainability (Switzerland)*, *12*(1). Advance online publication. DOI: 10.3390/su1201018

Chang, Y., Iakovou, E., & Shi, W. (2020). Blockchain in global supply chains and cross border trade: A critical synthesis of the state-of-the-art, challenges and opportunities. *International Journal of Production Research*, *58*(7), 2082–2099. DOI: 10.1080/00207543.2019.1651946

Chan, H., & Wahab, M. I. M. (2024). A machine learning framework for predicting weather impact on retail sales. *Supply Chain Analytics*, *5*, 100058. DOI: 10.1016/j.sca.2024.100058

Chari, A., Niedenzu, D., Despeisse, M., Machado, C. G., Azevedo, J. D., Boavida-Dias, R., & Johansson, B. (2022). Dynamic capabilities for circular manufacturing supply chains—Exploring the role of Industry 4.0 and resilience. *Business Strategy and the Environment*, *31*(5), 2500–2517.

Chava, Shri. V. K., & Dharmavaram, V. G. (2025). Al-Driven Predictive Maintenance in Shipyards: Enhancing Project Management Efficiency and Operational Cost Reduction through Statistical, Data-Driven Strategies for MRO Services. *Journal of Information Systems Engineering & Management*, *10*(12s), 63–75. DOI: 10.52783/jisem.v10i12s.1707

Chen, A. P. S., Huang, Y. F., & Do, M. H. (2022). Exploring the challenges to adopt green initiatives to supply chain management for manufacturing industries. *Sustainability*, *14*(20), 13516. DOI: 10.3390/su142013516

Chen, D. Q., Preston, D. S., & Swink, M. (2021). How big data analytics affects supply chain decision-making: An empirical analysis. *Journal of the Association for Information Systems*, *22*(5), 1224–1244.

Chen, Q., Lei, Y., & Jasin, S. (2024). Real-time spatial–intertemporal pricing and relocation in a ride-hailing network: Near-optimal policies and the value of dynamic pricing. *Operations Research*. Advance online publication. DOI: 10.1287/opre.2022.2425

Chen, W., Men, Y., Fuster, N., Osorio, C., & Juan, A. A. (2024). Artificial intelligence in logistics optimization with sustainable criteria: A review. *Sustainability*, *16*(21), 9145. DOI: 10.3390/su16219145

Chen, Y.-C., & Hasan, M. K. (2023). Impacts of liner shipping connectivity and global competitiveness on logistics performance: The mediating role of the quality of port and infrastructure. *Transport*, *38*(2), 87–104. DOI: 10.3846/transport.2023.19372

Chen, Y., Zhang, X., Ji, J., & Zhang, C. (2024). Cold chain transportation energy conservation and emission reduction based on phase change materials under dual-carbon background: A review. *Journal of Energy Storage*, *86*, 111258. DOI: 10.1016/j.est.2024.111258

Cheung, K., Bell, M. G., & Bhattacharjya, J. (2021). Cybersecurity in logistics and supply chain management: An overview and future research directions. *Transportation Research Part E, Logistics and Transportation Review*, *146*, 102217. DOI: 10.1016/j.tre.2020.102217

Chidukwani, A., Zander, S., & Koutsakis, P. (2022). A Survey on the Cyber Security of Small-to-Medium Businesses: Challenges, Research Focus and Recommendations. *IEEE Access : Practical Innovations, Open Solutions*, *10*, 85701–85719. DOI: 10.1109/ACCESS.2022.3197899

Choi, S.-B., Ahn, Y.-H., Ma, J.-H., & Dar, Q. F. (2025). Blockchain-Based Revision of Korea's E-Bill of Lading Act in Line with Rotterdam Rules. *Journal of Korea Trade*, *29*(1), 25–51. DOI: 10.35611/jkt.2025.29.1.25

Choi, T. M., Wallace, S. W., & Wang, Y. (2018). Big Data Analytics in Operations Management. *Production and Operations Management*, *27*(10). Advance online publication. DOI: 10.1111/poms.12838

Choi, T., Kumar, S., Yue, X., & Chan, H. (2022). Disruptive Technologies and Operations Management in the Industry 4.0 Era and Beyond. *Production and Operations Management*, *31*(1), 9–31. DOI: 10.1111/poms.13622

Chowdhury, A., Karmakar, G., Kamruzzaman, J., Jolfaei, A., & Das, R. (2020). Attacks on Self-Driving Cars and Their Countermeasures: A Survey. *IEEE Access : Practical Innovations, Open Solutions*, *8*, 207308–207342. DOI: 10.1109/ACCESS.2020.3037705

Chowdhury, P., Paul, S. K., Kaisar, S., & Moktadir, M. A. (2021). COVID-19 pandemic related supply chain studies: A systematic review. *Transportation Research Part E, Logistics and Transportation Review*, *148*, 102271. PMID: 33613082

Christidis, K., & Devetsikiotis, M. (2016). Blockchains and Smart Contracts for the Internet of Things. In *IEEE Access* (Vol. 4). https://doi.org/DOI: 10.1109/ACCESS.2016.2566339

Christopher, M. (2016). *Logistics and Supply Chain Management: Logistics & Supply Chain Management*. Pearson UK.

Chung, S. H. (2021). Applications of smart technologies in logistics and transport: A review. *Transportation Research Part E, Logistics and Transportation Review*, *153*, 102455. Advance online publication. DOI: 10.1016/j.tre.2021.102455

Cichosz, M., Wallenburg, C. M., & Knemeyer, A. M. (2020). Digital transformation at logistics service providers: Barriers, success factors and leading practices. *International Journal of Logistics Management*, *31*(2), 209–238. DOI: 10.1108/IJLM-08-2019-0229

Cirillo, V., Massimo, F. S., Rinaldini, M., Staccioli, J., & Virgillito, M. E. (2024). Monopoly Power upon the World of Work: A Workplace Analysis in the Logistics Segment Under Automation. *Review of Political Economy*, •••, 1–33. DOI: 10.1080/09538259.2024.2419611

Colucciello, A. (2025). *Drivers and Barriers to the implementation of the Digital Product Passport* [Master's Thesis in Sustainability Transition Management, University of Bologna]. https://amslaurea.unibo.it/id/eprint/34334/1/TesiMagistrale_Albino_Colucciello.pdf

Costantini, F., Thomopoulos, N., Steibel, F., Curl, A., Lugano, G., & Kováčiková, T. (2020). *Autonomous vehicles in a GDPR era: An international comparison* (pp. 191–213). https://doi.org/DOI: 10.1016/bs.atpp.2020.02.005

Coza, H. (2024). Architectural approaches in the production process of logistics spaces. In *Theories and practices for sustainable urban logistics* (pp. 215–233). IGI Global., DOI: 10.4018/979-8-3693-1447-0.ch011

Crosby, M., Nachiappan, Pattanayak, P., Verma, S., & Kalyanaraman, V. (2016). Blockchain Technology - BEYOND BITCOIN. *Berkley Engineering*.

Crouhy, M., Galai, D., & Wiener, Z. (2021). The Impact of Fintechs on Financial Intermediation: A Functional Approach. *The Journal of FinTech*, *01*(01), 2031001. DOI: 10.1142/S270510992031001X

Cuervo-Cazurra, A., & Li, C. (2021). State ownership and internationalization: The advantage and disadvantage of stateness. *Journal of World Business*, *56*(1), 101112. DOI: 10.1016/j.jwb.2020.101112

Cunneen, M., Mullins, M., Murphy, F., Shannon, D., Furxhi, I., & Ryan, C. (2020). Autonomous Vehicles and Avoiding the Trolley (Dilemma): Vehicle Perception, Classification, and the Challenges of Framing Decision Ethics. *Cybernetics and Systems*, *51*(1), 59–80. DOI: 10.1080/01969722.2019.1660541

Czachorowski, K., Brezočnik, M., & Trkman, P. (2019). The role of blockchain technology in improving maritime systems and reducing cybercrime. *Maritime Policy & Management*, *46*(8), 1024–1039. DOI: 10.1080/03088839.2019.1644318

da Costa, T. P., Gillespie, J., Cama-Moncunill, X., Ward, S., Condell, J., Ramanathan, R., & Murphy, F. (2022). A Systematic Review of Real-Time Monitoring Technologies and Its Potential Application to Reduce Food Loss and Waste: Key Elements of Food Supply Chains and IoT Technologies. *Sustainability*, *15*(1), 614. DOI: 10.3390/su15010614

Da Silva, E. R., Lohmer, J., Rohla, M., & Angelis, J. (2023). Unleashing the circular economy in the electric vehicle battery supply chain: A case study on data sharing and blockchain potential. *Resources, Conservation and Recycling*, *193*, 106969.

Dabees, A., Barakat, M., Elbarky, S. S., & Lisec, A. (2023). A Framework for Adopting a Sustainable Reverse Logistics Service Quality for Reverse Logistics Service Providers: A Systematic Literature Review. *Sustainability*, *15*(3), 1755. DOI: 10.3390/su15031755

Dabo, A.-A. A., & Hosseinian-Far, A. (2023). An Integrated Methodology for Enhancing Reverse Logistics Flows and Networks in Industry 5.0. *Logistics (Basel)*, *7*(4), 97. DOI: 10.3390/logistics7040097

Dadashzada, I., Garza-Reyes, J. A., Roy Ghatak, R., & Gonzalez-Aleu, F. (2024). An investigation into the major barriers to the adoption of electric vehicles in last-mile deliveries for sustainable transport. *International Journal of Logistics Management*. Advance online publication. DOI: 10.1108/IJLM-01-2024-0007

Dangsawang, B., & Nuchitprasitchai, S. (2024). A machine learning approach for detecting customs fraud through unstructured data analysis in social media. *Decision Analytics Journal*, *10*, 100408. DOI: 10.1016/j.dajour.2024.100408

Dasaklis, T. K., & Tsoulfas, G. T. (2024). *The Future of Healthcare Supply Chains: Integrating Industry 4.0 Technologies for Improved Resilience and Sustainability* (pp. 533–551). https://doi.org/DOI: 10.1007/978-3-031-70292-1_25

Dattero-Snell, D. (2023). *Appraisal of electric vehicle retrofit for transport decarbonization within agriculture: Whole system approach* (Doctoral dissertation, Cardiff University).

Davenport, T. H., & Rajeev, R. (2018). *Artificial intelligence for the real world*. Boston Business Journal. https://www.bizjournals.com/boston/news/2018/01/09/hbr-artificial-intelligence-for-the-real-world.html

de Almeida Pais, J. E., Raposo, H. D. N., Farinha, J. T., Cardoso, A. J. M., & Marques, P. A. (2021). Optimizing the Life Cycle of Physical Assets through an Integrated Life Cycle Assessment Method. *Energies*, *14*(19), 6128. DOI: 10.3390/en14196128

De Mattos Nascimento, D. L., de Oliveira-Dias, D., Moyano-Fuentes, J., Maqueira Marín, J. M., & Garza-Reyes, J. A. (2024). Interrelationships between circular economy and Industry 4.0: A research agenda for sustainable supply chains. *Business Strategy and the Environment*, *33*(2), 575–596.

De Vass, T., Shee, H., & Miah, S. (2021). IoT in supply chain management: Opportunities and challenges for businesses in early industry 4.0 context. *Operations and Supply Chain Management*, *14*(2), 148–161. DOI: 10.31387/oscm0450293

Del Giudice, M., Chierici, R., Mazzucchelli, A., & Fiano, F. (2021). Supply chain management in the era of circular economy: The moderating effect of big data. *International Journal of Logistics Management*, *32*(2), 337–356.

Deloitte. (2020). *Hyperautomation-The next frontier* (pp. 1–21). https://www2.deloitte.com/in/en/pages/technology-media-and-telecommunications/articles/hyperautomation-the-next-frontier.html

Dey, P. K., Malesios, C., De, D., Budhwar, P., Chowdhury, S., & Cheffi, W. (2022). Circular economy to enhance sustainability of small and medium sized enterprises. In *Supply chain sustainability in small and medium sized enterprises* (pp. 10–45). Routledge.

Di Battista, A., Grayling, S., Hasselaar, E., Leopold, T., Li, R., Rayner, M., & Zahidi, S. (2023). *Future of job report 2023*. World Economic Forum. https://www.weforum.org/publications/the-future-of-jobs-report-2023/

Di Vaio, A., Boccia, F., Landriani, L., & Palladino, R. (2020). Artificial intelligence in the agri-food system: Rethinking sustainable business models in the COVID-19 scenario. *Sustainability*, *12*(12), 4851.

Díaz-Rodríguez, N., Del Ser, J., Coeckelbergh, M., López de Prado, M., Herrera-Viedma, E., & Herrera, F. (2023). Connecting the dots in trustworthy Artificial Intelligence: From AI principles, ethics, and key requirements to responsible AI systems and regulation. *Information Fusion*, *99*, 101896. DOI: 10.1016/j.inffus.2023.101896

Dimri, S. C., Indu, R., Bajaj, M., Rathore, R. S., Blazek, V., Dutta, A. K., & Alsubai, S. (2024). Modeling of traffic at a road crossing and optimization of waiting time of the vehicles. *Alexandria Engineering Journal*, *98*, 114–129. DOI: 10.1016/j.aej.2024.04.050

Ding, Y., Jin, M., Li, S., & Feng, D. (2021). Smart logistics based on the internet of things technology: An overview. *International Journal of Logistics Research and Applications*, *24*(4), 323–345. DOI: 10.1080/13675567.2020.1757053

Dobrovnik, M., Herold, D., Fürst, E., & Kummer, S. (2018). Blockchain for and in Logistics: What to Adopt and Where to Start. Logistics, 2, 18. Consultado en https://www.mdpi.com/2305-6290/2/3/18

Dong, C., Akram, A., Andersson, D., Arnäs, P.-O., & Stefansson, G. (2021). The impact of emerging and disruptive technologies on freight transportation in the digital era: Current state and future trends. *International Journal of Logistics Management*, *32*(2), 386–412. DOI: 10.1108/IJLM-01-2020-0043

Dong, L., Jiang, P., & Xu, F. (2023). Impact of traceability technology adoption in food supply chain networks. *Management Science*, *69*(3), 1518–1535.

Donta, P. K., Murturi, I., Casamayor Pujol, V., Sedlak, B., & Dustdar, S. (2023). Exploring the Potential of Distributed Computing Continuum Systems. *Computers*, *12*(10), 198. DOI: 10.3390/computers12100198

Du Plessis, M. J., Gerber, R., Goedhals-Gerber, L. L., & Van Eeden, J. (2025). Shaping the future of freight logistics: Use cases of artificial intelligence. *Sustainability*, *17*(4), 1355. DOI: 10.3390/su17041355

Dubey, R., Bryde, D. J., Blome, C., Dwivedi, Y. K., Childe, S. J., & Foropon, C. (2024). Alliances and digital transformation are crucial for benefiting from dynamic supply chain capabilities during times of crisis: A multi-method study. *International Journal of Production Economics*, *269*, 109166.

Dubey, R., Gunasekaran, A., Childe, S. J., Papadopoulos, T., Luo, Z., Wamba, S. F., & Roubaud, D. (2019). Can big data and predictive analytics improve social and environmental sustainability? *Technological Forecasting and Social Change*, *144*, 534–545.

Dubey, R., Gunasekaran, A., Papadopoulos, T., Childe, S. J., Shibin, K. T., & Wamba, S. F. (2017). Sustainable supply chain management: Framework and further research directions. *Journal of Cleaner Production*, *142*, 1119–1130.

Durach, C. F., Peers, Y., Wang, Y., & Repasky, T. (2024). Mitigating upstream disruptions: Effects of extended inventories in first-and second-tier suppliers. *Journal of Operations Management*, *70*(8), 1261–1285. DOI: 10.1002/joom.1332

Durán, C., Yazdi, A. K., Derpich, I., & Tan, Y. (2024). Leveraging Blockchain for Maritime Port Supply Chain Management through Multi-criteria Decision Making. *Mathematics*, *12*(10), 1511. DOI: 10.3390/math12101511

Dutta, P., Choi, T.-M., Somani, S., & Butala, R. (2020). Blockchain technology in supply chain operations: Applications, challenges and research opportunities. *Transportation Research Part E, Logistics and Transportation Review*, *142*, 102067. DOI: 10.1016/j.tre.2020.102067 PMID: 33013183

Dwivedi, Y. K., Hughes, L., Ismagilova, E., Aarts, G., Coombs, C., Crick, T., & Williams, M. D. (2021). Artificial intelligence (AI): Multidisciplinary perspectives on emerging challenges, opportunities, and agenda for research, practice, and policy. *International Journal of Information Management*, *57*, 101994. DOI: 10.1016/j.ijinfomgt.2019.08.002

El Boudali, J., Qbadou, M., & Mansouri, K. (2022). Designing of the reverse logistics network for returnable packaging. *2022 14th International Colloquium of Logistics and Supply Chain Management (LOGISTIQUA)*, 1–6. https://doi.org/DOI: 10.1109/LOGISTIQUA55056.2022.9938079

El Moussaoui, A. E. (2025). Impact of logistics pooling on reduction of CO 2 emissions in last-mile logistics. *Management & Sustainability: An Arab Review*, *4*(2), 383–401. DOI: 10.1108/MSAR-04-2024-0023

Elkington, J. (1997). The triple bottom line. *Environmental management: Readings and cases, 2*, 49-66.

Elkington, J. (1997). *The Triple Bottom Line of 21st Century Business*. Capstone.

Ellahi, R. M., Wood, L. C., & Bekhit, A. E. D. A. (2023). Blockchain-Based Frameworks for Food Traceability: A Systematic Review. In *Foods* (Vol. 12, Issue 16). https://doi.org/DOI: 10.3390/foods12163026

Ellithy, K., Salah, M., Fahim, I. S., & Shalaby, R. (2024). AGV and Industry 4.0 in warehouses: A comprehensive analysis of existing literature and an innovative framework for flexible automation. *International Journal of Advanced Manufacturing Technology*, *134*(1–2), 15–38. DOI: 10.1007/s00170-024-14127-0

Emon, M. M. H., Khan, T., Rahman, M. A., Hamid, A. B. A., & Yaakub, N. I. (2025). GreenTech Revolution: Navigating Challenges and Seizing Opportunities. In *AI and Green Technology Applications in Society* (pp. 63–90). IGI Global Scientific Publishing. https://doi.org/DOI: 10.4018/979-8-3693-9879-1.ch003

Emon, M. M. H. (2023). A Systematic Review of the Causes and Consequences of Price Hikes in Bangladesh. *Review of Business and Economics Studies*, *11*(2), 49–58. DOI: 10.26794/2308-944X-2023-11-2-49-58

Emon, M. M. H. (2025). The Mediating Role of Supply Chain Responsiveness in the Relationship Between Key Supply Chain Drivers and Performance: Evidence from the FMCG Industry. *Brazilian Journal of Operations & Production Management*, *22*(1), 2580. DOI: 10.14488/BJOPM.2580.2025

Emon, M. M. H., & Khan, T. (2024). A Systematic Literature Review on Sustainability Integration and Marketing Intelligence in the Era of Artificial Intelligence. *Review of Business and Economics Studies*, *12*(4), 6–28. DOI: 10.26794/2308-944X-2024-12-4-6-28

Emon, M. M. H., & Khan, T. (2024). Unlocking Sustainability through Supply Chain Visibility: Insights from the Manufacturing Sector of Bangladesh. *Brazilian Journal of Operations & Production Management*, *21*(4), 2194. DOI: 10.14488/BJOPM.2194.2024

Emon, M. M. H., & Khan, T. (2025a). The mediating role of attitude towards the technology in shaping artificial intelligence usage among professionals. *Telematics and Informatics Reports*, *17*, 100188. DOI: 10.1016/j.teler.2025.100188

Emon, M. M. H., & Khan, T. (2025b). The transformative role of Industry 4.0 in supply chains: Exploring digital integration and innovation in the manufacturing enterprises. *Journal of Open Innovation*, *11*(2), 100516. DOI: 10.1016/j.joitmc.2025.100516

Emon, M. M. H., & Khan, T. (2025c). The Role of Traditional Media in Crisis Amplification: How Mainstream Media Magnifies Fake News and Ethical Dilemmas in Supply Chain Crises. In *Mass Media and Impact of Fake News on Supply Chains* (pp. 59–90). IGI Global., DOI: 10.4018/979-8-3373-2175-2.ch003

Emon, M. M. H., & Khan, T. (2025d). The Rise of Circular Supply Chains: Recycling and Closed-Loop Systems Could Mitigate Inflationary Pressures. In *Supply Chain Disruptions and Impact on Global Inflation* (pp. 195–226). IGI Global., DOI: 10.4018/979-8-3373-1982-7.ch008

Ermini, C., Visintin, F., & Boffelli, A. (2024). Understanding supply chain orchestration mechanisms to achieve sustainability-oriented innovation in the textile and fashion industry. *Sustainable Production and Consumption*, *49*, 415–430. DOI: 10.1016/j.spc.2024.07.008

Eslamipoor, R., & Sepehriyar, A. (2024). Promoting green supply chain under carbon tax, carbon cap and carbon trading policies. *Business Strategy and the Environment*, *33*(5), 4901–4912. DOI: 10.1002/bse.3721

Esmaeilian, B., Sarkis, J., Lewis, K., & Behdad, S. (2020). Blockchain for the future of sustainable supply chain management in Industry 4.0. *Resources, Conservation and Recycling*, *163*. Advance online publication. DOI: 10.1016/j.resconrec.2020.105064

Fani, V., Bucci, I., Bandinelli, R., & Da Silva, E. R. (2025). Sustainable reverse logistics network design using simulation: Insights from the fashion industry. *Cleaner Logistics and Supply Chain*, *14*, 100201. DOI: 10.1016/j.clscn.2024.100201

Fareed, A. G., De Felice, F., Forcina, A., & Petrillo, A. (2024). Role and applications of advanced digital technologies in achieving sustainability in multimodal logistics operations: A systematic literature review. *Sustainable Futures : An Applied Journal of Technology, Environment and Society*. Advance online publication. DOI: 10.1016/j.sftr.2024.100278

Fariba, S. (2025). A Review of Advances in Retail Product Return Management: The Role of AI and Digital Technologies in Enhancing Sustainability. *Marketing in Service of Nature and Humanity, 36*, 806–823. https://www.researchgate.net/profile/Bente-Fatema-3/publication/389051849

Fatorachian, H., Kazemi, H., & Pawar, K. (2025). Enhancing smart city logistics through IoT-Enabled Predictive Analytics: A digital twin and cybernetic feedback approach. *Smart Cities*, *8*(2), 56. DOI: 10.3390/smartcities8020056

Fedosovsky, M. E., Uvarov, M. M., Aleksanin, S. A., Pyrkin, A. A., Colombo, A. W., & Prattichizzo, D. (2022). Sustainable Hyperautomation in High-Tech Manufacturing Industries: A Case of Linear Electromechanical Actuators. *IEEE Access : Practical Innovations, Open Solutions*, *10*, 98204–98219. DOI: 10.1109/ACCESS.2022.3205623

Felsberger, A. (2018). *An overview of measurement approaches for evaluating the impact of the digital transformation on sustainable supply chain management* (Doctoral dissertation, Alpen-Adria-Universität Klagenfurt).

Feng, Y., Lai, K. H., & Zhu, Q. (2022). Green supply chain innovation: Emergence, adoption, and challenges. *International Journal of Production Economics*, *248*, 108497. DOI: 10.1016/j.ijpe.2022.108497

Ferdaus, M. M., Dam, T., Anavatti, S., & Das, S. (2024). Digital technologies for a net-zero energy future: A comprehensive review. *Renewable & Sustainable Energy Reviews*, *202*, 114681. DOI: 10.1016/j.rser.2024.114681

Fernandez de Arroyabe, I., Watson, T., & Phillips, I. (2024). Cybersecurity Maintenance in the Automotive Industry Challenges and Solutions: A Technology Adoption Approach. *Future Internet*, *16*(11), 395. DOI: 10.3390/fi16110395

Ferraris, A., Santoro, G., & Pellicelli, A. C. (2020). "Openness" of public governments in smart cities: Removing the barriers for innovation and entrepreneurship. *The International Entrepreneurship and Management Journal*, *16*(4), 1259–1280. DOI: 10.1007/s11365-020-00651-4

Ferreira, B., & Reis, J. (2023). A Systematic Literature Review on the Application of Automation in Logistics. *Logistics (Basel)*, *7*(4), 80. DOI: 10.3390/logistics7040080

Filom, S., & Vanhassel, E. (2020). *Blockchain application for shipping industry documents.* 19. https://www.researchgate.net/profile/Siyavash-Filom/publication/343417519_Blockchain_application_for_shipping_industry_documents/links/5f29365aa6fdcccc43a8abe2/Blockchain-application-for-shipping-industry-documents.pdf

Firoozi, A. A., Tshambane, M., Firoozi, A. A., & Sheikh, S. M. (2024). Strategic load management: Enhancing eco-efficiency in mining operations through automated technologies. *Results in Engineering*, *24*, 102890. DOI: 10.1016/j.rineng.2024.102890

Foroughi, A. (2021). Supply chain workforce training: Addressing the digital skills gap. *Higher Education. Skills and Work-Based Learning*, *11*(3), 683–696. DOI: 10.1108/HESWBL-07-2020-0159

Foster, M. N., & Rhoden, S. L. N. H. (2020). The integration of automation and artificial intelligence into the logistics sector. *Worldwide Hospitality and Tourism Themes*, *12*(1), 56–68.

Francisco, K., & Swanson, D. (2018). The Supply Chain Has No Clothes: Technology Adoption of Blockchain for Supply Chain Transparency. *Logistics (Basel)*, *2*(1). Advance online publication. DOI: 10.3390/logistics2010002

Frederico, G. F. (2021). From supply chain 4.0 to supply chain 5.0: Findings from a systematic literature review and research directions. *Logistics (Basel)*, *5*(3), 49. DOI: 10.3390/logistics5030049

Freeman, R. E. (2010). *Strategic management: A stakeholder approach.* Cambridge university press.

Frei, R., Jack, L., & Brown, S. (2020). Product returns: A growing problem for business, society and environment. *International Journal of Operations & Production Management*, *40*(10), 1613–1621. DOI: 10.1108/IJOPM-02-2020-0083

Frikha, R., & Hlali, A. (2023). The evolution of logistics management toward the digital transition. *International Journal of Commerce. Industry and Entrepreneurship Studies*, *3*(1), 66–75.

Frikha, R., & Hlali, A. (2023). The Evolution Of Logistics Management Toward The Digital Transition. International Journal of Commerce. *Industry and Entrepreneurship Studies*, *3*, 66–75.

Frontoni, E., Marinelli, F., Rosetti, R., & Zingaretti, P. (2020). Optimal stock control and procurement by reusing of obsolescences in manufacturing. *Computers & Industrial Engineering*, *148*, 106697. DOI: 10.1016/j.cie.2020.106697

Gafsi, N. (2025). Analysing the impact of renewable energy use, CO_2 emissions, oil production, and oil prices on sustainable economic growth: Evidence from Saudi Arabia using the ARDL approach. *Edelweiss Applied Science and Technology*, *9*(5), 2317–2326. DOI: 10.55214/25768484.v9i5.7465

Gafsi, N. (2025). Machine Learning Approaches to Credit Risk: Comparative Evidence from Participation and Conventional Banks in the UK. *Journal of Risk and Financial Management*, *18*(7), 345. DOI: 10.3390/jrfm18070345

Gafsi, N. (2025). The Role of Customer and Market Orientation in Enhancing Islamic Insurance Performance: Evidence from Tunisia. *Journal of Ecohumanism*, *4*(2), 2429. DOI: 10.62754/joe.v4i2.6636

Gafsi, N., & Louhichi, L. (2025). Role of green finance in sustainable energy transition and economic growth in MENA region. *Edelweiss Applied Science and Technology*, *9*(6), 1704–1717. DOI: 10.55214/25768484.v9i6.8216

Galvez, J. F., Mejuto, J. C., & Simal-Gandara, J. (2018). Future challenges on the use of blockchain for food traceability analysis. In *TrAC - Trends in Analytical Chemistry* (Vol. 107). https://doi.org/DOI: 10.1016/j.trac.2018.08.011

Gandhi, S., Strohmer, M. F., Lakner, M., Hickerson, T., & He, S. (2024). Strong supply chains through resilient operations: Five principles for leaders to win in a volatile world. Wiley.

Ganne, E., & Patel, D. (2019). Blockchain & DLT in trade: A Reality Check. Obtenido de World Trade Organization: https://www.wto.org

Gao, H., Kou, G., Liang, H., Zhang, H., Chao, X., Li, C. C., & Dong, Y. (2024). Machine learning in business and finance: A literature review and research opportunities. *Financial Innovation*, *10*(1), 86. DOI: 10.1186/s40854-024-00629-z

Gardner, T. A., Benzie, M., Börner, J., Dawkins, E., Fick, S., Garrett, R., & Wolvekamp, P. (2019). Transparency and sustainability in global commodity supply chains. *World Development*, *121*, 163–177. PMID: 31481824

Gartner. (2019). *Top 10 strategic technology trends for 2020*. https://www.gartner.com/smarterwithgartner/gartner-top-10-strategic-technology-trends-for-2020

Gartner. (2021). *From automation to autonomy: The supply chain 2035 roadmap* (pp. 1–5). https://www.gartncr.com/en/supply-chain/trends/supply-chain-automation

Gartner. (2022). *The top 8 supply chain technology trends* (pp. 1–7). https://www.gartner.com/en/supply-chain/trends/supply-chain-technology-trends

Geissdoerfer, M., Morioka, S. N., de Carvalho, M. M., & Evans, S. (2018). Business models and supply chains for the circular economy. *Journal of Cleaner Production*, *190*, 712–721.

Genovese, A., Acquaye, A. A., Figueroa, A., & Koh, S. L. (2017). Sustainable supply chain management and the transition towards a circular economy: Evidence and some applications. *Omega*, *66*, 344–357.

George, A. S., George, A. H., Baskar, T., & Sujatha, V. (2023). The rise of hyper-automation: A new frontier for business process automation. *Partners Universal International Research Journal*, *2*(4), 13–35.

Gerakoudi-Ventouri, K. (2022). Review of studies of blockchain technology effects on the shipping industry. *Journal of Shipping and Trade*, *7*(1), 2. DOI: 10.1186/s41072-021-00105-2

Gevaers, R., Van de Voorde, E., & Vanelslander, T. (2009). Characteristics of innovations in last-mile logistics–using best practices, case studies and making the link with green and sustainable logistics. *Association for European Transport and contributors*, 1, 21.

Ghadge, A., Bourlakis, M., Kamble, S., & Seuring, S. (2023). Blockchain implementation in pharmaceutical supply chains: A review and conceptual framework. In *International Journal of Production Research* (Vol. 61, Issue 19). https://doi.org/DOI: 10.1080/00207543.2022.2125595

Ghobadian, A., Talavera, I., Bhattacharya, A., Kumar, V., Garza-Reyes, J. A., & O'Regan, N. (2020). Examining legitimatisation of additive manufacturing in the interplay between innovation, lean manufacturing and sustainability. *International Journal of Production Economics*, *219*, 457–468. DOI: 10.1016/j.ijpe.2018.06.001

Gholipour, A., Sadegheih, A., Mostafaeipour, A., & Fakhrzad, M. B. (2024). Designing an optimal multi-objective model for a sustainable closed-loop supply chain: A case study of pomegranate in Iran. *Environment, Development and Sustainability*, *26*(2), 3993–4027. PMID: 36687734

Giannakos, M. N., Mikalef, P., & Pappas, I. O. (2022). Systematic Literature Review of E-Learning Capabilities to Enhance Organizational Learning. *Information Systems Frontiers*, *24*(2), 619–635. DOI: 10.1007/s10796-020-10097-2 PMID: 33551669

Goel, R., Singla, J., & Kumar, S. (2025). The Digital Circular Economy: Advancing Sustainable Innovation through Technological Integration. In *Sustainability, Innovation, and Consumer Preference* (pp. 441-480). IGI Global Scientific Publishing.

Gogoi, N., Saikia, D., & Neog, P. (2021). Influence of Covid-19 Pandemic on Clothing Interests of Working Women. *International Journal of Current Microbiology and Applied Sciences, 10*(01), 509–516. DOI: 10.20546/ijcmas.2021.1001.062

Gohar, A., & Nencioni, G. (2021). The Role of 5G Technologies in a Smart City: The Case for Intelligent Transportation System. *Sustainability, 13*(9), 5188. DOI: 10.3390/su13095188

Gölgeci, I., Gligor, D. M., Tatoglu, E., & Arda, O. A. (2019). A relational view of environmental performance: What role do environmental collaboration and cross-functional alignment play? *Journal of Business Research, 96*, 35–46.

Golicic, S. L., & Smith, C. D. (2013). A meta-analysis of environmentally sustainable supply chain management practices and firm performance. *The Journal of Supply Chain Management, 49*(2), 78–95.

Gomber, P., Koch, J.-A., & Siering, M. (2017). Digital Finance and FinTech: Current research and future research directions. *Journal of Business Economics, 87*(5), 537–580. DOI: 10.1007/s11573-017-0852-x

Goni, K. M., Mohammed, A., Sundararajan, S., & Kassim, S. I. (2024). Proactive risk management in smart manufacturing: A comprehensive approach to risk assessment and mitigation. In *Artificial Intelligence Solutions for Cyber-Physical Systems*. Auerbach Publications.

Goodarzi, A. H., Jabbarzadeh, A., Fahimnia, B., & Paquet, M. (2024). Evaluating the sustainability and resilience of an intermodal transport network leveraging consolidation strategies. *Transportation Research Part E, Logistics and Transportation Review, 188*, 103616. DOI: 10.1016/j.tre.2024.103616

Govindan, K., Khodaverdi, R., & Jafarian, A. (2013). A fuzzy multi criteria approach for measuring sustainability performance of a supplier based on triple bottom line approach. *Journal of Cleaner Production, 47*, 345–354.

Govindan, K., Rajeev, A., Padhi, S. S., & Pati, R. K. (2020). Supply chain sustainability and performance of firms: A meta-analysis of the literature. *Transportation Research Part E, Logistics and Transportation Review, 137*, 101923.

Gözaçan, N., & Lafci, C. (2020). Evaluation of key performance indicators of logistics firms. *Logistics, Supply Chain. Sustainability and Global Challenges, 11*(1), 24–32. DOI: 10.2478/jlst-2020-0002

Graf, L., & Anner, F. (2021). *Autonomous Vehicles as the Ultimate Efficiency Driver in Logistics.*, DOI: 10.1007/978-3-030-61093-7_15

Greenberg, A. (2018). *The Untold Story of NotPetya, the Most Devastating Cyberattack in History*. Wired.

Gruchmann, T. (2018). Advanced green logistics strategies and technologies. In *Operations, logistics and supply chain management* (pp. 663–686). Springer., DOI: 10.1007/978-3-319-92447-2_29

Gumzej, R. (2021). *Intelligent Logistics Systems for Smart Cities and Communities*. Springer International Publishing., DOI: 10.1007/978-3-030-81203-4

Gunisity, S. R. (2024). Evolution of Automation to Hyperautomation: Leveraging RPA, AI ML, NLP for Optimal Operational Efficiency. *International Journal of Computer Trends and Technology - IJCTT, 72*. https://doi.org//DOI: 10.14445/22312803

Guo, H., & Yu, X. (2022). A survey on blockchain technology and its security. *Blockchain: Research and Applications*, *3*(2). Advance online publication. DOI: 10.1016/j.bcra.2022.100067

Gupta, A., & Singh, R. K. (2020). Managing operations by a logistics company for sustainable service quality: Indian perspective. *Management of Environmental Quality*, *31*(5), 1309–1327.

Gupta, B. B., & Quamara, M. (2020). An overview of Internet of Things (IoT): Architectural aspects, challenges, and protocols. *Concurrency and Computation*, *32*(21). Advance online publication. DOI: 10.1002/cpe.4946

Gupta, S., & Mukherjee, S. K. (2025). Advancing AYUSH Exports Through Sustainability and Ethical Practices: A Path to Global Leadership. https://doi.org/DOI: 10.5281/ZENODO.14929371

Gurtu, A., & Johny, J. (2021). Supply chain risk management: Literature review. *Risks*, *9*(1), 16.

Hackius, N., & Petersen, M. (2017). Blockchain in logistics and supply chain: trick or treat? Digitalization in Supply Chain Management and Logistics (pp. 3-18). Consultado en https://tore.tuhh.de/bitstream/11420/1447/1/petersen_hackius_blockchain_in_scm_and_logistics_hicl_2017.pdf

Hackius, N., & Petersen, M. (2017). Blockchain in logistics and supply chain: Trick or treat? In Digitalization in Supply Chain Management and Logistics (Vol. 23, pp. 3–18). *epubli GmbH*, https://doi.org/ DOI: 10.15480/882.1444

Hadhi, A. (2017). MOL, NYK and K Line to develop trade data sharing platform using blockchain. Lloyd's List. Available at: https://lloydslist.maritimeintelligence.informa.com/LL111092/MOL-NYK-and-K-Line-to-develop-trade-data-sharing-platform-using-blockchain

Haghshenas, S. S., Astarita, V., Haghshenas, S. S., & Guido, G. (2024). Artificial Intelligence-Powered Driver Behavior Analysis for Fuel Consumption Optimization: A Pathway to Greener Roads. *2024 10th International Conference on Control, Decision and Information Technologies (CoDIT)*, 116–122. https://doi.org/DOI: 10.1109/CoDIT62066.2024.10708512

Haleem, A., Javaid, M., Singh, R. P., Rab, S., & Suman, R. (2021). Hyperautomation for the enhancement of automation in industries. *Sensors International*, *2*, 100124. DOI: 10.1016/j.sintl.2021.100124

Han, H., Liu, Z., Wang, X., & Li, S. (2021). Research of the relations among cloud computing, Internet of Things, big data, artificial intelligence, block chain and their application in maritime field. *Journal of Physics: Conference Series*, *1927*(1), 12026.

Hanumantu, D. (2024). Logistics 5.0: The next evolution of logistics systems. *International Journal of Physical Distribution & Logistics Management*, *54*(1), 34–48.

Hardik, N. (2024). Digitalisation promotes adoption of soft information in SME credit evaluation: The case of Indian banks. *Digital Finance*. Advance online publication. DOI: 10.1007/s42521-023-00078-w PMID: 37362067

Harreis, H., Koullias, T., Roberts, R., & Te, K. (2023, March 8). Generative AI: Unlocking the future of fashion. https://www.mckinsey.com/industries/retail/our-insights/generative-ai-unlocking-the-future-of-fashion

Hasan, M. K., Lei, X., Hlali, A., & Bian, Z. (2024). Modelling capability factors of logistics industry based on ISM-MICMAC. *Heliyon*, *10*(22), e40539. DOI: 10.1016/j.heliyon.2024.e40539 PMID: 39641072

Hasan, M. K., Lei, X., Tang, W., Nishi, N. N., & Latif, Z. (2025). *Exploring logistics performance index (LPI) from global perspective: A study based on network analysis (NA)*. Operations Management Research., DOI: 10.1007/s12063-025-00550-3

Hassija, V., Chamola, V., Mahapatra, A., Singal, A., Goel, D., Huang, K., Scardapane, S., Spinelli, I., Mahmud, M., & Hussain, A. (2024). Interpreting Black-Box Models: A Review on Explainable Artificial Intelligence. *Cognitive Computation*, *16*(1), 45–74. DOI: 10.1007/s12559-023-10179-8

Heckmann, I., Comes, T., & Nickel, S. (2015). A critical review on supply chain risk–Definition, measure and modeling. *Omega*, *52*, 119–132.

Helo, P., & Shamsuzzoha, A. H. M. (2020). Real-time supply chain—A blockchain architecture for project deliveries. *Robotics and Computer-Integrated Manufacturing, 63*(November 2019), 101909. https://doi.org/DOI: 10.1016/j.rcim.2019.101909

Helo, P., & Thai, V. V. (2024). Logistics 4.0–digital transformation with smart connected tracking and tracing devices. *International Journal of Production Economics*. Advance online publication. DOI: 10.1016/j.ijpe.2024.109336

Henrich, J., Li, J., Mazuera, C., & Perez, F. (2022). Future-proofing the supply chain. *McKinsey & Company*.

Hensher, D. A., & Wei, E. (2024). Energy and environmental costs in transitioning to zero and low emission trucks for the Australian truck Fleet: An industry perspective. *Transportation Research Part A, Policy and Practice*, *185*, 104108. DOI: 10.1016/j.tra.2024.104108

Herm, L.-V., Janiesch, C., Helm, A., Imgrund, F., Hofmann, A., & Winkelmann, A. (2023). A framework for implementing robotic process automation projects. *Information Systems and e-Business Management*, *21*(1), 1–35. DOI: 10.1007/s10257-022-00553-8

Hervani, A. A., Nandi, S., Helms, M. M., & Sarkis, J. (2022). A performance measurement framework for socially sustainable and resilient supply chains using environmental goods valuation methods. *Sustainable Production and Consumption*, *30*, 31–52.

Hlali, A., Ablanedo-Rosas, J. H., & Ruiz-Torres, A. J. (2023). Operational efficiency of major cargo seaports in some developing regions: Results from a bootstrap DEA. International Journal of Shipping and Transport Logistics, 16(3/4), 1 290-319. https://doi.org/DOI: 10.1504/IJSTL.2023.129874

Hlali, A. (2017). Efficiency of the 26 major container ports in 2015: Comparative analysis with different models. International Journal of Economics & Strategies. *Management of Business*, (10), 15–20.

Hlali, A. (2023). Impact of logistics and economic structure on seaport infrastructure: A case of Mediterranean countries. *Australian Journal of Maritime and Ocean Affairs*, *16*(13). Advance online publication. DOI: 10.1080/18366503.2023.2217584

Hlali, A., & Gafsi, N. (2024). Analysis of Digitalization and Sustainable Development in Africa. *Perspectives on Global Development and Technology*, *22*(5-6), 415–428. DOI: 10.1163/15691497-12341668

Hlali, A., & Wanis, A. (2020). Theoretical highlights in container port logistics systems. *Journal of Marine and Island Cultures*, *9*(2). Advance online publication. DOI: 10.21463/jmic.2020.09.2.13

Hoang, T.-H., Tran, T.-T., Huynh, L. N. T., Vo, D. K., Huynh, B. G., Tran, T. M. T., & Le Nguyen, N. D. (2025). Advances and barriers in promoting green logistics 4.0 from a multi-stakeholder perspective–a systematic review. *Environment Systems & Decisions*, *45*(2), 14. DOI: 10.1007/s10669-025-10006-5

Hofmann, E., Strewe, U. M., & Bosia, N. (2017). Supply chain finance and blockchain technology. In *SpringerBriefs in finance*. https://doi.org/DOI: 10.1007/978-3-319-62371-9

Hofmann, E. (2010). Linking corporate strategy and supply chain management. *International Journal of Physical Distribution & Logistics Management*, *40*(4), 256–276.

Hong, W., Xu, Z., Liu, W., Wu, L., & Pu, X. (2021). Queuing theory-based optimization research on the multi-objective transportation problem of fourth party logistics. *Proceedings of the Institution of Mechanical Engineers. Part B, Journal of Engineering Manufacture*, *235*(8), 1327–1337. DOI: 10.1177/0954405420969266

Horsthemke, J., & Böhm, E. (2025). Different Keep Rewards in Product Return Management. *Marketing in Service of Nature and Humanity*, *36*, 837–840. https://www.researchgate.net/profile/Bente-Fatema-3/publication/389051849

Hosseini-Motlagh, S.-M., Johari, M., Nematollahi, M., & Pazari, P. (2023). Reverse supply chain management with dual channel and collection disruptions: Supply chain coordination and game theory approaches. *Annals of Operations Research*, *324*(1–2), 215–248. DOI: 10.1007/s10479-022-04909-8

Hosseini, Z. S., Flapper, S. D., & Pirayesh, M. (2022). Sustainable supplier selection and order allocation under demand, supplier availability and supplier grading uncertainties. *Computers & Industrial Engineering*, *165*, 107811.

Huang, R., & Mao, S. (2024). Carbon Footprint Management in Global Supply Chains: A Data-Driven Approach Utilizing Artificial Intelligence Algorithms. *IEEE Access : Practical Innovations, Open Solutions*, *12*, 89957–89967. DOI: 10.1109/ACCESS.2024.3407839

Hutton, M., Corus, C., Dorsey, J., Minton, E., Roux, C., Blocker, C. P., & Zhang, J. Z. (2022). Getting real about consumer poverty: Deep processes for transformative action. *The Journal of Consumer Affairs*, *56*(3), 1332–1355. DOI: 10.1111/joca.12479

IBM. (2020). *Blockchain for business: A practical guide*. Retrieved from IBM.

IBM. (2020). *TradeLens: A Blockchain-based Shipping Solution*. Retrieved from IBM.

Ibn-Mohammed, T., Mustapha, K. B., Godsell, J., Adamu, Z., Babatunde, K. A., Akintade, D. D., & Koh, S. C. L. (2021). A critical analysis of the impacts of COVID-19 on the global economy and ecosystems and opportunities for circular economy strategies. *Resources, Conservation and Recycling*, *164*, 105169. PMID: 32982059

Idrees, H., Xu, J., & Andrianarivo Andriandafiarisoa Ralison, N. A. (2023). Green entrepreneurial orientation and knowledge creation process as enablers of green innovation performance: The moderating role of resource orchestration capability. *European Journal of Innovation Management*. Advance online publication. DOI: 10.1108/EJIM-02-2023-0143

Ilango, V. (2025). Challenges and future trends in the hyperautomation of sustainable agriculture. In Singh, S., Sood, V., Srivastav, A. L., & Ampatzidis, Y. (Eds.), *Hyperautomation in Precision Agriculture* (pp. 289–298). Academic Press., DOI: 10.1016/B978-0-443-24139-0.00024-2

Inigo, E. A., & Albareda, L. (2016). Understanding sustainable innovation as a complex adaptive system: A systemic approach to the firm. *Journal of Cleaner Production*, *126*, 1–20. DOI: 10.1016/j.jclepro.2016.02.043

Irannezhad, E., & Faroqi, H. (2023). Addressing some of bill of lading issues using the Internet of Things and blockchain technologies: A digitalized conceptual framework. *Maritime Policy & Management*, *50*(4), 428–446. DOI: 10.1080/03088839.2021.1930223

Irannezhad, E., Mahmud, K., & Islam, T. (2020). Blockchain technology in logistics and transportation: Challenges and opportunities. *Journal of Transportation and Logistics*, *8*(2), 123–135. DOI: 10.1016/j.tra.2019.11.007

Islam, M. S., Moeinzadeh, S., Tseng, M. L., & Tan, K. (2021). A literature review on environmental concerns in logistics: Trends and future challenges. *International Journal of Logistics Research and Applications*, *24*(2), 126–151. DOI: 10.1080/13675567.2020.1732313

Islam, R., Ansari, M. E., Dewan, M. A., Sultana, S., & Rivin, M. A. H. (2024). Supply Chain Management Analysis and Design for a Variety of Economic Scenarios, Including Data and System Administration. *Journal of Software Engineering and Applications*, *17*(10), 770–785.

ISO. (2025). *Reverse Logistics*. 3.5.14 Reverse Logistics - International Standards Organization. https://www.iso.org/obp/ui/en/#iso:std:iso:59004:ed-1:v1:en

Issaoui, Y., Khiat, A., Bahnasse, A., & Ouajji, H. (2019). Smart logistics : Study of the application of blockchain technology. *Procedia Computer Science, 160*(2018), 266–271. https://doi.org/DOI: 10.1016/j.procs.2019.09.467

Iva, B. (2019, December 16). *N*ew TechA Theory—New Technology Acceptance Theory. https://www.linkedin.com/pulse/new-techa-theory-technology-acceptance-iva-blazecki/

Ivanov, D. (2018). Revealing interfaces of supply chain resilience and sustainability: A simulation study. *International Journal of Production Research*, *56*(10), 3507–3523.

Ivanov, D. (2022). Viable supply chain model: Integrating agility, resilience and sustainability perspectives—lessons from and thinking beyond the COVID-19 pandemic. *Annals of Operations Research*, *319*(1), 1411–1431. PMID: 32836614

Ivanov, D., & Dolgui, A. (2021). A digital supply chain twin for managing the disruption risks and resilience in the era of Industry 4.0. *Production Planning and Control*, *32*(9), 775–788.

Ivascu, L., Domil, A. E., Artene, A. E., Bogdan, O., Burcă, V., & Pavel, C. (2022). Psychological and Behavior Changes of Consumer Preferences During COVID-19 Pandemic Times: An Application of GLM Regression Model. *Frontiers in Psychology*, *13*, 879368. DOI: 10.3389/fpsyg.2022.879368 PMID: 35572289

Jabbar, K., & Bjørn, P. (2018). Infrastructural Grind: Introducing Blockchain Technology in the Shipping Domain. *Proceedings of the 2018 ACM Conference on Supporting Groupwork*, 297–308. https://doi.org/DOI: 10.1145/3148330.3148345

Jabbour, C. J. C., & de Sousa Jabbour, A. B. L. (2016). Green human resource management and green supply chain management: Linking two emerging agendas. *Journal of Cleaner Production*, *112*, 1824–1833.

Jacobsen, M. (2023). Mediating Infrastructural Discipline: Established Practices and Changing Structures of Dar es Salaam's Transport Sector. *Urban Forum, 34*(4), 481–500. https://doi.org/DOI: 10.1007/s12132-022-09477-5

Jain, P., Tandon, A., & Bansal, R. C. (2025). *Integration of Renewable Energy Sources (RES) into Electric Vehicle (EV) Charging Infrastructure: State-of-the-Art Review* (pp. 171–214). https://doi.org/DOI: 10.1007/978-981-96-0361-9_9

Jain, G., Sharma, N., & Shrivastava, A. (2021). Enhancing training effectiveness for organizations through blockchain-enabled training effectiveness measurement (BETEM). *Journal of Organizational Change Management*, *34*(2), 439–461. DOI: 10.1108/JOCM-10-2020-0303

Jain, R., Singh, S. K., Palaniappan, D., & Parmar, K.. (2023). Data-Driven Civil Engineering: Applications of Artificial Intelligence, Machine Learning, and Deep Learning. *Turkish Journal of Engineering*, *9*(2), 354–377. DOI: 10.31127/tuje.1581564

Jaouad, K. (2017). Développement des stratégies Supply chain par la mise en place des concepts Lean-Application dans le domaine industriel marocain de la transformation plastique.

Javaid, M., Haleem, A., Singh, R. P., Suman, R., & Khan, S. (2022). A review of Blockchain Technology applications for financial services. *BenchCouncil Transactions on Benchmarks. Standards and Evaluations*, *2*(3), 100073. DOI: 10.1016/j.tbench.2022.100073

Jayarathna, C. P., Agdas, D., & Dawes, L. (2023). Exploring sustainable logistics practices toward a circular economy: A value creation perspective. *Business Strategy and the Environment*, *32*(1), 704–720. DOI: 10.1002/bse.3170

Jayaratne, P. (2024). Technological Advancements and Cost Reduction in 3PL Sector. In *Transforming Logistics in a Developing Nation* (pp. 465–499). Springer Nature Singapore., DOI: 10.1007/978-981-97-7819-5_17

Jean, G. (2024). Supply Chain Visibility and Transparency. ResearchGate. Available at:https://www.researchgate.net/publication/384335325_Supply_Chain_Visibility_and_Transparency/citation/download

Jensen, T., Hedman, J., & Henningsson, S. (2019). How TradeLens delivers business value with blockchain technology. *MIS Quarterly Executive*, *18*(4), 221–243.

Jeyalakshmi, R., & Sagarika, V. (2024). A Study on Reverse Logistics in Customer Satisfaction through Sustainable Supply Chain. *IJMRSET, 7*(12). https://www.researchgate.net/profile/Jeyalakshmi-R/publication/388916839

Jiang, F., Wei, K. K., Ng, S.-P., Amin, M., Herjanto, H., & Liu, J. (2023). How blockchain technology hyperautomatically affects corporate performance by green supply chain? *Enterprise Information Systems*, *17*(10), 2204305. DOI: 10.1080/17517575.2023.2204305

Jiang, T., Wu, X., & Yin, Y. (2023). Logistics Efficiency Evaluation and Empirical Research under the New Retailing Model: The Way toward Sustainable Development. *Sustainability*, *15*(20), 15028.

Ji-Hyland, C., White, D., & Khavdarov, R. (2025). The impact of circular economy practices on sustainable logistics performance. *International Journal of Logistics Research and Applications*, 1–27. https://doi.org/DOI: 10.1080/13675567.2025.2465579

Jing, Z., Lu, S., Zhao, Y., & Zhou, J. (2023). Economic policy uncertainty, corporate investment decisions and stock price crash risk: Evidence from China. *Accounting and Finance*, *63*(S1), 1477–1502. DOI: 10.1111/acfi.13077

Jithin, P., Arayankalam, J., Rajesh, S. P., & Tiwari, A. K. (2024). Decoding the digital leap: Exploring the role of global value chains in driving country-level digitalization. *Journal of Cleaner Production*, *454*, 142208. DOI: 10.1016/j.jclepro.2024.142208

John, L., Patro, R., Padmakala, S., & Madhumala, R. B. (2024). *E-Mobility as a Service and Its Economic Impact.*, DOI: 10.4018/979-8-3693-2611-4.ch003

Jović, M., Filipović, M., Tijan, E., & Jardas, M. (2019). A Review of Blockchain Technology Implementation in Shipping Industry. *Pomorstvo*, *33*(2), 140–148. DOI: 10.31217/p.33.2.3

Jović, M., Tijan, E., Žgaljić, D., & Aksentijević, S. (2020). Improving Maritime Transport Sustainability Using Blockchain-Based Information Exchange. *Sustainability*, *12*(21), 8866. DOI: 10.3390/su12218866

K.V. T., Rattan, P., & Nair, R. R. (2025). Greening the Click-Environmental Initiatives in Global E-Commerce Marketing. In *Green Marketing Perspectives* (pp. 261–272). Emerald Publishing Limited. https://doi.org/DOI: 10.1108/978-1-83608-772-420251021

Kakade, P., Patil, N., Shete, A., Roy, A., & Kalyani, Y. (2024). Digital Apparel Try-Ons: A Technological Odyssey into the World of Virtual Dressing Rooms and Consumer Engagement. [IRJAEM]. *International Research Journal on Advanced Engineering and Management*, *2*(02), 12–19. DOI: 10.47392/IRJAEM.2024.0003

Kalmykova, Y., Sadagopan, M., & Rosado, L. (2018). Circular economy–From review of theories and practices to development of implementation tools. *Resources, Conservation and Recycling*, *135*, 190–201.

Kalubanga, M., & Mbekeka, W. (2024). Compliance with government and firm's own policy, reverse logistics practices and firm environmental performance. *International Journal of Productivity and Performance Management*, *73*(5), 1427–1478. DOI: 10.1108/IJPPM-09-2022-0463

Kamargianni, M., Li, W., Matyas, M., & Schäfer, A. (2016). A critical review of new mobility services for urban transport. *Transportation Research Procedia*, *14*, 3294–3303. DOI: 10.1016/j.trpro.2016.05.277

Kamath, R. (2018). Food Traceability on Blockchain: Walmart's Pork and Mango Pilots with IBM. *The Journal of the British Blockchain Association*, *1*(1). Advance online publication. DOI: 10.31585/jbba-1-1-(10)2018

Kamble, S. S., Gunasekaran, A., & Sharma, R. (2020). Modeling the blockchain enabled traceability in agriculture supply chain. International Journal of Information Management, 52, 101967. Elsevier. https://doi.org/DOI: 10.1016/j.ijinfomgt.2019.05.023

Kamble, S., Gunasekaran, A., & Arha, H. (2019). Understanding the Blockchain technology adoption in supply chains-Indian context. *International Journal of Production Research, 57*(7). Advance online publication. DOI: 10.1080/00207543.2018.1518610

Kamble, S., Pandit, P., & Sansare, S. (2025). The economics of autonomous freight and logistics systems. *International Journal for Multidisciplinary Research*, *7*(2).

Kamewor, F. T., Kwateng, K. O., & Mensah, J. (2024). Green logistics practices: A bibliometric and systematic methodological review and future research opportunities. *Journal of Cleaner Production, 143735*. Advance online publication. DOI: 10.1016/j.jclepro.2024.143735

Kandasamy, J., K E K, V., Ethirajan, M., & Murali, N. (2025). *Circular Supply Chain Management: A Sustainability Approach*. Springer Nature Switzerland. https://doi.org/DOI: 10.1007/978-3-031-81750-2

Kang, T.-J. (2017). HMM completes pilot blockchain voyage with reefer-laden boxship. Lloyd's List. Available at: https://lloydslist.maritimeintelligence.informa.com/LL111275/HMM-completes-pilot-blockchain-voyage-with-reefer-laden-boxship

Kang, P. S., Wang, X., Son, J. Y., & Jat, M. (2024). *Service 4.0*. Springer Nature Switzerland., DOI: 10.1007/978-3-031-63875-6

Kaplan, R. S. (1996). *The balanced scorecard: translating strategy into action*. Harvard Business Review Press.

Karp, V., Burko, I., Murenets, I., Polynyak, V., & Krysovatyy, I. (2024). Enhancing competitive advantage through digital innovation and organisational culture in the logistics sector. *Salud Ciencia Y Tecnología - Serie De Conferencias, 3*. https://doi.org/DOI: 10.56294/sctconf2024.1165

Karulkar, Y., Shah, A., & Naik, R. (2024). AI-powered business evolution. In *Advances in Business Information Systems and Analytics* (pp. 39–72). IGI Global.

Kasap, A. (2025). Sustainable e-commerce: Examining green logistics and digitalization strategies. *Asya Studies*, *9*(31), 261–290. DOI: 10.31455/asya.1622024

Kashem, M. A., Shamsuddoha, M., & Nasir, T. (2024). Digital-Era Resilience: Navigating Logistics and Supply Chain Operations after COVID-19. *Businesses*, *4*(1), 1–17.

Kaswan, K. S., Dhatterwal, J. S., Malik, V., & Rajani. (2025). Hyper Automation 2.0 and Ecosystem Collaboration: Paradigm Shift in SCM. In A. Pandey & F. Al-Turjman (Eds.), *Transformation of Supply Chain Ecosystems* (pp. 281–301). Emerald Publishing Limited. https://doi.org/DOI: 10.1108/978-1-83549-246-820251017

Kaur, H., & Singh, S. P. (2019). Sustainable procurement and logistics for disaster resilient supply chain. *Annals of Operations Research*, *283*(1), 309–354.

Kaushik, V., Kumar, A., Gupta, H., & Dixit, G. (2022). Modelling and prioritizing the factors for online apparel return using BWM approach. *Electronic Commerce Research*, *22*(3), 843–873. DOI: 10.1007/s10660-020-09406-3

Kavaliauskas, Ž., Šajev, I., Blažiūnas, G., Gecevičius, G., & Kazlauskas, S. (2024). Development and Investigation of a Smart Impact Detector for Monitoring the Shipment Transport Process. *Applied Sciences (Basel, Switzerland)*, *14*(16), 7102. DOI: 10.3390/app14167102

Kayikci, Y., Gozacan-Chase, N., & Rejeb, A. (2024). Blockchain entrepreneurship roles for circular supply chain transition. *Business Strategy and the Environment*, *33*(2), 197–222.

Keivanpour, S. (2022). Sustainability balanced scorecard approach to Internet of Things enabled logistics systems. *Engineering Management Journal*, *34*(3), 450–474.

Khan, T., Emon, M. M. H., & Nath, A. (2024). Quantifying the Effects of AI-Driven Inventory Management on Operational Efficiency in Online Retail. *2024 27th International Conference on Computer and Information Technology (ICCIT)*, 2092–2097. https://doi.org/DOI: 10.1109/ICCIT64611.2024.11021996

Khan, T., Emon, M. M. H., & Rahman, S. (2024b). Marketing Strategy Innovation via AI Adoption: A Study on Bangladeshi SMEs in the Context of Industry 5.0. *2024 6th International Conference on Sustainable Technologies for Industry 5.0 (STI)*, 1–6. https://doi.org/DOI: 10.1109/STI64222.2024.10951050

Khan, T., Emon, M. M. H., Rahman, M. A., Hamid, A. B. A., & Yaakub, N. I. (2025). Bridging the Gap: Realizing GreenTech Potential. In *AI and Green Technology Applications in Society* (pp. 91–122). IGI Global Scientific Publishing. https://doi.org/DOI: 10.4018/979-8-3693-9879-1.ch004

Khan, A., Chen, C. C., Suanpong, K., Ruangkanjanases, A., Kittikowit, S., & Chen, S. C. (2021). The impact of CSR on sustainable innovation ambidexterity: The mediating role of sustainable supply chain management and second-order social capital. *Sustainability*, *13*(21), 12160.

Khan, A., Jhanjhi, N., Abdulhabeb, G. A. A., Ray, S. K., Ghazanfar, M. A., & Humayun, M. (2024). *Securing IoT Devices Using Generative AI Techniques.*, DOI: 10.4018/979-8-3693-5415-5.ch007

Khan, M., Ajmal, M. M., Jabeen, F., Talwar, S., & Dhir, A. (2023). Green supply chain management in manufacturing firms: A resource-based viewpoint. *Business Strategy and the Environment, 32*(4), 1603–1618.

Khan, M., Alshahrani, A. N., & Jacquemod, J. (2023). Digital Platforms and Supply Chain Traceability for Robust Information and Effective Inventory Management: The Mediating Role of Transparency. *Logistics (Basel), 7*(2). Advance online publication. DOI: 10.3390/logistics7020025

Khan, M., Parvaiz, G. S., Dedahanov, A. T., Abdurazzakov, O. S., & Rakhmonov, D. A. (2022). The Impact of Technologies of Traceability and Transparency in Supply Chains. *Sustainability (Switzerland), 14*(24). Advance online publication. DOI: 10.3390/su142416336

Khanna, K., Kuik, S., & Ban, J. (2025). Circular Supply Chain Management: Bridging Business Innovation and Sustainability Through Best Practices. *Circular Economy, 3*(1). Advance online publication. DOI: 10.55845/VLHS2148

Khanra, S., Kaur, P., Joseph, R. P., Malik, A., & Dhir, A. (2022). A resource-based view of green innovation as a strategic firm resource: Present status and future directions. *Business Strategy and the Environment, 31*(4), 1395–1413.

Khan, S. A. R., Godil, D. I., Jabbour, C. J. C., Shujaat, S., Razzaq, A., & Yu, Z. (2021). Green data analytics, blockchain technology for sustainable development, and sustainable supply chain practices: Evidence from small and medium enterprises. *Annals of Operations Research*, •••, 1–25.

Khan, S. A., Mubarik, M. S., Kusi-Sarpong, S., Gupta, H., Zaman, S. I., & Mubarik, M. (2022). Blockchain technologies as enablers of supply chain mapping for sustainable supply chains. *Business Strategy and the Environment, 31*(8), 3742–3756.

Khan, S., Singh, R., Sta, J. C., Santos, G., & Ferreira, L. P. (2022). Modelling of determinants of logistics 4.0 adoption: Insights from developing countries. *Machines (Basel), 10*(12), 1242. DOI: 10.3390/machines10121242

Khan, T., & Emon, M. M. H. (2025). Supply chain performance in the age of Industry 4.0: Evidence from manufacturing sector. *Brazilian Journal of Operations & Production Management, 22*(1), 2434. DOI: 10.14488/BJOPM.2434.2025

Khan, T., Emon, M. M. H., & Rahman, M. A. (2024a). A systematic review on exploring the influence of Industry 4.0 technologies to enhance supply chain visibility and operational efficiency. *Review of Business and Economics Studies*, *12*(3), 6–27. DOI: 10.26794/2308-944X-2024-12-3-6-27

Khan, Y., Su'ud, M. B. M., Alam, M. M., & Ahmad, S. F., Ahmad (Ayassrah), A. Y. A. B., & Khan, N. (2022). Application of Internet of Things (IoT) in Sustainable Supply Chain Management. *Sustainability*, *15*(1), 694. DOI: 10.3390/su15010694

Khaw, K. W., & Alnoor, A., AL-Abrrow, H., Tiberius, V., Ganesan, Y., & Atshan, N. A. (2023). Reactions towards organizational change: A systematic literature review. *Current Psychology (New Brunswick, N.J.)*, *42*(22), 19137–19160. DOI: 10.1007/s12144-022-03070-6 PMID: 35431526

Kicova, E., Rosnerova, Z., Ponisciakova, O., & Gajanova, L. (2023). Concept for the Customer Perspective of the Balanced Scorecard (BSC) System in Bus Transport Companies in the Slovak Republic. *Systems*, *11*(12), 575.

Kin, B., Hopman, M., & Quak, H. (2021). Different Charging Strategies for Electric Vehicle Fleets in Urban Freight Transport. *Sustainability*, *13*(23), 13080. DOI: 10.3390/su132313080

Kneipp, J. M., Gomes, C. M., Zaluski, F. C., Pontelli, G. E., & Favarin, R. R. (2023). The relationship between adopting sustainability-oriented innovation practices and the business models of Brazilian industrial companies. *International Journal of Environment and Sustainable Development*, *22*(3), 349–367. DOI: 10.1504/IJESD.2023.132090

Kocaoglu, B. (2024). Enterprise Applications in Logistics. *Data Processing*, •••, 121–180. DOI: 10.1007/978-3-031-60290-0_5

Kofar Kudu, U. B., & Karia, N. (2024). The effects of the factors affecting sustainability of Nigerian humanitarian logistics firms: The mediation effect of the leadership. *Global Business and Management Research*, •••, 16.

Kong, D. (2024). 4D Golf Apparel Wear Simulation for Improved Online Shopping Experience. *Conference: Bridging the Divide*, https://doi.org/DOI: 10.31274/itaa.17382

Kopnina, H., Padfield, R., & Mylan, J. (2023). Strategic change for sustainability. In *Sustainable Business* (pp. 148–164). Routledge., DOI: 10.4324/9781003266150-10

Korpela, K., Hallikas, J., & Dahlberg, T. (2017). Digital supply chain transformation toward blockchain integration. *Supply Chain Management*, *22*(3), 251–264. DOI: 10.1108/SCM-02-2016-0046

Kouhizadeh, M., Saberi, S., & Sarkis, J. (2021). Blockchain technology and the sustainable supply chain: Theoretically exploring adoption barriers. *International Journal of Production Economics*, *231*. Advance online publication. DOI: 10.1016/j.ijpe.2020.107831

Kouhizadeh, M., & Sarkis, J. (2018). Blockchain and the Circular Economy: A New Paradigm for Sustainable Supply Chain Management. *Resources, Conservation and Recycling*, *135*, 1–6. DOI: 10.1016/j.resconrec.2018.02.014

Kouhizadeh, M., & Sarkis, J. (2018). Blockchain practices, potentials, and perspectives in greening supply chains. *Sustainability (Switzerland)*, *10*(10). Advance online publication. DOI: 10.3390/su10103652

Kouhizadeh, M., & Sarkis, J. (2018). Blockchain practices, potentials, and perspectives in greening supply chains. *Sustainability*, *10*(10), 3652.

Kshetri, N. (2014). The emerging role of Big Data in key development issues: Opportunities, challenges, and concerns. *Big Data & Society*, *1*(2). Advance online publication. DOI: 10.1177/2053951714564227

Kshetri, N. (2017). Can Blockchain Strengthen the Internet of Things? *IT Professional*, *19*(4). Advance online publication. DOI: 10.1109/MITP.2017.3051335

Kshetri, N. (2018). Blockchain's roles in meeting key supply chain management objectives. *International Journal of Information Management*, *39*, 80–89. DOI: 10.1016/j.ijinfomgt.2017.12.005

Kshetri, N. (2018). Blockchain's roles in strengthening cybersecurity and protecting privacy. *Journal of International Management*, *24*(3), 251–263.

Kujawski, A., & Nürnberg, M. (2023). Analysis of the potential use of unmanned aerial vehicles and image processing methods to support road and parking space management in urban transport. *Sustainability*. Advance online publication. DOI: 10.3390/su15043285

Kumar, A., Shukla, S., & Dwivedi, Y. K. (2019). A comprehensive framework for adopting blockchain in supply chains. *Journal of Cleaner Production*, *231*, 271–282. DOI: 10.1016/j.jclepro.2019.05.273

Kumar, D., Kr Singh, R., Mishra, R., & Fosso Wamba, S. (2022). Applications of the internet of things for optimizing warehousing and logistics operations: A systematic literature review and future research directions. *Computers & Industrial Engineering*, *171*, 108455. DOI: 10.1016/j.cie.2022.108455

Kumar, M., Raut, R. D., Jagtap, S., & Choubey, V. K. (2023). Circular economy adoption challenges in the food supply chain for sustainable development. *Business Strategy and the Environment*, *32*(4), 1334–1356.

Kumar, P. J. S., Petla, R. K., Elangovan, K., & Kuppusamy, P. G. (2022). Artificial Intelligence Revolution in Logistics and Supply Chain Management. In *Artificial Intelligent Techniques for Wireless Communication and Networking* (pp. 31–45). Wiley., DOI: 10.1002/9781119821809.ch3

Kumar, V. (2020). Global implications of cause-related loyalty marketing. *International Marketing Review*, *37*(4), 747–772. DOI: 10.1108/IMR-06-2019-0160

Kumar, V. (2022). Product Recalls in European Textile and Clothing Sector—A Macro Analysis of Risks and Geographical Patterns. *Stats*, *5*(4), 1044–1061. DOI: 10.3390/stats5040062

Kurniadi, W. (2025). Digital transformation in the transportation and logistics industry. *Siber Journal of Transportation and Logistics*, *3*(1), 1–6. DOI: 10.38035/sjtl.v3i1.429

Kusiak, A. (1990). Intelligent manufacturing systems. *The Journal of Technology Transfer*, *15*(4), 49–51. DOI: 10.1007/bf02371524

Kusiak, A. (2020). Open manufacturing: A design-for-resilience approach. *International Journal of Production Research*, *58*(15), 4647–4658. DOI: 10.1080/00207543.2020.1770894

Kusiak, A. (2023). Predictive models in digital manufacturing: Research, applications, and future outlook. *International Journal of Production Research*, *61*(17), 6052–6062. DOI: 10.1080/00207543.2022.2122620

Kusiak, A. (2024). Hyper-automation in manufacturing industry. *Journal of Intelligent Manufacturing*, *35*(1), 1–2. DOI: 10.1007/s10845-023-02265-3

Kusi-Sarpong, S., Gupta, H., & Sarkis, J. (2019). A supply chain sustainability innovation framework and evaluation methodology. *International Journal of Production Research*, *57*(7), 1990–2008.

Kwak, D. W., Rodrigues, V. S., Mason, R., Pettit, S., & Beresford, A. (2018). Risk interaction identification in international supply chain logistics: Developing a holistic model. *International Journal of Operations & Production Management*, *38*(2), 372–389.

Kyaw, A. Y. (2024). Application of Advanced Technology on Transport Ships as a Technological Revolution in the Maritime Industry. *Maritime Park Journal of Maritime Technology and Society*, 1–7. https://doi.org/DOI: 10.62012/mp.v3i2.35384

Lambourdiere, E., & Corbin, E. (2020). Blockchain and maritime supply-chain performance: dynamic capabilities perspective. Worldwide Hospitality and Tourism Themes, 12(1), pp. 24-34. Emerald Publishing Limited. https://doi.org/DOI: 10.1108/whatt-10-2019-0069

Landini, S. (2020). *Ethical Issues*. Cybersecurity and Automated Vehicles., DOI: 10.1007/978-3-030-27386-6_14

Lasso-Rodriguez, G., & Winkler, K. (2020). Hyperautomation to fulfil jobs rather than executing tasks: The BPM manager robot vs human case. *Romanian Journal of Information Technology and Automatic Control*, *30*(3), 7–22. DOI: 10.33436/v30i3y202001

Lasswell, H. D. (1932). The triple-appeal principle: A contribution of psychoanalysis to political and social science. *American Journal of Sociology*, *37*(4), 523–538. DOI: 10.1086/215791

Latif, Z., Riaz, A., Mahmood, S., & Hameed, R. M. (2023). An Exploration of Moral Identity's Role in Mitigating the Impact of Despotic Leadership on Organizational Culture and Organizational Agility in the Public Sector of Pakistan. *Foundation University Journal of Business & Economics*, *8*(2), 142–168. DOI: 10.33897/fujbe.v8i2.816

Lazzaris, J., Carvalho, A. M., & Carvalho, M. S. (2022). Supply chain quality management and industry 5.0: A literature review and analysis. *2022 IEEE International Conference on Industrial Engineering and Engineering Management (IEEM)*, 285–289. https://doi.org/DOI: 10.1109/IEEM55944.2022.9989770

Leal, T. L. M. D. C., Araújo, J. C. G. D., & Rodrigues, L. B. (2025). Avaliação dos acordos setoriais de logística reversa como mecanismos de promoção da economia circular. *Brazilian Journal of Production Engineering*, *11*(1), 192–212. DOI: 10.47456/bjpe.v11i1.46051

Lee, I. (2019). The Internet of Things (IoT). In *Securing the Internet of Things* (pp. 1557–1574). IGI Global.

Lee, K. H., & Wu, Y. (2014). Integrating sustainability performance measurement into logistics and supply networks: A multi-methodological approach. *The British Accounting Review*, *46*(4), 361–378.

Lee, V. H., Foo, P. Y., Cham, T. H., Hew, T. S., Tan, G. W. H., & Ooi, K. B. (2024). Big data analytics capability in building supply chain resilience: The moderating effect of innovation-focused complementary assets. *Industrial Management & Data Systems*, *124*(3), 1203–1233.

Leng, C. (2023). Information sharing in supply chain based on products return and game theory. In Batista, P., & Zhang, Y. (Eds.), *Second International Conference on Applied Statistics, Computational Mathematics, and Software Engineering (ASCMSE 2023)* (p. 81). SPIE. https://doi.org/DOI: 10.1117/12.2692080

Leung, T. C. H., Guan, J., & Lau, Y.-Y. (2023). Exploring environmental sustainability and green management practices: Evidence from logistics service providers. *Sustainability Accounting. Management and Policy Journal*, *14*(3), 461–489. DOI: 10.1108/SAMPJ-03-2022-0133

Li, G., & Li, W. (2015). The Analysis of Return Reverse Logistics Management Strategy Based on B2C Electronic Commerce. *Proceedings of the 2015 International Conference on Economics, Social Science, Arts, Education and Management Engineering*. 2015 International Conference on Economics, Social Science, Arts, Education and Management Engineering, Xi'an, China. https://doi.org/DOI: 10.2991/essaeme-15.2015.162

Li, A., Zhuang, S., Yang, T., Lu, W., & Xu, J. (2024). Optimization of logistics cargo tracking and transportation efficiency based on data science deep learning models. *Applied and Computational Engineering*, *69*, 71–77. DOI: 10.54254/2755-2721/69/20241522

Li, J., Han, D., Weng, T.-H., Wu, H., Li, K.-C., & Castiglione, A. (2025). A secure data storage and sharing scheme for port supply chain based on Blockchain and Dynamic searchable encryption. *Computer Standards & Interfaces*, *91*, 103887. DOI: 10.1016/j.csi.2024.103887

Li, K., Gharehgozli, A., & Lee, J.-Y. (2023). Smart technologies and port operations: Optimal adoption strategy with network externality consideration. *Computers & Industrial Engineering*, *184*, 109557. DOI: 10.1016/j.cie.2023.109557

Li, L., & Zhou, J. (2025). Blockchain Effects and Investment Strategies in the Maritime Supply Chain Under Perishable Goods Loss. *Systems*, *13*(3), 196. DOI: 10.3390/systems13030196

Lin, H.-F. (2024). Blockchain adoption in the maritime industry: Empirical evidence from the technological-organizational-environmental framework. *Maritime Policy & Management*, *51*(7), 1474–1496. DOI: 10.1080/03088839.2023.2175063

Lin, H.-F. (2025). Examining the determinants of Blockchain technology-enabled maritime supply chain system adoption intention: Does market turbulence play a moderating role? *Marine Policy*, *174*, 106616. DOI: 10.1016/j.marpol.2025.106616

Li, Q., Cui, Y., Song, T., & Zheng, L. (2023). Federated Multiagent Actor–Critic Learning Task offloading in Intelligent Logistics. *IEEE Internet of Things Journal*, *10*(13), 11696–11707. DOI: 10.1109/jiot.2023.3244783

Liu, A., Zhu, Q., Xu, L., Lu, Q., & Fan, Y. (2021). Sustainable supply chain management for perishable products in emerging markets: An integrated location-inventory-routing model. *Transportation Research Part E, Logistics and Transportation Review*, *150*, 102319. DOI: 10.1016/j.tre.2021.102319

Liu, H., Zhou, L., Zhao, J., Wang, F., Yang, J., Liang, K., & Li, Z. (2022). Deep-Learning-Based Accurate Identification of Warehouse Goods for Robot Picking Operations. *Sustainability*, *14*(13), 7781. DOI: 10.3390/su14137781

Liu, J. (2022). *Development and Prospects of International Logistics in China Under the New Development Paradigm.*, DOI: 10.1007/978-981-19-5833-5_10

Li, X., Zhou, Y., & Yuen, K. F. (2024). Blockchain implementation in the maritime industry: Critical success factors and strategy formulation. *Maritime Policy & Management*, *51*(2), 304–322. DOI: 10.1080/03088839.2022.2119614

Li, Z., Wang, L., Wang, G., Xin, X., Chen, K., & Zhang, T. (2024). Investment and subsidy strategy for low-carbon port operation with blockchain adoption. *Ocean and Coastal Management*, *248*, 106966. DOI: 10.1016/j.ocecoaman.2023.106966

Li, Z., Wang, W. M., Liu, G., Liu, L., He, J., & Huang, G. Q. (2018). Toward open manufacturing a cross-enterprises knowledge and services exchange framework based on blockchain and edge computing. *Industrial Management & Data Systems*, *118*(1). Advance online publication. DOI: 10.1108/IMDS-04-2017-0142

Loklindt, C., Moeller, C., & Kinra, A. (2020). How blockchain enables sustainable supply chain innovation: Insights from container shipping. *International Journal of Physical Distribution & Logistics Management*, *50*(5), 602–625. DOI: 10.1108/IJPDLM-03-2020-0104

López-Gálvez, F., Gómez, P. A., Artés, F., Artés-Hernández, F., & Aguayo, E. (2021). Interactions between microbial food safety and environmental sustainability in the fresh produce supply chain. *Foods*, *10*(7), 1655. PMID: 34359525

Lorenc, A. (2023). How to Find Disruptions in Logistics Processes in the Cold Chain and Avoid Waste of Products? *Applied Sciences (Basel, Switzerland)*, *14*(1), 255. DOI: 10.3390/app14010255

Loske, D., Klumpp, M., Keil, M., & Neukirchen, T. (2021). Logistics Work, Ergonomics and Social Sustainability: Empirical Musculoskeletal System Strain Assessment in Retail Intralogistics. *Logistics (Basel)*, *5*(4), 89. DOI: 10.3390/logistics5040089

Lu, B., Lu, H., & Wang, H. (2024). Design and value analysis of the blockchain-based port logistics financial platform. *Maritime Policy & Management*, *51*(6), 1037–1061. DOI: 10.1080/03088839.2023.2205870

Lu, H., Zhao, G., & Liu, S. (2024). Integrating circular economy and Industry 4.0 for sustainable supply chain management: A dynamic capability view. *Production Planning and Control*, *35*(2), 170–186.

Lustenberger, M., & Spychiger, F. (2025). Blockchain in supply chains: An unfulfilled promise. *Supply Chain Management*. Advance online publication. DOI: 10.1108/SCM-03-2024-0192

Luthra, S., Kumar, A., Zavadskas, E. K., Mangla, S. K., & Garza-Reyes, J. A. (2020). Industry 4.0 as an enabler of sustainability diffusion in supply chain: An analysis of influential strength of drivers in an emerging economy. *International Journal of Production Research*, *58*(5), 1505–1521.

Madhura, M., & Raghavendra, D. (2024). Leveraging IoT for smarter supply chain management and logistics: A comprehensive review and future perspectives. In *Futuristic Trends in IOT Volume 3 Book 8* (pp. 159–170). Iterative International Publishers, Selfypage Developers Pvt Ltd.

Madupati, B. (2021). Blockchain in day-to-day life: Transformative applications and implementation. *International Journal for Multidisciplinary Research*, *3*(1).

Majeed, M., Gideon, A., & Tijani, A. (2025). Green Warehousing Practices for Firms. In M. Majeed, K. Agarwal, & A. Tijani, *Green Supply Chain Management* (1st ed., pp. 133–152). Apple Academic Press. https://doi.org/DOI: 10.1201/9781003560845-8

Malladi, S. S., Christensen, J. M., Ramírez, D., Larsen, A., & Pacino, D. (2022). Stochastic fleet mix optimization: Evaluating electromobility in urban logistics. *Transportation Research Part E, Logistics and Transportation Review*, *158*, 102554. DOI: 10.1016/j.tre.2021.102554

Manda, V. K., & Polisetty, A. (2018). Status Check on Blockchain Implementations in India. SSRN *Electronic Journal*. https://doi.org/DOI: 10.2139/ssrn.3265654

Manda, V. K., Sagi, S., & Yadav, A. (2024). Blockchain in Advertising and Marketing: Revolutionizing the Industry Through Transparency and Trust. In Tarnanidis, T. K., & Sklavounos, N. (Eds.), (pp. 89–112). Advances in Marketing, Customer Relationship Management, and E-Services. IGI Global., DOI: 10.4018/979-8-3693-2754-8.ch005

Mandegari, M., Ebadian, M., van Dyk, S., & Saddler, J. (John). (2023). Decarbonizing British Columbia's (BC's) marine sector by using low carbon intensive (CI) biofuels. *Biofuels, Bioproducts & Biorefining*, *17*(4), 1101–1114. DOI: 10.1002/bbb.2495

Mann, S., Potdar, V., Gajavilli, R. S., & Chandan, A. (2018). Blockchain technology for supply chain traceability, transparency and data provenance. *ACM International Conference Proceeding Series*, 22–25. https://doi.org/DOI: 10.1145/3301403.3301408

Marabelli, M., Newell, S., & Handunge, V. (2021). The lifecycle of algorithmic decision-making systems: Organizational choices and ethical challenges. *The Journal of Strategic Information Systems*, *30*(3), 101683. DOI: 10.1016/j.jsis.2021.101683

Martins, V. W., Anholon, R., Quelhas, O. L., & Leal Filho, W. (2019). Sustainable practices in logistics systems: An overview of companies in Brazil. *Sustainability*, *11*(15), 4140. DOI: 10.3390/su11154140

Martyushev, N. V., Malozyomov, B. V., Kukartsev, V. V., Gozbenko, V. E., Konyukhov, V. Y., Mikhalev, A. S., Kukartsev, V. A., & Tynchenko, Y. A. (2023). Determination of the Reliability of Urban Electric Transport Running Autonomously through Diagnostic Parameters. *World Electric Vehicle Journal*, *14*(12), 334. DOI: 10.3390/wevj14120334

Mashayekhy, Y., Babaei, A., Yuan, X.-M., & Xue, A. (2022). Impact of internet of things (IoT) on inventory management: A literature survey. *Logistics (Basel)*, *6*(2), 33.

Matenga, A., & Mpofu, K. (2023). Blockchain-based Product Lifecycle Management using Supply Chain Management for Railcar Remanufacturing. *Procedia CIRP*, *116*, 486–491. DOI: 10.1016/j.procir.2023.02.082

Mathew, D., Brintha, N. C., & Jappes, J. T. W. (2023). *Artificial Intelligence Powered Automation for Industry 4.0* (pp. 1–28). https://doi.org/DOI: 10.1007/978-3-031-20443-2_1

Mathur, A., Dabas, A., & Sharma, N. (2022). Evolution From Industry 1.0 to Industry 5.0. *2022 4th International Conference on Advances in Computing, Communication Control and Networking (ICAC3N)*, 1390–1394. https://doi.org/DOI: 10.1109/ICAC3N56670.2022.10074274

Mathur, T., & RV College of Engineering. (2024). reviewing optimization techniques in supply chains: AI and blockchain perspectives. International journal of scientific research in engineering and management, *08*(06), 1–5.

Ma, Z., Yang, X., Miao, R., & Yue, Y. (2024). Sustainable development of low-carbon supply chain economy based on the Internet of Things and environmental responsibility. *Economics - The Open-Access. Open-Assessment Journal*, *18*(1), 1–18. DOI: 10.1515/econ-2022-0099

Melchers, S. J. (2024). Military Supply Chain: Analysis Designing an Information Sharing System for Enhancing Efficiency in Military Supply Chain Operations [Master Thesis, Eindhoven University of Technology]. https://pure.tue.nl/ws/portalfiles/portal/351901285/Master_Thesis_Stijn_Melchers.pdf

Mendling, J., Weber, I., Van Der Aalst, W., Vom Brocke, J., Cabanillas, C., Daniel, F., Debois, S., Di Ciccio, C., Dumas, M., Dustdar, S., Gal, A., García-Bañuelos, L., Governatori, G., Hull, R., La Rosa, M., Leopold, H., Leymann, F., Recker, J., Reichert, M., & Zhu, L. (2018). Blockchains for business process management - Challenges and opportunities. *ACM Transactions on Management Information Systems*, *9*(1). Advance online publication. DOI: 10.1145/3183367

Mentzer, J. T., DeWitt, W., Keebler, J. S., Min, S., Nix, N. W., Smith, C. D., & Zacharia, Z. G. (2001). Defining supply chain management. *Journal of Business Logistics*, *22*(2), 1–25.

Mettler, M. (2016). Blockchain technology in healthcare: The revolution starts here. *2016 IEEE 18th International Conference on E-Health Networking, Applications and Services, Healthcom 2016*. https://doi.org/DOI: 10.1109/HealthCom.2016.7749510

Miles, M. B., & Huberman, A. M. (2003). *Analyse des données qualitatives*. De Boeck Supérieur.

Min, H., & Kim, I. (2012). Green supply chain research: Past, present, and future. *Logistics Research*, *4*, 39–47.

Mishra, A., Dutta, P., & Gottipalli, N. (2024). An optimization model for the downstream supply chain network, considering consolidated warehouses and the selection of transportation mode. *International Journal of Productivity and Performance Management*, *73*(3), 912–942. DOI: 10.1108/IJPPM-05-2022-0231

Mishra, A., Dutta, P., Jayasankar, S., Jain, P., & Mathiyazhagan, K. (2023). A review of reverse logistics and closed-loop supply chains in the perspective of circular economy. *Benchmarking*, *30*(3), 975–1020.

Mittelstadt, B. D., Allo, P., Taddeo, M., Wachter, S., & Floridi, L. (2016). The ethics of algorithms: Mapping the debate. *Big Data & Society*, *3*(2), 1–21. DOI: 10.1177/2053951716679679

Modgil, S., Singh, R. K., & Hannibal, C. (2022). Artificial intelligence for supply chain resilience: Learning from Covid-19. *International Journal of Logistics Management, 33*(4), 1246–1268.

Mohamed B. F., Yussuf A., Haithem M., Syed A. S., Omar A. M., Sandy T., Xavier B., Raouf Abozariba, M. I., Adel A. (2024). A survey on blockchain technology in the maritime industry: Challenges and future perspectives, 157(1), 618-637. https://doi.org/DOI: 10.1016/j.future.2024.03.046

Mohammad, A. S., Khanfar, I. A., Oraini, B. A., Vasudevan, A., Suleiman, I. M., & Fei, Z. (2024). Predictive analytics on artificial intelligence in supply chain optimization. *Data & Metadata, 3*, 395. DOI: 10.56294/dm2024395

Mohanta, B. K., Jena, D., Panda, S. S., & Sobhanayak, S. (2019). Blockchain technology: A survey on applications and security privacy Challenges. In *Internet of Things (Netherlands)* (Vol. 8). https://doi.org/DOI: 10.1016/j.iot.2019.100107

Mohrman, S. A., & Bartunek, J. M. (2023). *How Can ODC Help Accomplish a Sustainable Future? A Joint Reflection* (pp. 1–26). https://doi.org/DOI: 10.1108/S0897-301620220000030003

Mohsen, B. M. (2024). AI-Driven Optimization of Urban Logistics in Smart Cities: Integrating Autonomous Vehicles and IoT for Efficient Delivery Systems. *Sustainability, 16*(24), 11265. DOI: 10.3390/su162411265

Monios, J., & Bergqvist, R. (2020). Logistics and the networked society: A conceptual framework for smart network business models using electric autonomous vehicles (EAVs). *Technological Forecasting and Social Change, 151*, 119824. DOI: 10.1016/j.techfore.2019.119824

Morcillo-Bellido, J., & Duran-Heras, A. (2020). Sustainability governance mechanisms in supply chains: An application in the retail sector. *Sustainability, 12*(17), 6911.

Morkunas, V. J., Paschen, J., & Boon, E. (2019). How blockchain technologies impact your business model. *Business Horizons, 62*(3). Advance online publication. DOI: 10.1016/j.bushor.2019.01.009

Mougayar, W. (2016). *The Business Blockchain: Promise, Practice, and the Application of the Next Internet Internet Internet.* Wiley.

Mourtzis, D., Vlachou, E., & Milas, N. (2016). Industrial Big Data as a Result of IoT Adoption in Manufacturing. *Procedia CIRP, 55*. Advance online publication. DOI: 10.1016/j.procir.2016.07.038

Mubarik, M. S., & Khan, S. A. (2024). Digital Supply Chain Transformation: Adoption and Approaches. In *The Theory, Methods and Application of Managing Digital Supply Chains* (pp. 107–120). Emerald Publishing Limited. https://doi.org/ DOI: 10.1108/978-1-80455-968-020241007

Mulligan, C., Morsfield, S., & Cheikosman, E. (2024). Blockchain for sustainability: A systematic literature review for policy impact. *Telecommunications Policy*, *48*(2), 102676.

Murphy, P. R., & Poist, R. F. (2000). Green logistics strategies: An analysis of usage patterns. *Transportation Journal*, ●●●, 5–16.

Mustafa, G., Rafiq, W., Jhamat, N., Arshad, Z., & Rana, F. A. (2025). Blockchain-based governance models in e-government: A comprehensive framework for legal, technical, ethical and security considerations. *International Journal of Law and Management*, *67*(1), 37–55. DOI: 10.1108/IJLMA-08-2023-0172

Mvelase, L., & Ferrer, S. (2024). The economywide impact of bioethanol production in South Africa. *Energy Conversion and Management*, *X*. Advance online publication. DOI: 10.1016/j.ecmx.2024.100729

Mwanyota, J. L. (2021). Reverse Logistics, Process Innovation, Operational Performance and Competitive Advantage of Manufacturing Firms in Kenya [Thesis, University of Nairobi]. https://erepository.uonbi.ac.ke/handle/11295/155696

Nag, A., Hassan, M. M., Das, A., Sinha, A., Chand, N., Kar, A., Sharma, V., & Alkhayyat, A. (2024). Exploring the applications and security threats of Internet of Thing in the cloud computing paradigm: A comprehensive study on the cloud of things. *Transactions on Emerging Telecommunications Technologies*, *35*(4). Advance online publication. DOI: 10.1002/ett.4897

Nakamoto, S. (2008). Bitcoin: A Peer-to-Peer Electronic Cash System | Satoshi Nakamoto Institute. *Bitcoin.Org*.

Nakamoto, S. (2008). Bitcoin: A Peer-to-Peer Electronic Cash System. Retrieved from Bitcoin.org.

Nakamoto, S. (2009). Bitcoin open source implementation of P2P currency, P2P Foundation, https://p2pfoundation.ning.com/forum/topics/bitcoin-open-source

Nand, A., Sohal, A., Fridman, I., Hussain, S., & Wallace, M. (2023). An exploratory study of organisational and industry drivers for the implementation of emerging technologies in logistics. *Industrial Management & Data Systems*, *123*(5), 1418–1439. DOI: 10.1108/IMDS-08-2022-0467

Nantee, N., & Sureeyatanapas, P. (2021). The impact of Logistics 4.0 on corporate sustainability: A performance assessment of automated warehouse operations. *Benchmarking*, *28*(10), 2865–2895. DOI: 10.1108/BIJ-11-2020-0583

Naradda Gamage, S. K., Ekanayake, E. M. S., Abeyrathne, G., Prasanna, R., Jayasundara, J., & Rajapakshe, P. S. K. (2020). A review of global challenges and survival strategies of small and medium enterprises (SMEs). *Economies*, *8*(4), 79.

Narayanan, A., Bonneau, J., Felten, E., Miller, A., & Goldfeder, S. (2016). Bitcoin and Cryptocurrency Technologies: A Comprehensive Introduction. In *Bitcoin and Cryptocurrency Technologies: A Comprehensive Introduction*. Princeton University Press.

Nasir, M. H. A., Genovese, A., Acquaye, A. A., Koh, S. C. L., & Yamoah, F. (2017). Comparing linear and circular supply chains: A case study from the construction industry. *International Journal of Production Economics*, *183*, 443–457.

Negri, M., Cagno, E., Colicchia, C., & Sarkis, J. (2021). Integrating sustainability and resilience in the supply chain: A systematic literature review and a research agenda. *Business Strategy and the Environment*, *30*(7), 2858–2886.

Neri, A., Cagno, E., Lepri, M., & Trianni, A. (2021). A triple bottom line balanced set of key performance indicators to measure the sustainability performance of industrial supply chains. *Sustainable Production and Consumption*, *26*, 648–691.

Neu, D. A., Lahann, J., & Fettke, P. (2022). A systematic literature review on state-of-the-art deep learning methods for process prediction. *Artificial Intelligence Review*. Advance online publication. DOI: 10.1007/s10462-021-09960-8

Newton, E. (2023). Packaging Has an Undeniably Powerful Impact on Customer Experience. https://parcelindustry.com/article-6208-Packaging-Has-an-Undeniably-Powerful-Impact-on-Customer-Experience.html

Ngo, V. M., Quang, H. T., Hoang, T. G., & Binh, A. D. T. (2024). Sustainability-related supply chain risks and supply chain performances: The moderating effects of dynamic supply chain management practices. *Business Strategy and the Environment*, *33*(2), 839–857.

Nguyen, S., Leman, A., Xiao, Z., Fu, X., Zhang, X., Wei, X., Zhang, W., Li, N., Zhang, W., & Qin, Z. (2023). Blockchain-Powered Incentive System for JIT Arrival Operations and Decarbonization in Maritime Shipping. *Sustainability*, *15*(22), 15686. DOI: 10.3390/su152215686

Niedzielski, B., Buła, P., & Yang, M. (2024). Hyperautomation as a vital optimization tool in organizations: Cognitive approach with the use of Euler circles. *Journal of Electronic Business &amp. Digital Economics*, *3*(1), 61–73. DOI: 10.1108/JEBDE-02-2023-0004

Nikseresht, A., Golmohammadi, D., & Zandieh, M. (2024). Sustainable green logistics and remanufacturing: A bibliometric analysis and future research directions. *International Journal of Logistics Management*, *35*(3), 755–803. DOI: 10.1108/IJLM-03-2023-0085

Nimmagadda, S. L., Wood, L. C., Namugenyi, C., Mani, N., Singh, A., & Vishnu, T. (2025). Information System Guided Reverse Logistics – Managing the Green Industry Environments. *Pre-ICIS Workshop Proceedings 2024*. https://aisel.aisnet.org/sprouts_proceedings_siggreen_2024/7/

Nnabuife, S. G., Hamzat, A. K., Whidborne, J., Kuang, B., & Jenkins, K. W. (2025). Integration of renewable energy sources in tandem with electrolysis: A technology review for green hydrogen production. *International Journal of Hydrogen Energy*, *107*, 218–240. DOI: 10.1016/j.ijhydene.2024.06.342

Notheisen, B., Hawlitschek, F., & Weinhardt, C. (2017). Breaking down the blockchain hype – Towards a blockchain market engineering approach. *ECIS 2017 Proceedings*.

Notteboom, T. (2016). The adaptive capacity of container ports in an era of mega vessels: The case of upstream seaports Antwerp and Hamburg. *Journal of Transport Geography*, *54*, 295–309. DOI: 10.1016/j.jtrangeo.2016.06.002

Notteboom, T., Pallis, A., & Rodrigue, J.-P. (2021). *Port Economics, Management and Policy* (1st ed.). Routledge., DOI: 10.4324/9780429318184

Ntanis, G., Aggelakakis, A., Boile, M., Tsaganos, L.-N., Papaefthimiou, K., Baroutsi, M., Chatzinikolaou, S., Paven, D., Vlascici, M., & Binchiciu, E. (2025). *Innovative Adaptation of Predictive Maintenance Familiarization Content to Address Contemporary Requirements in Transportation Sector.*, DOI: 10.1007/978-3-031-82818-8_15

Nugroho, B. Y., Shariff, S. R., Fathurahman, H., & Haris, M. H. (2025). Determining Priority Factors for Executing of Reverse Logistics in Palm Oil Industry of Indonesia. *Journal of Ecohumanism*, *4*(2). Advance online publication. DOI: 10.62754/joe.v4i2.6382

O'Dwyer, M., Filieri, R., & O'Malley, L. (2023). Establishing successful university–industry collaborations: Barriers and enablers deconstructed. *The Journal of Technology Transfer*, *48*(3), 900–931. DOI: 10.1007/s10961-022-09932-2

OECD, & EUIPO. (2019). Trends in Trade in Counterfeit and Pirated Goods. *Illicit Trade*.

Olufemi-Phillips, A. Q., Ofodile Onyeka Chrisanctus and Toromade, A. S., Eyo-Udo, N. L., & Adewale, T. T. (2024). Optimizing FMCG supply chain management with IOT and cloud computing integration. *International Journal of Management & Entrepreneurship Research*, *6*(11), 3685–3722.

Om P, Bashir A, Vinay T, Surendra S, (2021). Key management for blockchain technology. 7(1), 76-80. https://doi.org/DOI: 10.1016/j.icte.2019.08.002

Omol, E. J. (2024). *Organizational digital transformation: from evolution to future trends*. Digital Transformation and Society.

Onyeji-Nwogu, I., Bazilian, M., & Moss, T. (2020). Big data and the electricity sector in African countries. *World Development Perspectives*, *17*, 100170. DOI: 10.1016/j.wdp.2020.100170

Onyeka, N. C., & Chikwendu, O. C. (2025). Circular economy strategies in industrial engineering: From theory to practice. *International Journal of Multidisciplinary Research and Growth Evaluation*, *6*(1), 1773–1782.

Opoku, R. K., & Li, X. (2025). Sustainable management practices, operational and sustainable performance in manufacturing contexts: Empirical evidence from a developing economy. *Journal of Responsible Production and Consumption*, *2*(1), 48–82. DOI: 10.1108/JRPC-07-2024-0035

Oriekhoe, O. I., Oyeyemi, O. P., Bello, B. G., Omotoye, G. B., Daraojimba, A. I., & Adefemi, A. (2024). Blockchain in supply chain management: A review of efficiency, transparency, and innovation. *International Journal of Science and Research Archive*, *11*(1), 173–181. DOI: 10.30574/ijsra.2024.11.1.0028

Osman, A., Fowowe, O. O., Agboluaje, R., & Orekha, P. O. (2025). Integrating machine learning in business analytics consulting for proactive decision-making and innovation. *World Journal of Advanced Research and Reviews*, *25*(1), 1817–1836. DOI: 10.30574/wjarr.2025.25.1.0251

Oyedijo, A., Kusi-Sarpong, S., Mubarik, M. S., Khan, S. A., & Utulu, K. (2024). Multi-tier sustainable supply chain management: A case study of a global food retailer. *Supply Chain Management*, *29*(1), 68–97.

Oyekanlu, E. A., Smith, A. C., Thomas, W. P., Mulroy, G., Hitesh, D., Ramsey, M., Kuhn, D. J., Mcghinnis, J. D., Buonavita, S. C., Looper, N. A., Ng, M., Ng'oma, A., Liu, W., Mcbride, P. G., Shultz, M. G., Cerasi, C., & Sun, D. (2020). A Review of Recent Advances in Automated Guided Vehicle Technologies: Integration Challenges and Research Areas for 5G-Based Smart Manufacturing Applications. *IEEE Access : Practical Innovations, Open Solutions*, *8*, 202312–202353. DOI: 10.1109/ACCESS.2020.3035729

Ozdenizci Kose, B. (2020). Digital transformation of supply chains with mobile IoT. In *Advances in Business Information Systems and Analytics* (pp. 156–184). IGI Global.

Pachar, N., Darbari, J. D., Govindan, K., & Jha, P. C. (2022). Sustainable performance measurement of Indian retail chain using two-stage network DEA. *Annals of Operations Research*, *315*(2), 1477–1515.

Paiva, S., Ahad, M., Tripathi, G., Feroz, N., & Casalino, G. (2021). Enabling Technologies for urban smart mobility: Recent trends, opportunities and challenges. *Sensors (Basel)*, *21*(6), 2143. DOI: 10.3390/s21062143 PMID: 33803903

Pajić, V., Radivojević, G., & Kilibarda, M. (2021). Influence of KPI of logistics processes on logistics costs. *International Journal for Traffic & Transport Engineering*, 11(4), https://doi.org/ (4).09DOI: 10.7708/ijtte2021.11

Pal, K. (2023). Drivers of sustainable supply chain management using internet of things-based blockchain technology. In *Advances in Logistics, Operations, and Management Science* (pp. 171–201). IGI Global.

Pal, S. (2023). Integrating AI in sustainable supply chain management: A new paradigm for enhanced transparency and sustainability. *International Journal for Research in Applied Science and Engineering Technology*, *11*(6), 2979–2984.

Pandey, S. C., & P, V. K. (2025). Adaptive AI-Driven Toll Management: Enhancing traffic flow and sustainability through Real-Time prediction, allocation, and task optimization. *Future Transportation*, *5*(1), 21. DOI: 10.3390/futuretransp5010021

Paparini, S., Papoutsi, C., Murdoch, J., Green, J., Petticrew, M., Greenhalgh, T., & Shaw, S. E. (2021). Evaluating complex interventions in context: Systematic, meta-narrative review of case study approaches. *BMC Medical Research Methodology*, *21*(1), 225. DOI: 10.1186/s12874-021-01418-3 PMID: 34689742

Park, A., & Li, H. (2021). The Effect of Blockchain Technology on Supply Chain Sustainability Performances. *Sustainability*, *13*, 1726.

Paśko, Ł., Mądziel, M., Stadnicka, D., Dec, G., Carreras-Coch, A., Solé-Beteta, X., Pappa, L., Stylios, C., Mazzei, D., & Atzeni, D. (2022). Plan and Develop Advanced Knowledge and Skills for Future Industrial Employees in the Field of Artificial Intelligence, Internet of Things and Edge Computing. *Sustainability*, *14*(6), 3312. DOI: 10.3390/su14063312

Pasupuleti, M. K. (2025). AI and IoT for the smart economy: Transforming manufacturing and service industries. In *AI and IoT in the Smart Economy: Revolutionizing Manufacturing and Services* (pp. 21–30). National Education Services.

Pasupuleti, V., Thuraka, B., Kodete, C. S., & Malisetty, S. (2024). Enhancing supply chain agility and sustainability through machine learning: Optimization techniques for logistics and inventory management. *Logistics (Basel)*. Advance online publication. DOI: 10.3390/logistics8030073

Patil, K., Garg, V., Gabaldon, J., Patil, H., Niranjan, S., & Hawkins, T. (2024). Firm performance in digitally integrated supply chains: A combined perspective of transaction cost economics and relational exchange theory. *Journal of Enterprise Information Management*, *37*(2), 381–413. DOI: 10.1108/JEIM-09-2022-0335

Pattanayak, S., Ramkumar, M., Goswami, M., & Rana, N. P. (2024). Blockchain technology and supply chain performance: The role of trust and relational capabilities. *International Journal of Production Economics*, *271*, 109198. DOI: 10.1016/j.ijpe.2024.109198

Pautassi, P. (2024). Algorithmic Pricing in the digital age.

Pauzuolienė, J., Kavecke, I., & Pyra, M. (2024). Smart technologies integration and challenges in the context of logistics companies. *European Research Studies Journal*, 0(Special A), 999–1018. https://ideas.repec.org/a/ers/journl/vxxviiy2024ispecialap999-1018.html

Pejić Bach, M., Klinčar, A., Aleksić, A., Rašić Jelavić, S., & Zeqiri, J. (2023). Supply chain management maturity and business performance: The balanced scorecard perspective. *Applied Sciences (Basel, Switzerland)*, *13*(4), 2065.

Pejovic, C., & Lee, U. (2022). UNCITRAL Model Law on Electronic Transferable Records as a Potential Legal Regime for the Use of Electronic Bills of Lading. European Transport Law, 57(1), 13-32. Available @ https://kyushu-u.elsevierpure.com/en/publications

Pekkala, M. (2023). Sustainable supply chain management practices in retailing: Qualitative content analysis based on sustainability reports.

Penrose, E. T. (2009). *The Theory of the Growth of the Firm*. Oxford university press.

Peronja, I., Gračan, D., & Hlača, B. (2020). Blockchain technologies for freight cost optimization in maritime trade. *Maritime Economics & Logistics*, *22*(3), 453–472. DOI: 10.1057/s41278-020-00152-x

Peters, G. W., & Panayi, E. (2016). *Understanding modern banking ledgers through blockchain technologies: Future of transaction processing and smart contracts on the internet of money*. New Economic Windows., DOI: 10.1007/978-3-319-42448-4_13

Pfaff, Y. M., Birkel, H., & Hartmann, E. (2023). Supply chain governance in the context of industry 4.0: Investigating implications of real-life implementations from a multi-tier perspective. *International Journal of Production Economics*, *260*, 108862. DOI: 10.1016/j.ijpe.2023.108862

Pham, T. Y. (2023). A smart port development: Systematic literature and bibliometric analysis. *The Asian Journal of Shipping and Logistics*, *39*(3), 57–62. DOI: 10.1016/j.ajsl.2023.06.005

Plakantara, S. P., Karakitsiou, A., & Mantzou, T. (2024). *Managing Risks in Smart Warehouses from the Perspective of Industry 4.0* (pp. 1–47). https://doi.org/DOI: 10.1007/978-3-031-58919-5_1

Politou, E., Alepis, E., & Patsakis, C. (2018). *Forgetting personal data and revoking consent under the GDPR: Challenges and proposed solutions. Journal of Cybersecurity, 4(1)*. Academic., DOI: 10.1093/cybsec/tyy001

Ponis, S. T., & Efthymiou, O. K. (2020). Cloud and IoT Applications in Material Handling Automation and Intralogistics. *Logistics (Basel)*, *4*(3), 22. DOI: 10.3390/logistics4030022

Poongodi, T., Lucia Agnesbeena, T., Janarthanan, S., & Balusamy, B. (2020). Accelerating data acquisition process in the pharmaceutical industry using Internet of Things. In *An Industrial IoT Approach for Pharmaceutical Industry Growth* (pp. 117–152). Elsevier., DOI: 10.1016/B978-0-12-821326-1.00005-X

Porter, M. E. (1985). Technology and competitive advantage. *The Journal of Business Strategy*, *5*(3), 60–78.

Prakash, J., Murali, L., Manikandan, N., Nagaprasad, N., & Ramaswamy, K. (2024). RETRACTED ARTICLE: A vehicular network based intelligent transport system for smart cities using machine learning algorithms. *Scientific Reports*, *14*(1), 468. DOI: 10.1038/s41598-023-50906-7 PMID: 38172149

Pu, S., & Lam, J. S. L. (2021). Blockchain adoptions in the maritime industry: A conceptual framework. *Maritime Policy & Management*, *48*(6), 777–794. DOI: 10.1080/03088839.2020.1825855

Pushpamali, N., Agdas, D., Rose, T. M., & Yigitcanlar, T. (2021). Stakeholder perception of reverse logistics practices on supply chain performance. *Business Strategy and the Environment*, *30*(1), 60–70. DOI: 10.1002/bse.2609

Putra, A. R., Kopot, C., & Zhao, L. (2024). *Cultural Differences in Apparel Product Return Behavior: An Exploratory Study of Indonesia and USA E-Commerce Consumers. Bridging the Divide*. Bridging the Divide., DOI: 10.31274/itaa.17473

Putri, A. R., Tusadiah, W., Rizaldy, W., & Alfaridi, N. (2024). Analysis of Barrier Reverse Logistics Practices in Courier Companies in Indonesia. *Advances in Transportation and Logistics Research*. GROSTLOG 2024. https://proceedings.itltrisakti.ac.id/index.php/ATLR/article/download/691/731

Qian, X., Shen, L., Wang, Y., Lin, J., Jin, Z., Ge, Y.-E., & George Haddad, S. S. (2025). Stability analysis of maritime logistics alliance based on Blockchain. *Transport Policy*, *163*, 219–231. DOI: 10.1016/j.tranpol.2024.12.025

Qiu, F., Chen, M., Wang, L., Ying, Y., & Tang, T. (2023). The architecture evolution of intelligent factory logistics digital twin from planning, implement to operation. *Advances in Mechanical Engineering*, *15*(9). Advance online publication. DOI: 10.1177/16878132231198339

Qorri, A., Mujkić, Z., & Kraslawski, A. (2018). A conceptual framework for measuring sustainability performance of supply chains. *Journal of Cleaner Production*, *189*, 570–584.

Queiroz, M. M., Telles, R., & Bonilla, S. H. (2019). Blockchain and supply chain management integration: a systematic review of the literature. Supply Chain Management: An International Journal, 25(2), pp. 241-254. Emerald Publishing Limited. https://doi.org/DOI: 10.1108/scm-03-2018-0143

Queiroz, M. M., & Fosso Wamba, S. (2019). Blockchain adoption challenges in supply chain: An empirical investigation of the main drivers in India and the USA. *International Journal of Information Management*, *46*, 70–82.

Quesado, P., Costa Oliveira, H., & Silva, R. (2025). Integrating sustainability goals into the balanced scorecard: A bibliometric analysis of the sustainability balanced scorecard. *Measuring Business Excellence*.

Rahmanifar, G. (2025). Green vehicle routing and logistics optimization: IoT-driven solutions for modern urban challenges [Dipartimento Di Ingegneria Civile, Edile E Ambientale]. https://tesidottorato.depositolegale.it/handle/20.500.14242/188585

Raja Santhi, A., & Muthuswamy, P. (2022). Influence of Blockchain Technology in Manufacturing Supply Chain and Logistics. In *Logistics* (Vol. 6, Issue 1). https://doi.org/DOI: 10.3390/logistics6010015

Raman, R., Lathabhai, H., Pattnaik, D., Kumar, C., & Nedungadi, P. (2024). Research contribution of bibliometric studies related to sustainable development goals and sustainability. *Discover Sustainability*, *5*(1), 7.

Ramesh, K., Renjith, P. N., Balasubramani, S., Anto Bennet, M., Saritha, S., Pandey, D., & Kanike, U. K. (2024). Leveraging cutting-edge technologies and innovative strategies to optimize the IoT and AI integration in supply chain management. In *Utilization of AI Technology in Supply Chain Management* (pp. 159–173). IGI Global.

Rashid, H. (2019). Integrating Circular Economy Principles in Logistics to Drive Sustainable Warehousing Practices. *IJIRMPS*, *7*(5), 1–9.

Rashid, N., Imtiaz, A., Ali, J., & Sorooshian, S. (2025). Mitigating The Impact of Purchase Uncertainty on Reverse Supply Chain Through Impulsive Consumer Buying with Moderation of Lenient Return Policies. *Cleaner Logistics and Supply Chain*, *14*, 100207. DOI: 10.1016/j.clscn.2025.100207

Ratanabanchuen, R., Saengchote, K., Nakavachara, V., Amonthumniyom, T., Parinyavuttichai, P., & Vinaibodee, P. (2024). The test of investors' behavioral bias through the price discovery process in cryptoasset exchange" Transactional-level evidence from Thailand. *arXiv preprint arXiv:2406.02878.*

Raza, Z., Woxenius, J., Vural, C. A., & Lind, M. (2023). Digital transformation of maritime logistics: Exploring trends in the liner shipping segment. *Computers in Industry*. Advance online publication. DOI: 10.1016/j.compind.2022.103811

Rebs, T., Brandenburg, M., & Seuring, S. (2019). System dynamics modeling for sustainable supply chain management: A literature review and systems thinking approach. *Journal of Cleaner Production*, *208*, 1265–1280.

Rehman Khan, S. A., Yu, Z., Sarwat, S., Godil, D. I., Amin, S., & Shujaat, S. (2022). The role of block chain technology in circular economy practices to improve organisational performance. *International Journal of Logistics Research and Applications*, *25*(4–5), 605–622. DOI: 10.1080/13675567.2021.1872512

Rejeb, A., Keogh, J. G., Leong, G. K., & Treiblmaier, H. (2021). Potentials and challenges of augmented reality smart glasses in logistics and supply chain management: A systematic literature review. *International Journal of Production Research*, *59*(12), 3747–3776. DOI: 10.1080/00207543.2021.1876942

Rejeb, A., Rejeb, K., Simske, S., & Treiblmaier, H. (2021). Humanitarian Drones: A Review and Research Agenda. *Internet of Things : Engineering Cyber Physical Human Systems*, *16*, 100434. DOI: 10.1016/j.iot.2021.100434

Rethlefsen, M. L., & Page, M. J. (2022). PRISMA 2020 and PRISMA-S: Common questions on tracking records and the flow diagram. *Journal of the Medical Library Association: JMLA*, *110*(2), 253. PMID: 35440907

Reza, T., Pejvak, O., Vahid, S., Pankaj, C. P., & Rana, M. (2022). Block by block: A blockchain-based peer-to-peer business transaction for international trade. *Technological Forecasting and Social Change*, *180*(1). Advance online publication. DOI: 10.1016/j.techfore.2022.121714

Riofrancos, T. (2023). The security–sustainability nexus: Lithium onshoring in the Global North. *Global Environmental Politics*, *23*(1), 20–41.

Ripple. (2020). Blockchain in ship finance: Leveraging Ripple's technology for secure transactions. Ripple Case Studies.

Rodrigue, J. (2020). The geography of transport systems. In *Routledge eBooks*. https://doi.org/DOI: 10.4324/9780429346323

Rodrique, J.-P. (2020). Routledge, New York, 456 pages, ISBN 978-0-367-36463-2.

Rong, Y., & Wan, G. (2025). An Integrated Fermatean Fuzzy Group Decision Method based on Sugeno-Weber Operators for the Selection of Reverse Logistics Supplier. *Computer and Decision Making: An International Journal*, *2*, 508–529. DOI: 10.59543/comdem.v2i.10537

Ruiz-Torres, A. J., Mahmoodi, F., Ohmori, S., & Hlali, A. (2022). Suppliers portfolio and returner incentive decisions in closed-loop remanufacturing systems under multiple stochastic scenarios. *International Journal of Sustainable Engineering*, *15*(1), 208–225. DOI: 10.1080/19397038.2022.2110330

Rukanova, B., van Engelenburg, S., Ubacht, J., Tan, Y.-H., Geurts, M., Sies, M., Molenhuis, M., Slegt, M., & van Dijk, D. (2023). Public value creation through voluntary business to government information sharing enabled by digital infrastructure innovations: A framework for analysis. *Government Information Quarterly*, *40*(2), 101786. DOI: 10.1016/j.giq.2022.101786

Rusch, M., Schöggl, J. P., & Baumgartner, R. J. (2023). Application of digital technologies for sustainable product management in a circular economy: A review. *Business Strategy and the Environment*, *32*(3), 1159–1174.

Ryzhkov, Y. (2024). Maritime Radio Communication: Language Challenges and How to handle them. *Humanities Science Current Issues*, *2*(82), 392–395. DOI: 10.24919/2308-4863/82-2-55

Saberi, S., Kouhizadeh, M., Sarkis, J., & Shen, L. (2019). Blockchain technology and its relationships to sustainable supply chain management. *International Journal of Production Research*, *57*(7), 2117–2135. DOI: 10.1080/00207543.2018.1533261

Sabir, H. (2020). Pratiques de la grande distribution alimentaire et performance de la logistique urbaine: Revue de littérature. *Revue Internationale du Chercheur*, *1*(2).

Sadiq, M., Ali, S. W., Terriche, Y., Mutarraf, M. U., Hassan, M. A., Hamid, K., Ali, Z., Sze, J. Y., Su, C.-L., & Guerrero, J. M. (2021). Future Greener Seaports: A Review of New Infrastructure, Challenges, and Energy Efficiency Measures. *IEEE Access : Practical Innovations, Open Solutions*, *9*, 75568–75587. DOI: 10.1109/ACCESS.2021.3081430

Safety4sea (2018). Port of Antwerp works on blockchain pilot project – SAFETY-4SEA. Available at: https://safety4sea.com/port-of-antwerp-works-on-blockchain-pilot-project/

Sahoo, S., Kumar, S., Sivarajah, U., Lim, W. M., Westland, J. C., & Kumar, A. (2024). Blockchain for sustainable supply chain management: Trends and ways forward. *Electronic Commerce Research*, *24*(3), 1563–1618.

Sainath, K. L. (2024). Robots in Logistics: Apprehension of current status and future trends in Indian warehouses. In *Lecture notes in electrical engineering* (pp. 201–211). https://doi.org/DOI: 10.1007/978-981-97-8031-0_21

Sakaguchi, M., & Aoki, E. (2022). Study on the comparison of consumer impression of e-commerce and real stores in the fashion tech era, and the effectiveness of VR utilization. In *Lecture notes in networks and systems* (Vol. 497, pp. 528–537). Springer., DOI: 10.1007/978-3-031-08812-4_51

Sallam, K., Mohamed, M., & Mohamed, A. W. (2023). Internet of Things (IoT) in supply chain management: Challenges, opportunities, and best practices. *Sustainable Machine Intelligence Journal*, *2*, 3–1. DOI: 10.61185/SMIJ.2023.22103

Sánchez-Flores, R. B., Cruz-Sotelo, S. E., Ojeda-Benitez, S., & Ramírez-Barreto, M. E. (2020). Sustainable supply chain management—A literature review on emerging economies. *Sustainability*, *12*(17), 6972.

Sandilands, D. (2014). Bivariate Analysis. In Michalos, A. C. (Ed.), *Encyclopedia of Quality of Life and Well-Being Research* (pp. 416–418). Springer Netherlands., DOI: 10.1007/978-94-007-0753-5_222

Sarkis, J. (2012). A boundaries and flows perspective of green supply chain management. *Supply Chain Management, 17*(2), 202–216. DOI: 10.1108/13598541211212924

Savin, A. (2020). Blockchain, Digital Transformation and the Law: What Can We Learn from the Recent Deals? University of San Francisco Maritime Law Journal, 31(2), 107-113. https://heinonline.org/HOL/Page?collection=journals&handle=hein.journals/usfm31&id=2&men_tab=srchresults

Scholten, K., Stevenson, M., & van Donk, D. P. (2019). Dealing with the unpredictable: Supply chain resilience. *International Journal of Operations & Production Management, 40*(1), 1–10. DOI: 10.1108/IJOPM-01-2020-789

Seele, P., Dierksmeier, C., Hofstetter, R., & Schultz, M. D. (2021). Mapping the ethicality of algorithmic pricing: A review of dynamic and personalized pricing. *Journal of Business Ethics, 170*, 697–719. DOI: 10.1007/s10551-019-04371-w

Sekarini, S., & Selvabaskar, S. (2024). *AI-Powered Branding.*, DOI: 10.4018/979-8-3693-7122-0.ch002

Selvakumar, P., Shanthi, M., Pitchiah, R., Sharma, M., Dahake, P. S., & T. C., M. (2025). *The Role of Artificial Intelligence in Business Model Innovation* (pp. 219–246). https://doi.org/DOI: 10.4018/979-8-3693-9571-4.ch009

Senna, P. P., Ferreira, L. M. D. F., Barros, A. C., Roca, J. B., & Magalhaes, V. (2022). Prioritizing barriers for the adoption of Industry 4.0 technologies. *Computers & Industrial Engineering, 171*, 108428.

Şerbetçioğlu, C., & Oflaç, B. S. (2024). Emerging Trends in Supply Chain Resilience: A Systematic Literature review. *Markets Globalization & Development Review, 9*(4). Advance online publication. DOI: 10.23860/mgdr-2024-09-04-04

Sgarbossa, F., Arena, S., Tang, O., & Peron, M. (2023). Renewable hydrogen supply chains: A planning matrix and an agenda for future research. *International Journal of Production Economics, 255*, 108674.

Shaban, A., Saraeva, A., Rose, S., & Clark, M. (2024). The invisible hand of touch: Testing a tactile sensation-choice satisfaction model in online shopping. *Journal of Sensory Studies, 39*(1), e12897. DOI: 10.1111/joss.12897

Shahin, M., Maghanaki, M., Hosseinzadeh, A., & Chen, F. F. (2024). Improving operations through a lean AI paradigm: A view to an AI-aided lean manufacturing via versatile convolutional neural network. *International Journal of Advanced Manufacturing Technology, 133*(11–12), 5343–5419. DOI: 10.1007/s00170-024-13874-4

Shahrjerdi, R. (2024). Rethinking the Secondhand Supply Chain: A Technological and Sustainable Approach. *Advances in Industrial Engineering, Online First*. https://doi.org/DOI: 10.22059/aie.2024.380818.1904

Sha, K., Taeihagh, A., & De Jong, M. (2024). Governing disruptive technologies for inclusive development in cities: A systematic literature review. *Technological Forecasting and Social Change*, *203*, 123382. DOI: 10.1016/j.techfore.2024.123382

Sharma, V. (2025). Impact of automation on Retail Logistics: AI-powered solutions for efficient supply chains. *International journal of scientific research in engineering and management, 09*(02), 1–8.

Sharma, N. K., Kumar, V., Verma, P., & Luthra, S. (2021). Sustainable reverse logistics practices and performance evaluation with fuzzy TOPSIS: A study on Indian retailers. *Cleaner Logistics and Supply Chain*, *1*, 100007.

Sharma, N., Saraswat, C., Sharma, J., Mittal, M. L., & Keprate, A. (2024a). Multi-Objective Optimization for Economic and Environmental Sustainability in Apparel E-commerce Reverse Logistics. *International Journal of Mathematical. Engineering and Management Sciences*, *9*(1), 111–128. DOI: 10.33889/IJMEMS.2024.9.1.00

Sharma, V., Raut, R. D., Mangla, S. K., Narkhede, B. E., Luthra, S., & Gokhale, R. (2021). A systematic literature review to integrate lean, agile, resilient, green, and sustainable paradigms in the supply chain management. *Business Strategy and the Environment*, *30*(2), 1191–1212. DOI: 10.1002/bse.2679

Shee, H. K., Miah, S. J., & De Vass, T. (2021). Impact of smart logistics on smart city sustainable performance: An empirical investigation. *International Journal of Logistics Management*, *32*(3), 821–845. DOI: 10.1108/IJLM-07-2020-0282

Shi, H., & Wang, X. (2021). Research on Electronic Bill of Lading of Container Shipping Based on Blockchain Technology. *Journal of Physics: Conference Series*, *2029*(1), 012123. DOI: 10.1088/1742-6596/2029/1/012123

Shi, J. (2022). Research on Optimization of Cross-Border e-Commerce Logistics Distribution Network in the Context of Artificial Intelligence. *Mobile Information Systems*, *2022*, 1–11. DOI: 10.1155/2022/3022280

Shin, S., Wang, Y., Pettit, S., & Abouarghoub, W. (2024). Blockchain application in maritime supply chain: A systematic literature review and conceptual framework. *Maritime Policy & Management*, *51*(6), 1062–1095. DOI: 10.1080/03088839.2023.2234896

Siems, E., Seuring, S., & Schilling, L. (2023). Stakeholder roles in sustainable supply chain management: A literature review. *Journal of Business Economics*, *93*(4), 747–775.

Silva, Ó., Cordera, R., González-González, E., & Nogués, S. (2022). Environmental impacts of autonomous vehicles: A review of the scientific literature. *The Science of the Total Environment*, *830*, 154615. DOI: 10.1016/j.scitotenv.2022.154615 PMID: 35307440

Simon, H. A. (1962). The Architecture of Complexity [Reprinted in: Herbert A. Simon, The Sciences of the Artificial, M.I.T Press, Cambridge, Massachusetts, 1969, pp. 84-118]. *Proceedings of the American Philosophical Society*, *106*, 467–482.

Sindiramutty, S. R., Jhanjhi, N. Z., Tan, C. E., Khan, N. A., Shah, B., & Manchuri, A. R. (2024). *Cybersecurity Measures for Logistics Industry*., DOI: 10.4018/979-8-3693-3816-2.ch001

Singh, D., Lanka, K., & Gopal, P. R. C. (2021). Predicting Sustainable Supply Chain Performance Based on GRI Metrics and Multilayer Perceptron Neural Networks. *Emerging Frontiers in Operations and Supply Chain Management: Theory and Applications*, 159-180.

Singh, G. (2024). Blockchain-based smart contracts. In *Advances in Computational Intelligence and Robotics* (pp. 183–203). IGI Global.

Singh, A., Goel, A., Chauhan, A., & Singh, S. K. (2025). Sustainability of electronic product manufacturing through e-waste management and reverse logistics. *Sustainable Futures : An Applied Journal of Technology, Environment and Society*, *9*, 100490. DOI: 10.1016/j.sftr.2025.100490

Singh, S. K., & Bansal, A. (2016). Multimodal Interpretation and Analysis of Traffic Survey Data. *International Journal of Innovative Research in Science, Engineering and Technology*, *5*(5), 7040–7048. https://www.ijirset.com/upload/2016/may/59_Multimodal.pdf

Singh, S. K., & Gupta, T. (2021). Critical Analysis and Feasibility of PRT for Gurgaon City. *International Journal of Scientific Research in Science, Engineering and Technology*, *8*(1), 83–86. DOI: 10.32628/IJSRSET21812

Singh, S. K., Jain, R., Palaniappan, D., & Parmar, K.. (2025). Future of Mobility: Potential Challenges and Ethical Considerations. In *AIoT for Smart Transportation: Transforming the Future of Mobility*. IET Publishers., DOI: 10.1049/PBTR047E_ch12

Singh, S. K., & Prabhakar, K. (2017). Statistical Analysis of Traffic of Rotary Intersection. *International Journal of Engineering Sciences & Research Technology*, *6*(2), 327–334. DOI: 10.5281/zenodo.290268

Singh, S. K., & Saraswat, A. (2019). Design service volume, capacity, level of service calculation and forecasting for a semi-urban city. *Revue d'Intelligence Artificielle*, *33*(2), 139–143. DOI: 10.18280/ria.330209

Skalli, D., Cherrafi, A., Charkaoui, A., Chiarini, A., Shokri, A., Antony, J., Garza-Reyes, J. A., & Foster, M. (2024). Integrating Lean Six Sigma and Industry 4.0: Developing a design science research-based LSS4.0 framework for operational excellence. *Production Planning and Control*, •••, 1–27. DOI: 10.1080/09537287.2024.2341698

Snyder, H. (2019). Literature review as a research methodology: An overview and guidelines. *Journal of Business Research*, *104*, 333–339.

Song, H. (2022). Intelligent supply chain and tech-enabled supply chain finance. In *Smart Supply Chain Finance* (pp. 89–148). Springer., DOI: 10.1007/978-981-16-5997-3_3

Song, Y., Yu, F. R., Zhou, L., Yang, X., & He, Z. (2020). Applications of the Internet of Things (IoT) in smart logistics: A comprehensive survey. *IEEE Internet of Things Journal*, *8*(6), 4250–4274. DOI: 10.1109/JIOT.2020.3034385

Sorooshian, S., Khademi Sharifabad, S., Parsaee, M., & Afshari, A. R. (2022). Toward a Modern Last-Mile Delivery: Consequences and Obstacles of Intelligent Technology. *Applied System Innovation*, *5*(4), 82. DOI: 10.3390/asi5040082

Spellmeier, J. P., Rosa, C. B., Rigo, P. D., Mello, M. F., & Hoss, M. (2025). Design of a Business Model for Competitive End-of-Life Performance of Photovoltaic Systems in Brazil. *Renewable Energy*, *122755*. Advance online publication. DOI: 10.1016/j.renene.2025.122755

Srivastava, A., Pandey, P., Pandey, A., Gupta, A., Manglick, A., & Mahajan, N. (2025). Sustaining supply chain with automation and robotics. In Pandey, A., & Al-Turjman, F. (Eds.), *Transformation of Supply Chain Ecosystems* (pp. 173–188). Emerald Publishing Limited., DOI: 10.1108/978-1-83549-246-820251011

Srivastava, S. K. (2007). Green supply-chain management: A state-of-the-art literature review. *International Journal of Management Reviews*, *9*(1), 53–80. DOI: 10.1111/j.1468-2370.2007.00202.x

Stanford, V. I., Buc, L., Houck, A., & Jost, E. (2023). *Using Pricing as a Tool to Achieve Carbon Neutrality*. Implications for the United States Postal Service., DOI: 10.1007/978-3-031-25362-1_16

Stankov, S. P. (2024). DEVELOPMENT OF AUTOMATION IN THE DIRECTION OF HYPERAUTOMATION. *Annals of the Faculty of Engineering Hunedoara*, *22*(1), 179–184.

Stevenson, A. B., & Rieck, J. (2024). Investigating Returns Management across E-Commerce Sectors and Countries: Trends, Perspectives, and Future Research. *Logistics (Basel)*, *8*(3), 82. DOI: 10.3390/logistics8030082

Stöcker, B., Baier, D., & Brand, B. M. (2021). New insights in online fashion retail returns from a customers' perspective and their dynamics. *Journal of Business Economics*, *91*(8), 1149–1187. DOI: 10.1007/s11573-021-01032-1

Stoica, M. (2021). Green Marketing Communication Strategies: An Integrative Literature Review. *The Annals of the University of Oradea. Economic Sciences*, *30*(30 (1)), 388–396. DOI: 10.47535/1991AUOES30(1)043

Strubell, E., Ganesh, A., & McCallum, A. (2020). Energy and Policy Considerations for Modern Deep Learning Research. *Proceedings of the AAAI Conference on Artificial Intelligence*, *34*(09), 09. Advance online publication. DOI: 10.1609/aaai.v34i09.7123

Sturgeon, T. J. (2021). Upgrading strategies for the digital economy. *Global Strategy Journal*, *11*(1), 34–57. DOI: 10.1002/gsj.1364

Sun, X., Yu, H., & Solvang, W. D. (2022). Towards the smart and sustainable transformation of Reverse Logistics 4.0: A conceptualization and research agenda. *Environmental Science and Pollution Research International*, *29*(46), 69275–69293. DOI: 10.1007/s11356-022-22473-3 PMID: 35972653

Sun, X., Yu, H., Solvang, W. D., Wang, Y., & Wang, K. (2022). The application of Industry 4.0 technologies in sustainable logistics: A systematic literature review (2012–2020) to explore future research opportunities. *Environmental Science and Pollution Research International*, ●●●, 1–32. DOI: 10.1007/s11356-021-17693-y PMID: 34893953

Sun, Y., Ma, A., Cui, X., & Gu, Y. (2023). Effective risk assessment and management with IoT in supply chains. *Frontiers in Management Science*, *2*(5), 50–57.

Surur, F. M., Mamo, A. A., Gebresilassie, B. G., Mekonen, K. A., Golda, A., Behera, R. K., & Kumar, K. (2025). *Unlocking the power of machine learning in big data: A scoping survey*. Data Science and Management., DOI: 10.1016/j.dsm.2025.02.004

Susanto, H., & Kemaluddin, N. (2023). Innovative Blockchain-Based Tracking Systems, A Technology Acceptance for Cross-Border Runners During and Post-Pandemic. *Sustainability*, *15*(8), 6519. DOI: 10.3390/su15086519

Su, Y., Duan, H., Wang, Z., Song, G., Kang, P., & Chen, D. (2020). Characterizing the environmental impact of packaging materials for express delivery via life cycle assessment. *Journal of Cleaner Production, 274*, 122961. DOI: 10.1016/j.jclepro.2020.122961

Szelągowski, M., & Berniak-Woźny, J. (2023). The impact of hyperautomation on business processes in SMEs. *International Journal of Process Management and Benchmarking, 13*(3), 384–400. DOI: 10.1504/IJPMB.2023.129646

Tadayonrad, Y., & Ndiaye, A. B. (2023). A new key performance indicator model for demand forecasting in inventory management considering supply chain reliability and seasonality. *Supply Chain Analytics, 3*, 100026. DOI: 10.1016/j.sca.2023.100026

Tahir, B., & Tariq, M. (2024). Federated learning for Supply Chain Management 5.0. In *Federated Learning for Multimedia Data Processing and Security in Industry 5.0* (pp. 181–201). https://doi.org/DOI: 10.1049/pbpc066e_ch9

Tan, W. Z. (2017). Antwerp to use blockchain technology in container handling operations. Lloyd's List. Available at: https://lloydslist.maritimeintelligence.informa.com/LL108882/Antwerp-to-use-blockchain-technology-in-container-handling-operations

Tan, W. Z. (2017). PIL and PSA jump on the blockchain bandwagon with IBM. Lloyd's List. Available at: https://lloydslist.maritimeintelligence.informa.com/LL110930/PIL-and-PSA-jump-on-the-blockchain-bandwagon-with-IBM

Tan, T. M., & Saraniemi, S. (2023). Trust in blockchain-enabled exchanges: Future directions in blockchain marketing. *Journal of the Academy of Marketing Science, 51*(4), 914–939.

Tapscott, D., & Tapscott, A. (2018). Blockchain Revolution: How the Technology Behind Bitcoin and Other Cryptocurrencies Is Changing the World. In *Sage Publications, Inc.*

Tariq, M. U. (2024). *Emerging Trends and Innovations in Blockchain-Digital Twin Integration for Green Investments.*, DOI: 10.4018/979-8-3693-1878-2.ch007

Tarnanidis, T., Papathanasiou, J., Ismyrlis, V., & Kittu Manda, V. (Eds.). (2024). *Multiple-Criteria Decision-Making (MCDM) Techniques and Statistics in Marketing*. IGI Global., DOI: 10.4018/979-8-3693-9122-8

Teece, D. J., Pisano, G., & Shuen, A. (1997). Dynamic capabilities and strategic management. *Strategic Management Journal, 18*(7), 509–533.

Tennakoon, G. A., Rameezdeen, R., & Chileshe, N. (2025). Understanding the Limited Uptake of Reprocessed Construction Materials: A Pro-Environmental Behaviour Perspective. *Sustainable Development*, sd.3400. https://doi.org/DOI: 10.1002/sd.3400

Thanigaivel, S., Priya, A. K., Dutta, K., Rajendran, S., & Vasseghian, Y. (2022). Engineering strategies and opportunities of next generation biofuel from microalgae: A perspective review on the potential bioenergy feedstock. *Fuel*, *312*, 122827. DOI: 10.1016/j.fuel.2021.122827

Thornton, M. (2025). *Management Strategies and Processes for Improving Product Returns* [Doctoral Study, Walden University]. https://www.proquest.com/openview/3d9098519ccb2be1cd0ea0198a306901/1

Thürer, M., Li, S. S., & Qu, T. (2022). Digital Twin Architecture for Production Logistics: The Critical role of Programmable Logic Controllers (PLCS). *Procedia Computer Science*, *200*, 710–717. DOI: 10.1016/j.procs.2022.01.269

Tian, F. (2016). An agri-food supply chain traceability system for China based on RFID & blockchain technology. *2016 13th International Conference on Service Systems and Service Management, ICSSSM 2016*. https://doi.org/DOI: 10.1109/ICSSSM.2016.7538424

Tijan, E., Aksentijević, S., Ivanić, K., & Jardas, M. (2019). Blockchain technology implementation in logistics. *Sustainability*, *11*(4), 1185. DOI: 10.3390/su11041185

Tiwari, S., Sharma, P., Choi, T. M., & Lim, A. (2023). Blockchain and third-party logistics for global supply chain operations: Stakeholders' perspectives and decision roadmap. *Transportation Research Part E, Logistics and Transportation Review*, *170*, 103012. DOI: 10.1016/j.tre.2022.103012

Torchio, F. (2023). Survey on automated systems for smart warehouses (Doctoral dissertation, Politecnico di Torino). https://doi.org/DOI: 10.6092/polito/amsphd/2023/001

Tranfield, D., Denyer, D., & Smart, P. (2003). Towards a methodology for developing evidence-informed management knowledge by means of systematic review. *British Journal of Management*, *14*(3), 207–222.

Treiblmaier, H. (2018). The impact of the blockchain on the supply chain: A theory-based research framework and a call for action. *Supply Chain Management*, *23*(6). Advance online publication. DOI: 10.1108/SCM-01-2018-0029

Trstenjak, M., Mustapić, M., Gregurić, P., & Opetuk, T. (2023). Use of green Industry 5.0 technologies in logistics activities. *Tehnički glasnik, 17*(3), 471–477. https://doi.org/DOI: 10.31803/tg-20230518185836

Trung, C. T., Xuan, T. P. T., & Thanh, H. T. (2024). *Application of Artificial Intelligence in Reverse Logistics: A Case Study of Seafood Enterprises in The Mekong Delta*. 9. https://www.researchgate.net/profile/Chuyen-Tran-Trung-2/publication/388860284

Tsang, Y. P., Fan, Y., & Feng, Z. P. (2023). Bridging the gap: Building environmental, social and governance capabilities in small and medium logistics companies. *Journal of Environmental Management, 338*, 117758. DOI: 10.1016/j.jenvman.2023.117758 PMID: 36996566

Tseng, J. H., Liao, Y. C., Chong, B., & Liao, S. W. (2018). Governance on the drug supply chain via gcoin blockchain. *International Journal of Environmental Research and Public Health, 15*(6). Advance online publication. DOI: 10.3390/ijerph15061055 PMID: 29882861

Tseng, M. L., Ha, H. M., Lim, M. K., Wu, K. J., & Iranmanesh, M. (2022). Sustainable supply chain management in stakeholders: Supporting from sustainable supply and process management in the healthcare industry in Vietnam. *International Journal of Logistics Research and Applications*, *25*(4-5), 364–383.

Tsiulin, S., Reinau, K. H., Hilmola, O.-P., Goryaev, N., & Karam, A. (2020). Blockchain-based applications in shipping and port management: A literature review towards defining key conceptual frameworks. *Rev. Int. Bus. Strateg.*, *30*, 201–224.

Tsiulin, S., Reinau, K. H., Hilmola, O.-P., Goryaev, N., & Karam, A. (2020). Blockchain-based applications in shipping and port management: A literature review towards defining key conceptual frameworks. *Review of International Business and Strategy*, *30*(2), 201–224. DOI: 10.1108/RIBS-04-2019-0051

Tsymbal, L., Natsvlishvili, T., & Verdenhofa, O. (2023). One Belt, One Road project: The impact of smart technologies on infrastructure and logistics. *Baltic Journal of Economic Studies*, *9*(3), 214–221. DOI: 10.30525/2256-0742/2023-9-3-214-221

Tubis, A. A., & Rohman, J. (2023). Intelligent Warehouse in Industry 4.0—Systematic Literature review. *Sensors (Basel)*, *23*(8), 4105. DOI: 10.3390/s23084105 PMID: 37112446

Tubis, A. A., Ryczyński, J., & Żurek, A. (2021). Risk assessment for the use of drones in warehouse operations in the first phase of introducing the service to the market. *Sensors (Basel)*, *21*(20), 6713. DOI: 10.3390/s21206713 PMID: 34695924

Tyagi, A. K. (2023). Blockchain and artificial intelligence for cyber security in the era of internet of things and industrial internet of things applications. In *Advances in Computational Intelligence and Robotics* (pp. 171–199). IGI Global.

Uda, S., & Basrowi, B. (2024). Environmental education using SARITHA-Apps to enhance environmentally friendly supply chain efficiency and foster environmental knowledge towards sustainability. *Uncertain Supply Chain Management, 12*(1), 359–372.

Udeh, E. O., Amajuoyi, P., Adeusi, K. B., & Scott, A. O. (2024). The role of IoT in boosting supply chain transparency and efficiency. *Magna Scientia Advanced Research and Reviews, 12*(1), 178–197. DOI: 10.30574/msarr.2024.11.1.0081

Ullah, I., & Havinga, P. J. M. (2023). Governance of a Blockchain-Enabled IoT Ecosystem: A Variable Geometry Approach. *Sensors (Basel), 23*(22), 9031. DOI: 10.3390/s23229031 PMID: 38005419

UN SDG. (2025). The 17 Goals—Sustainable Development. https://sdgs.un.org/goals

UNCTAD. (2017). Report on maritime transport available at https://unctad.org/system/files/official-document/rmt2017_en.pdf

UNCTAD. (2021). *Technology and innovation report 2021- catching technological waves: Innovation with equity.* https://unctad.org/publication/technology-and-innovation-report-2021

Upadhyay, N. (2020). Demystifying blockchain: A critical analysis of challenges, applications and opportunities. *International Journal of Information Management, 54*, 102120.

Vashishth, T. K., Sharma, V., Sharma, K. K., Kumar, B., Chaudhary, S., & Panwar, R. (2025). Digital twins solutions for smart logistics and transportation. In *Digital Twins for Smart Cities and Villages* (pp. 353–376). Elsevier., DOI: 10.1016/B978-0-443-28884-5.00016-6

Vasiulis Ferreira Rodrigues, N., De Camargo Fiorini, P., Piato, É. L., Lopes de Sousa Jabbour, A. B., & Chiappetta Jabbour, C. J. (2024). Resources and capabilities for logistics 4.0 and sustainable value creation: A study of logistics service providers in an emerging market. *International Journal of Logistics Management.* Advance online publication. DOI: 10.1108/IJLM-11-2023-0471

Vegter, D., van Hillegersberg, J., & Olthaar, M. (2023). Performance measurement system for circular supply chain management. *Sustainable Production and Consumption, 36*, 171–183.

Verbivska, L., Zhygalkevych, Z., Fisun, Y., Chobitok, I., & Shvedkyi, V. (2023). Digital technologies as a tool of efficient logistics. *Revista de la Universidad del Zulia, 14*(39), 492–508. DOI: 10.46925//rdluz.39.28

Vidal, N. G., Spetic, W., Croom, S., & Marshall, D. (2023). Supply chain stakeholder pressure for the adoption of sustainable supply chain practices: Examining the roles of entrepreneurial and sustainability orientations. *Supply Chain Management, 28*(3), 598–618.

Vienažindienė, M., Tamulienė, V., & Zaleckienė, J. (2021). Green Logistics Practices Seeking Development of Sustainability: Evidence from Lithuanian Transportation and Logistics Companies. *Energies, 14*(22), 7500. DOI: 10.3390/en14227500

Vijaykumar, V., Mercy, P., Lucia Agnes Beena, T., Leena, H. M., & Savarimuthu, C. (2024). Convergence of IoT, Artificial Intelligence and Blockchain Approaches for Supply Chain Management. In *Blockchain, IoT, and AI Technologies for Supply Chain Management* (pp. 45–89). Apress. https://doi.org/DOI: 10.1007/979-8-8688-0315-4_2

Villacis, M. Y., Merlo, O. T., Rivero, D. P., & Towfek, S. K. (2024). Optimizing sustainable inventory management using an improved big data analytics approach. *Journal of Intelligent Systems and Internet of Things, 11*(1), 55–64. DOI: 10.54216/JISIoT.110106

Villar, A., Paladini, S., & Buckley, O. (2023). Towards Supply Chain 5.0: Redesigning supply chains as resilient, sustainable, and human-centric systems in a post-pandemic world. *Operations Research Forum, 4*(3), 60. Springer International Publishing. https://doi.org/DOI: 10.1007/s43069-023-00234-3

Vintimilla Alvarez, P., & Alarcón Valero, F. (2025). A framework for facility layout problem characterization in a bi-directional logistics context. *Journal of Industrial Engineering and Management, 18*(1), 130. DOI: 10.3926/jiem.8573

Visconti, P., Rausa, G., Del-Valle-Soto, C., Velázquez, R., Cafagna, D., & De Fazio, R. (2025). Innovative Driver Monitoring Systems and On-Board-Vehicle Devices in a Smart-Road Scenario Based on the Internet of Vehicle Paradigm: A Literature and Commercial Solutions Overview. *Sensors (Basel), 25*(2), 562. DOI: 10.3390/s25020562 PMID: 39860930

Vlachos, I., Pascazzi, R. M., Ntotis, M., Spanaki, K., Despoudi, S., & Repoussis, P. (2024). Smart and flexible manufacturing systems using Autonomous Guided Vehicles (AGVs) and the Internet of Things (IoT). *International Journal of Production Research, 62*(15), 5574–5595. DOI: 10.1080/00207543.2022.2136282

Vudugula, S. (2025). Sustainable smart supply chains: A review of green technologies and their impact on logistics. *American Journal of Scholarly Research and Innovation*, *4*(01), 1–32.

Vural, C. A., Roso, V., Halldórsson, Á., Ståhle, G., & Yaruta, M. (2020). Can digitalization mitigate barriers to intermodal transport? An exploratory study. *Research in Transportation Business & Management*, *37*, 100525. DOI: 10.1016/j.rtbm.2020.100525

Wachter, S., Mittelstadt, B., & Floridi, L. (2017). Transparent, explainable, and accountable AI for robotics. *Science Robotics*, *2*(6), eaan6080. Advance online publication. DOI: 10.1126/scirobotics.aan6080 PMID: 33157874

Walmart. (2019). Walmart and IBM: Food Safety and Traceability. Retrieved from Walmart.

Wang, Y., Han, J. H., & Beynon-Davies, P. (2019). Understanding blockchain technology for future supply chains: a systematic literature review and research agenda. In *Supply Chain Management* (Vol. 24, Issue 1). https://doi.org/DOI: 10.1108/SCM-03-2018-0148

Wang, Y., Singgih, M., Wang, J. et Rit, M. (2019). Making sense of blockchain technology: How will it transform supply chains?. International Journal of Production Economics, 211: 221– 236. 241. https://doi.org/DOI: 10.1016/j.ijpe.2019.02.002

Wang, J., Guo, Q., & Sun, H. (2024). Planning approach for integrating charging stations and renewable energy sources in low-carbon logistics delivery. *Applied Energy*, *372*, 123792. DOI: 10.1016/j.apenergy.2024.123792

Wang, J., Liu, J., Wang, F., & Yue, X. (2021). Blockchain technology for port logistics capability: Exclusive or sharing. *Transportation Research Part B: Methodological*, *149*, 347–392. DOI: 10.1016/j.trb.2021.05.010

Wang, L., & Hui, M. (2020). Research on joint emission reduction in supply chain based on carbon footprint of the product. *Journal of Cleaner Production*, *263*, 121086. DOI: 10.1016/j.jclepro.2020.121086

Wang, R. (2024). Safeguarding Enterprise Prosperity: An In-depth Analysis of Financial Management Strategies. *Journal of the Knowledge Economy*, *15*(4), 17676–17704. DOI: 10.1007/s13132-024-01752-z

Wang, S., Wan, J., Li, D., & Zhang, C. (2016). Implementing smart factory of Industrie 4.0: An outlook. *International Journal of Distributed Sensor Networks*, *12*(1), 1–10. DOI: 10.1155/2016/3159805

Wang, T., Hu, S., & Jiang, Y. (2021). Predicting shared-car use and examining non-linear effects using gradient boosting regression trees. *International Journal of Sustainable Transportation, 15*(12), 893–907. DOI: 10.1080/15568318.2020.1827316

Wang, Y., Gunasekaran, A., Ngai, E. W. T., & Papadopoulos, T. (2019). Big Data in Logistics and Supply Chain Management: Antecedents and Consequences. *Transportation Research Part E, Logistics and Transportation Review, 99*, 212–228. DOI: 10.1016/j.tre.2016.01.013

Wang, Y., Han, J. H., & Beynon-Davies, P. (2019). Understanding blockchain technology for future supply chains: A systematic literature review and research agenda. *Supply Chain Management, 24*(1), 62–84.

Wang, Y., & Jotikasthira, N. (2024). A Quantitative Study of The Impact of Supply Chain Management on Customer Satisfaction. *Frontiers in Business, Economics and Management, 12*(3), 3. Advance online publication. DOI: 10.54097/vteg6mls

Wang, Y., Yang, Y., Qin, Z., Yang, Y., & Li, J. (2023). A literature review on the application of digital technology in achieving green supply chain management. *Sustainability, 15*(11), 8564.

Wang, Y., Yu, B., & Chen, J. (2023). Factors affecting customer intention to return in online shopping: The roles of expectation disconfirmation and post-purchase dissonance. *Electronic Commerce Research*. Advance online publication. DOI: 10.1007/s10660-023-09769-3

Waqas, A., Bui, M. M., Glassy, E. F., El Naqa, I., Borkowski, P., Borkowski, A. A., & Rasool, G. (2023). Revolutionizing digital pathology with the power of generative artificial intelligence and foundation models. *Laboratory Investigation, 100255*(11), 100255. DOI: 10.1016/j.labinv.2023.100255 PMID: 37757969

Weerapong, P., & Singhdong, P. (2024). Assessment of sustainability in supply chain management: Literature study. *Social Science Innovation and Applied Management (SIAM).*

Weingarten, J., & Spinler, S. (2021). Shortening Delivery Times by Predicting Customers' Online Purchases: A Case Study in the Fashion Industry. *Information Systems Management, 38*(4), 287–308. DOI: 10.1080/10580530.2020.1814459

Wenig, C., & Hamann, J. (2025). Increasing Supply Chain Resilience with Reverse Logistics: Hypotheses for a Value Model. *Industry 4.0 Science, 41*(1), 34–40.

WHO. (2023). Substandard and Falsified Medical Products. In *MCN: The American Journal of Maternal/Child* (Vol. 44, Issue 6).

Widdis, R. W. (2024). Back to the Future: Winnipeg's Reinvention from Borderland Trade and Transportation Gateway to Globalized Trade and Transportation Hub. *Journal of Borderlands Studies*, •••, 1–24. DOI: 10.1080/08865655.2024.2363198

Wilhelm, M. M., Blome, C., Bhakoo, V., & Paulraj, A. (2016). Sustainability in multi-tier supply chains: Understanding the double agency role of the first-tier supplier. *Journal of Operations Management*, *41*, 42–60.

Williams, L. D. (2021). Concepts of Digital Economy and Industry 4.0 in Intelligent and information systems. *International Journal of Intelligent Networks*, https://doi.org/DOI: 10.1016/j.ijin.2021.09.002

Wilson, M., Paschen, J., & Pitt, L. (2022). The circular economy meets artificial intelligence (AI): Understanding the opportunities of AI for reverse logistics. *Management of Environmental Quality*, *33*(1), 9–25. DOI: 10.1108/MEQ-10-2020-0222

Wiredu, J., Yang, Q., Sampene, A. K., Gyamfi, B. A., & Asongu, S. A. (2024). The effect of green supply chain management practices on corporate environmental performance: Does supply chain competitive advantage matter? *Business Strategy and the Environment*, *33*(3), 2578–2599.

World Bank. (2021). *Accelerating Digitalization Across the Maritime Supply Chain*. https://www.worldbank.org/en/topic/transport/publication/accelerating-digitalization-across-the-maritime-supply-chain

Wu, D., & Pi, Y. (2023). Digital technologies and product-service systems: A synergistic approach for manufacturing firms under a circular economy. *Journal of Digital Economy*, *2*, 37–49. DOI: 10.1016/j.jdec.2023.04.001

Wu, J. (2022). Sustainable development of green reverse logistics based on blockchain. *Energy Reports*, *8*, 11547–11553. DOI: 10.1016/j.egyr.2022.08.219 PMID: 36089958

Xia, D., Yu, Q., Gao, Q., & Cheng, G. (2017). Sustainable technology selection decision-making model for enterprise in supply chain: Based on a modified strategic balanced scorecard. *Journal of Cleaner Production*, *141*, 1337–1348.

Yadav, Anuradha, Shivani, Shivani, Manda, Vijaya Kittu, & Sangwan, Vikramaditya, & Demkiv, A. (2024). Blockchain technology for ecological and environmental applications. *Ecological Questions*, *35*(4), 1–20. DOI: 10.12775/EQ.2024.050

Yang, M., Fu, M., & Zhang, Z. (2021). The adoption of digital technologies in supply chains: Drivers, process and impact. *Technological Forecasting and Social Change*, *169*, 120795.

Yang, Z., & Lin, Y. (2020). The effects of supply chain collaboration on green innovation performance: An interpretive structural modeling analysis. *Sustainable Production and Consumption*, *23*, 1–10. DOI: 10.1016/j.spc.2020.03.010

Yele, S., & Litoriya, R. (2024). Blockchain-based secure dining: Enhancing safety, transparency, and traceability in food consumption environment. *Blockchain: Research and Applications*, *5*(2), 100187. DOI: 10.1016/j.bcra.2023.100187

Yiannas, F. (2018). A New Era of Food Transparency Powered by Blockchain. *Innovations: Technology, Governance, Globalization*, *12*(1–2). Advance online publication. DOI: 10.1162/inov_a_00266

Yin, R. K. (2018). Case study research and applications.

Yin, Y., Chu, F., Dolgui, A., Cheng, T. C. E., & Zhou, M. C. (2022). Big data analytics in production and distribution management. In *International Journal of Production Research* (Vol. 60, Issue 22). https://doi.org/DOI: 10.1080/00207543.2022.2130589

Ying, P. (2023). A study of enterprise warehouse management based on intelligent logistics. In *Advances in Social Science, Education and Humanities Research* (pp. 829–835). Atlantis Press SARL.

Ying, F., Tookey, J., & Seadon, J. (2018). Measuring the invisible: A key performance indicator for managing construction logistics performance. *Benchmarking*, *25*(6), 1921–1934. DOI: 10.1108/BIJ-11-2016-0176

Yli-Huumo, J., Ko, D., Choi, S., Park, S., & Smolander, K. (2016). Where is current research on Blockchain technology? - A systematic review. *PLoS One*, *11*(10). Advance online publication. DOI: 10.1371/journal.pone.0163477 PMID: 27695049

Yusuf, Z., Yusuf, F., Nuryanto, U., & Basrowi, B. (2024). Assessing organizational commitment and organizational citizenship behavior in ensuring the smoothness of the supply chain for medical hospital needs towards a green hospital: Evidence from Indonesia. *Uncertain Supply Chain Management*, *12*(1), 181–194.

Zafar, F. (2024). Examining the effect of Internet of Things (IoT) adoption on supply chain performance. *South Asian Journal of Operations and Logistics*, *3*(2), 282–294.

Zafar, S., Bhatti, K. M., Shabbir, M., Hashmat, F., & Akbar, A. H. (2022). Integration of blockchain and Internet of Things: Challenges and solutions. *Annales des Télécommunications*, •••, 1–20.

Zaid, O., Arif, J., & Jawab, F. (2024). Human-centric supply chain management towards Industry 5.0. In *2024 IEEE 15th International Colloquium on Logistics and Supply Chain Management (LOGISTIQUA)* (pp. 1–7). IEEE. https://doi.org/DOI: 10.1109/LOGISTIQUA61063.2024.10571421

Zambujal-Oliveira, J., Franco, A., & Fernandes, B. (2025). Aligning Financing Strategies With Circular Business Principles: A Multicriteria Decision Framework. *Business Strategy and the Environment*, bse.4199. https://doi.org/DOI: 10.1002/bse.4199

Zekhnini, K., Benabdellah, A. C., Bag, S., & Gupta, S. (2024). Supply chain 5.0 digitalization: An integrated approach for risk assessment. *Management Decision*. Advance online publication. DOI: 10.1108/MD-12-2023-2329

Zelbst, P. J., Green, K. W., Sower, V. E., & Bond, P. L. (2019). The impact of RFID, IIoT, and Blockchain technologies on supply chain transparency. *Journal of Manufacturing Technology Management*, *31*(3), 441–457. DOI: 10.1108/JMTM-03-2019-0118

Zeng, X. (2017). HMM completes first blockchain pilot voyage. Fairplay IHS Markit. Available at: https://fairplay.ihs.com/container/article/4291331/hmm-completes-first-blockchain-pilot-voyage

Zhang, A., Venkatesh, V. G., Liu, Y., Wan, M., Qu, T., & Huisingh, D. (2019). Barriers to smart waste management for a circular economy in China. *Journal of Cleaner Production*, *240*, 118198.

Zhang, A., Zhong, R. Y., Farooque, M., Kang, K., & Venkatesh, V. G. (2020). Blockchain-based life cycle assessment: An implementation framework and system architecture. *Resources, Conservation and Recycling*, *152*, 104512.

Zhang, F., Liao, Y., & Ding, Y. (2024). Development and application of smart logistics management service platform under big data technology. *Proceedings of the 4th International Conference on Economic Management and Big Data Applications.*

Zhang, H., Sun, X., Dong, K., Sui, L., Wang, M., & Hong, Q. (2022). Green Innovation in Regional Logistics: Level Evaluation and Spatial Analysis. *International Journal of Environmental Research and Public Health*, *20*(1), 735. PMID: 36613056

Zhang, J., Peng, S., Gao, Y., Zhang, Z., & Hong, Q. (2023). APMSA: Adversarial Perturbation Against Model Stealing Attacks. *IEEE Transactions on Information Forensics and Security*, *18*, 1667–1679. DOI: 10.1109/TIFS.2023.3246766

Zhang, X., Chen, H., Hao, Y., & Yuan, X. (2024). A low-carbon route optimization method for cold chain logistics considering traffic status in China. *Computers & Industrial Engineering, 110304*. Advance online publication. DOI: 10.1016/j.cie.2024.110304

Zheng, Z., Xie, S., Dai, H., Chen, X., & Wang, H. (2017). An Overview of Blockchain Technology: Architecture, Consensus, and Future Trends. *Proceedings - 2017 IEEE 6th International Congress on Big Data, BigData Congress 2017*. https://doi.org/DOI: 10.1109/BigDataCongress.2017.85

Zhou, K., Liu, T., & Zhou, L. (2015). Industry 4.0: Towards future industrial opportunities and challenges. *2015 12th International Conference on Fuzzy Systems and Knowledge Discovery (FSKD)* (pp. 2147–2152). IEEE. https://doi.org/DOI: 10.1109/FSKD.2015.7382284

Zhou, P., Song, F. M., & Huang, X. (2023). Environmental regulations and firms' green innovations: Transforming pressure into incentives. *International Review of Financial Analysis*, *86*, 102504. DOI: 10.1016/j.irfa.2023.102504

Zhu, Y., Long, L., Liu, W., Shu, P., & Chen, S. (2023). How and when does authentic leadership reduce employee resistance to change? An explanation from uncertainty management theory. *Leadership and Organization Development Journal*, *44*(8), 969–993. DOI: 10.1108/LODJ-03-2023-0155

Zuro, Z. (2024, April). Stakeholder Theory And Corporate Sustainability: The Silent Stakeholder Problem. In *Economic and Social Development (Book of Proceedings), 110th International Scientific Conference on Economic and Social* (Vol. 5, p. 29).

Zutshi, A., Grilo, A., & Nodehi, T. (2021). The value proposition of blockchain technologies and its impact on Digital Platforms. *Computers & Industrial Engineering*, *155*, 107187. DOI: 10.1016/j.cie.2021.107187

Zyskind, G., Nathan, O., & Pentland, A. S. (2015). Decentralizing privacy: Using blockchain to protect personal data. *Proceedings - 2015 IEEE Security and Privacy Workshops. SPW, 2015*. Advance online publication. DOI: 10.1109/SPW.2015.27

About the Contributors

Arbia Hlali is a doctor of economics science from the Faculty of Economics and Management of Sfax, University of Sfax, Tunisia. She holds a master of transport and logistics sciences from the higher Institute of industrial management of Sfax, Tunisia. Currently, she is an Assistant Professor at Taibah University, Saudi Arabia. She has international experience in teaching, earlier worked at University of Puerto Rico at Rio Piedras, San Juan, Puerto Rico, and prior to that at different Universities in Tunisia. Her research interests include Logistics, Supply Chain, Transport Economics, Management, Maritime Transport, Transport Management, Transportation Science, Containers port, Port Management, Advanced Econometrics, Standard Statistical Analysis, Operation Management, strategic Management, Sustainability, among others. She is a prolific researcher and has several publications in renowned journals and books. She works also as editor and reviewer in several international journals.

***

Shivasharana is an Associate Professor at the REVA Business School, REVA University. He has altogether 35 years of experience that includes both Industry and Teaching. In the field of Academics (Teaching), he has worked in various capacities as a Lecturer, Sr. Lecturer, Reader, Assistant Professor, and Head of the Department. He is a Doctorate in the field of Management (Specialized in Operations and Systems). He has taught various subjects and in continuation too. He has published/presented papers at national and international conferences. He is a self-directed, action-oriented professional with over 25 years of experience in education. His educational qualifications are M.Sc. (Mathematics'), MBA (Operations and Systems'), M.Phil. (Management), PGCCA (Computers), Masters in Induction Programming, and Ph.D. (Logistics and Supply Chain Management).

Munir Ahmad is a seasoned professional in the realm of Spatial Data Infrastructure (SDI), Geo-Information Productions, Information Systems, and Information Governance, boasting over 25 years of dedicated experience in the field. With a PhD in Computer Science, Dr. Ahmad's expertise spans Spatial Data Production, Management, Processing, Analysis, Visualization, and Quality Control. Throughout his career, Dr. Ahmad has been deeply involved in the development and deployment of SDI systems specially in the context of Pakistan, leveraging his proficiency in Spatial Database Design, Web, Mobile & Desktop GIS, and Geo Web Services Architecture. His contributions to Volunteered Geographic Information (VGI) and Open Source Geoportal & Metadata Portal have significantly enriched the geospatial community. As a trainer and researcher, Dr. Ahmad has authored over 50 publications, advancing the industry's knowledge base and fostering innovation in Geo-Tech, Data Governance, and Information Infrastructure, and Emerging Technologies. His commitment to Research and Development (R&D) is evident in his role as a dedicated educator and mentor in the field.

Shah Afrin Billah Aka completed her bachelor's degree at Chongqing University of Technology in Chongqing, China, and currently she is pursuing a master's degree at Beijing Institute of Technology in Beijing, China. Her research interests include mining software repositories, exploring open-source software ecosystems, and enhancing software security.

Nasser Abdel Raheem Al Ali, he completed postgraduate studies PhD of international law at the Department of International Law at Peoples' Friendship University of Russia, and he is currently working as an Associate Professor at the Department of Maritime Law and International Law at the Russian University of Transport. he publish several papers in different international journals.

Lhoussaine Alla, professor in management sciences at the National School of Applied Sciences, researcher at the LAREMEF laboratory, Sidi Mohamed Ben Abdellah University, Fez, Morocco. Prof. Lhoussaine ALLA has invested more in scientific research in various themes inherent in marketing, finance, entrepreneurship, tourism, logistics. He is also editor of the journal "Management et Alternatives Economiques - AME". Prof. Lhoussaine ALLA has accumulated as many educational and scientific experiences, which he constantly mobilizes to catalyze a large team of researchers and experts in analysis, reflexivity and application of innovative and intelligent solutions from Data Engineering and AI in various management dimensions. Prof. Lhoussaine ALLA is a co-editor of collective works published by IGI Global: InteIntegrating Intelligence and Sustainability in Supply

Chains; Applying Qualitative Research Methods to Science and Management; Using Technology to Manage Territories.

Anorgul Atajanova is working as Department Head, Department of Primary Education Methodology, Urgench State Pedagogical Institute, Urgench, Uzbekistan

Naoual Bouhtati is a doctoral student in Business Management at the Ecole Nationale de Commerce et Gestion de Fès, Sidi Mohamed ben Abdellah University (Morocco), and a researcher at the LAREMEF Laboratory. Preparing a thesis in logistics management, the researcher has explored numerous questions on the subject, particularly in terms of determinants, measurement and management indicators, as well as studying numerous contexts such as mass retailing, small shops, hospitals and local produce. The doctoral student has published numerous articles and book chapters on these themes, in full collaboration with other Moroccan and international researchers.

Most. Sharmin Ara Chowdhury is a research practitioner with a strong focus on key areas such as Artificial Intelligence, strategic innovation, management information systems, and sustainability. Her research explores the intersection of emerging technologies and organizational strategy. By aligning innovation with practical needs, she addresses real-world challenges through applied and impactful research. Sharmin's work bridges academic theory and professional practice, making significant contributions to the evolving landscape of digital transformation and sustainable development.

Md Mehedi Hasan Emon is a research practitioner in Business and Management, with specialized in Supply Chain Management, Digital Transformation, Marketing, Information Systems, and Educational Technology (Edutech). His work bridges a diverse range of domains including Artificial Intelligence in Business, Human-Computer Interaction, Cognitive Behaviour, E-commerce, and Smart Logistics. His research extensively explores the integration of emerging technologies in business ecosystems focusing on AI-driven innovation, behavioral responses to technology adoption, and digital marketing strategies. He has also contributed significantly to sustainability-focused fields such as GreenTech, Green Finance, Renewable Energy, and Blockchain-enabled financial innovation. Additionally, his work in Smart Cities and IoT adoption emphasizes the importance of user trust, security, and operational efficiency. Emon has authored numerous peer-reviewed publications on topics including AI adoption intention, supply chain visibility, digital learning acceptance, and crisis-resilient supply chains. Many of his studies adopt behavioral and cognitive perspectives to understand how professionals and consumers interact with technology highlighting the psychological and user-centric aspects of digital transformation. He has participated in several research initiatives funded by the University Grants Commission of Bangladesh and the European Union. His work aligns closely with the United Nations Sustainable Development Goals (SDGs), particularly in areas such as poverty reduction, access to quality education, clean and affordable energy, inclusive economic growth, sustainable industrialization, responsible consumption, climate resilience, and ocean sustainability. His work also reflects a commitment to reducing inequalities and fostering international partnerships for sustainable development. In addition to his research contributions, he serves as a peer reviewer for several high-impact academic journals and is widely recognized for promoting academic rigor and ethical scholarship. As a prolific author, he continues to shape the discourse on sustainability, innovation, and digital advancement through his research, writing, and knowledge dissemination.

Radwan Eskhita (LLM, PhD) is a lecturer and researcher specializing in Cyber Security, Privacy, and Information Technology Law at Lucerne University of Applied Sciences and Arts (Switzerland). He teaches courses on networking, regulation, and privacy & cyber security and actively explores the intersection of law and technology. His research focuses on data protection laws, extraterritorial regulatory effects, and the legal implications of digital markets.

Nesrine Gafsi is an assistant Professor of Finance at Imam Mohammad Ibn Saud Islamic University - Saudi Arabia

Ankit Garg is associated with Ajay Kumar Garg Institute of Management, Ghaziabad, boosting over 13+ years of experience in teaching and research. He holds a Ph.D. in Management, an MBA, an M. Com, and a B.E. His expertise spans MS Office, Excel, SPSS, Python, R, Power BI, and Tableau. He has multiple certifications, including IBM Data Analyst and Google Analytics. Dr. Garg has published research papers, patents, books, and book chapters in reputed journals. He is an active conference presenter and serves as a Guest Editor for peer-reviewed and ABDC-listed journals.

Jaishri Gothania is an academician, author, researcher, and data scientist with over 9 years of experience. She has published 12 research articles, presented 6 conference papers, and holds multiple patents. Her work bridges data science and innovation, contributing significantly to academia, research, and technological advancement.

Mohammad Kamrul Hasan obtained a Ph.D. in Management Science and Engineering from Shijiazhuang Tiedao University, Hebei, China, in 2024. Before getting his Ph.D., he obtained 2nd Master degree in Business Administration in

China. Currently, he is working in School of Business Administration and involved in teaching & research in Tongling University, Tongling, Anhui, China. His research interests mainly include logistics management, green and sustainable logistics, and qualitative and quantitative research methodologies. He has already published a few papers in WoS and SCOPUS-indexed journals.

Aziz Hmioui received his PhD in Industrial Economics and is a Professor at Sidi Mohammed Ben Abdellah University, Fez. His research focuses on tourism, logistics and territorial attractiveness. He is the author of numerous scientific articles. He has participated in numerous international scientific events (Algeria, Brazil, Canada, Egypt, Spain, France, Tunisia and Vietnam). He is a member of several scientific committees of international journals and conferences.

Asma Imran is serving as an Associate Professor in the Department of Management papersSciences at the COMSATS University Islamabad, Lahore Campus. She holds a PhD in Management Sciences. She has more than 12 years of experience teaching at the graduate level. She has also published a number of in her area of specialization. Her area of research and specialization include HRM and management.

Rituraj Jain is currently working in the Department of Information Technology, Marwadi University, Rajkot, Gujarat, India. He has published many papers in International Journals and Conferences. He has published 4 books. He is an Oracle Database SQL Certified Expert. He is also associated with professional bodies like the Indian Society of Technical Education (ISTE), Computer Science Teachers Association (CSTA), Academy & Industry Research Collaboration Center (AIRCC), International Association of Computer Science and Information Technology (IACSIT), International Association of Engineers (IAENG). His research interests include Cloud Computing, Machine Learning, Deep Learning, Fuzzy Logic, IoT, Genetic Algorithms, Big Data and Software Engineering.

Tahsina Khan is serving as Deputy Director (Research) at the Centre for Higher Studies and Research in Bangladesh University of Professionals (BUP). In addition, she is also serving as the Assistant Editor of the BUP Journal. She is an Academician in Business Studies with more than 14 years of teaching, research & consulting experience in Higher Education Institutions. Over the years, she has successfully supervised multilateral academic programs in collaboration with the Government, NGOs, and Corporations from the Business sector. As a Visiting Lecturer, she has taught in the MBA program of the University of Gavle, Sweden. She has worked as Director of the research projects funded by the University Grants Commission (UGC) under the Ministry of Education. Her research papers were presented in

National and International Conferences in Canada, France, Malaysia and Indonesia. As Session Chair, she presided over the conference organized by Higher Education and Innovation Group (HEAIG). She has also been invited as a resource speaker at the United Nations affiliated conference at the Yonsei University in Wonju, South Korea. She has published a number of peer-reviewed articles in reputed international journals and her policy brief paper on Rural Development has been included in the knowledge hub of the UN Task Force on SDG implementation. She is a member of International Sociological Association (ISA) which is associated with UNESCO, Economic & Social Council of the United Nations.

Zahid Latif obtained MS in Management Sciences from Allama Iqbal Open University, Pakistan in 2023. Before getting his MS, he obtained an MBA degree with a major in Human resources management from the same institution. Currently, he is serving as a Court Associate and engaged in administrative & judicial tasks at Lahore High Court, Lahore, Pakistan. His research interests mainly include leadership, organizational behavior and I/O psychology, qualitative and quantitative research methodologies. He has already published a few papers in WoS and SCOPUS-indexed journals.

Mohammed Majeed is a Senior Lecturer (PhD) at Tamale Technical University, Tamale Ghana. He is the current Head of Department for Marketing. His current research interest includes branding, Hospitality and Tourism, social media in service organizations. Majeed holds Doctor of Philosophy (PhD) and Doctor of Business Administration (DBA), MPhil and MBA Marketing, Postgraduate Diploma, HND Marketing. He lectures part time in many Ghanaian public Universities and a reviewer to many Journals in Management, hospitality, and marketing. Majeed has also published in good journals like Journal of Hospitality and Tourism Insights (Emerald), Springer, Palgrave, Cogent Business & Management, Journal of African Business (Taylor & Francis). Furthermore, Dr. Majeed has authored over 40 book chapters, solidifying his influence as a scholar and thought leader in his field. His citations on Google Scholar is 556 as at 10-07-2025, Hindex 9 and 10index of 8.

Vijaya Kittu Manda has nearly 13+ years of experience in capital markets, financial planning, and investing. He is a Researcher at PBMEIT, India. He is an Advocate, a technocrat, an academician, a book writer, and a stock market enthusiast. He has 11 University Postgraduate Degrees in various disciplines. He is a Ph.D. in Financial Management. His thesis on Mutual Funds and their Market Competition won the prestigious NSE-IEA Best Thesis Award in 2023. He is currently pursuing his second Ph.D. in Computer Science with focus on Blockchain. He contributed over 785 articles to various magazines and has over 110+ Google Scholar and 30+

Scopus-indexed publications. He is the Chief Editor for a Management Book Series, Editor of several books, a Peer Reviewer and is a Certified Peer Review Supervisor. He sits as a Session Chair and an Advisor for various academic and industrial conferences. He writes Research Papers and Case Studies, and sits on Editorial Boards of various publishers. He is a guest speaker for colleges and universities. He serves as the host for a research talk show called PBMEIT Expert Insights.

Kirubhakaran Marisamy is working as an Assistant Professor in the Department of Artificial Intelligence and Data Science at Nehru Institute of Engineering and Technology, Coimbatore, India

Nwoloziri Chinyeaka Nwokodi is a lecturer in the Department Of Maritime Science, Faculty of Science, Rivers State University, Port Harcourt, Nigeria. He studied at the Federal University of Technology, Owerri Imo State, Nigeria, obtaining a Bachelor of Technology Degree in Transport Management Technology, a Master of Science (MSc) in Maritime Management Technology, and a PhD in Maritime Management Technology. He also holds a Postgraduate Diploma in Education (PGDE) from the National Open University of Nigeria. Dr. Nwoloziri is a professional seafarer and has many years of sea and industry experience in the maritime industry. He has occupied many positions in the university as an academic adviser, a member of the ad-hoc committee on course design and development, and a planning committee on NUC accreditation. He has authored over 50 research papers published in national and international journals, including Scopus-indexed journals. He has participated in and presented various maritime transport and logistics papers at many conferences, seminars, and workshop training programs.

Balakrishnan R is a passionate and dynamic academician, seamlessly blending over 7 years of industry leadership with 6 years of academic excellence in Hotel Management & Catering Technology. Beginning his journey as a Lecturer, he now serves as an Assistant Professor, known for his student-centric approach, effective mentoring, and engaging teaching style. He has guided students to national accolades, including second place at an all-India paper-writing competition. With granted patents in India and the UK, he has authored various book chapters and published in high-impact international journals. His Ph.D. research focused on the integration of Augmented Reality (AR) in hospitality training, aiming to revolutionize industry training methodologies and enhance service standards in the evolving hospitality landscape. A sought-after resource person and workshop facilitator, he actively bridges the gap between academia and industry. His dedication to transformative learning continues to shape the future of hospitality education and training on a global scale.

Ravikumar is an experienced educator with 11+ years of teaching in Computer Science across India and overseas. Currently an Assistant Professor at Marwadi University, Rajkot, he specializes in Advanced Java, Machine Learning, Data Science, and AI. He holds a Mini MBA from the Swiss eLearning Institute (2015), an M.E. in Computer Science Engineering from VMRF University (2013), and a B.E. from Anna University (2010). Completed PhD at Amity University, Jaipur, he is dedicated to research, professional development, and advancing education through technology.

Aarthi S is a dedicated Assistant Professor in Computer Science with over six years of teaching experience. She is currently pursuing her Ph.D. at Marwadi University, Gujarat, and holds an M.Phil. and MCA from Bharathiar University, Tamil Nadu. Throughout her academic career, Aarthi has specialized in programming languages such as C++, Java, and C, and contributed to research in recommender systems and AI-related data privacy. She has published journal articles, contributed to book chapters, and actively participated in technical workshops. Known for her student mentorship and engagement in academic events, Aarthi remains committed to fostering innovation and excellence in computer science education.

Nimit Sharma is working as an assistant professor in School of Commerce at REVA University, India. Her research focus is on Reverse Logistics and on Supply Chain. She bring a wealth of experience in teaching, research, and professional development, with a special interest in finance, supply chain management, and business strategy. moderated and chaired sessions at international conferences, demonstrating her leadership and communication skills. She is a strong advocate for continuous learning and have completed numerous certifications and FDPs from prestigious institutions like IITs, IIMs, covering areas like supply chain management, finance, marketing, and leadership. She is also an NPTEL Star (Believers, Achievers and Enthusiasts Certificates) felicitated by IIT Madras for her contributions. She has been awarded by the Education Minister of Karnataka for being one of the top scorers in the State Eligibility Test (SET). She has also qualified UGC NET in commerce.

Sitesh Kumar Singh is an accomplished academic and Chartered Engineer with a Ph.D. in Civil Engineering and over nine years of diverse experience in education, research, consultancy, and educational administration. Currently serving as an Assistant Professor in the Department of Civil and Environmental Engineering at the National University of Science and Technology, Muscat, Sultanate of Oman, he specializes in Civil and Transportation Engineering, Project Management, and Data Analytics. Dr. Singh holds multiple advanced degrees including M.Tech, B.Tech, PGDIPR, and PGDUPDL. His career encompasses curriculum development, research supervision, quality assurance, and strategic academic planning. He has supervised over 40 postgraduate and 2 doctoral students, contributing to academic leadership through workshops, conferences, and editorial roles, and has published over 40 research articles, several patents, and authored books and book chapters.

Surabhi Singh, PhD in Digital Marketing and Consumer Behaviour from AMU, is a Professor and Head–International Relations at GLBIMR, Greater Noida. With 24 years in academics and administration, she has authored 3 books, edited 10, and published over 100 papers in reputed journals. A TEDx speaker and international presenter, she has also served as President of WICCI Ghaziabad City Council. Dr. Singh is an Associate Editor and board member of several journals, PhD guide, and advisor in education and urban infra. Her research spans marketing, analytics, emerging tech, and strategy.

Lei Xunping is currently the dean of School of Business Administration, Tongling University. He has published so many SCI, SSCI, and Scopus indexed research papers. His research interests mainly include logistics management, green and sustainable logistics, and qualitative and quantitative research methodologies.

Index

A

B

C

D

E

F

G

H

I

K

L

M

N

O

P

R

S

T

W

www.ingramcontent.com/pod-product-compliance
Lightning Source LLC
LaVergne TN
LVHW080353011026
849161LV00009B/2291